Business Ethics

Decision-Making for Personal Integrity and Social Responsibility

McGraw-Hill Books by Laura P. Hartman and Joseph DesJardins

Business Ethics: Decision-Making for
Personal Integrity and Social Responsibility
By Laura Hartman and Joseph DesJardins
ISBN: 0073136867, © 2008

Perspectives in Business Ethics,
3rd Edition
By Laura Hartman
ISBN: 0072881461, © 2005

Employment Law for Business,
5th Edition
By Dawn Bennett-Alexander and Laura Hartman
ISBN: 0073028959, © 2007

An Introduction to Business Ethics,
2nd Edition
By Joseph DesJardins
ISBN: 0072989009, © 2006

business ethics:

Decision-Making for Personal Integrity & Social Responsibility

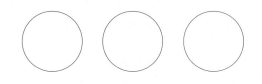

Laura P. Hartman
DePaul University

Joe DesJardins
College of St. Benedict/St John's University

Boston   Burr Ridge, IL   Dubuque, IA   New York   San Francisco
St. Louis   Bangkok   Bogotá   Caracas   Lisbon   London   Madrid
Mexico City   Milan   New Delhi   Seoul   Singapore   Sydney   Taipei   Toronto

BUSINESS ETHICS: DECISION-MAKING FOR PERSONAL INTEGRITY & SOCIAL RESPONSIBILITY

1 2 3 4 5 6 7 8 9 0 DOC DOC 0 9 8

ISBN-13: 978-0-07-726403-1
ISBN-10: 0-07-726403-7

Custom Publishing Specialist: Michael Hemmer
Production Editor: Nicole Baumgartner
Printer/Binder: BR Printing

To Rachel and Emma.

*Once you are Real, you can't become unreal
again. It lasts for always.*
– *The Velveteen Rabbit*, by Margery Williams

—Laura Hartman

To Michael and Matthew.

—Joe DesJardins

About the Authors

Laura P. Hartman *DePaul University*

Laura P. Hartman is a Professor of Business Ethics and Legal Studies at DePaul University's College of Commerce and is Associate Vice President for Academic Affairs at the University. She has been an invited professor at INSEAD (France), HEC (France) the Université Paul Cezanne Aix Marseille III, among other European universities, and previously held the Grainger Chair in Business Ethics at the University of Wisconsin–Madison. Her other books include *Rising above Sweatshops: Innovative Management Approaches to Global Labor Challenges, Employment Law for Business, Perspectives in Business Ethics*, and *The Legal Environment of Business: Ethical and Public Policy Contexts*. Hartman graduated from Tufts University and received her law degree from the University of Chicago Law School.

Joe DesJardins *College of St. Benedict/St. John's University*

Joe DesJardins is a Professor of Philosophy at the College of St. Benedict and St. John's University in Minnesota and serves as Interim Academic Dean and Associate Provost. He is also the Executive Director of the Society for Business Ethics. His other books include: *Environmental Ethics: An Introduction to Environmental Philosophy; An Introduction to Business Ethics* (McGraw Hill); and *Business, Ethics, and the Environment: Ethics for the Next Industrial Revolution*. He received his Ph.D. from the University of Notre Dame and taught for many years at Villanova University before moving to Minnesota.

Preface

As recently as the mid-1990s, articles in such major publications as *The Wall Street Journal, Harvard Business Review,* and *U.S. News and World Report* questioned the legitimacy and value of teaching classes in business ethics. Yet, in the post-Enron world of business, the questions today are less about *whether* ethics should be a part of business strategy than they are about *which* values and principles should guide business decisions and *how* ethics should be integrated within business.

This textbook provides a comprehensive yet accessible introduction to the ethical issues arising in business. Students unfamiliar with ethics will find themselves as unprepared for careers in business as students who are unfamiliar with accounting and finance. It is fair to say that students will not be fully prepared, even within traditional disciplines such as accounting, finance, human resource management, marketing, and management, unless they are sufficiently knowledgeable about the ethical issues that arise specifically within those fields.

While other solid introductory textbooks are available, several major features make this book distinctive. We emphasize a **decision-making approach** to ethics and we provide **strong pedagogical support** for both teachers and students throughout the entire book. In addition, we bring both of these strengths to the students through a pragmatic discussion of issues with which they are already often familiar, thus approaching them through subjects that have already generated their interest.

Why a Decision Making Model?

Ethics is all about making decisions: What should we do? How should we act? What type of life should we live? What type of organization and society ought we to create? Who should we be? By providing a decision-making model early in this text and revisiting and reinforcing this model through Decision Points and discussions of case studies in each chapter, we hope to accomplish several important goals.

First, an emphasis on decision making avoids the nagging challenge of relativism without succumbing to dogmatic preaching. Our decision-making model teaches students to think for themselves and to build a case in support of their own conclusions, conclusions that are rationally defensible precisely because they are the result of a rational decision-making process. In this way, students become active learners by taking responsibility for their points of view.

A decision-making emphasis also offers the promise of life-long lessons. Long after students have forgotten the specific content of this course, the reasoning skills and habits developed here will continue to influence their everyday personal and professional lives. The purpose of the text is to encourage readers to explore

their own values and then to apply a logical process to reach a well-reasoned conclusion regarding an appropriate course of action. This process will be relevant no
matter the circumstances, profession involved, or stage in life as students proceed
beyond the course within which it is taught.

The significance of the decision-making model also makes this text inherently
compatible with diverse and global perspectives in a way that could not be achieved
by a discussion that focused only on specific ethical values and principles. This
inclusivity allows the model greater power of application across borders, subjects,
and even time, than a value-based orientation would allow.

Finally, the decision-making model introduced here is easily transferred into
other contexts and other courses. Many scholars now realize that business ethics
should be integrated across the entire range of business disciplines. The strength
of our decision-making model is that students and teachers can use it in any business course as a means for addressing ethical issues that arise in other fields. This
is not a text that students will leave on the bookshelves. This is one that they will
need to consult for each of their courses and, one would hope, for each of the
issues they might also face in the business environment outside of the educational
environment as well.

Pedagogical Support

Business ethics creates distinct challenges for both students and teachers. One
would naturally assume that business ethics requires familiarity with the concepts
and categories of two diverse fields, business and ethics. For many business students, a class in ethics will be unlike any other class in their experience. Faculty
trained in business disciplines are challenged to master ethics; and those trained
in ethics are equally challenged to master business concepts. This challenge will
be increasing as more and more business school faculty are asked to teach ethics
as part of the recognition of the critical importance and consequent integration of
ethics in the business school curriculum. This evolution demands a textbook that
provides strong pedagogical support for both student learners and teachers.

As if the challenge of teaching an interdisciplinary field is not enough, accred-
iting agencies are increasingly requiring that faculty demonstrate student learning, and the assessment of student learning will be required at both the program
and individual instructor level.

This text offers a range of pedagogical elements to support both students and
teachers. Each chapter in introduced with a **Decision Point**, a short case that raises
issues that will be introduced and examined in the chapter. The Decision Point
provides a topic through which to begin discussion and to ease students into the
issues to follow, and it also includes a set of questions that demonstrate how to
explore each decision using the ethical decision-making model proposed early in
the book. A follow-up discussion of these Decision Points concludes each chapter,
offering the opportunity to reflect on the opening case as a means to summarize
and reflect upon the chapter. Decision Points are also sprinkled throughout each
chapter as a way to help refine students' critical thinking skills.

Each chapter begins with a specific list of **Chapter Objectives**, which serve as the student learning goals as well as the organizational framework of the chapter, and concludes with a list of **Key Terms** introduced within the chapter. Key Terms are in color in the chapter text where they first appear, then included with comprehensive definitions at the end of the book in a full glossary.

Also integrated within each chapter are **Reality Checks**, which highlight real-life situations of business applications. They are examples of how these particular processes are applied in a timely, straight from the headlines business situation. The Reality Checks provide another application of the text material and keep students aware of issues and questions they will need to grapple with in this course.

The end-of-chapter material contains **Discussion and Project Questions** that go beyond recall questions to also include further research and application. The end-of-chapter **Readings** present a variety of provocative takes on the issues just raised in each chapter so that students become familiar with new perspectives, the subtle ethical implications of business actions, and the need for clarity of vision in engaging in business activity.

The **Instructor's Resource CD (IRCD)** for this text includes additional support for instructors, comprising the **Instructor's Manual**, with outlines and teaching tips for each chapter, as well as notes on how to use the chapter Decision Points, Reality Checks, and readings. The **Test Bank** includes 75 questions per chapter across a range of question types (true/false, fill-in, multiple choice, short answer, and essay) and is completely editable. The **PowerPoint Presentations** include two different sets: a shorter, outline-based presentation and a longer, more comprehensive presentation with notes for the instructor, links to relevant content, and discussion questions to address in class.

This text also includes a complimentary **DVD** for instructors who wish to use video cases to enliven course discussions and give your students a taste of how ethics plays out in real companies. Cases are selected by the authors from the McGraw-Hill/Irwin video library to dovetail with each chapter, and include news footage and mini-documentaries on various companies' practices. **Video Notes** are included in the Instructor's Manual to offer suggestions on how to use the cases in your classes.

The **Online Learning Center** for this book, *www.mhhe.com/busethics*, has two portals: instructors can download the IM, Video Files and Notes, Weblinks to related research sites, PPT files, and Sample Syllabi. Students can access the basic PPT files, Glossary pages, Video Files, Weblinks to Suggested Resources, and Chapter Review Quizzes.

By striving to speak to the students in language that is accessible to them, providing them with a framework within which to respond to even the most complicated ethical challenges, and by equipping them with theories that allow them a breadth of perspective and insight, the text offers the support that students need to ensure their voices will be heard in the business environment they are entering or have entered. Articulate, persuasive students with integrity and conviction will be business leaders of action. Our objective is to provide students with the tools they will require to ensure their action is effective, valuable, and sustainable.

Acknowledgments

A textbook should introduce students to the cutting-edge of the scholarly research that is occurring within a field. As in any text that is based in part on the work of others, we are deeply indebted to the work of our colleagues who are doing this research. We are especially grateful to those scholars who graciously granted us personal permission to reprint their materials in this text:

Denis Arnold

Norm Bowie

Martin Calkins

Michael Cranford

Jon Entine

Andrew Kluth

Philip Kotler

Dennis Moberg

Lisa Newton

Mark Pincus

Tara Radin

Ed Romar

Penelope Washbourne

Partricia Werhane

Our book is a more effective tool for both students and faculty because of their generosity. In addition, we wish to express our deepest gratitude to the reviewers and others whose efforts served to make this manuscript infinitely more effective:

Denis Arnold,
University of Tennessee

John Bennett,
Park University

Francisco Benzoni,
Duke University

Sam Bruton,
University of Southern Mississippi

Brian Burton,
Western Washington University

Joe DiPoli,
Curry College

Paul Govekar,
Ohio Northern University

Francine Guice,
Indiana-Purdue University–Fort Wayne

Andra Gumbus,
Sacred Heart University

Nancy Hauserman,
University of Iowa

Anita Leffel,
University of Texas–San Antonio

Jeff Leon,
University of Texas–Austin

Anne Levy,
Michigan State University

Dan Marin,
Louisiana State University

Paul Melendez,
University of Arizona

Patricia Murray,
Virginia Union University

Patricia Parker,
Maryville University

Sandra Powell,
Sacred Heart University

Ed Romar,
University of Massachusetts–Boston

Lindsay Thompson,
Johns Hopkins University

Frank Walker,
Lee University

Roger Ward,
Georgetown University

Our thanks also go out to the team at McGraw-Hill/Irwin who helped this book come into existence:

John Biernat
Editorial Director

Andy Winston
Publisher

Kelly Lowery
Senior Sponsoring Editor

Dana Woo
Sponsoring Editor

Kirsten Guidero
Developmental Editor

Kelly Odom
Marketing Manager

Harvey Yep
Project Manager

Debra Sylvester
Production Supervisor

Jillian Lindner
Design Coordinator

Sue Lombardi
Media Project Manager

Brief Contents

Table of Contents

1

Ethics and Business

Good people do not need laws to tell them to act justly, while bad people will find a way around the laws.

Plato

It is difficult to get a man to understand something when his salary depends upon his not understanding it.

Upton Sinclair

1−17
24−31

Opening Decision Point
Loyalty after a Crisis: Should Aaron Feuerstein Rebuild and Pay His Employees in the Meantime?

During the early evening hours of December 11, 1995, a fire broke out in a textile mill in Lawrence, Massachusetts. By morning, the fire had destroyed most of Malden Mills, the manufacturer of Polartec fabric. The fire seemed a disaster to the company, its employees, its customers, and the surrounding communities.

Malden Mills was a family-owned business, founded in 1906 and run by the founder's grandson Aaron Feuerstein. Polartec is a high-quality fabric well known for its use in the outdoor apparel featured by such popular companies as L.L. Bean, Lands' End, REI, J. Crew, and Eddie Bauer. The disaster promised many headaches for Malden Mills and for the numerous businesses that depend on its products.

But the fire also was a disaster for an entire community. The towns surrounding the Malden Mills plant have long been home to textile manufacturing. But the industry effectively died during the middle decades of the twentieth century when outdated factories and increasing labor costs led many companies to abandon the area and relocate, first to the nonunionized South, and later to foreign countries such as Mexico and Taiwan. As happened in many northern manufacturing towns, the loss of major industries, along with their jobs and tax base, began a long period of economic decline from which many have never recovered. Malden Mills was the last major textile manufacturer in town, and with 2,400 employees it supplied the economic lifeblood for the surrounding communities. With both its payroll and taxes, Malden Mills contributed approximately $100 million a year into the local economy.

As CEO and president, Aaron Feuerstein faced some major decisions. He could have used the fire as an opportunity to follow his local competitors and relocate to a more economically attractive area. He certainly could have found a location with lower taxes and cheaper labor and thus have maximized his earning potential. He could have simply taken the insurance money and decided not to reopen at all. Instead, as the fire was still smoldering, Feuerstein pledged to rebuild his plant at the same location and keep the jobs in the local community. But even more surprising, he promised to continue paying his employees and extend their medical coverage until they could come back to work.

- What do you think of Feuerstein's decision? What would you have done had you been in his position?
- What facts would be helpful as you make your judgments about Feuerstein?
- How many different ethical values are involved in this situation? What kind of man is Feuerstein? How would you describe his actions after the fire? Can you describe the man and his actions without using ethical or evaluative words?
- Whose interests should Feuerstein consider in making this decision? How many different people were affected by the fire and the decision?
- What other options were available for Feuerstein? How would these alternatives have affected the other people involved?
- Were Feuerstein's actions charitable, or was this something he had a duty or obligation to do? What is the difference between acts of charity and obligatory acts?

Chapter Objectives

After reading this chapter, you will be able to:

1. Explain why ethics is important in the business environment.
2. Explain the nature of business ethics as an academic discipline.
3. Distinguish the ethics of personal integrity from the ethics of social responsibility.
4. Distinguish ethical norms and values from other business-related norms and values.
5. Distinguish legal responsibilities from ethical responsibilities.
6. Explain why ethical responsibilities go beyond legal compliance.
7. Distinguish ethical decision making from other practical decision situations.

Introduction: Making the Case for Business Ethics

From the time Enron Corporation collapsed in 2001, business ethics has seldom strayed from the front pages of the press. The list of corporations and business leaders that have been involved with legal and ethical wrongdoing is, sadly, incredibly long. Reflect for a moment on the businesses that have been involved in recent scandals: Enron, WorldCom, Tyco, Adelphia, Cendant, Rite Aid, Sunbeam, Waste Management, HealthSouth, Global Crossing, Arthur Andersen, Ernst & Young, Imclone, KPMG, JPMorgan, Merrill Lynch, Morgan Stanley, Citigroup Salomon Smith Barney, Marsh & McLennan, Credit Suisse First Boston, and even the New York Stock Exchange itself. Individuals implicated in ethical scandals include Martha Stewart, Kenneth Lay, Jeffrey Skilling, Andrew Fastow, Dennis Kozlowski, John J. Rigas, Richard M. Scrushy, Samuel Waksal, Richard Grasso, and Bernard Ebbers. Beyond these well-known scandals, consumer boycotts based on allegations of unethical conduct have targeted such well-known firms as Nike, McDonald's, Home Depot, Gap, Shell Oil, Levi-Strauss, Donna Karen, Kmart, and Wal-Mart.

This chapter will introduce business ethics as a process of responsible decision making. Simply put, the scandals and ruin experienced by all the institutions and every one of the individuals just mentioned were brought about by ethical failures. This text provides a decision-making model that, we hope, can help individuals understand such failures and avoid future business and personal tragedies. As an introduction to that decision-making model, this chapter reflects on the nature of ethics and business.

Ethical decision making in business is not limited to the type of major corporate decisions with dramatic social consequences listed above. At some point every worker, and certainly everyone in a managerial role, will be faced with an issue that will require ethical decision making. Not every decision can be covered by economic, legal, or company rules and regulations. More often than not, responsible decision making must rely on the personal values and principles of the individuals involved. Individuals will have to decide for themselves what type of person they want to be.

At other times, of course, decisions will involve significant general policy issues that affect entire organizations, as happened in all the well-known corporate scandals and in the Malden Mills case described at the start of this chapter. The managerial role especially involves decision making that establishes organizational precedents and has organizational and social consequences. Hence, both of these types of situations—the personal and the organizational—are reflected in the title of this book: *Business Ethics: Decision Making for Personal Integrity and Social Responsibility.*

As recently as the mid-1990s, articles in such major publications as *The Wall Street Journal*, the *Harvard Business Review*, and *U.S. News and World Report* questioned the legitimacy and value of teaching classes in business ethics. Few disciplines face the type of skepticism that commonly confronted courses in business ethics. Many students believed that, like "jumbo-shrimp," "business ethics" was an oxymoron. Many also viewed ethics as a mixture of sentimentality and personal opinion that would interfere with the efficient functioning of business. After all, who is to say what's right or wrong?

Throughout the 1980s and 1990s, this skeptical attitude was as common among business practitioners as it was among students. But this simply is no longer the case in contemporary business. The questions today are less about *why* or *should* ethics be a part of business, than they are about *which* values and principles should guide business decisions and *how* ethics should be integrated within business.[1] Students unfamiliar with the basic concepts and categories of ethics will find themselves as unprepared for careers in business as students who are unfamiliar with accounting and finance. Indeed, it is fair to say that students will not be fully prepared even within fields such as accounting, finance, human resource management, marketing, and management unless they are familiar with the ethical issues that arise within those specific fields. You simply will not be prepared for a career in accounting, finance, or any area of business if you are unfamiliar with the ethical issues that commonly occur in these fields.

OBJECTIVE

To understand the origins of this change, consider the range of people who were harmed by the collapse of Enron. Stockholders lost over $1 billion in stock value. Thousands of employees lost their jobs, their retirement funds, and their health care benefits. Consumers in California suffered from energy shortages and blackouts that were caused by Enron's manipulation of the market. Hundreds of businesses that worked with Enron as suppliers suffered economic loss with the loss of a large client. Enron's accounting firm, Arthur Andersen, went out of business as a direct result. The wider Houston community was also hurt by the loss of a major employer and community benefactor. Families of employees, investors, and suppliers were also hurt. Many of the individuals directly involved will themselves suffer criminal and civil punishment, including prison sentences for some. Indeed, it is hard to imagine anyone who was even loosely affiliated with Enron

Today, business executives have many reasons to be concerned with the ethical standards of their organizations. Perhaps the most straightforward reason is that the law requires it. In 2002, the U.S. Congress passed the Sarbanes-Oxley Act to address the wave of corporate and accounting scandals. Section 406 of that law, "Code of Ethics for Senior Financial Officers," requires that corporations have a Code of Ethics "applicable to its principal financial officer and comptroller or principal accounting officer, or persons performing similar functions." The Code must include standards that promote:

1. Honest and ethical conduct, including the ethical handling of actual or apparent conflicts of interest between personal and professional relationships.

2. Full, fair, accurate, timely, and understandable disclosure in the periodic reports required to be filed by the issuer.

3. Compliance with applicable governmental rules and regulations.

who was not harmed as a result of the ethical failings there. Multiply that harm by the dozens of other companies implicated in similar scandals and you get an idea of why ethics is no longer dismissed as irrelevant. The consequences of unethical behavior and unethical business institutions are too serious for too many people to be ignored.

This description of the consequences of the Enron collapse, along with the opening description of the Malden Mills case, demonstrates the significant impacts that business decisions can have on a very wide range of people. Both cases dramatically affected the lives of thousands of people: employees, stockholders, management, suppliers, customers, and surrounding communities. For better or for worse, the decisions a business firm makes will affect many more people than just the decision maker. Ethically responsible business decision making therefore must move beyond a narrow concern with stockholders to consider the impact that decisions will have on a wide range of stakeholders. In a general sense, a business *stakeholder* will be anyone affected, for better or worse, by decisions made within the firm.

The preceding Reality Check describes some legal requirements that have been created since the Enron fiasco. Beyond these specific legal obligations, contemporary business managers have many other reasons to be concerned with ethical issues. Unethical behavior not only creates legal risks for a business, it creates financial and marketing risks as well. Managing these risks requires managers and executives to remain vigilant about their company's ethics. It is now clearer than ever that a company can lose in the marketplace, it can go out of business, and its employees can go to jail if no one is paying attention to the ethical standards of the firm. A firm's ethical reputation can provide a competitive advantage or disadvantage in the marketplace and with customers, suppliers, and employees. The consumer boycotts of such well-known firms as Nike, McDonald's, Home

---

Reality Check *Why Be Good?*

The Institute for Business, Technology and Ethics suggests the following "Nine Good Reasons" to run a business ethically:

1. Litigation/indictment avoidance
2. Regulatory freedom
3. Public acceptance
4. Investor confidence
5. Supplier/partner trust
6. Customer loyalty
7. Employee performance
8. Personal pride
9. It's right

Source: Institute for Business, Technology and Ethics, *Ethix*, no. 22 (March/April 2002), p. 11.

Depot, and Wal-Mart mentioned previously give even the most skeptical business leader reason to pay attention to ethics. Managing ethically can also pay significant dividends in organizational structure and efficiency. Trust, loyalty, commitment, creativity, and initiative are just some of the organizational benefits that are more likely to flourish within ethically stable and credible organizations (see the Reality Check above).

For business students, the need to study ethics should be as clear as the need to study the other subfields of business education. Without this background, students simply will be unprepared for a career in contemporary business. But even for students not anticipating a career in business management or business administration, familiarity with business ethics is just as crucial. After all, it was not only the managers at Enron who suffered because of their ethical lapses. Our lives as employees, as consumers, and as citizens are affected by decisions made within business institutions, and therefore everyone has good reasons for being concerned with the ethics of those decision makers.

The case for business ethics is by now clear and persuasive. Business must take ethics into account and integrate ethics into its organizational structure. Students need to study business ethics. But what does this mean? What is "ethics," and what is the point of a class in business ethics?

Business Ethics as Ethical Decision Making

As the title of this book suggests, our approach to business ethics will emphasize ethical decision making. No book can magically create ethically responsible people or change behavior in any direct way. But students can learn and practice responsible ways of thinking and deliberating. We assume decisions that follow from a process of thoughtful and conscientious reasoning will be more responsible and ethical decisions. In other words, responsible decision making and deliberation will result in more responsible behavior.

So what is the point of a business ethics course? On one hand, *ethics* refers to an academic discipline with a centuries-old history, and we might expect knowledge about this history to be among the primary goals of a class in ethics. Thus, in an ethics course, students might be expected to learn about the great ethicists of history such as Aristotle, John Stuart Mill, and Immanuel Kant. As in many other courses, this approach to ethics would focus on the *informational content* of the class.

Yet, according to some observers, learning about ethical theories and gaining knowledge about the history of ethics is beside the point. Many people, ranging from businesses looking to hire college graduates to business students and teachers themselves, expect an ethics class to address ethical *behavior*, not just information and knowledge about ethics. After all, shouldn't an ethics class help prevent future Enrons? Ethics refers not only to an academic discipline, but to that arena of human life studied by this academic discipline, namely, how human beings should properly live their lives.

OBJECTIVE

Yet, a caution about influencing behavior within a classroom is appropriate. Part of the hesitation about teaching ethics involves the potential for abuse; expecting teachers to influence behavior may be viewed as permission for teachers to impose their own views on students. Many believe that teachers should remain value-neutral in the classroom and respect a student's own views. Another part of this concern is that the line between motivating students and manipulating students is a narrow one. There are many ways to influence someone's behavior, including threats, guilt, pressure, bullying, and intimidation. Some of the executives involved in the worst of the recent corporate scandals were very good at using some of these means to motivate the people who worked for them. Presumably, none of these approaches belong in a college classroom, and especially not in an ethical classroom.

But not all forms of influencing behavior raise such concerns. There is a major difference between manipulating someone and persuading someone, between threats and reasons. This textbook resolves the tension between knowledge and behavior by emphasizing ethical judgment, ethical deliberation, ethical decision making. We agree with those who believe that an ethics class should strive to produce more ethical behavior among the students who enroll. But we believe that the only academically and ethically legitimate way to do this is through careful and reasoned decision making. Our fundamental assumption is that a process of rational decision making, a process that involves careful thought and deliberation, can and will result in behavior that is both more reasonable and more ethical.

Perhaps this view is not surprising after all. Consider any course within a business school curriculum. Doesn't a management course aim to create better managers? Wouldn't we judge as a failure any finance or accounting course that denied a connection between the course material and financial or accounting practice? Every course in a business school assumes a connection between what is taught in the classroom and appropriate business behavior. Classes in management, accounting, finance, and marketing all aim to influence students' behavior. All assume that the knowledge and reasoning skills learned in the classroom will lead to better decision making and therefore better behavior within a business context. A business ethics class is no different.

While few teachers think that it is our role to *tell* students the right answers and *proclaim* what they ought to think and how they ought to live, fewer still think that there should be no connection between knowledge and behavior. Our role should not be to preach ethical dogma to a passive audience, but to treat students as active learners and engage them in an active process of thinking, questioning, and deliberating. Taking Socrates as our model, philosophical ethics rejects the view that passive obedience to authority or the simple acceptance of customary norms is an adequate ethical perspective. Teaching ethics must, in this view, involve students *thinking for themselves.* The decision-making model that will be presented in the next chapter offers one such process of ethical analysis, deliberation, and reasoning.

Business Ethics as Personal Integrity and Social Responsibility

Another aspect of ethical behavior that deserves mention is the fact that social circumstances also have a significant influence over behavior. An individual may have carefully thought through a situation and decided what is right and may be motivated to act accordingly, but the corporate or social context surrounding the individual may create serious barriers to do so. As individuals, we need to recognize that our social environment will greatly influence the range of options that are open to us and can significantly influence our behavior. Otherwise good people can, in the wrong circumstances, do bad things and less ethically motivated individuals can, in the right circumstances, do the right thing. Business leaders therefore have a responsibility for the business environment, what we shall later refer to as the corporate culture, to encourage or discourage ethical behavior. Ethical business leadership is exactly this skill: to create the circumstances in which good people are able to do good, and bad people are prevented from doing bad.

Again, the Enron case provides an example. Sherron Watkins, an Enron vice president, seemed to understand fully the corruption and deception that was occurring within the company, and she took some small steps to address the problems. But when it became clear that her boss might use her concerns against her, she backed off. So, too, with some of the Arthur Andersen auditors involved. When some individuals raised concerns about Enron's accounting practices, their supervisors pointed out that the $100 million annual revenues generated by the Enron account provided good reasons to back off. The Decision Point that follows exemplifies the culture present at Enron during the heat of its downfall.

OBJECTIVE

At its most basic level, ethics is concerned with how we act and how we live our lives. Ethics involves what is perhaps the most monumental question any human being can ask: How *should* we live? Ethics is, in this sense, *practical*, having to do with how we act, choose, behave, do things. Philosophers often emphasize that ethics is normative, in that it deals with our reasoning about how we *should* act. Social sciences such as psychology and sociology also examine human decision making and actions, but these sciences are descriptive, rather than normative. They provide an account of how and why people *do* act the way they do; as a normative discipline, ethics seeks an account of how and why people *should* act, rather than how they *do* act.

Following is a portion of the famous memo that Sherron Watkins, an Enron vice president, sent to CEO Kenneth Lay as the Enron scandal began to unfold. As a result of this memo, Watkins became famous as the Enron "whistleblower."

Has Enron become a risky place to work? For those of us who didn't get rich over the last few years, can we afford to stay? Skilling's [former Enron CEO Jeffrey Skilling] abrupt departure will raise suspicions of accounting improprieties and valuation issues. . . . The spotlight will be on us, the market just can't accept that Skilling is leaving his dream job. . . . It sure looks to the layman on the street that we are hiding losses in a related company and will compensate that company with Enron stock in the future. . . .

I am incredibly nervous that we will implode in a wave of accounting scandals. My eight years of Enron work history will be worth nothing on my résumé, the business world will consider the past successes as nothing but an elaborate accounting hoax. Skilling is resigning now for "personal reasons" but I would think he wasn't having fun, looked down the road and knew this stuff was unfixable and would rather abandon ship now than resign in shame in two years.

Is there a way our accounting gurus can unwind these deals now? I have thought and thought about a way to do this, but I keep bumping into one big problem—we booked the Condor and Raptor deals in 1999 and 2000, we enjoyed wonderfully high stock price, many executives sold stock, we then try and reverse or fix the deals in 2001, and it's a bit like robbing the bank in one year and trying to pay it back two years later. Nice try, but investors were hurt, they bought at $70 and $80 a share looking for $120 a share and now they're at $38 or worse. We are under too much scrutiny and there are probably one or two disgruntled "redeployed" employees who know enough about the "funny" accounting to get us in trouble. . . . I realize that we have had a lot of smart people looking at this and a lot of accountants including AA & Co. [Arthur Andersen] have blessed the accounting treatment. None of that will protect Enron if these transactions are ever disclosed in the bright light of day. (Please review the late 90's problems of Waste Management (news/quote)—where AA paid $130 million plus in litigation re questionable accounting practices.) . . .

I firmly believe that executive management of the company must . . . decide one of two courses of action: 1. The probability of discovery is low enough and the estimated damage too great; therefore we find a way to quietly and quickly reverse, unwind, write down these positions/transactions. 2. The probability of discovery is too great, the estimated damages to the company too great; therefore, we must quantify, develop damage containment plans and disclose. . . . I have heard one manager-level employee from the principal investments group say, "I know it would be devastating to all of us, but I wish we would get caught. We're such a crooked company." These people know and see a lot.

After the collapse of Enron, Watkins was featured on the cover of *Time* magazine and honored as a corporate whistleblower, despite the fact that she never shared these concerns with anyone other than Kenneth Lay. Was Watkins an ethical hero in taking these steps?

- What facts wuld you want to know before making a judgment about Watkins?
- What ethical issues does this situation raise?

(continued)

- Besides Kenneth Lay, who else might have had an interest in hearing from Watkins? Who else might have had a right to be informed? Did Watkins have a responsibility to anyone other than Lay?
- Other than her informing Lay, what other alternatives might have been open to Watkins?
- What might the consequences of each of these alternatives had been?
- From this section of the memo, how would you characterize Watkins' motivation? What factors seem to have motivated her to act?
- If you were Ken Lay and had received the memo, what options for next steps might you have perceived? Why might you have chosen one option over another?
- Do you think Watkins should have taken her concerns beyond Kenneth Lay to outside legal authorities?

How should we live? This fundamental question of ethics can be interpreted in two ways. "We" can mean each one of us individually, or it might mean all of us collectively. In the first sense, this is a question about how I should live my life, how I should act, what I should do, what kind of person I should be. This meaning of ethics is sometimes referred to as morality, and it is the aspect of ethics that we refer to by the phrase "personal integrity." There will be many times within a business setting where an individual will need to step back and ask: What should I do? How should I act?

In the second sense, "How should we live?" refers to how we live together in a community. This is a question about how a society and social institutions such as corporations ought to be structured and about how we ought to live together. This area is sometimes referred to as social ethics and it raises questions of justice, public policy, law, civic virtues, organizational structure, and political philosophy. In this sense, business ethics is concerned with how business institutions ought to be structured, about corporate social responsibility, and about making decisions that will impact many people other than the individual decision maker. This aspect of business ethics asks us to examine business institutions from a social rather than an individual perspective. We refer to this broader social aspect of ethics as decision making for social responsibility.

In essence, managerial decision making will always involve both aspects of ethics. Each decision a business manager makes not only involves a personal decision, but also involves making a decision on behalf of, and in the name of, an organization that exists within a particular social, legal, and political environment. Thus, our book's title makes reference to both aspects of business ethics. Within a business setting, individuals will constantly be asked to make decisions affecting both their own personal integrity and their social responsibilities.

Expressed in terms of how we should live, the major reason to study ethics becomes clear. Whether we explicitly *examine* these questions or not, each and every one of us *answers* them every day in the course of living our lives. Whatever decisions business managers make, they will have taken a stand on ethical issues, at least

Imagine that you are examining this chapter's opening scenario in one of your classes on Organizational Behavior or Managerial Finance. What advice would you offer to Aaron Feuerstein? What judgment would you make about this case from a financial perspective? After offering your analysis and recommendations, reflect on your own thinking and describe what values underlie those recommendations.

- What facts would help you make your decision?
- Does the scenario raise values that are particular to a management class?
- What stakeholders should be involved in your advice?
- What values do you rely on in offering your advice?
- How, if at all, does your advice differ from Feuerstein's decision?

implicitly. The actions each one of us takes and the lives we lead give very practical and unavoidable answers to fundamental ethical questions. Our only real choice is whether we answer them deliberately or unconsciously. Philosophical ethics simply asks us to step back from these unavoidable everyday decisions to examine and evaluate them. Thus, Socrates gave the philosophical answer to why you should study ethics over 2000 years ago: "The unexamined life is not worth living."

To distinguish ethics from other practical decisions faced within business, consider two approaches to the Malden Mills scenario that opened this chapter. This case could just as well be examined in a management, human resources, or organizational behavior class as in an ethics class. The more social-scientific approach common in management or business administration classes would examine the situation and the decision by asking questions such as, What factors led to one decision rather than another? Why did this manager act the way he did?

A second approach to Malden Mills, from the perspective of ethics, steps back from the facts of the situation to raise such questions as, What *should* the manager do? What *rights and responsibilities* are involved? What advice *ought* Feuerstein's tax accountant or human resource manager offer? What *good* will come from this situation? Is Feuerstein being *fair, just, virtuous, kind, loyal, trustworthy*? This normative approach to business is at the center of business ethics. Ethical decision making involves the basic categories, concepts, and language of ethics: *shoulds, oughts, rights and responsibilities, goodness, fairness, justice, virtue, kindness, loyalty, trustworthiness, honesty,* and the like.

To say that ethics is a *normative* discipline is to say that it deals with norms, those standards of appropriate and proper (or "normal") behavior. Norms establish the guidelines or standards for determining what we should do, how we should act, what type of person we should be. Another way of expressing this point is to say that norms appeal to certain values that would be promoted or attained by acting in a certain way. Normative disciplines presuppose some underlying values.

But to say that ethics is a normative discipline is not to say that all normative disciplines involve ethics. After all, isn't business management and business

OBJECTIVE

administration itself normative? Aren't there norms for business managers that presuppose a set of business values? One could add accounting and auditing to this list, as well as economics, finance, politics, and the law. Each of these disciplines appeals to a set of values to establish the norms of appropriate behavior within each field.

These examples suggest that there are many different types of norms and values. In general, we can think of values as those beliefs that incline us to act or to choose one way rather than another. Thus, the value that I place on an education leads me to study rather than play video games. I believe that education is more worthy, or valuable, than playing games. I choose to spend my money on groceries rather than on a vacation because I value food more than relaxation. A company's core values, for example, are those beliefs and principles that provide the ultimate guide in its decision making.

Understood in this way, many different types of values can be recognized: financial, religious, legal, historical, nutritional, political, scientific, and aesthetic. Individuals can have their own personal values and, importantly, institutions also have values. Talk of a corporation's "culture" is a way of saying that a corporation has a set of identifiable values that establish the expectations for what is "normal" within that firm. These norms guide employees, implicitly more often than not, to behave in ways that the firm values and finds worthy. One important implication of this, of course, is that an individual or a corporation can have a set of *unethical* values. The corporate culture at Enron, for example, seems to have been committed to pushing the envelope of legality as far as possible to get away with as much as possible in pursuit of as much money as possible. Values? Yes. Ethical values? No.

One way to distinguish these various types of values is in terms of the ends they serve. Financial values serve monetary ends, religious values serve spiritual ends, aesthetic values serve the end of beauty, legal values serve law, order, and justice, and so forth. Different types of values are distinguished by the various ends served by those acts and choices. So, how are ethical values to be distinguished from these other types of values? What ends does ethics serve?

Values, in general, were earlier described as those beliefs that incline us to act or choose in one way rather than another. Consider again the harms attributed to the ethical failures at Enron. Thousands of innocent people were hurt by the decisions made by some individuals seeking their own financial and egotistical aggrandizement. This example reveals two important elements of ethical values. First, ethical values serve the ends of human well-being. Acts and choices that aim to promote human welfare are acts and choices based on ethical values. Controversy may arise when we try to specify more precisely what is involved in human well-being, but we can start with some general observations. Happiness certainly is a part of it, as is respect, dignity, integrity, and meaning. Freedom and autonomy surely seem a part of human well-being, as do companionship and health.

Second, the well-being promoted by ethical values is not a personal and selfish well-being. After all, the Enron scandal resulted from many individuals seeking to promote their own well-being. Ethics requires that the promotion of human well-being be done impartially. From the perspective of ethics, no one person's welfare is to count as more worthy than any other's. Ethical acts and choices should be acceptable and reasonable from all relevant points of view. Thus, we can offer an initial characterization of ethics and ethical values. Ethical values are those beliefs and principles that impartially promote human well-being.

Ethics and the Law

OBJECTIVE

Any discussion of norms and standards of proper behavior would be incomplete without considering the law. Deciding what one *should do* in business situations often requires reflection on what the law requires, expects, or permits. The law provides a very important guide to ethical decision making, and this text will integrate legal considerations throughout. But legal norms and ethical norms are not identical nor do they always agree. Some ethical requirements, such as treating one's employees with respect, are not legally required though they may be ethically warranted. Conversely, some actions that can be legally allowed, such as firing an employee for no reason, would fail ethical standards.

A common view, perhaps more common prior to the scandals of recent years than after, holds that a business fulfills its social responsibility simply by obeying the law. From this perspective, an ethically responsible business decision is merely one that complies with the law; there is no responsibility to do anything further. Individual businesses may decide to go beyond the legal minimum, as when a business supports the local arts, but such choices are voluntary. A good deal of management literature on corporate social responsibility centers on this approach, contending that ethics requires obedience to the law; anything beyond that is a matter of corporate philanthropy and charity, something praiseworthy and allowed, but not required.

Over the last decade, many corporations have established ethics programs and hired ethics officers who are charged with managing corporate ethics programs. Ethics officers do a great deal of good work, but it is fair to say that much of it focuses on compliance issues. The Sarbanes-Oxley Act created a dramatic and vast new layer of legal compliance issues. But is compliance with the law all that is required for behaving ethically? Though we will address this issue in greater detail in Chapter 5, let us briefly explore at this point several persuasive reasons for thinking that it is not sufficient in order to move forward to our discussion of ethics as perhaps a more effective guidepost for decision making.

First, holding that obedience to the law is sufficient to fulfill one's ethical duties begs the question of whether or not the law itself is ethical. Dramatic examples from history, Nazi Germany and apartheid in South Africa being the most obvious, demonstrate that one's ethical responsibility may run counter to the law. On a more practical level, this question can have significant implications in a global economy in which businesses operate in countries with legal systems different from those of their home country. Some countries make child labor or sexual discrimination legal, but businesses that choose to adopt such practices do not escape ethical responsibility for doing so. From the perspective of ethics, you do not forgo your ethical responsibilities by a blind obedience to the law.

Second, societies that value individual freedom will be reluctant to legally require more than just an ethical minimum. Such liberal societies will seek legally

Reality Check *Ethics: Essential to Governance?*

In 2003, Deloitte polled 5,000 directors of the top 4,000 publicly traded companies and reported that 98 percent believed that an ethics and compliance program was an essential part of corporate governance. Over 80 percent had developed formal codes of ethics beyond those required by Sarbanes-Oxley, and over 90 percent included statements concerning the company's obligations to employees, shareholders, suppliers, customers, and the community at large in their corporate code of ethics. Ethics clearly has gone mainstream. Further, corporate leaders have come to recognize that their responsibilities are much wider than previously thought. In practice, if not yet in theory, corporate America has adopted the stakeholder model of corporate social responsibility. Contemporary business now takes seriously its ethical responsibilities to a variety of stakeholders other than its shareholders.

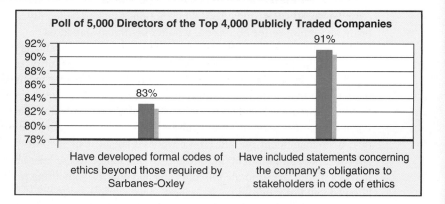

Poll of 5,000 Directors of the Top 4,000 Publicly Traded Companies

Source: "Business Ethics and Compliance in the Sarbanes-Oxley Era," A Survey by Deloitte and *Corporate Board Member Magazine*, July 2003 (www.deloitte.com/dtt/cda/doc/content/ethicsCompliance_f.pdf).

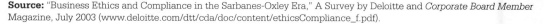

to prohibit the most serious ethical harms, but they will not legally require acts of charity, common decency, and personal integrity that may otherwise comprise the social fabric of a developed culture. The law can be an efficient mechanism to prevent serious harms, but it is not very effective at promoting goods. Even if it were, the cost in human freedom of legally requiring such things as personal integrity would be too high. Imagine a society that legally required parents to love their children, or even a law prohibiting lying.

Third, on a more practical level, telling business that its ethical responsibilities end with obedience to the law is just inviting more and more legal regulation. Consider the difficulty of trying to create laws to cover each and every possible business challenge; the task would require such specificity that the number of regulated areas would become unmanageable. Additionally, it was the failure of personal ethics among such companies as Enron and WorldCom, after all, that led to the creation of the Sarbanes-Oxley Act and many other legal reforms. If business restricts its ethical responsibilities to obedience to the law, it should not be surprised to find a new wave of government regulations that require what were formerly voluntary actions.

Fourth, the law cannot possibly anticipate every new dilemma businesses might face, so often there may not be a regulation for the particular dilemma confronting a business leader. For example, when workplace e-mail was in its infancy, laws regarding who actually owned the e-mail transmissions, the employee or the employer, were not yet in place. As a result, one had no choice but to rely on the ethical decision-making processes of those in power to respect the appropriate boundaries of employee privacy while also adequately managing the workplace (see Chapter 7 for a more complete discussion of the legal implications of workplace monitoring). When new quandaries arise, one must be able to rely on ethics since the law might not yet—or might never—provide a solution.

Finally, the perspective that compliance is enough relies on a misleading understanding of law. To say that all a business needs to do is obey the law suggests that laws are clear-cut, unambiguous rules that can be easily applied. This rule model of law is very common, but not very accurate. If the law was clear and unambiguous, there wouldn't be much of a role for lawyers and courts.

Consider one law that has significant impact of business decision making: the Americans with Disabilities Act. This law requires employers to make reasonable accommodations for employees with disabilities. But what counts as a disability and what counts as a reasonable accommodation? Over the years, claims have been made that relevant disabilities include obesity, depression, dyslexia, arthritis, hearing loss, high blood pressure, facial scars, and the fear of heights. Whether or not such conditions are covered under the law will depend on a number of factors, including how severe the illness is and how it affects the employee's ability to work. Imagine that you are a corporate human resource manager and an employee asks that you make reasonable accommodations for her allergy. How would you decide if allergies and hay fever are disabilities under the Americans with Disabilities Act?

The legal answer is ambiguous. The law offers general rules that get specified in case law. Most of the laws that concern business are based on past cases that establish legal precedents. Each precedent applies general rules to the specific circumstances of an individual case. In most business situations, asking "Is this legal?" is really to ask "Are these circumstances similar enough to past cases that the conclusions reached in those cases will also apply here?" Since there will always be some differences between cases, this will always remain an open question. Thus, there is no unambiguous answer to the conscientious business manager who wishes only to obey the law. One simply cannot find the applicable rule, apply it to the situation, and deduce a decision from it.

It is worth remembering that many of the people involved in the wave of recent corporate scandals were lawyers. In the Enron case, for example, corporate attorneys and accountants were encouraged to "push the envelope" of what was legal. Especially in civil law where much of the law is established by past precedent, there is always room for ambiguity in applying the law. Further, in civil law there is a real sense in which one has not done anything illegal unless and until a court decides that one has. This means that if no one files a lawsuit to challenge an action, it is legal.

As some theories of corporate social responsibility suggest, if a corporate manager is told that she has a responsibility to maximize profits within the law, a competent manager will go to her corporate attorneys and tax accountants to ask what the law allows. A responsible attorney or accountant will advise how far she can reasonably go before she would do something obviously illegal. In this situation, it would seem a manager has a responsibility to "push the envelope" of legality in pursuit of profits.

Most of the cases of corporate scandal mentioned at the start of this chapter involved attorneys and accountants who advised their clients that what they were doing could be defended in court. The off-book partnerships that were at the heart of the collapse of Enron and Arthur Andersen were designed with the advice of attorneys who thought that, if challenged, they had at least a reasonable chance of winning in court. At this point, the decision to "push the envelope" becomes more a matter of risk assessment and cost-benefit analysis than a matter of ethics. On this model, there is a strong incentive to assess the likelihood of being challenged in court, the likelihood of losing the case, the likelihood of settling for financial damages, and a comparison of those costs against the financial benefits of taking the action.

Because the law is ambiguous, because in many cases it simply is not clear what the law requires, business managers will often face decisions that will rely on their ethical judgments. To suggest otherwise is simply to hold a false picture of corporate reality. Thus, the fundamental ethical questions will confront even the businessperson who is committed to obeying the law. What should I do? How should I live?

As suggested previously, whether we step back and explicitly ask these questions or not, each one of us implicitly answers these questions every time we make a decision about how to act. Responsible decision making requires that we do step back to reflect upon and consciously choose the values by which we make decisions. No doubt, this is a daunting task. Fortunately, we are not alone in meeting this challenge. The history of ethics is the history of how some of the most insightful human beings have sought to answer these questions. Before turning to the range of ethical challenges awaiting each of us in the world of business, we will review some of the major traditions in ethics. Chapter 3 provides an introductory survey of several major ethical traditions that have much to offer in business settings.

Ethics as Practical Reason

OBJECTIVE

In a previous section, ethics was described as *practical* and *normative,* having to do with our actions, choices, decisions and *reasoning* about how we should act. In light of this, we will describe ethics as a part of **practical reason,** reasoning about what we should do, and distinguish it from **theoretical reason,** which is reasoning about what we should *believe.* This book's perspective on ethical decision making is squarely within this understanding of ethics as a part of practical reason.

Opening Decision Point Revisited

Loyalty after a Crisis: Should Aaron Feuerstein Rebuild in Malden and Pay His Employees in the Meantime?

Malden Mills has been a favorite case of business ethics courses for many years. On the surface it provides a clear, if extreme, example of a business leader who was willing to make significant financial sacrifices for the well-being of his employees and community. Aaron Feuerstein could have made many other decisions that would have been financially beneficial, although at a great costs to employees and the surrounding towns. To many people, he was a true hero.

Yet, the case eventually became more complex. One important fact is that Malden Mills was privately owned. Had Feuerstein been CEO of a publicly traded corporation, his responsibilities would have been significantly different. Because of this fact, some observers describe Feuerstein's decisions as a simple case of personal generosity, but not a helpful model for other corporate executives. As it was, Malden Mills was unable to recover financially from the losses associated with both the fire and Feuerstein's decisions and eventually entered bankruptcy. Critics claim that this fact demonstrates the real costs of such generosity.

Theoretical reason is the pursuit of truth, which is the highest standard for what we should believe. According to this tradition, science is the great arbiter of truth. Science provides the methods and procedures for determining what is true. Thus, the scientific method can be thought of as the answer to the fundamental questions of theoretical reason: What should we believe? So the question arises, is there a comparable methodology or procedure for deciding what we should do and how we should act?

The simple answer is that there is no single methodology that can in every situation provide one clear and unequivocal answer to that question. But there are guidelines that can provide direction and criteria for decisions that are more or less reasonable and responsible. We suggest that the traditions and theories of philosophical ethics can be thought of in just this way. Over thousands of years of thinking about the fundamental questions of how human beings should live, philosophers have developed and refined a variety of approaches to these ethical questions. These traditions, or what are often referred to as ethical theories, explain and defend various norms, standards, values, and principles that contribute to responsible ethical decision making. Ethical theories are patterns of thinking, or methodologies, to help us decide what to do.

The following chapter will introduce a model for making ethically responsible decisions. This can be considered as a model of practical reasoning in the sense that, if you walk through these steps in making a decision about what to do, you would certainly be making a reasonable decision. In addition, the ethical traditions and theories that we describe in Chapter 3 will help flesh out and elaborate upon this decision procedure. Other approaches are possible, and this approach will not guarantee one single and absolute answer to every decision. But this is a helpful beginning in the development of responsible, reasonable, and ethical decision making.

Questions, Projects, and Exercises

1. Other than ethical values, what values might a business manager use in reaching decisions? Are there classes in your college curriculum, other than ethics, which advise you about proper and correct ways to act and decide?

2. Why might legal rules be insufficient for fulfilling one's ethical responsibilities? Can you think of cases in which a business person has done something legally right, but ethically wrong? What about the opposite—are there situations in which a business person might have acted in a way that was legally wrong but ethically right?

3. What might be some benefits and costs of acting unethically in business? Distinguish between benefits and harms to the individual and benefits and harms to the firm.

4. Review the distinction between personal morality and matters of social ethics. Can you think of cases in which some decisions would be valuable as a matter of social policy, but bad as a matter of personal ethics? Something good as a matter of personal ethics and bad as a matter of social policy?

5. As described in this chapter, the Americans with Disabilities Act requires firms to make reasonable accommodations for employees with disabilities. Consider such conditions as obesity, depression, dyslexia, arthritis, hearing loss, high blood pressure, facial scars, and the fear of heights. Imagine that you are a business manager and an employee comes to you asking that accommodations be made for these conditions. Under what circumstances might these conditions be serious enough impairments to deserve legal protection under the ADA? What factors would you consider in answering this question? After making these decisions, reflect on whether your decision was more a legal or ethical decision.

6. Do an Internet search on Malden Mills and research the present status of the business and Aaron Feuerstein's ownership. How much of a difference would it make if Malden Mills was a publicly traded corporation rather than privately owned? Can any lessons be drawn from the present situation?

7. Construct a list of all the people who were adversely affected by the collapse of Enron. Who, among these people, would you say had their rights violated? What responsibilities, if any, did the managers of Enron have to each of these constituencies?

8. What difference, if any, exists between ethical reasons and reasons of self-interest? If a business performs a socially beneficial act in order to receive good publicity, or if it creates an ethical culture as a business strategy, has the business acted in a less than ethically praiseworthy way?

Key Terms

After reading this chapter, you should have a clear understanding of the following Key Terms. The page numbers refer to the point at which they were discussed in the chapter. For a more complete definition, please see the Glossary.

descriptive ethics, *p. 8*	normative ethics, *p. 8*	social ethics, *p. 10*
ethical values, *p. 12*	norms, *p. 11*	theoretical reasoning,
ethics, *p. 7*	practical reasoning, *p. 16*	*p. 16*
morality, *p. 10*	stakeholders, *p. 5*	values, *p. 12*

Endnotes

1. A persuasive case for why this shift has occurred can be found in *Value Shift* by Lynn Sharp Paine (New York: McGraw-Hill, 2003).

Value Shift

Lynn Sharp Paine

Business has changed dramatically in the past few decades. Advances in technology, increasing globalization, heightened competition, shifting demographics—these have all been documented and written about extensively. Far less notice has been given to another, more subtle, change—one that is just as remarkable as these more visible developments. What I have in mind is the attention being paid to values in many companies today.

When I began doing research and teaching about business ethics in the early 1980s, skepticism about this subject was pervasive. Many people, in business and in academia, saw it as either trivial or altogether irrelevant. Some saw it as a joke. A few were even hostile. The whole enterprise, said critics, was misguided and based on a naïve view of the business world. Indeed, many had learned in their college economics courses that the market is amoral.

Back then, accepted wisdom held that "business ethics" was a contradiction in terms. People joked that an MBA course on this topic would be the shortest course in the curriculum. At that time, bookstores offered up volumes with titles like *The Complete Book of Wall Street Ethics* consisting entirely of blank pages. The most generous view was that business ethics had something to do with corporate philanthropy, a topic that might interest executives *after* their companies became financially successful. But even then, it was only a frill—an indulgence for the wealthy or eccentric.

Today, attitudes are different. Though far from universally embraced—witness the scandals of 2001 and 2002—ethics is increasingly viewed as an important corporate concern. What is our purpose? What do we believe in? What principles should guide our behavior? What do we owe one another and the people we deal with—our employees, our customers, our investors, our communities? Such classic questions of ethics are being taken seriously in many companies around the world, and not just by older executives in large, established firms. Managers of recently privatized firms in transitional economies, and even some far-sighted high-technology entrepreneurs, are also asking these questions.

Ethics, or what has sometimes been called "moral science," has been defined in many ways—"the science of values," "the study of norms," "the science of right conduct," "the science of obligation," "the general inquiry into what is good." In all these guises, the subject matter of ethics has made its way onto management's agenda. In fact, a succession of definitions have come to the forefront as a narrow focus on norms of right and wrong has evolved into a much broader interest in organizational values and culture. Increasingly, we hear that values, far from being irrelevant, are a critical success factor in today's business world.

The growing interest in values has manifested itself in a variety of ways. In recent years, many managers have launched ethics programs, values initiatives, and cultural change programs in their companies. Some have created corporate ethics offices or board-level ethics committees. Some have set up special task forces to address issues such as conflicts of interest, corruption, or electronic data privacy. Others have introduced educational programs to heighten ethical awareness and help employees integrate ethical considerations into their decision processes. Many have devoted time to defining or revising their company's business principles, corporate values, or codes of conduct. Still others have carried out systematic surveys to profile their company's values and chart their evolution over time.

A survey of U.S. employees conducted in late 1999 and early 2000 found that ethics guidelines and training were widespread. About 79 percent of the respondents said their company had a set of written ethics guidelines, and 55 percent said their company offered some type of ethics training, up from 33 percent in 1994. Among those employed by organizations with more than 500 members, the proportion was 68 percent.

Another study—this one of 124 companies in 22 countries—found that corporate boards were becoming more active in setting their companies' ethical standards. More than three-quarters (78 percent) were involved in 1999, compared to 41 percent in 1991 and 21 percent in 1987. Yet another study found that more than 80 percent of the *Forbes* 500 companies that had adopted values statements, codes of conduct, or corporate credos had created or revised these documents in the 1990s.

During this period, membership in the Ethics Officer Association, the professional organization of corporate ethics officers, grew dramatically. At the beginning of 2002, this group had 780 members, up from 12 at its founding 10 years earlier. In 2002, the association's roster included ethics officers from more than half the *Fortune* 100.

More companies have also undertaken efforts to strengthen their reputations or become more responsive to the needs and interests of their various constituencies. The list of initiatives seems endless. Among the most prominent have been initiatives on diversity, quality, customer service, health and safety, the environment, legal compliance, professionalism, corporate culture, stakeholder engagement, reputation management, corporate identity, cross-cultural management, work–family balance, sexual harassment, privacy, spirituality, corporate citizenship, cause-related marketing, supplier conduct, community involvement, and human rights. A few companies have even begun to track and report publicly on their performance in some of these areas. For a sampling of these initiatives, see Figure 1.1.

To aid in these efforts, many companies have turned to consultants and advisors, whose numbers have increased accordingly. A few years ago, *BusinessWeek* reported that ethics consulting had become a billion-dollar business. Though perhaps somewhat exaggerated, the estimate covered only a few segments of the industry, mainly misconduct prevention and investigation, and did not include corporate culture and values consulting or consulting focused in areas such as diversity, the environment, or reputation management. Nor did it include the public relations and crisis management consultants who are increasingly called on to help companies handle values-revealing crises and controversies such as product recalls, scandals, labor disputes, and environmental disasters. Thirty or 40 years ago, such consultants were a rare breed, and many of these consulting areas did not exist at all. Today, dozens of firms—perhaps hundreds, if we count law firms and the numerous consultants specializing in specific issue areas—offer companies expertise in handling these matters. Guidance from nonprofits is also widely available.

What's Going On?

A thoughtful observer might well ask "What's going on?" Why the upsurge of interest in ethics and values? Why have companies become more attentive to their stakeholders and more concerned about the norms that guide their own behavior? In the course of my teaching, research, and consulting over the past two decades, I have interacted with executives

Figure 1.1 **Values in Transition**

CORPORATE INITIATIVES—A SAMPLER	
COMPREHENSIVE (APPLYING TO ALL ACTIVITIES AND FUNCTIONS)	*Internally Oriented:* Ethics programs Compliance programs Mission and values initiatives Business principles initiatives Business practices initiatives Culture-building initiatives Cross-cultural management programs Crisis prevention and readiness *Externally Oriented:* Reputation management programs Corporate identity initiatives Corporate brand-building initiatives Stakeholder engagement activities Societal alignment initiatives Nonfinancial-performance reporting initiatives
FOCUSED (APPLYING TO PARTICULAR ISSUES OR CONSTITUENCIES)	*Employee Oriented:* Diversity initiatives Sexual harassment programs Work–family initiatives Workplace environment initiatives *Customer Oriented:* Product and service quality initiatives Customer service initiatives Product safety initiatives Cause-related marketing *Supplier Oriented:* Supplier conduct initiatives *Investor Oriented:* Corporate governance initiatives *Community Oriented:* Environmental initiatives Corporate citizenship initiatives Community involvement initiatives Strategic philanthropy *Issue Oriented:* Electronic privacy Human rights initiatives Anticorruption programes Biotechnology issues

and managers from many parts of the world. In discussing these questions with them, I have learned that their motivating concerns are varied:

An Argentine executive sees ethics as integral to transforming his company into a "world-class organization."

A group of Thai executives wants to protect their company's reputation for integrity and social responsibility from erosion in the face of intensified competition.

A U.S. executive believes that high ethical standards are correlated with better financial performance.

An Indian software company executive sees his company's ethical stance as important for building customer trust and also for attracting and retaining the best employees and software professionals.

A Chinese executive believes that establishing the right value system and serving society are key components in building a global brand.

The executives of a U.S. company see their efforts as essential to building a decentralized organization and entrepreneurial culture around the world.

Two Nigerian entrepreneurs want their company to become a "role model" for Nigerian society.

A Swiss executive believes the market will increasingly demand "social compatibility."

An Italian executive wants to make sure his company stays clear of the scandals that have embroiled others.

A U.S. executive believes that a focus on ethics and values is necessary to allow his company to decentralize responsibility while pursuing aggressive financial goals.

A U.S. executive answers succinctly and pragmatically, "*60 Minutes.*"

These responses suggest that the turn to values is not a simple phenomenon. Individual executives have their own particular reasons for tackling this difficult and sprawling subject. Even within a single company, the reasons often differ and tend to change over time. A company may launch an ethics initiative in the aftermath of a scandal for purposes of damage control or as part of a legal settlement. Later on, when the initiative is no longer necessary for these reasons, a new rationale may emerge.

This was the pattern at defense contractor Martin Marietta (now Lockheed Martin), which in the mid-1980s became one of the first U.S. companies to establish what would later come to be called an "ethics program." At the time, the entire defense industry was facing harsh criticism for practices collectively referred to as "fraud, waste, and abuse," and Congress was considering new legislation to curb these excesses. The immediate catalyst for Martin Marietta's program, however, was the threat of being barred from government contracting because of improper billing practices in one of its subsidiaries.

According to Tom Young, the company president in 1992, the ethics program began as damage control. "When we went into this program," he explained, "we didn't anticipate the changes it would bring about. . . . Back then, people would have said, 'Do you really need an ethics program to be ethical?' Ethics was something personal, and you either had it or you didn't. Now that's all changed. People recognize the value." By 1992, the ethics effort was no longer legally required, but the program was continued nonetheless. However, by then it had ceased to be a damage control measure and was justified in terms of its business benefits: problem avoidance, cost containment, improved constituency relationships, enhanced work life, and increased competitiveness.

A similar evolution in thinking is reported by Chumpol NaLamlieng, CEO of Thailand's Siam Cement Group. Although Siam Cement's emphasis on ethics originated in a business philosophy rather than as a program of damage control, Chumpol recalls the feeling he had as an MBA student—that "ethics was something to avoid lawsuits and trouble with the public, not something you considered a way of business and self-conduct." Today, he says, "We understand corporate culture and environment and see that good ethics leads to a better company."

Siam Cement, one of the first Thai companies to publish a code of conduct, put its core values into writing in 1987 so they "would be more than just words in the air," as one executive explains. In 1994, shortly after the company was named Asia's "most ethical" in a survey conducted by *Asian Business* magazine, Chumpol called for a thorough review of the published code. The newly appointed CEO wanted to make sure that the document remained an accurate statement of the company's philosophy and also to better understand whether the espoused values were a help or hindrance in the more competitive environment of the 1990s. In 1995, the company reissued the code in a more elaborate form but with its core principles intact. The review had revealed that while adhering to the code did in some cases put the company at a competitive disadvantage, it was on balance a plus. For example, it helped attract strong partners and employees and also positioned the company, whose largest shareholder was the Thai monarchy's investment arm, as a leader in the country.

A very different evolution in thinking is reported by Azim Premji, chairman of Wipro Ltd., one of India's leading exporters of software services and, at the height of the software boom in 2000, the country's largest company in terms of market capitalization. Wipro's reputation for high ethical standards reflects a legacy that began with Premji's father, M.H. Hasham Premji, who founded the company in 1945 to make vegetable oil. The elder Premji's value system was based on little more than personal conviction—his sense of the right way to do things. Certainly it did not come from a careful calculation of business costs and benefits. In fact, his son noted, "It made no commercial sense at the time."

When his father died in 1966, Azim Premji left Stanford University where he was an undergraduate to assume responsibility for the then-family-owned enterprise. As he sought to expand into new lines of business, Premji found himself repeatedly having to explain why the company was so insistent on honesty when it was patently contrary to financial interest. Over time, however, he began to realize that the core values emphasized by his father actually made for good business policy. They imposed a useful discipline on the company's activities while also helping it attract quality employees, minimize transaction costs, and build a good reputation in the marketplace. In 1998, as part of an effort to position Wipro as a leading supplier of software services to global corporations, the company undertook an intensive self-examination and market research exercise. The result was a reaffirmation and rearticulation of the core values and an effort to link them more closely with the company's identity in the marketplace.

Managers' reasons for turning to values often reflect their company's stage of development. Executives of large, well-established companies typically talk about *protecting* their company's reputation or its brand, whereas entrepreneurs are understandably more likely to talk about *building* a reputation or *establishing* a brand. For skeptics who wonder whether a struggling start-up can afford to worry about values, Scott Cook, the founder of software maker Intuit, has a compelling answer. In his view, seeding a company's culture with the right values is "the most powerful thing you can do." "Ultimately," says Cook, "[the culture] will become more important to the success or failure of your company than you are. The culture you establish will guide and teach all your people in all their decisions."

In addition to company size and developmental stage, societal factors have also played a role in some managers' turn to values. For example, executives in the United States are more likely than those who operate principally in emerging markets to cite reasons related to the law or the media. This is not surprising, considering the strength of these two institutions in American society and their relative weakness in many emerging-markets countries. Since many ethical standards are upheld and reinforced through the legal system, the linkage between ethics and law is a natural one for U.S. executives. In other cases, executives offer reasons that mirror high-profile issues facing their industries or countries at a given time—issues such as labor shortages, demographic change, corruption, environmental problems, and unemployment. Antonio Mosquera, for example, launched a values initiative at Merck Sharp & Dohme Argentina as part of a general improvement program he set in motion after being named managing director in 1995. Mosquera emphasized, however, that promoting corporate ethics was a particular priority for him because corruption was a significant issue in the broader society.

Despite the many ways executives explain their interest in values, we can see in their comments several recurring themes. Seen broadly, their rationales tend to cluster into four main areas:

Reasons relating to *risk management*

Reasons relating to *organizational functioning*

Reasons relating to *market positioning*

Reasons relating to *civic positioning*

A fifth theme, somewhat less salient but nevertheless quite important for reasons we will come back to later, has to do with the idea simply of "a better way." For some, the rationale lies not in some further benefit or consequence they are seeking to bring about but rather in the inherent worth of the behavior they are trying to encourage. In other words, the value of the behavior resides principally in the behavior itself. For these executives, it is just *better*—full stop—for companies to be honest, trustworthy, innovative, fair, responsible, or good citizens. No further explanation is necessary any more than further explanation is required to justify the pursuit of self-interest or why more money is better than less.

Source: From *Value Shift*, by Lynn Sharp Paine, Copyright © 2004, The McGraw-Hill Companies. Reproduced by permission of the publisher.

Reading **1-2**

An Ethical Hero or a Failed Businessman?
The Malden Mills Case Revisited
Penelope Washbourne

Introduction

At the annual meeting of the Society for Business Ethics in Boston in 1997 the guest speaker was Aaron Feuerstein, the acclaimed CEO of Malden Mills, who brought tears to the eyes of skeptical academics with his tales of the mill fire in 1995 and his generous actions towards his employees. I had written a case about him during the winter of 1996 and suggested him as a guest speaker for the annual meeting. After the meeting, I was given a guided tour of the gleaming rebuilt factory in Lawrence, Mass., and was duly impressed by the state of the art manufacturing technology used to make that cozy fleece, Polartec, which is made from recycled plastic. Aaron Feuerstein's star continued to shine in the business press, and even in 2004, as a hero who paid his employees for a number of months after the fire destroyed their jobs.

As many noted then and now, here was a true man of virtue, an ethical giant in a business world of massive layoffs such as those at AT&T and Sunbeam, and when compared with colossal failures in leadership in many huge corporations.

I taught this case over the years, with video clips from the national media, in my business ethics courses and was subsequently told by students that the case had made a powerful impression on them. Maybe it was the pictures of those desperately anxious mill workers with their tears and gratitude responding to Feuerstein's announcement after the fire that he was going to continue to pay his workers for another month. "You're a saint" said one. Or maybe it was Feuerstein's own tears that affected my students?

The case touched a deep nerve: here was a business man who put the care of his workers above the bottom line. My goal in writing and teaching about this case was to demonstrate that it is better to teach business ethics with examples of ethical leadership than to continue to focus on, as most of our case books do, the multiple failures in moral leadership in corporate life. Even formerly exemplary companies can fall under an ethical cloud.

Subsequently, though I read that Malden Mills had gone bankrupt, since the tenth year anniversary of the fire was in 2005, I decided to take another look at what the effect had been on the local community of Aaron Feuerstein's actions after the fire. My reading of the events that have taken place since the fire raises an important dilemma for teaching this tale of ethical virtue. What has been the aftermath? It would be nice to say that the gleaming new mill saved the jobs in the community and that Aaron Feuerstein is still in charge of his grandfather's firm, well loved by his workers and local politicians for preserving the one remaining industry in an area of high unemployment.

It would be nice to say that not only is virtue its own reward, but also that it is indeed rewarded by the world. For Aaron Feuerstein and his family firm, unfortunately this is not the case. The actual story is more complex than that, as is often the case in real life.

To describe it briefly: Aaron borrowed money to rebuild the mill, beyond the money he would finally receive from the insurance company. He built a large facility, counting on the expansion of his Polartec fleece lines and the continuation of his brand of upholstery fabrics. His debt was more than his final insurance settlement, the upholstery business proved a failure and he decided to get out of it, cheap competition and an unseasonably warm winter cut into his Polartec sales and he had to declare bankruptcy in 2001. The firm remained under bankruptcy protection until 2003, but Aaron lost control of the company and GE Capital, the main creditor with 16.6 percent, became its largest shareholder, with a dominant influence on the new board. In July 2004 the board hired a new executive. A new manufacturing operation has been opened in China. Jobs in Lawrence and nearby New Hampshire have declined. In the meantime, Aaron and his son Daniel with a group of investors and a commitment to keep jobs in the local communities, attempted to buy back the firm. Their offers were rejected.

How indeed will I teach this case now? Were Aaron's actions after the fire virtuous or reckless? Did his hope for the future and his commitment to the local community blind him to the economic realities of the industry at the time and cause him to overbuild, and so put the whole company in jeopardy? From a utilitarian perspective, did he do the right thing? What was the long-term effect of his actions on the community?

I decided that I had to get close to the source and elected to spend a few days in Lawrence, Massachusetts, and I was able to interview Aaron Feuerstein in his home in Boston. When I interviewed Aaron in November 2004, he said he felt he had failed.

Lawrence, Massachusetts

In fall 2004, the main impression of Lawrence as a community to a visitor unfamiliar with depressed mill towns in New England was decay. The massive empty mill buildings along the Merrimack River have forlorn signs for "Space Available," as if the next high-tech boom was going to transform this now virtual ghost town into a thriving business community.

Along the main street with its closed businesses, even the Goodwill center was shuttered. The one remaining open facility was a large Headstart center with its brightly colored plastic play structures. The impression was that this must be a city that is heavily funded with federal grant monies for low income families.

Though large trash receptacles ready for collection lined the narrow residential streets the day I was there, they did not contain the abandoned sofas and junk in the empty lots. The local community newspaper, printed in Spanish and English, spoke of the challenge of trash as a neighborhood problem. The mayor wanted to put awnings over the shops in the main streets, to attract business downtown. Among the nail salons and the few ethnic food establishments, one set of buildings, and one alone, remained a viable concern, Malden Mills Inc. Located next to the Arlington section of town, one of the poorest neighborhoods, the mill is the only sizable employer in Lawrence, Massachusetts.

Five hundred of its employees live in a five mile radius of the mill and many walk to work. It would be fair to say that the economic well-being of Lawrence and its nearby community in New Hamphire, depressed as they are, is intimately connected to the well-being of the one remaining manufacturing facility paying union wages at an average rate in 2004 of $12.50 an hour, with benefits. The unemployment rate in Lawrence has remained at two and a half to three times the state average for the last 20 years , between 10 and 15 percent since 1983. The academic standings of the local schools are the lowest in the state.

My trip to Lawrence answered my question: Why did Aaron Feuerstein feel and still feel today such a fierce loyalty and sense of obligation to the community of Lawrence and its neighboring towns? What did it mean to those communities that he decided to rebuild the mill and committed to pay his employees for several months after the fire? As he told me, the tears of the workers after the fire were not tears of gratitude towards him, but recognition that without the mill there was nothing left for them, their future, or their community.

The 72,000 People of Lawrence and Their History

This city calls itself the "city of immigrants." It claims that 45 different nationalities and ethnicities have lived in Lawrence. It was founded as a mill town in 1842 to establish woolen and cotton mills and to exploit the new technology of water power along the swift-flowing rivers. The large labor pool required for the factories was imported, and consisted largely of women and immigrants, who lived in dormitories and boarding houses. At its peak, between 1890 and 1915, there were 90,000 residents in Lawrence.

Lawrence was the site of the famous "Bread and Roses" strike in 1912 when after nine weeks of a strike for better conditions during a harsh winter, the company bosses brought the state militia out to attempt to force the 30,000 strikers into submission and prevent them from shipping their children out to relatives and sympathetic families in other communities.

Thus, over the years, Lawrence became known for being in the forefront of the struggle for workers' rights and for the right to organize unions. Now earlier generations of Scots and Irish and Eastern European immigrants have been been replaced by Puerto Ricans and first-generation immigrants from Central America. Their mill jobs allow them the ability to function in their native languages, a rare option in high-paying employment where knowledge of English is often a necessity.

Though most of Lawrence's jobs have disappeared as the mills finally closed after World War II, Aaron Feuerstein's commitment to continuing his operation in this immigrant, unionized town is unique. It stems from a recognition of the value of his own family's history and his grandfather's legacy. As a Hungarian Jewish immigrant in New York City at the turn of the century, his grandfather sold dry goods and eventually moved to Massachusetts and began the family firm in 1907. Aaron remembers his roots and the history of earlier generations of immigrant labor who formed the economic engine that brought succeeding generations to a better way of life. His antipathy to shipping jobs South and to offshoring manufacturing jobs at the expense of domestic workers comes from a profound respect for the skills of those who worked hard to build a future for their families in this country.

Though Aaron had indeed laid off workers due to business conditions, nevertheless he believes we owe these workers in this community an opportunity to perform on the job, for themselves and the community. This is a relationship of mutual respect and obligation that has been carried through three generations of Feuersteins towards their union workers and their communities in Massachusetts and New Hampshire. Aaron spoke proudly of never having had a strike over the years and of having tough but fair negotiations with the unions during his tenure in the company.

Knowing of Aaron's commitment to keep jobs in the local community, the union leadership had hoped that the Feuersteins would be successful in their efforts to regain control of the company. Since the advent of the new company management, the union threatened a strike last fall in November 2004, but finally settled on a new contract.

Aaron had resurrected himself once before when he went bankrupt in the 1980s. His technological innovations captured a new market in fleece material which he branded under the name of Polartec for garments for outdoor enthusiasts. His workers had come through for him in that difficult time. Once again he believed he could resurrect his company from the ashes. Could he do it again?

Aaron's sense of failure, at this point in his life (he was 80 in 2005), paternalistic though it may sound, may have to do with failing to live up to the legacy of the family firm that had been handed to him, failing the very community he had pledged to support with good jobs, and failing to protect them from the cost-cutting strategies in which wages are just an expense.

The Business Strategy and Hope for Lawrence

When fleece was invented it filled a wonderful need in the market for garments that did not become wet with moisture and perspiration, as cotton did, but were wickable, allowing the person to stay warm. Aaron's strategy was to pursue research and development and create high-end, high-quality products that could be recognized as a brand: "Polartec." Since its first invention the number of different weights, colors, and features has exploded, with windproof features and even designs for children's outerwear. Aaron believed that Malden Mills could stay ahead of increasing competition of offshore manufacturers and the "commodification" of the industry by staying ahead of the innovation curve. Fleece was soon everywhere, not just in high-quality jackets for climbers and winter sports enthusiasts, but in regular articles of clothing for adults and children, as well as blankets and throws.

After the fire, even though one of his main customers, Lands' End, initially showed support and featured the story of the mill's fire and Aaron's actions towards his employees in its spring 1996 catalogue, Aaron eventually lost major customers, including Lands' End, which sought other suppliers. Along with the interruption in supply, apparently the Polartec brand did not have the power in the general market, except in specialized high-end products, to withstand the flood of cheaper goods coming from Asia.

After the fire another of his product lines, jacquard upholstery velvet, proved to be unsuccessful in earning a brand identity. Furniture manufacturers were unwilling to pay the premium for a branded fabric and in 1998, Aaron got out of that business. It represented about 50 percent of the company's business at the time of the fire, and its production lines were hard hit by the fire and took longer to resume operation than the polarfleece lines.

One business strategy implemented after the fire by one of the company's former executives, Cesar Aguilar, who spent an uncomfortable weekend in wet clothing as part of his military reserve training, is beginning to pay off for the company and for the community, however. Malden Mills is supplying warm winter clothing to the troops in Afghanistan and Iraq as well as conducting research into new lightweight electronic high-tech fabrics that soldiers can wear next to their skin and that can monitor their vital signs and be of assistance in determining injuries. Another innovation is a next-to-skin fabric that would prevent the growth of bacteria and odor for soldiers who are out in the field. The U.S. military approved $21 million for Polartec garments for 2005, a portion of which goes to the garment manufacturer. That figure includes $1.5 million for research.

The military contracts offer a ray of hope for the company. Not only must all products made for the U.S. Armed Services be made in the United States, but the innovations in new products designed for military use can be developed into commercial applications in the future. In addition, according to a company spokesman the military business is not seasonal, which makes it easier to balance the workload. The military contract currently represents about 20 percent of Malden Mills' business.

What Went Wrong?

After a traumatic event such as the fire, one's decision making capacity is impaired. I know this from personal experience, having escaped from the Oakland Hills fire in 1991 where almost 3,000 homes were destroyed and 24 people ultimately died. I think my interest in this case certainly was influenced by having had this common experience. After a fire, "post-traumatic distress" is an important factor. Aaron even witnessed his factory burning down. In the aftermath of the fire, the shock and sense of loss are enormous, and yet major decisions that have a long-term impact must be made immediately. Relations with family and friends are strained. In Aaron's case, he had a huge sense of responsibility for the injured workers, several of whom were badly burned, though luckily none died, and for those who risked their lives to save parts of the buildings that were not so heavily engulfed. In addition, the fire happened just before Christmas. Though some members of his board, which included members of his own family who worked in the company, opposed it, Feuerstein generously offered to pay his idled workers for the following month, even though he was not required to do so. He said he did not do it for the publicity, but because he was firmly convinced it was the right thing to do. But in hindsight, was it the right thing to do?

Feuerstein renewed his pledge to his 1,500 employees for another three months. As the news spread of his actions he received about $1 million in donations, from small to large checks from all around the country. By the end of a month some of his operations were up and running again as they shifted equipment undamaged by the fire to other locations. Some of the manufacturing facilities for Polartec had been spared.

Was Feuerstein's generosity to his employees a costly decision that ultimately put his company in jeopardy? It cost about $15 million. One view is that by itself it may not have been a foolhardy decision, given the growing business he was in. Sales of Polartec had been growing by 50 percent anually at the time of the fire. Aaron also knew that if his business was going to have a chance to rebuild, he was going to have to rely heavily on his workers to put in an extraordinary effort to get him up and running again.

After three months the remaining workers who were still out of work were supported by unemployment and special funds from the gifts that had been donated.

The outpouring of support, both financial and in the public arena, surprised Feuerstein. He was a private man, an owner of a small family firm, little known outside of New England,

and now all of a sudden he was in front of the cameras, making statements about the state of American business. He was invited to sit behind Hillary Clinton at President Clinton's State of the Union Address in January 1996. The names of Malden Mills and Aaron Feuerstein were in all the press and created a flood of goodwill for the company.

He was lauded not only for paying his workers after the fire, but for his immediate commitment to rebuild the factory in the same location. As he said so frequently in interviews after the fire, he and his father had not moved the operation to the South as many other mills did in search of cheaper labor in the 1950s and 1960s, so why would he abandon Lawrence now? He continues to believe that highly skilled labor can produce the best quality products, which in turn can differentiate a company from its competition, and that there is still a place for manufacturing in this country. This commitment earned him enormous political support from the local politicians, the governor, Senators Kennedy and Kerry, and New Hampshire representatives.

The Decision to Rebuild

At issue seems to be not the fact of rebuilding in Lawrence , but the manner in which Aaron Feuerstein proceeded on this project.

Aaron knew that he was "fully insured." What he did not know, what no claimant after a loss knows, is what the actual payout amount will be. He would not know that for many months of negotiations with the insurer. At the point of a claim, the relationship with the insurer turns from one of being, as it were, "in good hands" to one that is adversarial in nature.

The insurer tries to keep the settlement as low as possible and the claimant wants to replace the buildings that burned. The insurer AGI was a tough negotiator, settling well after the newly rebuilt factory had been completed in 1997. The final insurance settlement was about $300 million, covering only 75 percent of the $400 million in rebuilding costs that Feuerstein had borrowed to put his factory in operation.

Was Aaron's decision to rebuild in the immediate aftermath of the fire one of an emotion-driven "survival instinct"? The firm's famous clock tower had been saved during the fire. How could Aaron not see that as a symbol of the firm's commitment to rise from the ashes? Was the idea of renting or renovating facilities, or scaling down the size, never seriously considered? Was the promise of all that cash that would allow him to replace aging equipment with brand new machines, to build a new state of the art facility to deal with the overbearing heat in summer and accommodate the new computerized methodologies, a license to spend more than he should?

Even within the context of rebuilding it was clear that Aaron thought big and wanted the best. There was dispute among the members of the board and with his own son about the scale of the rebuilding. The insurance coverage did not specify that the buildings had to be rebuilt at all or require a minimal square footage, but Aaron opted for the best. He replaced almost all of the space that had been lost, anticipating that his Polartec sales would continue to grow, even though his son was advising him to scale back the square footage. He later admitted that maybe his building plans had been overly extravagant, even to the point of buying new equipment, whereas before the fire he would have bought used. While the mill was being rebuilt, he had leased space for some of his operations in neighboring towns, but now it was he who was to have excess space as the business turned down.

What was Aaron's failure? Did he fail to anticipate the great gap between his rebuilding costs and his final insurance settlement? Did he fail to anticipate that in spite of great attention and support on one level from all the media, months of interruption of his supply would enable his competitors to gain an edge and win customers? Was his attention so focused on recovery from the fire and its aftermath, the insurance claims, and the lawsuits against the company from injured employees, that he failed to see the business risks? Was he imprudent or unlucky that a warm winter depressed fleece sales just at the time his upholstery line was floundering? Was Aaron Feuerstein trying to singlehandedly buck the inexorable pressure on the costs of manufacturing and prices that eventually led the new board after the bankruptcy to a partnership with a mill in China? In 2004 this outsourced production was at about 10 percent of production, but that figure is likely to rise due to the expiration of the textile tariffs with China in January 2005.

The Legacy

Under the special arrangements of the bankruptcy settlement, Aaron and his sons had an opportunity to bid on the firm for another year, but their bids were rejected by the current owners. His group of financial investors, along with the Import-Export Bank, which had guaranteed a loan, had plans to develop the excess mill space into mixed income housing units and retain jobs in the local area. Though Aaron at 79 had surgery on his heart in July 2004, his determination to regain control over the company remained undimmed. He feared it would become another commodity company and the original vision of investing in innovative products that require a highly skilled workforce would be lost. He did not want to run the mill as CEO, but he wanted to resurrect the legacy of the family firm, committed to the goal of continuing to provide high-quality, well-paying jobs to the people of Massachusetts and New Hampshire.

If it were dependent solely on the force of his personality, it would have happened. Aaron is an obstinate man. The local politicians were supporting him, hoping that he could be given the chance to preserve the jobs in the local area.

Since Aaron failed to regain control of the family firm, has he failed? He believes that he has. But as a former journalist at the *Boston Globe* assures him, "You have won, Aaron, no matter what happens!" His ethical legacy is independent of whether or not his family regains control of Malden Mills.

Though his enterprise may have failed, he rebuilt the mill in Lawrence and gave the community hope that there is a future for their families. The new owners currently repeat their commitment to the community, though they state that more jobs will probably be offshored in the future.

What Aaron did was indeed an example of virtue ethics since it was in his character to be concerned for his employees. Examples of his prior support for them, such as giving assistance to help buy a house or send a child to college, were recounted by workers after the fire. However, what Aaron did in paying his workers after the fire was more a demonstration of Carol Gilligan's "Ethic of Care," shaped by the importance of preserving relationships. When faced with the decision of what he could do for his workers he asked himself the question, not what was his duty to do, but what was the most loving thing to do?

This act has called American business leaders to consider again the employment relationship between an enterprise and its workers, not as being exclusively an economic one, but also a personal and communal one. Aaron Feuerstein's acts, which put his workers' needs above his own economic self-interest, were grounded in his religious convictions as an orthodox Jew. He believes he has a responsibility to them as individuals and to the common good. He had the unique chance to show that rather than pursuing the course of the moral minimum, he chose the moral maximum. As he said to me, "*At the end of the day, at the Final Judgment, will it be enough to say, 'I have been the CEO of a company and made a lot of money?' After your basic needs are met, what is the point of all that activity, if not to do some good? … on Judgment Day what do you amount to?*"

In the retail outlet at Malden Mills among the colorful bolts of cloth and remnants are two images that caught my attention. One was a portrait of Aaron Feuerstein made out of different colored cotton spools, a diffuse image made by an employee.

The other was a wall hanging embroidered by children at a synagogue school as a gift in thanks to Aaron for his support of them. What is his legacy? He is clearly loved.

Aaron is a unique businessman: He lives modestly and his heavily thumbed Bible sits on his table beside his two volumes of Shakespeare's comedies and tragedies.

He reads them frequently.

Is this a tragic tale? Maybe, but for Shakespeare's best tragic heroes, their defeat at the hands of fate is not the end. The truth of their life lives on.

Source: Copyright © Penelope Washbourne. Used by permission of the author.

Reading **1-3**

Do You Need an Ethics Officer?

Jon Entine

"We Have Seen the Enemy and He May Be Us"

Frank Daly has steered an unusual career path. A devout Catholic, the Boston native went to seminary before going to Rome to study at the Gregorian University. He became a priest and for eight years served as an assistant pastor. For a time, he was a university chaplain. He dedicated his life to living in God's reflection.

So how did Frank Daly end up as a corporate director at Northrop Grumman, the southern California–based defense contractor? Daly is an "ethics officer," one of a new generation of corporate managers who believe that "business ethics" need not be an oxymoron.

An ethics officer? After all, isn't business war? Or as professor Theodore Levitt once wrote in the *Harvard Business Review*, "Business must fight as if it were at war. And, like a good war, it should be fought gallantly, daringly, and above all not morally."

Times have changed. The renewed focus on corporate ethics has come about as a response to the public outcry and avalanche of lawsuits that accompanied the business scandals of the anything-goes go-go '80s: Dennis Levine, Ivan Boesky, Charles Keating, Michael Milken, international bribery. The movement to hire ethical officers gathered steam with the extension of the Federal Sentencing Guidelines to executives in 1991—they now face the prospect of jail time as a result of wrongdoing by subordinates.

Companies have learned that ethical programs can avoid expensive litigation and keep skeletons off the front page of *The Wall Street Journal*—which pays off handsomely in company loyalty and burnishes a corporation's reputation. That goes right to the bottom line.

In response to embarrassing disclosures such as toilet seats and hammers costing hundreds of dollars, and with the design in part to ward off more government oversight, military contractors launched an initiative in the '80s to bolster legal and ethical compliance. The southern California region is peppered with defense-related companies that have full-time ethics officers: Northrop Grumman, which has a plant in Oxnard; Whittaker in Simin Valley; Lockheed Martin, whose companywide ethics office is in Westlake Village; and Litton in Woodland Hills. The former head of the defense industry initiative was recently hired by Columbia HCA, which runs Las Robles Hospital, to clean up its scandal-tinged operation. Other area companies with ethics officers include Southern California Edison, Avery Dennison, and Earthlink.

"The goal of an ethics officer, my goal, is not only to insure that that we are operating in legal compliance but that we bring a strong, personal sense of values to our everyday experience in the workplace," says Daly. "Corporations are publicly owned, after all. They no longer act—they no longer should act—as if they have no accountability. I think we're making some real progress."

To many, this rings of public relations fluffery. But Daly is anything but a spin artist. After leaving the priesthood, he went to work in Massachusetts politics, first in the Dukakis administration and then as an aid to Paul Tsongas. The ethics initiatives at Northrop caught Daly's attention. He signed on as division manager of communications and public relations and was promoted to director of ethics and business conduct. Shortly thereafter, a crisis rocked the company, prompting an agonizing appraisal of its corporate culture.

Back in 1987, Northrop's Pomona, California, operation was making flight data transmitters for cruise missiles and sensors to stabilize the AV-8B Harrier Jump Jet. Northrop's tests indicated that the parts functioned perfectly. But in the real world, both parts failed miserably. Operating on an anonymous tip, the FBI raided the plant, eventually charging 11 individuals and Northrop itself with 189 counts of fraud and conspiracy.

What had gone wrong?

It turns out that Pomona engineers had long recognized that the equipment used to test the missile components occasionally malfunctioned. When this happened, they substituted a printout from a prior successful test. As for the Harrier Jump Jet, the chief engineer would later confess that they had falsified vibration-level tests. Pomona managers said they felt pressure to find a way to pass the units even without adequate testing equipment. They had convinced themselves that their futures and millions of company dollars were on the line.

Ironically, and unfortunately for them, they were right. The Pomona plant was subsequently shuttered, most of the managers fired, and in 1989, Northrop paid a $17 million fine.

President Kent Kresa was apoplectic. "This isn't the case of a few rotten apples," he fumed. It was a corrupted corporate culture. "I think we have to blame our own process," he said. "It could be a problem in the future if we don't stamp it out." Northrop employees at division headquarters in suburban Boston joined in the outrage at the betrayal in Pomona.

"We found errors principally of management," Air Force investigators agreed. "Not so much of employees not being concerned about ethical conduct but the failure of the management system to open these up, bring them to light."

Part crisis manager, part corporate theologian, Daly was called upon to do nothing less than to address employee doubts about the internal ethics of the company and institute constructive, long-term solutions. He wasn't looking for legal Band-Aids but to overhaul the corporate culture and introduce higher standards of accountability. The challenge tapped into Daly's lifelong passion for personal responsibility.

"We aren't in the business of teaching people how to be ethical," said Daly. "We're teaching ethical people how to make a good decision when it could be difficult."

It's easy for people to say they would not cut corners when presented with the choice faced by the engineers in Pomona. But as with most real-life dilemmas, the pressures can be overwhelming to those in the ethical crucible. They feared for their jobs and had convinced themselves that no one would be the wiser for their short-cuts. In fact, they had no place to turn—there were no clear companywide ethical standards, no ethical hotline, and no ombudsmen to take their concerns to.

Daly helped draw up a code of ethics that was both inspirational and practical—not just bromides about "doing the right thing." With the backing of Kresa, who navigated the crisis and was later named CEO of the merged Northrop Grumman, Daly oversaw the "Northrop

Leadership Inventory," which attempts to evaluate the linkage of behavior, values, and leadership conflict resolution. To help employees make tough ethical calls, the company distributes guidelines that it calls "When to Challenge" and "When to Support." Employees also can call an ethics hotline, which is both confidential and responsive. Some 30 percent of the calls allege actual wrongdoing, about half of which check out. "Mostly, the hotline offers an outlet for employees to diffuse potential crises before they lead to unethical or unlawful behavior," Daly says.

At many corporations, crisis management, ethics, and brand management are now closely intertwined. Twenty years ago, says Daly, many businesses did not believe they had a duty beyond the minimum dictates of the law. "That just doesn't work today," he says. "A small number of wayward employees can sink an organization. We've learned that the hard way at Northrop Grumman. For companies to survive, they have to learn to be pro-active in the gray areas of business. That's where the tough decisions are made. That's when ethics pays off."

Source: Copyright © Jon Entine. Used by permission of the author.

Chapter  2

Ethical Decision Making: Personal and Professional Contexts

This above all: to thine own self be true, and it must follow, as the night the day, Thou canst not then be false to any man.

Shakespeare

To be nothing but yourself, in a world which is doing its best to make you everybody else, means to fight the hardest battle which any human being can fight, and never stop fighting.

e.e. cummings

From here that looks like a bucket of water, but from an ant's point of view, it's a vast ocean; from an elephant's point of view, it's just a cool drink; and to a fish, of course, it's home.

Norton Juster, The Phantom Toll Booth

I am not afraid of storms, for I am learning to build my ship.

Louisa May Alcott

Imagine that you are the first person to arrive for your business ethics class. As you sit down at your desk, you notice an iPod on the floor underneath the adjacent seat. You pick it up and turn it on. It works just fine, and it even has some of your favorite music listed. Looking around, you realize that you are still the only person in the room and that no one will know if you keep it.

Not being able to decide immediately, and seeing that other students are beginning to enter the room, you place the iPod down on the floor next to your own backpack and books. As the class begins, you realize that you have the full class period to decide what to do.

What would you think about as you sat there trying to decide what to do?

What would you do?

Now let us change the scenario. Instead of being the person who finds the iPod, imagine that you are a friend who sits next to that person. As class begins, your friend leans over, tells you what happened, and asks for advice.

The lesson for today's business ethics class is Chapter 2 of your textbook, *Business Ethics: Decision Making for Personal Integrity and Social Justice.*

Finally, imagine that you are a student representative on the judicial board of your school. This student decides to keep the iPod and is later accused of stealing. How would you make your decision?

- What are the key facts that you should consider before making a decision, as either the person who discovered the iPod, the friend, or the judicial board member?
- Is this an ethical issue? What exactly are the ethical aspects involved in your decision?
- Who else is involved, or should be involved, in this decision? Who has a stake in the outcome?
- What alternatives are available to you? What are the consequences of each alternative?
- How would each of your alternatives affect the other people you have identified as having a stake in the outcome?
- Where might you look for additional guidance to assist you in resolving this particular dilemma?

 ## Chapter Objectives

After reading this chapter, you will be able to:

1. Describe a process for ethically responsible decision making
2. Apply this model to ethical decision points.
3. Explain the reasons why "good" people might engage in unethical behavior.
4. Explore the impact of managerial roles on the nature of our decision making.

Introduction

Chapter 1 introduced our approach to business ethics as a form of practical reasoning, a process for decision making in business. Putting ethics into practice requires not simply decision making, but *accountable* decision making. Chapter 1 also suggested that, even if a person does not consciously think about a decision, her or his own actions will involve making a choice and taking a stand. If you find a lost iPod, you cannot avoid making an ethical decision. Whatever you do with the iPod, you will have made a choice that will be evaluated in ethical terms.

The previous chapter provided a general context for thinking about business ethics; in the current chapter, we begin to bring this topic to a more practical level by examining ethical decision making as it occurs in everyday life and within business contexts. We will examine various elements involved in individual decision making and apply those concepts to the decisions individuals make every day in business. This chapter also examines various ways in which ethical decision making can go wrong, as well as the ways in which effective business leaders can model the very best ethical decision making.

A Decision-Making Process for Ethics

Let us consider an initial sketch of an **ethical decision-making process.** How would you decide what to do in the iPod case? First, you might wonder how the iPod ended up under the desk. Was it lost? Perhaps someone intentionally discarded the iPod. Wouldn't that fact make a big difference in the ethical judgment you would make? Or, suppose the person who discovered the iPod actually saw it fall from another student's backpack. Would that make a difference in your judgment about that person?

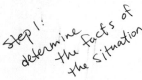 *Step 1: determine the facts of the situation*

OBJECTIVE

Perhaps the first step in making decisions that are ethically responsible is to *determine the facts* of the situation. Making an honest effort to understand the situation, to distinguish facts from mere opinion, is essential. **Perceptual differences** in how individuals experience and understand situations can explain many ethical disagreements. Knowing the facts and carefully reviewing the circumstances can go a long way to resolving disagreements at an early stage. For example, disagreements about Aaron Feuerstein's responsibilities might depend on the facts of local unemployment rates. One person might think that his decision does not pose a significant ethical question because the employees involved can always get other jobs. Someone else might hold the opposite view precisely because high unemployment rates will mean that few employees will, in fact, be able to find other jobs.

Let us turn to the iPod case. What facts would be useful to know before making a decision? Suppose you already owned an iPod. Would that make a difference? Suppose you knew who sat at the desk in the previous class. Imagine that, in fact, the iPod had been in a place not easily seen and you had observed it there over the course of several days. Suppose the iPod did not work and, instead of being discovered underneath a seat, you found it in a wastebasket. How would your decision change as any of these facts changed? Can you imagine a situation in which what looks like an ethical disagreement turns out to be a disagreement over the facts?

Given the general importance of determining the facts, there is a role for science (and theoretical reason) in any study of ethics. An ethical judgment made in light of a diligent determination of the facts is a more reasonable ethical judgment that one made without regard for the facts. A person who acts in a way that is based upon a careful consideration of the facts has acted in a more ethically responsible way than a person who acts without deliberation. The sciences, and perhaps especially the social sciences, can help us determine the facts surrounding our decisions. For a business example, consider what facts might be relevant for making a decision regarding child labor. Consider how the social sciences of anthropology and economics, for example, might help us understand the facts surrounding employing children in the workplace within a foreign country.

A second step in responsible ethical decision making requires the ability to recognize a decision or issue as an ethical decision or ethical issue. It is easy to be led astray by a failure to recognize that there is an ethical component to some decision. *Identifying the ethical issues involved* is the next step in making responsible decisions.

In the iPod case, imagine that the student claims he simply discovered a lost item and kept it. He denies that this is even an ethical issue at all because, after all, he didn't steal the iPod. What is the difference between stealing and finding a lost item? Similarly, in many business situations, what appears to be an ethical issue for one person will be judged as a simple financial decision by others. How does one determine that a question raises an ethical issue at all? When does a business decision become an ethical decision?

First, of course, we need to recognize that "business" or "economic" decisions and ethical decisions are not mutually exclusive. Just because a decision is made on economic grounds does not mean that it does not involve ethical considerations as well. Being sensitive to ethical issues is an important characteristic that needs to be cultivated in ethically responsible people. Beyond sensitivity, we also need to ask how our decisions will impact the well-being of the people involved. Chapter 1 described ethical values as concerned with the impartial promotion of human well-being. To the degree that a decision affects the well-being—the happiness, health, dignity, integrity, freedom, respect—of the people involved, it is a decision with ethical implications.

In business contexts, it can be easy to become so involved in the financial aspects of decisions that one loses sight of the ethical aspects. Some writers have called this inability to recognize ethical issues **normative myopia,** or short-sightedness about values.[1] Normative myopia does not occur only in business. See the Reality Check that follows.

The third step involved in ethical decision making involves one of its more vital elements. We are asked to *identify and consider all of the people affected by a decision, the people often called "stakeholders."* "Stakeholders" in this general

Identifying the issues involved

Identify & consider Stakeholders

Reality Check *Is There an Ethics of Writing Papers?*

Perhaps the most common ethical issue that students and teachers deal with involves plagiarism. From the academic perspective, there is no more serious offense than plagiarizing the work of others. Yet, many students seem honestly surprised to learn that what they believed was research is interpreted as unethical behavior by their teachers.

Many students rely on Internet sources in writing their school papers. It is very easy to "cut and paste" sections of an online source into one's own writing assignment. No doubt, some of this is intentional cheating, such as when a student downloads or purchases an entire paper from an Internet source. But, in many cases, students seem honestly perplexed

that their teacher treats an unattributed "cut and paste" passage as cheating. Few teachers have not experienced situations in which they have had to explain to a student why this practice is unethical.

Such cases are not rare. People often make bad ethical decisions because they fail to understand that there is an ethical issue involved. Typically they have not thought through the implications of their decision and have not stepped back from their situation to reflect on their choice and consider their decision from other points of view. Often they are simply too involved in the immediate situation to think about such things. We can think of such condition as "normative myopia."

sense include all of the groups and/or individuals affected by a decision, policy, or operation of a firm or individual. Considering issues from a variety of perspectives other than one's own, and other than what local conventions suggest, helps make one's decisions more reasonable and responsible. To the contrary, thinking and reasoning from a narrow and personal point of view virtually guarantees that we will not understand the situation fully. Making decisions from a narrow and personal point of view likewise guarantees that we are likely to make a decision that does not give due consideration to other persons and perspectives.

One helpful exercise for considering the affects of a decision on others is to shift one's role. Rather than being in the position of the person who discovers the iPod, what would you think of this case if you were the person who lost it? How does that impact your thinking? What would your judgment be if you were the friend who was asked for advice? A long tradition in philosophical ethics argues that a key test of ethical legitimacy is whether or not a decision would be acceptable from the point of view of all parts involved. If you could accept a decision as legitimate no matter whose point of view you take, that decision would be fair, impartial, and ethical. If you acknowledge that you would not accept the legitimacy of keeping the iPod were you the person who lost it rather than the person who found it, then that is a strong indication that the decision to keep it is not a fair or ethical one.

Consider Aaron Feuerstein's decisions on the night of his factory fire, as described in Chapter 1. In his position, some people might think first of how the fire would affect their own personal well-being. The financial status of the owner and his family was seriously threatened by the fire, but a decision that considered only the owner's point of view would not be a responsible decision. The fire also had a great impact on the lives of employees, thousands of whom were about to lose their only source of income. In addition, the fire would have serious consequences for the wider community, a community already harmed by business relocations and vulnerable to any further economic downturn. Customers were also vulnerable to harms caused by the loss of the exclusive supplier of an important product. In the case of every stakeholder, the harms were undeserved. That is, no one had done anything wrong, no one was at fault, yet all stood to suffer serious harms. The following Reality Check explores later implications.

The fact that many decisions will involve the interests of multiple stakeholders also helps us to understand a major challenge to ethical decision making. The very fact that there are many perspectives and interests at stake means that ethical decisions often involve dilemmas. Each alternative will impose costs on some stakeholders and offer benefits to others. Deciding on a way that benefits one group often means that other stakeholders are denied benefits.

Once we have examined the facts, identified the ethical issues involved, and identified the stakeholders, we need to *consider the available alternatives*. Creativity in identifying options – also called "moral imagination" – is one element that distinguishes good people who make ethically responsible decisions from good people who do not.[2] It is important not only to consider the obvious options with regard to a particular dilemma, but also the much more subtle ones that might not be evident at first blush. When reviewing the Malden Mills circumstances, ask yourself how many people would have even thought about paying employees while the factory was being rebuilt. Aaron Feuerstein utilized moral imagination in doing so.

Or consider the less dramatic case of discovering a lost iPod. One person might decide to keep it because she judges that the chances of discovering the true owner are slim and that if she doesn't keep it, the next person to discover it will. Another person is able to think of some alternatives. For example, she could return early for the next class to see who is sitting at the desk, or she could find out who teaches the previous class and ask that teacher for help in identifying the owner. Moral imagination might be something as simple as checking in a lost and found department. How would the school community be changed if students went out of their way to return lost items rather than keeping them for their own use?

The next step in the decision-making process is to *compare and weigh the alternatives*—create a mental spreadsheet that evaluates the impact of each alternative you have devised on each stakeholder you identified. Perhaps the most helpful way to accomplish this is to try to place oneself in the other person's position. Understanding a situation from another's point of view, making an effort to "walk a mile in their shoes," contributes significantly to responsible ethical decision making. Weighing the alternatives will involve predicting the likely, the foreseeable, and the possible consequences to all the relevant stakeholders. A critical element of this evaluation will be the consideration of ways to mitigate, minimize, or compensate for any possible harmful consequences or to increase and promote beneficial consequences.

Ethicists sometimes ask the decision maker to consider whether he would feel proud or ashamed if *The Wall Street Journal* (or whatever is your relevant

Reality Check *With Friends Like These . . .*

Is Aaron Feuerstein a model for every business leader? Unfortunately, the Malden Mills case did not have a completely happy ending. Initially, all went well. Malden Mills was able to rebuild its factory and reopen sections within a year. Employees came back to work and the community seemed to recover. But Malden Mills couldn't recover fully. Insurance covered only three-fourths of the $400 million cost of rebuilding and by 2001 Malden Mills filed for bankruptcy protection. During the summer of 2004, Malden Mills emerged from bankruptcy but its board of directors was now controlled by its creditors, led by GE Commercial Finance Division.

The new board replaced Aaron Feuerstein as CEO and board chairman, although he retained the right to buy back the controlling interest if he could raise sufficient financing. In October of 2004, the board rejected Feuerstein's offer to buy back the company. In response to the company's contract offer that included cuts in health care benefits, the union representing the remaining 1,000 workers at Malden Mills voted to authorize a strike in December 2004, the first in company history. Are strong ethical values and ethically praiseworthy decisions good for business? The only reasonable answer might be that sometimes they are and sometimes they are not.

daily newspaper) printed this decision as a front page article, or whether he could explain it to a 10-year-old child so the child thinks it is the right decision, or whether it will stand the test of time. Note that in the iPod case, the student was described as looking around to see if anyone else noticed his discovery. Would your behavior change if other people knew about it? The point of this exercise is to recognize that a fully responsible decision should be explainable and justifiable to the entire range of people involved. Typically, it is the irresponsible decisions that we wish to keep hidden.

But consequences or justifications are not the only means for comparing alternatives. Some alternatives might concern matters of principles, rights, or duties that override consequences. Aaron Feuerstein believed that the long-term loyalty of his employees created a special duty not to abandon them in times of crisis. Within business settings, individuals will often have specific duties associated with their position. A purchasing manager for a large retail store has a duty associated with her role that directs her to avoid conflicts of interest in dealing with suppliers. Are duties associated with company rules, professional codes of conduct, business roles, or legal duties involved? Perhaps guidance is available in specific circumstances from these sources or others.

One additional factor in comparing and weighing alternatives requires consideration of the effects of a decision on one's own integrity and character. Understanding one's own character and values should play a role in decision making. By all accounts, Aaron Feuerstein was a deeply religious and moral man who, in many ways, could not have acted differently than he did. A responsible person will ask: "What type of person would make this decision? What kind of habits would I be developing by deciding in one way rather than another? What type of corporate culture am I creating and encouraging? How would I, or my family, describe a

FIGURE 2.1
An Ethical Decision-Making Process

Determine the facts

- Identify the ethical issues involved
- Identify stakeholders and consider the situation from their point of view
- Consider the available alternatives – also called "moral imagination"
- Consider how a decision affects stakeholders, comparing and weighing the alternatives, based on:
  - Consequences
  - Duties, rights, principles
  - Implications for personal integrity and character
- Make a decision
- Monitor outcomes

person who decides in this way? Is this a decision that I am willing to defend in public?" Such questions truly go to the heart of ethical business leadership. An honest person might not even think about retaining the iPod; keeping it for oneself is simply not an option for such a person.

Once you have explored the above variables, it is time to *make a decision.* However, the process is not yet complete. To be accountable in our decision making, it is not sufficient to deliberate over this process, only to later throw up our hands once the decision is made: "It's out of my hands now!" Instead, we have the ability as humans to learn from our experiences. That ability creates a responsibility to then evaluate the implications of our decisions, to *monitor and learn from the outcomes*, and to modify our actions accordingly when faced with similar challenges in the future. The following Decision Point gives us a chance to put this decision-making process into practice.

OBJECTIVE

The ethical traditions and theories that we describe in the next chapter will help us flesh out and elaborate upon this decision procedure. Other approaches to ethically responsible decision making are possible, and this approach will not guarantee one single and absolute answer to every decision. But it is a helpful beginning in the development of responsible and ethical decision making.

When Ethical Decision Making Goes Wrong: Why Do "Good" People Engage in "Bad" Acts?

To say that each individual has the capability to follow a similar decision-making process or possesses the capacity to make autonomous decisions is not to say that every individual always does so. There are many ways in which responsible decision making can go wrong and many ways in which people fail to act in accordance with the ethical judgments they make. Sometimes, of course, people can simply choose to do something unethical. We should not underestimate the real possibility of immoral choices and unethical behavior.

Let's give it a try: Should Richard Grasso give back any of the $139.5 million he received in his final year as chairman of the New York Stock Exchange?

Consider how one might begin to use this model to deliberate about an ethical issue in business. Richard Grasso is the former chairman of the New York Stock Exchange. During his last year as chairman, he received total compensation of $140 million and was slated to receive approximately another $48 million in retirement benefits. This compensation package was determined by the employment contract he had signed with the NYSE board of directors. Mr. Grasso resigned in the face of public criticism of this pay package and, at least initially, agreed to forgo the final $48 million. What is your judgment about this situation?

What facts might be relevant? Presumably you would want to know what work he had done to earn this salary. What were his responsibilities? You might also want to know who decided that he should receive so much money and under what circumstances this decision was made.

As it turned out, the board of directors for the NYSE approved the compensation package, but some of those responsible for setting his pay, including the director of the NYSE human resources department who made the pay recommendation to the board's compensation committee, were friends of Grasso. He had appointed them to their positions and he played a role is determining their own pay. The facts also are that the NYSE is a nonprofit organization, which functions to regulate publicly traded companies. The companies being regulated by the NYSE ultimately were the very same companies that were paying Grasso.

What ethical issues does this case raise? At first glance, concerns over conflicts of interest, deception, fraud, misallocation of funds, and theft, as well as such personal ethical questions as greed and arrogance, come to mind.

If one thinks that the only people involved in this case are the NYSE board as the employer, and Mr. Grasso as employee, one might be tempted to conclude that this was a private business matter between an employer and an employee. But the stakeholders involved here include not only members of the board and other employees, but quite literally every company whose securities are traded on the NYSE and every investor who relies on the integrity of the NYSE to oversee and regulate the sale of securities. Because so much of the stock exchange's work must depend on investor confidence and trust in the system and because this case worked to undermine that confidence and trust, many other people have something at stake in its outcome.

The available options will depend on who the decision maker is. Ultimately, the New York State Attorney General sued both the NYSE and Richard Grasso to recover some of the money paid as salary. As an individual investor, one might not have much of an option in responding to this event. But as citizens, we have other options.

But at other times, well-intentioned people fail to choose ethically. What factors determine which companies or individuals engage in ethical behavior and which do not? Why do people we consider to be "good" do "bad" things? This does not mean that these unethical decisions or acts are excusable but that the individuals who engage in the unethical behavior may have done so for a variety of reasons. As it turns out, there are many stumbling blocks to responsible decision making and behavior.

OBJECTIVE

Some stumbling blocks to responsible action are cognitive or intellectual. As the model of ethical decision making outlined above suggests, a certain type of ignorance can account for bad ethical choices. Sometimes that ignorance can be almost willful and intentional. After you discover a lost iPod, you might rationalize to yourself that no one will ever know, that no one is really going to be hurt, that an owner who is so careless deserves to lose the iPod. You might try to justify the decision by telling yourself that you are only doing what anyone else would do in this circumstance. You might even choose not to think about it and try to put any guilty feelings out of your mind.

Another cognitive barrier is that we sometimes only consider limited alternatives. When faced with a situation that suggests two clear alternative resolutions, we often consider only those two clear paths, missing the fact that other alternatives might be possible. Upon discovering a lost iPod, you might conclude that if you don't take it, someone else will. Because the original owner will lose out in both cases, it is better that you benefit from the loss than someone else. Responsible decision making would require that we discipline ourselves to explore additional methods of resolution.

We also generally feel most comfortable with simplified decision rules. Having a simple rule to follow can be reassuring to many decision makers. For example, assume you are a business manager who needs to terminate a worker in order to cut costs. Of course, your first thought may be to uncover alternative means by which to cut costs instead of firing someone, but assume for the moment that cutting the workforce is the only viable possibility. It may be easiest and most comfortable to terminate the last person you hired, explaining, "I can't help it; it must be done, last in/first out, I have no choice…." Or, in the iPod case, "finders keepers, losers weepers" might be an attractive rule to follow. Using a simple decision rule might appear to relieve us of accountability for the decision, even if it may not be the best possible decision.

We also often select the alternative that satisfies minimum decision criteria, otherwise known as "satisficing." We select the option that suffices, the one that people can live with, even if it might not be the best. Imagine a committee at work that needs to make a decision. They spend hours arriving at a result and finally reach agreement. At that point it is unlikely that someone will stand up and say, "Whoa, wait a minute, let's spend another couple of hours and figure out a *better* answer!" The very fact that a decision was reached by consensus can convince everyone involved that is must be the most reasonable decision.

Other stumbling blocks are less intellectual or cognitive than they are a question of motivation and willpower. As author John Grisham explained in his book *Rainmaker*, "Every (lawyer), at least once in every case, feels himself crossing a line he doesn't really mean to cross. It just happens." Sometimes it is simply easier to do the wrong thing. After all, who wants to go through all the trouble of finding the lost and found office and walking across campus to return the iPod? Consider how you would answer the questions asked in the following Reality Check.

Reality Check *The Ethics of Cheating*

In a 1991 study, researchers determined that business undergraduate students are the most likely to have cheated on a test, when compared with prelaw students and the general population.[3] In response to a statement claiming that *not* cheating is the best way to get ahead in the long run, business students claimed, "This is the Nineties. You snooze, you lose."[4] Does this mean that, perhaps, there is a failure in ethics in the business arena because the people who go into business already cheat? Or is it that business students are aware that the business arena demands this type of unethical conduct so they prepare themselves for it from the start? Competitiveness might blur the border between ethical and unethical. Either way, as our parents have told us, simply because an environment is replete with a certain type of behavior does not mean that we must follow suit, nor does it relieve us of our responsibility for actions in that environment (thus the common parental question, "If Janie jumps off a bridge, are you going to follow?").

Unfortunately, we do not always draw the lines for appropriate behavior in advance, and even when we do, they are not always crystal clear. As Grisham suggests, it is often easy to do a little thing that crosses the line, and the next time it is easier, and the next easier still. One day, you find yourself much further over your ethical line than you thought you would ever be.

People also sometimes make decisions they later regret because they lack the courage to do otherwise. It is not always easy to make the right decision; you might lose income, your job, or other valuable components of your life. Sherron Watkins was only one of many Enron employees who explained their reluctance to push their concerns by reference to the culture of intimidation and fear that characterized upper management at Enron.

Of course, the usual suspects for explaining unethical conduct are still very much apparent in the scandals that make the front pages every day. The enormous amounts of corporate executive compensation, lack of oversight of corporate executive decisions, significant distance between decision makers and those they impact, financial challenges, and a set of ethical values that has not yet caught up to technological advances – all of these factors can create an environment rife with ethical challenges and unethical decisions. We can benefit from unethical acts, from gaining something as simple as an iPod, to something as significant as a salary package of $180 million. Temptation is often all around us and any person can succumb to it. The questions that are most difficult to answer are often those that are most important to answer in defining who we are. Give it a try in the following Decision Point.

Making ethically responsible decisions throughout one's life is perhaps the most serious challenge we all face. The easiest thing to do would be to remain passive and simply conform to social and cultural expectations, to "go with the flow." But such passivity is exactly the sort of unexamined life that Socrates claimed was not worth living. To live a meaningful human life, we must step back and reflect on our decisions, assuming the responsibility of autonomous beings.

Before leaving this discussion it is worth reflecting on those people who do not succumb to temptations and who may not even deliberate in the face of an

All around us there is a breakdown of values ... It is not just the overpowering greed that pervades our business life. It is the fact that we are not willing to sacrifice for the ethics and values we profess. For an ethics is not an ethics and a value is not a value without some sacrifice to it. Something given up, something not taken. Something not gained.

Jerome Kohlberg, Jr., addressing investors at his retirement from his private equity firm, Kohlberg, Kravis, Roberts & Co. (May 18, 1987)

What values are most important to you? What are you willing to sacrifice to maintain your own values? What is important? What are your priorities?

Questions to Ask Yourself:

Are there any values that you would quit a job over?
What would you be willing to die for?
What do you stand for, personally and professionally?

Is it not important to consider the answers to these questions *before* you are actually faced with a decision?

ethical dilemma. In the following chapter, we will describe an ethical tradition that emphasizes ethical character and virtues. For many people, finding a lost iPod would not raise much of a dilemma at all. Many people would not have to deliberate about what to do or go through a decision-making process before acting. Many people have developed a certain type of character, a set of ethical habits, that will incline them, without deliberation, to act ethically. For every Richard Grasso, there are many business executives who could, but do not, take exorbitant salaries, scheme to manipulate stock options, and otherwise seek to enrich themselves. Developing such habits, inclinations, and character is an important aspect of living an ethical life.

Ethical Decision Making in Managerial Roles

At several points already in this text we have acknowledged that individual decision making can be greatly influenced by the social context in which it occurs. Social circumstances can make it easier or more difficult to act in accordance with one's own judgment. Within business, an organization's context sometimes makes it difficult for even the best-intentioned person to act ethically, or it can make it difficult for a dishonest person to act unethically. Responsibility for the circumstances that can encourage ethical behavior and discourage unethical behavior falls to the business management and executive team. Chapter 4 will examine this issue in more detail as we introduce the concepts of corporate culture and ethical leadership, but it will be helpful to introduce this topic here.

Applying our decision-making model to the iPod case, we would first try to determine the facts. Knowing that the iPod functioned perfectly would be good evidence for concluding that it was left behind accidentally rather than intentionally discarded. Knowing the actual cost of the iPod would also be evidence that it is something likely to be highly valued and not something easily discarded. The cost, as well as your own understanding of private property, makes it clear that this situation raises ethical issues of rights, happiness, personal integrity, and honesty.

Most obviously, this would seem to involve two major stakeholders: the true owner and yourself. But upon reflection, you can understand that whatever decision you make will have broader implications. People will talk about the stolen iPod or the iPod that had been returned, and this can encourage or diminish a campus culture of trust and honesty.

Imagining yourself in the position of the student who lost the iPod or of the student who might sit in judgment at a campus judicial hearing can provide a perspective easily missed if you think only of yourself. Imagining the results of keeping the iPod and then having that fact discovered and publicized is another helpful step. How would you try to justify that decision to others? Considering the number of hours someone might have to work at an on-campus job in order to earn enough money to buy another iPod introduces another important perspective. Finally, a concern with personal integrity would encourage you to reflect on the type of person who keeps another's property and to ask yourself if this is who you really are and want to be.

Given all these steps, it would be difficult to imagine that one could justify a decision to keep the iPod.

The decision-making model introduced in this chapter develops from the point of view of an individual who finds herself in a particular situation. Personal integrity lies at the heart of such individual decision making: What kind of person am I? What are my values? What do I stand for? But every individual also fills a variety of social roles, and these roles carry with them a range of expectations, responsibilities, and duties. Within a business setting, individuals must consider the ethical implications of both personal and professional decision making. Some of our roles are social: friend, son or daughter, spouse, citizen, neighbor. Some are institutional: manager, teacher, student body president. Among the major roles and responsibilities that we will examine in this text are those associated with specific professions: attorneys, accountants, auditors, financial analysts, and the like. Decision making in these contexts raises broader questions of social responsibilities and social justice.

OBJECTIVE

Consider how different roles might impact your judgment about the discovery of the iPod. Your judgment about the iPod might differ greatly if you knew that your friend had lost it, or if you were a teacher in the class, or if you were a member of the campus judicial board. Our judgment about Richard Grasso might change when we learn that his professional responsibility included oversight of a regulatory body that governed the very companies that were paying his salary.

In a business context, individuals fill roles of employees, managers, senior executives, and board members. Managers, executives, and board members have the ability to create and shape the organizational context in which all employees make decisions. They therefore have a responsibility to promote organizational arrangements that encourage ethical behavior and discourage unethical behavior.

The following three chapters develop these topics. Chapter 3 will provide an overview of how some major ethical traditions might offer guidance both to individual decision-makers and to those who create and shape social organizations. Chapter 4 will examine topics of corporate culture, ethical organizations, and ethical leadership. Chapter 5 examines corporate social responsibility, the ends towards which ethical organizations and ethical leaders should aim.

Questions, Projects, and Exercises

1. Consider your own personal values and explain where they originated. Can you pinpoint their derivation? To what degree have you chosen your own values? To what degree are your own values products of your family, your religious or cultural background, or your age? Does it matter where values originate?

2. Identify an activity that is outside of your "zone of comfort"; in other words, do something that you might not otherwise do, experience something that you might not otherwise experience. Before engaging in this activity, consider what your expectations are (i.e., how do you think you will feel, what do you think it will be like?). Then, subsequent to the experience, write a description of the experience and whether the reality matched your expectations, considering in particular your original perceptions and expectations and whether they were accurate.

3. What issue, challenge, or idea do you care about most in the world? Share it in a brief essay, then convince your reader why it is so important that she or he should also care about that issue to the same extent. It may be effective to use the theories discussed in prior chapters to persuade your reader of the value of your argument.

4. Your CEO recognizes you as having extraordinary skills in decision making and communications, so she asks for guidance on how to best communicate her plans for an imminent reduction in force. What are some of the key strategies you will suggest she employ in reaching such a decision and making the announcement?

5. Describe the qualities you believe are necessary in an "ethical leader." Provide support for your contentions and explain why a leader should evidence these qualities in order to be considered "ethical" from your perspective. Then identify someone you believe embodies these qualities in her or his leadership and provide examples. Finally, provide an example of someone who you believe does not possess these qualities and describe that person's leadership.

6. How can your global firm best ensure that it is taking into account the perceptual differences that may exist as a result of diverse cultures, religions, ethnicities, and other factors when creating a worldwide marketing plan?

7. Describe an event or decision that you would judge to be clearly unethical. Can you imagine any circumstances in which it would be ethical? Can you imagine a situation in which you yourself would do something unethical?

8. As a class exercise, write a brief account of any unethical or ethically questionable experience you have witnessed in a work context. Read and discuss the examples in class, keeping the authors anonymous. Consider how the organization allowed or encouraged such behavior and what might have been done to prevent it.

Key Terms

After reading this chapter, you should have a clear understanding of the following Key Terms. The page numbers refer to the point at which they were discussed in the chapter. For a more complete definition, please see the Glossary.

ethical decision-making process, *p. 37*

moral imagination, *p. 40*

normative myopia, *p. 38*

perceptual differences, *p. 37*

personal and professional decision making, *p. 47*

Endnotes

1. The concept of normative myopia as applied to business executives can be found in Diane Swanson, "Toward an Integrative Theory of Business and Society," *Academy of Management Review,* vol. 24, no. 3 (July 1999) pp. 506–521.

2. For a far more in-depth analysis of moral imagination, please see Patricia H. Werhane, *Moral Imagination and Management Decision Making* (New York: Oxford University Press, 1999).

3. Rick Tetzeli, "Business Students Cheat Most," *Fortune*, July 1, 1991, p. 14. See also James Stearns and Shaheen Borna, "A Comparison of the Ethics of Convicted Felons and Graduate Business Students: Implications for Business Practice and Business Ethics Education," *Teaching Business Ethics* 2 (1998), pp. 175–195. This research found that MBA students were more likely to cheat than convicted felons.

4. Stearns and Borna, "A Comparison of the Ethics of Convicted Felons and Graduate Business Student," p. 18.

Readings

Reading **2-1**

Abandoning the "Just School" Myth

Tara Radin

Have you ever cheated on a test? Perhaps you just glanced over your shoulder and happened to notice a classmate's answer on a question that was giving you trouble. Have you ever seen someone else cheat? During an exam, have you ever looked around and noticed other students paying unusually close attention to their cell phones or PDAs? Advances in technology have created new opportunities for cheaters and are making it increasingly difficult for professors to proctor their exams.

The Internet has also introduced new challenges regarding paper assignments. Students can purchases papers online on almost any subject. Of course, technology also makes it easier to catch cheaters. Turnitin, for example, is an Internet-based subscription service that helps to identify attempts at plagiarism by comparing submissions to multiple databases including its own repository of tens of millions of previously submitted student papers; millions of commercial pages from books, newspapers, and journals; and publicly available Internet information.

What Is It?

Cheating occurs when a person obtains an unfair advantage. Plagiarism is one type of cheating. It occurs when a person attempts to pass off someone else's work as his or her own by using someone else's words or ideas without citing the source. More than 75 percent of college students admit to having cheated in school, and this number appears to be increasing.

This is a real problem and it is about much more than grades on quizzes and tests. If we, as a society, condone this sort of behavior in schools, explicitly or implicitly, by not putting an end to it, it makes it all the more difficult for us to maintain vibrant, trusting communities as adults. How did Enron happen? What about WorldCom or Tyco? It is ironic that we ask those questions as if the answers are mysteries. Some people throw stones at the business schools—"They are not teaching business ethics appropriately!"

Why Do I Care?

The problem, though, is much deeper: students cannot be taught ethics if they are not willing to learn—and this willingness to learn has to be rooted deeper than in the requirements for a program of study. In order for undergraduate or graduate business ethics teaching to be successful, students have to begin with their own sets of values. Values are not learned in the classroom like math and science; values are acquired over time. Children develop their sense of "right" and "wrong" according to what they learn at home from their parents, what their religion teaches, and what they see day-to-day in the world around them.

Numerous studies emphasize the importance of families regularly eating dinner together. These studies show that children perform better in school and are better adjusted overall as teens and adults when they come from families that have eaten together regularly. If you stop to think about it, this makes sense. The dinner table is not just about the meal, but also about conversation. Regular dinners ensure that children have face time with their parents and siblings, and accompanying this are innumerable opportunities for children to hear about and see values in action, which they often acquire by osmosis.

What Are Others Doing?

Schools, particularly high schools, can help to reinforce in students the values they learn at home. In fact, a number of high schools, colleges, and universities have honor codes that do just this.

The University of Virginia (UVa) has a model honor code, which has been in existence for more than 150 years. In fact, it is the country's oldest student-run system. The premise of UVa's Honor System is that the university represents people who choose to live together in a community of trust. One of the conditions for living in that community is "honor." UVa does not claim to teach honor; rather, it is assumed that community members are honorable—or, at least, agree to live as honorable people—in order to preserve trust. If a new member wants to join the community, he or she is required to agree to abide by the honor code. Before entering UVa, students must pledge not to lie, cheat, or steal at UVa, in Charlottesville or Albemarle County, or anywhere where he or she represents him- or herself as a UVa student. Thus the honor code not only encompasses academic fraud but also has been interpreted to cover the writing of bad checks and the use of fake IDs.

UVa's honor code is extreme. Either community members live honorably or they are asked to leave. In other words, there is only a single sanction. If a student admits to an honor infraction or is found guilty of an act of lying, cheating, or stealing by a jury of his or her student peers, that student is asked (required) to leave UVa. No matter how insignificant the infraction, the student is no longer welcome in the community.

The Honor System remains alive and well at UVa. Although it is challenged periodically by student leaders and the full student body, the Honor System and its single sanction continue to withstand scrutiny as student referenda repeatedly reaffirm its reliability and importance.

The Honor System at UVa is one example of how a community can combat cheating. It is not the only way, and it is far from perfect. Cheating still unfortunately occurs at UVa, but the system does provide a strong deterrent. Studies show that cheating occurs significantly less on campuses with honor codes.

UVa's Honor System also includes a requirement that students report suspected instances of lying, cheating, and stealing. This, like the single sanction, attracts a significant amount of controversy. Children are taught not to "tattle," and college students resent the imposition of this sort of burden. The reality is that there is no way to enforce this provision, and it is likely that numerous suspected incidents remain unreported. UVa has nevertheless instituted a procedure through which incidents can be reported anonymously to attempt to make it easier for students to report suspected incidents.

What Can I Do?

Although many students attempt to rationalize their dishonorable behavior by saying, "It's just school," the reality is that behavior in the classroom mirrors what happens in the so-called "real world." The student who sits behind you in class becomes the co-worker sitting next to you in the office or the sales representative with whom you negotiate a purchase for your office.

An important first step involves abandoning the "just school" myth: it is not "just school." How you behave in one sphere of your life influences how you behave in others. While you cannot necessarily control how others act, you can control how you act. If you choose to cheat, recognize that it is a choice and there are consequences, even if you are never "caught."

A second step involves deciding what you will tolerate and deem acceptable from others. Even if you choose not to report suspected honor infractions (as a student) or violations of the law (as an adult), how you respond matters. If a friend grabs you after an exam and laughs about how he or she was able to cheat without the professor noticing, how do you respond? Do you laugh along with your friend? Or do you let him or her know how wrong the behavior was?

The question you should perhaps be asking is, "Do I want to live in a community of trust?" You alone cannot create a community of trust, but do you want to live in one? If so, then you need to create one by being a trusting, honorable person. Like UVa, you can say that you want to deal only with others like you, who are trustworthy. When someone acts dishonorably, you can then choose not to continue interacting with that person. Some might argue that you could end up with a very small community. If, however, enough people make that choice, the communities of trust will eventually get larger. The choice is yours.

Source: Copyright © Tara Radin. Reprinted by permission of the author.

Reading **2-2**

The Parable of the Sadhu

Bowen H. McCoy

Last year, as the first participant in the new six-month sabbatical program that Morgan Stanley has adopted, I enjoyed a rare opportunity to collect my thoughts as well as do some traveling. I spent the first three months in Nepal, walking 600 miles through 200 villages in the Himalayas and climbing some 120,000 vertical feet. My sole Western companion on the trip was an anthropologist who shed light on the cultural patterns of the villages that we passed through.

During the Nepal hike, something occurred that has had a powerful impact on my thinking about corporate ethics. Although some might argue that the experience has no relevance to business, it was a situation in which a basic ethical dilemma suddenly intruded into the lives of a group of individuals. How the group responded holds a lesson for all organizations, no matter how defined.

The Sadhu

The Nepal experience was more rugged than I had anticipated. Most commercial treks last two or three weeks and cover a quarter of the distance we traveled.

My friend Stephen, the anthropologist, and I were halfway through the 60-day Himalayan part of the trip when we reached the high point, an 18,000-foot pass over a crest that we'd have to traverse to reach the village of Muklinath, an ancient holy place for pilgrims.

Six years earlier, I had suffered pulmonary edema, an acute form of altitude sickness, at 16,500 feet in the vicinity of Everest base camp, so we were understandably concerned about what would happen at 18,000 feet. Moreover, the Himalayas were having their wettest spring in 20 years, hip-deep powder and ice had already driven us off one ridge. If we failed to cross the pass, I feared that the last half of our once-in-a-lifetime trip would be ruined.

The night before we would try the pass, we camped in a hut at 14,500 feet. In the photos taken at that camp, my face appears wan. The last village we'd passed through was a sturdy two-day walk below us, and I was tired.

During the late afternoon, four backpackers from New Zealand joined us, and we spent most of the night awake, anticipating the climb. Below, we could see the fires of two other parties, which turned out to be two Swiss couples and a Japanese hiking club.

To get over the steep part of the climb before the sun melted the steps cut in the ice, we departed at 3:30 A.M. The New Zealanders left first, followed by Stephen and myself, our porters and Sherpas, and then the Swiss. The Japanese lingered in their camp. The sky was clear, and we were confident that no spring storm would erupt that day to close the pass.

At 15,500 feet, it looked to me as if Stephen were shuffling and staggering a bit, which are symptoms of altitude sickness. (The initial stage of altitude sickness brings a headache and nausea. As the condition worsens, a climber may encounter difficult breathing, disorientation, aphasia, and paralysis.) I felt strong—my adrenaline was flowing—but I was very concerned about my ultimate ability to get across. A couple of our porters were also suffering from the height, and Pasang, our Sherpa sirdar (leader), was worried.

Just after daybreak, while we rested at 15,500 feet, one of the New Zealanders, who had gone ahead, came staggering down toward us with a body slung across his shoulders. He dumped the almost naked, barefoot body of an Indian holy man, a sadhu, at my feet. He had found the pilgrim lying on the ice, shivering and suffering from hypothermia. I cradled the sadhu's head and laid him out on the rocks. The New Zealander was angry. He wanted to get across the pass before the bright sun melted the snow. He said, "Look, I've done what I can. You have porters and Sherpa guides. You care for him. We're going on!" He turned and went back up the mountain to join his friends.

I took a carotid pulse and found that the sadhu was still alive. We figured he had probably visited the holy shrines at Muklinath and was on his way home. It was fruitless to question why he had chosen this desperately high route instead of the safe, heavily traveled caravan route through the Kali Gandaki gorge. Or why he was shoeless and almost naked, or how long he had been lying in the pass. The answers weren't going to solve our problem.

Stephen and the four Swiss began stripping off their outer clothing and opening their packs. The sadhu was soon clothed from head to foot. He was not able to walk, but he was very much alive. I looked down the mountain and spotted the Japanese climbers, marching up with a horse.

Without a great deal of thought, I told Stephen and Pasang that I was concerned about withstanding the heights to come and wanted to get over the pass. I took off after several of our porters who had gone ahead.

On the steep part of the ascent where, if the ice steps had given way, I would have slid down about 3,000 feet, I felt vertigo. I stopped for a breather, allowing the Swiss to catch up with me. I inquired about the sadhu and Stephen. They said that the sadhu was fine and that Stephen was just behind them. I set off again for the summit.

Stephen arrived at the summit an hour after I did. Still exhilarated by victory, I ran down the slope to congratulate him. He was suffering from altitude sickness—walking 15 steps, then stopping, walking 15 steps, then stopping. Pasang accompanied him all the way up. When I reached them, Stephen glared at me and said: "How do you feel about contributing to the death of a fellow man?"

I did not completely comprehend what he meant. "Is the sadhu dead?" I inquired.

"No," replied Stephen, "but he surely will be!"

After I had gone, followed not long after by the Swiss, Stephen had remained with the sadhu. When the Japanese had arrived, Stephen had asked to use their horse to transport the sadhu down to the hut. They had refused. He had then asked Pasang to have a group of our porters carry the sadhu. Pasang had resisted the idea, saying that the porters would have to exert all their energy to get themselves over the pass. He believed they could not carry a man down 1,000 feet to the hut, reclimb the slope, and get across safely before the snow melted. Pasang had pressed Stephen not to delay any longer.

The Sherpas had carried the sadhu down to a rock in the sun at about 15,000 feet and pointed out the hut another 500 feet below. The Japanese had given him food and drink. When they had last seen him, he was listlessly throwing rocks at the Japanese party's dog, which had frightened him.

We do not know if the sadhu lived or died.

For many of the following days and evenings, Stephen and I discussed and debated our behavior toward the sadhu. Stephen is a committed Quaker with deep moral vision. He said, "I feel that what happened with the sadhu is a good example of the breakdown between the individual ethic and the corporate ethic. No one person was willing to assume ultimate responsibility for the sadhu. Each was willing to do his bit just so long as it was not too inconvenient. When it got to be a bother, everyone just passed the buck to someone else and took off. Jesus was relevant to a more individualistic stage of society, but how do we interpret his teaching today in a world filled with large, impersonal organizations and groups?"

I defended the larger group, saying, "Look, we all cared. We all gave aid and comfort. Everyone did his bit. The New Zealander carried him down below the snow line. I took his pulse and suggested we treat him for hypothermia. You and the Swiss gave him clothing and got him warmed up. The Japanese gave him food and water. The Sherpas carried him down to the sun and pointed out the easy trail toward the hut. He was well enough to throw rocks at a dog. What more could we do?"

"You have just described the typical affluent Westerner's response to a problem. Throwing money—in this case, food and sweaters—at it, but not solving the fundamentals!" Stephen retorted.

"What would satisfy you?" I said. "Here we are, a group of New Zealanders, Swiss, Americans, and Japanese who have never met before and who are at the apex of one of the most powerful experiences of our lives. Some years the pass is so bad no one gets over it. What right does an almost naked pilgrim who chooses the wrong trail have to disrupt our lives? Even the Sherpas had no interest in risking the trip to help him beyond a certain point."

Stephen calmly rebutted, "I wonder what the Sherpas would have done if the sadhu had been a well-dressed Nepali, or what the Japanese would have done if the sadhu had been a well-dressed Asian, or what you would have done, Buzz, if the sadhu had been a well-dressed Western woman?"

"Where, in your opinion," I asked, "is the limit of our responsibility in a situation like this? We had our own well-being to worry about. Our Sherpa guides were unwilling to jeopardize us or the porters for the sadhu. No one else on the mountain was willing to commit himself beyond certain self-imposed limits."

Stephen said, "As individual Christians or people with a Western ethical tradition, we can fulfill our obligations in such a situation only if one, the sadhu dies in our care; two, the sadhu demonstrates to us that he can undertake the two-day walk down to the village; or three, we carry the sadhu for two days down to the village and persuade someone there to care for him."

"Leaving the sadhu in the sun with food and clothing—where he demonstrated hand-eye coordination by throwing a rock at a dog—comes close to fulfilling items one and two," I answered. "And it wouldn't have made sense to take him to the village where the people appeared to be far less caring than the Sherpas, so the third condition is impractical. Are you really saying that, no matter what the implications, we should, at the drop of a hat, have changed our entire plan?"

The Individual versus the Group Ethic

Despite my arguments, I felt and continue to feel guilt about the sadhu. I had literally walked through a classic moral dilemma without fully thinking through the consequences. My excuses for my actions include a high adrenaline flow, a superordinate goal, and a once-in-a-lifetime opportunity—common factors in corporate situations, especially stressful ones.

Real moral dilemmas are ambiguous, and many of us hike right through them, unaware that they exist. When, usually after the fact, someone makes an issue of one, we tend to resent his or her bringing it up. Often, when the full import of what we have done (or not done) hits us, we dig into a defensive position from which it is very difficult to emerge. In rare circumstances, we may contemplate what we have done from inside a prison.

Had we mountaineers been free of stress caused by the effort and the high altitude, we might have treated the sadhu differently. Yet isn't stress the real test of personal and corporate values? The instant decisions that executives make under pressure reveal the most about personal and corporate character.

Among the many questions that occur to me when I ponder my experience with the sadhu are: What are the practical limits of moral imagination and vision? Is there a collective or institutional ethic that differs from the ethics of the individual? At what level of effort or commitment can one discharge one's ethical responsibilities?

Not every ethical dilemma has a right solution. Reasonable people often disagree; otherwise there would be no dilemma. In a business context, however, it is essential that managers agree on a process for dealing with dilemmas.

Our experience with the sadhu offers an interesting parallel to business situations. An immediate response was mandatory. Failure to act was a decision in itself. Up on the mountain we could not resign and submit our résumés to a headhunter. In contrast to philosophy, business involves action and implementation—getting things done. Managers must come up with answers based on what they see and what they allow to influence their decision-making processes. On the mountain, none of us but Stephen realized the true dimensions of the situation we were facing.

One of our problems was that as a group we had no process for developing a consensus. We had no sense of purpose or plan. The difficulties of dealing with the sadhu were so complex that no one person could handle them. Because the group did not have a set of preconditions that could guide its action to an acceptable resolution, we reacted instinctively as individuals. The cross-cultural nature of the group added a further layer of complexity. We had no leader with whom we could all identify and in whose purpose we believed. Only Stephen was willing to take charge, but he could not gain adequate support from the group to care for the sadhu.

Some organizations do have values that transcend the personal values of their managers. Such values, which go beyond profitability, are usually revealed when the organization is under stress. People throughout the organization generally accept its values, which, because they are not presented as a rigid list of commandments, may be somewhat ambiguous. The stories people tell, rather than printed materials, transmit the organization's conceptions of what is proper behavior.

For 20 years, I have been exposed at senior levels to a variety of corporations and organizations. It is amazing how quickly an outsider can sense the tone and style of an organization and, with that, the degree of tolerated openness and freedom to challenge management.

Organizations that do not have a heritage of mutually accepted, shared values tend to become unhinged during stress, with each individual bailing out for himself or herself. In the great takeover battles we have witnessed during past years, companies that had strong cultures drew the wagons around them and fought it out, while other companies saw executives—supported by golden parachutes—bail out of the struggles.

Because corporations and their members are interdependent, for the corporation to be strong the members need to share a preconceived notion of correct behavior, a "business ethic," and think of it as a positive force, not a constraint.

As an investment banker, I am continually warned by well-meaning lawyers, clients, and associates to be wary of conflicts of interest. Yet if I were to run away from every difficult situation, I wouldn't be an effective investment banker. I have to feel my way through conflicts. An effective manager can't run from risk either; he or she has to confront risk. To feel "safe" in doing that, managers need the guidelines of an agreed-upon process and set of values within the organization.

After my three months in Nepal, I spent three months as an executive-in-residence at both the Stanford Business School and the University of California at Berkeley's Center for Ethics and Social Policy of the Graduate Theological Union. Those six months away from my job gave me time to assimilate 20 years of business experience. My thoughts turned often to the meaning of the leadership role in any large organization. Students at the seminary thought of themselves as antibusiness. But when I questioned them, they agreed that they distrusted all large organizations, including the church. They perceived all large organizations as impersonal and opposed to individual values and needs. Yet we all know of organizations in which people's values and beliefs are respected and their expressions encouraged. What makes the difference? Can we identify the difference and, as a result, manage more effectively?

The word *ethics* turns off many and confuses more. Yet the notions of shared values and an agreed-upon process for dealing with adversity and change—what many people mean when they talk about corporate culture—seem to be at the heart of the ethical issue. People who are in touch with their own core beliefs and the beliefs of others and who are sustained by them can be more comfortable living on the cutting edge. At times, taking a tough line or a decisive stand in a muddle of ambiguity is the only ethical thing to do. If a manager is indecisive about a problem and spends time trying to figure out the "good" thing to do, the enterprise may be lost.

Business ethics, then, has to do with the authenticity and integrity of the enterprise. To be ethical is to follow the business as well as the cultural goals of the corporation, its owners, its employees, and its customers. Those who cannot serve the corporate vision are not authentic businesspeople and, therefore, are not ethical in the business sense.

At this stage of my own business experience, I have a strong interest in organizational behavior. Sociologists are keenly studying what they call corporate stories, legends, and heroes as a way organizations have of transmitting value systems. Corporations such as Arco have even hired consultants to perform an audit of their corporate culture. In a company, a leader is a person who understands, interprets, and manages the corporate value system. Effective managers, therefore, are action-oriented people who resolve conflict, are tolerant of ambiguity, stress, and change, and have a strong sense of purpose for themselves and their organizations.

If all this is true, I wonder about the role of the professional manager who moves from company to company. How can he or she quickly absorb the values and culture of different organizations? Or is there, indeed, an art of management that is totally transportable? Assuming that such fungible managers do exist, is it proper for them to manipulate the values of others?

What would have happened had Stephen and I carried the sadhu for two days back to the village and become involved with the villagers in his care? In four trips to Nepal, my most interesting experience occurred in 1975 when I lived in a Sherpa home in the Khumbu for five days while recovering from altitude sickness. The high point of Stephen's trip was an invitation to participate in a family funeral ceremony in Manang. Neither experience had to do with climbing the high passes of the Himalayas. Why were we so reluctant to try the lower path, the ambiguous trail? Perhaps because we did not have a leader who could reveal the greater purpose of the trip to us.

Why didn't Stephen, with his moral vision, opt to take the sadhu under his personal care? The answer is partly because Stephen was hard-stressed physically himself and partly because, without some support system that encompassed our involuntary and episodic community on the mountain, it was beyond his individual capacity to do so.

I see the current interest in corporate culture and corporate value systems as a positive response to pessimism such as Stephen's about the decline of the role of the individual in large organizations. Individuals who operate from a thoughtful set of personal values provide the foundation for a corporate culture. A corporate tradition that encourages freedom of inquiry, supports personal values, and reinforces a focused sense of direction can fulfill the need to combine individuality with the prosperity and success of the group. Without such corporate support, the individual is lost.

That is the lesson of the sadhu. In a complex corporate situation, the individual requires and deserves the support of the group. When people cannot find such support in their organizations, they don't know how to act. If such support is forthcoming, a person has a stake in the success of the group and can add much to the process of establishing and maintaining a corporate culture. Management's challenge is to be sensitive to individual needs, to shape them, and to direct and focus them for the benefit of the group as a whole.

For each of us the sadhu lives. Should we stop what we are doing and comfort him; or should we keep trudging up toward the high pass? Should I pause to help the derelict I pass on the street each night as I walk by the Yale Club en route to Grand Central Station? Am I his brother? What is the nature of our responsibility if we consider ourselves to be ethical persons? Perhaps it is to change the values of the group so that it can, with all its resources, take the other road.

When Do We Take a Stand?

I wrote about my experiences purposely to present an ambiguous situation. I never found out if the sadhu lived or died. I can attest, though, that the sadhu lives on in his story. He lives in the ethics classes I teach each year at business schools and churches. He lives in the classrooms of numerous business schools, where professors have taught the case to tens of thousands of students. He lives in several casebooks on ethics and on an educational video. And he lives in organizations such as the American Red Cross and AT&T, which use his story in their ethics training.

As I reflect on the sadhu now, 15 years after the fact, I first have to wonder, What actually happened on that Himalayan slope? When I first wrote about the event, I reported the experience in as much detail as I could remember, but I shaped it to the needs of a good classroom discussion. After years of reading my story, viewing it on video, and hearing others discuss it, I'm not sure I myself know what actually occurred on the mountainside that day!

I've also heard a wide variety of responses to the story. The sadhu, for example, may not have wanted our help at all—he may have been intentionally bringing on his own death as a way to holiness. Why had he taken the dangerous way over the pass instead of the caravan route through the gorge? Hindu businesspeople have told me that in trying to assist the sadhu, we were being typically arrogant Westerners imposing our cultural values on the world.

I've learned that each year along the pass, a few Nepali porters are left to freeze to death outside the tents of the unthinking tourists who hired them. A few years ago, a French group even left one of their own, a young French woman, to die there. The difficult pass seems to demonstrate a perverse version of Gresham's law of currency: The bad practices of previous travelers have driven out the values that new travelers might have followed if they were at home. Perhaps that helps to explain why our porters behaved as they did and why it was so difficult for Stephen or anyone else to establish a different approach on the spot.

Our Sherpa sirdar, Pasang, was focused on his responsibility for bringing us up the mountain safe and sound. (His livelihood and status in the Sherpa ethnic group depended on our safe return.) We were weak, our party was split, the porters were well on their way to the top with all our gear and food, and a storm would have separated us irrevocably from our logistical base.

The fact was, we had no plan for dealing with the contingency of the sadhu. There was nothing we could do to unite our multicultural group in the little time we had. An ethical dilemma had come upon us unexpectedly, an element of drama that may explain why the sadhu's story has continued to attract students.

I am often asked for help in teaching the story. I usually advise keeping the details as ambiguous as possible. A true ethical dilemma requires a decision between two hard choices. In the case of the sadhu, we had to decide how much to sacrifice ourselves to take care of a stranger. And given the constraints of our trek, we had to make a group decision, not an individual one. If a large majority of students in a class ends up thinking I'm a bad person because of my decision on the mountain, the instructor may not have given the case its due. The same is true if the majority sees no problem with the choices we made.

Any class's response depends on its setting, whether it's a business school, a church, or a corporation. I've found that younger students are more likely to see the issue as black-and-white, whereas older ones tend to see shades of gray. Some have seen a conflict between the different ethical approaches that we followed at the time. Stephen felt he had to do everything he could to save the sadhu's life, in accordance with his Christian ethic of compassion. I had a utilitarian response: Do the greatest good for the greatest number. Give a burst of aid to minimize the sadhu's exposure, then continue on our way.

The basic question of the case remains, When do we take a stand? When do we allow a "sadhu" to intrude into our daily lives? Few of us can afford the time or effort to take care of every needy person we encounter. How much must we give of ourselves? And how do we prepare our organizations and institutions so they will respond appropriately in a crisis? How do we influence them if we do not agree with their points of view?

We cannot quit our jobs over every ethical dilemma, but if we continually ignore our sense of values, who do we become? As a journalist asked at a recent conference on ethics, "Which ditch are we willing to die in?" For each of us, the answer is a bit different. How we act in response to that question defines better than anything else who we are, just as, in a collective sense, our acts define our institutions. In effect, the sadhu is always there, ready to remind us of the tensions between our own goals and the claims of strangers.

Reading 2-3

When Good People Do Bad Things at Work
Rote Behavior, Distractions, and Moral Exclusion Stymie Ethical Behavior on the Job

Dennis J. Moberg

The news is full of the exploits of corporate villains. We read about how officials at Lincoln Savings and Loan bilked thousands out of their customers' retirement nest eggs. There are stories of the lies Brown and Williamson Tobacco executives told about the addictive nature of cigarettes and the company's subsequent campaign to destroy whistle-blower Jeffrey Wigant. Also in the news are the top managers at Time Warner who looked the other way rather than forgo millions from the sale of rap music with lyrics that advocated violence directed at women and the police. Such acts are hard to forgive. Scoundrels such as these seem either incredibly weak or dangerously flawed.

Yet not all corporate misdeeds are committed by bad people. In fact, a significant number of unethical acts in business are the likely result of foibles and failings rather than selfishness and greed. Put in certain kinds of situations, good people inadvertently do bad things.

For those of us concerned about ethical actions and not just good intentions, the problem is clear. We must identify the situational factors that keep people from doing their best and eliminate them whenever we can.

Problem No. 1: Scripts

One factor is something psychologists call scripts. This term refers to the procedures that experience tells us to use in specific situations. When we brush our teeth or congratulate a friend on the arrival of a new grandchild, we probably use scripts.

Unlike other forms of experience, scripts are stored in memory in a mechanical or rote fashion. When we encounter a very familiar situation, rather than actively think about it, we reserve our mental energy for other purposes and behave as though we are cruising on automatic pilot.

In a classic psychological experiment, people approached someone at an office machine making copies and asked, "May I please make just one copy because …" The person at the machine generally complied with this request, but the really interesting finding was that the likelihood of compliance was totally independent of the reasons stated. In fact, superfluous reasons such as "because I need to make a copy" were just as successful as good reasons such as "because my boss told me she needed these right away." Apparently, we have all experienced this situation so often that we don't give the reasons our full attention, not to mention our careful consideration.

One ethical lapse clearly attributable to scripts was Ford Motor Co.'s failure to recall the Pinto in the 1970s. The Pinto was an automobile with an undetected design flaw that made the gas tank burst into flames on impact, resulting in the death and disfigurement of scores of victims. Dennis Gioia, the Ford recall coordinator at the time, reviewed hundreds of accident reports to detect whether a design flaw was implicated. Later, he recalled,

> When I was dealing with the first trickling-in of field reports that might have suggested a significant problem with the Pinto, the reports were essentially similar to many others that I was dealing with (and dismissing) all the time…. I was making this kind of decision automatically every day. I had trained myself to respond to prototypical cues, and these didn't fit the relevant prototype for crisis cases.

Situations like this occur frequently in the work world. Repetitive jobs requiring vigilance to prevent ethical lapses can be found in quality control, customer service, and manufacturing. In this respect, consider what happened when a nurse with a script that called for literal obedience to a doctor's written orders misread the directions to place ear drops in a patient's right ear as "place in Rear." Good people can inadvertently do very bad things.

Scripts may also be at work when we come face to face with those who are suffering. In situations where we observe the pain of those in need, scripts permit us to steel ourselves against feelings of empathy. Most of us have been approached by the homeless on the street, exposed to horrific images on the television news, and asked for donations on behalf of the victims of natural disasters.

According to research at the University of Kansas, scripts allow people to avoid responsibility for the suffering of others in situations when providing help appears costly. In work contexts, this might explain why businesspeople do not always respond philanthropically to documented cases of human suffering. What appears to be calculated indifference may actually not be calculated at all.

Whenever there is repetition, there are likely to be scripts. Accordingly, the best way to eliminate the potential of scripts to result in unethical behavior is to keep people out of highly repetitive situations. Technology can and has been used to eliminate highly routine tasks, but job rotation is also an option. For example, the *Daily Oklahoman* newspaper of Oklahoma City cross-trains most of its editors and schedules them to switch roles often. This helps keep the editors mentally sharp.

One editor who often switches roles from night to night commented: "You're fresh when you come to a particular job. Like last night I did inside [design], and it was a long and torturous night because of the large paper. But then again I turn around and do something thoroughly different tonight, so I don't feel like I'm trudging back to the same old rut again."

Oklahoman News Editor Ed Sargent thinks editing quality has improved because those who switch roles are exposed to the different approaches their colleagues take to the job. "Every editor has different opinions, obviously, about what's a big error and what's a little error," he said. Although the original intent of the role switching was to distribute stress more evenly, a side effect is that the paper is probably less prone to ethical lapses.

Problem No. 2: Distractions

Scripts are cognitive shortcuts that take the place of careful thinking. A similar human tendency is our mindless treatment of distractions. Think for a moment about the last time you drove to a very important meeting. Once there, were you able to recall any details of your journey? Most of us cannot, which demonstrates that when concentrating on completing an involving task, we don't deal well with distractions.

This inattention to what is happening on the periphery can get us into trouble with our spouses and significant others, and it can also result in ethical lapses. In one very telling experiment, divinity students were told that they had to deliver a lecture from prepared notes in a classroom across campus. Half the students were told they had to hurry to be on time, and the other half were told they had more than ample time.

On the way, the students came across a person in distress (actually an actor), who sat slumped motionless in a doorway, coughing and groaning. Shockingly, only 16 of the 40 divinity students stopped to help, most of them from the group that had ample time. To those in a hurry, the man was a distraction, a threat to their focus on giving a lecture. Ironically enough, half of them had been asked to discuss the parable of "The Good Samaritan."

Mindlessness about distractions at work is most pronounced when employees, with limited means of gaining perspective, are encouraged to be focused and driven. The best way to combat this tendency is for senior managers to model the virtue of temperance. If the president of a company is a workaholic, it is difficult to convince employees to be open to problems on the outskirts of their commitments. In contrast, an organizational culture that facilitates work–family balance or encourages employee involvement in the community may move experiences that should not be seen as mere distractions onto the center stage of consciousness.

Problem No. 3: Moral Exclusion

A final problem that brings out the worst in good people is the very human tendency to morally exclude certain persons. This occurs when individuals or groups are perceived as outside the boundary in which moral values and considerations of fairness apply. The most striking example occurs during warfare when the citizens of a country readily perceive their enemies in demonic terms. Yet, this tendency to discount the moral standing of others results in us discounting all kinds of people, some of them as close as coworkers and valued customers.

Greater awareness and extensive training have reduced some of the exclusion women and people of color have historically experienced. More work needs to be done in this area, as well as in other equally insidious forms of exclusion.

One way such exclusion shows up is in our use of pronouns. If *we* are in marketing and *they* are in production, the chances are that the distance may be great enough for us to be morally indifferent to what happens to them. Similarly, if we use stereotypic terms like *bean counter* or sneer when we say *management*, then it is clear that people in these categories don't count.

Not surprisingly, one way to expand the scope of justice is to promote direct contact with individuals who have been morally excluded. One company that applied this notion in an intriguing way is Eisai, a Japanese pharmaceutical firm. In the late 1980s, Haruo Naito had recently become CEO, and his closest advisers expressed concern that his managers and employees lacked an understanding of the end users of Eisai's products.

Hearing this, Naito decided to shift the focus of attention from the customers of his company's products—doctors and pharmacists—to *their* customers—patients and their families. Eisai managers, he decided, needed to identify better with end users and then infuse the insights from this sense of inclusion throughout the organization. This was a revolutionary idea for this company of 4,500 employees, but Naito believed his employees needed a more vivid reason to care deeply about their work.

"It's not enough to tell employees that if they do something, the company will grow this much or their salary will increase this much. That's just not enough incentive," says Naito. "You have to show them how what they are doing is connected to society, or exactly how it will help a patient." Accordingly, Naito decided to send 100 managers to a seven-day seminar: three days of nursing-home training and four days of medical care observation.

These managers were then sent to diverse regions throughout Japan, where they had to deal with different people, many of whom were in critical condition. They met patients with both physical and emotional problems; some of the patients they came in contact with died during their internships.

This pilot program grew to include more than 1,000 Eisai employees. Pretty soon, even laboratory support personnel had to leave their benches and desks and meet regularly with pharmacists and hospital people.

"Getting them out of the office was a way to activate human relationships," says Naito. Another way was to institute hotlines, which have generated product ideas. As a consequence, many new Eisai drugs were produced, including some that have promise in dealing with Alzheimer's disease. Clearly, moral inclusion was stimulated at Eisai, at least insofar as the end users of its products are concerned.

Failing to Bother

Jesuit scholar James F. Keenan reminds us that "sinners in the New Testament are known not for what they did, but for what they failed to do—for failing to bother." We are all prone to this failure, but not necessarily because we are sinners. Repetition, distractions, and our natural tendency to exclude those unfamiliar to us cloud our best thinking and forestall the expression of our virtues. We owe it to ourselves to resist these pernicious influences, and we owe it to those in our work communities to help them to do the same.

Source: Issues in Ethics 10, no. 2 (Fall 1999), Markkula Center for Applied Ethics, (http://www.scu.edu/ethics/publications/iie/v10n2/peopleatwork.html).

Further Reading

Cooper, R. K., and A. Sawaf, *Executive EQ: Emotional Intelligence in Leadership and Organizations* (New York: Grosset/ Putnam, 1996).

Craig, D., "Cross-training, Rotation Leads to Less Stress," *The American Editor* 788 (January 1998), pp. 16–17.

Gioia, D. A., "Pinto Fires and Personal Ethics: A Script Analysis of Missed Opportunities," *Journal of Business Ethics* 11 (1992), pp. 379–389.

Opotow, S., "Moral Exclusion and Injustice: An Introduction," *Journal of Social Issues* 46 (1990), pp. 120.

Shaw, Laura L., C. Daniel Batson, and Matthew R. Todd, "Empathy Avoidance: Forestalling Feeling for Another in Order to Escape the Motivational Consequences," *Journal of Personality and Social Psychology* 67, no. 5 (1994), pp. 879–887.

Chapter 3

Philosophical Ethics and Business

Rules cannot substitute for character.

Alan Greenspan

Hell begins the day that God grants you the vision to see all that you could have done, should have done, and would have done, but did not do.

Goethe

The purchasing departments of major retail firms are responsible for deciding which products their stores will stock and which suppliers will provide these products. In many cases, retail stores develop long-term relationships with their suppliers that can work in the best interests for both companies.

In the global economy, it has become increasingly attractive for major retail stores to turn to foreign suppliers who can sell products comparable to those produced domestically for much lower costs. This practice allows the retailer to pass on savings to the consumer and remain competitive in the marketplace. This choice has also resulted in a significant loss of business for many domestic suppliers, and, in some cases, suppliers have been forced out of business. Imagine the following conversation between a supplier and the purchasing manager for a large retail store.

Supplier: You can't cancel your order with us. If you do, I'll have to lay off many of my employees and I don't even know if the company will survive. We already have done as much as we can to cut costs; our employees have not had a pay increase in years and some wages and benefits have been reduced. Yet, the costs of our own materials, especially our energy costs, have risen significantly, and our taxes remain high. We have always been reliable, cooperative, and accommodating to your needs. Don't you feel any loyalty to us, to our employees, to fellow American citizens?

Purchasing manager: I am not happy doing this, but I do have a responsibility to my own company, to its stockholders, and to our customers. I have a responsibility to purchase our products at the lowest costs. We have always been loyal to you, too, but loyalty is not the issue. Our relationship is a business and contractual relationship only. Besides, we both know what economists and politicians say about foreign trade. Our entire society will benefit if we seek the lowest cost products: Consumers benefit from lower costs, our economy grows when consumer purchasing power increases as a result, and this growing economy will provide jobs to American workers. Further, economic growth in foreign countries will increase their imports from the United States and, once again, lead to more jobs domestically.

Supplier: That may sound good in theory, but I know my employees will not think it is very fair for them to lose real jobs now for possible jobs for other people in the future. Besides, it is not as if your own company and its owners have not already made billions of dollars. Maybe it's time they reduced their profits to keep loyal suppliers in business.

- How would you describe the decision faced by the purchasing manager? Is it an ethical issue at all? Why or why not?
- Are there any factual questions that you would want to resolve before making such a decision?

(continued)

(concluded)

- What alternatives are available for the purchasing manager?
- What role, if any, should the principle of loyalty play in business decisions?
- Do you agree that employees have a duty to seek the greatest profits for their companies? What values are promoted by such a duty?
- What duties does the purchasing manager have? To whom does the purchasing manager owe responsibility; who are the stakeholders involved?
- Assume that it is true that foreign trade will produce greater long-term overall economic consequences. Is it fair for some individuals to lose their jobs so that other individuals will benefit in the future?
- Does a business have responsibilities to suppliers that are not specified in their contracts? What other alternatives are available to the purchasing manager and how do these alternatives impact each stakeholder or group of stakeholders?
- Is it fair that loyal suppliers be treated this way?
- Is there anywhere else you can look for assistance or guidance?

 ## Chapter Objectives

After reading this chapter, you will be able to:

1. Explain the ethical tradition of utilitarianism.
2. Describe how utilitarian thinking underlies much economic and business decision making.
3. Explain how free markets might serve the utilitarian goal of maximizing the overall good.
4. Explain strengths and weaknesses of utilitarian decision making.
5. Explain principle-based, or deontological, ethical traditions.
6. Explain the concept of moral rights.
7. Distinguish moral rights from legal rights.
8. Explain the Rawlsian theory of justice as fairness.
9. Describe and explain virtue-based theories of ethical character.

Introduction: Ethical Theories and Traditions

Chapters 1 and 2 introduced ethics as a form of practical reasoning in support of decision making about how we should live our lives. Ethics involves what is perhaps the most significant question any human being can ask: How *should* we live our lives? But, of course, this question is not new; every major philosophical, cultural, political, and religious tradition in human history has grappled with it. In light of this, it would be imprudent to ignore these traditions as we begin to examine ethical issues in business. In particular, several traditions in Western ethics have had a significant influence on the development of contemporary business and economics.

Nevertheless, discussions of philosophical ethics can appear intimidating or too abstract to many students. Discussion of ethical "theories" often seems to be too *theoretical* to be of much relevance to business. Throughout this chapter, we hope to suggest a more accessible understanding of ethical theories, one that will shed some light on the practical and pragmatic application of these theories to actual problems businesspeople face.

An ethical theory is nothing more than an attempt to provide a systematic answer to the fundamental ethical question: How should human beings live their lives? Not only do ethical theories attempt to answer the question of how we should live, but they also provide *reasons* to support their answer. As the previous chapter suggested, accountable decision making requires giving reasons to justify our actions. Ethical theories seek to provide a rational justification for *why* we should act and decide in a particular way. Anyone can offer prescriptions for what you should do and how you should act, but *philosophical* ethics answers the "Why?" question as well by connecting its prescriptions with an underlying account of a good and meaningful human life.

Many people and cultures across the world base their ethical views on certain religious or theological foundations. The biggest practical problem with this approach, of course, is that people differ widely in their religious beliefs. If ethics is based only on religious principles, and if people disagree about those religious starting points, then ethics would never escape the predicament of relativism.

Unlike theological ethics, which explains human well-being in religious terms, philosophical ethics provides justifications that must be applicable to all people, regardless of their religious starting points. Philosophical ethics seeks foundations that all reasonable people can accept, regardless of their religious convictions. Thus, for example, "you should contribute to disaster relief because it will reduce human suffering" is a philosophical justification for an ethical judgment, whereas "you should contribute to disaster relief because God commands it," or "because it will bring you heavenly rewards" is not.

This chapter will introduce several ethical frameworks that have proven influential in the development of business ethics: **utilitarianism,** an ethical tradition that directs us to decide based on overall consequences of our act; **deontological** ethical traditions, which direct us to act on the basis of moral principles such as respecting human **rights;** a theory of social justice that takes fairness as the primary social principle; and **virtue ethics,** which directs us to consider the moral **character** of individuals and how various character traits can contribute to, or obstruct, a happy and meaningful human life.

Are you an ethical relativist? Ethical relativists hold that ethical values are relative to particular people, cultures, or times. The relativist denies that there can be any rationally justified or objective ethical judgments. When ethical disagreements occur between people or cultures, the ethical relativist concludes that there is no way to resolve that dispute and to prove that one side is right or more reasonable than the other.

Do you believe that there is no way to decide what is right or wrong? Imagine a teacher returns an assignment to you with a grade of "F." When you ask for an explanation, you are told that, frankly, the teacher does not believe that people "like you" (e.g., women, Christians, African Americans) are capable of doing good work in this field (e.g., science, engineering, math, finance). When you object that this is unfair and wrong, the teacher offers a relativist explanation. "Fairness is a matter of personal opinion," the professor explains. "Who determines what is fair or unfair?" you ask. Your teacher claims that his view of what is fair is as valid as any other. Because all people are entitled to their own personal opinions, he is entitled to fail you since, in his personal opinion, you do not deserve to succeed.

- Would you accept this explanation and be content with your failing grade? If not, how would you defend your own, opposing view?
- Are there any relevant facts you would rely on to support your claim?
- What values are involved in this dispute?
- What alternatives are available to you?
- Besides you and your teacher, should any other people, any other stakeholders, be involved in this situation?
- What reasons would you offer to the dean in an appeal to have the grade changed?
- What consequences would this professor's practice have on education?
- If reasoning and logical persuasion do not work, how else could this dispute be resolved?

Utilitarianism: Making Decisions Based on Ethical Consequences

OBJECTIVE

The first ethical tradition that we will discuss, utilitarianism, has its roots in 18th- and 19th-century social and political philosophy. Utilitarianism was part of the same social movement that gave rise to modern democratic market capitalism. Much of neoclassical economics, and the model of business and management embedded in it, has its roots in utilitarian thinking. (See the Reality Check that follows.)

Utilitarianism begins with the conviction that we should decide what to do by considering the *consequences* of our actions. Utilitarianism tells us that we should act in ways that produce better overall consequences than the alternatives we are considering. "Better" consequences are those that promote human well-being: the happiness, health, dignity, integrity, freedom, and respect of all the people affected.

Reality Check *Adam Smith, Utilitarianism and the Invisible Hand of Free Markets*

The roots of contemporary market capitalism are commonly traced to Adam Smith's book, *The Wealth of Nations* (1776). Smith's ethical goals were decidedly utilitarian: Economic institutions should be arranged in ways that would promote the overall wealth of a nation, rather than the personal wealth of the monarch or the aristocracy. Smith argued that if society adopted certain economic principles—the principles of what we have come to understand as market capitalism—then the pursuit of individual self-interest alone would, as if "led by an invisible hand," result in greater overall prosperity. Smith was a utilitarian who concluded that a free market economy was the most efficient means to attain the utilitarian goal.

In what is perhaps the most famous passage from Smith's *Wealth of Nations,* he writes:

> As every individual, therefore, endeavours as much as he can both to employ his capital in the support of domestic industry, and so to direct that industry that its produce may be of the greatest value; every individual necessarily labours to render the annual value of society as great as he can. He generally, indeed, neither intends to promote the public interest, nor knows how much he is promoting it. By preferring the support of domestic to that of foreign industry, he intends only his own security; and by directing that industry in such a manner as its produce may be of the greatest value, he intends only his own gain, and he is in this, as in many other cases, led by an invisible

hand to promote an end which was no part of his intention. Nor is it always the worse for the society that it was no part of it. By pursuing his own interest he frequently promotes that of society more effectually than when he really intends to promote it. I have never known much good done by those who affected to trade for the public good. It is an affectation, indeed, not very common among merchants, and very few words need be employed in dissuading them from it.

Contrary to what is often thought, Smith did not believe that humans were selfish nor did he believe that self-interest alone was sufficient to secure the ethical ends of maximum overall happiness. Sympathy, empathy, fellow-feeling were just as basic human motivations as self-interest. Human nature is such that we naturally imagine ourselves in the place of others, we agonize with their suffering and feel joy at their happiness. These motivations are as real and as effective as self-interest. Smith's economic conclusion was simply that we do not need sympathy and altruism to achieve beneficial overall consequences:

> It is not from the benevolence of the butcher, the brewer, or the baker that we expect our dinner, but from their regard to their own interest. We address ourselves, not to their humanity but to their self-love, and never talk to them of our own necessities but of their advantages.

If a basic human value is individual happiness, then an action that promotes more of that than an alternative does is more reasonable and more justified from an ethical point of view. A decision that promotes the greatest amount of these values for the greatest number of people is the most reasonable decision from an ethical point of view.

The emphasis on producing the greatest good for the greatest number makes utilitarianism a social philosophy that provides strong support for democratic institutions and policies and opposes those policies that aim to benefit only a small social, economic, or political minority. Therefore, it could be said that the economy and economic institutions are utilitarian in that they exist to provide the highest standard of living for the greatest number of people, not simply to create wealth for a privileged few.

For a business-related example, consider the case of child labor, discussed in further detail in Chapter 6. In judging the ethics of child labor, utilitarian thinking would advise us to consider all the likely consequences of employing young children in factories. Obviously, the practice has many problematic consequences: Children suffer physical and psychological harms, they are denied opportunities for education, their low pay is not enough to escape a life of poverty, and so forth. But these consequences must be compared to the consequences of alternative decisions. What are the consequences if children in poor regions are denied factory jobs? These children would still be denied opportunities for education; they would live in worse poverty; and they would have less money for food and family support. In many cases, the only alternatives for obtaining any income available to young children who are prohibited from joining the workforce might include crime, drugs, and prostitution. Further, we should consider not only the consequences to the children themselves, but to the entire society. Child labor can have beneficial results for bringing foreign investment and money into a poor country. In the opinion of some observers, allowing children to work for pennies a day under sweatshop conditions produces better overall consequences than the available alternatives. Thus, one might argue on utilitarian grounds that such labor practices are ethically permissible because they produce better overall consequences than the alternatives.

This example highlights several important aspects of utilitarian reasoning. Because utilitarians decide on the basis of consequences, and because the consequences of our actions will depend on the specific facts of each situation, utilitarians tend to be very pragmatic thinkers (but not egoistic; see the Reality Check that follows). No act is ever absolutely right or wrong in all cases in every situation; right and wrong will always depend on the consequences. For example, lying is neither right nor wrong in itself, according to utilitarians. In some situations, lying may produce greater overall good than telling the truth. In such a situation, it would be ethically justified to tell a lie.

Utilitarian reasoning also usually supplies some support for each competing available alternative. For example, the utilitarian might argue for banning child labor as harmful to the overall good or allowing child labor as contributing to the overall good. Deciding on the ethical legitimacy of alternative decisions requires that we make judgments about the likely consequences of our actions. How do we do this? The utilitarian tradition has a strong inclination to rely on the social sciences for help in making such predictions. After all, social science studies the causes and consequences of individual and social actions. Who is better situated than a social scientist to help us predict the social consequences of our decisions? Consider, as an example, how the fields of economics, anthropology, political science, sociology, public policy, psychology, and medical and health sciences could help determine the likely consequences of child labor in a particular culture. We will return to examine this example further in Chapter 6.

Reality Check *Is Utilitarianism Egoistic?*

While the imperative to maximize pleasure or happiness sounds selfish and egoistic, utilitarianism differs from *egoism* in important ways. Egoism is also a consequentialist theory, but it focuses on the happiness of the individual. In other words, instead of determining the "greatest good for the greatest number," egoism seeks "the greatest good for me"!

Utilitarianism judges actions by their consequences for the general and overall good. Consistent with the utilitarian commitment to democratic equality, however, the general good must take into consideration the well-being of each and every individual affected by the action. In this way utilitarianism serves the ultimate goal of ethics: the impartial promotion of human well-being. It is impartial because it considers the consequences for everyone, not just for the individual. People who act in ways to maximize only their own happiness, or the happiness of their company, are not utilitarians, they are egoists.

Utilitarianism and Business: Profit Maximization versus Public Policy Approaches

OBJECTIVE

Utilitarianism answers the fundamental questions of ethics—what should we do?—by reference to a rule: Maximize the overall happiness. But another question remains to be answered: *How* do we achieve this goal? What is the best means for attaining the utilitarian goal of maximizing the overall good? Two answers prove especially relevant in business and business ethics.

One movement within utilitarian thinking invokes the tradition of Adam Smith, claiming that free and competitive markets are the best means for attaining utilitarian goals. This version would promote policies that deregulate private industry, protect property rights, allow for free exchanges, and encourage competition. In such situations, decisions of rationally self-interested individuals would result, as if led by "an invisible hand" in Adam Smith's terms, in the maximum satisfaction of individual happiness.

OBJECTIVE

Given this utilitarian goal, neoclassical free market economics advises us that the most efficient economy is structured according to the principles of free market capitalism. This requires that business managers, in turn, should seek to maximize profits. This idea is central to one common perspective on corporate social responsibility. By pursuing profits, business insures that scarce resources go to those who most value them and thereby insures that resources will provide optimal overall satisfaction. Thus, these economists see competitive markets as the most efficient means to the utilitarian end of maximizing happiness. For an example of this applied in practice, see the Reality Check that follows.

A second influential version of utilitarian policy turns to policy experts who can predict the outcome of various policies and carry out policies that will attain utilitarian ends. These experts, usually trained in the social sciences such as economics, political science, and public policy, are familiar with the specifics of how society works, and they therefore are in a position to determine which policy will maximize the overall good.

This approach to public policy underlies one theory of the entire administrative and bureaucratic side of government and organizations. From this view, the

Reality Check *Utilitarian Experts in Practice*

Consider how the Federal Reserve Board sets interest rates. There is an established goal, a public policy "good," that the Federal Reserve takes to be the greatest good for the country. (This goal is something like the highest sustainable rate of economic growth compatible with minimal inflation.) The Fed examines the relevant economic data and makes a judgment about the present and future state of the economy. If economic activity seems to be slowing down, the Fed might decide to lower interest rates as a means of stimulating economic growth. If the economy seems to be growing too fast and the inflation rate is increasing, the Fed might choose to raise interest rates. Lowering or raising interest rates in itself is neither good nor bad; the rightness of the act depends on the consequences. The role of public servants is to use their expertise to judge the likely consequences and make the decision that is most likely to produce the best result.

legislative body (from Congress to local city councils) establishes the public goals that we assume will maximize overall happiness. The administrative side (presidents, governors, mayors) executes (administers) policies to fulfill these goals. The people working within the administration know how the social and political system works and use this knowledge to carry out the mandate of the legislature. The government is filled with such people, typically trained in such fields as economics, law, social science, public policy, and political science. This utilitarian approach, for example, would be sympathetic with government regulation of business on the grounds that such regulation will insure that business activities do contribute to the overall good.

The dispute between these two versions of utilitarian policy, what we might call the "administrative" and the "market" versions of utilitarianism, characterizes many disputes in business ethics. One clear example concerns regulation of unsafe or risky products. (Similar disputes involve worker health and safety, environmental protection, regulation of advertising, and almost every other example of government regulation of business.) One side argues that questions of safety and risk should be determined by experts who then establish standards that business is required to meet. Government regulators (for example, the Consumer Products Safety Commission) are then charged with enforcing safety standards in the marketplace.

The other side argues that the best judges of acceptable risk and safety are consumers themselves. A free and competitive consumer market will insure that people will get the level of safety that they want. Individuals calculate for themselves what risks they wish to take and what trade-offs they are willing to make in order to attain safety. Consumers willing to take risks likely will pay less for their products than consumers who demand safer and less risky products. The very basic economic concept of efficiency can be understood as a placeholder for the utilitarian goal of maximum overall happiness. Thus, market-based solutions will prove best at optimally satisfying these various and competing interests and will thereby serve the overall good. The following Decision Point tests the efficacy of this approach with regard to consumer safety.

Decision Point

Should Consumer Product Safety Be Left to Individual Bargaining?

The free market version of utilitarian decision making would conclude that standards for consumer product safety are best left to the workings of the market. From this perspective, individual consumers should be left alone to bargain for the level of safety in products that they find acceptable and to make trade-offs with other benefits such as price or convenience. According to free market theory, the result of this policy would be an optimal distribution of risks and benefits. This recommendation underlies the traditional policy of *caveat emptor*, or "let the buyer beware." Do you agree that such decisions are best left to the market?

- What facts are relevant in answering this question? Does it matter what type of consumer product is involved? Does it matter who the consumer is? Why?
- What values support a policy of *caveat emptor*? What values count against it?
- Other than consumers and producers, what other stakeholders might be affected by product safety issues?
- What alternative might there be to a policy of *caveat emptor* and what impact would your alternatives have on each stakeholder?

Problems of Utilitarian Ethics

4
OBJECTIVE

Because utilitarian thinking is so common in business settings, it is important that we are aware of some of its problems. For instance, if utilitarianism advises that we make decisions by comparing the consequences of alternative actions, then we must have a method for making such comparisons. In practice, however, some comparisons and measurements are very difficult. How, after all, can we count, measure, compare, and quantify happiness? One problem that follows is that, because of these difficulties, there will be a tendency to ignore the consequences, especially the harmful consequences, to anyone other than those closest to us.

This problem is intensified when we recognize that our actions may impact the happiness not only of ourselves and those people surrounding us, but unknown and untold people in distant places and in the distant future. The action of the purchasing agent described in our opening Decision Point will affect not only her own business and the employees of her supplier, but workers and their families living in distant countries. Some utilitarians argue that the happiness of future generations ought to be considered; others include animals and all living beings capable of feeling pleasure and pain. The more expansive the list we should consider, the less practical utilitarian thinking becomes.

A second challenge goes directly to the core of utilitarianism. The essence of utilitarianism is its reliance on consequences. Ethical and unethical acts are determined by their consequences. In short, the end justifies the means. But this seems to deny one of the earliest ethical principles that many of us have learned: The ends do not justify the means.

This challenge can be explained in terms of ethical principles. When we say that the ends do not justify the means, what we are saying is that there are certain decisions we should make or certain rules we should follow no matter what the consequences. To put it another way, we have certain duties or responsibilities that we ought to obey, even when doing so does not produce a net increase in overall happiness. Examples of such duties are those required by such principles as justice, loyalty, and respect, as well as the responsibilities that flow from our social or institutional roles as parent, spouse, friend, citizen, employee, or professional.

Several examples can be used to explain why this is a serious criticism of utilitarian reasoning. Since utilitarianism focuses on the overall consequences, utilitarianism seems willing to sacrifice the good of individuals for the greater overall good. So, for example, it might turn out that the overall happiness would be increased if a small minority of a population were held as slave labor. Utilitarians would object to slavery or to child labor, not as a matter of principle, but only if and to the degree that it detracts from the overall good. If it turns out that slavery and child labor increase the net overall happiness, utilitarianism would have to support these practices. In the judgment of many people, such a decision would violate fundamental ethical principles of justice, equality, and respect. Consider the issue of torture posed in the following Decision Point.

A similar counterexample that can be raised against utilitarianism looks to specific relationships and commitments that we all make. For example, as parents we love our children and have certain duties to them. Utilitarians would seem to be committed to parental love and duty only to the degree that such love and duty contribute to the overall good. Parents should love their children because this contributes to the overall good of society. (And if it doesn't? What of the evildoer's parents–should they stop loving their child? The torturer's mother?) But surely this misrepresents (and insults) the nature of parental love. We do not love our children because of the consequences that this might have for society. Other ethicists would argue that we make certain commitments, we have certain duties, that should not be violated even if doing so would increase the net overall happiness. Violating such commitments and duties would require individuals to sacrifice their own integrity for the common good.

Such commitments and duties play a large role in business life. Contracts and promises are exactly the commitments that one ought to honor even if the consequences turn out unfavorable. The duties that one takes on as a professional function in a similar way. Arthur Andersen's auditors should not have violated their professional duties simply to produce greater overall beneficial consequences. Teachers should not violate their professional duties by failing students they do not like. Aaron Feuerstein might claim that despite bad overall consequences, he had to remain loyal to his employees as a matter of principle. We will consider similar professional commitments and duties when later chapters examine the role of professional responsibilities within business institutions.

Nevertheless, utilitarian ethics does contribute to responsible decision making in several important ways. First, and most obviously, we are reminded of the significance of consequences. Responsible decision making requires that we consider the consequences of our acts. But, as an ethical theory, utilitarianism also reminds us that we must consider the consequences to the well-being of all people affected by our decisions. Clearly, part of the fault of the Enron executives and

A major ethical and political controversy arose in recent years over the treatment of hundreds of prisoners captured during the fighting in Afghanistan and Iraq. The government argued that these were dangerous individuals who posed a significant threat to the United States and that this threat justified the treatment they received. Government attorneys even argued that because these individuals were not members of the military of a recognized country, they were not protected by international law and prohibitions against torture. The government argued that it was justified in using severe treatment that bordered on torture to extract information from these prisoners if this information could prevent future attacks on the United States.

Critics argued that some actions, torture among them, are so unethical that they should never be used, even if the result is lost opportunity to prevent attacks. Many critics argued that all people, even terrorists, deserve fundamental rights of a trial, legal representation, and due process.

Do the *ends* of preventing attacks on the United States ever, under any circumstances, justify the *means* of torture?

Arthur Andersen auditors is that they considered only their own short-term and narrow interests when making decisions and failed to consider the consequences to other stakeholders.

But the shortcomings of utilitarian reasoning must also be kept in mind. It is difficult to know everyone who will be affected by our decisions and how they are impacted. Utilitarian reasoning demands rigorous work to calculate all the beneficial and harmful consequences of our actions. Perhaps more important, utilitarian reasoning does not exhaust the range of ethical concerns. Consequences are only a part of the ethical landscape. Responsible ethical decision making also involves matters of duties, principles, and personal integrity. We turn to such factors in the following sections.

Deontology: Making Decisions Based on Ethical Principles

OBJECTIVE

Making decisions based upon the consequences certainly should be a part of responsible ethical decision making. But this approach must be supplemented with the recognition that some decisions should be matters of principle, not consequences. In other words, the ends do not always justify the means. But how do we know what principles we should follow and how do we decide when a principle should trump beneficial consequences? Principle-based, or "deontological," ethical theories, work out the details of such questions.

The language of "deontology" and "deontological ethics" is very abstract and is likely to strike many students as academic gobbledygook. But the ideas behind this approach are based in common sense. Ethical principles can simply be thought of as types of rules, and this approach to ethics tells us that there are some rules we ought to follow, even if doing so prevents good consequences from happening or even if it results in some bad consequences. Rules or principles (e.g., "obey the law," "keep your promises") create duties that bind us to act or decide in certain ways. For example, many would argue that there is an ethical rule prohibiting child labor, even if this practice would have beneficial economic consequences for society.

Sources of Rules

The law is one example of a type of rule that we ought to follow, even when it does not promote happiness. We have a duty to pay our taxes, even if the money might be more efficiently spent on our children's college education. I ought to stop at a red light, even if no cars are coming and I could get to my destination that much sooner. I ought not to steal my neighbor's property, even if he will never miss it and I will gain many benefits from it. Decision making within a business context will involve many situations in which one ought to obey legal rules even when the consequences, economic and otherwise, seem to be undesirable.

Other rules are derived from various institutions in which we participate or from various social roles that we fill. I ought to read each student's research paper carefully and diligently, even if they will never know the difference and their final grade will not be affected. In my role as teacher and university faculty member, I have taken on certain responsibilities that accompany those roles that cannot be abandoned whenever it is convenient for me to do so. As the referee in a sporting event, I have the duty to enforce the rules fairly, even when it would be easier not to do so. Similar rule-based duties follow from our roles as friends (do not gossip about your friends), family members (do your chores at home), students (do not plagiarize), church member (contribute to the church's upkeep), citizens (vote), and good neighbors (do not operate your lawn mower before 8:00 A.M.).

There will be very many occasions in which such role-based duties arise in business. As an employee, one takes on a certain role that creates duties. Every business will have a set of rules that employees are expected to follow. Sometimes these rules are explicitly stated in a code of conduct, other times in employee handbooks, still others simply by managers. Likewise, as a business manager, one ought to follow many rules in respect to stockholders, employees, suppliers, and other stakeholders.

Perhaps the most dramatic example of role-based duties concerns the work of professionals within business. Lawyers, accountants, auditors, financial analysts, and bankers have important roles to play within political and economic institutions. Many of these roles, often described as "gatekeeper functions," insure the integrity and proper functioning of the economic, legal, or financial system. Chapter 2

Reality Check *Ethical Principles at Compaq*

Ethical principles are often integrated within corporate codes of conduct. For example, Compaq Corporation's Code of Conduct mentions six fundamental duties:

> Compaq Computer Corporation is committed to promoting integrity and maintaining the highest standard of ethical conduct in all of its activities. Our business success is dependent on trusting relationships, which are built on this foundation of integrity. Our reputation is founded on the personal integrity of the company's personnel and our dedication to:

Honesty in communicating within the company and with our suppliers and customers, while at the same time protecting the company's confidential information and trade secrets

Quality in our products and services, by striving to provide defect-free products and services to our customers

Responsibility for our words and actions, confirms our commitment to do what we say

Compassion in our relationships with our employees and the communities affected by our business

Fairness to our fellow employees, shareholders, customers and suppliers through adherence to all applicable laws, regulations and policies, and a high standard of behavior

Respect for our fellow employees, shareholders, customers and suppliers while showing willingness to solicit their opinions and value their feedback

introduced the idea of professional responsibilities within the workplace, and this theme will be developed further in Chapter 8.

The Enron and Arthur Andersen case provides a helpful example for understanding professional duties. While examining Enron's financial reports, the auditors at Arthur Andersen knew that diligent application of strict auditing standards required one decision, but that the consequences of this diligent application would be harmful to Arthur Andersen's business interests. A fair analysis of this aspect of the Enron–Arthur Andersen scandal would point out that Andersen's auditors failed in their ethical duties precisely because they did not follow the rules governing their professional responsibilities and allowed beneficial consequences to override their professional principles. (See the Reality Check that follows.)

So far we have mentioned legal rules, organizational rules, role-based rules, and professional rules. We can think of these rules as part of a social agreement, or social contract, which functions to organize and ease relations between individuals. No group could function if members were free at all times to decide for themselves what to do and how to act. By definition, any cooperative activity requires cooperation; that is, it requires rules that each member follows.

Reality Check *Ethical Rules as a Check on Misguided Consequences*

The Enron and Arthur Andersen case also demonstrates one of the major vulnerabilities of the consequentialist approach. Utilitarians would rightfully point out that Andersen's auditors did not make decisions according to strict utilitarian ethical principles. The auditors calculated the consequences, but only those to their *own* firm and their *own* well-being. Had they truly calculated the *overall* consequences of their decisions, as utilitarianism would require, Andersen's auditors may very well have made the right ethical decision. Instead, they thought only about the $100 million of business generated by Enron and decided to allow this influence to override their principles. But this shows the difficulty in calculating consequences. Because it is so difficult to know all the consequences of our actions, it will always be tempting to consider only the consequences to ourselves and the stakeholders in our close professional or personal circles. To avoid the slide from a consideration of overall consequences to a consideration of purely individualistic, egoistic (and nonethical) consequences, deontological ethics advises us instead to *follow the rules*, regardless of consequences.

Moral Rights and Duties

OBJECTIVE

Are there *any* rules we should follow, decisions we should make, no matter what the consequences? The foremost advocate of this tradition in ethics, the 18th-century German philosopher Immanuel Kant, argued that there is essentially one such fundamental ethical principle: respect the dignity of each individual human being.

Kant claimed that this duty to respect human dignity could be expressed in several ways. One version directs us to act according to those rules that could be universally agreed to by all people. (This is the first form of the famous "Kantian categorical imperative.") Another, less abstract version requires us to treat all persons as ends in themselves and never only as means to our own ends. In other words, our fundamental duty is to treat people as subjects capable of living their own lives and not as mere objects that exist for our purposes. To use the familiar subject/object categories from grammar, humans are subjects because they make decisions and perform actions rather than being objects that are acted upon. Humans have their own ends and purposes and therefore should not be treated simply as a means to the ends of others.

Since every person has this same fundamental duty towards others, each of us can be said to have fundamental moral rights: the right to be treated with respect, to expect that others will treat us as an end and never as a means only, the right to be treated as an autonomous person. Perhaps this offers a new perspective on some of the issues we have already addressed. Consider the following Decision Point.

This perspective on ethical duties is particularly relevant to employment issues. Examine the language of *human resource management,* which suggests that humans are "resources" to be managed (akin to natural resources that are managed?). To return to an earlier example, the Kantian would object to child labor

Let us reconsider the Decision Point on utilitarianism from earlier in the chapter. We explored the question of whether the *ends* of preventing attacks on the United States ever justified the *means* of torture.

Recall that critics argued that all people, even terrorists, deserve fundamental rights of a trial, legal representation, and due process. If we now approach the question from a Kantian perspective, does this offer us any greater insights or ability to articulate support for the arguments of these critics?

because such practices violate our duty to treat children with respect. We violate the rights of children when we treat them as mere means to the ends of production and economic growth. We are treating them merely as means because, as children, they have not rationally and freely chosen their own ends. We are simply using them as tools or objects.

In this way, the concept of a moral right is central to the deontological tradition. The inherent dignity of each individual means that we cannot do just anything we choose to another person. Moral rights protect individuals from being treated in ways that would violate their dignity and that would treat them as mere objects or means. Moral rights imply that some acts and some decisions are "off-limits." Accordingly, our fundamental moral duty (the "categorical imperative") is to respect the fundamental moral rights of others. Our rights establish limits on the decisions and authority of others.

So what rights do we have? We can at least sketch a general account of rights by returning to the original idea of respect and the elements of **autonomy** and dignity on which it is based. What human characteristic justifies the assumption that humans possess a special dignity? Why would it be wrong to treat humans as mere means or objects, rather than as ends or subjects?

The most common answer offered through the Western ethical tradition is that the human capacity to make free and rational choices is the distinctive human characteristic. Humans do not act only out of instinct and conditioning; they make free choices about how they live their lives, about their own ends. In this sense, humans are said to have *autonomy*. Humans are subjects in the sense that they originate action, they choose, they act for their own ends. To treat them as a means or as an object is to deny them this distinctive and essential human characteristic; it would be to deny them their very humanity.

From this we can see how two related rights have emerged as fundamental within philosophical ethics. If autonomy, or "self-rule," is a fundamental characteristic of human nature, then the freedom to make our own choices deserves special protection as a basic right. But since all humans possess this fundamental characteristic, equal treatment and equal consideration are also fundamental rights.

In summary, we can say that rights offer protection of certain central human interests, prohibiting the sacrifice of these interests merely to provide a net increase in the overall happiness. But interests, as opposed to desires, are connected to human well-being in an objective manner. Human nature, characterized as the capacity for free and autonomous choice, provides the grounds for

Reality Check *Are Fundamental Human Rights Universally Accepted?*

In 1948, the United Nations adopted the Universal Declaration of Human Rights. Since that time, this declaration has been translated into more than 300 languages and dialects. The declaration contains 30 articles outlining basic human rights. In part, the declaration includes the following:

PREAMBLE

Recognition of the inherent dignity and of the equal and inalienable rights of all members of the human family is the foundation of freedom, justice and peace in the world.

Article 1.
All human beings are born free and equal in dignity and rights. They are endowed with reason and conscience and should act towards one another in a spirit of brotherhood.

Article 2.
Everyone is entitled to all the rights and freedoms set forth in this Declaration, without distinction of any kind, such as race, colour, sex, language, religion, political or other opinion, national or social origin, property, birth or other status.

Article 3.
Everyone has the right to life, liberty and security of person.

Article 4.
No one shall be held in slavery or servitude; slavery and the slave trade shall be prohibited in all their forms.

Article 5.
No one shall be subjected to torture or to cruel, inhuman or degrading treatment or punishment.

Article 9.
No one shall be subjected to arbitrary arrest, detention or exile.

Article 10.
Everyone is entitled in full equality to a fair and public hearing by an independent and impartial tribunal, in the determination of his rights and obligations and of any criminal charge against him.

Article 18.
Everyone has the right to freedom of thought, conscience and religion; this right includes freedom to change his religion or belief, and freedom, either alone or in community with others and in public or private, to manifest his religion or belief in teaching, practice, worship and observance.

Article 19.
Everyone has the right to freedom of opinion and expression; this right includes freedom to hold opinions without interference and to seek, receive and impart information and ideas through any media and regardless of frontiers.

Article 23.
(1) Everyone has the right to work, to free choice of employment, to just and favourable conditions of work and to protection against unemployment.
(2) Everyone, without any discrimination, has the right to equal pay for equal work.
(3) Everyone who works has the right to just and favourable remuneration ensuring for himself and his family an existence worthy of human dignity, and supplemented, if necessary, by other means of social protection.
(4) Everyone has the right to form and to join trade unions for the protection of his interests.

Article 25.
(1) Everyone has the right to a standard of living adequate for the health and well-being of himself and of his family, including food, clothing, housing and medical care and necessary social services, and the right to security in the event of unemployment, sickness, disability, widowhood, old age or other lack of livelihood in circumstances beyond his control.

Article 26.
(1) Everyone has the right to education.

distinguishing central interests from mere wants. Our fundamental ethical rights, and the duties that follow from them, are derived from our nature as free and rational beings. They are, according to much of this tradition, "natural rights" that are more fundamental and persistent than the legal rights created by governments and social contracts.

Distinguishing between Moral Rights and Legal Rights

OBJECTIVE

It will be helpful at this point to distinguish between moral rights and legal rights. To illustrate this distinction, let us take employee rights as an example. Three senses of employee rights are common in business. First, there are those *legal* rights granted to employees on the basis of legislation or judicial rulings. Thus, employees have a right to a minimum wage, equal opportunity, to bargain collectively as part of a union, to be free from sexual harassment, and so forth. Second, employee rights might refer to those goods that employees are entitled to on the basis of contractual agreements with employers. In this sense, a particular employee might have a right to a specific health care package, a certain number of paid holidays, pension funds, and the like. Finally, employee rights might refer to those moral entitlements to which employees have a claim independently of any particular legal or contractual factors. Such rights would originate with the respect owed to them as human beings.

To expand on this understanding, consider how legal and contractual rights interact. In general, both parties to an employment agreement bargain over the conditions of work. Employers offer certain wages, benefits, and working conditions and in return seek worker productivity. Employees offer skills and abilities and seek wages and benefits in return. Thus, employment rights emerge from contractual promises. However, certain goods are legally exempt from such negotiation. An employer cannot make a willingness to submit to sexual harassment or acceptance of a wage below the minimum established by law a part of the employment agreement. In effect, legal rights exempt certain interests from the employment contract. Such legal rights set the basic legal framework in which business operates. They are established by the legal system in which business operates and, in this sense, are part of the price of doing business.

So, too, moral rights lie outside of the bargaining that occurs between employers and employees. Unlike the minimum wage, moral rights are established and justified by moral, rather than legal, considerations. Moral rights establish the basic moral framework for the legal environment itself, and more specifically for any contracts that are negotiated within business. Thus, as described in the United States Declaration of Independence, governments and laws are created in order to secure fundamental natural moral rights. The rights outlined on the previous page in the excerpt from the United Nations fit this conception of fundamental moral rights.

Social Justice: Rawlsian Justice as Fairness

We have introduced and examined utilitarianism as a theory that guides decisions based on the consequential outcomes of our actions and a second theory that guides us to explore the moral principles implicated by our decisions. We will now examine a third important approach that will provide insights into our decision-making process, a theory of social justice based on fairness as its primary social principle.

The American philosopher John Rawls has developed one of the most powerful and influential accounts of justice. Rawls offers a contemporary version of the social contract theory that understands basic ethical rules as part of an implicit contract necessary to insure social cooperation. Rawls's theory has proven influential in political theory, economics, and the law. Rawls's theory of justice consists of two major components: a method for determining the principles of justice that should govern society, and the specific principles that are derived from that method.

The method itself is a version of the hypothetical social contract, which can be a valuable tool for our own ethical decision making. Imagine rational and self-interested individuals having to choose and agree on the fundamental principles for their society. The image of members of a constitutional convention is a helpful model for this idea. To ensure that the principles are fair and impartial, imagine further that these individuals do not know the specific details or characteristics of their own lives. They do not know their abilities or disabilities and talents or weaknesses; they have no idea about their position in the social structure of this new society. They are, in Rawls's terms, behind a **"veil of ignorance"** and must choose principles by which they will abide when they come out from behind the veil. To ensure that each individual is treated as an end and not as a means, imagine finally that these individuals must *unanimously* agree on the principles. These initial conditions of impartiality, what Rawls calls the "original position," guarantee that the principles chosen are fair—the primary value underlying Rawls's concept of justice.

The idea of this "original position," of having to make decisions behind a veil of ignorance, is at the heart of Rawls's theory that fairness is the central element of a just decision or just organization. He contends that our decisions *ought* to be made in such a way, and our social institutions *ought* to be organized in such a way, that they would prove acceptable to us *no matter whose point of view we take*. A fair decision is an impartial decision. Rawls would argue that the only way we can reach this conclusion is to seek out the original perspective from behind a veil of ignorance, to imagine ourselves ignorant with regard to our position and strive toward impartiality. See the Pie Chart Reality Check that follows for a demonstration of how this is applied.

The specific principles of justice that emerge from this decision procedure are also valuable tools for thinking about economics and business institutions. Rawls derives two fundamental principles of justice from this original position. The first principle states that each individual is to have an equal right to the most extensive system of liberties. In the original position, individuals would demand as much freedom as possible, but no rational or self-interested individual would be willing to sacrifice his own equality simply to secure more freedom for others. This first principle therefore argues that equal rights are a fundamental element of social justice.

The second principle that is derived from the veil of ignorance holds that benefits and burdens of a society should generally be distributed equally. An unequal distribution could be justified only if it would benefit the least advantaged members of society and only if those benefits derive from positions for which each person has an equal opportunity. Thus Rawls's justice as fairness would imply

Reality Check *A Pie Chart Demonstration*

A simple example can be demonstrated with your favorite dessert. If you are charged with cutting a pie before the arrival of the guests, you might not know which slice will be yours once your guests are allowed to choose theirs first. This is comparable to having to decide behind the veil of ignorance. Therefore, you are likely to cut each slice the same size to ensure that you will at least end up with a slice as large as everyone else's. The same will be true, Rawls would argue, with the distribution of goods and services in a social group. If you are not certain in which group you might fall once the hypothetical veil is lifted, you are most likely to treat each group with the greatest care and equality in case that is the group in which you later find yourself.

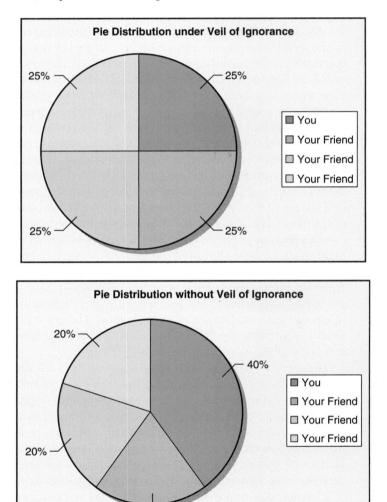

very specific conclusions regarding such business and social issues as tax policy, affirmative action, executive compensation, and government regulation.

Virtue Ethics: Making Decisions Based on Integrity and Character

OBJECTIVE

For the most part, utilitarian and deontological approaches to ethics focus on rules and principles that we might follow in deciding what we should do, both as individuals and as citizens. These approaches conceive of practical reason in terms of deciding how to act and what to do. Chapter 1 pointed out, however, that ethics also involves questions about the type of person one should become. Virtue ethics is a tradition within philosophical ethics that seeks a full and detailed description of those character traits, or virtues, that would constitute a good and full human life. See the Reality Check on the next page for a discussion of the language used to describe those traits.

To understand how virtue ethics differs from utilitarian and deontological approaches, consider the problem of egoism. As mentioned above, egoism is a view that holds that people act only out of self-interest. Many economists, for example, assume that all individuals always act out of self-interest; indeed, many assume that rationality itself should be defined in terms of acting out of self-interest. The biggest challenges posed by egoism and, according to some, the biggest challenge to ethics, is the apparent gap between self-interest and altruism, or between motivation that is "self-regarding" and motivation that is "other-regarding." Ethics requires us, at least at times, to act for the well-being of others. Yet, some would claim that this is not possible, that humans act only from self-interested motives. (See the Reality Check on page 85.)

An ethics of virtue shifts the focus from questions about what a person should *do*, to a focus on who that person *is*. This shift requires not only a different view of ethics but, at least as important, a different view of ourselves. Implicit in this distinction is the recognition that our identity as a person is constituted in part by our wants, beliefs, values, and attitudes. A person's character—those dispositions, relationships, attitudes, values, and beliefs that popularly might be called a "personality"—is not a feature independent of that person's identity. Character is not like a suit of clothes that you step into and out of at will. Rather, the self is identical to a person's most fundamental and enduring dispositions, attitudes, values, and beliefs.

Note how this shift to an emphasis on the individual changes the nature of justification in ethics. If, as seems true for many people, an ethical justification of some act requires that it be tied to self-interest, we should not be surprised to find that this justification often fails. Ethical controversies often involve a conflict between self-interest and ethical values. Why should I do the ethical thing if it would require me to give up a lot of money? For a personality that does not already include a disposition to be modest, the only avenue open for justification would involve showing how the disposition serves some other interest of that person. Why should an executive turn down a multimillion dollar bonus? The only

Reality Check   *Virtues in Practice*

The language of virtues and vices may seem old-fashioned or quaint for modern readers, but this was a dominant perspective on ethics in the Western world for centuries. If you develop a list of adjectives that describe a person's character, you will find that the language of virtues and vices is not as outdated as it may seem.

The ancient Greeks identified four primary virtues: courage, moderation, wisdom, and justice. Early Christians described the three cardinal virtues of faith, hope, and charity. Boys Scouts pledge to be trustworthy, loyal, helpful, friendly, courteous, kind, obedient, cheerful, thrifty, brave, clean, and reverent.

According to ancient and medieval philosophers, the virtues represented a balanced mean, the "golden mean," between two extremes, both of which would be considered vices. Thus, for example, a brave person finds the balance between too little courage, which is cowardice, and too much courage, which would be reckless and foolhardy.

The virtues are those character traits, or habits, that would produce a good, happy, and meaningful life. Practicing such virtues and habits, and acting in accord with one's own character, is to live a life of integrity.

way to answer this question appears to be to show how it would be in his self-interest to do so. But this is at times unlikely.

On the other hand, for the person already characterized by modest and unaffected desires, the question of justifying a smaller salary is less relevant. If I am the type of person who had moderate and restrained desires for money, then there is no temptation to be unethical for the sake of a large bonus. For many people, the "self" of self-interest is a caring, modest, unaffected, altruistic self. For these people, there simply is no conflict between *self*-interest and altruism.

The degree to which we are capable of acting for the well-being of others therefore seems to depend on a variety of factors such as our desires, our beliefs, our dispositions, and our values; in short, it depends on our character or the type of person we are. For those who are caring, empathetic, charitable, and sympathetic, the challenge of selfishness and egoism is simply not a factor in their decision making.

Virtue ethics emphasizes the more affective side of our character. Virtue ethics recognizes that our motivations—our interests, wants, desires—are not the sorts of things that each one of us chooses anew each morning. Instead, human beings act in and from character. By adulthood, these character traits typically are deeply ingrained and conditioned within us. Given that our character plays such a deciding role in our behavior, and given the realization that our character can be shaped by factors that are controllable (by conscious individual decisions, by how we are raised, by the social institutions in which we live, work, and learn), virtue ethics seeks to understand how those traits are formed and which traits bolster and which undermine a meaningful, worthwhile, and satisfying human life so that we can take responsibility for the person we become.

Virtue ethics can offer us a more fully textured understanding of life within business. Rather than simply describing people as good or bad, right or wrong, an ethics of virtue encourages a fuller description. For example, we might describe Aaron Feuerstein as heroic and courageous. He is a man of integrity, who sympathizes

Reality Check *Is Selfishness a Virtue?*

Does ethics demand that we sacrifice our own interests for others? If so, is this reasonable? Is it even possible?

The tension between ethics and self-interest has been central to philosophical ethics since at least the time of Socrates and Plato. Ethical responsibilities certainly seem to require that we sometimes restrict our own actions out of consideration for the interests of other people. Yet, some thinkers have concluded that such a requirement is unreasonable and unrealistic. It is unreasonable because it would be too much to ask people to act against their own self-interest; and it would be unrealistic because, in fact, it is simply part of human nature to be selfish.

Twentieth-century philosopher Ayn Rand argued that selfishness is a virtue. Rand denied that altruism, acting for the interests of others, was an ethical virtue. Altruism too easily makes people predisposed to sacrifice for others and ignore their own basic interests. Instead, she argued that ethically responsible persons should be motivated by a concern with their own interests. From this perspective, selfishness is a virtue; people who act out of consideration for their own interests will live more fulfilling and happy human lives.

This philosophical starting point has led many thinkers, including Rand herself, to adopt a political and social philosophy of libertarianism. This is the view that the fundamental right of individuals is the right to liberty, understood as the right to be free from interference by others. Libertarianism also provides philosophical support for free market capitalism and is often the ethical view implicit in the thinking of people in business. Free markets are the economic system that best serve the libertarian goal of protecting individual rights of liberty.

But even Rand recognized that selfishness in this philosophical sense is not the same as what is commonly understood as selfish behavior. Simply doing whatever one wants will not necessarily advance one's own self-interest. The behavior of the stereotypical selfish and self-centered person who is antagonistic to others is not likely to lead to a happy, secure, and meaningful life. Rand recognized that self-interest, properly understood, may sometimes demand that we restrict and regulate our own desires. Further, since the virtue of selfishness applies equally to all people, our own self-interest is limited by the equal rights of others.

Thus, Rand's version of libertarianism is not as extreme as it might first appear. No ethical tradition expects people to live a life of total self-sacrifice and self-denial. But even those who might be described as ethical egoists concede that rational self-interest does create ethical limits to our own actions and that narrowly selfish people are unethical.

with employees and cares about their well-being. Other executives might be described as greedy or ruthless, proud or competitive. Faced with a difficult dilemma, we might ask what a person with integrity would do. What would an honest person say? Do I have the courage of my convictions? In other words, you might consider someone you believe to be virtuous and ask yourself what that person would do in a specific situation. What would a virtuous person do?

But virtue ethics seeks more than a detailed description of business life. Like all ethical theories, virtue ethics is also prescriptive in offering advice on how we should live. Virtue ethics calls on us to reflect on two deeper questions. Given a more detailed and textured description of moral behavior, which set of virtues are more likely to embody a full, satisfying, meaningful, enriched, and worthy human life? Business provides many opportunities for behavior that is generous or greedy, ruthless or compassionate, fair or manipulative. Given these opportunities, each one of us must ask which character traits are likely to help us live a good life and which are likely to frustrate this. What type of person are we to be?

Besides connecting the virtues to a conception of a fuller human life, virtue ethics also reminds us to examine how character traits are formed and conditioned. By the time we are adults, much of our character is formed by such factors as our parents, schools, church, friends, and society. But powerful social institutions such as business and especially our own places of employment and our particular social roles within them (e.g., manager, professional, trainee) have a profound influence on shaping our character. Consider an accounting firm that hires a group of trainees fully expecting that fewer than half will be retained and anticipating that only a very small group will make partner. That corporate environment encourages motivations and behavior very different from a firm that hires fewer people but gives them all a greater chance at long-term success. A company that sets unrealistic sales goals will find it creates a different sales force than one that understands sales more as customer service. Virtue ethics reminds us to look to the actual practices we find in the business world and ask what type of people these practices are creating. Many individual moral dilemmas that arise within business can best be understood as arising from a tension between the type of person we seek to be and the type of person business expects us to be.

Consider an example described by a researcher conducting empirical studies of the values found in marketing firms and advertising agencies. This person reported that, on several occasions, advertising agents told her they would never allow their own children to watch the television shows and advertisements that their firm was producing. By their own admission, the ads for such shows aim to manipulate children into buying, or getting their parents to buy, products that had little or no real value. In some cases, the ads promoted beer drinking and the advertisers themselves admitted, as their "dirty little secret," that they were intended to target the teenage market. Further, their own research evidenced the success of their ads in increasing sales.

Independent of the ethical questions we might ask about advertising aimed at children, a virtue ethics approach would look at the type of person who is so able to disassociate himself and his own values from his work, and the social institutions and practices that encourage it. What kind of person is willing to subject others' children to marketing practices that are unacceptable for his own children? Such a person seems to lack even the most elementary form of personal integrity. What kind of institution encourages people to treat children in ways that they willingly admit are indecent? What kind of person does one become working in such an institution?

A Decision-Making Model for Business Ethics Revisited

This chapter provided a detailed introductory survey of ethical theory. While some of these topics might appear esoteric and too abstract for a business ethics class, they have a very practical aim. Understanding the philosophical basis of ethics will enable you to become more aware of ethical issues, better able to recognize the impact of your decisions, and more likely to make better informed and more reasonable decisions. In addition, the theories allow us to better and more articulately explain why we have made or wish to make a particular decision. While a statement such as "we should engage in this practice because it is right" might

Reality Check *Can Virtue Be Taught?*

Plato's famous dialogue the *Meno* opens with the title character asking Socrates this basic question: Can virtue be taught? If ethics involves developing the right sort of character traits and habits, as the virtue theorist holds, then the acquisition of those traits becomes a fundamental question for ethics. Can we teach people to *be* honest, trustworthy, loyal, courteous, moderate, respectful, and compassionate?

Meno initially cast the question in terms of two alternatives: either virtue is taught, or it is acquired naturally. In modern terms, this is the question of nurture or nature, environment or genetics. Socrates' answer is more complicated. Virtue cannot simply be taught by others, nor is it acquired automatically through nature. Each individual has the natural potential to become virtuous, and learning from one's surroundings is a part of this process. But, ultimately, virtues must be developed by each individual through a complex process of personal reflection, reasoning, practice, and observation, as well as social reinforcement and conditioning.

Virtues are habits, and acquiring any habit is a subtle and complex process.

Parents confront this question every day. I know my children will lead happier and more meaningful lives if they are honest, respectful, cheerful, and moderate and not greedy, envious, gloomy, arrogant, or selfish. Yet, simply telling my children to be honest and to avoid greed is insufficient. Nor can I remain passive and assume that these traits will develop naturally. Instilling these character traits and habits is a long-term process that develops over time.

Business institutions also have come to recognize that character formation is both difficult and unavoidable. Employees come to business with certain character traits and habits, and these can be shaped and reinforced in the workplace. Hire a person with the wrong character traits, and there will be trouble ahead. Designing a workplace, creating a corporate culture, to reinforce virtues and discourage vice is one of the greatest challenges for an ethical business.

seem a bit vague or unpersuasive, an alternate explanation such as "we should engage in this practice because more people will be better off than harmed if we do so" could be tremendously effective and convincing. When a decision leader asks you why you support or oppose a specific proposal, your response now has comprehensive substance behind it and will therefore be more sophisticated, credible, and influential.

These ethical theories and traditions also provide important ways to develop the decision-making model introduced in Chapter 2. These ethical theories, after all, provide systematic and sophisticated ways to think and reason about ethical questions. By analyzing dilemmas with the theories presented in this chapter and revisited throughout the text, one is better able to gain insights, to observe perspectives that might have otherwise gone unnoticed, to be empathetic to the impact of a decision on others, to be sensitive to the protection of fundamental rights and duties, and to remain cognizant of one's duty to one's self and one's own integrity and values.

We now can offer a more detailed version of our decision-making model, one in which ethical theories are integrated into an explicit decision procedure. The decision-making process introduced here aims, above all else, to help you make ethically responsible business decisions. To summarize, we next review that decision-making process in more detail.

1. **Determine the facts.** Gather all of the relevant facts. It is critical at this stage that we do not unintentionally bias our later decision by gathering only those facts in support of one particular outcome.

2. **Identify the ethical issues involved.** What is the ethical dimension? What is the ethical issue? Often we do not even notice the ethical dilemma. Avoid normative myopia.

3. **Identify stakeholders.** Who will be affected by this decision? What are their relationships, their priorities to me, and what is their power over my decision or results? Who has a stake in the outcome? Do not limit your inquiry only to those stakeholders to whom you believe you owe a duty; sometimes a duty arises as a result of the impact. For instance, you might not necessarily first consider your competitors as stakeholders; however, once you understand the impact of your decision on those competitors, an ethical duty may arise.

4. **Consider the available alternatives.** Exercise "moral imagination." Are there creative ways to resolve conflicts? Explore not only the obvious choices, but also those that are less obvious and that require some creative thinking or moral imagination to create. Imagine how the situation appears from other points of view.

5. **Consider how a decision affects stakeholders.** Take the point of view of other people involved. How is each stakeholder affected by my decision? Imagine a decision that would prove acceptable to all parties. Compare and weigh the alternatives: Ethical theories and traditions can help here. Consider the following issues:

   What are the consequences, both beneficial and harmful?

   Who gets the benefits? Who bears the costs?

   What duties, rights, and principles are involved?

   What does the law say?

   Are professional duties involved?

   Which principles are obligatory?

   How are people being treated?

   What is a fair and impartial decision?

   What are the implications for personal integrity and character?

   What type of person am I becoming through this decision?

   What are my own principles and purposes?

   Can I live with public disclosure of this decision?

6. **Guidance.** Can you discuss the case with relevant others? Can you gather additional opinions or perspectives? Are there any guidelines, codes, or other external sources that might shed light on the dilemma?

7. **Assessment.** Have you built in mechanisms for assessing your decision and making possible modifications, if necessary? Make sure you learn from each decision and utilize that increased knowledge as you face similar decisions in the future or as your current situation changes.

One crucial lesson this Decision Point raises is that many business decisions implicitly involve a wide range of ethical issues. The purchasing manager may well believe that the decision to outsource suppliers is simply a financial decision. The manager is behaving as the business, financial, and economic system expects. But it should be clear that financial and ethical considerations are not mutually exclusive. Business decisions often involve both. One does not avoid ethical responsibility by making a financial decision. Finance and business management are not value-neutral.

If pressed for an ethical rationale, the manager might also cite an economic justification in terms of overall job growth, economic efficiency, and lower prices to consumers. The manager would also likely refer to the duty to maximize return for stockholders. But these, too, are clearly ethical factors. At their base, many of these economic justifications are utilitarian. Economic efficiency is the best policy because it will lead to the greater overall good. Managers also have duties to stockholders because of their ownership rights in the company.

Implicit within the financial and economic framework taught in business schools is a very clear ethical perspective. Those who deny a place for ethics in a business school curriculum often lose sight of this fact. The economic theory of market capitalism, and the theories of business management, finance, marketing, and accounting implied by that economic theory, already presuppose a range of ethical values. The utilitarian goal of economic growth and economic efficiency, along with the rights and duties associated with private and corporate property, are inevitably involved in business decisions. Ethical decision making requires only that such values be made explicit and that other ethical values also be acknowledged.

Loyalty surely has a place in personal and social relationships. But does it have a role in business relationships? Some would argue that loyalty is seldom a two-way street in business. A company may ask for or expect loyalty from employees, by asking them to sacrifice free time on the weekend to work, for example. But companies may not be as willing to sacrifice for employees in return. Citizens are expected to be loyal to their own country, but are corporations citizens? If the law treats a corporation as a legal person, does this imply that the corporation has a specific duty of loyalty to the country? Should a company sacrifice profits by declining to outsource jobs and production?

Questions, Projects, and Exercises

1. What makes an ethical decision or issue *ethical*? How would you explain the differences between ethical/nonethical and ethical/unethical? What ethical issues or dilemmas have you experienced in the workplace? Are any ethical issues or dilemmas presently being discussed at your school?

2. Are some ethical values or principles relative to one's own culture, religion, or personal opinion? Are some ethical values not culturally relevant? What makes them different?

3. Do an Internet search on international human rights and/or fundamental moral rights. Can you make the argument that any moral rights are universally acknowledged?

4. Why might the political goal of economic growth be considered a utilitarian goal?

5. Some political philosophers consider the ethical foundations of legislatures to be utilitarian, while the ethical foundation of the judiciary is deontological. How would you explain this distinction?

6. Do people have a right to do whatever they want? If not, in what sense can people have a right to liberty or personal freedom?

7. Can such character traits as honesty, loyalty, trustworthiness, compassion, and humility be taught? Do people learn to be selfish, greedy, and aggressive, or do these traits come naturally?

8. Do professionals such as accountants and lawyers have duties and obligations that other people do not? From where would such duties come?

Key Terms

After reading this chapter, you should have a clear understanding of the following Key Terms. The page numbers refer to the point at which they were discussed in the chapter. For a more complete definition, please see the Glossary.

autonomy, *p. 78*
categorical imperative, *p. 77*
character, *p. 66*
consequentialist theories, *p. 70*

deontological ethics, *p. 66*
duties, *p. 73*
egoism, *p. 83*
loyalty, *p. 64*
rights, *p. 66*

social contract theory, *p. 76*
utilitarianism, *p. 66*
veil of ignorance, *p. 81*
virtue ethics, *p. 66*

Readings

Reading 3-1: "The Justification of Human Rights," by Denis Arnold, *p. 90*
Reading 3-2: "Do CEO's Get Paid Too Much?," by Jeffrey Moriarty, *p. 95*
Reading 3-3: "Caux Principles for Business," *p. 105*

Reading 3-1

The Justification of Human Rights

Denis G. Arnold

Human rights are moral rights that apply to all persons in all nations, regardless of whether the nation in which a person resides acknowledges and protects those rights. It is in this sense that human rights are said to be *inalienable*. In order to think about human rights in a meaningful way, it is necessary to answer certain philosophical questions about their nature. Three of the most basic questions are the following: How can human rights be justified? What specific human rights exist? How do human rights differ from other rights, such as legal rights? Let us consider each question in turn.

Philosophical Foundations

Human rights are rights enjoyed by humans not because we are members of the species *Homo sapiens,* but because fully functional members of our species are persons. Personhood is a metaphysical category that may or may not be unique to *Homo sapiens.* To be a person one must be capable of reflecting on one's desires at a second-order level, and one must be capable of acting in a manner consistent with one's considered preferences (Dworkin, 1988; Frankfurt, 1988). First-order desires are the assortment of desires that occupy one's conscious mind and compete for one's attention. Second-order desires are desires about those first-order desires. When one embraces a particular first-order desire at a second-order level, it becomes a preference. A mundane example will help to illustrate this concept. Each of us is likely to have found ourselves staring at a bedside clock after having turned off an early morning alarm. Lying comfortably in bed, one might reflect on one's immediate desires: to get up and go for a run; to get up and prepare for an early morning meeting; or to roll over and return to sleep. The process of reflecting on these competing desires takes place at a second-order level of consciousness. It is the capacity to reflect on one's competing desires and to act in a manner consistent with our second-order preferences that distinguishes persons from mere animals. This is not to say that one cannot sometimes fail to act in a manner consistent with one's better judgment and still be regarded as a person. Indeed, most of us are intimately familiar with such weakness of the will. The point is that we enjoy this capacity, and we are capable of acting in a manner consistent with this capacity. Furthermore, if a human were constitutionally incapable of acting in a manner consistent with his or her second-order preferences, he or she would not be properly described as a person. It is in this sense that the idea of personhood is properly understood as metaphysical rather than biological (Melden, 1977).

Theorists with a wide range of commitments readily agree that persons enjoy a basic right to individual freedom, and that other persons have a duty not to restrict or constrain the freedom of others without strong justification (Nozick, 1974; Lomasky; O'Neill). This right is grounded in Kant's second formulation of the categorical imperative: "Act so that you treat humanity, whether in your own person or in that of another, always as and end and never as a means only" (Kant, 1990, p. 46). The popular expression of this principle is that morality requires that we respect people. Kant provides a sustained defense of the doctrine of respect for persons, and he and his interpreters specify in detail its practical implications. Respecting other persons requires that one refrain from interfering with their decisions and actions. Typically one person is justified in limiting the freedom of another only when her own freedom is unjustly restricted by that person. One traditional way of capturing this sense of a liberty right is that individuals should be free to have as much liberty or freedom as is compatible with like liberty or freedom for all.

There is little controversy regarding the negative right to liberty or freedom. However, there is significant controversy over whether or not there are positive rights to certain economic and social goods. Positive rights entail not merely negative obligations on the part of others to refrain from certain actions, but a positive obligation to fulfill the right of the rights holder. For example, if individuals have a right to employment or health care in order to ensure their subsistence and well-being, then others have an obligation to provide them with health care or employment. The state may be called upon to fulfill these duties, but in weak or corrupt states such duties may be neglected. And in states where market values trump consideration for basic human rights, such rights may also be neglected. Under such conditions the burden of fulfilling such obligations seems to fall on individuals, but most individuals are not well positioned to meet such obligations. Furthermore, even in cases where the state does meet such alleged obligations, traditional libertarians would argue that it is illegitimate to tax some citizens in order to ensure the subsistence and well-being of others (Nozick, 1974). Have we reached an impasse?

Arguably there are at least two philosophically sound reasons for thinking that we can move beyond this apparent impasse. First, there is an influential and persuasive argument against the idea that the distinction between negative and positive rights is unsustainable. Second, there is a widely influential set of positive arguments that can be used to support both a right to freedom and minimal welfare rights such as the right to subsistence. Let us consider each argument in turn.

Henry Shue has famously argued that the very distinction between negative and positive rights that the preceding analysis presumes is artificial and inconsistent with social reality (1996). For example, consider the right to physical security (i.e., the right not to be harmed). It is possible to avoid violating a person's right not to be harmed by refraining from certain actions. However, it is not possible to protect a person from harm without taking proactive steps. At a minimum, law enforcement agencies and a criminal justice system are required so that individuals are not left to defend themselves against forces that they are unable to defeat on their own. The existence of these social institutions is predicated on positive actions in the forms of design, implementation, administration, and taxation. In this way it can be seen that the protection of a prototypical negative right requires positive actions, and not merely the avoidance of particular actions. Since negative rights entail both negative and positive duties, the notion of negative versus positive rights loses its meaning. There are only rights and corresponding obligations, but the obligations that correspond to these rights are both negative and positive. There is then a strong argument against a theory of rights that includes negative but not positive rights.

Much of the most important and influential work on human rights has been produced by Kantians. Rather than beginning with rights claims, Kantians begin with obligations or duties to respect other persons. These duties constrain the pursuit of ends, whether they are self-interested goals or projects pursued on behalf of other parties such as shareholders. Respecting persons involves both negative obligations, such as refraining from using others as mere tools via physical force, coercion, or manipulation, and positive obligations such as supporting physical well-being and the development of basic human capacities. When they stand in the appropriate relationship to an obligation-bearer, persons have rationally justified rights-claims against them. Rights take the form of side-constraints that bound the moral space in which agents may pursue ends without unjustified interference by other agents or institutions. For example, a minor child has legitimate rights-claims against her parents regarding her physical well-being and the development of her human capacities by virtue of her relation to them. The morally legitimate ends of parents do not include actions that substantially undermine the physical well-being or normal development of their child. Similarly, a convenience store owner has a rights-claim against those in his community to be free from assault and robbery. The morally legitimate ends of other community members do not include actions that would undermine the freedom of the store owner.

Wherever corporations do business they are already in special relationships with a variety of stakeholders, such as workers, customers, and local communities. In their global operations and in their global supply chains, corporations have a duty to respect those with whom they have relationships. Corporate managers, then, have obligations both to ensure that they do not illegitimately undermine the liberty of any persons, and the additional obligation to help ensure that minimal welfare rights to physical well-being and the development of basic human capacities are met within their spheres of influence. For example, corporations have sufficient power and coercive influence to ignore the labor and environmental laws in many developing nations. These host nations typically lack the police and judicial infrastructure necessary to enforce such laws. Host nation governments may also be fearful that if they enforce their own laws, then the corporations may move their operations to nations that are willing to ignore local laws. However, such laws are essential for the protection of the basic rights of the citizens of developing nations. For this reason, corporate managers have an obligation to ensure that local host nations' laws are respected.

Human Rights versus Legal Rights

Human rights differ from legal rights in that, unlike legal rights, the existence of human rights is not contingent upon any institution. Many nations grant their citizens certain constitutional or legal rights via foundational documents or legal precedent. However, the rights that are protected vary among nations. Some nations ensure that the rights of citizens are protected via effective policing and an independent judiciary. Frequently, however, poor citizens and disfavored groups are not provided with the same level of protection for their legal rights as the economic and political elite. Persons who are deprived of their rights do not thereby cease to have those rights. As A.I. Melden has argued (1977, pp. 167–168):

> … the complaint that persons are deprived of their human rights when, for example, they are subjected to forced indenture by their employers, is a complaint that their rights have been violated and implies, clearly, that they have rights they are unjustly prevented from exercising. If one were deprived of one's rights in the sense in which one would be deprived of things in one's physical possession by having them taken away, one would no longer have the rights, and there would be no grounds for the complaint. So it is with the denial of a person's right—this does not consist in denying that he has the right but, rather, in denying him, by withholding from him, that to which he has the right or the means or opportunity for its exercise.

Employers may deny employees or other stakeholders their inalienable right to freedom and well-being, whether or not local governments are complicit, but in doing so they in no way diminish the legitimacy of the claims of their employees to those rights. However, by virtue of their failure to properly respect these stakeholders, such employers succeed in diminishing their own standing in the community of rights holders.

In the weak and failed states where many multinational corporations operate, they are often the most powerful institutions in existence. In such cases, corporate managers are uniquely situated to help ensure that the basic rights of individuals within their spheres of influence are protected. Many corporations have embraced this obligation. For example, Mattel ensures that all of the factories in its global supply chains meet basic human rights standards. Nike provides micro-loans to community members in the areas where it has large contract factories, thus providing additional help to improve the economic well-being of these communities. And Adidas ensures that the basic rights of workers in its contract factories are respected, while using its occupational safety expertise to help noncontract factories in those same communities improve working conditions.

Are Human Rights a Western Concept?

At this point in our discussion, it is worthwhile to consider an objection to the foregoing argument concerning human rights. This criticism stems from the observation that the idea of human rights emerged from the Western philosophical tradition, but is taken to be universal in its applicability. The claim is then made that human rights are of less importance in the value systems of other cultures. For example, it is argued that "Asian values" emphasize order, discipline, and social harmony, as opposed to individual rights. In this view, the freedom and well-being of individuals should not be allowed to interfere with the harmony of the community, as might be the case, for example, when workers engage in disruptive collective action in an effort to secure their rights. This view might also be used to defend the claim that the moral norms that govern Asian factory operations should emphasize order and discipline, not freedom and well-being.

Several points may be made in reply to this objection. First, Asia is a large region with a vast and heterogeneous population. As Amartya Sen and others have argued, to claim that all, or even most, Asians share a uniform set of values is to impose a level of uniformity that does not exist at present and has not existed in the past (Donnely, 1999; Sen, 1999a, 2000; Tatsuo, 1999). Second, in secular, democratic Asian societies such as India, respect for individual rights has a long tradition. Indeed, there are significant antecedents in the history of the civilizations of the Indian subcontinent that emphasize individual freedom and well-being. For example, in the third century BC, the Emperor Ashoka granted his citizens the freedom to embrace whatever religious or philosophical system they might choose, while at the same time he emphasized the importance of tolerance and respect for philosophical and religious beliefs different than one's own (Sen, 1999a). Third, even if it was the case that Asian cultures shared a uniform set of values that de-emphasized human rights, this would not by itself provide good reasons for denying or disrespecting the rights to freedom and well-being. This is because the justification of human rights provided above is grounded in rational arguments that are valid across cultures. Jack Donnely makes a similar point in his recent defense of universal human rights (1999, p. 87):

> One of the things that makes us human is our capacity to create and change our culture. Cultural diversity has in recent years increasingly come to be valued in itself. Westerners have in recent centuries been especially insensitive in their approach to such differences. Nonetheless, the essential insight of human rights is that the worlds we make for ourselves, intentionally and unintentionally, must conform to relatively universal requirements that rest on our common humanity and seek to guarantee equal concern and respect from the state for every person.

The critic is likely to retort that such a view reflects Western prejudices grounded in Enlightenment ideals. This response is unpersuasive. Diverse intellectual traditions have emphasized the importance of values derived from reason, rather than mythology, traditionalism, mere sentiment, or some other source. For example, in the sixteenth century the Moghul Emperor Akbar wrote (Sen, 2000, p. 37):

> The pursuit of reason and rejection of traditionalism are so brilliantly patent as to be above the need for argument. If traditionalism were proper, the prophets would merely have followed their own elders (and not come with new messages).

Akbar arranged to have philosophers representing diverse religious and philosophical beliefs engage in rational discussions regarding the merits of their competing views, and sought to identify the most persuasive features of each view. In so doing, Akbar was able to emphasize the power and force of rational analysis. Given that a similar emphasis on rational analysis concerning values may be found in the histories of other non-Western cultures, the claim that such analysis is uniquely Western is unpersuasive.

References

Arnold, Denis G., *The Ethics of Global Business* (Malden, MA: Blackwell Publishers, 2007).

Donnely, Jack, "Human Rights and Asian Values: A Defense of 'Western' Universalism," in Joanne R. Bauer and Daniel A. Bell (eds.), *The East Asian Challenge for Human Rights* (Cambridge, UK: Cambridge University Press, 1999), pp. 60–87.

Dworkin, Gerald, *The Theory and Practice of Autonomy* (Cambridge, UK: Cambridge University Press, 1988).

Frankfurt, Harry, *The Importance of What We Care About* (Cambridge, UK: Cambridge University Press, 1988).

Hartman, Laura, Denis G. Arnold, and Richard E. Wokutch, *Rising Above Sweatshops: Innovative Approaches to Global Labor Challenges* (Westport, CT Praeger Publishers, 2003).

Lomasky, Loren, *Persons, Rights, and the Moral Community* (New York: Oxford University Press, 1987).

Melden, A.I., *Rights and Persons* (Berkeley, CA: University of California Press, 1977).

Nozick, Robert, *Anarchy, State, and Utopia* (New York: Basic Books, 1974).

O'Neill, Onora, *Bound of Justice* (Cambridge: Cambridge University Press, 2000).

Sen, Amartya, "Human Rights and Asian Values," in Tibor Machan (ed.), *Business Ethics in the Global Marketplace* (Stanford, CA: Hoover Institution Press, 1999), pp. 37–62.

_____, "East and West: The Reach of Reason," *The New York Review of Books*, July 20, 2000, pp. 33–38.

Shue, Henry, *Basic Rights: Subsistence, Affluence, and U.S. Foreign Policy*, 2nd ed. (Princeton: Princeton University Press, 1996).

Tatsuo, Inoue, 'Liberal Democracy and Asian Orientalism,' in Joanne R. Bauer and Daniel A. Bell (eds.), *The East Asian Challenge for Human Rights* (Cambridge, UK: Cambridge University Press, 1999), pp. 27–59.

Reading 3-2

Do CEOs Get Paid Too Much?[1]

Jeffrey Moriarty

America's corporate executives get paid huge sums of money. *BusinessWeek* estimates that, in 2003, CEOs of the 365 largest U.S. corporations were paid on average $8 million, 301 times as much as factory workers. CEOs' pay packages, including salary, bonus, and restricted stock and stock option grants, increased by 340 percent from 1991 to 2001, while workers' paychecks increased by only 36 percent. What, if anything, is wrong with this?

* * * *

This paper attempts to advance the philosophical discussion of executive compensation. What is needed, I suggest, is an ethical framework for thinking about justice in pay. After elaborating this framework, I will argue that CEOs get paid too much.

* * * *

Three Views of Justice in Wages

To decide whether CEOs make too much money, we first need to consider what, in general, makes a wage just. In this section I will sketch three views of justice in wages, each of which is based on a widely recognized moral value . . . . According to what I will call the "agreement view," just prices for goods are obtained through arm's-length negotiations between informed buyers and informed sellers. In our case, the good is the CEO's services, the seller is the CEO, and the buyer(s) is (are) the company's owner(s). Provided there are no imperfections (e.g., fraud, coercion) in the bargaining process, the agreement view says, the wage that comes out of it is just. Owners are free to do what they want with their money, and CEOs are free to do what they want with their services.

The "desert view" appeals to independent standards for justice in wages. It says that people deserve certain wages for performing certain jobs, whatever they might agree to accept for performing them. The wages people deserve may depend on facts about their jobs (e.g., their difficulty or degree of responsibility), people's performances in them (e.g., how much effort they expend, how much they contribute to the firm), or both. According to the desert view, the CEO should be paid $8 million per year if and only if he deserves to be paid $8 million per year.

What I will call the "utility view" conceives of wages not as rewards for past work, but as incentives for future work. The purpose of wages on this view is to maximize firm wealth by attracting, retaining, and motivating talented workers. If, in our case, the CEO's position is not compensated adequately, few talented candidates will apply or remain on the job for long, and the company as a whole will suffer. On the other hand, an expensive CEO can easily earn his keep through even small increases in the price of the company's stock. According to the utility view, then, a compensation package of $8 million per year is just if and only if it maximizes firm wealth by attracting, retaining, and optimally motivating a talented CEO.

* * * *

The Agreement View

According to this view, a just price for the CEO's services is one that results from an arm's-length negotiation between an informed CEO and informed owners. I will show that these negotiations are not, in general, conducted at arm's-length. If they were, CEOs would be paid on average less than $8 million per year.

The problem occurs mainly on the "buy" side of the equation, so we will focus our attention there. Since there are potentially tens of thousands of shareholders, there are potentially tens of thousands of buyers of the CEO's services. This many people cannot effectively participate in negotiations with the CEO. Shareholders need representatives. The agreement view tells us that, to be legitimate, the representatives must meet two conditions. First, they must be independent of the CEO (the "arm's-length" condition). If they have something to gain from advancing the CEO's interests, they are likely to pay too much for his services. Second, they must be informed (the "informed buyer" condition). If they do not know what kind of talent it takes to run their firm, and how rare that talent is, they are liable either to overpay a mediocre CEO or to underpay an exceptional one.

* * * *

Traditionally, shareholders are represented in negotiations with the CEO by a subset of the members of the company's board of directors. This may seem promising to those who appeal to the agreement view to justify the current level of CEO pay. Since directors are usually elected by shareholders, they might say, it is likely that the directors who negotiate with the CEO—those who form the board's "compensation committee"—are in fact independent and informed. If shareholders did not elect independent and informed directors, they would risk paying too much to an incompetent CEO, or too little to an exceptional one.

This hope is unfounded. First, there is no guarantee that shareholders would choose independent and informed representatives in a democratic election. Although parties who own large amounts of stock might be motivated to determine which of the candidates is independent and informed, many will not. Voters who do not familiarize themselves with the candidates have little chance of picking the right ones. Second, and more importantly, shareholders do not as a matter of fact elect directors in any meaningful way. When a seat on the board opens up, usually there is just one person who "runs" in the "election." Once a candidate is nominated, her election is a formality. What matters, then, is the nomination process. The group that controls it controls the board's membership. But in most cases this is not the shareholders but the board itself, whose chairman in 84 percent of American firms is the firm's CEO. Although there has been a trend away from direct CEO involvement in the nominating process in recent years most CEOs still wield considerable informal influence over it.

This is worrisome. Whereas shareholders may elect, out of apathy or ignorance, directors who are unfamiliar with the industry and friendly with the CEO, CEOs can encourage the appointment of such directors. Do they? The fact that CEOs who are appointed before the appointment of their compensation committee chairs are paid more, on average, than CEOs who are appointed after suggests that they do. Examining the composition of boards of directors more carefully, we see that, in general, directors may be informed, but they are not independent.

Three factors compromise directors' independence from their CEOs. The first is gratitude. The board member's job is prestigious, lucrative, and undemanding. Directors of the 200 largest American corporations receive on average $179,000 for twenty days of work per year. They may also be given life and medical insurance, retirement benefits, and the use of company property such as automobiles and vacation homes. In addition, there is the considerable "social capital" directors acquire in the form of connections with influential people. Thus getting an appointment to a board is like getting a large gift. This is problematic, for it is natural for gift recipients to feel grateful to gift givers.

* * * *

Self-interest is the second factor compromising the independence of directors in pay negotiations with CEOs. To determine how much to pay their CEO, the board will usually find out how much CEOs of comparable firms are being paid. The more those CEOs make, the more the board will pay. This is good from the point of view of having knowledgeable directors. But CEO-directors have a self-interested reason to increase the pay of the CEO with whom they are negotiating. Suppose CEO A sits on CEO B's board, and A and B run comparable firms. The more pay A agrees to give to B, the more pay A himself will later receive. For when it comes time to determine A's pay package, B's pay package will be used as one of the reference points.

The third factor is not a reason directors have to favor CEOs; it is the absence of a reason directors should have to favor shareholders. Since they are paying with their own money, shareholders have a powerful incentive not to overpay the CEO. The more they pay the CEO, the less they have for themselves. Directors, by contrast, are not paying with their own money. Although they are often given shares in the company as compensation, directors are rarely required to buy them. So their incentive not to overpay the CEO is less powerful. It might be wondered whether shareholders can make it more powerful by threatening to recall overly generous directors. They cannot. Shareholders in most firms lack this power. In fact, not only will directors have nothing to fear if they do overpay the CEO, they will have something to fear if they do not. Shareholders cannot recall generous directors, but CEOs can use their power to force them out.

While admitting that these influences are problematic, it might be objected that they compromise the independence of directors only if directors are "on their own" in negotiations with CEOs. But they are not. Directors are usually assisted by compensation consultants who can make accurate and bias-free assessments of a CEO's worth. On this view, provided that the board acts on the consultant's recommendation, the wage it agrees to pay the CEO will be just.

This objection fails. The reason, according to the agreement view, the pay agreements between CEOs and shareholders' representatives are unfair is that the latter group is not sufficiently independent of the former. But compensation consultants are hired to make sure boards are informed, not to make sure they are independent. Consultants can offer directors a variety of facts about CEO pay, and this will help them to avoid making obviously bad deals with the CEO. But, because of gratitude, self-interest, and lack of financial penalties, boards will still give CEOs a substantial benefit of the doubt when it comes to pay.

The Desert View

A familiar complaint about CEO pay—that it has increased in years when firms have performed badly—is grounded in the desert view of justice in wages. This complaint assumes that a CEO should get the wage he deserves, that the wage a CEO deserves is determined by his contribution to the firm, and that the proper measure of contribution is firm performance. If the firm performs worse in year two than in year one, the argument goes, the CEO deserves to make less, and therefore should make less, in year two than in year one. The agreement and utility views of justice in wages cannot account, except indirectly, for this intuition.

Two Problems

To determine whether CEOs deserve to make $8 million per year, we must formulate, at least in part, a theory of desert of wages. Let us begin by discussing two of the problems we will face.

The first is identifying the standard(s) for deservingness. One cannot be deserving for no reason at all; there must be some reason for, or basis of, that desert. Economists sometimes write as if it were obvious that CEO pay, and pay generally, should be based on contribution, as measured by firm performance. This is far from clear. Philosophers have written extensively on the nature of desert, and have offered a variety of possible desert-bases for pay, including (i) the physical effort exerted by the worker, (ii) his contribution to the firm, (iii) the amount of ability, skill, or training his job requires, (iv) its difficulty, stress, dangerousness, risk, or unpleasantness, and (v) its degree of responsibility or importance. Some think a person's desert of pay is determined by only one of these factors; others think it is determined by a combination of them.

How does the CEO's job fare? Compared to the jobs of ditch diggers and coal miners, it requires (i) relatively little physical effort. It is not unpleasant or dangerous in the way these jobs are, but it can be (iv) a considerable source of stress. Some writers suggest that CEOs are more prone to stress-related illness and burnout than average workers. According to one study CEOs work on average thirteen hours per day, including time spent traveling to meetings.

The CEO's job is also difficult in the sense that it requires the performance of a variety of complex tasks, such as negotiating deals, processing information, and meeting with subordinates and clients in leadership and ceremonial roles. The fact that CEOs wield significant power within already powerful organizations means that their jobs have (v) high degrees of responsibility. Decisions they make about budgets, personnel, and plant (re)location can affect thousands of people's lives. For the same reason, CEOs are in a position to make (ii) large contributions to their firms. What does it take to perform this job? Most CEOs have (iii) some formal education and many years of experience. Over 90 percent have college degrees; 50 percent hold advanced degrees. Of those who hold advanced degrees, 68 percent hold an MBA. The average CEO is fifty-three years old, and worked for his firm for thirteen years before becoming CEO. We see, then, that the CEO's job rates highly in some categories but not in others. So, depending on how the first problem is solved, we will get different answers to the question of how much CEOs deserve to be paid.

The second problem is connected to the first. Once we identify the base(s) for desert of wages, we must find a way of matching desert levels to pay levels. In other words, after determining what makes a person deserving, and how deserving he is, we have to decide what he deserves. Suppose effort is the basis of desert, and suppose the CEO works 3,000 hours in a year. How much does he deserve to be paid: $300,000 or $3 million? Or suppose contribution is the basis of desert, and suppose the firm's profits increase 20 percent in a year. We might think the CEO deserves a 20 percent raise. But what should his initial salary have been? Without a way of matching desert levels to pay levels, we have no way of answering this question.

This difficulty can be used to cast doubt on some of the traditional evidence that CEOs are overpaid. Consider again the complaint that CEO pay has risen while stock prices have fallen. Suppose the drop in a company's stock price is due directly to a decline in its CEO's performance. The fact that the CEO is contributing less now to his company than before does not mean that he is being paid too much now. It may mean that he was being paid too little before. Or consider the complaint that American CEOs make several times more than their foreign counterparts—roughly twenty-two times more than Japanese CEOs and six times more than British CEOs. A skeptic may say that British and Japanese CEOs make too little, not that American CEOs make too much. Again, if we cannot map desert-creating behavior onto pay, we cannot say for sure exactly how much CEOs deserve to be paid.

* * * *

In response, I will argue that, however much money CEOs deserve to make absolutely, they do not deserve to make 301 times as much as their employees. Given that their employees make on average $27,000 per year, CEOs do not deserve to make on average $8 million per year. CEOs are not 301 times as deserving as their employees.

Why CEOs Deserve Less Than They Get

Most of those who endorse the desert view of justice in wages think that the sole desert-base for wages is productive contribution. Let us begin with this view. We will consider other desert-bases below.

Under the assumption that contribution is the sole desert-base for pay, the CEO deserves to be paid 301 times what the average employee is paid if and only if his contribution to the firm is 301 times as valuable as the employee's. For every $1 in revenue the employee generates, the CEO must generate $301. To appreciate this idea, it may be helpful to think about it in another way. Suppose a manufacturing company M has 10,000 employees, 9,999 of whom engage in the (identical) assembly-line work that generates its products. And suppose in one year M generates $1 billion in revenue. For M's CEO to deserve 301 times the pay of M's average assembly-line worker, he must generate $29.2 million in revenue compared to the worker's $97,100. If we imagine, more realistically, that M employs not only assembly-line workers and a CEO but also several middle managers, the result is not too different. If each of 100 middle managers generates $500,000 in revenue, the CEO must generate $27.8 million in revenue compared to the worker's $92,200. Does this happen?

* * * *

We have not argued that no version of the desert view can be used to justify the current disparity between CEO and worker pay. There are other desert-bases to consider. It takes only a moment to see, however, that none of these desert-bases succeeds where this one fails.

Consider first physical effort. The job of the CEO requires less physical effort than many other jobs in the firm. So a desert view according to which effort is the sole desert-base for pay will not support the claim that the CEO deserves to be paid 301 times what the average worker is paid.

Consider next skill and difficulty. The average CEO is a highly skilled individual; his job requires the performance of complex tasks and can be a source of considerable stress. But is the CEO 301 times as skilled as the average employee? Is his job 301 times as difficult and stressful? The answer to these questions is no. Some may doubt this, perhaps because they have a very low opinion of most people's jobs. Consider, then, the job of a scientist in the company's research and development department. The scientist might be paid $150,000 per year—1/53 the pay of the CEO. For the CEO to deserve to make $8 million per year while the scientist makes $150,000 per year, the CEO would have to be 53 times as skilled, perform tasks 53 times as difficult, or feel 53 times as much stress as the scientist. This is not the case. Often the scientist will be more skilled, and will perform more difficult tasks than the CEO. And the jobs of CEOs are not the only stressful jobs. According to one study, 25 percent of all employees report experiencing a "great deal" of stress of work.

The final possible desert-base is degree of responsibility. Initially, this may seem attractive to the defender of the status quo, for CEOs' decisions can affect the lives of thousands of people both inside and outside the firm. But it will not work either. The decisions of lower-level workers can be equally important. Had the Exxon Valdez's captain stayed sober, millions of gallons of oil might not have been spilled into the sea. Had a few maintenance personnel in Bhopal taken countermeasures instead of running from the scene, thousands might not have died. Some of the decisions of airplane pilots, bus drivers, and engineers can have as much riding on them as the decisions of the CEOs who run their companies.

* * * *

So far we have been comparing the pay of CEOs to the pay of lower-level employees within their firms. Additional evidence that CEOs do not deserve, by any standard of deservingness, to be paid $8 million per year is found by comparing their pay to the pay of professionals in other fields. The average CEO makes roughly 53 times what a medical doctor, a military general, or a federal district court judge makes. But he is not 53 times as deserving as them. These jobs require similar amounts of physical effort. They all require extensive training, are difficult to perform, and have a high degree of responsibility. And the people who perform them are in a position to make significant contributions to their organizations as well as to society as a whole. Thus we can believe either that medical doctors, military generals, and federal judges get paid far less than they deserve, or that CEOs get paid far more. The latter belief is more plausible.

I conclude—in the case of contribution, tentatively—that there is no standard of deservingness according to which CEOs deserve to make 301 times as much as their employees. If I am right, the desert view of justice in wages condemns the current disparity between CEO and employee pay. I did not argue that CEOs do not deserve to make $8 million per year simpliciter. Perhaps they do. But then employees deserve to make more than $27,000 per year. If employee pay cannot be drastically increased, then the desert view demands that CEO pay be drastically reduced.

The Utility View

Having seen that neither the agreement view nor the desert view can be used to justify the current level of CEO pay, in this section I will examine the utility view. The recent actions of American Airlines provide a stark example of utility-based reasoning about pay. After a $1.04 billion loss in the first quarter of 2003, the company's management requested significant concessions in pay from its employee unions. At the same time, its board gave the CEO a $1.6 million "retention bonus." They did so not to honor a clause in his contract, or to reward him for past performance. Their goal was to convince him to stay. The board believed that, without this bonus, the CEO would leave, and then the company would be even worse off. The utility view generalizes this reasoning. According to it, a just wage is one that maximizes firm wealth by attracting talented workers, retaining them in the face of competing offers, and motivating them to do their best. $8 million per year is a just wage on this view if and only if it accomplishes these tasks.

The utility view should not be confused with the desert view. The utility view may recommend, as a way of motivating employees, offering bonuses to those who make contributions to the firm. According to one version of the desert view, people's deserts are determined by their contributions. Since both views can recommend rewarding contribution, it may seem that they are not really different. This appearance is misleading. The reason, according to the utility view, productive employees should be rewarded is that doing so will lead to future benefits for the firm. The reason, according to the desert view, productive employees should be rewarded is that they have made contributions to the firm—and that is all. Suppose, for example, that an employee makes a significant contribution to his firm. If giving him a higher salary is not necessary to make him stay, and will not cause him (or anyone else in the firm) to make a future contribution that he (or they) otherwise would not make, then the utility view says he should not be given a higher salary. The firm has nothing to gain by doing so. The desert view, on the other hand, leaves it open that this employee should receive a higher salary, provided his contribution is significant enough.

Note also that while the utility view recommends rewarding successful CEOs, it does not recommend paying them whatever they want. The wealth created by the CEO must be weighed against the cost of his services. Suppose that A and B apply for an open CEO job. Both are talented, but A is more so. Suppose further that A demands $5 million more in pay than B. The utility view recommends hiring A over B only if A will generate at least $5 million more in revenue for the firm than B. Otherwise it recommends hiring B. The utility view does not recommend getting the most talented person. It recommends getting the person who creates the most benefit for the lowest cost—the most "bang for the buck."

This helps us to see what a utility-based justification of the current level of CEO pay must look like. It cannot claim merely that offering $8 million per year will attract, retain, and motivate a person talented enough to be the CEO. It must claim that $8 million per year is the most cost-effective wage to offer—that it maximizes firm wealth. When this is understood, many will begin to doubt that a utility-based justification of the current level of CEO pay can be provided. They are right to be skeptical. But utility-based arguments are the ones most often appealed to by boards of directors to justify the pay packages they give to their CEOs. Against this, I will give reason to believe that firm wealth is maximized by paying CEOs less than $8 million per year. I begin by discussing pay as a tool of attraction and retention. I then consider its role in motivation.

Attraction and Retention

Several of the desert-bases discussed above might be cited as reasons an employer has to pay more, or can pay less, to fill a certain job. The most important of these, it seems to me, are effort, skill, and difficulty (including stress, dangerousness, risk, and unpleasantness). Since, other things equal, employees will choose the easier job over the harder job, employers will have to make other things unequal, by offering higher wages for the harder job. Similarly, employers will have to offer higher wages for jobs that require rare and valuable skills or long periods of training, and for jobs that are comparatively difficult.

The CEO's job has some of these characteristics. It does not require much physical effort, but it requires skill and training, and it is difficult and stressful. The question, of course, is not if the CEO's job has these characteristics, but to what degree it has them. Is the CEO's job so difficult and stressful, and does it require so much skill and training, that offering $8 million per year is necessary to get talented people to become CEOs? Those convinced by my argument that CEOs do not deserve to be paid 301 times what their employees are paid may think not. But we are now asking a different question: not what people deserve for performing the CEO's job, but what would make them willing to perform it.

The answer, however, is similar. There is no evidence that offering $8 million per year is necessary to get talented people to become CEOs. Indeed, we have reason to believe that much less will do. Consider the jobs of university presidents and U.S. military generals. They are no less difficult, and require no less skill and training, than the jobs of CEOs. But the wages offered to presidents and generals are many times lower than the wages offered to CEOs. The median compensation of presidents of private research universities is $385,000; U.S. military generals earn $143,000 per year. Despite this, there is no shortage of talented university presidents and military generals. The fact that people can be attracted to difficult, specialized, and high-skill managerial jobs that pay "only" several hundred thousand dollars per year suggests that talented people will still want to become CEOs even if they are paid less than $8 million per year.

* * * *

Motivation

Attraction and retention are not the only utility-based reasons for paying employees certain wages. There is also motivation. Employees who are talented and motivated create more wealth for their firms than employees who are only talented. There are three ways paying CEOs $8 million per year might be thought—mistakenly, I will argue—to maximize firm wealth through motivation.

First, it might motivate the CEO himself. The CEO knows that, if he does not do an excellent job, he will be fired. Since he wants to keep making $8 million per year, he will work as hard as he can. If CEOs were paid less money, they would work less hard, and firms would be worse off.

In this respect also, pay matters: it motivates people to work hard. It is thus arguable that the CEO who is paid $8 million per year will work harder than the CEO who is paid $1 million per year. But this, as we know by now, is not what needs to be shown. What needs to be shown is that the extra amount of hard work put in by the $8-million-per-year CEO is worth an extra $7 million. It is unlikely that it is. There is no guarantee that extra hard work will translate into extra revenue, and there is only so hard an executive can work. One might think that an extra $7 million per year would be worth it if one thought that CEOs would put in very little effort if they were paid only $1 million per year. But this takes a pessimistic view of CEOs' characters, as if only money—and only a lot of it—could get them to do anything. There is no empirical evidence to support this view. To the contrary, studies show that money is not the only, or even the primary, reason people work hard. Instead of trying to further motivate their CEOs with more money, then, firms would do better to use the extra money to increase revenue in other ways, such as advertising more.

The second motivation-based reason for paying CEOs $8 million per year is, in effect, a slightly different version of the first. It has been said that CEOs' compensation packages should be structured so that CEOs' and owners' interests are aligned. Owners want the stock price to go up. So CEOs should be paid in a way that makes them want the stock price to go up. This is typically achieved by paying CEOs mostly in restricted stock and stock options. Since, it is assumed, the CEO wants to make more money rather than less, this will give him an incentive to try to make the company's stock price go up. The idea not just to make sure that CEOs do what investors want, but to make sure that they do only what investors want. If the CEO is paid mostly in stock, he has little to gain from pursuing alternative courses of action.

Let us grant, for the sake of argument, that CEOs' interests should be aligned exclusively with investors' interests. Let us also grant that offering CEOs $5 million per year in restricted stock and stock options accomplishes this. Does this prove that CEOs should be paid $5 million in stock? It does only if there is no cheaper way of achieving this goal. But there is: monitoring and dismissal. The interests of most employees are aligned with investors' interests this way. Employees are monitored. If they promote interests other than those (ultimately) of the investors, they are dismissed. Would anyone seriously propose, as an alternative to this practice, giving each employee several million dollars in stock options? To be sure, doing so would align their interests with investors' interests. But it is expensive and unnecessary. The same is true of paying CEOs $5 million in stock. There is no reason to give away so much of the firm's wealth when the CEO can simply be fired for poor performance. Owners could secure the same level of loyalty at a fraction of the price.

We have examined two ways that paying CEOs $8 million per year might maximize firm wealth through motivation. Both focus on the effects of high pay on the CEO. The third focuses on the effects of high pay on other employees. According to some, a firm's job hierarchy can be seen as a tournament, with the CEO's job as top prize. Many of the firm's employees, they say, want this prize and will work hard to get it. The better the prize is, the harder they will work. If the CEO is paid $8 million per year, the rest of the employees will work very hard indeed. The consequent increase in productivity will be good for the firm as a whole. Ehrenberg and Bognanno find evidence for this hypothesis in the field of professional golf. They observe that golfers' scores are negatively correlated with potential earnings. The larger the tournament's purse is, and hence the more money the golfers could win, the better they play.

This is perhaps the most plausible of the utility-based attempts to justify the current level of CEO pay. Still, the argument in its present form has several problems. In the first place, not every employee wants to be CEO, no matter how much the job pays. So paying the CEO

$8 million per year provides an incentive to work hard to only some of the firm's employees. Second, there is evidence that this practice will have unintended negative effects. Since there is only one CEO's job, employees must compete with each other to get it. The more the job pays, the more intense the competition will be. This is problematic, for competition fosters jealousy and hostility, which can hinder communication and cooperation. This will not matter to golfers; they play alone. But employees often work together; a decline in communication and cooperation may lead to a decline in productivity. In support of this, Cowherd and Levine find that pay inequality between workers and managers is negatively correlated with product quality. They explain: "interclass pay equity affects product quality by influencing employee commitment to managerial goals, effort, and cooperation." Thus, while paying CEOs $8 million per year may increase hard work, it may also increase competition. The benefit of the former may be outweighed by the cost of the latter.

Even if it is not, this does not suffice to prove that CEOs should be paid $8 million per year. My objection is familiar. That is, while paying CEOs $8 million per year might be an effective motivational tool, it is likely not a cost-effective one. Above we said that the $8-million-per-year CEO is likely to be only slightly more productive than the $1-million-per-year CEO. Similar reasoning suggests that $8-million-per-year CEO hopefuls are likely to be only slightly more productive than $1-million-per-year CEO hopefuls. From the point of view of utility, then, firms would do better to use the extra $7 million to increase revenue in other ways.

Let me clarify the nature of my conclusions. I think I have amply demonstrated my negative claim: there are no good utility-based arguments in favor of the current level of CEO pay. But I put forward a positive claim as well: according to this view of justice in wages, CEOs get paid too much. In light of what we now know about attracting, retaining, and motivating managerial talent, and how important that talent is, we have reason to believe that paying CEOs $8 million per year does not maximize firm wealth. Talented people could be attracted to the CEO's job, retained in the face of competing offers, and motivated to work hard, with less than $8 million per year. This part of my argument is less secure. New research could undermine the conclusions upon which I have relied. This would be surprising, but it has not been ruled out.

Conclusion

In the meantime, what should be done? CEO pay should be kept from increasing; ideally, it should decrease. In poorly governed firms, CEOs set their own pay. Even in well governed ones, they can refuse exorbitant pay packages. Thus the most direct way of achieving this goal is to appeal to CEOs themselves. They should be pressured to accept less pay. This may not work, for various reasons. Another tactic is to enact laws which limit CEO pay. Just as minimum wage laws provide a floor for wages, we might create "maximum wage" laws to provide a ceiling for them. This approach will seem heavy-handed to some. There is, however, a middle road. This is to ensure that all firms are better governed with respect to pay.

Determining what such firms will look like is not a matter for a priori reflection. There is a large literature that links characteristics of boards of directors to CEO pay. Drawing on it, I offer the following two suggestions.

First, CEOs should be removed from the director election process. Directors feel obligated to those who put them on the board. If this is the CEO, they will feel obligated to him, and be more inclined to overpay him. Directors should feel obligated to the people they are actually representing: the shareholders. Letting shareholders elect them will help to create this feeling. It is possible that it will also make being a director a more demanding job. It may end the era in which an individual can serve on several corporate boards and still hold a full time job. This would be a good thing. Being a director is an important job: directors oversee entities whose actions can impact the welfare of thousands of people. It should feel like one.

Second, directors should be required to make meaningful financial investments in the firms which they direct. They need not all own a certain percentage of the firm's total stock. What matters is that they own an amount that is meaningful for them. This promotes the first objective: directors will feel more obligated to shareholders if they are themselves shareholders. It is useful for another reason as well. Above we said that a problem with the pay negotiations between directors and CEOs is that directors feel as if they are not paying with their own money. Making them buy stock would help to ameliorate this problem. An implication of this view is that other kinds of compensation that seem "free" to directors should be eliminated. This includes stock options insofar as they are not counted against firm earnings. If options are given as compensation, they should be expensed.

Implementing these suggestions will, I believe, help to reduce the pay of CEOs. But it will not guarantee that they receive wages that are just. More attention needs to be paid to the fundamental question of what makes a wage just. The subject of wages has received far more attention by economists, organizational theorists, and consultants than by philosophers. This paper has provided a framework for thinking about the moral dimensions of wages. They cannot be ignored.

Source: Copyright © Jeffrey Moriarty. A draft of this paper was presented at Georgetown University. The author wishes to thank members of that audience, and also George Brenkert, Edwin Hartman, Kelly Moriarty, Jeffrey Wilder, and two anonymous *Business Ethics Quarterly* referees for helpful comments and discussion.

1. Editors' note: This essay provides a fine example of philosophical analysis in which the principles and theories of philosophical ethics are applied to an ethical controversy in contemporary business. Students should note that the logical reasoning process developed throughout this essay provides an admirable model of ethical decision making and analysis. What follows is an edited version of a longer essay that appeared in *Business Ethics Quarterly* 15, no. 2, pp. 257–281, and has been reprinted by permission. Notes and references have been deleted.

Reading 3-3

Caux Principles for Business

Introduction

The Caux Round Table believes that the world business community should play an important role in improving economic and social conditions. As a statement of aspirations, this document aims to express a world standard against which business behavior can be measured. We seek to begin a process that identifies shared values, reconciles differing values, and thereby develops a shared perspective on business behavior acceptable to and honored by all.

These principles are rooted in two basic ethical ideals: *kyosei* and human dignity. The Japanese concept of *kyosei* means living and working together for the common good, enabling cooperation and mutual prosperity to coexist with healthy and fair competition. "Human dignity" refers to the sacredness or value of each person as an end, not simply as a means to the fulfillment of others' purposes or even majority prescription.

The General Principles in Section 2 seek to clarify the spirit of kyosei and "human dignity," while the specific Stakeholder Principles in Section 3 are concerned with their practical application.

In its language and form, the document owes a substantial debt to The Minnesota Principles, a statement of business behavior developed by the Minnesota Center for Corporate Responsibility. The Center hosted and chaired the drafting committee, which included Japanese, European, and United States representatives.

Business behavior can affect relationships among nations and the prosperity and well-being of us all. Business is often the first contact between nations and, by the way in which it causes social and economic changes, has a significant impact on the level of fear or confidence felt by people worldwide. Members of the Caux Round Table place their first emphasis on putting one's own house in order, and on seeking to establish what is right rather than who is right.

Section 1. Preamble

The mobility of employment, capital, products and technology is making business increasingly global in its transactions and its effects.

Law and market forces are necessary but insufficient guides for conduct.

Responsibility for the policies and actions of business and respect for the dignity and interests of its stakeholders are fundamental.

Shared values, including a commitment to shared prosperity, are as important for a global community as for communities of smaller scale.

For these reasons, and because business can be a powerful agent of positive social change, we offer the following principles as a foundation for dialogue and action by business leaders in search of business responsibility. In so doing, we affirm the necessity for moral values in business decision making. Without them, stable business relationships and a sustainable world community are impossible.

Section 2. General Principles

Principle 1. The Responsibilities of Businesses: *Beyond Shareholders toward Stakeholders*

The value of a business to society is the wealth and employment it creates and the marketable products and services it provides to consumers at a reasonable price commensurate with quality. To create such value, a business must maintain its own economic health and viability, but survival is not a sufficient goal. Businesses have a role to play in improving the lives of all their customers, employees, and shareholders by sharing with them the wealth they have created. Suppliers and competitors as well should expect businesses to honor their obligations in a spirit of honesty and fairness. As responsible citizens of the local, national, regional and global communities in which they operate, businesses share a part in shaping the future of those communities.

Principle 2. The Economic and Social Impact of Business: *Toward Innovation, Justice and World Community*

Businesses established in foreign countries to develop, produce or sell should also contribute to the social advancement of those countries by creating productive employment and helping to raise the purchasing power of their citizens. Businesses also should contribute to human rights, education, welfare, and vitalization of the countries in which they operate.

Businesses should contribute to economic and social development not only in the countries in which they operate, but also in the world community at large, through effective and prudent use of resources, free and fair competition, and emphasis upon innovation in technology, production methods, marketing and communications.

Principle 3. Business Behavior: *Beyond the Letter of Law toward a Spirit of Trust*

While accepting the legitimacy of trade secrets, businesses should recognize that sincerity, candor, truthfulness, the keeping of promises, and transparency contribute not only to their own credibility and stability but also to the smoothness and efficiency of business transactions, particularly on the international level.

Principle 4. Respect for Rules

To avoid trade frictions and to promote freer trade, equal conditions for competition, and fair and equitable treatment for all participants, businesses should respect international and domestic rules. In addition, they should recognize that some behavior, although legal, may still have adverse consequences.

Principle 5. Support for Multilateral Trade

Businesses should support the multilateral trade systems of the GATT/World Trade Organization and similar international agreements. They should cooperate in efforts to promote the progressive and judicious liberalization of trade and to relax those domestic measures that unreasonably hinder global commerce, while giving due respect to national policy objectives.

Principle 6. Respect for the Environment

A business should protect and, where possible, improve the environment, promote sustainable development, and prevent the wasteful use of natural resources.

Principle 7. Avoidance of Illicit Operations

A business should not participate in or condone bribery, money laundering, or other corrupt practices: indeed, it should seek cooperation with others to eliminate them. It should not trade in arms or other materials used for terrorist activities, drug traffic or other organized crime.

Section 3. Stakeholder Principles

Customers

We believe in treating all customers with dignity, irrespective of whether they purchase our products and services directly from us or otherwise acquire them in the market. We therefore have a responsibility to:

- provide our customers with the highest quality products and services consistent with their requirements;
- treat our customers fairly in all aspects of our business transactions, including a high level of service and remedies for their dissatisfaction;

- make every effort to ensure that the health and safety of our customers, as well as the quality of their environment, will be sustained or enhanced by our products and services;
- assure respect for human dignity in products offered, marketing, and advertising; and respect the integrity of the culture of our customers.

Employees

We believe in the dignity of every employee and in taking employee interests seriously. We therefore have a responsibility to:

- provide jobs and compensation that improve workers' living conditions;
- provide working conditions that respect each employee's health and dignity;
- be honest in communications with employees and open in sharing information, limited only by legal and competitive constraints;
- listen to and, where possible, act on employee suggestions, ideas, requests and complaints;
- engage in good faith negotiations when conflict arises;
- avoid discriminatory practices and guarantee equal treatment and opportunity in areas such as gender, age, race, and religion;
- promote in the business itself the employment of differently abled people in places of work where they can be genuinely useful;
- protect employees from avoidable injury and illness in the workplace;
- encourage and assist employees in developing relevant and transferable skills and knowledge; and
- be sensitive to the serious unemployment problems frequently associated with business decisions, and work with governments, employee groups, other agencies and each other in addressing these dislocations.

Owners / Investors

We believe in honoring the trust our investors place in us. We therefore have a responsibility to:

- apply professional and diligent management in order to secure a fair and competitive return on our owners' investment;
- disclose relevant information to owners/investors subject to legal requirements and competitive constraints;
- conserve, protect, and increase the owners/investors' assets; and
- respect owners/investors' requests, suggestions, complaints, and formal resolutions.

Suppliers

Our relationship with suppliers and subcontractors must be based on mutual respect. We therefore have a responsibility to:

- seek fairness and truthfulness in all our activities, including pricing, licensing, and rights to sell;
- ensure that our business activities are free from coercion and unnecessary litigation;

- foster long-term stability in the supplier relationship in return for value, quality, competitiveness and reliability;
- share information with suppliers and integrate them into our planning processes;
- pay suppliers on time and in accordance with agreed terms of trade; and
- seek, encourage and prefer suppliers and subcontractors whose employment practices respect human dignity.

Competitors

We believe that fair economic competition is one of the basic requirements for increasing the wealth of nations and ultimately for making possible the just distribution of goods and services. We therefore have a responsibility to:

- foster open markets for trade and investment;
- promote competitive behavior that is socially and environmentally beneficial and demonstrates mutual respect among competitors;
- refrain from either seeking or participating in questionable payments or favors to secure competitive advantages;
- respect both tangible and intellectual property rights; and
- refuse to acquire commercial information by dishonest or unethical means, such as industrial espionage.

Communities

We believe that as global corporate citizens we can contribute to such forces of reform and human rights as are at work in the communities in which we operate. We therefore have a responsibility in those communities to:

- respect human rights and democratic institutions, and promote them wherever practicable;
- recognize government's legitimate obligation to the society at large and support public policies and practices that promote human development through harmonious relations between business and other segments of society;
- collaborate with those forces in the community dedicated to raising standards of health, education, workplace safety and economic well-being;
- promote and stimulate sustainable development and play a leading role in preserving and enhancing the physical environment and conserving the earth's resources;
- support peace, security, diversity and social integration;
- respect the integrity of local cultures; and
- be a good corporate citizen through charitable donations, educational and cultural contributions, and employee participation in community and civic affairs.

Source: www.cauxroundtable.org.

Chapter  4

The Corporate Culture—Impact and Implications

Our plans miscarry because they have no aim. When a person does not know what harbor he [or she] is making for, no wind is the right wind.

Seneca

A leader knows what's best to do; a manager merely how best to do it.

Ken Adelman

Imagine that you work in the Human Resources department of your company. Your CEO has asked the HR department to develop an ethics program for the firm, and you have been assigned responsibility for creating it. You have been asked to report back to your CEO in two weeks with a draft version of a code of ethics for the company, a summary of other elements that the ethics program will include, and a proposal for how you will be able to assess whether the program is working. Your CEO also asks that you come prepared to explain to her what role she can play in promoting ethics and in insuring the success of the ethics program.

In beginning your research, you discover that the Ethics & Policy Integration Centre (EPIC) suggests seven potentially desirable outcomes of effective ethics programs and the extent to which they have been achieved:

1. Discovering unethical/illegal behavior.
2. Generating awareness of ethical and legal issues.
3. Providing a resource for guidance and advice.
4. Reporting wrongdoing.
5. Incorporating values in decision processes.
6. Developing greater employee commitment to the organization.
7. Meeting external and internal stakeholder needs.

Play the role of this HR person in several different types of businesses: a fast-food restaurant, an automobile dealership, a retail store selling consumer electronics, a government agency, and a large international corporation.

- List the issues you think should be addressed in a code of ethics.
- Other than a code of ethics, what other elements would you include in an ethics program?
- How will you define "success"? Are there any facts that you will need to gather to make this judgment?
- How would you measure success? How will you measure whether your ethics program is "working"?
- Who will you define as your primary stakeholders?
- What are their interests in your program and what are the impacts of your program on each stakeholder? How might the measurement of the program's success influence the type of people attracted to the firm or who are most motivated within your organization?
- How will you answer the CEO's questions about her own role in promoting ethics?

Source: EPIC, "Measuring Organizational Integrity and the Bottom Line Results One Can Expect," http://www.epic-online.net/quest_7.html.

Chapter Objectives

After reading this chapter, you will be able to:

1. Define corporate culture.
2. Explain how corporate culture impacts ethical decision making.
3. Discuss the differences between a compliance culture and a values-based culture.
4. Discuss the role of corporate leadership in establishing the culture.
5. Explain the difference between effective leaders and ethical leaders.
6. Discuss the role of mission statements and codes in creating an ethical corporate culture.
7. Explain how various reporting mechanisms such as ethics hotlines and ombudsmen can help integrate ethics within a firm.
8. Discuss the role of assessing, monitoring, and auditing the culture and ethics program.
9. Explain how culture can be enforced via governmental regulation.

What Is Corporate Culture?

This chapter will consider ways in which corporations might develop ethical cultures, cultures in which individuals are encouraged and supported in making ethically responsible decisions. The decision-making model of ethics that we have introduced in the opening chapters emphasizes the responsibility of individuals for the decisions they make in business. These decisions impact one's own personal integrity as well as having consequences for many stakeholders with whom business organizations interact.

But personal decision making does not exist in a vacuum. Decision making within a firm is influenced, limited, shaped, and in some cases virtually determined by the corporate culture of the firm. Individuals can be hindered or helped in making the right, or the wrong, decision by the expectations, values, and structure of the organization in which they live and work. This chapter surveys some of the major issues surrounding the development, influence, and management of a corporate culture and the role of business leaders in creating and preserving ethical cultures.

Even in this age of decentralized corporations and other institutions, there remains a sense of culture in organizations. This is especially true in small local firms, but it is just as true of major global corporations. Despite the fact that corporations have many locations, with diverse employee bases and management styles, an individual working for a large global firm in one country will share various aspects of her or his working culture with someone working for the same firm halfway around the world. This is not to say that their working environments cannot be wholly different in many regards; the culture, however, survives the distance and differences.

So, what do we mean by *corporate culture?* Every organization has a culture, fashioned by a shared pattern of beliefs, expectations, and meanings that influence

OBJECTIVE

Reality Check *Built to Last*

Does a corporate culture matter? James Collins and Jerry Porras, authors of the best-selling book *Built to Last: Successful Habits of Visionary Companies*, researched dozens of very successful companies looking for common practices that might explain their success. These companies not only outperformed their competitors in financial terms; they have outperformed their competition over the long term. On average, the companies Collins and Porras studied were founded in 1897. Among their key findings was the fact that the truly exceptional and enduring companies all placed great emphasis on a set of core values. These core values are described as the "essential and enduring tenets" that help define the company and are "not to be compromised for financial gain or short-term expediency."[1]

Collins and Porras cite numerous examples of core values that the founders and CEOs of such companies as IBM, Johnson & Johnson, Hewlett-Packard, Procter & Gamble, Wal-Mart, Merck, Motorola, Sony, Walt Disney, General Electric, and Philip Morris articulated and promoted. Some companies made a commitment to customers their core value, while others focused on employees, their products, innovation, or even risk taking. The common theme was that core values and a clear corporate purpose, what together are described as the organization's core ideology, were essential elements of enduring and financially successful companies.

Talk of a corporation's "culture" is a way of saying that a corporation has a set of identifiable values. All the companies Collins and Porras described are known for having strong corporate cultures and a clear set of values.

and guide the thinking and behaviors of the members of that organization. This culture shapes the people who are members of the organization. Consider how your own company, organization or school, dormitory, or fraternity/sorority differs from a similar one. Is there a "type" of person stereotypical of your organization, dormitory, or fraternity/sorority? Are there unspoken but still influential standards and expectations that shape students at your school? How would you be different if you had chosen a different institution, or had joined a different fraternity or sorority, or had participated in a different organization?

Businesses also have unspoken yet influential standards and expectations. IBM was once famous for a culture in which highly starched white shirts and ties (for it was a very male culture) were part of the required dress code. Many software and technologies companies have reputations for a culture of informality and playfulness. Some companies have a straight nine-to-five work schedule; others expect employees to work long hours and weekends. A person who enters the second type of firm with a nine-to-five attitude, intending to leave as the clock strikes five, might not "fit" and is likely not to last long. The same might hold true for a firm's values. If you join a firm with a culture that supports other values than those with which you are comfortable, there will be values conflicts – for better or worse.

No culture, in business or elsewhere, is static. Cultures change; but modifying culture—indeed, having any impact on it at all—is a bit like moving an iceberg. The iceberg is always moving and, if you ignore it, will continue to float with whatever currents hold sway at the moment. One person cannot alter its course alone, but strong leaders can have a significant impact on a culture, and a strong business leader can certainly have a significant impact on a corporate culture.

FIGURE 4.1

Source: Illustration copyright © Nancy Margulies, St. Louis, MO. Reprinted with permission of the artist.

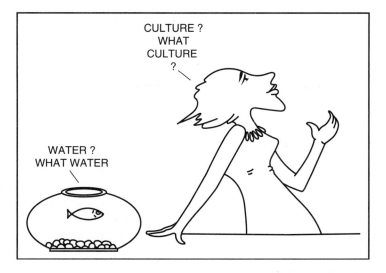

A firm's culture can be its sustaining value – that which offers it direction and stability during challenging times. It can, however, also serve to constrain an organization in the common ways of managing issues, as in the typical phrases "that's how things have always been done here" or "that's our prevailing climate." The stability that can be a benefit at one time can be a barrier to success at another.

Defining the specific culture within an organization is not an easy task since it is partially based on each participant's perception of the culture. In fact, perception may actually impact the culture in a circular way—a culture exists, we perceive it to be a certain type of culture, we respond to the culture on the basis of our perception, and we thereby impact others' experience of the culture. Several of the elements that are easiest to perceive, such as attitudes and behaviors, are only a small fraction of the elements that comprise the culture. In addition, culture is present in and can be determined by exploring any of the following, among others:

• Tempo of work.
• The organization's approach to humor.
• Methods of problem solving.
• The competitive environment.
• Incentives.
• Individual autonomy.
• Hierarchical structure.

Even with this list of cultural elements, it can be difficult for individuals in a firm to identify the specific characteristics of the culture within which they work. That phenomenon is best illustrated by the cartoon in Figure 4.1: Culture becomes so much a part of the environment that participants do not even notice its existence. Consider the culture you experience within your family. Oftentimes it is only when you first move away from your family, when you go off to college, for example, that you can even recognize that your family has its own culture. As you delve into the quirky particularities of your family's relationships, choices, preferences, communication styles, even gift-giving practices, you will notice that each family has a culture that is distinct and self-perpetuating. So, too, with business.

Culture and Ethics

How, exactly, does the notion of culture connect with ethics? More specifically, what role does corporate culture play in business ethics? We can answer these questions by reflecting on several topics introduced previously.

2

OBJECTIVE

In Chapter 1, we considered the law's limitations in ensuring ethical compliance. For example, the law requires business to make reasonable accommodations for employees with disabilities. But the law can be ambiguous in determining if a business should make a reasonable accommodation for an employee with allergies, depression, dyslexia, arthritis, hearing loss, or high blood pressure. In situations where the law is an incomplete guide for ethical decision making, the business culture is likely to be the determining factor in the decision. Ethical businesses must find ways to encourage, to shape, and to allow ethically responsible decisions. We can understand a corporate culture as the sum total of all the corporate practices that encourage, shape, or allow some types of decisions and discourage others.

Each of the factors in the decision-making model we introduced in previous chapters, from fact gathering through moral imagination to assessment, can be helped or hindered by the decision maker's social environment. An ethical culture would be one in which employees are empowered and expected to act in ethically responsible ways even when the law does not require it. A corporate culture sets the expectations and norms that will determine which decisions are made.

Later in this chapter we will examine types of cultures and various ways in which a corporation can create a culture that encourages ethical action. But to understand that cultures can encourage some types of behaviors and discourage others, consider as an example two organizational approaches to the relief efforts following hurricane Katrina in September 2005.

On one hand, the Federal Emergency Management Agency (FEMA) was charged with overall responsibility for the government's response to the hurricane. FEMA was created in 1979 when several governmental agencies ranging from fire prevention to insurance to civil defense were merged into one larger agency. FEMA itself was later subsumed into the federal Department of Homeland Security. By all accounts at the time of the hurricane, FEMA was a bureaucratic, hierarchical organization. Established rules and procedures were to be followed in making decisions. Many decisions required approval from people in authority. At one point, emergency personnel were delayed in reaching the hurricane area for days because FEMA required that they first attend mandatory training sessions on preventing sexual harassment in the workplace.

Despite years of preparation and plans, the magnitude of the hurricane and resultant flooding overwhelmed FEMA's ability to respond. When the situation did not fit plans and the rules no longer applied, FEMA's bureaucracy seemed incapable of acting. Temporary homes and supplies, despite being stored nearby, were not moved into the area for months after the storm because those in authority had not yet given approval. Decisions were made, then retracted. Days after the hurricane, while television reports showed thousands of people stranded at the New Orleans convention center, FEMA director Michael Brown claimed that he had learned of these survivors only from a reporter's question. Apparently no one had told the director of FEMA of the problem, therefore he couldn't make a decision, and therefore thousands of people went without help. The organization seemed unable to move information up to decision makers, and lower-level managers lacked authority to decide for themselves.

On the other hand, the United States Coast Guard is another organization with similar responsibilities for search and rescue during emergency situations. FEMA director Brown was eventually removed from his position and replaced by a Coast Guard admiral. The Coast Guard has a reputation for being a less bureaucratic organization. The unofficial motto is to "rescue first, and get permission later." The Coast Guard empowers frontline individuals to solve problems without waiting for superiors to make decisions or give directions. Imagine how the same person working in either of these organizations would approach a decision and you will have some idea of the importance of organizational culture.

It is fair to say that FEMA and the Coast Guard are two very similar organizations with similar missions, rules, and legal regulations, but with very different cultures. The decisions made throughout both organizations reflect the culture of each. The attitudes, expectations, and habits encouraged and reinforced in the two agencies reflect the differences of culture.

FIGURE 4.2

Source: Adapted from Rushworth Kidder, Institute for Global Ethics, "Overcoming Ethical Nonchalance in the Boardroom," *Ethics Newsline* 7, no. 22 (June 1, 2004), p. 1.

<table>
<tr><td colspan="2" align="center">If ignored . . .
Additional costly examples</td></tr>
<tr><td>•</td><td>(During one two-week period)</td></tr>
<tr><td>•</td><td>Lucent Technologies:</td></tr>
<tr><td></td><td>– Settled a class-action suit for misleading investors ($517 million) and was then fined for obstructing the probe ($25 million).</td></tr>
<tr><td>•</td><td>Pfizer:</td></tr>
<tr><td></td><td>– Found guilty of aggressively marketing one of its drugs to doctors for "off-label" use in unapproved ways ($430 million).</td></tr>
<tr><td>•</td><td>Citigroup:</td></tr>
<tr><td></td><td>– Liable for loan abuses to low-income and high-risk borrowers ($70 million), one week after it settled a class-action suit for biasing its brokerage advice in urging investors to buy WorldCom stock ($2.65 billion).</td></tr>
<tr><td>•</td><td>NEC:</td></tr>
<tr><td></td><td>– Fined for fraud under its contract to provide Internet access to the nation's poor schools ($20.7 million).</td></tr>
</table>

The notion of expectations and habits suggests a second previous topic that is relevant for our discussion of corporate culture. Chapter 3 introduced the ethics of virtue and described the virtues as character traits and habits. The cultivation of habits, including the cultivation of ethical virtue, is greatly shaped by the culture in which one lives.

When we talk about decision making, it is easy to think in terms of a rational, deliberative process in which a person consciously deliberates about and weighs each alternative before acting. But the virtue ethics tradition reminds us that our decisions and our actions are very often less deliberate than that. We are as likely to act out of habit and based on character than we are to act after careful deliberations. So the question of where we get our habits and character is all-important.

Part of the answer surely is that we can choose to develop some habits rather than others. But it is also clear that our habits are shaped and formed by education and training—by culture. This education takes place in every social environment, ranging from families and religions to entire societies and cultures. It also takes place in the workplace, where individuals quickly learn appropriate and expected behaviors. Intentionally or not, business institutions provide an environment in which habits are formed and virtues, or vices, are created. To talk of such an environment is to talk of an ethical corporate culture.

Besides these more abstract considerations, an ethical culture can also have a direct and practical impact on the bottom line. If attended to and supported, a strong ethical culture can serve as a deterrent to stakeholder damage and improve bottom line sustainability. If ignored, the culture could instead reinforce a perception that "anything goes," and "any way to a better bottom line is acceptable," destroying long-term sustainability. Responsibility for creating and sustaining such ethical corporate cultures rests on business leaders.

Collins and Porras' book *Built to Last: Successful Habits of Visionary Companies* explains the power of a corporate culture to shape the individuals who work within it. While it may be true that individuals can shape an organization, and perhaps charismatic leaders can do this especially well, it is equally true, if not more so, that organizations shape individuals. Imagine spending a 20-, 30-, or even 40-year career in the same organization. The person you become, your attitudes, values, expectations, mind-set, and habits, will all be significantly determined by the culture of the organization in which you work.

Compliance and Value-Based Cultures

OBJECTIVE

In the 1990s, a distinction came to be recognized in types of corporate culture: some firms were classified as compliance-based cultures (the traditional approach) while others were considered to be values-based or integrity-based cultures. These latter cultures are perceived as more flexible and far-sighted corporate environments. The distinction between compliance-based and values-based cultures is best applied in accounting and auditing situations, but it can also be used more generally to understand wider corporate cultures.

TABLE 4.1
The Evolution of Compliance Programs into Values-Based Programs

Source: Reprinted from Paul Lindow and Jill Race, "Beyond Traditional Audit Techniques," *Journal of Accountancy Online,* July 2002. http://www.aicpa. org/PUBS/JOFA/jul2002/lindow.htm.

Traditional	Progressive (best practices)
Audit focus	Business focus
Transaction-based	Process-based
Financial account focus	Customer focus
Compliance objective	Risk identification, process improvement objective
Policies and procedures focus	Risk management focus
Multiyear audit coverage	Continual risk-reassessment coverage
Policy adherence	Change facilitator
Budgeted cost center	Accountability for performance improvement results
Career auditors	Opportunities for other management positions
Methodology: Focus on policies, transactions, and compliance	Methodology: Focus on goals, strategies, and risk management processes

As the name suggests, a compliance-based culture emphasizes obedience to the rules as the primary responsibility of ethics. A compliance-based culture will empower legal and audits offices to mandate and monitor compliance with the law and with internal codes. A values-based culture is one that reinforces a particular set of values rather than a particular set of rules. Certainly, these firms may have codes of conduct; but those codes are predicated on a statement of values and it is presumed that the code includes mere examples of the values' application. Integrating these values into the firm's culture encourages a decision-making process that uses the values as underlying principles to guide employee decisions rather than as hard-and-fast rules.

The argument in favor of a values-based culture is based on the fact that a compliance culture is only as strong and as precise as the rules with which workers are expected to comply. A firm can only have a certain number of rules and the rules can never unambiguously apply to every conceivable situation. A values-based culture recognizes that where a rule does not apply, the firm must rely on the personal integrity of its workforce when decisions need to be made.

This is not to say that values-based organizations do not include a compliance structure. In fact, an Ethics Resource Center study found that "strict compliance and audit programs are often springboards for implementing more comprehensive programs addressing ethical values. When this occurs, compliance goals typically do not diminish. Rather a focus on ethical values adds important priorities and incentives."[2] The goals of a traditional compliance-oriented program may include meeting legal and regulatory requirements, minimizing risks of litigation and indictment, and improving accountability mechanisms.

The goals of a more evolved and inclusive ethics program may entail a broader and more expansive application to the firm, including maintaining brand and reputation, recruiting and retaining desirable employees, helping to unify a firm's global operations, creating a better working environment for employees, and doing the right thing in addition to doing things right. You should notice the more comprehensive implications of the latter list for the firm, its sustainability, and its long-term bottom line.

If a firm were to make a determination that it prefers the benefits and structure of a values-based orientation to its ethics program, the next question is how it can integrate ethics into the compliance environment to most effectively prevent these common dilemmas and to create a "culture" of ethics. That question is addressed in the next section.

Ethical Leadership and Corporate Culture

If the goal of corporate culture is to cultivate values, expectations, beliefs, and patterns of behavior that best and most effectively support ethical decision making, it becomes the primary responsibility of corporate leadership to steward this effort. Leaders are charged with this duty in part because stakeholders throughout the organization are guided to a large extent by the "tone at the top."

Merck's CEO, Raymond Gilmartin, explains, "In thought, word, and deed, a company's leaders must clearly and unambiguously both advocate and model ethical behavior."[3] If a leader is perceived to be shirking her or his duties, misusing corporate assets, misrepresenting the firm's capabilities, or engaging in other inappropriate behavior, stakeholders receive the message that this type of behavior is not only acceptable, but perhaps expected and certainly the way to get ahead in that organization. Instead, if a leader is clearly placing her or his own ethical behavior above any other consideration, stakeholders are guided to follow that role model and to emulate that priority scheme.

OBJECTIVE

● Beyond personal behavior, leadership sets the tone through other mechanisms such as the dedication of resources. Ethical business leaders not only talk about ethics and act ethically on a personal level, but they also allocate corporate resources to support and promote ethical behavior. There is a long-standing credo of management: "budgeting is all about values." More common versions are "put your money where your mouth is" and "walk the talk."

For example, when **ethics officers** were first introduced to the corporate structure in the early 1990s, a clear indication of their relevance and influence within the organization was reflected in the extent to which they were supported financially. It was clear that ethics was not a priority if the general counsel served as the ethics officer in her "spare time," and no additional resources were allocated to that activity. On the contrary, ethics may hold a different position in the firm if a highly skilled individual is hired into an exclusive position as ethics officer and is given a staff and a budget to support the work required. Similarly, if a firm mandates ethical decision making from its workers through the implementation of a code of conduct, extending the same standard for its vendors, suppliers, and other contractors is a symbol of how seriously the firm takes the code.

One study of the nature of ethical leadership emphasized the importance of being perceived as a people-oriented leader, as well as the importance of leaders engaging in visible ethical action. Traits that were also important included receptivity,

---

Reality Check *Priorities at the Top*

The Business Roundtable Institute for Corporate Ethics listed the following as the top five ethics priorities for corporate leaders, as identified by CEOs in a survey:

1. Regaining the public trust.

2. Effective company management in the context of today's investor expectations.

3. Ensuring the integrity of financial reporting.

4. Fairness of executive compensation.

5. Ethical role-modeling by senior management.

Source: Business Roundtable Institute for Corporate Ethics, "Mapping the Terrain" Study (June 2004), www. corporate-ethics.org. Reprinted with permission.

---

listening, and openness, in addition to the more traditionally considered traits of integrity, honesty, and trustworthiness. Finally, being perceived as having a broad ethical awareness, showing concern for multiple stakeholders, and using ethical decision processes are also important.[4] Those perceived as ethical leaders do many of the things "traditional leaders" do (e.g., reinforce the conduct they are looking for, create standards for behavior, and so on), but they do that within the context of an ethics agenda. People perceive that the ethical leader's goal is not simply job performance, but performance that is consistent with a set of ethical values and principles. Finally, ethical leaders demonstrate caring for people (employees and external stakeholders) in the process.

However, as mentioned above, all of these traits and behaviors must be visible. If an executive is "quietly ethical" within the confines of the top management team, but more distant employees don't know about it, she or he is not likely to be perceived as an ethical leader. Traits and behaviors must be socially visible and understood in order to be noticed and influence perceptions.[5] People notice when an executive walks the talk and acts on concerns for the common good, society as a whole, and long-term business prospects. Executives are expected to be focused on the financial bottom line and the short-term demands of stock analysts, but it is noteworthy when they focus on these broader and longer-term concerns. Finally, making courageous decisions in tough situations represents another way ethical leaders get noticed. Ethical leaders are "courageous enough to say 'no' to conduct that would be inconsistent with [their] values."

Effective Leadership and Ethical Leadership

Being perceived as a leader plays an important role in a leader's ability to create and transform an ethical corporate culture. Key executives have the capability of transforming a business culture for better or worse. If the corporate culture has significant impact on ethical decision making within the firm, then leaders have the responsibility for shaping that environment so that ethical decision making might flourish. But what is it to be a "leader," and, more important, what is it to be an ethical leader?

What do we mean by an "ethical" leader? It is important to make a distinction between good leaders and ethical leaders. A good leader is simply anyone who

Good leader

does well what leaders do. Since leaders guide, direct, and escort others towards a destination, a good leader is someone who does this successfully and, presumably, efficiently. Good leaders are effective at getting followers to their common destination. But not every good leader is an ethical leader.

In the corporate context, Ken Lay and Jeffrey Skilling were good and effective business leaders. They were able to transform Enron from a small oil and gas pipeline company into one of the largest corporations in the world. By many accounts, they were inspirational, imaginative, and creative leaders who could motivate their staff to attain very high levels of success. They were also unethical leaders. So, what is the difference between effective leaders and ethical leaders?

OBJECTIVE 5

One key difference lies with the means used to motivate others and achieve one's goals. Skilling was said to be a very difficult person to work for. Effective leaders might be able to achieve their goals through threats, intimidation, harassment, and coercion. One can also lead using more attractive means such as modeling ethical behavior, persuasion, or simply using one's institutional role.

Some of the discussions in the literature on leadership suggest that ethical leadership is determined solely by the methods used in leading. Promoters of certain styles of leadership want to suggest that their style is a superior style of leadership. Consequently, they tend to identify a method of leading with "true" leadership in an ethical sense. On this line, for example, Robert Greenleaf's "Servant Leadership" suggests that the best leaders are nonhierarchical individuals who lead by the example of serving others. Other discussions similarly suggest that "transformative" or "transactional" leaders employ methods that empower subordinates to take the initiative and solve problems for themselves and that this constitutes the best ethical leaders.

Certainly ethically appropriate methods of leadership are central to becoming an ethical leader. Creating a corporate culture in which employees are empowered and expected to make ethically responsible decisions is a necessary part of being an ethical business leader. But while some means may be ethically better than others (e.g., persuasion rather than coercion), it is not the method alone that establishes a leader as ethical. While perhaps necessary, ethical means of leading others are not sufficient for establishing ethical leadership. The other element of ethical leadership involves the end or goal towards which the leader leads.

One cannot be a leader, and there cannot be followers, unless there is a direction or goal towards which one is heading. In the business context, productivity, efficiency, and profitability are minimal goals. A business executive who leads a firm into bankruptcy is unlikely to qualify as an effective or good leader. An executive who transforms a business into a productive, efficient, and profitable business will be judged as an effective business leader. One who does this in a way that respects subordinates or empowers them to become creative and successful is, at least at first glance, both an effective and ethical leader. But is profitability and efficiency accomplished through ethical means alone enough to make a business leader an ethical leader?

Imagine a business leader who empowers his subordinates, respects their autonomy by consulting and listening, but who leads a business that publishes child pornography or pollutes the environment or sells weapons to radical organizations. Would the method alone determine the ethical standing of such a leader?

The Ethics Officers Association was established in 1992 by a dozen companies to provide ethics officers with training and a variety of venues to exchange best-practices information. The EOA now has over 1,000 members and is the largest peer-to-peer multi-industry organization for ethics and compliance practitioners.

The Ethics Practitioners' Association of Canada, another professional association for ethics officers, has established a Competency Profile of Ethics Practitioners that is designed to establish a common standard for those who work in the industry. In particular, it addresses the functions practitioners carry out, the standard knowledge base, and the skills they should possess. It can be found at http://www.epac-apec.ca/cont-ang/competency-profile.htm.

If you were to develop standards of practice for ethics officers, what might be some of the principles you would be sure to include? Consider the following questions:

- What are the ethical issues involved in this task?
- What process would you use to develop these standards of practice?
- How would you reach your decision on what to include?
- Would you anticipate developing standards based on the identification of responsibilities and protection of rights? Are you more likely to develop a code that defines desirable or undesirable outcomes, or would you instead define the characteristics of an "ethical" ethics officer? If you focus the code on a statement of rights or values, how will you suggest they be prioritized?
- Who are the stakeholders of a code such as this one? How will your decision on what to include impact the stakeholders involved?
- Do you have any external guidance? Does the law offer any guidance?
- How would you measure the success of the standards developed?

Beyond the goal of profitability, other socially responsible goals might be necessary before we conclude that the leader is fully ethical. Chapter 5 will pick up on this theme as we examine corporate social responsibility.

Building a Values-Based Corporate Culture

As in the iceberg example we discussed earlier, each individual in an organization has an impact on the corporate culture, although, except for perhaps the key leadership, no one individual can build or change the culture alone. Culture derives from leadership, integration, and assessment/monitoring.

Mission Statements, Codes of Conduct, and Statements of Values

One of the key manifestations of ethical leadership is the articulation of values for the organization. Of course, this articulation may evolve after an inclusive process of values identification—it need not simply mimic the particular values of one chief executive. However, it is that leader's responsibility to ensure that the firm

Reality Check *Do Codes Make a Difference?*

As a result of its quick and effective handling of its experience with tainted Tylenol in both 1982 and 1986, Johnson & Johnson has often been viewed as one of the most admired firms in the world. J&J had sales in 2001 of $33 billion, almost triple those of the previous decade and representing its 69th year of consecutive sales increases. It has had 17 consecutive years of double-digit earnings increases and 39 consecutive years of dividend increases. Its market value ended 2001 at more than $180 billion, up from $38 billion in 1991, evidence that a firm that lives according to its strong values and a culture that supports those values not only can survive but sustains profit over the long term. CEO Ralph Larsen credits these successes directly to the J&J Credo: "it's the glue that holds our decentralized company together . . . For us, the credo is our expression of managing the multiple bottom lines of products, people, planet and profits. It's the way we conceptualize our total impact on society."[6]

The Johnson & Johnson Credo and History

At Johnson & Johnson there is no mission statement that hangs on the wall. Instead, for more than 60 years, a simple, one-page document—Our Credo—has guided our actions in fulfilling our responsibilities to our customers, our employees, the community and our stockholders. Our worldwide Family of Companies shares this value system in 36 languages spreading across Africa, Asia/Pacific, Eastern Europe, Europe, Latin America, Middle East and North America.

Our Credo History

General Robert Wood Johnson, who guided Johnson & Johnson from a small, family-owned business to a worldwide enterprise, had a very perceptive view of a corporation's responsibilities beyond the manufacturing and marketing of products.

As early as 1935, in a pamphlet titled TRY REALITY, he urged his fellow industrialists to embrace what he termed "a new industrial philosophy." Johnson defined this as the corporation's responsibility to customers, employees, the community and stockholders.

But it was not until eight years later, in 1943, that Johnson wrote and first published the Johnson & Johnson Credo, a one-page document outlining these responsibilities in greater detail. Johnson saw to it that the Credo was embraced by his company, and he urged his management to apply it as part of their everyday business philosophy.

The Credo, seen by business leaders and the media as being farsighted, received wide public attention and acclaim. Putting customers first, and stockholders last, was a refreshing approach to the management of a business. But it should be noted that Johnson was a practical minded businessman. He believed that by putting the customer first the business would be well served, and it was.

The Corporation has drawn heavily on the strength of the Credo for guidance through the years, and at no time was this more evident than during the TYLENOL® crises of 1982 and 1986, when the McNeil Consumer & Specialty Pharmaceuticals product was adulterated with cyanide and used as a murder weapon. With Johnson & Johnson's good name and reputation at stake, company managers and employees made countless decisions that were inspired by the philosophy embodied in the Credo. The company's reputation was preserved and the TYLENOL® acetaminophen business was regained.

Today the Credo lives on in Johnson & Johnson stronger than ever. Company employees now participate in a periodic survey and evaluation of just how well the company performs its Credo responsibilities. These assessments are then fed back to the senior management, and where there are shortcomings, corrective action is promptly taken.

Over the years, some of the language of the Credo has been updated and new areas recognizing the environment and the balance between work and family have been added. But the spirit of the document remains the same today as when it was first written.

When Robert Wood Johnson wrote and then insti-tutionalized the Credo within Johnson & Johnson, he never suggested that it guaranteed perfection. But its principles have become a constant goal, as well as a source of inspiration, for all who are part of the Johnson & Johnson Family of Companies.

More than 60 years after it was first introduced, the Credo continues to guide the destiny of the world's largest and most diversified health care company.

Our Credo

We believe our first responsibility is to the doctors, nurses and patients, to mothers and fathers and all others who use our products and services. In meeting their needs everything we do must be of high quality. We must constantly strive to reduce our costs in order to maintain reasonable prices. Customers' orders must be serviced promptly and accurately. Our suppliers and distributors must have an opportunity to make a fair profit.

We are responsible to our employees, the men and women who work with us throughout the world. Everyone must be considered as an individual. We must respect their dignity and recognize their merit. They must have a sense of security in their jobs. Compensation must be fair and adequate, and working conditions clean, orderly and safe. We must be mindful of ways to help our employees fulfill their family responsibilities. Employees must feel free to make suggestions and complaints. There must be equal opportunity for employment, development and advancement for those qualified. We must pro-vide competent management, and their actions must be just and ethical.

We are responsible to the communities in which we live and work and to the world community as well. We must be good citizens – support good works and charities and bear our fair share of taxes. We must encourage civic improvements and better health and education. We must main-tain in good order the property we are privileged to use, protecting the environment and natural resources.

Our final responsibility is to our stockholders. Busi-ness must make a sound profit. We must experi-ment with new ideas. Research must be carried on, innovative programs developed and mistakes paid for. New equipment must be purchased, new facilities provided and new products launched. Reserves must be created to provide for adverse times. When we operate according to these prin-ciples, the stockholders should realize a fair return.

Source: Courtesy of Johnson & Johnson, http://www. jnj.com/our_company/our_credo_history/index.htm and http://www.jnj.com/our_company/our_credo/index.htm.

is guided by some set of organizing principles that can guide employees in their decision-making processes.

OBJECTIVE

Before impacting the culture through a code of conduct or statement of val-ues, a firm must first determine its mission. In the absence of other values, the only value is profit—at any cost. Therefore, without additional guidance from the top, a firm is sending a clear message that a worker should do whatever it takes to reap profits. A code of conduct then may more specifically delineate this foundation both for internal stakeholders such as employees and for external stakeholders such as customers. The code has the potential, therefore, to both enhance corporate reputation and provide concrete guidance for internal decision making, thus creat-ing a built-in risk management system. When David Packard passed away, Bill Hewlett, his business partner in creating HP, commented, "as far as the company is concerned, the greatest thing he left behind him was a code of ethics known as 'the HP Way."[7] The vision can be inspiring—indeed it *should be* inspiring. Jim Collins, author of *Built to Last* and *Good to Great,* explains, "Contrary to business school doctrine, we did not find 'maximizing shareholder wealth' or 'profit maximization' as the dominant driving force or primary objective through the history of most of the visionary companies. They have tended to produce a cluster of objectives, of which money is only one—and not necessarily the primary one."[8] By establishing (especially through a participatory process) the core tenets on which a company is built, corporate leadership is effectively laying down the law with regard to the basis and objectives for all future decisions.

The 1990s brought a proliferation of corporate codes of conduct and mission statements as part of the corporate response to the Federal Sentencing Guidelines (see below), and a 2002 survey found that 75 percent of these mention the word *ethics*.[9] How successful these codes are depends in large part on the process by which they are conceived and written, as well as their implementation. As with the construction of a personal code or mission, it is critical to first ask yourself what you stand for or what the company stands for. Why does the firm exist, what are its purposes, and how will it implement these objectives? Once you make these determinations, how will you share them and encourage a commitment to them among your colleagues and subordinates?

The second step in the development of guiding principles for the firm is the articulation of a clear vision regarding the firm's direction. Why have a code? Bobby Kipp, PricewaterhouseCoopers' global ethics leader, explains that "we felt it was important for all our clients, our people and other stakeholders to understand exactly what we stand for and how they can expect us to conduct ourselves . . . The code doesn't change the basic nature of the business we undertake, but instead it articulates the way we strive to conduct ourselves. The code shows how we apply our values to our daily business practices."[10]

The third step in this process is to identify clear steps as to how this cultural shift will occur. You have a code, but you can't simply "print, post and pray," as Ethics Resource Center President Stuart Gilman has referred to Enron's experience. Do you just post a sign on the wall that says, "let's make more profits!" Of course not; you need to have processes and procedures in place that support and then sustain that vision.

TABLE 4.2
Ethics Code Guidelines

Source: Ethics Resource Center, "Code Construction and Content," http://www.ethics.org/printable_code_outline.html. Reprinted with permission of Ethics Resource Center.

The Ethics Resource Center provides the following guidelines for writing an ethics code:

1. Be clear about the objectives the code is intended to accomplish.
2. Get support and ideas for the code from all levels of the organization.
3. Be aware of the latest developments in the laws and regulations that affect your industry.
4. Write as simply and clearly as possible. Avoid legal jargon and empty generalities.
5. Respond to real-life questions and situations.
6. Provide resources for further information and guidance.
7. In all its forms, make it user-friendly because ultimately a code fails if it is not used.[11]

You are a corporate vice president of one of the largest units in your organization. Unfortunately, you have noticed over the past few years that your unit has developed a singular focus on profits since employees' performance appraisals and resulting compensation increases are based in significant part on "making the numbers." Though the unit has done well in this regard, you have noticed that people have been known to cut corners, to treat others less respectfully than you would like, and to generally disregard other values in favor of the bottom line. While this might be beneficial to the firm in the short run, you have grave concerns about the long-term sustainability of this approach.

- What are the ethical issues involved in striving to define or impact the culture of a unit?
- How might you go about defining the culture of your unit so that employees might be able to understand your concerns?
- What will be the most effective means by which to alter this culture?
- What stakeholders would be involved in your suggestion in response to the previous question? How might the different stakeholder groups be impacted by your decision on this process?
- How can you act in order to ensure the most positive results? How will you measure those results or determine your success? Will you measure inputs or outcomes, responsibilities, and rights?

Finally, to have an effective code that will successfully impact culture, there must be a belief throughout the organization that this culture is actually possible, achievable. If conflicts remain that will prevent certain components from being realized, or if key leadership is not on board, no one will have faith in the changes articulated.

Ethics Hotlines, Ombudsmen, and Integrating Ethical Culture

OBJECTIVE

Recalling Gilman's warning not to "print, post and pray," business firms must have mechanisms in place that allow employees to come forward with questions, concerns, and information about unethical behavior. Integrating an ethical culture throughout a firm and providing means for enforcement is vitally critical both to the success of any cultural shift and to the impact on all stakeholders. Integration can take a number of different forms, depending both on the organizational culture and the ultimate goals of the process.

One of the most determinative elements of integration is communication because without it, there is no clarity of purpose, priorities, or process. Communication of culture must be incorporated into the firm's vocabulary, habits, and attitudes to become an essential element in the corporate life, decision making, and determination of success. In the end, the Ethics & Policy Integration Centre contends that communication patterns describe the organization far better than organization charts!

To explore the effectiveness of a corporation's integration process, consider whether incentives are in the right place to encourage ethical decision making

---

Reality Check *Examples of Culture Integration*

- Lockheed Martin offers its Chairman's Award, which is bestowed upon the employee who most fully represents the spirit of the culture. In addition, the company coordinates an ethics film festival that encourages workers—on their own time and without financial assistance—to create short videos on ethics at the firm.

- DuPont strives to reinforce the message in a slightly different way. The firm has decided to publicize compliance transgressions (omitting the names to protect privacy) and the results of discipline. Though this "tell all" method might have its lawyers quaking in their seats, DuPont believes that, without it, workers have no idea what is acceptable and unacceptable behavior.

---

and whether ethical behavior is evaluated during a worker's performance review. It is difficult to reward people for doing the right thing, such as correctly filing an expense report, but as the Lockheed Martin Chairman's Award2 shows, incentives such as appropriate honors and positive appraisals are possible. Are employees comfortable raising questions relating to unethical behavior? Are multiple and varied reporting mechanisms in place? Do employees believe their reports will be free from retaliation? What can be done to ensure that employees who violate the company code are disciplined appropriately, even if they are good performers?

How does communication about ethical matters occur? The fact of the matter is that reporting ethically suspect behavior is a difficult thing to do. Childhood memories of "tattletales" or "snitches," along with a general social prohibition against informing on others, create barriers to reporting unethical behavior. More ominously, individuals often pay a real cost when they report on unethical behavior, especially if workplace superiors are involved.

"Whistleblowing" is one of the classic issues in business ethics. Whistleblowing involves the disclosure of unethical or illegal activities to someone who is in the position to take action to prevent or punish the wrongdoing. Whistleblowing can expose and end unethical activities, but it can also seem disloyal, it can harm the business, and it can extract significant costs on the whistleblower.

Whistleblowing can occur internally, as when Sherron Watkins reported her concerns to Ken Lay (see p. 9). It can occur externally, as when Jeffrey Wigand (as portrayed in the movie *The Insider*), reported to *60 Minutes* about Brown & Williamson's activities in not only concealing and knowingly misleading the public about the harmful effects of cigarettes, but also using additives that increased the potential for harm. Whistleblowing can also occur externally when employees report wrongdoing to legal authorities, as when rocket engineer Roger Boisjoly reported the activities of his employer Morton Thiokol and NASA prior to the launch of the space shuttle Challenger.

Because whistleblowing to external groups such as the press and the legal authorities can be so harmful to both the whistleblower and the firm itself, internal

Reality Checl *Whistleblowing in Different Languages – International Approaches*

By Tara Radin and Martin Calkins[12]

Whistleblowing is often considered American. In fact, the term "whistleblowing" is derived from the policeman's blowing a whistle to alert others to a wrongdoing. It refers to "the disclosure by organizational members (former or current) of illegal, immoral, or illegitimate practices under the control of their employers, to persons or organizations that may be able to effect action." Whistleblowing technically refers to occasions where members of an organization go outside the bounds of their organizations in order to report and find a remedy for suspected wrongdoing evidenced by questionable behavior. Today, in the United States and elsewhere, the term "whistleblowing" is increasingly being used to refer to situations where employees report questionable behavior within their organizations as well as to those who seek assistance externally.

INTERNATIONAL RAMIFICATIONS

In the United States, the response to deterrents to whistleblowing has been largely legislative. The majority of states have passed laws specifically protecting the rights of whistleblowers. While this does not necessarily provide a strong impetus for many potential whistleblowers, it does help to remove one potential obstacle, that is, the fear of direct retaliation. Further, government agencies have heightened regulation and inspection in particularly sensitive areas. For example, Congress passed the controversial Patriot Act in response to fears regarding terrorism in the wake of 9/11. This allows the American government to intervene in situations that could jeopardize public safety.

In the international workplace, legislation is often unavailable. In Malaysia, for example, there is no specific legislation. In Malaysia, where there is a tradition of poor treatment of workers, "[i]t is difficult in the Malaysian context because the concept of whistle-blowing is not there. One problem is, who do you whistle-blow to?" Treatment of workers has improved a bit, but is still part of Malaysia's history. Whistleblower legislation does exist in China, however, but it is largely ineffective—as is much of the legislation in China as a result of the existing cultural and landscape. Hotlines have been created by individual companies to field reports from whistleblowers, but getting people to understand the purpose and security of the hotlines is another issue. Effective legal protection for whistleblowers exists only in countries such as Australia, the United Kingdom, and, believe it or not, South Africa. In South Africa, for example, whistleblowing plays a significant role. According to a recent survey, "more than 60% of companies polled said whistleblowers had helped them detect wrongdoing, far higher than the 27% global average."

External monitoring therefore offers an alternative to whistleblowing in many instances. As companies have increasingly turned to outsourcing in order to remain competitive, they have opened themselves up to a new array of potential problems. This is a particularly prevalent phenomenon in the garment industry. Companies such as Levi Strauss & Co. have instituted complex monitoring procedures through which they keep a watchful eye on the business practices of their outsourcing partners. Other companies, such as Chiquita, have endorsed the value of external monitors. Chiquita owns the majority of its farms, but, considering the span of operations over multiple developing countries in Latin America, the company has found that external monitors can help preserve the integrity of those operations and the company's overall image.

Whistleblowing continues to suffer from the taint of association with wrongdoing. The view is that revealing a problem is harmful. Even though Johnson & Johnson's legacy in the wake of the Tylenol scare of the 1980s was that apologizing and taking responsibility can transform a company into an admired industry leader, people still cling to the fear that it could work the other way. In general, businesses are anxious to hide their flaws from their fickle fans.

Chiquita publishes an annual Corporate Responsibility Report, available to stockholders and the general public, in which the company reports the findings of its annual audits. Although Chiquita values transparency and considers it a business necessity, this runs against the common view that acknowledging that you have problems shows undesirable weakness. Chiquita's view is that the company is

(continued)

not pointing out problems—over the long term, these reports will show how Chiquita has remedied potential problems.

BUSINESS SOLUTIONS

Business can support the voices of potential whistleblowers by creating internal mechanisms through which they can be heard. Increasingly popular in China, for example, are whistleblower hotlines. The creation of confidential hotlines, mailboxes, or complete departments through which people can seek advice as well as report incidents represents an essential step toward encouraging whistleblowers to come forward. At the same time, record-keeping plays an integral role. Even where specifics are not identified, it is important that companies keep records of the information that is collected, and that people inside the organization are made aware that reported incidents are addressed. Making this sort of information available to employees will give them a reason to come forward. At the managerial level, it is important that managers train their subordinates properly, and that they provide subordinates outlets through which they can vent frustration. As much as a manager would prefer that his or her subordinates come to him or her directly with problems, it is essential that managers recognize that not all employees do and that they need to provide accessible alternatives.

For businesses in general, supporting local laws, governments, and nongovernmental organizations can prove extremely beneficial. Whistleblowing does not have to translate into exposing wrong-doing to the public. The media has usurped the role of seeking out instances of wrongdoing, because no one else was doing it. Silence enables sweatshops to blossom around the world; the press has effectively curbed their growth and changed behavior in many instances. The presence of effective and willing local external organizations can provide whistleblowers an alternative to the press. By supporting laws, businesses can ensure that competitors are behaving appropriately, and this can affect past or future employees of that business. By advocating other organizations as possible resources, businesses can help create a community through which problems can be addressed.

It is important to keep in mind that our goal is not to increase whistleblowing for its own sake. On the contrary, we recognize the imperfection of businesses and managers coupled with the vulnerability of internal and external stakeholders. The goal, then, is to increase whistleblowing in order to decrease the harmful decision making of the business leaders in whom we place considerable trust and who are responsible for our financial, emotional, and physical safety. As more and more companies endeavor to become world-class competitive, it is essential that these companies acknowledge their fallibility in order to protect the stakeholders that will either propel them forward or prevent them from achieving their goals.

mechanisms for reporting wrongdoing are preferable for all concerned. But the internal mechanisms must be effective, they must allow anonymity, and they also must protect the rights of the accused party. In addition to or as part of ethics and compliance officers' responsibilities, many firms have created ethics ombudsman and ethics hotlines. These mechanisms allow employees to report wrongdoing and create mechanisms for follow-up and enforcement.

Assessing and Monitoring the Corporate Culture: Audits

OBJECTIVE

Unfortunately, if one cannot measure something, it often declines in importance. The same result occurs with regard to culture. If we cannot measure, assess, or monitor culture, it is difficult to encourage others throughout the organization to pay attention to it. Yet, monitoring and an ongoing ethics audit allow organizations to uncover silent vulnerabilities that could pose challenges later to the firm,

Reality Check *Warning Signs!*

PricewaterhouseCoopers (PwC) offers a list of early warning signs of an ethically troubled organization that might, though do not necessarily, indicate areas of concern regarding fraud, conflicts of interest, ineffective controls, imbalance of power, inappropriate pressure, or other areas, among them these:

1. An inability to generate positive cash flows despite positive earnings and growth.
2. Unusual pressure to achieve accounting-based financial objectives.
3. Compensation tied closely or only to financial results.
4. Debt covenants that have been violated (or are close to being so).
5. Increased liabilities with no apparent source of funding.
6. Off–balance sheet transactions.
7. Complex or creative structures.
8. Ratios/trends that buck expectations or industry trends.
9. Large returns or revenue credits after the close of the period.
10. A large number of nonstandard adjusting entries.
11. A history of unreliable accounting estimates.
12. Numerous related-party transactions.
13. Transactions with no or questionable business purposes.

In addition, PwC suggests the following organizational signals:

1. An unusually complex organizational structure; numerous entities with unclear purpose.
2. Insufficient management depth in key positions, especially positions that manage risks.
3. Rapid growth or downsizing that places stress on organizational resources.
4. Resignations of management or board members for reasons other than retirement, health, or conflict of interest.
5. A member of the board or senior management who was possibly involved in or aware of financial manipulation that resulted in restatement is still connected with the organization.
6. An understaffed finance/accounting staff.
7. Undersized or understaffed internal audit department.
8. No audit committee or ineffective committee.
9. Management conveys a lifestyle beyond their financial means.
10. The scope of internal audit seems too narrow.
11. Failure to address weaknesses in controls or process.

On the other hand, the Institute for Business, Technology and Ethics cites the following eight traits of a healthy organization culture:

1. Openness and humility from top to bottom of the organization.
2. An environment of accountability and personal responsibility.
3. Freedom from risk taking within appropriate limits.
4. A fierce commitment to "doing it right."
5. A willingness to tolerate and learn from mistakes.
6. Unquestioned integrity and consistency.
7. A pursuit of collaboration, integration, and holistic thinking.
8. Courage and persistence in the face of difficulty.

thus serving as a vital element in risk assessment and prevention. By engaging in an ongoing assessment, organizations are better able to spot these areas before other stakeholders (both internal and external) spot them. But how do you detect a potentially damaging or ethically challenged corporate culture—sometimes

FIGURE 4.3
Sources of Culture

> **Review: Culture Derives from Leadership,**
> **Integration, and Assessment/Monitoring**
>
> 1. **Leadership** (and maintenance) of the control
>   environment
>   - Through high-level commitment and management
>   responsibility, leaders set the standard and the tone
> 2. **Control activities, information, and communication**
>   - Statements, policies, operating procedures,
>   communications and training
>   - Constant/consistent integration into business practices
> 3. **Review, assessment, ongoing monitoring**
>   - Monitoring, evaluation, historical accountability

referred to as a "toxic" culture? The first clear sign would be a lack of any generally accepted base values for the organization, as discussed above. In addition, warning signs can occur in the various component areas of the organization. How does the firm treat its customers, suppliers, clients, and workers? The management of its internal and external relationships is critical evidence of its values. How does the firm manage its finances? Of course, a firm can be in a state of financial disaster without engaging in even one unethical act (and vice versa), but the manner in which it manages and communicates its financial environment is telling.

Mandating and Enforcing Culture: The Federal Sentencing Guidelines

OBJECTIVE

When internal mechanisms for creating ethical corporate cultures prove inadequate, the business community can expect governmental regulation to fill the void. The United States Sentencing Commission (USSC), an independent agency in the United States Judiciary, was created in 1984 to regulate sentencing policy in the federal court system. Prior to that time, disparity in sentencing, arbitrary punishments, and crime control had been significant congressional issues. By using the USSC to mandate sentencing procedures, Congress has been able to incorporate the original purposes of sentencing in federal court procedures, bringing some of these challenges under control.

Beginning in 1987, the USSC prescribed mandatory Federal Sentencing Guidelines that apply to individual and organizational defendants in the federal system, bringing some amount of uniformity and fairness to the system. These prescriptions, based on the severity of the offense, assign most federal crimes to one of 43 "offense levels." Each offender also is placed into a criminal history category based upon the extent and recency of past misconduct. The court then inputs this information into a sentencing grid and determines the offender's sentence guideline range (ranges are either in six-month intervals or 25 percent of the sentence, whichever is greater), subject to adjustments. In its October 2004 decision in *U.S.* v. *Booker,* however, the Supreme Court severed the "mandatory" element of the guidelines from their advisory role, holding that their mandatory nature violated the Sixth Amendment right to a jury trial. Accordingly, though no longer mandatory, a sentencing court is still required to consider guideline ranges, but it is also permitted to tailor a sentence in light of other statutory concerns. This modification has not come without confusion. "Judges are still generally following the guidelines with new cases. But figuring out what to do with all the cases that have been sentenced under the old guidelines is the closest thing to chaos you can describe," says Douglas Berman, a law professor.[13]

The relevance of these guidelines to our exploration of ethics and, in particular, to our discussion of the corporate proactive efforts to create an ethical workplace is that the USSC strived to use them to create both a legal and an ethical corporate environment. The Sarbanes-Oxley legislation instructed the USSC to consider and review its guidelines for fraud relating to securities and accounting, as well as to obstruction of justice, and specifically asked for severe and aggressive deterrents. In recognition of the enormous impact of corporate culture on ethical decision making, the USSC updated the guidelines in 2004 to include references not only to compliance programs but to "ethics and compliance" programs. In addition, the criteria for an effective program, which used to be outlined in the guidelines' commentary, are now found in a separate guideline.

The guidelines seek to reward corporations that create an effective ethics and compliance system so that they are not penalized (or the penalty is reduced) if they have an effective program but they find themselves in court as a result of a bad apple or two. On the other hand, firms that did not have effective ethics and compliance systems would be sentenced additionally to a term of probation and ordered to develop a program during that time.

The USSC notes that

> [d]ue diligence and the promotion of desired organizational culture are indicated by the fulfillment of seven minimum requirements, which are the hallmarks of an effective program that encourages compliance with the law and ethical conduct.

The guidelines identify those specific acts of an organization that can serve as due diligence in preventing crime and the minimal requirements for an effective compliance and ethics program. These include the following actions:

1. Establish compliance standards and procedures (reasonably designed, implemented and enforced so that it will generally be effective in preventing and detecting violations of law).[14]
2. Governing body (board) has a duty to act prudently, to be knowledgeable about the content and operation of the compliance and ethics program, and must undergo ongoing and consistent training.

Protecting confidentiality is one of the most effective tools in creating a corporate culture in which illegal and unethical behavior can be uncovered. Corporate ethics officers, ombudsman, and ethics hotlines typically guarantee that any reports of illegal or unethical behavior will be held in strictest confidence. Ethics officers promise anonymity to whistleblowers, and those who report wrongdoing trust that this promise of confidentiality will be upheld.

However, Federal Sentencing Guidelines can create real ethical dilemmas for corporations that promise anonymity and confidentiality. The guidelines call for significantly reduced punishment for firms that immediately report potential wrongdoing to government authorities. Failure to report evidence of wrongdoing can mean the difference between a significant penalty and exoneration. Of course, failure to promise confidentiality can also be evidence of an ineffective ethics and compliance system, itself a potential risk for receiving stiffer legal penalties.

Should ethics officers guarantee confidentiality to those who report wrongdoing, and should they violate that confidence to protect the firm from prosecution?

- What facts would you want to know before making this decision?
- Can you imagine any creative way out of this dilemma?
- To whom does the ethics officer owe duties?
- What are the likely consequences of either decision?

3. Assign specific high level person to oversee compliance and to be responsible for the day-to-day operations of the program. This individual shall report directly to the board or other governing authority and shall have sufficient resources.

4. Use due care not to delegate important responsibilities to known high risk persons.

5. Communicate its program effectively to all employees and agents. In addition to the board, training must be conducted throughout the organizational leadership, employees and, where appropriate, its agents.

6. Monitor and audit program operation for effectiveness and to detect criminal activity, and establish a retribution-free, anonymous or confidential means for employees and agents to report possible violations to management or to seek guidance.

7. Create an incentive and disincentive structure to encourage performance in accordance with the program, including consistent discipline for employee violations.

8. Respond promptly and appropriately to any offenses and remedy any program deficiencies.[15]

Though these steps are likely to lead to an effective program, "[such a program] is more than checking off the items on a list. This concept of 'due diligence' is a restless standard, as flexible as changing events reflected in the day's

You have developed and implemented an ethics program. But how do you know whether the ethics program is "working"? How will you define "success"? Who do you define as your primary stakeholders? What are their interests in your program and what are the impacts of your program on each stakeholder? How could you modify your program to ensure even greater success?

This Decision Point asks you to define the "success" of an ethics program, an extraordinary challenge even for those in this business for many years. One way to look at the inquiry would be to consider the measures by which you might be willing to be evaluated, since this is your project. Overall, you will need to explore whether there are pressures in your environment that encourage worker misconduct. You will need to consider whether there are systematic problems that encourage bad decisions. Have you identified all the major legal, ethical, and reputational risks that your organization faces, and have you determined the means by which to remediate those risks?

Because you will encourage the performance that you plan to measure, it is important to determine whether you will be most concerned with the end results or consequences, or with the protection of particular values articulated by your program or codes. If you measure outcomes alone, you will have a singular focus on the achievement of those outcomes by decision makers. If you measure the protection of rights alone, you may be failing to consider the long-range implications of decisions in terms of their costs and benefits to the firm.

headlines and as creative as the minds of potential wrongdoers."[16] For instance, the guidelines require an investigation in response to a report of wrongdoing; but they also seem to require more than that. A firm must learn from its mistakes and take steps to prevent recurrences such as follow-up investigation and program enhancements. The USSC also mandates consideration of the size of the organization, the number and nature of its business risks, and the prior history of the organization; mitigating factors such as self-reporting of violations, cooperation with authorities, and acceptance of responsibility; and aggravating factors such as its involvement in or tolerance of criminal activity, a violation of a prior order, or its obstruction of justice. These standards are to be judged against applicable industry standards; however, this requires that each firm benchmark against comparable companies.

In a 1997 survey of members of the Ethics Officers Association, 47 percent of ethics officers reported that the guidelines were an influential determinant of their firm's commitment to ethics.[17] Another USSC study showed that the guidelines influenced 44.5 percent of these officers to enhance their existing compliance programs.[18]

To provide some context to this exploration, consider which offenses are most likely to lead to a fine for an organization. In 2001, the USSC received information on 238 organizations sentenced under Chapter 8 (a 21.7 percent decrease from the previous year). The sentenced organizations had pled guilty in 92.4 percent of the cases. Of the fines and restitution imposed, 30 percent were issued for cases of fraud, with antitrust offenses and import/export violations the next most common crimes at 6.7 percent each. Of those violations not included in the fine list, violations of environmental laws with regard to water topped the list at 13 percent. The mean restitution imposed was $4 million and the mean fine was $2 million.[19]

Questions, Projects, and Exercises

1. To help understand an organizational culture, think about some organization to which you belong. Does your company, school, or fraternity/sorority have its own culture? How would you describe it? How does it influence individual decision making and action? Would you be a different person had you attended a different school or joined a different fraternity/sorority? How would you go about changing your organization's culture?

2. Consider how you evaluate whether a firm is "one of the good guys" or not. What are some of the factors you use to make this determination? Do you actually know the facts behind each of those elements, or has your judgment been shaped by the firm's reputation? Identify one firm you believe to be decent or ethical and make a note of the bases for that conclusion. Next identify a second firm that you do not believe to be ethical or that you think has questionable values and write down the bases for that alternate conclusion. Now, using the Internet and other relevant sources, explore the firms' cultures and decisions, checking the results of your research against your original impressions of the firms. Try to evaluate the cultures and decisions of each firm as if you had no idea whether they were ethical. Were you accurate in your impressions or do they need to be modified slightly?

3. You will need to draft a memorandum to your chief executive identifying the value of a triple bottom line approach, which would represent an enormous shift from the firm's current orientation. What are the three key points that you could make and how would you best support this argument?

4. Now that you have an understanding of corporate culture and the variables that impact it, how would you characterize an ethically effective culture, one that would effectively lead to a profitable and valuable long-term sustainability for the firm?

5. One element that surely impacts a firm's culture is its employee population. While a corporate culture can shape an employee's attitudes and habits, it will do so more easily if people who have already developed those attitudes and habits are hired in the first place. How would you develop a recruitment and selection process that would most successfully allow you to hire the best workers for your particular culture? Should you get rid of employees who do not share the corporate culture? If so, how would you do that?

6. What are some of the greatest benefits and most deleterious costs of compliance-based cultures?

7. Assume you have a number of suppliers for your global apparel business. You have in place a code of conduct both for your workplace and for your suppliers. Each time you visit a particular supplier, even on unannounced visits, it seems as if that supplier is in compliance with your code. However, you have received communications from that supplier's employees that there are violations. What should you do?

8. You are aware of inappropriate behavior and violations of your firm's code of conduct throughout your operation. In an effort to support a collegial and supportive atmosphere, however, you do not encourage co-workers to report on their peers. Unfortunately, you believe that you must make a shift in that policy and institute a mandatory reporting structure. How would you design the structure and how would you implement the new program in such as way that the collegiality that exists is not destroyed?

9. A large United States–based corporation has decided to develop a mission statement and then conduct training on a new ethics program. It engages you to assist in these endeavors. What activities would you need to conduct in order to complete this project? What are some of the concerns you should be sure to consider?

10. Put yourself in the position of someone who is establishing an organization from the ground up. What type of leader would you want to be? How would you create that image or perception? Do you create a mission statement for the firm and/or a code of conduct? What process would you use to do so? Would you create an ethics and/or compliance program and how would you then integrate the mission statement and program throughout your organization? What do you anticipate might be your successes and challenges?

Key Terms

After reading this chapter, you should have a clear understanding of the following Key Terms. The page numbers refer to the point at which they were discussed in the chapter. For a more complete definition, please see the Glossary.

code of conduct, *p. 125*
compliance-based culture, *p. 118*
culture, *p. 113*
ethics officers, *p. 120*

Federal Sentencing Guidelines, *p. 132*
mission statement, *p. 126*
United States Sentencing Commission, *p. 132*

values-based culture, *p. 118*
whistleblowing, *p. 128*

Endnotes

1. James Collins and Jerry Porras, *Built to Last: Successful Habits of Visionary Companies* (New York: HarperCollins, 1994), p. 73.
2. Joshua Joseph, *Integrating Ethics and Compliance Programs* (Washington, DC: Ethics Resource Center 2001), p. 9.
3. Raymond Gilmartin, "Ethics and the Corporate Culture," *Raytheon Lectureship in Business Ethics,* November 10, 2003.
4. L. Trevino, M. Brown, and L. Hartman, "A Qualitative Investigation of Perceived Executive Ethical Leadership: Perceptions from Inside and Outside the Executive Suite," *Human Relations* 56, no. 1 (January 2003), pp. 5–37.
5. Trevino, Brown, and Hartman, "A Qualitative Investigation."
6. Ralph Larsen, "Leadership in a Values-Based Organization," Sears Lectureship in Business Ethics, Bentley College, February 7, 2002
7. James Collins and Jerry Porras, "Building Your Company's Vision," *Harvard Business Review,* September/October 1996.
8. Mark Satin, "We Need to Alter the Culture at Places Like Enron—Not Just Pass More Laws," *Radical Middle Newsletter,* March/April 2002, http://www.radicalmiddle/com.
9. *2002 Corporate Values Survey*, American Management Association Report, 2002.
10. PricewaterhouseCoopers, "Why Have a Code?" http://www.pwc.com/extweb/newcoatwork.nsf/docid/BCC554487E1C3BC680256C2B003115D5.

11. Ethics Resource Center, "Code Construction and Content," http://www.ethics.org/printable_code_outline.html.

12. References omitted but available from the authors.

13. Kris Axtman, "Cases Test New Flexibility of Sentencing Guidelines," *Christian Science Monitor,* February 18, 2005.

14. USSC, *Guidelines Manual,* sec. 8A1.2, comment (n. 3(k)) (2000).

15. USSC, *Guidelines Manual,* sec. 8A1.2, comment (n. 3(k)) (2000).

16. Joseph Murphy, "Lost Words of the Sentencing Guidelines," *Ethikos,* November/December 2002, p. 5.

17. Ethics Officer Association, 1997 Member Survey (2000), p. 9.

18. USSC, "Corporate Crime in America: Strengthening the 'Good Citizen' Corporation," 1995, pp. 123–191.

19. Data is from the United States Sentencing Commission, Office of Policy Analysis, 2001 Datafile, OPAFYOI.

Readings

Reading 4-1: "Good Business Sometimes Means the Customer Doesn't Come First," by Tara Radin, *p. 138*

Reading 4-2: "Assessment and Plan for Organizational Culture Change at NASA," by the Columbia Accident Investigation Board, *p. 143*

Reading 4-3: "Arthur Andersen Culture," by Sarah Smith, *p. 145*

Reading **4-1**

Good Business Sometimes Means the Customer Doesn't Come First

Tara Radin

Since the so-called "Tylenol scare" of the early 1980s, Johnson & Johnson (J&J) has been praised for its "customers first" approach to business. In 1982, seven people died after taking Tylenol (manufactured by J&J). It was subsequently determined that the capsules had been laced with cyanide poison by unknown culprits. The response by then CEO James Burke was to take full responsibility for the incident. According to Burke, it did not matter that a person or group of people had tampered with the capsules; because Tylenol was a J&J product, J&J considered itself accountable to anyone who used its products. Burke cited the J&J Credo, written in 1943 by General Robert Wood Johnson (son of founder, Robert Wood Johnson), which defines the company's focus: "We believe our first responsibility is to the doctors, nurses and patients, to mothers and fathers and all others who use our products and services." J&J issued an immediate, voluntary massive recall of Tylenol that cost the company more than $100 million. The company also initiated a nationwide advertising campaign to warn people not to use Tylenol.

Businesspeople, scholars, and textbooks commonly refer to J&J as an exemplary business—a model for how responsible business can be profitable. In the aftermath of the

Tylenol scare, although J&J market share initially dropped from 35 percent to 8 percent, the brand rebounded within a year. As recently as 2006, J&J ranked sixth on *Fortune*'s list of most admired companies in the United States.

While J&J's approach remains a successful model for business, it is only one model, not the only model. Too often businesspeople mistakenly conflate these two thoughts and assume customers must come first—as if there were some unwritten rule that specifies this. In fact, there is no such rule. All companies are answerable to a wide array of stakeholders, including but not limited to customers. It is incumbent upon each company to determine for itself how it will balance the many—often conflicting—stakeholder concerns. It makes sense for J&J to consider customers first, because that is what the J&J Credo specifies. Other companies might find it necessary or beneficial to prioritize other stakeholder interests—either upon occasion or as a rule—and should therefore be wary of following J&J's example without considering their own particular circumstances.

The Secret of Starbucks' Success

Take, for example, Starbucks. Starbucks is a company that has traditionally prioritized consideration for how employees are to be treated. Employees are considered "partners" at Starbucks. Indeed, partners receive preference even according to the company mission, which places partners first, above both customers and shareholders. "Our people come first, then customers, then shareholders," said Howard Schultz when CEO (currently Chairman and Chief Global Strategist). "It may sound out of order, but we can't exceed the expectations of our customers unless we exceed it for our employees first."

"Our only sustainable competitive advantage . . . is the quality of our work force," said Schultz. "We're building a national retail company by creating pride in—and a stake in—the outcome of our labor." Starbucks offers to all partners—full-time and part-time—a generous employee-benefits package that covers health care, stock options, training programs, career counseling, and product discounts. "No one can afford not to provide these kinds of benefits," added Schultz. "The desire to scrimp on these essentials helps reinforce the sense of mediocrity that seeps into many companies. Without them, people don't feel financially or spiritually tied to their jobs."

Starbucks takes pride in its partners. While Starbucks employees are treated well, they are required to earn that treatment, for partners are held up to very high standards. As of the early 1990s, only 19 people had qualified to roast coffee for Starbucks in 22 years. "Learning to roast is a tremendous privilege," said Schultz. And so, it appears, is being a "partner" at Starbucks. Today Starbucks employs more than 74,000 people across the globe.

"Latteland" and the Customer

In its stores, Starbucks offers regular and decaffeinated coffee beverages, Italian-style espresso beverages, cold blended beverages, cold and hot tea, and distinctively packaged roasted whole bean coffees. In addition, most locations have available a selection of pastries and light snacks; prepackaged candies, gifts, and other novelty items; and coffee-making equipment and accessories.

While partners are placed first, the goal is clearly customer satisfaction through a superior product and quality service. The tenet, "only perfection will do," lies at the heart of Starbucks' management.

A great deal of attention was paid to the presentation of this product. Indeed, there is an entire cachet created around the Starbucks offerings: "One double-tall skinny no foam, walking latte. Next. One decaf mocca Grande. Next. One short latte, hit of almond, with foam to go. Next . . ." The orders reverberate through the small stores. Customers hand over several dollars for each order, sprinkle their coffee with chocolate, nutmeg, or cinnamon powder, and dart to work.

Part of the mystique involves a specialized caffeine vocabulary that began in the Northwest but has become standard all over. Coffee preparers are "baristas," Italian for bartenders. In addition, drinks are ordered in three special sizes: short, tall, and grande. And two shots of espresso is a "doppio."

The Starbucks lingo underscores the recognized value of customers to Starbucks. This is clearly for good reason. More than 35 million customers pass through Starbucks stores' doors on a weekly basis in more than 10,000 locations around the world. Jean Godden, a columnist for the *Seattle Times,* dubbed Seattle "Latteland"; Schultz's dream was to turn the United States into an entire "Latteland" through Starbucks, which, in effect, is a dream he has realized.

Starbucks Sucks?

Starbucks' success is not universal, however. Jeremy Dorosin was once a loyal Starbucks customer. Today he considers himself "Starbucked," and he disseminates his dissatisfaction via www.starbucked.com.

In the early 1990s, Dorosin not only enjoyed Starbucks coffee, but he invested in a Starbucks-branded espresso machine as well. He remained a fan of Starbucks even after this espresso machine, a "Vapore," turned out to be defective. He returned it to the location where he bought it and Starbucks not only made sure it was repaired, but also provided him with a loaner to use free of charge while his machine was being serviced.

During this time, Dorosin happened to stop by Starbucks to buy another espresso machine—this time as a gift. Although the original coffee maker that he bought for himself was still being repaired, he was so impressed with the loaner, an "Estro 410," that he decided to buy one for a friend as a wedding present. The loaner cost only $169, as opposed to the $289 he had paid for his machine, but it seemed like a better machine.

Dorosin was initially somewhat concerned about his purchase. The box in which the espresso machine was packaged was visibly worn. "The box was dog-eared," Dorosin explained, "and the machine looked used, although the clerk assured me that packages from Europe often looked that way." According to the salesperson, said Dorosin, "they just got roughed up a little in transit." In light of the condition of the package, Dorosin was hesitant. When he was told it was the last model in stock, though, he decided to go ahead and make the purchase.

At the checkout counter, Dorosin experienced additional dissatisfaction. When he requested the complimentary half-pound of coffee that the store ordinarily included with coffee-maker purchases, the cashier refused. "You get nothing," said the cashier.

According to Dorosin, "It was humiliating to be in the store surrounded by other customers and be treated that way." He nevertheless made the purchase.

A few days later, Dorosin found out that the espresso machine purchased as a wedding gift was defective. There was no instruction manual, and Dorosin's friend indicated that the machine would not work properly—there was visible rust and there appeared to be missing parts.

Humiliated, Dorosin returned to Starbucks with the defective machine. He explained the situation to the store manager, but all the store manager offered was a refund. Dorosin refused. This was not a satisfactory solution to the inconvenience and embarrassment he felt he had suffered.

What Happened Next...

Dorosin then insisted that Starbucks make restitution by sending his friend a new, higher quality espresso machine to replace the defective wedding present. He also stated that the machine should be accompanied by a formal letter of apology. In addition, he demanded that his machine, which had broken for a second time, be replaced. When the situation was not resolved, he demanded that a top-of-the-line machine be sent to his friend. He threatened that, if the machine was not sent to his friend, he would place an ad in the *Wall Street Journal*.

In fact, Dorosin did live up to his threat. During the following weeks and months, Dorosin placed several negative ads in the *Wall Street Journal,* and he installed a toll-free (1-800) number for people to call to report their dissatisfaction with Starbucks. Radio stations, news shows, and newspapers around the country picked up the story. A Corporate Customer Relations Manager for Starbucks Coffee (a senior executive) spent several months endeavoring—albeit unsuccessfully—to reach a suitable compromise.

In spite of prolonged negotiations and considerable press coverage, the situation continued to escalate and was never resolved satisfactorily.

What Did Starbucks Do Wrong?

This situation illustrates what can happen if a company does not pay careful enough attention to its own principles. Starbucks initially tried to appease its customer (Dorosin), but clearly was not sufficiently committed to that end, for Starbucks did not satisfy Dorosin. At the same time, however, Starbucks did not adequately support the employees with whom Dorosin interacted and against whom he made accusations. It appeared that Starbucks was willing to apologize for the allegedly poor treatment he received without conducting any sort of proper investigation into the matter. Further, it became necessary for a senior executive to become involved—clearly the value of her time was worth more than it would have cost Starbucks to fulfill Dorosin's even most extreme demands.

There are at least three key points here. First, if Starbucks were truly aiming for customer satisfaction, then Starbucks should have satisfied Dorosin, regardless of the short-term cost. A loyal customer—particularly one who does not give up after repeat negative experiences—is a valuable customer indeed. The prolonged negotiations served merely to insult Dorosin and compound his dissatisfaction.

Second, the minute Dorosin issued an ultimatum, Starbucks should have taken a firm stand—either by succumbing to his demands then or by ceasing attempts at negotiations. The negotiations were neither successful nor remotely useful—on the contrary, they served merely to amplify Dorosin's dissatisfaction. In addition, it seems they were a waste of valuable time for the Starbucks employees (including the senior executive) involved.

Third, in its feeble attempts to appease Dorosin, Starbucks ignored any consideration of its so-called "partners." How respectful was it for Starbucks to treat Dorosin's complaints as legitimate without any sort of proper inquiry? Starbucks could, in this situation, simply have deferred to the partners involved and asserted confidence in how its partners must have acted. While this would have proved unsatisfactory to Dorosin, it would have made sense according to Starbucks' management philosophy and it would have represented a defensible course of action.

The Influence of Organizational Values and Culture

The customer does not always have to come first. It seems almost as if businesspeople today assume that the customer has to come first. While that approach has worked well for many companies, it is not the only way to do good business. Numerous stakeholders are almost always involved—customers, employees, stockholders, and so on. There is no universal rule about who or what comes first; companies have to decide for themselves how to balance and resolve conflicting stakeholder interests according to their missions and organizational cultures.

Nordstrom, like J&J, prioritizes customers. There is a story that has been passed along that, in the 1970s, a customer attempted to return a set of tires to Nordstrom. Nordstrom has a notably liberal return policy: customers are generally allowed to return anything that the store sells (that the customer could have bought there). The customer in question claimed to have bought the tires at the store that was in that location prior to Nordstrom. In accordance with the company's liberal policy, and since the customer had technically bought the tires at that physical location, Nordstrom accepted the return, even though the purchase took place prior to Nordstrom having begun operating at that location.

It could be argued that this decision, like Starbucks' treatment of Dorosin, was controversial. It made Nordstrom vulnerable to other idiosyncratic claims, and it placed salespeople on the front line in the position of dealing with these sorts of claims and associated complaints. At the same time, however, the decision was entirely consistent with Nordstrom's values and organizational culture.

In fact, hindsight reveals the benefits of this decision. Just as J&J was able to turn a crisis into a positive turning point, Nordstrom has used this story to continue to attract customers who are willing to pay extra for special treatment. There is no evidence that the fear of excessive returning was in any way warranted. This is not to say that Starbucks should have done the same; rather, the point is only that, whatever Starbucks chose to do, it should have done so firmly and straightforwardly.

The Customer Should Not Necessarily Always Come First

If there is a message here, it is that it is important to stick up for stakeholders. Like J&J and Nordstrom, it often makes sense to stick up for customers. An increasing number of companies are finding that this does not make sense for them. In fact, some are going so far as to "fire" customers.

Several years ago, a small, California-based public relations firm took a strong stance in favor of its employees by firing one of its clients. The client, traveling in New York City, called one of the firm's employees in California at 1 A.M. PST (4 A.M. EST) for assistance in getting a cab. The public relations firm subsequently notified the client that the firm was no longer interested in providing representation.

This is only one example of what is happening more and more. Firms are recognizing that customers are not their only important stakeholders. Good business decisions involve balancing and resolving stakeholder interests and cannot always be reduced to a formula that automatically prioritizes one stakeholder above all others.

In this instance, the decision to "fire" a client sent a strong message to the employee that he or she was valued by the firm. Chances are that this was not, and/or would not be, the only instance of such disrespectful behavior. This decision also signaled clients that they are not always and unequivocally right—that they will be treated with respect, and employees expect to be treated with respect as well.

Conclusion

The reality is that there is no formula. This is both unfortunate and fortunate. It is unfortunate in that it means that there is no easy, straightforward answer to how to resolve difficult situations. It is fortunate, however, in that it leaves lots of room open for managers to distinguish themselves and their companies by managing well.

Even in the absence of a formula, there is abundant guidance. Companies tend to have values and philosophies that are embedded in their mission statements and organizational cultures. A good, defensible business decision is simply one that is consistent with those values and philosophies.

If you confront a crazy customer or an exasperating employee, to figure out what you should do, you do not need to look any further than your own organization's values and culture.

Source: Copyright © Tara Radin. Reprinted by permission of the author.

Assessment and Plan for Organizational Culture Change at NASA

Editors' note: Following the accident that destroyed the Space Shuttle Columbia in 2003, the National Aeronautics and Space Administration (NASA) appointed the Columbia Accident Investigation Board (CAIB) to investigate the causes of the accident. The loss of Columbia came eighteen years after the Space Shuttle Challenger exploded during take-off. The CAIB report identified the organizational culture at NASA as having "as much to do with the accident as the External Tank foam." Following the CAIB report, NASA hired an outside consulting firm, Behavioral Science Technology (BST), to recommend changes in the organization. This reading is taken from the BST report of their investigation. As was the case following the Challenger disaster, responsibility for the accident was attributed as much to the culture and practices of NASA as it was to physical or mechanical causes.

Executive Summary

On February 1, 2003, the Space Shuttle Columbia and its crew of seven were lost during return to Earth. A group of distinguished experts was appointed to comprise the Columbia Accident Investigation Board (CAIB), and this group spent six months conducting a thorough investigation of the cause of the accident. The CAIB found that NASA's history and culture contributed as much to the Columbia accident as any technical failure.

As a result of the CAIB and related activities, NASA established the objective of completely transforming its organizational and safety culture. BST was selected to assist NASA in the development and implementation of a plan for changing the safety climate and culture

Agency-wide. The scope of this effort is to develop and deploy an organizational culture change initiative within NASA, with an emphasis on safety climate and culture.

The first task assigned to BST was to conduct an assessment of the current status and develop an implementation plan, both to be completed within 30 days. This report summarizes the assessment findings and the recommended implementation plan.

This assessment concluded that there are many positive aspects to the NASA culture. The NASA culture reflects a long legacy of technical excellence, a spirit of teamwork and pride, and a can-do approach to task achievement. In particular, culture attributes related to work group functioning at the peer level are among the strongest we have seen. These characteristics are consistent with NASA's rating in the 2003 Office of Personnel Management Survey at the top of the Best Places to Work in the Federal Government.

Despite these positive attributes, there are some important needs for improvement. The present NASA culture does not yet fully reflect the Agency's espoused core values of Safety, People, Excellence, and Integrity. The culture reflects an organization in transition, with many ongoing initiatives and lack of a clear sense at working levels of "how it all fits together."

- **Safety** is something to which NASA personnel are strongly committed in concept, but NASA has not yet created a culture that is fully supportive of safety. Open communication is not yet the norm and people do not feel fully comfortable raising safety concerns to management.

- **People** do not feel respected or appreciated by the organization. As a result, the strong commitment people feel to their technical work does not transfer to a strong commitment to the organization.

- **Excellence** is a treasured value when it comes to technical work, but is not seen by many NASA personnel as an imperative for other aspects of the organization's functioning (such as management skills, supporting administrative functions, and creating an environment that encourages excellence in communications.)

- **Integrity** is generally understood and manifested in people's work. However, there appear to be pockets where the management chain has (possibly unintentionally) sent signals that the raising of issues is not welcome. This is inconsistent with an organization that truly values integrity.

There is an opportunity and need to become an organization whose espoused values are fully integrated into its culture—an organization that "lives the values" by fostering cultural integrity. We recommend an initiative with that as its theme.

The recommended initiative should address working through existing leaders to instill behaviors consistent with the Agency's values and the desired culture, while also establishing the foundation for developing future leaders who will sustain that culture and individual contributors who reflect the desired culture in their actions. A long-term (three year) plan is identified with a specific series of actions identified in the first five months to launch this effort.

BST's first efforts were to understand the current culture and climate at NASA in order to identify focus areas for improvement. We approached this task with the belief that there was much that was positive about NASA's culture. Our challenge was to build from positive aspects of the existing culture, strengthening the culture and at the same time addressing the issue raised in the CAIB report.

By culture we mean the shared values and beliefs of an organization—commonly described as "the way we do things here." The culture can also be thought of as the shared norms for the behavior in the organization, often motivated by unstated assumptions.

Where organizational culture comprises unstated assumptions that govern how we do things within an organization, climate describes the prevailing influences on a particular area of functioning (such as safety) at a particular time. Thus, the culture is something that is more deeply embedded and long-term, taking longer to change and influencing organizational performance across many areas of functioning. Climate, on the other hand, changes faster and more immediately reflects the attention of leadership.

Culture influences behavior in that the group's shared norms and beliefs will influence what people do. However, leaders' behavior is an important influence on culture. Through the examples they set, the messages they send, and the consequences they provide, leaders influence the behaviors of others, as well as their beliefs about what is acceptable and what is valuable to the organization.

The CAIB had produced a detailed report on the causes of the Columbia accident, and explicitly addressed "organizational causes" as the critical contributor. Specifically, the CAIB identified the following organizational cause of the Columbia accident:

"The organizational causes of this accident are rooted in the Space Shuttle Program's history and culture, including the original compromises that were required to gain approval for the Shuttle Program, subsequent years of resource constraints, fluctuating priorities, schedule pressures, mischaracterizations of the Shuttle as operational rather than developmental, and lack of an agreed national vision. Cultural traits and organizational practices detrimental to safety and reliability were allowed to develop, including: reliance on past success as a substitute for sound engineering practices (such as testing to understand why systems were not performing in accordance with requirements/specifications); organizational barriers which prevented effective communication of critical safety information and stifled professional differences of opinion; lack of integrated management across program elements; and the evolution of an informal chain of command and decision-making processes that operated outside the organization's rules. In the Board's view, NASA's organizational culture and structure had as much to do with this accident as the External Tank foam. Organizational culture refers to the values, norms, beliefs, and practices that govern how an institution functions. At the most basic level, organizational culture defines the assumptions that employees make as they carry out their work. It is a powerful force that can persist through reorganizations and the reassignment of key personnel."

Source: The full Columbia Accident Investigation Board report is available at http://caib.nasa.gov/.

Reading **4-3**

Inside Arthur Andersen

Editors' note: The following item is taken from the online web log ("blog") of author Sarah Smith. Ms. Smith is a former employee of consulting firm Arthur Andersen who posted this article about her perspective on the Andersen culture to her personal blog after she no longer worked at the firm and subsequent to the firm's ultimate demise.

Sarah Smith

Once a highly respected limited liability financial services practice with more than 77,000 employees in offices worldwide, Arthur Andersen LLP achieved notoriety (and walking papers from most of its clients) in the wake of the Enron accounting scandal of 2002.

Technically speaking, Arthur Andersen is actually just plain Andersen—a change inaugurated in 2001, after AA won its nearly decade-long legal battle against former satellite Andersen Consulting to get it to change its name (it is now Accenture). In a gratifying failure of gratuitous marketing department wheel-spinning, this minor change has been almost entirely ignored by the media.

Frankly, I was delighted to see Andersen go down. Every time a new dire pronouncement is made on Marketplace or in the Journal in regard to its bleak future and/or general f**kuppery, I do a cross between the Snoopy Jig and the Touchdown Dance and chortle "BWA-HA-HA-HA!" in a delighted but somewhat deranged Evil Laugh.

I used to work for the firm as the lead proposal writer for the Boston office, and hated its corporate culture with a profound and visceral passion. I was so allergic to Andersen (having come to it from the far funkier ethos of high tech) that sometimes I would nearly swoon from dysphoria during meetings.

General characteristics of Andersen's corporate culture:

- Doublespeak that would give George Orwell a migraine.
- A Taliban-esque dress code: all clothing must be "professional"—i.e., boring and conservative, all skirts must be below the knee, no sheer fabrics even if layered, no open-toed shoes, no sleeveless shirts or dresses, no dangling jewelry, and (in a burst of bizarrely uncharacteristic specificity) no cowboy boots. I bought a pair while home in Kansas on vacation, and wore them often—praying to be fired over it so I could sue and retire to the South of France on the proceeds.
- Amusing illustrations of office-appropriate outfits are provided in the orientation handbook which I really wanted to force-feed the human resources wench.
- Pass the buck, then pass it again, then point and yell at the person behind you.
- "Neologisms Make Us Feel Smart!"(tm)
- A not-so-secret star chamber which actually ran the firm on a day to day basis, comprised of the big-haired and undereducated administrative assistants of the top partners. Andersen's "commitment" to supporting women employees actually led to some of these idiots acquiring prima facie power. Example: I had to work on occasion with a former administrative assistant turned (after 20 years of clawing/poisoning/undermining/etc., no doubt) Director of *xxx*. She couldn't be a manager or otherwise promoted because she had no education, not to mention some seriously enormous hair. Nevertheless, her primary corporate virtue (the mentality of a brain-damaged pit-bull with a poodle complex) helped her to damn well wield a great deal of spooky virtual wang energy. A less overt example of how the big-haired secretly ruled the roost: I had to work with media whippin' boy/ex-Andersen energy partner David Duncan on a Boston energy proposal. I never got to talk to him. All communications were entirely mediated by his admin, leading me to a certain nonplussed uncertainty as to whether or not the man existed as anything other than a virtual gender mask for this Manchurian Candidate chick.
- Staffers who are terribly fond of backbiting reality television shows and seemed determined to invest Andersen with the same kind of interpersonal dynamics found most typically on *Survivor* and *The Weakest Link.*
- Hysterical egomaniac accountants with poor impulse control, bad breath, terrible ties, and a tenuous grip on reality.

While I realize that all of the above (save, perhaps, the very last item) is pandemic in corporate culture in general, something about the inherently fantastical environment of a financial services firm magnifies these unpleasant characteristics of late stage capitalist white collar worker culture.

Goodbye to the circus.

Source: Copyright © Sarah Anne Smith. Reprinted by permission of the author.

5

Corporate Social Responsibility

Business has to take account of its responsibilities to society in coming to its decisions, but society has to accept its responsibilities for setting the standards against which those decisions are made.[1]

Sir Adrian Cadbury

By "social responsibility," we mean the intelligent and objective concern for the welfare of society that restrains individual and corporate behavior from ultimately destructive activities, no matter how immediately profitable, and leads in the direction of positive contributions to human betterment, variously as the latter may be defined.[2]

Kenneth R. Andrews

Fill your bowl to the brim
and it will spill.
Keep sharpening your knife
and it will be blunt.
Chase after money and security
and your heart will never unclench.
Care about people's approval
and you will be their prisoner.
Do your work, then step back.
The only path to serenity.
Tao Te Ching

You never expect justice from a company, do you? They neither have a soul to lose nor a body to kick.

Sydney Smith, 1771–1845, English writer, clergyman

Do you care about *why* a firm engages in a particularly socially conscious endeavor? Does it matter to you that a firm may choose to sponsor a particular event because it will result in good press? Are you actually more likely to purchase a product or service from a company because it sponsored an event you support? The LaSalle Bank sponsors the Chicago Marathon each year. Might you be more likely to use that bank because it supports the marathon? Though, at first blush, this might seem a question of slight import, the amount of money spent on corporate promotions on an annual basis can be exponential. The economic impact of an event like the Chicago Marathon can mean more than $100 million per event for a city. If you do not really notice the sponsor or if the sponsorship does not have an impact on your consumer, employment, or investment decisions, then wouldn't that be critical information for the bank to know when deciding whether to sponsor the event in the future? Or, on the contrary, do you believe that at least part of the bank's decision to support the marathon has nothing to do with its ultimate impact on you as a stakeholder but instead with the simple fact that the bank wishes to support the event? If the latter, what justification can you imagine the bank uses when explaining the expenditure to its stockholders?

- What are the key facts relevant to your judgment about the above issues?
- What is the ethical issue involved in a firm's decision to sponsor an event or an organization?
- Who are the stakeholders?
- What alternatives does a firm have with regard to the way it engages in sponsorship?
- How do the alternatives compare; how do the alternatives you have identified affect the stakeholders?
- Does the law provide any guidance whatsoever in connection with the source of funds for particular causes?
- What are the consequences of offering greater support to companies that support causes that are important to you? Who benefits from that perception and by your judgment?
- Do you simply respect the bank or feel that it is a good corporate citizen based on its choice of how to spend its money? Can a bank have "virtues" as understood by virtue ethics?

Chapter Objectives

After reading this chapter, you will be able to:

1. Define corporate social responsibility.
2. Discuss the three models of corporate social responsibility (CSR).

3. Discuss the challenge in identifying the object of a corporation's responsibility.
4. Distinguish key components or elements of the term *responsibility*.
5. Explain the role of reputation as one possible motivation behind CSR.
6. Evaluate the claims that CSR is "good" for business.

Introduction

This chapter addresses the critical questions of (1) whether a social responsibility of business exists and, if so, (2) how firms can meet and evidence their fulfillment of this responsibility. Central to this question is the underlying determination of what responsibility business has to anyone at all. Do you ask yourself whether your friends, colleagues, parents, or others have a responsibility to *society* or to the *community in which you live?* You probably do, at some point. You might see your colleague drop some trash on the floor and walk on. You might feel that this person should stop and pick it up instead of continuing. Your belief about the responsibility of business might be no more than this — a firm should clean up after itself, so to speak. On the other hand, some believe firms owe something more to the society that supports them and that this debt is greater than the debt of the individual members of society.

Is There a Social Responsibility of Business? If So, What Is Its Origin?

Before we define the concept of **corporate social responsibility** (CSR), it may be enlightening to consider a 1906 definition of the corporation by Ambrose Bierce in his *Devil's Dictionary*: A corporation is "an ingenious device for obtaining individual profit without individual responsibility." In fact, one of the reasons individuals who engage in business "incorporate" is to create a legal corporate shield by which to protect themselves from personal liability for the liabilities of the new corporation. Consider, however, how astonished Bierce would be over recent and often successful claims of individual liability for actions taken by corporate leaders in some American and European firms, as in the case of Kenneth Lay of Enron.

OBJECTIVE

In general terms, CSR encompasses the responsibilities that businesses have to the societies within which these businesses operate. The European Commission defines CSR as "a concept whereby companies decide voluntarily to contribute to a better society and a cleaner environment." Specifically, CSR suggests that a business identify its stakeholder groups and incorporate their needs and values within its strategic and operational decision-making process.

OBJECTIVE

Advocates for CSR have several bases for their contentions that a business should go above and beyond the maximization of profits or at least that CSR activities contribute to that objective. The arguments for CSR are based in both economics and ethics (or "citizenship"). These arguments are not meant to be exclusionary or all-encompassing; they simply assist us in discussing areas of differentiation.

First, some companies engage in CSR efforts solely for the public good and do not expect a commercial return on their contributions. These organizations believe that they play a particular role in the community and that their ability to do good—which derives from the profits they reap—creates a responsibility to do good. For example, Ben & Jerry's Ice Cream's most recent Social & Environmental Assessment [3] explains that it seeks to create a "broader, bolder vision of how it can leverage its reputation and its expertise to advance its Social Mission." This corporate citizenship model of CSR often exists where there is a strong leader with a sense of responsibility and connection to the community. Consider the history of Equal Exchange, Inc. discussed in the Reality Check that follows.

Second, some CSR proponents argue that corporations reap the benefits of serving as a community citizen and therefore owe a reciprocal obligation to that community. The social contract model of CSR holds that there is a corporate responsibility to respect the moral rights of various stakeholders. In a 2003 study, researchers found that 70 percent of the public believe that industry and commerce do not pay enough attention to these social responsibilities.[4]

Third, the enlightened self-interest model of CSR states that incorporating CSR can lead to differentiation and competitive market advantage for the business, something that can contribute to the company's brand for the present and future. Companies that have implemented a strong CSR policy and also have been successful in establishing a positive brand include firms such as BP and Nike. Under this larger economics umbrella, one would find arguments based in the reduction of risk, market reputation, brand image, stakeholder relationships, and long-term strategic interests. We will explore the connection between CSR and these more traditional business measurements in greater detail below.

Though Adam Smith was probably among the first to articulate this concept, Milton Friedman's classic 1970 *New York Times* article, "The Social Responsibility of Business Is to Increase Its Profits," is perhaps best known as an argument for this *profit-based* social responsibility of business. Contrary to popular belief, Friedman does not ignore ethical responsibility in his analysis; he merely suggests that decision makers are acting ethically if they follow their firm's self-interest. Friedman explains his view as follows:

> A corporate executive has a "responsibility is to conduct business in accordance
> with [his or her employer's] desires, which generally will be to make as much
> money as possible while conforming to the basic rules of society, *both those embod-
> ied in law and those embodied in ethical custom"* (emphasis added).

This common view of corporate social responsibility has its roots in the utilitarian tradition and in neoclassical economics (as discussed in Chapter 3). As the

Reality Check *Fairness in a Cup of Coffee:*

Example of the Corporate Citizenship Model

The corporate citizenship model is evidenced in a company called Equal Exchange (www.equalexchange.coop), which is a worker-owned and governed business committed to Fair Trade with small-scale coffee, tea, and cocoa farmers. Its "Vision of Fairness to Farmers" explains its model:

A Vision of Fairness to Farmers

Fairness to farmers. A closer connection between people and the farmers we all rely on. This was the essence of the vision that the three Equal Exchange founders—Rink Dickinson, Michael Rozyne, and Jonathan Rosenthal—held in their minds and hearts as they stood together on a metaphorical cliff back in 1986.

The three, who had met each other as managers at a New England food co-op, were part of a movement to transform the relationship between the public and food producers. At the time, however, these efforts didn't extend to farmers outside of the U.S.

The founders decided to meet once a week—and did so for three years—to discuss how best to change the way food is grown, bought, and sold around the world. At the end of this time they had a plan for a new organization called Equal Exchange that would be:

- *A social change organization that would help farmers and their families gain more control over their economic futures.*
- *A group that would educate consumers about trade issues affecting farmers.*

- *A provider of high-quality foods that would nourish the body and the soul.*
- *A company that would be controlled by the people who did the actual work.*
- *A community of dedicated individuals who believed that honesty, respect, and mutual benefit are integral to any worthwhile endeavor.*

No Turning Back

It was a grand vision—with a somewhat shaky grounding in reality. But Rink, Michael, and Jonathan understood that significant change only happens when you're open to taking big risks. So they cried "¡Adelante!" (rough translation from the Spanish: "No turning back!") and took a running leap off the cliff. They left their jobs. They invested their own money. And they turned to their families and friends for start-up funds and let them know there was a good chance they would never see that money again.

The core group of folks believed in their cause and decided to invest. Their checks provided the $100,000 needed to start the new company. With this modest financing in hand, Rink, Michael, and Jonathan headed into the great unknown. At best, the project, which coupled a for-profit business model with a nonprofit mission, was viewed as utopian; at worst it was regarded as foolish. For the first three years Equal Exchange struggled and, like many new ventures, lost money. But the founders hung on and persevered. By the third year they began to break even.

Source: http://www.equalexchange.coop/story.

agents of the owners of business, managers have primary responsibility to pursue maximum profits for shareholders. By pursuing profits, a business manager functions to allocate resources to their most efficient uses. Consumers who most value a resource will be willing to pay the most for it; thereby profit is the measure of

---

Reality Check *Putting Your Money Where Your Mouth Is?*

Do you make purchases based on a company's social contributions? Are you more or less likely to buy something if you know that a company supports causes that are (or are not) important to you? Research conducted by MORI in 2003 found that 84 percent of respondents to its survey said that a company's level of social responsibility was a "very important" or "fairly important" factor in their decision to purchase a particular product.

Perhaps more important is whether you believe that companies care about what is important to you.

In that same research, MORI found that 47 percent of those questioned believed that companies did not listen to the public or respond to public concerns about social and environmental issues.

Source: MORI, The Public's Views of Corporate Responsibility 2003 (London, UK: MORI), www.ipsos-mori.com/publications/jld/publics-views-of-corporate-responsibility.pdf, p. 2.

---

optimal allocation of resources (see the preceding Reality Check). Over time, the pursuit of profit will continuously work towards the optimal satisfaction of consumer demand, which in one interpretation of utilitarianism is the optimal social good.

But even Milton Friedman acknowledges that business managers have other responsibilities that should limit the pursuit of profit. Both the law and ethical custom function as constraints on business's pursuit of profits. In this narrow view of CSR, business has responsibilities to pursue profits within the law and within the boundaries of ethical custom.

A more expanded, long-term view of social responsibility was offered by Kenneth Dayton, former Chairman of the Dayton-Hudson Corporation:

> We are not in business to make maximum profit for our shareholders. We are in business . . . to serve society. Profit is our reward for doing it well. If business does not serve society, society will not long tolerate our profits or even our existence.[5]

In fact, this is not an argument in favor of social responsibility for society's sake but instead an argument for the sustainablility of an organization through meeting the needs of its supporting stakeholders! We will explore the various possible motivations for CSR later in this chapter.

Is There a Social Responsibility of Business? If So, Responsibility to Whom?

OBJECTIVE

Even among those who advocate a social responsibility for business, there remains disagreement about the meaning and implications of social responsibility. In what sense can business have "social responsibilities"? How can a company have a responsibility? If someone were to ask what your responsibilities are, a fair response would be to ask, responsibility to whom? The responsibilities you owe to your family or partner are different from your responsibilities to an employer, mortgage company, friends, or country. A responsibility is based on an aspect of some relationship and is empty of content until that relationship is described and specified. Thus, some skepticism about a "social" responsibility for business has to do with the fact that *social* is a fairly ambiguous term. How does a company have a relationship with a person?

Moreover, to whom does a firm owe responsibility? To the employees? The community? The consumers? All stakeholders? The local political or governmental body? The entire country? Firms exist in relationships with many stakeholders and these relationships can create a variety of responsibilities. As we have seen in many of the cases and examples mentioned previously, it may not be possible to satisfy the needs of each and every stakeholder in a situation. Therefore, social responsibility would require decisions to prioritize competing and conflicting responsibilities.

Consider the case of the old-growth redwood forests and the loggers in the Pacific Northwest: Logging presents a danger to the giant redwoods, but discontinuing logging poses a hardship on the logging communities and those connected to them. Many environmentalists consider the interests of society in preserving old-growth forests to be predominant, while others consider the interests of the loggers and their communities to be predominant. Whether you are persuaded by the fact that this is a conflict between humans and trees or by the fact that a species might be endangered, business's social responsibility in this case will depend on which stakeholders are given priority. The prioritization of stakeholders is often determined by a company's mission, practice, board, or custom. All too often, however, the prioritization is presumed rather than intentionally discussed and challenged, which might lead to entrenchment rather than enhancement of the firm.

Is There a Social Responsibility of Business? If So, What Is the Extent of the Responsibility?

Is profit, legally made, the only guiding principle of socially responsible business activities, or should the impact of a decision on others be considered, even where the law does not require it? Shell Oil, for example, spent $100 million in 1995 alone on projects in Nigeria and more than $20 million on roads, health clinics, schools, scholarships, water projects, and agricultural support projects to help the people of the region, actions that did not seem to have been motivated by any legal duty to act. Instead, Shell seemed to be acting for a socially beneficial end that went beyond legal requirements. However, interestingly enough, a 2000 appellate court decision held that a lawsuit against Shell for allegedly aiding and abetting in the torture and murder of Nigerian activists who opposed drilling on their lands was allowed to proceed.[6] In the time since the activities discussed in that case, Shell has strived to create an awareness regarding corporate social responsibility both for itself and in its industry. "Corporate citizenship is not a luxury, especially in these difficult times," said P.B. Watts, Chairman, Royal Dutch/Shell Group of Companies, UK, during a recent annual shareholder meeting. "It's a sensible part of doing business."[7]

In a legendary legal case in the United States (*Dodge v. Ford,* 1919), stock-holders sued Henry Ford seeking to answer this very same type of question. Henry Ford believed that Ford cars should be both made for and affordable by everyone in America. To accomplish this goal, Ford decided to charge a lower price than he might otherwise have charged. At the time of the lawsuit by the Dodge brothers, two of Ford's largest shareholders, Ford's decision on his priorities resulted in a reduction in the price of a Ford from $440 to $360 and a refusal to pay stock divi-dends. John and Horace Dodge believed that Ford's primary objective should be to make profit for its shareholders and filed a lawsuit to force him to do so.

"My ambition," said Ford, "is to employ still more men, to spread the benefits of this industrial system to the greatest possible number, to help them build up their lives and their homes. To do this, we are putting the greatest share of our profits back in the business."[8] Ford's counsel argued that "although a manufactur-ing corporation cannot engage in humanitarian works as its principal business, the fact that it is organized for profit does not prevent the existence of implied powers to carry on with humanitarian motives such charitable works as are incident to the main business of the corporation." The court was not persuaded that it should interfere with the reasonable business judgment of the Ford Motor Co., and it did not find that the alleged motives of the directors "menace the interests of the shareholders."

Ford seemingly convinced the court that it was a valid and perhaps laudable claim that "a Ford in every garage" might be an effective long-term business strat-egy. In fact, consider the long-term gains. If you bought your first car and it was a Ford, you might be more likely to stick with that particular manufacturer; and you might tell others how affordable the cars are, and so on. Investment in loyalty and shared beliefs between the manufacturer and its customers has been shown in countless industries to be a profitable profit-maximizing process. Note that, as their interests seemed to be more short-term than those evidenced by Mr. Ford, the Dodges eventually opened their own firm producing Dodge automobiles to compete directly with Ford.

To help us sort through these various answers to the question of the extent of business's social responsibility, let us turn to a general discussion of responsibili-ties and how they can be understood from an ethical perspective.

Ethics and Social Responsibility

OBJECTIVE

The words *responsible* and *responsibility* are used in several different ways and it will be helpful to sort through them. When we say that a business is responsible, we might mean that it is reliable, dependable, or trustworthy. Thus, we might say that a business is very responsible in providing good customer service. A second meaning of responsible involves attributing something as a cause for an event or action. For example, Hurricane Katrina was responsible for the flood in New Orleans, and the location of the gas tank was responsible for fires in the Ford Pinto. A third sense involves attributing liability or accountability for some event or action, creating a responsibility to make things right again. To say, for example, that a business is responsible for a polluted river is not only to say that the business caused the pollution, but that the business is at fault for it and should be held accountable. An unavoidable accident would be a case in which someone was responsible as the cause, but not responsible as being liable or at fault.

Laws regarding product safety and liability involve many of these meanings of being responsible. When a consumer is injured by a product, for example, a first question is to ask if the product was responsible for the injury, in the sense of having caused the injury. Was Vioxx responsible for causing heart attacks in some users? Once this causal question is settled, we might then go on to ask if the manufacturer is responsible in the sense of being at fault and therefore being liable for paying for the damages caused by the product. Both ethics and tort law involve the question of liability or fault for causing harm. But the law also recognizes cases in which a business is held responsible, in the sense of accountable, even when the business was not at fault. (These issues will be discussed further in Chapter 8.)

But reference to corporate social responsibility also denotes those duties or restrictions that bind us to act in one way rather than another. We can think of our responsibilities as those things that we ought, or should, do, even if we would rather not. Responsibilities bind, or compel, or constrain, or require us to act in certain ways. Thus, to talk about business's social responsibilities is to be concerned with society's interests that restrict or bind business's behavior. Social responsibility is what a business should or ought to do for the sake of society. Understood in this way, we see that businesses have several different types of social responsibilities.

First, of course, business has the social responsibility to obey the law. Legal responsibilities, both those established by statutory law and by the case precedents of civil law, establish constraints on business's behavior for the sake of society. The law is one area of business's social responsibility that is beyond dispute.

But beyond the law, are there other things that business should or should not do? Are there ethical ways to bind business or constrain its activities? Philosophers sometime distinguish between different types of responsibilities, on a scale from more to less demanding and binding. First, we have responsibilities not to cause harm to others. A second, perhaps less binding, responsibility is to prevent harm even in those cases where one is not the cause. Finally, there might be responsibilities to do good. Let us consider how each might suggest different social responsibilities for business.

Even when not explicitly prohibited by law, ethics would demand that we not cause avoidable harm. In practice, this ethical requirement is very close to the responsibilities established by the precedents of tort law. If a business causes harm to someone and if that harm could have been avoided by exercising due care or proper planning, then both the law and ethics would say that business should be held liable for violating its responsibilities. The idea of individual rights is one way to elucidate the types of harms that business ought not cause. Beyond the responsibility to obey the law, a second level of responsibilities would hold that business has a social responsibility not to violate anyone's rights.

But there are also cases in which business is not causing harms, but could easily prevent harms from occurring. A more inclusive understanding of corporate social responsibility would hold that business has a responsibility to prevent harms. Consider, as an example, the actions taken by the pharmaceutical firm Merck with its drug Mectizan. Mectizan is a Merck drug that prevents river blindness, a disease prevalent in tropical nations. River blindness infects millions of people annually, causing severe rashes, itching, and loss of sight. A single tablet of Mectizan administered once a year can relieve the symptoms and prevent the disease from progressing.

On the surface, Mectizan would not be a very profitable drug to bring to market. The once-a-year dosage limits the demand for the drug among those people who require it. Further, the individuals most at risk for this disease are among the poorest people living in the poorest regions of Africa, Asia, Central America, and South America. In 1987, Merck began a program that provides Mectizan free of charge to people at risk for river blindness. Cooperating with the World Heath Organization, UNICEF, and the World Bank, Merck's program has donated more than 700 million tablets of Mectizan, which have been distributed to 40 million people each year since 1987. The program has also resulted in the development of a health care system, necessary to support and administer the program, in some of the poorest regions of the world. By all accounts, Merck's Mectizan Donation Program has significantly improved the lives of tens of millions of the most vulnerable people on earth. Merck's actions were explained by reference to part of its corporate identity statement: "We are in the business of preserving and improving human life."[9]

Clearly Merck was not responsible for causing river blindness and therefore according to the previous standard of CSR discussed, Merck had no social responsibility in this case. But Merck itself saw the issue differently. Given the company's core business purpose and values, its managers concluded that they did have a social responsibility to prevent a disease easily controlled by their patented drug.

Perhaps the most wide-ranging standard of CSR would hold that business has a social responsibility to do good things and to make society a better place. Corporate philanthropy would be the most obvious cases in which business takes on a responsibility to do good. Corporate giving programs to support community projects in the arts, education, and culture are clear examples. Most corporations have a charitable foundation or office that deals with such philanthropic programs (see the following Reality Check). Small business owners in every town across America can tell stories of how often they are approached to give donations to support local charitable and cultural activities.

Many of the debates surrounding corporate social responsibility involve the question of whether business really has a responsibility to support such good causes. Some people argue that, like all cases of charity, this is something that deserves praise and admiration, but it is not something that every business ought to do. Philosophers sometimes distinguish between obligations/duties and responsibilities to make exactly this point. We may have a responsibility to be charitable, but it is not obligatory nor is it a duty. Others argue that business does have an obligation to support good causes and "give back" to the community. This sense of responsibility is more akin to a debt of gratitude and thankfulness—something less binding than a legal or contractual obligation perhaps, but more than a simple act of charity. Perhaps a clear way to understand the distinction is to compare it to your obligation to write a thank-you note to your grandmother for the extraordinary hand-knit sweater she sent you for your birthday gift. No, you might not have a legal requirement to send the note, but you nevertheless feel a strong duty to do so.

Exploring Enlightened Self-Interest: Motivation for CSR

OBJECTIVE

In addition to Kenneth Dayton's argument that CSR increases the sustainability of an organization by meeting the needs of its supporting constituencies, there are other arguments to motivate a socially responsible firm. Employees who are well treated in their work environments may prove more loyal and more effective and productive in their work. Liz Bankowski, director of social missions at Ben & Jerry's Homemade Ice Cream Company, claims that 80 to 90 percent of Ben & Jerry's employees work there because "they feel they are part of a greater good."[10] The impact on the bottom line, therefore, stems not only from customer preference but also from employee preference.

The problem with a focus on preference, however, is that social responsibility becomes merely social marketing. That is, a firm may use the image of social responsibility to garner customer support or employee loyalty while the facts do not evidence a true commitment. Are motivations relevant? Can a firm have only one motivation? Paul Hawken, cofounder of Smith & Hawken gardening stores and an advocate of business social responsibility, reminds us that:

> [y]ou see tobacco companies subsidizing the arts, then later you find out that there are internal memos showing that they wanted to specifically target the minorities in the arts because they want to get minorities to smoke. That's not socially responsible. It's using social perception as a way to aggrandize or further one's own interests exclusively.[11]

Reality Check *Enron: "Best in Show" or "Can't Judge a Book by Its Cover"?*

As a firm, would you rather be an unethical firm with a good reputation or an ethical firm with a reputation for injustice? Enron included the following laudatory praises in its 2000 Corporate Responsibility Annual Report. The list drives home the challenges incumbent in any awards mechanism that strives to reward a trait such as "most innovative" or "all-star, most admired" rather than an enduring, measurable element of the corporate environment. On the other hand, awards such as those below can serve as influential motivating factors in corporate financial decisions, so many executives in fields impacted by these honors would prefer they remain.

As Reported in Enron's 2000 Corporate Responsibility Annual Report:

"The Most Innovative Company in America"

— *Fortune* Magazine for six consecutive years

"100 Best Companies to Work for in America"

— *Fortune* Magazine for three consecutive years, ranked no. 22 in 2000

"All-Star List of Global Most Admired Companies"

— Fortune Magazine, ranked no. 25 in 2000

"100 Fastest Growing Companies"

— Fortune Magazine, ranked no. 29 in 2000

The report goes on to say:

The principles that guide our behavior are based on our vision and values and include the following:

- Respect
- Integrity
- Communication
- Excellence ...

In 2001, we will continue to develop a systematic approach toward corporate responsibility, refine our implementation strategy, formalize stakeholder engagement, and strengthen our risk management practices.

Source: 2000 Enron Corporate Responsibility Annual Report (2001), pp. 2–3.

Does Johnson & Johnson reap a financial benefit from being ranked as the most reputable company in America by Responsibility Inc.? When Philip Morris Co. spends $250 million on an advertising campaign that communicates its charitable activities, do you question why the company engaged in the charitable activities in the first place? As you read the opening Decision Point, did you care about *why* a firm supported a particular sporting event?

Consider Procter & Gamble Co., which was harshly criticized by respondents to a survey seeking to rank firms on the basis of their corporate philanthropy. Respondents contended that P&G did "absolutely nothing to help" after the September 11 tragedy.[12] However, in truth, P&G provided more than $2.5 million in cash and products, but simply did not publicize that contribution. The same held true for Honda Motor Co., which donated cash, all-terrain vehicles, and generators for use at the World Trade Center site. Seemingly unaware of these efforts, respondents instead believed these companies to lack compassion for their failure to support America.

The quandary presented by publicizing corporate good deeds is addressed in Ingeborg Wick's article "Workers' Tool or PR Ploy? A Guide to Codes of International Labor Practice."[13] Wick explains that many codes of conduct for global

Reality Check *Why Buy?*

Note that a reputation is relevant to many stakeholders – not just purchasing consumers. A survey conducted in the United Kingdom found that 33 percent of workers in that country are "very likely" to seek new employment during the next year because of their current employer's poor record on corporate social responsibility.[14] Employers are also more likely to seek out new hires with a demonstrated aware-ness of social and environmental responsibility – in fact, a *Wall Street Journal* survey found that 77 percent of corporate recruiters said it is important in their hiring decisions.[15] Moreover, investors are sinking almost $1.3 billion into socially responsible mutual funds, effectively putting their money where their mouths are.[16]

workers originally evolved in response to negative publicity about dangerous working conditions and the use of child labor, among other challenges. Are codes of conduct now simply a public relations tactic to soothe stakeholder concerns or can they actually serve the purpose that they purport to address? Wick concludes that codes can actually be useful tools to implement social standards rather than simply to encourage good press, as long as they adhere to certain criteria with regard to their substance, stakeholder participation, independent verification, transparency, and other requirements. Therefore, CSR efforts can serve both objectives as long as their social impact is assured within the context and substance of the activity involved.

In a recent *Economist* cover story and special section, Clive Crook questions what all of these activities actually amount to. "Even to the most innocent observer, plenty of CSR policies smack of tokenism and political correctness more than of a genuine concern to 'give back to the community.' Is CSR then mostly for show?"[17] Crook claims that the answer must be yes, with exceptions. However, it is interesting to note that Crook is not very concerned about this window-treatment of CSR since he believes that "capitalism does not need the fundamental reform that many CSR advocates wish for."

The practice of caring for the "image" of a firm is sometimes referred to as **reputation management**. There is nothing inherently wrong with managing a firm's reputation, but observers might challenge firms for engaging in CSR activities *solely* for the purpose of impacting their reputations. The challenge is based on the fact that reputation management often *works*! Figure 5.1 shows the elements that Harris Interactive considers to be critical to the construction of a reputation and the resulting benefits that attention to these elements can produce. If a firm creates a good image for itself, it builds a type of trust bank—consumers or other stakeholders seem to give it some slack if they then hear something negative about the firm. Similarly, if a firm has a negative image, that image may stick, regardless of what good the corporation may do. Plato explored this issue when he asked whether one would rather be an unethical person with a good reputation or an ethical person with a reputation for injustice. You may find that, if given the

FIGURE 5.1
The Construction of Corporate Reputation

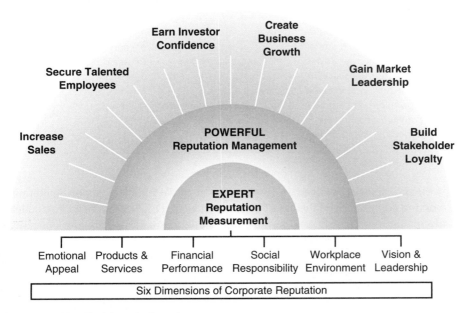

Source: Copyright © Harris Interactive Research.
Reprinted by permission from http://www.harrisinteractive.com/services/reputation.asp.

choice between the two, companies are far more likely to survive under the first conception than under the second. On the issue of reputation management and the impact of a variety of stakeholders on a firm's reputation, see the two preceding Reality Checks and check out the perspectives of various consumer and advocacy groups in connection with well-known businesses at any of the following Web sites:

- www.bankofamericafraud.org
- www.boycottameritech.com
- www.cokespotlight.org
- www.ihatestarbucks.com
- www.noamazon.com
- www.starbucked.com
- www.walmartsurvivor.com

In this way, reputation may often be more forceful than reality, as with the P&G and Honda cases mentioned previously. Shell Oil publicizes its efforts at good citizenship in Nigeria; but it has an unfortunate record in terms of the timing of its responsiveness to spills, and its community development projects have created community rifts in areas around oilfields. Similarly, British American

Tobacco heavily and consistently promotes its high health and safety standards, but it receives ongoing reports from contract farmers in Brazil and Kenya about ill health as a result of tobacco cultivation. Which image is more publicized and therefore remains in the stakeholders' conscience?

Does the "Enlightened Self-Interest" Model Work? Does "Good Ethics" Mean "Good Business"?

Look at a well-run company and you will see the needs of its stockholders, its employees, and the community at large being served simultaneously.

—*Arnold Hiatt, Former CEO, Stride Rite Corp.*

Good ethics is good business. Have you heard that before? Did you believe it? The third model of CSR, *enlightened self-interest,* presumes that corporations recognize the ultimate value to the organization in engaging in CSR activities. However, the long-term impact of participating in these efforts is not always so clear. A great deal of research therefore has concentrated on demonstrating this

TABLE 5.1

Multiple Bottom-Line Performance Indicators

Ten Measures of Business Success	Ten Dimensions of Corporate Sustainable Development Performance
Financial Performance	**Governance**
1. Shareholder value	1. Ethics, values, and principles
2. Revenue	2. Accountability and transparency
3. Operational efficiency	**General**
4. Access to capital	3. Triple bottom-line commitment
Financial Drivers	**Environment**
5. Customer attraction	4. Environmental process focus
6. Brand value and reputation	5. Environmental product focus
7. Human and intellectual capital	**Socioeconomic**
8. Risk profile	6. Socioeconomic development
9. Innovation	7. Human rights
10. License to operate	8. Workplace conditions
	Stakeholder Engagement
	9. Engaging business partners
	10. Engaging nonbusiness partners

Source: Adapted from Oliver Dudok van Heel, John Elkington, Shelly Fennell, and Franceska van Dijk, *Buried Treasure: Uncovering the Business Case for Corporate Sustainability* (London: SustainAbility, 2001).

connection. In fact, theorists continue to dispute whether ethical decisions lead to more significant profits than unethical decisions. While we are all familiar with examples of unethical decisions leading to high profits, there is general agreement that, in the long run, ethics pays off. However, it is the measurement of that payoff that is the challenge. Table 5.1 juxtaposes indicators of performance in the CSR arena with those traditionally used in the financial environment to provide some guidance in this area. Though those executives responsible for organizational measurement and risk assessment might be less familiar with the processes for assessing the elements included on the right side of the chart, they are by no means less measurable. Often, however, the long-term value is not as evident.

OBJECTIVE

Though there are many justifications for ethics in business, often the discussion returns to, well, returns—the business case for the return on investment. There is evidence that good ethics is good business; yet the dominant thinking is that, if you can't measure it, it is not important. Consequently, efforts have been made to measure the bottom-line impact of ethical decision making.

Measurement is critical since the business case is not without its detractors. David Vogel,[18] a political science professor at Berkeley, contends that, while there is a market for firms with strong CSR missions, it is a niche market and one that therefore caters to only a small group of consumers or investors. He argues that, contrary to a global shift in the business environment, CSR should instead be perceived as one option for a business strategy that might be appropriate for certain types of firms under certain conditions, such as those with well-known brand names, with reputations that are subject to threats by activists. He warns of the exposure a firm might suffer if it then does not live up to its CSR promises. He also cautions against investing in CSR when consumers are not willing to pay higher prices to support that investment. Though this perspective is persuasive, a review of the scholarly research on the subject suggests the contrary on numerous counts, most predominantly the overall return on investment to the corporation.

Persuasive evidence of impact comes from a recent study titled "Developing Value: The Business Case for Sustainability in Emerging Markets," based on a study produced jointly by SustainAbility, the Ethos Institute, and the International Finance Corporation. The research found that, in emerging markets, cost savings, productivity improvement, revenue growth, and access to markets were the most important business benefits of sustainability activities. Environmental process improvements and human resource management were the most significant areas of sustainability action. The report concludes that it does pay for businesses in emerging markets to pursue a wider role in environmental and social issues, citing cost reductions, productivity, revenue growth, and market access as areas of greatest return for multinational enterprises (MNEs).

In addition, studies have found that there are a number of expected—and measurable—outcomes to ethics programs in organizations. Some people look to the end results of firms that have placed ethics and social responsibility at

Reality Check *So They Say*

"Whether at the World Trade Organization, or at the OECD, or at the United Nations, an irrefutable case can be made that a universal acceptance of the rule of law, the outlawing of corrupt practices, respect for workers' rights, high health and safety standards, sensitivity to the environment, support for education and the protection and nurturing of children are not only justifiable against the criteria of morality and justice. The simple truth is that these are good for business and most business people recognize this."[19]

— Thomas d'Aquino, CEO of Canada's Business Council on National Issues

"We all pay for poverty and unemployment and illiteracy. If a large percentage of society falls into a disadvantaged class, investors will find it hard to source skilled and alert workers; manufacturers will have a limited market for their products; criminality will scare away foreign investments, and internal migrants to limited areas of opportunities will strain basic services and lead to urban blight. Under these conditions, no country can move forward economically and sustain development.... It therefore makes business sense for corporations to complement the efforts of government in contributing to social development."[20]

—J. Ayala II

"Our findings, both cross-sectional and longitudinal, indicate that there are indeed systematic linkages among community involvement, employee morale, and business performance in business enterprises. To the best of our knowledge, this is the first time that such linkages have been demonstrated empirically. Moreover, the weight of the evidence produced here indicates that community involvement is positively associated with business performance, employee morale is positively associated with business performance, and the interaction of community involvement—external involvement—with employee morale—internal involvement—is even more strongly associated with business performance than is either "involvement" measure alone."[21]

—Report of study by UCLA graduate school of business Professor David Lewin and J. M. Sabater (formerly IBM director of corporate community relations) in 1989 and 1991 involving in-depth, statistical research surveys of over 150 U.S.-based companies to determine whether there is a verifiable connection between a company's community involvement and its business performance

the forefront of their activities, while others look to those firms that have been successful and determine the role that ethics might have played. With regard to the former, consider Johnson & Johnson, known for its quick and effective handling of its experience with tainted Tylenol. As highlighted in a Reality Check in Chapter 4, J&J has had more than seven decades of consecutive sales increases, two decades of double-digit earnings increases, and four decades of dividend increases. Each of these quantifiable measurements can perhaps serve as proxies for success, to some extent, or at least would be unlikely to occur in a company permeated by ethical lapses.

Moreover, a landmark study by Professors Stephen Erfle and Michael Frantantuono found that firms that were ranked highest in terms of their records on a variety of social issues (including charitable contributions, community outreach programs, environmental performance, advancement of women, and promotion of minorities) had greater financial performance as well. Financial performance was better in terms of operating income growth, sales-to-assets ratios, sales growth, return on equity, earnings-to-asset growth, return on investment, return on assets, and asset growth.[22] The preceding Reality Check demonstrates that these perspectives are gaining traction worldwide.

Another study by Murphy and Verschoor reports that the overall financial performance of the 2001 *Business Ethics Magazine* Best Corporate Citizens was significantly better than that of the remaining companies in the S&P 500 index, based on the 2001 *BusinessWeek* ranking of total financial performance.[23] In addition, the researchers found that these same firms had a significantly better reputation among corporate directors, security analysts, and senior executives. The same result was found in a 2001 *Fortune* survey of most admired companies. The UK-based Institute of Business Ethics did a follow-up study to validate these findings and found that, from the perspectives of economic value added, market value added, and the price-earnings ratio, those companies that had a code of conduct outperformed those that did not over a five-year period.[24] The higher performance translated into significantly more economic value added, a less volatile price/earnings ratio (making the firm, perhaps, a more secure investment), and 18 percent higher profit/turnover ratios. The research concluded

> This study gives credence to the assertion that "you do business ethically because it pays." However, the most effective driver for maintaining a high level of integrity throughout the business is because it is seen by the board, employees and other stakeholders to be a core value and therefore the right thing to do . . . [A] sustainable business is one which is well managed and which takes business ethics seriously. Leaders of this type of business do not need any assurance that their approach to the way they do business will also enhance their profitability, because they know it to be true.[25]

This chapter sought to answer the question of whether there exists a social responsibility of business. Several sources of that responsibility were proposed. The responsibility may be based in a concept of good corporate citizenship, a social contract, or enlightened self-interest. Notwithstanding its origins, we then explored the challenge of how an inanimate entity like a corporation could actually have a responsibility to others and discussed the extent of that obligation, both in law and ethics.

Motivations for engaging in CSR are diverse and fluctuating. This chapter attempted to present that variety of perspective and explored objectively the concept of reputation management as it applies to CSR. Finally, we analyzed and evaluated the contention that good ethics is good business, the underlying foundation of the enlightened self-interest model of CSR.

No matter how one answers the several questions posed by this chapter, however, one thing is certain. It is impossible to engage in business today without encountering and addressing CSR. Despite substantial differences among companies, research demonstrates that almost all companies will confront CSR issues from stakeholders at some point in the near future.[26]

The opening Decision Point asks whether you care about *why* a firm engages in a particular socially conscious endeavor. The ethical decision-making process suggests that you make sure that you have all the relevant facts in order to reach a conclusion. Are we asking whether it is important to *know* a firm's motivation, or whether a particular motivation is better than another? If the latter, do you know the motivation behind a specific action of an organization? If you are going to judge whether you value the motivation, let's be sure that we are clear on what it is.

Next, if we care about the motivation, why do we care? Why is motivation important when we consider, for instance, a firm's decision to sponsor an event or an organization? If you are clear on why this is important to you, then you may be better prepared to find one motivation more desirable than another. Who are the stakeholders when we are considering a firm's motivation? Of course, the stakeholders might change depending on the specific action we are evaluating, but, in general, you have the firm itself, its direct stakeholders (such as employees, clients or customers, and investors), the recipient of the responsible behavior (the community, for example), the media (or the source of information about the activity). Can you think of a few others? We do not often think of competitors as stakeholders, but certainly they, too, are impacted by a firm's decision.

The next inquiry involves the alternatives a firm may have in the way in which it engages in sponsorship. One firm might opt to simply add its logo to a program or display a flag, while another firm might have its name on every element involved in the particular activity. Some firms might involve their own executives or employees in an activity, while others leave the hands-on involvement to a nongovernmental organization (NGO) or community organization. Do we respond differently, depending on the nature of the firm's involvement? Why? How do the alternatives compare; how do the alternatives you have identified affect the stakeholders?

What are the consequences of offering greater support to companies that support causes that are important to you? If you support a firm that, in turn, supports your causes, then you are encouraging it to continue to do that. There is an argument that the firm can have a larger impact than any one individual, so, by supporting the firm, you are going quite a way toward supporting your particular cause.

The chapter discussed several reasons why motivation might matter. Have you discovered any additional reasons? What is your conclusion? Do you care?

Questions, Projects, and Exercises

1. What is your overall perspective on CSR after reviewing this chapter? If the market does not encourage responsibility for social causes, should a firm engage in this behavior? Does social responsibility apply only to firms, or do we have a responsibility as well to support firms that take socially responsible action and withhold our support from firms that fail to exhibit socially responsible behavior? If we stand by and allow irresponsible actions to take place using profits made on our purchases, do we bear any responsibility?

   * How did you reach your decision? What key facts do you need to know in order to judge a firm's actions or your complicity in them by supporting a firm with your purchases or other choices?

   * How do you determine responsibility? Do you pay attention to these issues in your purchases and other choices?

   * Would you be more likely to support a company by purchasing its products or services if the company (a) donated a portion of the proceeds to a cause that was important to you; (b) paid its workers a "fair" wage (however you would define that concept); or (c) was a good investment for its stockholders? Which consequence is more influential to you? On the contrary, would you refrain from purchasing from a firm that failed in any of those areas?

   * How do the alternatives compare? Do you believe different purchasing decisions by consumers could really make a difference?

2. Which of the three models of CSR is most persuasive to you and why? Which do you believe is most prevalent among companies that engage in CSR efforts?

3. This chapter has asked in several ways whether the social responsibility of the companies you patronize has ever made any difference to your purchasing decisions. Will it make any difference in the future as a result of what you have learned? Consider your last three largest purchases. Go to the Web sites of the companies that manufacture the products you bought and explore those firms' social responsibility efforts. Are they more or less than what you expected? Do your findings make a difference to you in terms of how you feel about these firms, your purchases, and/or the amount of money you spent on these items?

4. One of the leading figures in the Enron debacle was company founder Kenneth Lay, who died in mid-2006 after his conviction for fraud and conspiracy but before he began serving his sentence. Prior to the events that led to the trial and conviction, Lay was viewed in Houston as one of its "genuine heroes" and Enron was a "shining beacon" according to a professor at Rice University in Houston. The Houston Astros' field was named after Enron when the company gave the Astros a large grant. Enron also gave money to local organizations such as the ballet and national organizations based in Houston such as United Way. The Lays individually supported Houston's opera and ballet, its Holocaust Museum, the University of Texas cancer center, and other charitable organizations. If you were on the jury, would *any* of this information be relevant to your decision about Mr. Lay's guilt or innocence? If your jury had determined that Mr. Lay was guilty, would *any* of this information be relevant to your decision about the sentence you would then impose? Defend your decision from an ethical perspective.

5. In 2005, Nestlé S.A. CEO Peter Braeck-Letmathe explained, "Companies shouldn't feel obligated to 'give back' to communities because they haven't taken anything away. Companies should only pursue charitable endeavors with the underlying intention of making money. It is not our money we're handing out but our investors'. A company's

obligation is simply to create jobs and make products. What the hell have we taken away from society by being a successful company that employs people?"[27] Which model of CSR would the Nestlé CEO advocate, and do you agree with his assessment?

6. Supermodel Kate Moss appeared in photos in a number of tabloid magazines and elsewhere using illegal drugs. Subsequent to the appearance of the photographs, several of her clients, including Chanel, H&M, and Burberry, cancelled their contracts (some only temporarily) with her or determined that they would not renew them when they became eligible for renewal. Other clients opted to retain her services, preferring to "stand by her" during this ordeal. Ms. Moss issued a statement that she had checked herself into a rehabilitation center for assistance with her drug use. Assume that you are the marketing vice president for a major global fashion label that is a client of Ms. Moss at the time of these events. Use the ethical decision-making process to evaluate how to respond to the situation. What is your decision on what to do?

7. What kind of organization would you like to work for? What would be the best? What would be the most realistic? Think about its structure, physical environment, lines of communication, treatment of employees, recruitment and promotion practices, policies towards the community, and so on. Consider also, however, what you lose because of some of these benefits (for example, if the company contributes in the community or offers more benefits for employees, there might be less money for raises).

8. Take another look at the quote earlier in this chapter by Paul Hawken. He seems to be saying that it is not acceptable to use social perception as a way to further one's own interests (exclusively). Now find the Smith & Hawken site on the Web and any additional information you can locate regarding Smith & Hawken or Paul Hawken and CSR. Would you identify Smith & Hawken as a firm interested in CSR? Would you identify Mr. Hawken as an individual interested in CSR or personal social responsibility? Which model of CSR would you suggest that Mr. Hawken supports?

9. Given the significant financial power that a retailer and sponsor like Nike can have in the sports world, does it have any obligation to use that power to do good in connection with its particular industry? A 2006 *New York Times* article[28] suggested that "(m)ore than television packages, more than attendance at the gate, track and field is driven by shoe company dough. Nike could, if it chose, threaten to pull its financial support from the coaches and trainers of athletes who are barred for doping violations. For years, the caretakers of the athletes have also been suspected as the doping pushers. Curiously, Nike hasn't fallen in line with everyone else calling for strict liability among coaches, trainers and athletes." The article instead suggests that Nike does not benefit when a star falls from glory so it tends to shy away from this area of oversight. In fact, it goes so far as to say that "Nike is the doping society's enabler." Can you make the argument that Nike has an obligation to intervene? Or, if you do not agree with an argument for its responsibility to do good, could you instead make an economic argument in favor of intervention?

Key Terms

After reading this chapter, you should have a clear understanding of the following Key Terms. The page numbers refer to the point at which they were discussed in the chapter. For a more complete definition, please see the Glossary.

corporate citizenship model of CSR, *p. 150*

corporate social responsibility (CSR), *p. 149*

enlightened self-interest model of CSR, *p. 150*

ethical custom, *p. 152*

reputation management, *p. 159*

social contract model of CSR, *p. 150*

Endnotes

1. Sir Adrian Cadbury, "Ethical Managers Make Their Own Rules," *Harvard Business Review* (September/October 1987).

2. Kenneth R. Andrews, *The Concept of Corporate Strategy* (Burr Ridge, IL: Irwin,1971), p. 120.

3. In late 2006, Ben & Jerry's made its 2004 Social and Environmental Assessment available at http://www.benjerry.com/our_company/about_us/social_mission/social_audits/2004/index.cfm.

4. C. Church, A. Cade, and A. Grant, "Corporate Social Responsibility: Attitudes of the British Public, 2," MORI (2003).

5. Stakeholder Alliance, http://www.stakeholderalliance.org/Buzz.html.

6. *Wiwa v. Royal Dutch Petroleum Co.,* 99-7223 (2000).

7. "Corporate Citizenship: A Luxury in Difficult Times?" World Economic Forum Knowledge Navigator (4/2/02).

8. *Dodge v. Ford Motor Co.,* 204 Mich. 459; 170 N.W. 668 (1919).

9. "Mission Statement: Our Values," http://www.merck.com/about/mission.html.

10. Joel Makower, *Beyond the Bottom Line* (New York: Simon & Schuster, 1994), p. 68.

11. Makower, *Beyond the Bottom Line,* p. 15.

12. Ronald Alsop, "For a company, charitable works are best carried out discreetly," *The Wall Street Journal,* January 16, 2002, Marketplace Section, p. 1.

13. Ingeborg Wick, *Workers' Tool or PR Ploy? A Guide to Codes of International Labor Practice,* 3rd ed. (Bonn: Friedrich-Ebert-Stiftung, Dept. for Development Policy, 2003).

14. The Work Foundation, "The Ethical Employee," http://www.theworkfoundation.com/research/publications/ethical.jsp (2002).

15. Ronald Alsop, "Corporations Still Put Profits First, but Social Concerns Gain Ground," *The Wall Street Journal*, October 30, 2001, p. B12.

16. A.J. Vogl, "Does It Pay to Be Good?" *Across the Board* (January 2003).

17. "The Good Company: A Survey of Corporate Social responsibility," *The Economist*, January 22, 2005.

18. David Vogel, *The Market for Virtue: The Potential and Limits of Corporate Social Responsibility* (Washington, DC: Brookings Institution, 2005).

19. Quoted in C. Forcese, "Profiting from Misfortune? The Role of Business Corporations in Promoting and Protecting International Human Rights," MA thesis, Norman Paterson School of International Affairs, Carleton University, Ottawa (1997), referred to in C. Forcese, Putting Conscience into Commerce: Strategies for Making Human Rights Business as Usual" (Montréal: International Centre for Human Rights and Democratic Development, 1997).

20. J. Ayala II, "Philanthropy Makes Business Sense," *Business Day* (Bangkok), September 25, 1995; J. Ayala II, "Philanthropy Makes Business Sense," *Ayala Foundation Inc. Quarterly* 4, no. 2 (July–September, October–Nov 1995), p. 3.

21. D. Lewin and J.M. Sabater, "Corporate Philanthropy and Business Performance," *Philanthropy at the Crossroads* (Bloomington: University of Indiana Press, 1996), pp. 105–26.

22. Makower, *Beyond the Bottam Line,* pp. 70–71

23. Curtis Verschoor and Elizabeth Murphy, "The Financial Performance of Large Firms and Those with Global Prominence: How Do the Best Corporations Rate?" *Business & Society Review* 107, no. 3 (2002), pp. 371–80. *See also* Elizabeth Murphy

and Curtis Verschoor, "Best Corporate Citizens Have Better Financial Performance," *Strategic Finance* 83, no. 7 (January 2002), p. 20.

24. Simon Webley and Elise More, *Does Business Ethics Pay?* (London: Institute of Business Ethics, 2003), p. 9.

25. Webley and More, *Does Business Ethics Pay?*, p. 33.

26. Margot Lobbezoo, "Social Responsibilities of Business," unpublished manuscript available from the author.

27. Jennifer Heldt Powell, "Nestlé Chief Rejects the Need to 'Give Back' to Communities," *Boston Herald,* March 9, 2005, p. 33, http://www.bc.edu/schools/csom/cga/executives/events/brabeck/ and http://www.babymilkaction.org/press/press22march05.html.

28. Selena Roberts, "Coaches Like Graham Still Have Their Sponsors," *The New York Times*, August 2, 2006.

Reading **5-1**

Rethinking the Social Responsibility of Business: A *Reason* Debate Featuring Milton Friedman, Whole Foods' John Mackey, and Cypress Semiconductor's T.J. Rodgers

Thirty-five years ago, Milton Friedman wrote a famous article for *The New York Times Magazine* whose title aptly summed up its main point: "The Social Responsibility of Business Is to Increase Its Profits." The future Nobel laureate in economics had no patience for capitalists who claimed that "business is not concerned 'merely' with profit but also with promoting desirable 'social' ends; that business has a 'social conscience' and takes seriously its responsibilities for providing employment, eliminating discrimination, avoiding pollution and whatever else may be the catchwords of the contemporary crop of reformers."

Friedman, now a senior research fellow at the Hoover Institution and the Paul Snowden Russell Distinguished Service Professor Emeritus of Economics at the University of Chicago, wrote that such people are "preaching pure and unadulterated socialism. Businessmen who talk this way are unwitting puppets of the intellectual forces that have been undermining the basis of a free society these past decades."

John Mackey, the founder and CEO of Whole Foods, is one businessman who disagrees with Friedman. A self-described ardent libertarian whose conversation is peppered with references to Ludwig von Mises and Abraham Maslow, Austrian economics and astrology, Mackey believes Friedman's view is too narrow a description of his and many other businesses' activities. As important, he argues that Friedman's take woefully under-sells the humanitarian dimension of capitalism.

In the debate that follows, Mackey lays out his personal vision of the social responsibility of business. Friedman responds, as does T.J. Rodgers, the founder and CEO of Cypress Semiconductor and the chief spokesman of what might be called the tough love school of laissez faire. Dubbed "one of America's toughest bosses" by *Fortune,* Rodgers argues that corporations add far more to society by maximizing "long-term shareholder value" than they do by donating time and money to charity.

Reason offers this exchange as the starting point of a discussion that should be intensely important to all devotees of free minds and free markets.

Putting Customers Ahead of Investors

John Mackey:

In 1970 Milton Friedman wrote that "there is one and only one social responsibility of business—to use its resources and engage in activities designed to increase its profits so long as it stays within the rules of the game, which is to say, engages in open and free competition without deception or fraud." That's the orthodox view among free market economists: that the only social responsibility a law-abiding business has is to maximize profits for the shareholders.

I strongly disagree. I'm a businessman and a free market libertarian, but I believe that the enlightened corporation should try to create value for *all* of its constituencies. From an investor's perspective, the purpose of the business is to maximize profits. But that's not the purpose for other stakeholders—for customers, employees, suppliers, and the community. Each of those groups will define the purpose of the business in terms of its own needs and desires, and each perspective is valid and legitimate.

My argument should not be mistaken for a hostility to profit. I believe I know something about creating shareholder value. When I co-founded Whole Foods Market 27 years ago, we began with $45,000 in capital; we only had $250,000 in sales our first year. During the last 12 months we had sales of more than $4.6 billion, net profits of more than $160 million, and a market capitalization over $8 billion.

But we have not achieved our tremendous increase in shareholder value by making shareholder value the primary purpose of our business. In my marriage, my wife's happiness is an end in itself, not merely a means to my own happiness; love leads me to put my wife's happiness first, but in doing so I also make myself happier. Similarly, the most successful businesses put the customer first, ahead of the investors. In the profit-centered business, customer happiness is merely a means to an end: maximizing profits. In the customer-centered business, customer happiness is an end in itself, and will be pursued with greater interest, passion, and empathy than the profit-centered business is capable of.

Not that we're only concerned with customers. At Whole Foods, we measure our success by how much value we can create for all six of our most important stakeholders: customers, team members (employees), investors, vendors, communities, and the environment . . . .

There is, of course, no magical formula to calculate how much value each stakeholder should receive from the company. It is a dynamic process that evolves with the competitive marketplace. No stakeholder remains satisfied for long. It is the function of company leadership to develop solutions that continually work for the common good.

Many thinking people will readily accept my arguments that caring about customers and employees is good business. But they might draw the line at believing a company has any responsibility to its community and environment. To donate time and capital to philanthropy, they will argue, is to steal from the investors. After all, the corporation's assets legally belong to the investors, don't they? Management has a fiduciary responsibility to maximize shareholder value; therefore, any activities that don't maximize shareholder value are violations of this duty. If you feel altruism towards other people, you should exercise that altruism with your own money, not with the assets of a corporation that doesn't belong to you.

This position sounds reasonable. A company's assets do belong to the investors, and its management does have a duty to manage those assets responsibly. In my view, the argument is not *wrong* so much as it is too narrow.

First, there can be little doubt that a certain amount of corporate philanthropy is simply good business and works for the long-term benefit of the investors. For example: In addition to the many thousands of small donations each Whole Foods store makes each year, we also hold five 5% Days throughout the year. On those days, we donate 5 percent of a store's total sales to a nonprofit organization. While our stores select worthwhile organizations to support, they also tend to focus on groups that have large membership lists, which are contacted and encouraged to shop our store that day to support the organization. This usually brings hundreds of new or lapsed customers into our stores, many of whom then become regular shoppers. So a 5% Day not only allows us to support worthwhile causes, but is an excellent marketing strategy that has benefited Whole Foods investors immensely.

That said, I believe such programs would be completely justifiable even if they produced no profits and no P.R. This is because I believe the entrepreneurs, not the current investors in a company's stock, have the right and responsibility to define the purpose of the company. It is the entrepreneurs who create a company, who bring all the factors of production together and coordinate it into viable business. It is the entrepreneurs who set the company strategy and who negotiate the terms of trade with all of the voluntarily cooperating stakeholders—including the investors. At Whole Foods we "hired" our original investors. They didn't hire us.

We first announced that we would donate 5 percent of the company's net profits to philanthropy when we drafted our mission statement, back in 1985. Our policy has therefore been in place for over 20 years, and it predates our IPO by seven years. All seven of the private investors at the time we created the policy voted for it when they served on our board of directors. When we took in venture capital money back in 1989, none of the venture firms objected to the policy. In addition, in almost 14 years as a publicly traded company, almost no investors have ever raised objections to the policy. How can Whole Foods' philanthropy be "theft" from the current investors if the original owners of the company unanimously approved the policy and all subsequent investors made their investments after the policy was in effect and well publicized?

The shareholders of a public company own their stock voluntarily. If they don't agree with the philosophy of the business, they can always sell their investment, just as the customers and employees can exit their relationships with the company if they don't like the terms of trade. If that is unacceptable to them, they always have the legal right to submit a resolution at our annual shareholders meeting to change the company's philanthropic philosophy. A number of our company policies have been changed over the years through successful shareholder resolutions.

Another objection to the Whole Foods philosophy is where to draw the line. If donating 5 percent of profits is good, wouldn't 10 percent be even better? Why not donate 100 percent of our profits to the betterment of society? But the fact that Whole Foods has responsibilities to our community doesn't mean that we don't have any responsibilities to our investors. It's a question of finding the appropriate balance and trying to create value for all of our stakeholders. Is 5 percent the "right amount" to donate to the community? I don't think there is a right answer to this question, except that I believe 0 percent is too little. It is an arbitrary percentage that the co-founders of the company decided was a reasonable amount and which was approved by the owners of the company at the time we made the decision. Corporate philanthropy is a good thing, but it requires the legitimacy of investor approval. In my experience, most investors understand that it can be beneficial to both the corporation and to the larger society.

That doesn't answer the question of why we give money to the community stakeholder. For that, you should turn to one of the fathers of free-market economics, Adam Smith. *The Wealth of Nations* was a tremendous achievement, but economists would be well served to read Smith's other great book, *The Theory of Moral Sentiments.* There he explains that human nature isn't just about self-interest. It also includes sympathy, empathy, friendship, love, and the desire for social approval. As motives for human behavior, these are at least as important as self-interest. For many people, they are more important.

When we are small children we are egocentric, concerned only about our own needs and desires. As we mature, most people grow beyond this egocentrism and begin to care about others—their families, friends, communities, and countries. Our capacity to love can expand even further: to loving people from different races, religions, and countries—potentially to unlimited love for all people and even for other sentient creatures. This is our potential as human beings, to take joy in the flourishing of people everywhere. Whole Foods gives money to our communities because we care about them and feel a responsibility to help them flourish as well as possible.

The business model that Whole Foods has embraced could represent a new form of capitalism, one that more consciously works for the common good instead of depending solely on the "invisible hand" to generate positive results for society. The "brand" of capitalism is in terrible shape throughout the world, and corporations are widely seen as selfish, greedy, and uncaring. This is both unfortunate and unnecessary, and could be changed if businesses and economists widely adopted the business model that I have outlined here.

To extend our love and care beyond our narrow self-interest is antithetical to neither our human nature nor our financial success. Rather, it leads to the further fulfillment of both. Why do we not encourage this in our theories of business and economics? Why do we restrict our theories to such a pessimistic and crabby view of human nature? What are we afraid of?

Making Philanthropy out of Obscenity

Milton Friedman:

> *By pursuing his own interest [an individual] frequently promotes that of the society more effectually than when he really intends to promote it. I have never known much good done by those who affected to trade for the public good.*

> —Adam Smith, *The Wealth of Nations*

The differences between John Mackey and me regarding the social responsibility of business are for the most part rhetorical. Strip off the camouflage, and it turns out we are in essential agreement. Moreover, his company, Whole Foods Market, behaves in accordance with the principles I spelled out in my 1970 *New York Times Magazine* article.

With respect to his company, it could hardly be otherwise. It has done well in a highly competitive industry. Had it devoted any significant fraction of its resources to exercising a social responsibility unrelated to the bottom line, it would be out of business by now or would have been taken over.

Here is how Mackey himself describes his firm's activities:

1. "The most successful businesses put the customer first, instead of the investors" (which clearly means that this is the way to put the investors first).
2. "There can be little doubt that a certain amount of corporate philanthropy is simply good business and works for the long-term benefit of the investors."

Compare this to what I wrote in 1970:

"Of course, in practice the doctrine of social responsibility is frequently a cloak for actions that are justified on other grounds rather than a reason for those actions.

"To illustrate, it may well be in the long run interest of a corporation that is a major employer in a small community to devote resources to providing amenities to that community or to improving its government . . .

"In each of these . . . cases, there is a strong temptation to rationalize these actions as an exercise of 'social responsibility.' In the present climate of opinion, with its widespread aversion to 'capitalism,' 'profits,' the 'soulless corporation' and so on, this is one way for a corporation to generate goodwill as a by-product of expenditures that are entirely justified in its own self-interest.

"It would be inconsistent of me to call on corporate executives to refrain from this hypocritical window-dressing because it harms the foundations of a free society. That would be to call on them to exercise a 'social responsibility'! If our institutions and the attitudes of the public make it in their self-interest to cloak their actions in this way, I cannot summon much indignation to denounce them."

I believe Mackey's flat statement that "corporate philanthropy is a good thing" is flatly wrong. Consider the decision by the founders of Whole Foods to donate 5 percent of net profits to philanthropy. They were clearly within their rights in doing so. They were spending their own money, using 5 percent of one part of their wealth to establish, thanks to corporate tax provisions, the equivalent of a 501c(3) charitable foundation, though with no mission statement, no separate by-laws, and no provision for deciding on the beneficiaries. But what reason is there to suppose that the stream of profit distributed in this way would do more good for society than investing that stream of profit in the enterprise itself or paying it out as dividends and letting the stockholders dispose of it? The practice makes sense only because of our obscene tax laws, whereby a stockholder can make a larger gift for a given after-tax cost if the corporation makes the gift on his behalf than if he makes the gift directly. That is a good reason for eliminating the corporate tax or for eliminating the deductibility of corporate charity, but it is not a justification for corporate charity.

Whole Foods Market's contribution to society—and as a customer I can testify that it is an important one—is to enhance the pleasure of shopping for food. Whole Foods has no special competence in deciding how charity should be distributed. Any funds devoted to the latter would surely have contributed more to society if they had been devoted to improving still further the former.

Finally, I shall try to explain why my statement that "the social responsibility of business [is] to increase its profits" and Mackey's statement that "the enlightened corporation should try to create value for all of its constituencies" are equivalent.

Note first that I refer to *social* responsibility, not financial, or accounting, or legal. It is social precisely to allow for the constituencies to which Mackey refers. Maximizing profits is an end from the private point of view; it is a means from the social point of view. A system based on private property and free markets is a sophisticated means of enabling people to cooperate in their economic activities without compulsion; it enables separated knowledge to assure that each resource is used for its most valued use, and is combined with other resources in the most efficient way.

Of course, this is abstract and idealized. The world is not ideal. There are all sorts of deviations from the perfect market—many, if not most, I suspect, due to government interventions. But with all its defects, the current largely free-market, private-property world seems to me vastly preferable to a world in which a large fraction of resources is used and distributed by 501c(3)s and their corporate counterparts.

Put Profits First

T.J. Rodgers:

John Mackey's article attacking corporate profit maximization could not have been written by "a free market libertarian," as claimed. Indeed, if the examples he cites had not identified him as the author, one could easily assume the piece was written by Ralph Nader. A more accurate title for his article is "How Business and Profit Making Fit into My Overarching Philosophy of Altruism."

Mackey spouts nonsense about how his company hired his original investors, not vice versa. If Whole Foods ever falls on persistent hard times—perhaps when the Luddites are no longer able to hold back the genetic food revolution using junk science and fear—he will quickly find out who has hired whom, as his investors fire him.

Mackey does make one point that is consistent with, but not supportive of, free market capitalism. He knows that shareholders own his stock voluntarily. If they don't like the policies of his company, they can always vote to change those policies with a shareholder resolution or simply sell the stock and buy that of another company more aligned with their objectives. Thus, he informs his shareholders of his objectives and lets them make a choice on which stock to buy. So far, so good.

It is also simply good business for a company to cater to its customers, train and retain its employees, build long-term positive relationships with its suppliers, and become a good citizen in its community, including performing some philanthropic activity. When Milton Friedman says a company should stay "within the rules of the game" and operate "without deception or fraud," he means it should deal with all its various constituencies properly in order to maximize long-term shareholder value. He does not mean that a company should put every last nickel on the bottom line every quarter, regardless of the long-term consequences.

My company, Cypress Semiconductor, has won the trophy for the Second Harvest Food Bank competition for the most food donated per employee in Silicon Valley for the last 13 consecutive years (1 million pounds of food in 2004). The contest creates competition among our divisions, leading to employee involvement, company food drives, internal social events with admissions "paid for" by food donations, and so forth. It is a big employee morale builder, a way to attract new employees, good P.R. for the company, and a significant benefit to the community—all of which makes Cypress a better place to work and invest in. Indeed, Mackey's own proud example of Whole Foods' community involvement programs also made a profit.

But Mackey's subordination of his profession as a businessman to altruistic ideals shows up as he attempts to negate the empirically demonstrated social benefit of "self-interest" by defining it narrowly as "increasing short-term profits." Why is it that when Whole Foods gives money to a worthy cause, it serves a high moral objective, while a company that provides a good return to small investors—who simply put their money into their own retirement funds or a children's college fund—is somehow selfish? It's the philosophy that is objectionable here, not the specific actions. If Mackey wants to run a hybrid business/charity whose mission is fully disclosed to his shareholders—and if those shareholder-owners want to support that mission—so be it. But I balk at the proposition that a company's "stakeholders" (a term often used by collectivists to justify unreasonable demands) should be allowed to control the property of the shareholders. It seems Mackey's philosophy is more accurately described by Karl Marx: "From each according to his ability" (the shareholders surrender money and assets); "to each according to his needs" (the charities, social interest groups, and environmentalists get what they want). That's not free market capitalism.

Then there is the arrogant proposition that if other corporations would simply emulate the higher corporate life form defined by Whole Foods, the world would be better off. After all, Mackey says corporations are viewed as "selfish, greedy, and uncaring." I, for one, consider free market capitalism to be a high calling, even without the infusion of altruism practiced by Whole Foods.

If one goes beyond the sensationalistic journalism surrounding the Enron-like debacles, one discovers that only about 10 to 20 public corporations have been justifiably accused of serious wrongdoing. That's about 0.1 percent of America's 17,500 public companies. What's the failure rate of the publications that demean business? (Consider the *New York Times* scandal involving manufactured stories.) What's the percentage of U.S. presidents who have been forced or almost forced from office? (It's 10 times higher than the failure rate of corporations.) What percentage of our congressmen has spent time in jail? The fact is that despite some well-publicized failures, most corporations are run with the highest ethical standards—and the public knows it. Public opinion polls demonstrate that fact by routinely ranking businessmen above journalists and politicians in esteem.

I am proud of what the semiconductor industry does—relentlessly cutting the cost of a transistor from $3 in 1960 to *three-millionths* of a dollar today. Mackey would be keeping his business records with hordes of accountants on paper ledgers if our industry didn't exist. He would have to charge his poorest customers more for their food, pay his valued employees less, and cut his philanthropy programs if the semiconductor industry had not focused so relentlessly on increasing its profits, cutting his costs in the process. Of course, if the U.S. semiconductor industry had been less cost-competitive due to its own philanthropy, the food industry simply would have bought cheaper computers made from Japanese and Korean silicon chips (which happened anyway). Layoffs in the nonunion semiconductor industry were actually good news to Whole Foods' unionized grocery store clerks. Where was Mackey's sense of altruism when unemployed semiconductor workers needed it? Of course, that rhetorical question is foolish, since he did exactly the right thing by ruthlessly reducing his recordkeeping costs so as to maximize his profits.

I am proud to be a free market capitalist. And I resent the fact that Mackey's philosophy demeans me as an egocentric child because I have refused on moral grounds to embrace the philosophies of collectivism and altruism that have caused so much human misery, however tempting the sales pitch for them sounds.

Profit Is the Means, Not End

John Mackey:

Let me begin my response to Milton Friedman by noting that he is one of my personal heroes. His contributions to economic thought and the fight for freedom are without parallel, and it is an honor to have him critique my article.

Friedman says "the differences between John Mackey and me regarding the social responsibility of business are for the most part rhetorical." But are we essentially in agreement? I don't think so. We are thinking about business in entirely different ways.

Friedman is thinking only in terms of maximizing profits for the investors. If putting customers first helps maximize profits for the investors, then it is acceptable. If some corporate philanthropy creates goodwill and helps a company "cloak" its self-interested goals of maximizing profits, then it is acceptable (although Friedman also believes it is "hypocritical"). In contrast to Friedman, I do not believe maximizing profits for the investors is the only acceptable justification for all corporate actions. The investors are not the only people who matter. Corporations can exist for purposes other than simply maximizing profits.

As for who decides what the purpose of any particular business is, I made an important argument that Friedman doesn't address: "I believe the entrepreneurs, not the current investors in a company's stock, have the right and responsibility to define the purpose of the company." Whole Foods Market was not created solely to maximize profits for its investors, but to create value for all of its stakeholders. I believe there are thousands of other businesses similar to Whole Foods (Medtronic, REI, and Starbucks, for example) that were created by entrepreneurs with goals beyond maximizing profits, and that these goals are neither "hypocritical" nor "cloaking devices" but are intrinsic to the purpose of the business.

I will concede that many other businesses, such as T.J. Rodgers' Cypress Semiconductor, have been created by entrepreneurs whose sole purpose for the business is to maximize profits for their investors. Does Cypress therefore have any social responsibility besides maximizing profits if it follows the laws of society? No, it doesn't. Rodgers apparently created it to maximize profits, and therefore all of Friedman's arguments about business social responsibility become completely valid. Business social responsibility should not be coerced; it is a voluntary decision that the entrepreneurial leadership of every company must make on its own. Friedman is right to argue that profit making is intrinsically valuable for society, but I believe he is mistaken that all businesses have only this purpose.

While Friedman believes that taking care of customers, employees, and business philanthropy are means to the end of increasing investor profits, I take the exact opposite view: Making high profits is the means to the end of fulfilling Whole Foods' core business mission. We want to improve the health and well-being of everyone on the planet through higher-quality foods and better nutrition, and we can't fulfill this mission unless we are highly profitable. High profits are necessary to fuel our growth across the United States and the world. Just as people cannot live without eating, so a business cannot live without profits. But most people don't live to eat, and neither must businesses live just to make profits.

Toward the end of his critique Friedman says his statement that "the social responsibility of business [is] to increase its profits" and my statement that "the enlightened corporation should try to create value for all of its constituencies" are "equivalent." He argues that maximizing profits is a private end achieved through social means because it supports a society based on private property and free markets. If our two statements are equivalent, if we really mean the same thing, then I know which statement has the superior "marketing power." Mine does.

Both capitalism and corporations are misunderstood, mistrusted, and disliked around the world because of statements like Friedman's on social responsibility. His comment is used by the enemies of capitalism to argue that capitalism is greedy, selfish, and uncaring. It is right up there with William Vanderbilt's "the public be damned" and former G.M. Chairman Charlie Wilson's declaration that "what's good for the country is good for General Motors, and vice versa." If we are truly interested in spreading capitalism throughout the world (I certainly am), we need to do a better job marketing it. I believe if economists and businesspeople consistently communicated and acted on my message that "the enlightened corporation should try to create value for all of its constituencies," we would see most of the resistance to capitalism disappear.

Friedman also understands that Whole Foods makes an important contribution to society besides simply maximizing profits for our investors, which is to "enhance the pleasure of shopping for food." This is why we put "satisfying and delighting our customers" as a core value whenever we talk about the purpose of our business. Why don't Friedman and other economists consistently teach this idea? Why don't they talk more about all the valuable contributions that business makes in creating value for its customers, for its employees, and for its communities? Why talk only about maximizing profits for the investors? Doing so harms the brand of capitalism.

As for Whole Foods' philanthropy, who does have "special competence" in this area? Does the government? Do individuals? Libertarians generally would agree that most bureaucratic government solutions to social problems cause more harm than good and that government help is seldom the answer. Neither do individuals have any special competence in charity. By Friedman's logic, individuals shouldn't donate any money to help others but should instead keep all their money invested in businesses, where it will create more social value.

The truth is that there is no way to calculate whether money invested in business or money invested in helping to solve social problems will create more value. Businesses exist within real communities and have real effects, both good and bad, on those communities. Like individuals living in communities, businesses make valuable social contributions by providing goods and services and employment. But just as individuals can feel a responsibility to provide some philanthropic support for the communities in which they live, so too can a business. The responsibility of business toward the community is not infinite, but neither is it zero. Each enlightened business must find the proper balance between all of its constituencies: customers, employees, investors, suppliers, and communities.

While I respect Milton Friedman's thoughtful response, I do not feel the same way about T.J. Rodgers' critique. It is obvious to me that Rodgers didn't carefully read my article, think deeply about my arguments, or attempt to craft an intelligent response. Instead he launches various ad hominem attacks on me, my company, and our customers. According to Rodgers, my business philosophy is similar to those of Ralph Nader and Karl Marx; Whole Foods Market and our customers are a bunch of Luddites engaging in junk science and fear mongering; and our unionized grocery clerks don't care about layoffs of workers in Rodgers' own semiconductor industry.

For the record: I don't agree with the philosophies of Ralph Nader or Karl Marx; Whole Foods Market doesn't engage in junk science or fear mongering, and neither do 99 percent of our customers or vendors; and of Whole Foods' 36,000 employees, exactly zero of them belong to unions, and we are in fact sorry about layoffs in his industry.

When Rodgers isn't engaging in ad hominem attacks, he seems to be arguing against a leftist, socialist, and collectivist perspective that may exist in his own mind but does not appear in my article. Contrary to Rodgers' claim, Whole Foods is running not a "hybrid business/charity" but an enormously profitable business that has created tremendous shareholder value.

Of all the food retailers in the *Fortune* 500 (including Wal-Mart), we have the highest profits as a percentage of sales, as well as the highest return on invested capital, sales per square foot, same-store sales, and growth rate. We are currently doubling in size every three and a half years. The bottom line is that Whole Foods stakeholder business philosophy works and has produced tremendous value for all of our stakeholders, including our investors.

In contrast, Cypress Semiconductor has struggled to be profitable for many years now, and their balance sheet shows negative retained earnings of over $408 million. This means that in its entire 23-year history, Cypress has lost far more money for its investors than it has made. Instead of calling my business philosophy Marxist, perhaps it is time for Rodgers to rethink his own.

Rodgers says with passion, "I am proud of what the semiconductor industry does—relentlessly cutting the cost of a transistor from $3 in 1960 to *three-millionths* of a dollar today." Rodgers is entitled to be proud. What a wonderful accomplishment this is, and the semiconductor industry has indeed made all our lives better. Then why not consistently communicate this message as the purpose of his business, instead of talking all the time about maximizing profits and shareholder value? Like medicine, law, and education, business has noble purposes: to provide goods and services that improve its customers' lives, to provide jobs and meaningful work for employees, to create wealth and prosperity for its investors, and to be a responsible and caring citizen.

Businesses such as Whole Foods have multiple stakeholders and therefore have multiple responsibilities. But the fact that we have responsibilities to stakeholders besides investors does not give those other stakeholders any "property rights" in the company, contrary to Rodgers' fears. The investors still own the business, are entitled to the residual profits, and can fire the management if they wish. A doctor has an ethical responsibility to try to heal her patients, but that responsibility doesn't mean her patients are entitled to receive a share of the profits from her practice.

Rodgers probably will never agree with my business philosophy, but it doesn't really matter. The ideas I'm articulating result in a more robust business model than the profit-maximization model that it competes against, because they encourage and tap into more powerful motivations than self-interest alone. These ideas will triumph over time, not by persuading intellectuals and economists through argument but by winning the competitive test of the marketplace. Someday businesses like Whole Foods, which adhere to a stakeholder model of deeper business purpose, will dominate the economic landscape. Wait and see.

Source: Copyright © Reason Magazine, http://www.reason.com/0510/fe.mf.rethinking. shtml, October 2005. Reprinted by permission.

Reading **5-2**

Why Should Corporate Responsibility Be Altruistic?

Andrew Kluth

For a business to commit money on an indefinite basis to activities that may have no direct material relationship to business operations at best is questionable and at worst destroys shareholder value.

For outsiders who want nonfinancial measures to be part of core business and therefore sustainable, altruism fails, as it cannot ensure commitment to corporate responsibility from a company through good and bad times.

Consider two companies. One defines itself by its embracing of corporate responsibility to its fullest in all that it does. It goes beyond either what law requires or what its stakeholders ask. It encourages staff to volunteer in community activities on company time. It sources raw materials for its products and services from sustainable, ethical, fair trade and organic sources whenever possible. It contributes a significant proportion of its profits to good causes.

It charges a premium for its products and services and investors know that they will get a lower-than-market return on their investment. The company does not justify these activities in business terms: they are simply "the right thing to do." The company publishes regular and detailed reports of its work and uses these activities as a differentiator in the marketplace. The company does not recognize collective bargaining, preferring instead a flat organizational structure where decisions are consulted throughout the workforce. While major decisions take time, they are achieved by consensus even when this may result in a less than optimal solution in pure business terms.

This company does not pay its senior managers full market rates. It states publicly that its people are motivated by more than money. It had no difficulty attracting keen young talent in its early development and grew rapidly at first. However, it has stalled in its efforts to increase market share. Market surveys suggest that a large number of people support the aims of the company but cannot or will not pay the high prices demanded by the company for its products and services.

The second company, like the first, adopts rigorous health, safety and environmental management systems that are externally audited and verified. But it only does so when it deems them to meet a regulatory, client or business need. It has a well-developed industrial relations process. It either demands verifiably robust performance from key (but not necessarily all) suppliers, or else conducts its own limited supply-chain audits.

The company measures and incentivises executives on regulatory compliance and quantified indicators, and rewards them well when they achieve. It runs community involvement schemes, but these are part of its business development, and are only done when marketing opportunities are available. The company is clear that it will not undertake any corporate-responsibility-related activities unless these have been justified on a cost-benefit analysis.

The analysis is risk and value based. Benefits that are implicit but cannot be quantified, such as share price impacts, are routinely discarded from the analysis. The firm charges competitive prices and is seen as a legally compliant, highly commercial, but fair organization. It lobbies for progressive health, safety, environment, employment, and company laws, but only when they work to its advantage in the marketplace. It does not publicize its activities as corporate responsibility but publishes analyses as part of its yearly reporting cycle with business justifications for why it is doing some things and not others.

Now consider which of these two companies is better able to claim that corporate responsibility is an integral part of its business. Which one is more likely to have sustained profit growth; to deliver consistently on its stated targets through good and bad times; to continue to pursue its activities when senior personnel change? Which one is more likely to convince its peer group, supply chain and other stakeholders that it has a credible, sustainable and profitable model?

The first company is vulnerable, because it does things without sound business reasons. It has not defined clearly where its business as a business ends. Its unbridled altruism makes it weak.

The second company, the hard-nosed, business-focused organization, is the more credible. It is the one more likely to create real corporate-responsibility benefits over an extended period. So: why should corporate responsibility be altruistic?

Source: Copyright © Andrew Kluth. Reprinted by permission of the author.

Reading **5-3**

Does It Pay to Be Good?

A.J. Vogl

Yes, say advocates of corporate citizen, who believe their time has come—finally.

Corporate citizenship: For believers, the words speak of the dawning of a new era of capitalism, when business, government, and citizen groups join forces for the greater good, to jointly tackle such problems as water shortages and air pollution, to do something about the 1.2 billion people who live on less than a dollar a day.

Corporate citizenship: For critics of today's capitalism, the words smack of hypocrisy, big business's cynical response to charges of greed and corruption in high places, intended to mollify those who say corporations have too much power and that they wield it shamelessly. Critics charge that corporate citizenship is a placebo to the enemies of globalization, a public-relations smoke screen, capitalism's last-ditch attempt to preserve itself by co-opting its opposition.

Corporate citizenship: For many, it remains a diffuse concept, but generally it speaks to companies voluntarily adopting a triple bottom line, one that takes into account social, economic, and environmental considerations as well as financial results. Though some associate corporate citizenship with charity and philanthropy, the concept goes further—it embraces a corporate conscience above and beyond profits and markets. David Vidal, who directs research in global corporate citizenship at The Conference Board, comments, "Citizenship is not, as some critics charge, window dressing for the corporation. It deals with primary business relationships that are part of a company's strategic vision, and a good business case can be made for corporate citizenship."

Whether you are a critic or believer, however, there is no question that corporate citizenship—a term that embraces corporate social responsibility (CSR) and sustainability— is no longer a concept fostered by idealists on the fringe. It has entered the mainstream.

* * * *

No Good Deed Goes Unpunished

As necessary as corporate citizenship may be, it still faces challenges from both inside and outside the corner office. Perhaps the most disheartening of these hurdles is that the most prominent corporate citizens rarely receive rewards commensurate with their prominence. As Hilton and Giles Gibbons, co-authors of the pro-CSR *Good Business: Your World Needs You,* point out, "Curiously, the companies whose hearts are most visibly fixed to their pinstriped sleeves tend to be the ones that attract the most frequent and venomous attacks from anti-business critics." Is this because critics feel that devious agendas lie behind the enlightened policies? Noreena Hertz, a British critic of corporate citizenship, wonders whether Microsoft, by putting computers in schools today, will determine how children learn tomorrow.

Is it that corporations haven't gotten their stories across properly, or that they have—and are still being vilified? The experience of McDonald's in this arena is revealing. In 2002, the fast-food chain published its first social-responsibility report, composed of 46 pages summarizing its efforts in four categories: community, environment, people, and marketplace. The efforts that went into that report were rewarded in some courts of public opinion: In 2000 and 2001 *Financial Times*/PricewaterhouseCoopers surveys of media and NGOs, McDonald's placed 14th among the world's most respected companies for environmental performance.

At the same time, few corporations have been attacked as savagely as McDonald's for its "citizenship." It has been portrayed as an omnivorous monster that destroys local businesses and culture, promotes obesity, treats its employees badly, and despoils the environment. McDonald's goes to great lengths to answer these charges in its social-responsibility report—which was itself widely criticized—but, like Nike, it can't help looking defensive. It will take a great deal more than a report of its good works to diminish the Golden Arches as a symbol of "capitalist imperialism" in the eyes of anti-globalists or to stanch the vitriol on such websites as Mcspotlight.

There's no question that the bar is set exceedingly high in the arena of corporate social involvement. Philip Morris Cos. spends more than $100 million a year, most conspicuously in a series of TV commercials, on measures to discourage underage smoking—and still critics charge that the Philip Morris campaign is a cynical PR stunt that actually encourages kids to smoke. The company has been accused of having "a profound conflict of interest that cannot be overcome."

Another tobacco company, BAT, the world's second-largest, put some members of the social-responsibility establishment in an uncomfortable position when, last July, it became the industry's first company to publish a social-responsibility report. Few knew what to think upon reading the tobacco company's blunt rhetoric—"[T]here is no such thing as a 'safe' cigarette . . . We openly state that, put simply, smoking is a cause of certain serious diseases" and the 18 pages devoted to the risks of smoking. BAT even had its report audited by an independent verifier. All this wasn't nearly enough to satisfy antismoking groups, of course—they continue to view the company with deep suspicion. Would anyone have predicted otherwise?

When accused of being overly suspicious, critics point to one company that, over the last six years, won numerous awards for its environmental, human rights, anti-corruption, anti-bribery, and climate-change policies; a company prominent on "most admired" and "best companies to work for" lists; a company that issued a report on the good deeds that supported its claim to be a top corporate citizen. That company was Enron.

No one would argue that Enron is typical, yet its debacle has tainted other companies. It also raises a difficult question about CSR: What is the link between how a company is managed—corporate governance—and corporate citizenship? Steve Hilton, speaking from London, says that the link is not really understood in the United Kingdom: "People here have not made the connection between the corporate governance, executive-compensation, and accounting-fraud issues in the United States and operational issues that come under the heading of corporate citizenship. I would argue they're all part of the same thing."

So would Transparency International's Frank Vogl, co-founder of the anti-corruption NGO. He believes that CSR has been undermined because it has been disconnected from corporate conduct issues. "Foreign public trust in Corporate America has been diminished," he said, "and there is scant evidence that U.S. business leaders recognize the global impact of the U.S. scandals."

Vogl says that, for most countries in the world, corruption is much more of a social-responsibility issue than either the environment or labor rights. "What U.S. businesspeople see as a facilitating payment may be seen in developing countries as a bribe," he comments, "and I think that provides some insight into why the United States ranks behind 12 other countries on the Transparency International Bribe Payers Index. To me, corporate citizenship means you don't bribe foreign officials. That's the worst kind of hypocrisy."

Will They Be Good in Bad Times?

The specter of hypocrisy raises its head in another quarter as well: Do employees of companies claiming to be good corporate citizens see their employer's citizenship activities as a diversion or cover-up to charges of bad leadership and poor management practices? Certainly, if recent surveys are a guide, top management needs to restore its credibility with employees. In a recent Mercer Human Resource Consulting study, only a third of the 2,600 workers surveyed agreed with the statement, "I can trust management in my organization to always communicate honestly." And a Walker Information survey of employees found that only 49 percent believe their senior leaders to be "people of high personal integrity." If CSR is perceived by employees merely as puffery to make top management look good, it will not get under an organization's cultural skin.

Even if there is a genuine management commitment, corporations have other obligations that may take precedence, begging the question: Will corporations be good citizens in bad times as well as good? The experience of Ford Motor Co. brings the question to earth. In August, Ford issued its third annual corporate-citizenship report. Previous reports had drawn plaudits from environmentalists, but this one, coming at a time when the automaker faced financial difficulties, was attacked by the same environmentalists for failing to set aggressive goals for reducing greenhouse-gas emissions or improving gas mileage. Sierra Club's executive director called it "a giant step in the wrong direction for Ford Motor Co., for American consumers, and for the environment."

Lingering tough economic conditions may impel other companies to take their own "giant steps" backward. An old business saw has it that when times get tough and cuts have to be made, certain budgets are at the top of the list for cutbacks—advertising for one, public relations for another. For companies in which corporate citizenship is seen as an extension of public relations, of "image building" or "reputation management," it may suffer this fate.

Which is as it should be, say some critics. As *The Wall Street Journal* lectured CEO William Ford on its editorial page: "We also hope Mr. Ford has learned from his mistake of ceding the moral and political high ground to environmentalists . . . Businesses needn't apologize for making products that other Americans want to buy. Their first obligation is to their shareholders and employees and that means above all making an honest profit."

Does the "Business Case" Really Have a Case?

But hold on: What about the so-called business case for corporate citizenship—that it contributes to making "an honest profit"? Unfortunately, it's difficult to quantify in cost-benefit terms what that contribution is. Not something to be concerned about, says Simon Zadek, CEO of AccountAbility, a London-based institute that has established CSR verification standards. "It is a fact that the vast majority of day-to-day business decisions are taken without any explicit cost-benefit analysis," he says, pointing to employee training as an example of a corporate expenditure that is difficult to quantify in cost-benefit terms. What he doesn't mention is that, when business is suffering, training is usually among the expenditures to be cut back or eliminated.

Ultimately, Zadek concedes that, in strictly quantifiable terms, one cannot make a cost-benefit case for corporate citizenship. "Although the question 'Does corporate citizenship pay?' is technically right, it is misleading in practice," he says. "Rephrasing the core question as 'In what ways does corporate citizenship contribute to achieving the core business strategy?' is far preferable."

To some hardheaded corporate types, Zadek's reasoning may seem disingenuous, but even the hardheads can't be dismissive—at least publicly. Moreover, they would probably acknowledge that corporate citizenship, in concept and practice, has come too far to be ignored.

In the future, it may well become what Steve Hilton calls a "hygiene factor," a condition of doing business. Hilton's firm, Good Business, consults with firms on citizenship issues. "I think business leaders are coming to realize CSR's potential to go beyond a compliance/risk-management issue into a genuine business tool," he says. "That's been the rhetoric all along, but the reality has been that it's been a slightly marginal issue. With few exceptions, it's been seen as an add-on, without being incorporated into core business decision making."

This is Zadek's point when he argues the case for what he calls "third-generation corporate citizenship." The first generation is defined by cause-related marketing and short-term reputation management.

The second occurs when social and environmental objectives become a core part of long-term business strategy; as an example, he points to automakers competing in the arena of emission controls. The third generation is based on collective action, where corporations join with competitors, NGOs, and government "to change the underlying rules of the game to ensure that business delivers adequate social and environmental results."

Changing the rules means, for one thing, a more level playing field. "In CSR," says AccountAbility COO Mike Peirce, "companies that are leaders might suffer a penalty if there's a big gap between themselves and laggards in the field, so they'd like everybody ticking along at at least a basic level." In other words, a socially responsible company does not want to be penalized financially for being socially responsible. Of course, a cynic might reply that if CSR indeed provides the competitive advantage that its proponents insist it does, then it is the laggards that should suffer the severest financial penalty.

To convince doubters, efforts are being made to schematically quantify corporate social responsibility. In a recent *Harvard Business* Review article titled "The Virtue Matrix: Calculating the Return on Corporate Responsibility," Roger L. Martin makes a point of treating corporate responsibility as a product or service like any other.

According to Martin, who is dean of the University of Toronto's Rotman School of Management, his matrix can help companies sort out such questions as whether a citizenship initiative will erode a company's competitive position.

Even if Martin's formula seems overly clinical, it supports the trend toward closer analysis of what social responsibility means and what it brings to corporations practicing it. But analysis will take you only so far. "[I]t is impossible to prove the direction of the flow of causality," writes Chad Holliday, chairman and CEO of DuPont and co-author of *Walking the Talk: The Business Case for Sustainable Development*. "Does a company become profitable and thus enjoy the luxury of being able to worry about environmental and social issues or does the pursuit of sustainability make a company more profitable?"

But for large public companies, the question of whether it truly pays to be good will be asked less and less; for them, it will be necessary to be good, if only to avoid appearing Neanderthal. That means that corporate social responsibility, itself nothing less than a growth industry today, will become "normalized" into corporate cultures.

Yes, there will be an effort to level the playing field in CSR, but, further, expect citizenship proponents to attempt to raise the field to a higher level by making corporate governance itself the issue. "Unless we make basic structural changes," says Marjorie Kelly, the editor of *Business Ethics* magazine and a frequent critic of CSR, "it'll be nothing but window dressing. The corporate scandals have given a real-world demonstration that business without ethics collapses, and that has given us an extraordinary opportunity to change the way we do business."

Investors Are Listening

For companies in sectors not considered exemplars of corporate citizenship—munitions, pornography, gambling, and tobacco (yes); liquor (probably); and oil (maybe)—there's good news: The market hasn't penalized them for their supposed lack of citizenship. For companies at the opposite end of the spectrum, there's also good news: Investors haven't penalized them for their expenditures on social causes.

On balance, the better news is for the socially responsible companies, who have long labored under the assumption that the investor automatically pays a price for investing in a socially responsible company or mutual fund—the price, of course, being a company or fund that doesn't perform as well as its peers that don't fly the socially responsible banner.

Investors appear to be listening. According to Financial Research Corp., investors added $1.29 billion of new money into socially responsible funds during the first half of 2002, compared to $847.1 million added during all of 2001. Over the year ending July 31, the average mutual fund—including stock, bond, and balanced funds—was down 13 percent, while comparable socially responsible funds were down 19 percent. But advocates point out that different indices—particularly the Domini Social Index, a capitalization-weighted market index of 400 common stocks screened according to social and environmental criteria, and the Citizen's Index, a market-weighted portfolio of common stocks representing ownership in 300 of the most socially responsible U.S. companies—have outperformed the S&P 500 over the last one, three, and five years.

While the $13 billion invested in socially responsible funds (according to Morningstar) comprises only about 2 percent of total fund assets, advocates expect this percentage to climb to 10 percent by 2012, says Barbara Krumsiek, chief executive of the Bethesda, Md.–based Calvert Group, a mutual-fund complex specializing in socially responsible investing. And others' tallies are far higher: The nonprofit Social Investment Forum counts more than $2 trillion in total assets under management in portfolios screened for socially concerned investors, including socially screened mutual funds and separate accounts managed for socially conscious institutions and individual investors.

Plus, recent corporate scandals may have raised many investors' consciousness: In the first half of 2002, socially responsible mutual funds saw their assets increase by 3 percent, while conventional diversified funds lost 9.5 percent in total assets. People may have decided that if their mutual-fund investments were going to lose money, it might as well be for a good cause.

* * * *

Attacked from All Sides

While many skeptics criticize the ways in which corporate social responsibility is enacted, some take matters a step further by asking if the concept should exist at all. Who would object to the idea of a company doing good, of moving beyond the traditional and literal bottom line, to take a larger view of the reason for its existence? You may be surprised: There are many critics, and they come from various and sometimes unpredictable directions.

First is a group that says corporate social responsibility is flawed at its heart because it's doing the right thing for the wrong reason. The right thing, they believe, is doing the right thing because it is right, as a matter of principle—not because it advances the firm's business interests. The rejoinder, of course, is that if a larger social or environmental good is met, we should not quibble about motivation. As corporate-governance activist Robert A.G. Monks points out: "You can get backing from institutional investors only if you talk a commercial idiom."

Next is a group of dissimilar critics who believe that, in attempting to pursue goals of corporate citizenship, companies are doing things that are none of their business. Paradoxically, these critics come from both the right and the left.

The right feels that the business of business should be business: As Michael Prowse argues in the *Financial Times,* the role of the corporation "is to provide individuals with the means to be socially responsible. Rather than trying to play the role of social worker, senior executives should concentrate on their statutory obligations. We should not expect benevolence of them, but we should demand probity: the socially responsible chief executive is the one who turns a profit without lying, cheating, robbing or defrauding anyone."

The left, on the other hand, feels that corporations are usurping the powers of government, to the detriment of the citizenry and democracy itself. Noreena Hertz, the British academic and broadcaster who wrote *The Silent Takeover: Global Capitalism and the Death of Democracy,* is not only dubious about business taking over responsibilities that she feels properly belong to government—she is skeptical about business's ability to handle them: "[M]anagers of multinationals operating in the third world are often overwhelmed by the social problems they encounter, and understandably find it difficult to know which causes to prioritize . . . Their contributions can be squandered, or diverted through corruption."

And what happens, she asks, when a corporation decides to pull out, if government has allowed private industry to take over its role? Worse still, she worries about situations in which a socially responsible corporation could use its position "to exact a stream of IOUs and quid pro quos, to demand ever more favorable terms and concessions from host governments."

Then there is a group of critics who see corporate citizenship as a diversionary ploy to placate a public outraged at dubious corporate practices. They will concede that Enron, WorldCom, and Tyco are egregious exceptions, but are other companies exemplars of probity? Hardly. Can companies be considered good corporate citizens when they move their headquarters to Bermuda to avoid taxes (and enrich their CEOs in the process)? Can companies like General Electric, Monsanto, Merck, SmithKline Beecham, and Chiquita Brands International claim the moral high ground when they have cut employee benefits in connection with mergers and spin-offs? And what of such companies as Wyeth, Wal-Mart, McKesson, and Merrill Lynch? Can they, ask the critics, be considered high-minded citizens when the top executives accumulate pots of money in their deferred-compensation accounts? This may be why PR eminence grise John Budd says, "For at least the next 18 post-Enron months, I certainly would not counsel any CEO to magically appear publicly as an enlightened champion of social responsibility. The circumstances make it automatic that it would be perceived as spinning."

Last, there is a group of critics that says that simply doing more good than we're doing now is not enough, that we have to rethink the nature of the beast—capitalism itself. Steven Piersanti, president of BerrettKoehler Publishers, is in the thick of this intellectual contretemps. Last fall, his firm published two books that took divergent views on the issue. The first, *Walking the Talk,* was written by Swiss industrialist Stephan Schmidheiny, along with two colleagues at the World Business Council for Sustainable Development, Chad Holliday of DuPont and Philip Watts of Royal Dutch/Shell. "It advances a reformist view that major changes are needed in our business world," says Piersanti, "but that these changes can best be achieved by reforms within our existing economic structures, institutions, and systems."

The second book, *Alternatives to Economic Globalization: A Better World Is Possible,* presents "an activist view that existing economic structures are insufficient and that new structures, institutions, and systems are needed in the world."

It's likely that doubts about the nature and purpose of corporate citizenship will continue to be raised from all quarters. But with social-responsibility reporting and verification initiatives in place and likely government regulation down the road, there's reason to think that their voices will become more isolated.

Source: *Across the Board*, vol. 40, no. 1 (January/February 2003): pp. 16–23. Copyright © 2003 by *Across the Board*. Reprinted with permission of the publisher, currently published as *The Conference Board Review*.

6

Ethical Decision Making: Employer Responsibilities and Employee Rights

We can invest all the money on Wall Street in new technologies, but we can't realize the benefits of improved productivity until companies rediscover the value of human loyalty.

Frederick Reichheld, Director, Bain & Co.

In 2003, clothing retailer Abercrombie & Fitch (A&F) was sued by current and past members of its sales force, as well as people who were denied jobs, claiming racial discrimination. The plaintiffs, in a class action lawsuit that grew to include 10,000 claimants, alleged that A&F favored whites in a variety of ways in order to project an image of the "classic American" look. This theme evolved from A&F's origins as the store that clothed both Theodore Roosevelt and Ernest Hemingway. Plaintiffs alleged that people of color were discouraged from applying for positions visible to the public and were instead steered to stockroom jobs. Managers were aware that they were going to be judged on whether their workforce fit the A&F image.

The suit was eventually settled in 2005 for $40 million (you'll find the details in the resolution at the end of this chapter), providing at least some evidence of a lack of diversity in the retailer's operation.

You might find this lack of diversity relevant as you consider some decisions A&F made in 2002, before the lawsuit was filed. A&F opted to produce a line of T-shirts designed to poke fun at particular ethnic groups. One of the shirts advertised the Wong Brothers Laundry Service and had images of two smiling men with bamboo rice-paddy hats, along with a motto, "Two Wongs Can Make it White."

Other shirts contained the following statements:

"Pizza Dojo: Eat in or wok out. You love long time."

"Wok-n-Bowl: Chinese food and bowl."

"Buddha Bash: Get your Buddha on the floor."

Images of the shirts can be viewed at http://www.sfgate.com/cgi-bin/object/article?f=/c/a/2002/04/18/MN109646.DTL&o=0 or at http://www.geocities.com/tarorg/shirts.html.

After protests from Asian-American groups, among others, and negative mail, company spokesman Hampton Carney responded, "We thought everyone would like these T-shirts. We're very, very, very sorry. It's never been our intention to offend anyone. The thought was that everyone would love them, especially the Asian community. We thought they were cheeky, irreverent and funny and everyone would love them. But that has not been the case."

- Do you see a connection between the subject of the lawsuit discussed above and the choices made for the T-shirt line?
- Do you feel that Abercrombie & Fitch did anything wrong in choosing to sell these T-shirts that would justify the protests and negative attention? What are the key facts relevant to your determination?
- What are the ethical issues involved in your decision?
- Who are the stakeholders in this scenario? Are the stakeholders' rights abridged? In what way?
- Even if you answer no to the first question above, evidently certain stakeholders believed that Abercrombie & Fitch acted inappropriately. Other than not selling the shirts at all, is there any other way to have prevented this from happening in the first place? What alternatives were originally available to the retailer? How would each of these new alternatives have affected each of the stakeholders you have identified?

(continued)

- As it moves forward from this point, what alternatives now exist for Abercrombie & Fitch to heal relationships with its stakeholders? What recommendations would you offer to Abercrombie & Fitch?

 ## Chapter Objectives

After reading this chapter, you will be able to:

1. Discuss the two distinct perspectives on the ethics of workplace relationships.
2. Explain the concept of due process in the workplace.
3. Define "employment at will" (EAW) and its ethical rationale.
4. Describe the costs of an EAW environment.
5. Explain how due process relates to performance appraisals.
6. Discuss whether it is possible to downsize in an ethical manner.
7. Explain the difference between intrinsic and instrumental value in terms of health and safety.
8. Describe the "acceptable risk" approach to health and safety in the workplace.
9. Describe the nature of an employer's responsibility with regard to employee health and safety and why the market is not the most effective arbiter of this responsibility.
10. Explain the basic arguments for and against regulation of the global labor environment.
11. Describe the argument for a market-based resolution to workplace discrimination.
12. Define diversity as it applies to the workplace.
13. Explain the benefits and challenges of diversity for the workplace.
14. Define affirmative action and explain the three ways in which affirmative action may be legally permissible.
15. Articulate the basic guidelines for affirmative action programs.

Introduction

Ethics in the employment context is perhaps the most universal topic in business ethics since nearly every person will have the experience of being employed. While legislators and the courts have addressed many aspects of the working environment, countless ethical issues remain that these regulatory and judicial bodies have left unresolved. The law provides guidance for thinking about ethical issues in the workplace, but such issues go well beyond legal considerations.

This chapter explores those areas of ethical decision making in the workplace where the law remains relatively fluid and where answers are not easily found by

Reality Check *Protecting Employee Rights through Unions*

In 1960, about one-third of the American workforce was represented by unions. Today, that figure is about 11 percent. Collective bargaining, established to protect the interests of workers, has led to some disappointments. Not surprisingly, federal and state regulations governing work practices have exploded as union membership has declined. The variety of protections is prodigious: anti-discrimination laws, wage and hour laws, worker safety laws, unemployment compensation, workers' compensation, and social security, to name a few.

simply calling the company lawyer. Issues may also arise where the law does seem clear but, for one reason or another, it is insufficient to protect the interests of all stakeholders. We will examine various ethical challenges that face the employee, whether a worker on an assembly line, the manager of a restaurant, or the CEO of a large corporation, and the nature of employer responsibilities. While individual perspectives may change, similar conflicts and stakeholders present themselves across business settings.

As you examine each issue raised in this chapter, consider how you might employ the ethical decision-making process we have discussed to reach the best possible conclusion for the stakeholders involved. Severe time constraints, limited information, and pressure usually accompany these challenging business decisions. However, though using the ethical decision-making process may seem cumbersome at the outset, once the process becomes embedded in the professional landscape and culture, its effectiveness and efficiency in resolving these issues will become apparent. In fact, utilizing an ethical decision-making process will avoid later hurdles, thus removing barriers to progress and momentum. Let us consider the issues that exist in the current workplace environment to test the effectiveness of the ethical decision-making process.

Ethical Issues in the Workplace: The Current Environment

We all have decisions to make about how we will treat others in the workplace and how we will ask to be treated. Ethics at work and in human resource management is about our relationships with others and with our organizations. Research demonstrates that "companies that place employees at the core of their strategies produce higher long-term returns to shareholders than do industry peers."[1]

The same holds true for interpersonal relationships. Notwithstanding these truths, less than half of U.S. workers feel a strong personal attachment to their organization or believe that the organization deserves their loyalty. Only one in four workers is truly loyal to their place of work. When asked about the greatest influence on their commitment, workers responded that the most important factor is fairness at work, followed by care and concern for employees—all key components of an ethical working environment.

Reality Check *Sears and Emotions*

Sears put the role of emotion in the workplace to the test when it asked its workers what is important to them. This is a sensitive question because, if a firm asks and then does not respond to those areas of importance, it is effectively ignoring the priorities of its workers. Sears did ask, though, and learned a great deal. The most important job factors to Sears employees include these:

- Whether they like their work.
- Whether their work gives them a sense of accomplishment.
- Whether they are proud to say they work at Sears.

- Their workload.
- Their working conditions.
- Their treatment by supervisors.
- Their optimism about the future of the company.
- Whether they feel Sears is competing effectively.
- Whether they understand the company's business strategy.
- Whether they see a connection between their work and the company's objectives.

Source: *Workforce Online*, "What's Most Important to Employees," http://workforceonline.com/sears/attitude.html (1999).

These observations call attention to the fact that there are two very distinct, and sometimes competing, perspectives on the ethics of workplace relationships. On one hand, employers might decide to treat employees well as a means to produce greater workplace harmony and productivity. (This consequentialist approach could be reminiscent of the utilitarian ethics discussed in Chapter 3 if couched in terms of the creation of a better workplace for all, though it also raises a question about moral motivation and instrumentalist, self-interested reasons for doing good that is similar to our discussion of corporate social responsibility in Chapter 5.) A comprehensive review of research by Jeffrey Pfeffer suggests that effective firms are characterized by a set of common practices, all of which involve treating employees in humane and respectful ways.[2]

OBJECTIVE

As an example of these concerns, consider the role of emotion in the workplace. Though it is a relatively new area of research, studies suggest that managers can have a significant impact on the emotions of their workers, and this impact can greatly affect productivity and loyalty, as well as perceptions of fairness, care, and concern. Scholars Neal Ashkanasy and Catherine Daus suggest that managers should pay attention to the emotional impact of various jobs within their workplace and model a positive emotional environment.[3]

Rewards and compensation structures can clearly impact the emotions of workers, as can the composition of teams or the power relationships within a workplace. Consider how Sears explored emotions in its workplace in the Reality Check on this page.

When employees see that a firm values their emotions, as well as exhibits values such as honesty, respect, and trust, they feel less pressure, more valued as employees, and more satisfied with their organizations. Since reporting to external stakeholders has become such a key issue in recent scandals, one might also want to consider whether a more satisfied employee is more or less likely to report misconduct to outside parties.

On the other hand, of course, employers might treat employees well out of a Kantian sense of duty and rights, regardless of the either utilitarian or self-interested productivity consequences. This deontological approach emphasizes the rights and duties of all employees, and treating employees well simply because "it is the right thing to do." Defenders of employee rights argue that rights should protect important employee interests from being constantly subjected to utilitarian and financial calculations. This sense of duty might stem from the law, professional codes of conduct, corporate codes of conduct, or such moral principles as fairness, justice, or human rights on the part of the organization's leadership.

Defining the Parameters of the Employment Relationship

The following section will explore the legal and ethical boundaries that will help us define the employment relationship based on some of the principles discussed above. "Employment," *per se,* implicates ethical issues because of the very nature of the relationship it implies. Consider the situation in which an individual agrees to work for another individual. This arrangement raises issues of power, obligation, responsibility, fair treatment, and expectations. In many circumstances, the livelihoods of both parties rely on each other's contributions to the relationship! Though legal requirements might serve to protect some interests, they can only go so far and cover so many bases. We will begin by looking to the ethics underlying the concepts of due process and fairness that help determine what is or is not acceptable behavior in the workplace. We will discover some of the ways in which employers might be able to remain true to these principles, even when specifically challenged by vexing circumstances such as a reduction in force. The relationship is further defined by the application of these principles to working conditions such as health and safety, both in domestic operations and abroad.

Note that the issues in the following sections are predominantly settled from an ethical perspective by their *justification.* In other words, people of goodwill would be likely to agree that an employee has a right to a safe and healthy workplace, for example. Disagreements do remain in discussions surrounding the implementation, interpretation, or extent of that right. In contrast, the second section of this chapter explores several issues that are not perceived as settled from either a legal or ethical point of view. Reasonable minds may differ not only as to whether the means to achieve the ends are justified but whether the ends themselves are just, fair, or ethical. An example of this latter issue would be affirmative action, a thorny matter for courts, managers, and philosophers alike.

Due Process and Just Cause

OBJECTIVE

Employment security—getting and keeping a job—is perhaps the most significant aspect of work from the employee's ethical perspective. Fundamental questions of justice arise because employees are subject to considerable harms from a lack of security in their jobs and do not have much power to create security. But should employers' rights and ability to hire, fire, or discipline employees therefore be restricted in order to prevent injustices? Are there any other means by which to protect against unethical behavior or unjust results?

Reality Check   *Rioting to Support Due Process in France*

As discussed in this chapter, a number of states maintain employment at will for employees. However, this is not the case in some other countries. In France, for instance, French labor laws protect all employees from arbitrary dismissal; employees cannot be fired as long as they maintain a good work record and as long as the firm is economically viable.

During the spring of 2006, protests and riots broke out across France in reaction to a proposed change in these laws. During one weekend alone, hundreds of thousands of protesters clashed with police in cities throughout France.

Ironically, the proposed change in law was itself a response to riots the previous year when unemployed young people, many of them immigrants living in poor neighborhoods, protested the lack of jobs. The French government sought to loosen job protection as a means of encouraging business to hire more young workers. The change would have exempted workers under the age of 25 from the legal job protections during their first two years of employment.

What was only a minor change in a law that, from the U.S. perspective, was already quite radical in protecting worker rights, resulted in massive riots. As a result of these protests, the French government withdrew its proposal.

Philosophically, the right of due process is the right to be protected against the arbitrary use of authority. In legal contexts, *due process* refers to the procedures that police and courts must follow in exercising their authority over citizens. Few dispute that the state, through its police and courts, has the authority to punish citizens. This authority creates a safe and orderly society in which we all can live, work, and do business. But that authority is not unlimited; it can be exercised only in certain ways and under certain conditions. Due process rights specify these conditions.

Similarly, due process in the workplace acknowledges an employer's authority over employees. Employers can tell employees what to do and when and how to do it. They can exercise such control because they retain the ability to discipline or fire an employee who does not comply with their authority. Because of the immense value that work holds for most people, the threat of losing one's job is a powerful motivation to comply. However, basic fairness—implemented through due process—demands that this power be used *justly*. It is the definition of basic fairness that remains the challenge. Review, for instance, the conflicting versions of fairness perceptions in France in 2006 in the Reality Check above.

OBJECTIVE

Ironically, the law has not always clearly supported this mandate of justice. Much employment law within the United States instead evolved in a context of a legal doctrine known as employment at will. Employment at will (EAW) holds that, absent a particular contractual or other legal obligation that specifies the length or conditions of employment, all employees are employed "at will." This means that, unless an agreement specifies otherwise, employers are free to fire an employee at any time and for any reason. In the words of an early court decision, "all may dismiss their employee at will, be they many or few, for good cause, for no cause, or even for cause morally wrong."[4] In the same manner, an EAW worker may opt to leave a job at any time for any reason, without offering any notice at all; so the freedom is *theoretically* mutual.

The ethical rationale for EAW, both historically and among contemporary defenders, has both utilitarian and deontological elements. EAW was thought to be an important management tool. Total discretion over employment gives managers the ability to make efficient decisions that should contribute to the greater overall good. It was thought that the manager would be in the best position to know what was best for the firm and that the law should not interfere with those decisions. Another basis for EAW was the rights of private property owners to control their property by controlling who works for them.

OBJECTIVE

Both legal and ethical analyses of these claims, however, demonstrate that there are good reasons to limit EAW. Even if EAW proved to be an effective management tool (though research of scholars such as Jeffrey Pfeffer suggests just the opposite), justice demands that such tools not be used to harm other people. Further, even if private property rights grant managers authority over employees, the right of private property itself is limited by other rights and duties. Also, though the freedom to terminate the relationship is theoretically mutual, the employer is often responsible for the employee's livelihood, while the opposite is unlikely to be true; the differential creates an unbalanced power relationship between the two parties.

Considerations such as these have led many courts and legislatures to create exceptions to the EAW rule (see Table 6.1). Civil rights laws, for example, prohibit firing someone on the basis of membership in certain prohibited classes, such as race, sex, disability, age, national origin, religion, or ethnic background. Labor laws prevent employers from firing someone for union activities. When the employer is the government, constitutional limitations on government authority are extended into the workplace to protect employees.

A crucial element to recognize with these exceptions, however, is the fact that EAW has priority unless the employee can prove that her or his case falls under one of the exceptions. That is, EAW is the default position on which courts will rely until and unless an exception can be demonstrated. The burden of proof lies with the dismissed employee to show that she or he was unjustly or illegally fired. Due process and just cause, whether instituted as part of internal corporate policy or through legislation, would reverse this burden of proof and require employers to show cause to justify the dismissal of an employee.

TABLE 6.1   Exceptions to the Doctrine of Employment at Will

States vary in terms of their recognition of the following exceptions to the doctrine of employment at will. Some states recognize one or more exceptions, while others might recognize none at all. In addition, the definition of these exceptions may vary from state to state.

- Bad faith, malicious or retaliatory termination in violation of *public policy.*
- Termination in breach of the *implied covenant of good faith and fair dealing.*
- Termination in breach of some other *implied contract term,* such as those that might be created by employee handbook provisions (in certain jurisdictions).
- Termination in violation of the doctrine of *promissory estoppel* (where the employee reasonably relied on an employer's promise, to the employee's detriment).
- Other exceptions as determined by *statutes* (such as the Worker Adjustment and Retraining Notification Act [WARN]).

OBJECTIVE

Due process issues arise in other employment contexts as well. Employees are constantly supervised and evaluated in the workplace, and such benefits as salary, work conditions, and promotions can also be used to motivate or sanction employees. Thus, being treated fairly in the workplace also involves fairness in such things as promotions, salary, benefits, and so forth. Because such decisions are typically made on the basis of performance appraisals, due process rights should also extend to this aspect of the workplace. Table 6.2 shows one model for making legally sound performance appraisals.

The ethical questions that remain in this EAW environment, therefore, are whether this atmosphere is one that is most fair and just to all stakeholders, whether it leads to the most effective employment outcomes, and whether it satisfactorily guards the rights and interests of both employers and employees. Relevant inquiries in reaching a conclusion on these matters will include those that comprise our decision-making framework. Consider the key facts relevant to issues of due process and fairness. What are the ethical issues involved in your decision and implementation? Who are the stakeholders involved in your decision? What alternatives are available to you? Might there be a way to safeguard the rights of the stakeholders involved while also protecting the interests of the decision makers? If you are, for instance, striving to serve the autonomy of the employer, could you perhaps serve the due process interests of the employee by offering additional notice of termination or more information about alternatives? Recall that due process is the right to be protected against the *arbitrary* use of authority. It is your role as decision maker to ensure protection against those arbitrary decisions. Employers should be fair in their implementation of judgments and just in their implementation of process in order to serve the above principles.

Downsizing

OBJECTIVE

One of the most emotional issues for both employees and corporate decision makers is the challenge not only of a single termination but letting many employees go when a firm makes a decision to "downsize." Terminating workers—whether

TABLE 6.2   **Procedural Recommendations for Legally and Ethically Sound Performance Appraisals**

Appraisal procedures should

1. Be standardized and uniform for all employees within a job group.
2. Be formally communicated to employees.
3. Provide notice of performance deficiencies and opportunities to correct them.
4. Provide access for employees to review appraisal results.
5. Provide formal appeal mechanisms that allow for employee input.
6. Use multiple, diverse, and unbiased raters.
7. Provide written instructions and training for raters.
8. Require thorough and consistent documentation across raters that includes specific examples of performance based on personal knowledge.
9. Establish a system to detect potentially discriminatory effects or abuses of the system overall.

Source: S.B. Malos, "Current Legal Issues in Performance Appraisal," in J.W. Smither (ed.), *Performance Appraisal: State-of-the-Art Methods for Performance Management* (San Francisco: Jossey-Bass, 1998), pp. 49–94. Reprinted with permission of the author.

one or one hundred—is not necessarily an unethical decision. However, the decision itself raises ethical quandaries since alternatives may be available to an organization in financial difficulty. Accordingly, the question of whether to resort to widespread terminations based on financial exigency in lieu of other options that may be available does not always lead to a clear answer. Once the decision has been made, are there ways in which an organization can act more ethically in the process of downsizing? How might our earlier discussion of due process and fairness offer some guidance and/or define limitations in a downsizing environment?

In a speech to the Ethics Officers Association, John Challenger suggested that we should consider the following factors in executing that process: planning, timing, notice, impact (on those who will go and those who will stay), and stakeholder perceptions.[5] We can make *better* choices, Challenger argues. In fact, our decision-making model offers significant guidance in a situation such as a downsizing.

First, the decision regarding downsizing should be made by a representative group so that all stakeholder interests can be considered and to earn the trust of those who will be impacted. The facts should be collected and issues should be determined. Since employees should be kept aware of business conditions, the need for a downsizing effort should not come as a great surprise. However, the question of notice is debatable.

It can be argued that a firm should give notice of an intent to downsize as soon as the need is determined, and let those who will be impacted know who will be let go as soon as that list is devised. On the other hand, the uncertainty and rumors that are sure to develop between the announcement of downsizing and the decision about who will be terminated may outweigh the benefits gained in early notification. In addition, allowing a worker to remain in a position for a period of time once she or he has been notified of impending termination might not be the best option. Workers may interpret early notice as an effort to get the most out of them before departure rather than an effort to allow them time to come to grips with the loss of their jobs.

Once the stakeholders are identified, it will be vital to enumerate any and all possible options with regard to the downsizing efforts and to catalog the impact of each option on each group of stakeholders. (See the following Reality Check for a discussion of options.) When a firm decides to downsize, as with any other termination, it is critical to lessen the impact as much as possible and to allow the terminated employees to depart with dignity (for example, unless there is some other reason for the decision, having a security guard follow terminated employees until they leave the building might not be the best option). Above all, during a time when relationships might be strained, it is critical to be honest and forthright and to be sensitive to the experiences of those who will be affected.

From a legal perspective, the decision about whom to include in a downsizing effort must be carefully planned. If the firm's decision is based on some criterion that seems to be neutral on its face, such as seniority, but the plan results in a different impact on one group than another, the decision may be suspect. For example, assume the firm does make termination decisions based on longevity with the organization. Also assume that those workers who are most senior are almost entirely male since women only entered this industry in recent years. If the firm moves forward with this process, the majority of those fired will be women and

Reality Check *Is It Really "Inevitable?"*

As inevitable as downsizing may seem during downturns in the economy, some firms have survived decade after decade without any layoffs. How do they do it? One firm, Nucor, has not laid off a worker in 20 years. However, it maintains a three-day workweek with an average wage of $8 per hour. When large contracts come in, the company expands to a seven-day workweek and $22 per hour wage. Other firms have entered into agreements with their workers under which the firm promises not to terminate workers for reasons of the economy as long as the workers agree to lower wages or decreased hours during tough periods. For instance, in December 1998, Volkswagen in Brazil was suffering under the collapse of that country's economy and the resulting 25 percent downturn in the Brazilian car market. It avoided terminations at its 20,000-worker plant by moving to a four-day workweek.

the majority of those remaining will be men. In this case, the effort may violate Title VII's prohibition against discrimination based on gender because the termination policy has a more significant—and negative—impact on women.

To avoid this result, firms should review both the fairness of their decision-making process and the consequence of that process on those terminated and the resulting composition of the workforce. One of the most effective philosophical theories to employ in downsizing decisions is John Rawls's theory of justice presented in Chapter 3. Under his formulation, you would consider what decision you would make—whether to downsize or how to downsize—if you did not know what role you would be playing following the decision. In other words, you might be the corporate executive with the secure position; you might be a terminated employee with years of seniority who was close to retirement; or you might be a worker who survives the termination slips. If you do not know which role you would be playing, Rawls contends that you are more likely to reach a decision that is relatively fairest to all impacted. Consider what facts might shift your decision in one way or another based on this formulation.

Health and Safety

The previous sections addressed ethics in the creation or termination of the employment relationship. The following discussion explores one particular responsibility within that relationship—the employer's role in protecting the employees' health and safety while at work. Within the United States and throughout many other countries with developed economies, there is a wide consensus that employees have a fundamental right to a safe and healthy workplace. In some other regions, employees lack even the most basic health and safety protections, such as in working environments that are often termed "sweatshops" (discussed later in this chapter). Even within the United States, this issue becomes quite complicated upon closer examination. Not only is the very extent of an employer's responsibility for workplace health and safety in dispute; there is also significant disagreement concerning the best policies to protect worker health and safety.

Like work itself, health and safety are "goods" that are valued both as a means for attaining other valuable ends and as ends in themselves. Whatever else we desire out of life, being healthy and safe makes it much more likely that we will

How do we measure the intrinsic value of a life, in addition to the instrumental value? Though perhaps an interesting mental exercise in which to engage, it is also a critical component of some business decisions and dilemmas. The following decision, though decades old, continues to teach us the hazards of considering only the instrumental value of a life. Though the instrumental calculation seems to make sense, and presumably it did at the time to those involved, you will see in hindsight that the "human element" seems to be missing.

In 1968, Ford Motor Company made a historic decision regarding the Ford Pinto, which was engineered with a rear gas tank assembly that had a tendency to explode in accidents that involved some rear-end collisions. The company allowed the Pinto to remain on the market after it determined that it would be more costly to engage in a recall effort than to pay out the costs of liability for injuries and deaths incurred. In an infamous memo, Ford's senior management calculated what the company would likely have to pay per life lost. It is noteworthy that these estimates were not Ford's alone but were based instead on figures from the National Highway Traffic Safety Administration.

Expected Costs of Producing the Pinto *with* Fuel Tank Modifications:

- Expected unit sales: 11 million vehicles (includes utility vehicles built on same chassis)
- Modification costs per unit: $11
- **Total Cost: $121 million [11 million vehicles × $11 per unit]**

Expected Costs of Producing the Pinto *without* Fuel Tank Modifications:

- Expected accident results (assuming 2,100 accidents):
  180 burn deaths
  180 serious burn injuries
  2,100 burned out vehicles

- Unit costs of accident results (assuming out of court settlements):
  $200,000 per burn death
  $67,000 per serious injury
  $700 per burned out vehicle

- **Total Costs: $49.53 million** [= (180 deaths × $200k) + (180 injuries × $67k) + (2,100 vehicles × $700 per vehicle)]

Using the figures above, the costs for recalling and modifying the Pinto were $121 million, while the costs for settling cases in which injuries were expected to occur would reach only $50 million.

If you were responsible for deciding whether to engage in the recall, how would you conduct the decision-making process? How would you account for the *intrinsic* as well as the *instrumental* value of a human life? Returning to the question that opened this Decision Point, consider how you would measure your own worth or the value of someone close to you. Who are your stakeholders and what is your value to each of them? How will you measure it—*financially*?

Would any of the following questions offer you a guidepost?

- How much would your stakeholders suffer if they lost you?

(continued)

- How much do you currently contribute to society and what would society lose if you were not here?
- How much would society benefit if you continued to survive?

Businesses have reasons to consider these issues, though extraordinarily difficult; how would you prefer that they reach conclusions in these areas?

be capable of attaining our ends. In this sense, health and safety have a very high instrumental value since part of their value derives from the fact that we use them to attain other things of value. Insurance therefore seeks to compensate workers for injuries they incur by paying the employees for the wages they lost as a result of being unable to work.

OBJECTIVE

Yet health and safety are also valuable in and of themselves. They have intrinsic value in addition to their instrumental value. To understand this distinction, consider how one might respond to the question of how much her or his life is worth. The life of one who dies in a workplace accident has instrumental value that can be measured, in part, by the lost wages that would have been earned had that person lived. But these lost wages do not measure the *intrinsic* value of the life, something that financial compensation simply cannot replace. The above Decision Point explores the measurement of intrinsic value.

What is the value of health and what does it mean to be healthy? When is a workplace safe? When is it unsafe? If "healthy" is taken to mean a state of flawless physical and psychological well-being, arguably no one is perfectly healthy. If "safe" means completely free from risk, certainly no workplace is perfectly safe. If health and safety are interpreted as ideals that are impossible to realize, then it would be unreasonable to claim that employees have a right to a healthy and safe workplace.

Health and Safety as Acceptable Risk

OBJECTIVE

Employers cannot be responsible for providing an ideally safe and healthy workplace. Instead, discussions in ethics about employee health and safety will tend to focus on the *relative* risks workers face and the level of *acceptable* workplace risk. In this discussion, "risks" can be defined as the probability of harm, and we determine "relative risks" by comparing the probabilities of harm involved in various activities. Therefore, scientists who compile and measure data can determine both risks and relative risks (see Figure 6.1). It is an easy step from these calculations to certain conclusions about acceptable risks. If it can be determined that the probability of harm involved in a specific work activity is equal to or less than the probability of harm of some more common activity, then we can conclude that this activity faces an "acceptable level of risk." From this perspective, *a workplace is safe if the risks are acceptable.*

Imagine if we generalize this conclusion and determine all workplace health and safety standards in this manner. Such an approach would place the responsibility for workplace safety solely on management. Business would hire safety engineers and other experts to determine the risks within their workplace. These experts would know the risk levels that are otherwise accepted throughout the society. These might involve the risks involved in driving a car, eating high-fat

FIGURE 6.1   Calculating Acceptable Level of Risk

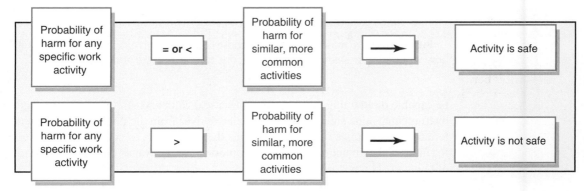

food, smoking, jogging, and so forth. Comparing these to the risks faced in the workplace, safety experts could perform a risk assessment and determine the relative risks of work. If the workplace were less risky than other common activities, management could conclude that they have fulfilled their responsibility to provide a healthy and safe workplace.

However, such an approach to workplace health and safety issues has several problems. First, this approach treats employees disrespectfully by ignoring their input as stakeholders. Such paternalistic decision making effectively treats employees like children and makes crucial decisions for them, ignoring their role in the decision-making process. Second, in making this decision, we assume that health and safety are mere preferences that can be traded off against competing values, ignoring the fundamental deontological right an employee might have to a safe and healthy working environment. Third, it assumes an equivalency between workplace risks and other types of risks when there are actually significant differences between them. Unlike many daily risks, the risks faced in the workplace may not be freely chosen, nor are the risks faced in the workplace within the control of workers. Fourth, it disregards the utilitarian concern for the consequences of an unsafe working environment on the social fabric, the resulting product or service created, the morale of the workforce, and the community, as well as other large-scale results of an unhealthy workplace.

Perhaps most important, unlike some daily risks each of us freely undertakes, the risks faced at work could be controlled by others, particularly by others who might stand to benefit by *not* reducing the risks. For instance, making the workplace safe may pose substantial costs to employers. Relative to the risks one might face by smoking, for example, working in a mill and inhaling cotton dust may not seem as risky. But, in the former case, the smoker chooses to take the risk and could take steps to minimize or eliminate them by herself or himself. In the latter case, the mill worker cannot avoid the risks as long as she or he wants to keep a job. Often someone else can minimize or eliminate these risks; but this other party also has a financial incentive not to do so. In one case, smoking, the decision maker freely chooses to take the risk, knowing that she or he can control it. In the other case, the worker's choices and control are limited. The challenges involved

TABLE 6.3   Challenges to the Acceptable Risk Approach to Health and Safety

- Treats employees disrespectfully by ignoring their input as stakeholders.
- Ignores the fundamental deontological right an employee might have to a safe and healthy working environment.
- Assumes an equivalency between workplace risks and other types of risks when there are significant differences between them.
- Improperly places incentives since the risks faced at work could be controlled by others who might stand to benefit by *not* reducing them.

in the acceptable risk approach to workplace health and safety are summarized in Table 6.3. Surely we need another approach.

Health and Safety as Market Controlled

Perhaps we can leave health and safety standards to the market. Defenders of the free market and the classical model of corporate social responsibility would favor individual bargaining between employers and employees as the approach to workplace health and safety.. On this account, employees would be free to choose the risks they are willing to face by bargaining with employers. Employees would balance their preferences for risk against their demand for wages and decide how much risk they are willing to take for various wages. Those who demand higher safety standards and healthier conditions presumably would have to settle for lower wages; those willing to take higher risks presumably would demand higher wages. In a competitive and free labor market, such individual bargaining would result in the optimal distribution of safety and income. Of course, the market approach can also support compensation to injured workers when it can be shown that employers were responsible for causing the harms. So an employer who fails to install fire-fighting equipment in the workplace can be held liable for burns an employee suffers during a workplace fire. The threat of compensation also acts as an incentive for employers to maintain a reasonably safe and healthy workplace. The following Decision Point considers whether it is therefore ethical for a company to outsource its most dangerous jobs to countries where the labor force is willing to accept low wages for unsafe conditions.

OBJECTIVE

This free market approach has a number of serious problems. First, labor markets are not perfectly competitive and free. Employees do not have the kinds of free choices that the free market theory would require in order to attain optimal satisfactions—though enlightened self-interest would be a valuable theory to introduce and apply in this environment, it is unrealistic to presume employees always have the choices available to them that make it possible. For example, risky jobs are often also the lowest-paying jobs, and people with the fewest employment choices hold them. Individuals are forced to accept the jobs because they have no choice but to accept; they are not actually "balancing their preferences for risk against their demand for wages" because they do not have options. Second, employees seldom, if ever, possess the kind of complete information efficient markets require. If employees do not know the risks involved in a job,

If one follows the market-based recommendation to allocate workplace risks on the basis of an optimal distribution of risks and benefits, one would conclude that, from a business perspective, dangerous jobs ought to be exported to those areas where wages are low and where workers are more willing to accept risky working conditions. The harms done by dangerous jobs, in terms of forgone earnings, are lower in regions with low wages and lower life expectancies. The benefits of providing jobs in regions with high unemployment would also outweigh the benefits of sending those jobs to regions with low unemployment. (See also the discussion of global labor markets, later in this chapter, and the discussion on exporting toxic wastes in Chapter 9.)

- What facts would you want to know before deciding whether the practice of exporting dangerous jobs was fair and responsible?
- What alternatives to exporting dangerous jobs exist for a firm?
- Who are the stakeholders of your decision? What is the impact of each alternative mentioned above on each stakeholder you have identified?
- Should local legal regulations govern the situation?
- What are the consequences of such a decision? What rights and duties are involved? If the consequences are effective and valuable to the majority but fundamental rights are implicated, how will you decide what to do?

they will not be in a position to freely bargain for appropriate wages and therefore they will not be in a position to effectively protect their rights or ensure the most ethical consequences. This is a particular concern when we recognize that many workplace risks are in no sense obvious. An employee may understand the dangers of heavy machinery or a blast furnace; but few employees can know the toxicity or exposure levels of workplace chemicals or airborne contaminants.

Such market failures can have deadly consequences when they involve workplace health and safety issues. Of course, market defenders argue, markets will, over time, compensate for such failures. Over time, employers will find it difficult to attract workers to dangerous jobs and, over time, employees will learn about the risks of every workplace. But this raises what we have previously described as the "first generation" problem. The means by which the market gathers information is by observing the harms done to the first generation exposed to imperfect market transactions. Thus, workers learn that exposure to lead is dangerous when some female workers exposed to lead suffer miscarriages or when others have children who are born with serious birth defects. We learn that workplace exposure to asbestos or cotton dust is dangerous when workers subsequently die from lung disease. In effect, markets sacrifice the first generation in order to gain information about safety and health risks. These questions of public policy, questions that after all will affect human lives, would never even be asked by an individual facing the choice of working at a risky job. To the degree that these are important questions that ought to be asked, individual bargaining will fail as an ethical public policy approach to worker health and safety. Table 6.4 summarizes the challenges inherent in the free market approach to health and safety.

Health and Safety – Government-Regulated Ethics

In response to such concerns, government regulation of workplace health and safety appears more appropriate from an ethical perspective. Mandatory government standards address most of the problems raised against market strategies. Standards can be set according to the best available scientific knowledge and thus overcome market failures that result from insufficient information. Standards prevent employees from having to face the fundamentally coercive choice between job and safety. Standards also address the first generation problem by focusing on prevention rather than compensation after the fact. Finally, standards are fundamentally a social approach that can address public policy questions ignored by markets.

In 1970, the U.S. Congress established the Occupational Safety and Health Administration (OSHA) and charged it with establishing workplace health and safety standards. Since that time, the major debates concerning workplace health and safety have focused on how such public standards ought to be set. The dominant question has concerned the appropriateness of using cost-benefit analysis to set health and safety standards.

When OSHA was first established, regulations were aimed at achieving the safest feasible standards. This "feasibility" approach allows OSHA to make trade-offs between health and economics, but it is prejudiced in favor of health and safety by placing the burden of proof on industry to show that high standards are not economically feasible. Health and safety standards are not required come what may; but an industry is required to meet the highest standards attainable within technological and economic reason.

Some critics charge that this approach does not go far enough and unjustly sacrifices employee health and safety. From that perspective, industries that cannot operate without harming the health and safety of its employees should be closed. But the more influential business criticism has argued that these standards go too far. Critics in both industry and government have argued that OSHA should be required to use cost-benefit analysis in establishing such standards. From this perspective, even if a standard is technologically and economically feasible, it would still be unreasonable and unfair if the benefits did not outweigh the costs. These critics argue that OSHA should aim to achieve the optimal, rather than highest feasible, level of safety.

Using cost-benefit analysis to set standards, in effect, returns us to the goals of the market-based, individual bargaining approach. Like that market approach,

---

TABLE 6.4 **Challenges with the Free Market Approach to Health and Safety**

- Labor markets are not perfectly competitive and free.
- Employees seldom if ever possess the kind of perfect information markets require.

We ignore important questions of social justice and public policy if we approach questions solely from the point of view of an individual.

Reality Check *Do Health and Safety Programs Cost Too Much?*

Evidence collected by the Occupational Safety and Health Administration suggests just the opposite: Safety and health programs *add* value and *reduce* costs. Even average companies can reduce injuries 20 to 40 percent by establishing safety and health programs. Several studies have estimated that safety and health programs save $4 to $6 for every dollar invested. Yet, only about 30 percent of U.S. work sites have established these programs. These savings result from a decrease in employee injuries and illnesses, lower workers' compensation costs, decreased medical costs, reduced absenteeism, lower turnover, higher productivity, and increased morale.

Source: Charles N. Jeffress, former assistant secretary for occupational safety and health, U.S. Department of Labor, "Future Directions for OSHA," speech delivered to National Safety Congress, New Orleans, October 19, 1999 (http://www.osha.gov/pls/oshaweb/owadisp.show_document?p table=SPEECHES&p_id=244).

this use of cost-benefit analysis faces serious ethical challenges. We should note, however, that rejecting cost-benefit analysis in setting standards is not the same as rejecting cost-effective strategies in implementing those standards. A commitment to cost-effectiveness would require that, once the standards are set, we adopt the least expensive and most efficient means available for achieving those standards. Cost-benefit analysis, in contrast, uses economic criteria in setting the standards in the first place. It is cost-benefit, not cost-effectiveness, analysis that is ethically problematic.

The use of cost-benefit analysis in setting workplace health and safety standards commits us to treating worker health and safety as just another commodity, another individual preference, to be traded off against competing commodities. It treats health and safety merely as an instrumental value and denies its intrinsic value. Cost-benefit analysis requires that an economic value be placed on one's life and bodily integrity. Typically, this would follow the model used by the insurance industry (where it is used in wrongful death settlements, for example) in which one's life is valued in terms of one's earning potential. Perhaps the most offensive aspect of this approach is the fact that since, in feasibility analysis, health and safety is already traded off against the economic viability of the industry, a shift to cost-benefit analysis entails trading off health and safety against profit margin. (Please see the above Reality Check for an application of cost-benefit analysis.)

The policies that have emerged by consensus within the United States seem to be most defensible. Employees have a legitimate ethical claim on mandatory health and safety standards within the workplace. To say that employees have a right to workplace health and safety implies that they should not be expected to make trade-offs between health and safety standards and job security or wages. Further, recognizing that most mandatory standards reduce rather than eliminate risks, employees should also have the right to be informed about workplace risks. If the risks have been reduced to the lowest feasible level and employees are fully aware of them, then a society that respects its citizens as autonomous decision makers has done its duty.

Global Applications: The Global Workforce and Global Challenges

As you consider the issues of due process, fairness, and health and safety raised thus far in the chapter, note that the law discussed here applies to workers who are employed in the United States. Workers outside of the United States may be subject to some U.S. laws if they work for an American-based organization, though enforcement is scattered. In some cases, workers in other countries are often protected by even more stringent laws than those in the United States. Many countries in the European Union, for example, have strong laws protecting workers' rights to due process and participation. But in many other cases, especially in certain developing countries, workers find themselves subject to conditions that U.S.-based workers would find appalling. While those of us who work in the United States may benefit from battles fought in years past for occupational safety and health, workers in certain Southeast Asian countries, for instance, are simply arguing for at-will bathroom breaks.

OBJECTIVE

The response to this stark contrast is not a simple one. Though few people, if any, would argue for the continuation of the circumstances described above, economists and others do not agree about a solution. Some contend that the exploitation of cheap labor allows developing countries to expand export activities and to improve their economies. This economic growth brings more jobs, which will cause the labor market to tighten, which in turn will force companies to improve conditions in order to attract workers (see Figure 6.2). In fact, several commentators argue that encouraging greater global production will create additional opportunities for expansion domestically, providing a positive impact on more stakeholders.[6] Though it is an unpopular sentiment with the general consuming public, many economists argue that the maintenance of sweatshops is therefore supported by economic theory. Indeed, even the term *sweatshops* remains open to debate.

On the other hand, opponents to this perspective argue that allowing this process to take its course will not necessarily lead to the anticipated result, just as voluntarily improving legal compliance, wages, and working conditions will not inevitably lead to the negative consequences the free market advocates threaten. As we examine ethical issues in the workplace, a helpful exercise is to consider the global dimension of an ethically responsible workplace. Certainly it is arguable that some minimum standards might apply and multinationals may have some core ethical obligations to employees. But how do we determine what those might be? Should the best employment practices in the United States set the standard for the global economy? That would mean concluding that the standards of one particular country are appropriate for all countries and cultures of the world, not necessarily the optimal conclusion.

Instead, some scholars have argued that Kantian universal principles should govern the employment relationship and that the ethical obligation of respect for persons should guide the employment interactions. "To fully respect a person, one must actively treat his or her humanity as an end, and not merely as a means to an end. This means that it is impermissible to treats persons like disposable tools."[7]

FIGURE 6.2

The Case *for* Sweatshops

Source: D. Arnold and L. Hartman, "Worker Rights and Low Wage Industrialization: How to Avoid Sweatshops," *Human Rights Quarterly*, vol. 28, no. 3 (August 2006), pp. 676–700. Reprinted by permission of *Human Rights Quarterly* and its publisher, the Johns Hopkins University Press.

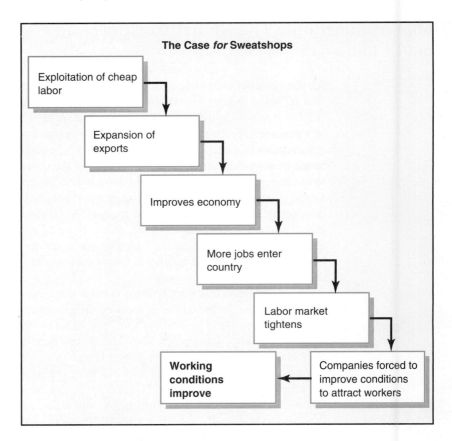

The Case *for* Sweatshops

Though different ethical theories may yield conflicting responses, it is arguable that a fundamental moral minimum set of standards exists that should be guaranteed to workers in all countries notwithstanding culture, stage of economic development, or availability of resources. Philosophers Arnold and Bowie contend that multinationals "must ensure the physical well-being of employees and refrain from undermining the development of their rational and moral capacities . . . [R]especting workers in global factories requires that factories of multinational corporations (MNCs), including contract factories, adhere to local labor laws, refrain from the use of coercion, provide decent working conditions, and provide wages above the overall poverty line for a 48-hour work week."[8] Others contend the list should also include a minimum age for child labor, nondiscrimination requirements (including the right to equal pay for equal work), and free association including the right to organize and to bargain collectively in contract negotiations.[9]

International nongovernmental organizations have also attempted to step into this fray to suggest voluntary standards to which possible signatory countries or organizations could commit. For instance, the International Labour Office has promulgated its Tripartite Declaration of Principles Concerning Multinational Enterprises and Social Policy, which offers guidelines for employment, training,

As you consider the discussion of child labor, consider the many stakeholders involved and the power each one holds (or lack thereof), the options available to the multinational corporations, and the options consumers have in determining from whom they will buy, what rights might be implicated and the consequences of protecting them, and how you would respond if you were a labor advocate seeking to determine the best next steps in the debate.

- What are the key facts relevant to your decision regarding child labor?
- What are the ethical issues involved in child labor? What incentives might be in place that would actively support or pose challenges to your response?
- Who are the stakeholders in connection with child labor?
- What alternative responses might you suggest?
- How would each of your alternatives affect each of the stakeholders you have identified?
- Is there any guidance available from global organizations to assist you in resolving this particular dilemma?

conditions of work and life, and industrial relations. The "Tripartite" part of the title refers to the critical cooperation necessary from governments, employers' and workers' organizations, and the multinational enterprises involved.

As mentioned above, the discussion of legal and ethical expectations and boundaries in this chapter is based on the law in the United States. However, awareness of the limitations of this analysis and sensitivity to the challenges of global implementation are critical in today's multinational business operations. We will revisit the quandary of varying ethical standards as applied to diverse economic and social environments in the next section with regard to the issue of child labor.

The Case of Child Labor

One of the key issues facing business in today's globalized economy is the potential for cultural or legal conflicts in connection with worldwide labor management. Though the issues stir our consciences, their resolution is not so clear. Let us consider, for example, the case of child labor. As we begin to understand the circumstances facing children worldwide, we can see that a simple prohibition might not offer us the best possible solution. But what options exist? (For a general inquiry, please see the Decision Point, above.)

According to International Labour Organization estimates, 250 million children between 5 and 17 years old currently work in developing countries, almost half of them on a full-time basis.[10] "Moreover, some 8.4 million children [a]re engaged in so-called 'unconditional' worst forms of child labor, which include forced and bonded labor, the use of children in armed conflict, trafficking in children and commercial sexual exploitation."[11] Because work takes children out of school, more than half of the child labor force will never be literate.[12] Substandard working conditions have an impact on growth; child employees will be physically smaller than those who did not work as children even into adulthood.[13] By the time child laborers become adults, most will irrevocably be sick or deformed, unlikely to live beyond fifty years old.[14]

Of course, many economically developed countries currently employ child labor, albeit with restrictions, so one should carefully review the social and economic structure within which the labor exists. While the easy answer may be to rid all factories of all workers under 18 years of age, that is often not the best answer for the children or the families involved. Prospects for working children in developing countries indeed appear bleak. Children may begin work as young as three years old. They not only may work in unhealthy conditions; they may also live in unhealthy conditions. The labor opportunities that exist almost always require children to work full time, thereby precluding them from obtaining an education.[15] However, if children are not working, their options are not as optimistic as those of children in developed economies. Sophisticated education systems or public schools are not always available. Often children who do not work in the manufacturing industry are forced to work in less hospitable "underground" professions, such as drug dealing or prostitution, simply to earn their own food each day.[16]

Moreover, even if educational alternatives are available in some environments, recommending removal of the child from the workplace completely ignores the financial impact of the child leaving his or her job. The income the youth worker generates may, at the very least, assist in supporting his or her fundamental needs (food, clothing, and shelter); at the most, it may be critical in supporting the entire family.

Rights and Responsibilities in Conflict: Discrimination, Diversity, and Affirmative Action

In the preceding sections, we explored the ethical environment of several elements of the employment relationship. As explained earlier, the ethical issues discussed in the first section of this chapter are, for the most part, settled. Though our discussion addressed particular areas of outstanding contention, the underlying rights have been established.

In the following section, we consider several matters that scholars, jurists, and corporate leaders continue to debate. The focus is on those subtle areas where the law may not yet be completely settled, where it remains open to diverse cultural interpretations, strong minority opinions, and value judgments. Though the courts have been forced to render judgment in these areas, their decisions might not be unanimous or might reverse a strong lower court opinion representing a contrary perspective.

From a Kantian, deontological perspective, agreement on the fundamental rights implied by the following issues and on their appropriate prioritization is not yet universal. From a utilitarian viewpoint, reasonable minds engaged in these ethical issues do not always agree on which resolution might lead towards the greatest common good, or even what that good should ultimately be. Distributive justice does not provide a clear-cut solution as each camp can often make an argument for fairness. Our purpose here is to articulate and apply the ethical decision-making process to

Decision Point

Who Needs Ethics? Can the Market "Fix" Discrimination?

One approach towards discrimination in employment calls for no corporate or governmental intervention. Defenders of the market argue that if the market were left to its own devices, we could expect discrimination to fall by the wayside. That is, if a firm hires its employees on the basis of prejudices and discriminatory views (such as that women cannot do a certain job), then it is limiting its pool of possible employees. Another firm that does not discriminate can choose from the larger pool and is more likely to obtain the *most* qualified individual for the job. There is therefore an opportunity cost to discrimination. Labor is clearly a factor of production; when we leave productive resources unused, the entire economy suffers. The human capital of women and minorities is lost when we deny them opportunities in the economy. Judge Richard Posner explains the economic impact of this theory in terms of race discrimination as follows:

> In a market of many sellers, the intensity of the prejudice against blacks will vary considerably. Some sellers will have only a mild prejudice against them. These sellers will not forgo as many advantageous transactions with blacks as their more prejudiced competitors (unless the law interferes). Their costs will therefore be lower, and this will enable them to increase their share of the market. The least prejudiced sellers will come to dominate the market in much the same way as people who are least afraid of heights come to dominate occupations that require working at heights: they demand a smaller premium.[17]

Should corporate policy makers and government leave such issues to the market? Should employees' fears or concerns about workplace discrimination be relieved upon understanding Judge Posner's theory? Why or why not?

- What key facts do you need to determine whether the market can solve this challenge? Under what circumstances would Posner's argument fail? What market failures might prevent economic forces from efficiently ending discrimination?
- What are some of the other ethical issues that come to mind when you consider this proposed "solution"? What is the effect of regulation such as Title VII on Posner's argument? Even if the market could work against discrimination, is this matter sufficiently important from an ethical perspective that society should address it more actively through legislation?
- Who are the stakeholders involved in this particular issue?
- What alternative responses could you propose? Are you more comfortable with management through legislation or a free market? Consider the implications if the discriminating firm held a monopoly on its good or service.
- How would each of your alternatives affect each of the stakeholders you have identified?
- Where might you look for additional guidance to assist you in resolving this particular dilemma?

the challenges presented, provide a cross section of the arguments the advocates involved make, and explore the insights that ethical theory might supply.

Discrimination

The courts have carefully construed legal precedent in the decades since Title VII of the United States Civil Rights Act was passed in 1964 and created the prohibited classes of discrimination. Though several specific areas of delicate and subtle quandaries remain, many of the original legal and ethical debates have been fought, offering business decision makers arguably clear guidance on appropriate behavior in the workplace. For instance, while the advent of sexual harassment as a basis for a legal complaint was new to the court system during the last century, seldom does a new recruit begin employment at a large company today without standard sexual harassment training. When the issue was first raised in U.S. workplaces, employees were at a loss about what was or was not acceptable. Today the Equal Employment Opportunity Commission (EEOC),[18] as well as a host of other sources, provides explicit guides and resources detailing appropriate behavior as well as offering legal direction and parameters for both employees and employers.

As we have stated throughout this text, though, the law can only go so far. While it is not our purpose to explore in detail the law relating to workplace discrimination, suffice it to say that the law allows employers to make decisions on *any basis* other than those prohibited by the Constitution, precedent, and several statutes (such as age, religion, race, disability, gender, national origin, and color). Some commentators would contend that this broad mandate allows employers enormous autonomy in their employment decisions while many employers still bemoan any regulation of their workplaces.

Widespread disagreement on a global basis remains about the rights of employees with regard to discrimination, the extent of protected classes, and the more specific subtopics such as diversity and affirmative action that we will examine shortly. Even in the United States, the concept of discrimination remains one of the most intensely debated issues today. Employers continue to advocate for their rights to manage the workplace and to be permitted to hire, retain, and terminate employees without external influence or control. Employees fear unfair treatment and a loss of power based on reasons completely outside their control. Judge Richard Posner argues in the previous Decision Point how the market might be able to relieve employees of some of these fears—*at least in theory*.

OBJECTIVE

Without diminishing the impact of overt acts of discrimination or their continuation in the workplace, covert forms of discrimination are also widely prevalent though they often go unnoticed. For instance, University of Chicago scholars Marianne Bertrand and Sendhil Millainathan found that there remains discrimination simply on the basis of one's name.[19] In order to determine the extent of discrimination in the labor market on the basis of the racial sound of a name, these researchers answered help-wanted ads in Boston and Chicago newspapers by submitting résumés that were exactly the same in their substance, but that used different names. The number of callbacks for each résumé differed significantly. Names that were traditionally associated with Caucasians (such as Jill, Allison, Neil, and Brad) drew 50

How would this same story about gender coaching sound if it had to do with one race acting too much like another? Or, how would you feel about the story if it suggested that a certain group of people should "know their place" or people will not want to work with them? What would you think of a program that offered coaching to men on how to be "more like women" because the program suggested that women were put off by boorish, insensitive males?

- What key facts are relevant to the issue of coaching?
- What are the origins of coaching and what challenges have served to create a need for it?
- In addition to the race question raised above, what are some of the other ethical issues that come to mind when you consider this practice?
- Who are the stakeholders involved in this particular issue?
- What alternative responses are available?
- How would each of your alternatives affect each of the stakeholders you have identified?
- Where might you look for additional guidance to assist you in resolving this particular dilemma?

percent more callbacks than did those traditionally associated with African Americans (such as Aisha, Ebony, Tremayne, and Leroy). Even when the researchers increased the quality of the résumés, higher quality résumés from candidates who sounded African American received no more callbacks than the original résumé. The only bright spot in the research was the finding that Chicago employers in African American neighborhoods discriminated less than those in other communities.

We often do not recognize areas of Western culture that contain or perpetuate covert discrimination. In the article "White Privilege: Unpacking the Invisible Knapsack,"[20] Peggy McIntosh identifies a number of daily conditions a white person in Western society can count on:

- I can go shopping alone most of the time, pretty well assured that I will not be followed or harassed.
- I can open a newspaper or turn on the television and see people of my race represented positively.
- I can do well in a challenging situation without being called a credit to my race.
- I am never asked to speak for all of the people in my racial group.

McIntosh explains that these privileges are like "an invisible weightless knapsack of provisions, maps, passports, codebooks, visas, clothes, tools and blank checks."

Discrimination not only persists in the United States with regard to race, but also in connection with gender. Women often face challenges that are distinct from those faced by men. For instance, women and men are both subject to gender stereotyping, but suffer from different expectations in that regard. A woman who is aggressive in the workplace is often considered a bully, while a man is deemed to be doing what he needs to do to get ahead. In fact, a corporate coaching program exists for women who are considered to be "bullies" called "Bully Broads." The program is designed to help women understand how their conception of what it takes to get ahead (often learned through interactions with men) might cause co-workers to view them negatively. Its goal is to boost productivity because "it is difficult to produce if others do not want to work with you." Can you imagine a similar program for men? Probably not. Aggressive men are viewed in positive terms: going after what they want, not letting anything get in their way, and so on. (See the Decision Point on the previous page for another perspective on coaching.)

An article discussing the above coaching program failed to mention how women's behavior might have been learned or whether it *should* be all right for women to engage in behavior similar to that of their male counterparts.[21]

Diversity

The Bully Broads idea that "it is difficult to produce if others do not want to work with you" might not have been relevant even just a few decades ago since the U.S. workforce today is significantly more diverse than ever before and all data suggest that this will continue. Efforts towards eliminating discrimination in employment over the past 30 years are partially responsible for this change. But a changing population is also a major factor in the increasingly diverse workplace.

OBJECTIVE

Diversity refers to the presence of differing cultures, languages, ethnicities, races, affinity orientations, genders, religious sects, abilities, social classes, ages, and national origins of the individuals in a firm. Ninety percent of employees in U.S. businesses believe they work in a diverse workplace.[22] This is not surprising since the pool of eligible and interested workers is becoming more and more diverse as well. It is estimated that, by 2010, only 20 percent of the workforce will be white men under 45.[23] As one might expect, the management composition at firms with diversity programs is significantly more diverse than those at firms that do not have such programs, and 79 percent of senior managers at those firms say that cultivating a more diverse workforce is part of the organization's overall business strategy. The positive impact on the overall strategy is not insignificant, as the following Reality Check indicates.

OBJECTIVE

Diversity has brought benefits to the workplace, but diversity efforts have also created new conflicts. Recall the definition of diversity above: Diversity refers to the presence of differing cultures, languages, ethnicities, races, affinity orientations, genders, religious sects, abilities, social classes, ages, and national origins of the individuals in a firm. When a firm brings together individuals with these (or other) differences—often exposing these individuals to such differences for the first time—areas of tension and anxiety may emerge. In addition, the organization is likely to ask its employees to work together toward common goals, on teams, in supervisory or subordinate roles, and in power relationships, all requests that might lead to conflicts or tension even without additional stressors such as cultural challenges.

Diversity can potentially increase several areas of values tension. Where differences are new or strong, *and* where negative stereotypes previously ruled interactions between particular groups, sensitivity to the potential for conflict is necessary.

Reality Check *Diversity = $$?*

A groundbreaking study by Catalyst in 2004 evidenced a strong link between gender diversity in top management teams and corporate financial performance. The study's authors contend that the link is based on the fact that employers who pay attention to diversity have a larger and more capable applicant pool from whom to choose the best workers. These organizations are also better positioned to respond more effectively to a diverse consumer population. In addition, these firms evidence better decision-making, production and other critical success factors.

- The group of companies with the highest representation of women on their top management teams experienced better financial performance than the group of companies with the lowest women's representation.

- In four out of the five industries analyzed, the group of companies with the highest women's representation on their top management teams experienced a higher total return to shareholders than the group of companies with the lowest women's representation.

Source: Catalyst, Inc., "The Bottom Line: Connecting Corporate Performance and Gender Diversity" (2004), http://www.catalystwomen.org/knowledge/titles/title.php?page=lead_finpertf_04.

Another concern involves integrating diverse viewpoints with a preexisting corporate culture. There seems nothing inappropriate about seeking to ensure that workers will support the particular values of a firm, but it might be difficult to do this while also encouraging diversity. Diversity, which might be the source of positive gains for the organization, might also be the source of fundamental differences in values that must be balanced. Some scholars suggest that job applicants be screened with regard to their values, but how can employers do so? Hiring is not an area to be taken lightly, but most firms go with a "gut" instinct about whether or not a job applicant will "fit in." In the same way that you might apply the "can you sleep at night" test to an ethical dilemma after considering all the implications of a decision, you might trust an employment choice to the same test.

It is not discriminatory to refuse to hire someone about whom you simply have a "bad feeling," unless that bad feeling is based on their difference in race or gender. On the other hand, it is vital to be wary of prejudgments based solely on differences in interpretations of culturally based standards. While variance in fundamental standards might justify a sense of a "bad fit" between a potential employer and employee, divergence in culturally based standards such as attire, hair styles, or manner of speaking might instead be treated differently. Efforts at understanding multiculturalism, such as acknowledging and promoting diversity through celebration and appreciation of various cultures in the workplace, can serve both to educate and to encourage the benefits linked to diversity efforts.

On the other hand, the cost of ignoring diversity is high, not only in terms of losses of productivity, creativity, and other performance-based measures, but also in terms of legal liability. Texaco experienced what insiders refer to simply as "the crisis" in 1996 when the company was required to pay $175 million to settle a racial discrimination lawsuit. The settlement was based on taped conversations of executives using racist language as well as documented compensation

Chevron Texaco includes case studies in its annual Corporate Responsibility Reports. The following appeared in its 2002 report in a discussion about diversity. As you read above, several years prior, Texaco settled a large discrimination suit and knew it had to make some changes in this area. As you review the statistics above and the case study below, consider these questions:

- What do you believe is Chevron Texaco's motivation?
- Who are its key stakeholders for this particular communication and for the program itself?
- Do you believe the program seems like it is or will be a successful one or, if you might need additional information, what do you believe would be the key components to make this program successful?

DIVERSITY MENTORING PROGRAM

ChevronTexaco Global Lubricants (CTGL) markets more than 3,500 lubricants and coolants around the globe and is ranked among the top three global lubricants companies. CTGL believes that its success depends not just on product quality but also on developing a workforce that mirrors the global diversity of its customers. "Having a diversity of backgrounds and views gives us a unique advantage," says Shariq Yosufzai, president of Global Marketing for Downstream. "The varied perspectives of our colleagues help us better anticipate market challenges and forge better solutions. We must look and think like our customers."

An innovative mentoring process helps CTGL cultivate a diverse management team. Each of the 15 members of the Global Lubricants Leadership Team mentors up to three visibly or globally diverse employees. The goal is to increase the number of diverse candidates for leadership positions around the world, while also providing those leaders continued support to ensure that they, as well as the business, succeed.

discrimination against minority employees, hundreds of whom were being paid below the minimum salary for their job level.

A firm often reaches its depths before it emerges anew, and Texaco's subsequent numbers tell a much different story. In 2002, minority hires accounted for 46 percent of all new employees, including some key senior executives, and more than 20 percent of promotions, and 34 percent of new hires were women. Texaco pledged to spend at least $1 million with minority and women contractors within five years of the settlement and, of course, diversity training is now mandated for all workers, with management compensation tied to the attainment of success in implementing new initiatives. (See above Decision Point for additional information about Chevron Texaco programs.)

Affirmative Action

Throughout this chapter, we have discussed the means by which to protect employer interests and employee rights. With regard to the latter, we have focused on employee rights to fair treatment and due process in the workplace. A question arises, however, when we consider balancing those rights with competing employee rights, as may occur in the case of affirmative action. The question regarding affirmative action is not necessarily whether a person has a right to fair process in connection with employment but instead whether one has a right to the job in the first place. Does one person deserve a position *more* than another person? For instance, efforts to encourage greater diversity may also be seen as a form of "reverse discrimination": discrimination against those traditionally considered to be in power or the majority, such as white men. A business that intentionally seeks to hire a candidate from an underrepresented group might be seen as discriminating against white males, for example.

The arguments on both sides of this issue have a tendency towards emotional persuasion. Imagine you are hiring a social worker to serve an overwhelmingly African American community that is currently facing issues, among others, of teen pregnancy. Not only might you argue that you want to hire someone who is African American; you might also want a female social worker who might be better able to speak with the teenage women in that community. On the other hand, in front of you is a 40-year-old white male with a master's degree from an extraordinarily valuable program. He has years of experience in the field and in fact has an adopted African American daughter himself. He claims he can handle the job. In fact, he claims he *deserves* the job. Does he? Does it matter whether he deserves it, has a *right* to the job? Assume you still want the younger African American woman you know is next on your interview list. What is the fairest decision? Fair to whom? Fairest to the young women of your community, to the applicants you are interviewing, or to other stakeholders? How should you decide? What will be the consequences of your decision?

Diversity issues raise other less apparent problems. For example, consider a report by the U.S. Commission on Civil Rights that addresses the unique predicament of Asian Americans. The report documents widespread discrimination against Asian Americans, who have long been seen as having escaped the national origin barriers that face other cultures. The report contends that the typical Asian stereotype of being hardworking, intelligent, and successful is actually a detriment to Asian Americans. This stereotype results in the problems of overlooking poor Asians and preventing successful Asian Americans from becoming more successful. It also places undue pressure on young Asian Americans to succeed in school, and it discredits other minorities by arguing that "if Asian Americans can succeed, so can other minorities."[24] In an article highlighting the report, *Fortune* magazine contends that the problem is really that the commission is "being driven crazy by the fact that Asian Americans have been succeeding essentially *without the benefit of affirmative action.* The ultimate problem is not that they may make other minorities look bad—it is that they are making the civil rights bureaucracy look irrelevant."[25] Some theorists argue that formal affirmative action measures have often served to create a greater divide rather than to draw people closer.

Let us take a closer look at affirmative action to explore the ethical issues it raises. The term *affirmative action* refers to a policy or a program that tries to respond to instances of past discrimination by implementing proactive measures to ensure equal opportunity today. It may take the form of intentional inclusion of previously excluded groups in employment, education, or other environments.

OBJECTIVE

The use of affirmative action policies in both business and universities has been controversial for decades. (For the latest facts and figures, see the Reality Checks that follow.) In its first discussion of affirmative action in employment, the U.S. Supreme Court found that employers could intentionally include minorities (and thereby exclude others) in order to redress past wrongs. However, the holding was not without restrictions, which have caused confusion. Even today, the law is not clear, and we must turn to values systems to provide direction, which we will discuss shortly.

Affirmative action arises in the workplace in three ways. The first way is through legal requirements. Much of the law relating to affirmative action applies only to about 20 percent of the workforce, however: those employees of federal contractors with 50 or more employees who are subject to Executive Order 11246, which requires affirmative action efforts to ensure equal opportunity. Where Executive Order 11246 does not apply, courts may also require what is termed "judicial affirmative action" in order to remedy a finding of past discrimination. A third form of affirmative action involves voluntary affirmative action plans employers undertake to overcome barriers to equal opportunity. These might include training plans and programs, focused recruiting activity, or the elimination of discrimination that might be caused by hiring criteria that exclude a particular group. A demonstrated underrepresentation of a particular group or a finding of past discrimination is required to justify affirmative action efforts under either of these latter two options.

OBJECTIVE

After a number of legal opinions, employers are left with some basic guidelines for creating these programs and policies. Consider how the following *legal* constraints to an affirmative action program are in line with deontological and teleological frameworks that also support ethical decision making:

1. The affirmative action efforts or policy may not unnecessarily infringe upon the majority employees' rights or create an absolute bar to their advancement.
2. The affirmative action effort or policy may not set aside any positions for women or minorities and may not be construed as quotas to be met.
3. It should unsettle no legitimate, firmly rooted expectation of employees.
4. It should be only temporary in that it is for the purpose of attaining, not maintaining, a balanced workforce.
5. It should represent a minimal intrusion into the legitimate, settled expectations of other employees.

Opponents to affirmative action contend that the efforts do more harm than good, that affirmative action creates ill will and poor morale among workforces. They argue that it translates into current punishment of past wrongs and therefore is inappropriately placed because those who "pay" for the wrongs are unfairly burdened and should not bear the responsibility for the acts of others. Not only white males make this claim. Ward Connerly, an African American regent of the University of California, discussed affirmative action during a *60 Minutes* interview and stated, "Black Americans are not hobbled by chains any longer. We're free to compete. We're capable of competing. It is an absolute insult to suggest that we can't."

Reality Check *Affirmative Action Facts*

- According to the U.S. Census, 23 percent of the workforce is minority, up from 10.7 percent in 1964.
- In 2003, white women's median weekly earnings were 76 percent those of white men. Black women's earnings were 66 percent of the earnings of white men, and Latina women's earnings were 55 percent of white men's earnings.
- Black women with bachelor's degrees make only $1,545 more per year than white males who have only completed high school.
- In an important longitudinal study of black and white women ages 34 to 44, only one-fifth of the gap between their wages could be explained by education and experience. The study found that while women are segregated into lower-paying jobs, the impact is greater on black women than white women.
- Research indicates that as the percentage of females and the percentage of minorities in a job increases, average pay falls, even when all other factors are held steady.
- Black men with professional degrees receive 79 percent of the salary paid to white men with the same degrees and comparable jobs. Black women earn 60 percent.
- A study conducted by the U.S. Department of Labor found that women and minorities have made more progress breaking through the glass ceiling at smaller companies. Women comprise 25 percent of the managers and corporate officers in smaller establishments, while minorities represent 10 percent. But among *Fortune* 500 companies, women held 18 percent of the managerial jobs, with minorities holding 7 percent.
- The federal Glass Ceiling Commission found that white women made up close to half the workforce, but held only 5 percent of the senior level jobs in corporations. Blacks and other minorities account for less than 3 percent of top jobs (vice president and above).
- Cecelia Conrad, associate professor of economics at Barnard College in New York, examined whether affirmative action plans had hurt worker productivity. She found "no evidence that there has been any decline in productivity due to affirmative action." She also found no evidence of improved productivity due to affirmative action.
- A study of Standard & Poor's 500 companies found firms that broke barriers for women and minorities reported stock market records nearly 2.5 times better than comparable companies that took no action.

Source: D. Bennett-Alexander and L. Hartman, *Employment Law for Business*, 5th ed. (McGraw-Hill/Irwin: Burr Ridge, IL 2005), p. 186. Copyright © 2006 by The McGraw-Hill Companies, Inc. Reprinted by permission of the publisher.

In its first ruling on this issue in more than a decade, the Supreme Court addressed affirmative action again through a case of "reverse discrimination" in 2003. While this particular case involved university admissions, American business was a stakeholder in the case as well. The University of Michigan Law School relied on an admissions policy that took into account the ability of each applicant to contribute to the school's social and intellectual life. As part of this criterion, the school considered the applicant's race, on the assumption that a diverse student body would contribute to the goals of the law school and that a critical mass of minority students was required to accomplish that goal. Thus, although scores from LSAT tests, undergraduate college grades, letters of recommendation, and other traditional factors were primarily used to grant admission, an applicant's race was also a factor. Two white females who were denied admission brought the

Reality Check *The White Male as Endangered Species?*

Some white males may feel that they under siege by the forces of affirmative action and multiculturalism. Still, *Newsweek* argues that being a white man remains a very comfortable role in contemporary America:

But is the white male truly an endangered species, or is he just being a jerk? It's still a statistical piece of cake being a white man, at least in comparison with being anything else. White males make up just 39.2 percent of the population, yet they account for 82.5 percent of the *Forbes* 400 (folks worth at least $265 million), 77 percent of Congress, 92 percent of state governors, 70 percent of tenured college faculty, almost 90 percent of daily-newspaper editors, 77 percent of TV news directors.

lawsuit, arguing that admission of minority students with lower grades and test scores violated their rights to equal treatment.

General Motors Corporation filed an *amicus curiae* ("friend of the court") brief in support of the law school's admission policy. By doing so, GM went out of its way at great expense to identify itself as a business stakeholder and argue publicly in support of affirmative action. In its brief, GM claimed that the need to ensure a racially and ethnically diverse student body was a compelling reason to support affirmative action policies. GM claimed that "the future of American business and, in some measure, of the American economy depends on it." In its own business experience, "only a well educated, diverse workforce, comprising people who have learned to work productively and creatively with individuals from a multitude of races and ethnic, religious, and cultural backgrounds, can maintain America's competitiveness in the increasingly diverse and interconnected world economy." Prohibiting affirmative action likely "would reduce racial and ethnic diversity in the pool of employment candidates from which the nation's businesses can draw their future leaders, impeding businesses' own efforts to achieve and obtain the manifold benefits of diversity in the managerial levels of their work forces."[26]

The court seemed to agree.

[D]iminishing the force of such stereotypes is both a crucial part of the Law School's mission, and one that it cannot accomplish with only token numbers of minority students. Just as growing up in a particular region or having particular professional experiences is likely to affect an individual's views, so too is one's own, unique experience of being a racial minority in a society, like our own, in which race unfortunately still matters. The Law School has determined, based on its experience and expertise, that a "critical mass" of underrepresented minorities is necessary to further its compelling interest in securing the educational benefits of a diverse student body.[27]

Do you believe that a diverse student body contributes to the ability of a school to accomplish its educational mission? Should the law prohibit, allow, or require affirmative action programs? Would General Motors be ethically correct in adopting a similar affirmative action hiring policy? Can you think of cases in which an employee's race or ethnic background would be a qualification—or a disqualification—for employment?

In the 2003 class action lawsuit against Abercrombie & Fitch, a settlement agreement was reached between A&F and more than 10,000 claimants who were Latino, African American, Asian American, and female applicants and employees of the company. Under the settlement, A&F agreed to pay claims ranging from several hundred dollars to thousands of dollars, depending on the claimant's particular damages and the extent to which they contributed to the prosecution of the case for a total of $50 million, including attorneys' fees. In addition, A&F also is required to institute policies and programs to promote diversity among its workforce and to prevent discrimination based on race or gender.

The following additional elements of the settlement agreement are important because they were included in order to promote diversity in A&F's workforce. Consider whether any of these elements might have helped A&F to avoid the challenging circumstances described at the beginning of this chapter. If it had instituted some of these prior to the T-shirt situation, maybe it would not have found itself in that hot water:

- "Benchmarks" for hiring and promotion of women, Latinos, African Americans, and Asian Americans (goals, rather than quotas).
- A prohibition on targeting fraternities, sororities, or specific colleges for recruitment purposes.
- Advertising available positions in publications that target minorities of both genders.
- A new Office of Diversity with its own vice president, responsible for reporting to the CEO on Abercrombie's progress toward fair employment practices.
- Hiring 25 recruiters who will focus on and seek women and minority employees.
- Equal Employment Opportunity (EEO) and Diversity Training for all employees with hiring authority.
- Revision of managers' performance evaluations, making progress toward diversity goals a factor in their bonuses and compensation.
- A new internal complaint procedure.
- Marketing materials that will reflect diversity by including members of minority racial and ethnic groups.[28]

Since the time of the settlement and in partial satisfaction of it, A&F has launched a new human resources campaign, "Diversity is who we are." Information about the campaign can be found at A&F's human resources general Web site at http://www.abercrombie.com/anf/hr/jobs/index2.html. The diversity link on the Web site includes photographs of multiracial couples rather than its traditional "American classic" look, images of people of color, and text from the chairman that explains, "**Diversity** and **inclusion** are key to our organization's success. We are determined to have a diverse culture, throughout our organization, that benefits from the perspectives of each individual." Ironically, the main "job opportunities" link on the human resources Web site continues to maintain the standard "American classic" imagery more traditional to A&F's original style.

(continued)

When one explores the impact of the T-shirt controversy it is interesting to consider both sides of the stakeholder opinions. Though one side expressed emotional pain and derided the perpetuation of historic discrimination, others felt that people have become too thin-skinned and that, as a society, we have moved beyond these issues to a point where poking fun at stereotypes is acceptable, hence A&F's response. One of the values in a diverse workforce is the ability to weigh varying stakeholder perspectives. While one group might consider a marketing campaign to be "poking fun," another might be brutally pained by the mockery. A greater diversity among decision makers certainly does not guarantee that all perspectives are represented, but it does ensure that a broader range of opinions might be considered.

A&F might benefit from a broader range of opinions on a variety of matters. In recent years, it has drawn criticism from Mothers Against Drunk Driving for its "Drinking 101" directions for "creative drinking" in its catalogs aimed at college students and from several family-oriented organizations for its children's thong underwear with the words "eye candy" and "wink wink" printed on the front. With headlines such as "Abercrombie Criticized for Sexy Undies,"[29] perhaps A&F again misjudged its audience. A&F responded that "the underwear for young girls was created with the intent to be lighthearted and cute," and placed any misunderstanding "purely in the eye of the beholder."

Questions, Projects, and Exercises

1. Maya confides in her friend and colleague, Alicia, "My husband Gene is very sick. I haven't shared this with anyone else at work because I didn't want them to think I couldn't manage my responsibilities. He was diagnosed last year with progressive Parkinson's and I thought it would move slowly, and that I could handle everything. Believe me, I am trying to keep everything under control, but our home life is just overwhelming me already. You couldn't imagine how hard this is—physically and emotionally—plus there's the added pressure of keeping it under wraps at work. You know they'll start diminishing my role on those larger projects if they knew my attention might be diverted, and Gene and I just can't risk the financial instability that might cause. I really appreciate being able to talk to you. I had to get this off my chest, and I knew I could trust you." Alicia offered her shoulder and told Maya that she could count on her to cover for her, if need be, or to support her in any way she needed. Three weeks later, Alicia and Maya are separately called into the president's office and told that they are both being considered for a more senior-level position. This new position would require a great commitment of both time and energy and would involve taking on a large number of subordinates for mentoring and development. Both women express a strong interest in the position and are told that they will learn of the president's decision within two weeks. What should Alicia do with the information Maya gave her, if anything? Notwithstanding your response to the previous question, if Alicia chooses to inform the president of Maya's current situation, would you consider that action to be wrong, unethical? If you were the president in this current scenario, what could you do to impact the corporate culture in order to ensure that your preferred result in this dilemma occurred in the future?

2. Review the discussion about global labor challenges, explore any additional resources (Web sites or otherwise), and offer your conclusions. In particular, which arguments do you find the most or least persuasive? Are you in favor of greater restrictions and regulations of MNCs and the treatment of their workforces, or would you advocate a more hands-off approach (sometimes described inappropriately as "pro-sweatshops")? Support your conclusions.

3. We can distinguish due process from just cause in the following way: Imagine a company wanted to abandon the arbitrary nature of employment at will and ensure that its employees were treated fairly in any termination decision. Can you imagine how the employment environment in that firm might be different than in other firms? One approach would be to specify the acceptable reasons for terminating an employee. Obvious candidates would include absenteeism, incompetent job performance, theft, fraud, and economic necessity. This approach might also identify unacceptable reasons for dismissal. Such a policy would be identified as a "just cause" practice, since it defines the factors that would justify dismissing an employee for cause. But creating such a list could be a challenge in that one would have to know beforehand all possible reasons for firing someone. As the common law clearly shows, one cannot anticipate all future ways in which something unjust could occur. As a result, a due process policy might be created to complement, or substitute for, a just cause policy. A policy guaranteeing due process, for example, would outline procedures that must be followed before an employee can be dismissed. The process itself is what determines a just dismissal. If an employer followed the process, the decision would be considered just; if the process was violated, then dismissal would be considered unjust. Such procedures might include regular written performance appraisals, prior warnings, documentation, probationary periods, rights to appeal, or response to accusations. Can you imagine other ways in which this hypothetical firm might change standard processes to ensure fairness?

   - What are the key facts relevant to issues of due process and fairness?
   - What are the ethical issues involved in your decision and implementation?
   - Who are the stakeholders involved in your decision?
   - What alternatives are available to you?
   - How would each of your alternatives affect each of the stakeholders you have identified?
   - Where might you look for additional guidance to assist you in resolving this particular dilemma?

4. What is the difference in your mind, and in your common usage, between a perception, a generalization, and a stereotype? Can you give an example of each? After doing so, go to the Web and find dictionary-equivalent definitions of the terms to determine whether your common understanding is the correct one. Are each or all consistently unethical judgments or are they sometimes or always ethically justified in their use and implementation? Under what conditions?

5. A particular research study provides some evidence that those born between 1979 and 1994 are perceived as "impatient, self-serving, disloyal, unable to delay gratification and, in short, feeling that they are entitled to everything without working for it." The study dubs this group the "entitlement generation." Do you know people born during those years? Is this true generally or would you consider the perception instead a stereotype? From where do you think it stems?

6. As a result of rising health care costs and the challenge to contain them, companies are trying to encourage employees to take better care of themselves, and some are even penalizing employees if they do not. One company, AstraZeneca, increased employees' health-insurance premium by $50 a month for each month they failed to complete an online health-risk assessment tool that asked for lifestyle details, then offered recommendations on ways live a more healthy lifestyle. In 2006, an internal Wal-Mart Stores Inc. memo was leaked publicly that suggested that it cut its health care costs by discouraging unhealthy people from applying for jobs. What do you think of businesses' attempts to decrease health care costs by helping employees to become healthier? What are the ethical issues associated with a firm's choice to cut health care costs by eliminating people who are unhealthy? What rights, duties, responsibilities, and consequences does this strategy imply? Do you think people who don't take care of themselves should be responsible for their increased health care costs? How would you feel personally if your past health conditions and current health practices were a part of an employment application?

7. You run a small consulting business that serves a relatively diverse community and have 24 employees in professional positions. You are not subject to Executive Order 11246. You are concerned that, of the employees in professional positions, your workplace has only one African American, no other employees of color, and three women. At this time, your upper-level management—the top six executives and yourself—are all white males. On the other hand, you have 15 support staff (secretaries and other clerical workers), of whom 14 are women and 11 are either African American or Latino.

8. You would very much like to better represent the community in which you do business and you believe a diverse workforce has significant business benefits. You therefore decide to institute a program that will increase the numbers of minorities and women in professional positions as soon as possible. Is this permissible? Do you have all the relevant facts you will need to answer this question? What steps will you undertake in your plan to increase these proportions and what pitfalls must you avoid?

9. You are a senior global human resources manager for a large apparel retailer that purchases goods from all over the world. The media have focused a great deal of attention on the conditions of your suppliers' workplaces and, for myriad reasons including a strong commitment to your values-based mission, as well as a concern for your reputation, you are paying close attention to the wages paid to the workers who construct your clothing. Your suppliers in several locations have agreed to talk with you about developing a policy that would apply throughout your operations—now and in the future, wherever you plan to do business—and would impose a minimum wage requirement for all factory workers. You begin to explore some of the resources publicly available to you, such as www.globalexchange.org, www.workersrights.org, www.fairlabor.org, and www.irrc.org, to find out what other firms are doing and what labor advocates recommend in terms of language for policies such as these. You explore Nike's Web site at www.nikebiz.com, http://www.adidas-group.com/en/home/welcome.asp, and others. Now it is time to begin constructing your own policy. What will you include, how specific will you make this policy, how will you determine what will be the "living wage" in each region, and what elements will it contain? Please draft a policy for your company on implementing a living wage worldwide.

Key Terms

After reading this chapter, you should have a clear understanding of the following Key Terms. The page numbers refer to the point at which they were discussed in the chapter. For a more complete definition, please see the Glossary.

affirmative action, *p. 215*

child labor, *p. 207*

discrimination, *p. 210*

diversity, *p. 212*

downsize, *p. 195*

due process, *p. 193*

employment at will (EAW), *p. 193*

just cause, *p. 194*

multiculturalism, *p. 213*

OSHA, *p. 203*

reverse discrimination, *p. 215*

sweatshops, *p. 205*

Endnotes

1. Walker Information, "Committed Employees Make Your Business Work," *Employee Relationship Report* (1999) http://www.walkerinfo.com/products/err/ee_study.cfm.

2. Jeffrey Pfeffer, *The Human Equation: Building Profits by Putting People First* (Boston, MA.: Harvard University Press, 1998).

3. Neal Ashkanasy and Catherine Daus, "Emotion in the Workplace," *Academy of Management Executive* 16, no. 1 (2002), p. 76.

4. *Payne* v. *Western & A.A.R. Co.,* 81 Tenn. 507 (1884).

5. John A. Challenger, "Downsizing: The Better Ways," *Ethikos* (January/February 2002), p. 7.

6. Craig Karmin, "Off-shoring Can Generate Jobs in the U.S.," *The Wall Street Journal,* March 16, 2004.

7. D. Arnold and L. Hartman, "Worker Rights and Low Wage Industrialization, How to Avoid Sweatshops," *Human Rights Quarterly*, vol. 28, no. 3 (August 2006), pp. 676–700.

8. Denis G. Arnold and Norman E. Bowie, "Sweatshops and Respect for Persons," *Business Ethics Quarterly* 221 (2003), pp. 223–224, cited in D. Arnold and L. Hartman, "Worker Rights."

9. L. Hartman, B. Shaw, R. Stevenson, "Exploring the Ethics and Economics of Global Labor Standards: A Challenge to Integrated Social Contract Theory," *Business Ethics Quarterly,* 13, no. 2 (2003), pp. 193–220.

10. Kebebew Ashagrie, *"Statistics on Working Children and Hazardous Child Labor in Brief"* (Geneva: ILO, 1998), (accessed July 29, 2006) at http://www.ilo.org/public/english/standards/ipec/simpoc/stats/child/stats.htm.

11. International Labour Office, *Every Child Counts* (Geneva: International Labour Organization, 2002), accessed July 29, 2006, at http://www.ilo.org/public/english/standards/ipec/simpoc/others/globalest.pdf.

12. International Labour Organization, *World Employment Report 1998-1999* (Geneva: International Labour Organization, 1999).

13. World Health Organization, *Children at Work: Special Health Risks, Technical Report Series No. 756* (Geneva: International Labour Organization, 1987); K. Satyanarayan et al., "Effect of Early Childhood Nutrition and Child Labour on Growth and Adult Nutritional Status of Rural Indian Boys around Hyderabad," *Human Nutrition: Clinical Nutrition*, no. 40 C (1986).

14. World Health Organization, *Children at Work, infra*, note 13.

15. See Lammy Betten, *International Labor Law* (1993), p. 316, which notes that child labor legislation may lead to a movement of child labor from the formal to the infor-

mal sectors of the economy. See also Ministry of Labour, Manpower and Overseas Pakistanis & SEBCON (Pvt) Ltd., *Qualitative Survey on Child Labour in Pakistan* (Islamabad: International Labour Organization/OPEC, 1996) The ILO study in Pakistan evidences that, among the child labourers interviewed, 72 percent had no access to education at all. Alan R. Myerson, "In Principle, a Case for More 'Sweatshops," *The New York Times* (June 22, 1997) (online version: http://www.ncpa.org/pd/pdint152. html); "Labor Secretary Herman Speaks Out against Child Labor,"*Apparel Industry Magazine* 58, no. 11 (November 1997), p. 12 [Mohammed Hafizul Islam Chowdhury, an apparel manufacturer from Bangladesh, asks, "Why are Americans against child labor? It's good in my country because it keeps children off the streets and out of prostitution."]; and Stephen Golub, "Are International Labor Standards Needed to Prevent Social Dumping?"*Finance & Development* (December 1997), pp. 20, 22, http://www. imf.org/external/pubs/ft/fandd/1997/12/pdf/golub.pdf.

16. However, some advocacy groups fail to consider all perspectives. For example, the Global Reporting Initiative's discussion on its Child Labour Indicators fails to take into account the impact of the termination of children beyond their removal from the workplace.

17. Richard A. Posner, *Economic Analysis of Law* (New York: Aspen, 2002), p. 616.

18. EEOC, "Sexual Harassment" (2006), http://www.eeoc.gov/types/sexual_harassment. html.

19. Marianne Bertrand and Sendhil Millainathan, "Are Emily and Brendan More Employable than Lakisha and Jamal?" University of Chicago, Graduate School of Business, unpublished paper, November 18, 2002.

20. Peggy McIntosh, "White Privilege: Unpacking the Invisible Knapsack," *Peace and Freedom* (July/August 1989), pp. 10–12.

21. *Good Morning America*, "Powerfully Nice," abcnews.com. July 16, 2001.

22. "Diversity Policies Have Positive Impact on Company Business Performance," *New York Times Company Press Release*, February 13, 2003.

23. Business in the Community, "Workplace," http://www.bitc.org.uk/resources/research/ statbank/workplace/index.html.

24. "Up from Inscrutable," Fortune, April 6, 1992, p. 20.

25. "Up from Inscrutable," *infra*, note 24.

26. General Motors, "Brief of General Motors as *Amicus Curiae* in support of Defendants" in *Gratz* v. *Bollinger,* 539 U.S. 244 (2003).

27. *Grutter* v. *Bollinger* 539 U.S. 306 (2003).

28. The actual consent decree (legal term for a settlement agreement) can be accessed at http://www.afjustice.com/pdf/20050422_consent_decree.pdf.

29. *CNN Money* (May 28, 2002), http://money.cnn.com/2002/05/22/news/companies/ abercrombie/.

Readings

Reading 6-1: "Worker Rights and Low Wage Industrialization: How to Avoid Sweatshops," *by Denis G. Arnold & Laura P. Hartman, p. 225.*

Reading 6-2: "Women in the Workplace: Freedom of Choice or Freedom from Choice?" *by Tara J. Radin, p. 235.*

Reading 6-3: "Employment-at-Will, Employee Rights, and Future Directions for Employment," *by Tara J. Radin and Patricia H. Werhane, p. 240.*

Reading **6-1**

Worker Rights and Low Wage Industrialization: How to Avoid Sweatshops

Denis G. Arnold and Laura P. Hartman

Abstract

Disputes concerning global labor practices are at the core of contemporary debates regarding globalization. Critics have charged multinational enterprises with the unjust exploitation of workers in the developing world. In response, some economists and "classical liberals" have argued that these criticisms are grounded in a naïve understanding of global economics. They contend instead that sweatshops constitute an inevitable and essential feature of economic development. To the contrary, we argue that there are persuasive theoretical and empirical reasons for rejecting the arguments of these defenders of sweatshops. In particular, we argue that respecting workers entails an obligation to adhere to local labor laws, and we demonstrate that it is feasible for multinational corporations (MNCs) to provide decent working conditions and fair wages to workers. The main conclusion of this essay is that there are compelling ethical and strategic reasons for MNCs to embrace voluntary codes of conduct.

I. Introduction

The use of global sweatshops for the manufacture of consumer goods is an important feature of contemporary debates concerning economic globalization.[1] On university campuses throughout the United States, student activists have successfully lobbied administrators to require that manufacturers of university-licensed apparel adhere to codes of conduct that protect factory workers from unjust exploitation. Human rights organizations and unions have led boycotts and have waged media campaigns against companies that they believe unjustly exploit factory workers in the interest of excessive profits. Consumers are becoming increasingly aware of the debate and are demanding changes to create greater alignment with the recommendations of intergovernmental organizations such as the International Labour Organization. Partially in response to such critics and inquiries, companies such as Nike and the Gap have made significant efforts to use their leverage to eliminate the worst forms of worker abuses from their contract factories. Meanwhile, some economists and proponents of "classical liberalism" wage a campaign of their own, arguing that these criticisms are grounded in a naïve understanding of global economics. They contend instead that not only do sweatshops constitute an inevitable and essential feature of economic development, but they also benefit the world's poor.

This essay provides an overview of arguments used to defend the existence and continued use of sweatshops. Section II argues that multinational corporations (MNCs) have an ethical obligation to respect the rights of their employees and contract workers. The next section argues that defenders of sweatshops fail to appreciate the range of ethical issues concerning working conditions. In particular, respecting workers entails an obligation to adhere to local labor laws, and it is feasible for MNCs to provide decent working conditions and fair wages to workers. Section IV argues that voluntarily improving legal compliance, working conditions, and wages will not inevitably lead to negative consequences. Section V argues that MNCs have good strategic reasons for embracing voluntary codes of conduct. The essay concludes that there are compelling ethical and strategic reasons for MNCs to respect local labor laws, to voluntarily improve working conditions, and to pay workers a living wage in their global factories.

II. The Case for Sweatshops

Many individuals who are concerned with the welfare of workers in developing nations nevertheless disagree with the conclusion that sweatshop conditions should be improved. These individuals argue, with varying degrees of sophistication, that improving sweatshop conditions will result in greater harm than good. They point out that the exploitation of cheap labor supplies allows developing countries to expand export activities and to improve their economies. This economic growth creates more jobs, causing the labor market to tighten, which in turn forces companies to improve conditions in order to attract additional workers. Though an unpopular sentiment with the general consuming public, many economists argue that the maintenance of sweatshop conditions is well supported by economic theory. Furthermore, proponents of sweatshops argue that people work in sweatshop conditions because it is the most rational means available to them for furthering their own ends.[2]

Frequently, these arguments are supplemented by the claim that the views of North American and European critics of sweatshops are simply naïve, or worse, their views are grounded merely in an aesthetic distaste for sweatshops. The defenders of sweatshops argue that, if these critics would only be less self-indulgent, they would recognize the positive role that sweatshops play in improving the lives of workers in the developing world. The following passages are typical of the arguments deployed by those who defend sweatshops:

> I have come to feel that campaigns against sweatshops are often counterproductive, harming the very Third World citizens that they are intended to help. The effect of these campaigns is to be twofold. First, in the short term they clearly raise the condition at existing factories producing branded merchandise for companies like Nike. Second, they raise labor costs and thus encourage mechanization, reducing the number of employees needed in the factories.[3]

> [H]igher wages and improved labor standards are not free. After all, the critics themselves attack companies for chasing cheap labor. It follows that, if labor in developing countries is made more expensive (say, as the result of pressures by critics), then those countries will receive less foreign investment, and fewer jobs will be created there. Imposing higher wages may deprive these countries of the one comparative advantage that they enjoy, namely low-cost labor.[4]

> You may say that the wretched of the earth should not be forced to serve as hewers of wood, drawers of water, and sewers of sneakers for the affluent. But what is the alternative? . . . Should their own governments provide more social justice? Of course—but they won't, or at least not because we tell them to. And as long as you have no realistic alternative to industrialization based on low wages, to oppose it means that you are willing to deny desperately poor people the best chance they have of progress for the sake of what amounts to an aesthetic standard—that is, the fact that you don't like the idea of workers being paid a pittance to supply rich Westerners with fashion items.[5]

> [Sweatshop critics seem] to ignore the well-established fact that multinational corporations commonly pay their workers more on average in comparison to the prevailing market wage for similar workers employed elsewhere in the economy. In cases where subcontracting is

involved, workers are generally paid no less than the prevailing market wage. We are concerned therefore that if MNCs are persuaded to pay even more to their apparel workers in response to what the ongoing studies by the anti-sweatshop organizations may conclude are appropriate wage levels, the net result would be shifts in employment that will worsen the collective welfare of the very workers in poor countries who are supposed to be helped.[6]

At least some of these claims are not baseless. For example, workers in these factories often do make more than workers in the informal sectors of developing economies. Furthermore, there is evidence that workers at these factories often make more than the going rate at nearby non-MNC factories.[7] In summary, defenders of sweatshops argue that, though one may not like some of what one sees in the labor conditions of developing nations, this is the market at work, and the market works to generate overall improvements for individuals and society as a whole. So, more, not fewer, sweatshops are needed.

There are, however, a number of perplexing features of pro-sweatshop arguments such as those outlined above. First, proponents of sweatshops seem to believe that MNCs and their contactors have no ethical obligations to workers in the developing world. Second, defenders of sweatshops typically do not distinguish between issues such as the health and safety conditions in the factories, the number of working hours of employees, compliance with local labor laws, wages, and benefits. Indeed, these defenders appear to assume that improvements in any one of these areas will result in inevitable and dire consequences for workers. However, such assumptions are unwarranted. Third, despite the significant scholarly accomplishments of some defenders of sweatshops, they have failed to provide detailed arguments or analyses in support of their conclusions. Instead they tend to invoke basic economic theory or "classical liberal" ideology as a basis for their claims. However, without more detailed, empirically grounded arguments that focus on the labor markets in specific economies and the practices of specific MNCs, their arguments are unpersuasive.[8] Furthermore, there are good reasons for thinking that many of the arguments used to defend sweatshops are flawed on both theoretical and empirical grounds. Section III of this essay will defend these contrary conclusions.

III. The Ethical Obligations of Multinational Corporations

A remarkable feature of many of the arguments used to defend current conditions in sweatshops is the assumption that MNC managers have no ethical obligations to employees in the developing world. Defenders of sweatshops appear to presume that the wages and working conditions in the factories of MNCs and their contractors are the inevitable outcome of global economic forces.[9] For example, economist Paul Krugman observes:

> Workers in those shirt and sneaker factories are, inevitably, paid very little and expected to
> endure terrible working conditions. I say "inevitably" because their employers are not in
> business for their (or their workers') health; they pay as little as possible, and that minimum
> is determined by the other opportunities available to workers.[10]

However, Krugman concedes too much. Insofar as business is a human activity, it is subject to the same rationally justifiable moral norms as any other human activity. While it is true that MNC managers have an ethical obligation to make a profit for the owners of the enterprise, this obligation does not automatically trump other ethical obligations. Indeed, one of the primary tasks of an ethical manager is to balance the competing ethical obligations of stakeholders. One core ethical obligation of MNC managers is to respect their employees. To fully respect a person, one must actively treat his or her humanity as an end, and not merely as a means to an end. This means that it is impermissible to treat persons like disposable tools. The Kantian basis for this claim is well established. Respecting people is an obligation that holds for every person qua person, whether in the personal realm or in the marketplace. Respecting people requires honoring their humanity; which is to say it requires treating them as ends in themselves. Thomas Hill argues that treating persons as ends in themselves requires supporting and developing certain human capacities, including the capacity to act on reason; the capacity to act on the basis of prudence or efficiency; the capacity to set goals; the capacity to accept categorical imperatives; and the capacity to understand the world and reason abstractly. In their recent discussion of the doctrine of respect for persons as it applies to global sweatshops, Denis Arnold and Norman Bowie make several additions to the list. They argue that treating people as ends in themselves requires that MNC managers and their contractors ensure the physical well-being of employees and refrain from undermining the development of their rational and moral capacities. They argue that respecting workers in global factories requires that MNC factories, including contract factories, adhere to local labor laws; refrain from the use of coercion; provide decent working conditions; and provide wages above the overall poverty line for a forty-eight-hour work week.

The application of a Kantian approach to problems concerning poverty and economic development in underdeveloped countries is similar to the capabilities approach developed by Amartya Sen. Sen has famously argued that development involves more than an increase in people's incomes and the gross national product of the country. He argues that one must be concerned with certain basic human capabilities, the most important of which is freedom. Sen's perspective is similar in important respects to the Kantian perspective because both are concerned with providing work that enhances the ability of workers to exercise core human capabilities. The United Nations utilizes both the Kantian view and the capabilities view as the dual theoretical foundation for its defense of human rights. Among the rights identified by the UN are freedom from injustice and violations of the rule of law; freedom to do decent work without exploitation; and the freedom to develop and realize one's human potential. The UN argues that all global actors, including MNCs, have a moral obligation to respect basic human rights. This general approach to poverty and development has recently been embraced by the World Bank. The World Bank identified "crucial gaps" in its efforts to encourage development and eliminate poverty through market liberalization. In particular, it notes its previous failure to pay "adequate attention to the quality and sustainability of growth." The World Bank now explicitly acknowledges that all major stakeholders have important roles to play in the process of promoting not merely economic growth, but sustainable economic growth that is sensitive to the needs of workers in developing nations. While holding that "[f]unctioning markets and liberalization are crucial" to poverty reduction, the World Bank acknowledges the "limits of the market" and the essential roles diverse stakeholders must play in the process. MNCs have significant interests in developing nations as sources of natural resources, inexpensive labor, and markets for their goods and services. As such, the World Bank properly recognizes MNCs as stakeholders with important moral obligations in the global reform process. Furthermore, it is not just non-governmental organizations (NGOs) that hold this view. Those familiar with the practice of business recognize that the view that MNCs have an ethical obligation to respect workers in their global factories has long been accepted and practiced by a select number of MNCs, including Motorola and Levi Strauss.

A second problematic feature of many of the arguments used to defend sweatshops is that they tend to blur the distinction between factories owned by MNCs and factories with which MNCs contract. Not all MNCs own their own factories; indeed, many MNCs use a substantial number of contractor factories to produce their products, and some use such contractors exclusively. Typically, employees of MNC contractor factories earn less than the employees of MNC-owned factories and work under more adverse conditions. Historically, most MNCs accepted responsibility only for that which fell within the boundaries of their own organizations and specifically did not regard themselves as accountable for those particular labor abuses that occurred within the operations of their contractors. This original conception of global supply chain systems was the outgrowth of traditionally insular domestic contracting relationships. When North American and European MNCs did business domestically, they were bound to domestic laws, as were their contractors and other stakeholders. When they began to globalize, most MNC managers did not at first consider the need to be accountable for the actions of their contractors since that was not the case in their domestic business operations, where comprehensive and well-enforced legal systems were already in place. In addition, part of the allure of overseas contracts was a lower cost structure, in part the result of fewer legal requirements and lax regulatory regimes. This conception of a global supply chain system changed for some MNC managers as awareness grew regarding working conditions in these factories and the lack of adequate legal protections for workers. The emerging alternative conception of supply chain systems involves a network of relationships among diverse stakeholders such as the MNCs, contractors, factory workers, NGOs, governments, and consumers. Each of these entities contributes to shaping the social-political and economic environments in which the MNCs operate, and helps define the boundaries within which the MNCs consider and reach decisions regarding the labor challenges they face. At the core of this new conception of the supply chain system is the recognition by MNCs that they have ethical obligations regarding the practices of their contractors. Defenders of sweatshops have tended to ignore these changes in the global supply chain.

The justification for the claim that MNCs have ethical obligations regarding the practices of their contractors is grounded in the moral claims discussed above, together with a recognition that the relationship of power between many MNCs and their contractors and suppliers is significantly imbalanced in favor of the MNCs. One researcher describes the relationship in the following way:

> [A]s more and more developing countries have sought to establish export sectors, local manufacturers are locked in fierce competitive battles with one another. The resulting oversupply of export factories allows U.S. companies to move from one supplier to another in search of the lowest prices, quickest turnaround, highest quality and best delivery terms, weighted according to the priorities of the company. In this context, large U.S. manufacturer-merchandisers and retailers wield enormous power to dictate the price at which they will purchase goods.[11]

MNCs that dictate the price at which they will purchase goods from contractors also have considerable influence regarding working conditions. In many cases, contract factory owners may not have the resources to improve working conditions and wages without assistance from the MNC.[12] Given this imbalance in power, MNC managers are well positioned to help ensure that the employees of its contractors are respected. In addition, MNCs can draw upon substantial economic resources, management expertise, and technical knowledge to assist their business partners in creating a respectful work environment.

Defenders of sweatshops tend to presume that there are only two choices: permit, or even encourage, existing sweatshops to maintain poor working conditions and wages in order to retain desperately needed jobs in developing economies, or mandate improvements in working conditions, allowing wages to drive up unemployment. As this essay will discuss, this is a false presumption. There is a third option. Morally imaginative MNCs can voluntarily opt to improve the conditions in their global factories, without laying off workers, while remaining competitive within their industry.

* * * *

V. Sweatshop Economics

Contrary to the contentions of the defenders of sweatshops, voluntarily improving legal compliance, working conditions, and wages will not inevitably lead to the negative consequences they predict. First, with regard to the lowest paid formal sector wage earners in developing countries, the assumption that productivity is independent of wage levels is mistaken. The wage which, if reduced, would make the firm worse off because of a decrease in worker productivity is known as the efficiency wage. The most obvious ways in which wages affect productivity are captured by nutrition models. Put simply, workers whose minimum daily dietary requirements are met and who have basic non-food needs met will have more energy and better attitudes at work; will be less likely to come to work ill; and will be absent less frequently. In order to ensure that workers' minimum daily caloric intake is met, it may be necessary to pay workers two to four times the amount necessary to purchase adequate food and health care for the employee. This is because the employer cannot prevent the worker from spending wages on food and health care for the employee's family.[13] A second economic model emphasizes the gift-exchange nature of employment relations, as opposed to the pure market exchange of such relations. On this model, employers who compensate workers at rates significantly higher than the wages demanded by the market are seen as bestowing a gift on workers, who reciprocate with greater productivity and greater loyalty. Increased productivity and employee loyalty alone may offset the cost spent to respect workers' basic rights through adherence to local labor laws, providing comparatively safe and healthy working conditions, and paying workers a living wage.

Second, it is economically feasible for MNCs to raise wages and to improve working conditions in factories in developing economies without causing increases in unemployment. MNCs may choose to improve wages and working conditions while maintaining existing employment levels. In cases where increased productivity and loyalty do not completely offset increased labor costs, these costs may be passed on to consumers. A recent study of this issue found that

> [l]arge mandated wage increases, as a feature of a decent labour standards regime in the
> apparel production industry, could be financed through increases in retail prices—certainly
> through price increases within the range that US consumers say they are willing to accept to
> ensure 'good' working conditions in apparel production.[14]

Increased labor cost may be offset by the value added to the good insofar as consumers demonstrate a preference for products produced under conditions in which the rights of workers are respected.

Third, it should also be noted that profit margins vary among products. For the manufacturers of brand name retail goods, a significant increase in labor costs may be readily absorbed as an operating expense, as in the case of Nike. However, there may be cases where increased labor costs are not offset by greater productivity, where the increase in costs cannot be passed on to consumers, and where the increased costs cannot be readily absorbed as an operating expense. For example, manufacturers of generic goods with low profit margins may find it difficult to absorb the cost of increased labor expenses. In such cases, the added cost of labor may instead be balanced by internal cost-cutting measures. One set of obvious targets for expense reduction is the cost of supporting significant numbers of home-country managers in the country of the supplier. While some presence may be necessary, it will often be more cost effective to employ host-country nationals in this capacity. Another attractive set of targets is executive perks. While such perks vary significantly among firms, it does appear morally inconsistent to argue that improving the welfare of the factory workers is cost prohibitive while executive perks remain substantial. Given the frequently fierce competition among the manufacturers of generic products targeted at cost-conscious consumers, it may be difficult for one retailer to remain competitive while raising prices to cover increased labor costs, while others do not. For this reason, industry-wide standards concerning labor practices may prove valuable as a way of distributing costs equitably. Finally, the cost may be passed on to the owners of the business enterprise via lower return on equity. In such cases, the costs of respecting workers must be regarded as a necessary condition of doing business. This point should not be problematic for any manager who recognizes the existence of basic human dignity. For insofar as one recognizes the dignity of workers qua persons, one has an obligation to respect that dignity.

VI. The Importance of Voluntary Codes

The best means by which to improve working conditions is through MNC adoption and implementation of voluntary codes of conduct. "Code of conduct" refers to the codification of a firm's values as they are interpreted and applied to the workplaces in which the firm's goods are produced. These codes are created voluntarily by MNCs and are not based on the laws of any one nation but are instead designed to help managers and suppliers embrace and implement a core set of values regarding the treatment of workers. These codes are intended to transcend cultural and geographical borders.

Sometimes the workplaces where the firm's goods are produced are wholly-owned by the MNC but, more often than not, they are owned and managed by third-party suppliers. Given the power differential discussed earlier, the MNC often has significant influence over the contractor that enables them to require adherence to the MNC's codes of conduct. Note that the mere drafting of a code of conduct is insufficient. Instead, it is the voluntary adoption and full-scale implementation of a code that is encouraged. A firm that merely produces a code without further action sends a message that the same lack of attention is all that is expected from its workers, suppliers, and other contractors. To the contrary, effective integration of a code throughout an organization's culture requires that a firm hold its contractors to the same standard regarding respect for employees to which it holds itself.

The remainder of this section explains the significant strategic value a firm can experience through the integration of a voluntary code of conduct for itself and its suppliers. Though this essay encourages an enlightened motivation for the development and integration of a code—one that respects and protects the basic rights of workers—this essay recognizes that some firms may simply proceed down this path on the assumption that cohesive, clear expectations about conduct and values through a code can support long-term business strategies and ultimately the firm's bottom line. Firms might also be motivated as a result of intense media scrutiny or other external pressure, or as a deterrent to the imposition of more stringent involuntary controls. Under any of these models, notwithstanding the basis or motivation for the code integration, the MNC as well as its suppliers and workers may still reap a benefit. However, a firm that undertakes code development and integration as part of a larger scheme of corporate global citizenship, and in an enlightened and concerted effort to recognize the rights of all workers involved in the production of its goods, is more likely to reap greater overall value from its effort than one that is limited to a basic adoption of the code itself in order to ensure positive bottom-line impact.

In her recent work on codes, Deborah Leipziger explains that effective codes can support a firm in the short-term (during crisis management), mid-term (perhaps prevent a crisis from arising), and long-term (enhance stakeholder value). In particular, effective codes can:

- Raise awareness about corporate responsibility within the company
- Help companies to set strategies and objectives
- Assist companies with implementation and control of values
- Help companies avoid risk
- Foster dialogue and partnerships between companies and key stakeholders and
- Enhance utility and identity among divergent companies

These benefits are reinforced by research and are repeatedly articulated as valid, credible results of successful code implementation. For instance, in its report, "Creating a Workable Company Code of Ethics," the Ethics Resource Center contends that "every organizations, regardless of size, focus or status, should have a code of conduct in place" for several reasons, including (1) communication with stakeholders and definition of desired behavior; (2) compliance with recent and anticipated legislation; (3) financial risk mitigation through a good faith effort to prevent illegal acts; and (4) benchmarks against which individual and organizational performance can be measured.

In recent years attempts have been made to measure the bottom-line impact of encouraging ethical decision making and, in particular, the financial returns on the development and implementation of a code of conduct. Researchers have found that in emerging markets, cost savings, productivity improvement, revenue growth, and access to markets were the most important business benefits of "sustainability activities"; and the role of codes of conduct in perpetuating these activities was found to be significant. Similarly, a landmark study found that firms that were ranked highest in terms of their records on a variety of social issues (including charitable contributions, community outreach programs, environmental performance, advancement of women, and promotion of minorities), which often find their foundations in codes of conduct, had greater financial performance as well. Financial performance was better in terms of operating income growth, sales-to-assets ratio, sales growth, return on equity, earnings-to-asset growth, return on investment, return on assets and asset growth.

In exploring the implementation of a voluntary code, research recently undertaken by the Human Rights Research and Education Centre shows that there are essentially five "generations" of issues of ethical and social responsibility dealt with in most business codes of conduct and corresponding management systems:

- First generation: conflict of interest.
- Second generation: commercial conduct.
- Third generation: employee and other third-party concerns.
- Fourth generation: community and environmental concerns.
- Fifth generation: accountability and social justice .

The business case for codes of conduct is related most closely to the third generation of issues and involves respect for employee rights as well as rights of others in direct relationship with the corporation: "[t]he business case for implementing these principles includes improved corporate relations, a motivated work force, and satisfied customers." The threshold issue is to determine whether the presence of a code is an accurate indicator of genuine ethical commitment. The Institute of Business Ethics conducted a study to validate this supposition by reviewing "good practices" at a sample of UK companies. They evaluated "good practices" by looking at (a) a rating for risk management; and (b) a peer evaluation which included, for example, competent management, financial soundness, and quality of goods and services and found a positive relationship. The second stage of their research was to determine the relationship between ethical commitment and financial performance:

- Regarding financial performance, it was found that those companies in the sample with a code of ethics had, over the period 1997–2001, out-performed a similar sized group who said they did not have a code.
- Companies with a code of ethics generated significantly more economic added value and market added value in the years 1997–2000, than those without codes.
- Companies with a code of ethics experienced far less P/E volatility over a four-year period than those without them. Other research has suggested that a stable P/E ratio tends to attract capital at below average cost; having a code may be said to be a significant indicator of consistent management.

This study gives credence to the assertion that "you do business ethically because it pays." However, the most effective driver for maintaining a high level of integrity throughout the business is "because it is seen by the board, employees and other stakeholders to be a core value and therefore the right thing to do … a sustainable business is one which is well managed and which takes business ethics seriously." Leaders of this type of business do not need any assurance that their approach to the way they do business will also enhance their profitability, because they know it to be true. The study concluded that "having a code . . . might, therefore, be said to be one hallmark of a well managed company." Defenders of sweatshops have yet to take seriously the positive role that a carefully crafted and well enforced voluntary code of conduct can have on the success of MNCs.

VII. Conclusions

There are persuasive theoretical and practical reasons for rejecting the arguments of the defenders of sweatshops. In particular, there are compelling ethical and strategic reasons for MNCs to respect local labor laws, to voluntarily improve working conditions, and to pay workers a living wage in their global factories. The evidence shows that MNCs can respect the rights of workers without decreasing overall welfare. However, there remain important areas for further research. For example, how can smaller firms that purchase only a portion of a supplier factory's production exert influence over that factory so that it adheres to the firm's code of conduct? To what extent will industrywide codes of conduct support or hinder respect for the rights of workers? How can firms that ignore workers' rights in the interest of economic efficiency best be identified and sanctioned? And how can those firms that actively seek to respect their workers best be identified and rewarded? These are some of the questions that remain to be taken up by scholars interested in enhancing the welfare of the global workforce.

Source: D. Arnold and L. Hartman, "Worker Rights and Low Wage Industrialization: How to Avoid Sweatshops," *Human Rights Quarterly*, vol. 28, no. 3 (August 2006), pp. 676–700. Reprinted by permission of *Human Rights Quarterly* and its publisher, the Johns Hopkins University Press.

Notes

1. For the purposes of this paper, we define the term *sweatshop* as any workplace in which workers are typically subject to two or more of the following conditions: income for a 48 hour workweek less than the overall poverty rate for that country; systematic forced overtime; systematic health and safety risks due to negligence or the willful disregard of employee welfare; coercion; systematic deception that places workers at risk; and underpayment of earnings. For an historical overview of the development of modern sweatshops, see Ellen I. Rosen, *Making Sweatshops: The Globalization of the U.S. Apparel Industry* (Berkeley, CA: University of California Press, 2002). For a overview of the contemporary issues regarding sweatshops see Theodore H. Moran, *Beyond Sweatshops: Foreign Direct Investment and Globalization in Developing Nations* (Washington, DC: Brookings Institution, 2002).

2. No one in this debate advocates forced labor.

3. Nicholas D. Kristof, "Brutal Drive," in Nicholas D. Kristof and Sheryl WuDunn, eds., *Thunder from the East: Portrait of a Rising Asia* (New York: Vintage Books 2000), p. 129.

4. Ian Maitland, "The Great Non-Debate over International Sweatshops," reprinted in Tom L. Beauchamp and Norman E. Bowie, eds., *Ethical Theory and Business,* 7th ed. (Upper Saddle River, NJ: Prentice Hall, 2004), p. 587.

5. Paul Krugman, *The Accidental Theorist and Other Dispatches from the Dismal Science* (New York: W.W. Norton & Co. 1999), p. 85.

6. Academic Consortium on International Trade, Letter to University Presidents, 29 July 2000, available at http://www.fordschool.umich.edu/rsie/acit/Documents/Anti-SweatshopLetterPage.html. For a reply to this letter from academics with a different stance on sweatshops, see statement by Scholars Against Sweatshops, Oct. 2001, available at http://www.umass.edu/peri/sasl/.

7   Linda Lim, *The Globalization Debate: Issues and Challenges* (2001). It is important to note that wages at many MNC factories have risen only in response to critics of low wages. Thus, it may not be reasonable to point to particular MNC factories with fair wages as evidence that the critics of low wages are mistaken. Those wages may have been increased to their current levels mainly because of public criticism.

8. For example, the Academic Consortium on International Trade sent its well-publicized letter defending sweatshops to university presidents in September 2000. In the preamble to that letter it promises to provide policy statements and papers defending sweatshops on its Web site. Four years later, the sum total of research presented on the ACIT Web site includes four newspaper opinion page pieces and six working papers on general issues concerning globalization. None are detailed, empirically grounded arguments that focus on the labor markets in specific economies and the practices of specific MNCs or their contractors (the link to a promised paper on living wages is non-functional). The most prominent follow-up work to the ACIT letter by one of its signatories is the recent book by Jagdish Bhagwati, *In Defense of Globalization* (2005). This article responds in detail to many of his arguments concerning sweatshops.

9. At least this was true at the early stages of the recent debate over sweatshops. The responses of MNCs such as Nike, Adidas, the Gap, Mattel, and many others that began in the late 1990s, and continue to this day, make it difficult for anyone familiar with these changes in corporate policy to hold that the treatment of workers in the

factories of MNCs and their suppliers in developing nations is merely at matter of economic forces.

10. Krugman, *The Accidental Theorist,* p. 83.

11. *The Sweatshop Quandary: Corporate Responsibility on the Global Frontier,* Pamela Varley, ed., p. 95.

12 Michael Santoro has defended a similar view concerning the duty of MNCs to ensure that their business partners respect employees by ensuring that human rights are not violated in the workplace. Santoro argues as follows: [M]ultinational corporations are morally responsible for the way their suppliers and subcontractors treat their workers. The applicable moral standard is similar to the legal doctrine of respondeat superior, according to which a principal is "vicariously liable" or responsible for the acts of its agent conducted in the course of the agency relationship. The classic example of this is the responsibility of employers for the acts of employees. Moreover, ignorance is no excuse. Firms must do whatever is required to become aware of what conditions are like in the factories of their suppliers and subcontractors, and thereby be able to assure themselves and others that their business partners don't mistreat those workers to provide a cheaper source of supply. Michael A. Santoro, *Profits and Principles: Global Capitalism and Human Rights in China* (Ithaca, NY: Cornell University Press, 2000), p. 161.

14 Although it is possible to provide meals and health care for the employee at work as part of an overall compensation package.

15 Robert Pollin, et al., "Global Apparel Production and Sweatshop Labour: Can Raising Retail Prices Finance Living Wages?," *Cambridge J. Econ.*, vol. 28 (2004), pp. 153, 169.

Reading **6-2**

Women in the Workplace: Freedom of Choice or Freedom from Choice?

Tara J. Radin

Diversity in the workplace, particularly gender diversity, poses numerous challenges. For decades businesses have grappled with sexual harassment and gender discrimination and have established policies to deal with both. These issues, however, merely scratch the surface of the problems that women confront in the workplace. Getting women hired is merely a preliminary first step. What about once they are hired? How do we ensure that workplaces not merely allow women but actually accommodate and support them?

An often overlooked yet pressing problem involves entrenched corporate policies that can hinder the professional advancement of women. This is a problem for women seeking careers as well as for firms that risk the loss of considerable talent as a result of antiquated systems that do not adequately handle the increasingly diverse needs and circumstances of the workforce.

An episode of the once popular FOX television series *Ally McBeal* illustrates some of the ways in which women struggle in the workplace for recognition, respect, and rights. Numerous gender-based concerns arise as firms wrestle with the competing demands of women who work outside the home.

The Partnership Track

In an episode of *Ally McBeal* entitled "Let's Dance," a woman sues the law firm where she worked for taking her off the partnership track. She had taken a leave of absence from the firm to have a child; after returning, she was no longer considered "partner material." While it is important to recognize that this is simply an episode of a television show and that television does not always mirror reality, the segment does adeptly capture some of the challenges women confront in the workplace as they attempt to juggle the competing demands of motherhood and a career. Although this episode is set in the specific context of law firms, it translates well into other venues such as accounting firms, investment banks, and so on.

To understand the problem better, some background information on the partnership track is perhaps helpful. Individuals join law firms as associates, where they spend anywhere from five to ten years (or more, depending upon region of country and size of firm) as junior and then senior associates before being considered for promotion to "partner." Many businesses operate similarly. During this time, associates work long hours—it is not uncommon for them regularly to put in 60- to 80-hour weeks—with little glory. They are generally judged in terms of the number of billable hours—hours billed to specific clients for work done—they log each week. To bill 40 hours a week, a person must work up to twice that amount of time because of the time he or she spends in non-billable activities, such as general administrative tasks.

Serving as an associate is not glamorous. They often do a lot of research and writing behind the scenes. While the common perception is that lawyers spend a great deal of time arguing in court, the reality is that associates spend most of their time in the office. It is, in fact, generally considered a rare honor for an associate to be invited just to sit in the court with partners during litigation.

While partnership is never a guarantee, the terms of what is expected tend to be fairly clear. During the past decade, it has become increasingly difficult for associates to "make partner." This is not a secret to associates (or to most entering law students, for that matter). As a result of the fierce competition for a limited number of openings, many associates move around a lot between firms, while others transition into corporate legal departments after acquiring several years of valuable, and valued, experience at law firms.

Despite the difficulties, "making partner" remains the goal for many associates. The chief reason for this is that it is only as "partner" that a member of the firm can share in the profits of the firm, assert authority, and exercise many of the legal abilities he or she has spent years developing. Once partner, he or she can meet with clients, try cases in court, and make pivotal decisions about the membership and direction of the firm.

From a financial perspective, the salaries of associates start high—well above six figures in most of the larger cities in the United States—but they grow relatively modestly thereafter. In New York City, for example, associate salaries at large firms typically start at more than $120K a year; the salaries of senior associates can be double that. Although this might seem exorbitant, it is important to keep in mind the number of hours associates are working. The associate working 60 hours per week, even at $240k per year, is only making about $80 per hour.

Partners, on the other hand, are often making millions. Many associates are willing to invest excessive hours in their career because of the chance to make partner. Eliminating the possibility of partnership therefore represents a significant loss for the associate.

Changes in the Workplace

In the *Ally McBeal* episode, the female plaintiff had been on partnership track prior to her maternity leave. Typical of associates, she joined the firm as a junior associate and worked alongside other associates for long hours in the office. She had performed equally well as, if not better than, her peers. She had received no complaints and, in fact, had been considered a model employee.

When the plaintiff returned from maternity leave, things noticeably changed in terms of her work performance. It was not that she had a child—it was the resulting lack of prioritization of her work—that caused concern at the firm. After she returned to work, her work was regarded as inferior to that done prior to her taking leave. While the quality of her work appeared consistent, the quantity of work and her manner of performing work were thought to have changed for the worse. Specifically, her level of billable hours decreased. She was still getting work done, but not as much as she had been prior to going on maternity leave. She claimed she was more efficient, but just was not putting in as much "face time" at the office. It appeared, too, that when she was at the office, she was often distracted and interrupted. She frequently received calls and pages, for or about her child, which demanded her attention and took her away from her work. The demands of motherhood also made her less predictable. It was not uncommon for her to arrive late or have to leave early to care for her child.

Concerns for the Firm

The combination of comparably low billable hours, recurring absences, and lack of dependability generated uneasiness on the part of the law firm. The firm was concerned about getting the high volume of work done and about making sure work was done properly—on time and with care. At the same time, the firm had an interest in maintaining some degree of internal equity. There was concern as to how not dealing with the plaintiff would affect other associates. Her absences meant that others had to pick up her slack. This resulted in a buildup of resentment that the firm considered necessary to address. To ignore the changes in her performance would risk setting a precedent that would be difficult to reverse; it would signal to other associates that such behavior was acceptable, which was not the case.

The plaintiff was cognizant of all these things and acknowledged the firm's concerns. She nevertheless contended that she was still getting the work done. While she sometimes had to juggle her job-related responsibilities to attend to unexpected situations at home, she claimed that she took work home with her and was still able to handle everything she needed to do. The "distractions," as others called them, were, in her view, simply part of motherhood. Moreover, she contended that firms must make allowances for motherhood; otherwise, women are effectively prevented from pursuing careers. Valuing diversity demands an understanding of the need for flexibility in promotion criteria. It requires changing the policies set to uphold traditional family models that have the male working and the female at home with the child. Such models no longer reflect the norm—today both members of many couples work. Attempting to force working parents to adapt to out-dated models creates an unnecessary strain on both work and family life.

Interestingly, in this episode of *Ally McBeal*, another female attorney spoke up in defense of the firm. She countered the female plaintiff and asserted that women are not denied anything; rather, they are given a choice: motherhood or a career. She explained that she (the attorney) had confronted that choice and chosen a career instead of motherhood.

Although it was a sacrifice for her, she made it freely. The woman at the law firm, in contrast, chose motherhood; she must likewise accept the consequences of her choice.

Motherhood, Choice, and the Workplace

Herein lies the crux of the more challenging issues: Is motherhood a situation that demands such consequences? Should it be so?

As firms reengineered and reexamined practices for the 21st century, they realized the extent to which diversity adds value to the workplace. Having a set of employees that reflects the diverse attributes of society enables firms to serve their constituents better. It puts them in closer touch with their stakeholders and gives them a more robust understanding of stakeholder concerns and considerations. Although such diversity extends beyond gender, gender is an attribute than cannot be ignored.

As women have entered the workplace in greater numbers during recent decades, the workplace has developed in unforeseen ways. Many of these developments have been positive, but there have also been a wide range of challenges that have not been anticipated or resolved adequately. Chief among these is the double role that women must play as career persons and as mothers.

While firms might prefer that women treat motherhood as an option, the reality is that motherhood is a non-negotiable. Only females can serve as mothers by bearing children. This places an inherent restriction on women, couples, and families. If only the female can carry and give birth to the child, and if she or the couple wants to have a child, she must make sacrifices to do so. The personal sacrifices, such as those to her health, are inevitable. The question that remains, though, is whether the sacrifices to her career should also be considered inevitable.

The easy answer is, "Yes." If a woman chooses to have a child, then she must accept the consequences of that choice. The child cannot raise itself. If she is not willing to hire someone to take care of the child (or make other such arrangements), it is often assumed that she will serve as the primary caregiver—particularly since she has already had to take time off to give birth. This is all known to the woman before she chooses to give birth.

A common response is that either the man or the woman could serve as the primary caregiver. Many people argue that the problem exists between the couple. If a mother is upset because she is not able to pursue a career, she is focusing her energy in the wrong direction. Instead of pressuring the firm, she should work within the family to find another suitable caregiver, such as her husband or her parents.

Whether or not the woman chooses to remain the primary caregiver is not the pivotal issue, however. Today it seems that the more important question involves the role the firm plays in supporting or penalizing caregivers—male or female. Should we compel firms, morally if not legally, to be considerate of the responsibilities of their employees (who are also parents) to their children? Or should we continue to accept firms' intentional blindness to the fact that employees are people—human beings—and, as such, they have connections outside the workplace that can affect their workplace performance?

Returning to the notion of motherhood as choice, is motherhood a choice? Do we want to treat motherhood as a choice similar to other daily choices: "Should I wear the red or blue shirt?" Interestingly, in law, motherhood is considered a right. The right to bear children is protected by the Constitution of the United States. Similarly, the right to work is protected. How, then, can we justify penalizing mothers in the workplace?

The typical firm answer is that women are not prohibited from working. If women are not able to rise within the firm, it is only because their external commitments inhibit their workplace performance. From the perspective of the firm, that is a personal problem, not a problem for the firm.

Interestingly, firms argue that they would be remiss in doing otherwise. Were they to make allowances for mothers, it would be unfair to nonmothers (men and women), and could potentially jeopardize other stakeholder interests. If a mother is not focused on her workplace responsibilities, then she could place firm business at risk. If a nonmother performs unsatisfactorily in the workplace, the firm punishes him or her, such as through reprimands, warnings, or even termination. Why, then, should a mother who performs similarly—such as through absences, tardiness, or distractedness—be rewarded?

The Problem

The problem is complex and goes beyond the simple choice a woman must make of whether or not to have a child. Forcing a woman to choose between her career aspirations and motherhood places her in a no-win situation. Moreover, it places society in a no-win situation. Workplaces are deprived of valuable members and families are stretched beyond reasonableness. It is not always financially an option for a parent to stay home. Life is expensive.

Our society feels the consequences of this tension. Women are waiting longer to have children. Firms are losing high-level employees on maternity leaves. And glass ceilings in many places, instead of being shattered, are becoming reinforced.

While there are benefits to having young mothers, there are also benefits to having more mature mothers. It can be argued that some of the consequences of firm behavior are positive, and helpful to the family unit in society. Whether these are positive or negative consequences is not the point. The point is, should we place our firms in the position of making such decisions for us?

In the *Ally McBeal* episode, the judge held that the plaintiff could not be denied partnership. He ruled that a firm cannot punish motherhood, implicitly or explicitly. In this fictitious situation, at least, the judgment was that it is not for firms to make choices for individuals by placing unreasonable obstacles in their paths. We, in other words, should be allowed to be the arbiters of our own destinies.

Although the *Ally McBeal* episode dealt specifically with a law firm, law firms are often set up similarly to business firms. In both professions, we expect a lot from our employees—long hours, huge effort, and valuable contributions, which we tend to measure in terms of visible results. In law, we use "billable hours" and "face time" to gage the worth of employees. In businesses, we have traditionally used similar measures. In both professions, working mothers have confronted obstacles.

In one sense, the situation presented in the *Ally McBeal* episode is flawed in that it is about what to do after *a* mother is denied promotion. Arguably, our interest should not lie with what to do after something goes wrong, but, rather, in creating a workplace where mothers can get promotions, or can at least know how to go about getting promotions. In *Ally McBeal*, there was no system in place for judging a mother as an associate. A large part of the problem, then, is not with the decision, but with the fact that the decision took place after the situation had played itself out. The responsibility for this should be shared by both the woman associate and the firm.

The argument here is not that working mothers should receive special treatment, but that we have to accept working parents as a reality and we need to prepare our workplaces for them. Where we have hierarchies in place that assume someone else is home with the children, we need to reexamine those hierarchies, and incorporate in hiring and promotion processes mechanisms to deal with and evaluate working parents.

Conclusion

There are a number of ways to handle diversity in the workplace, particularly those that stem from parenthood. Firms have experimented with *mommytracks* and *daddytracks* and some have instituted less structured programs that incorporate flexibility through work-at-home programs or variable work weeks. The technology is available to us; we just have to open up our thinking and explore our moral imagination to integrate new methods of performing and evaluating work in order to enable parents to keep pace with their peers without having to sacrifice the needs of their young children.

While the *Ally McBeal* episode highlighted the situation of a working mother, working fathers are equally at risk, if not more so. It is important for firms to make it possible for active parents to pursue successful careers. The first goal should lie in getting firms to be clear with their policies, so at least parents can know what lies ahead for them.

During this process, it is essential that individuals think carefully about their choices. A single decision affects innumerable others. It is thus imperative to take care in what we designate as a choice. In characterizing motherhood as a choice, it enables firms to punish mothers for creating our next generation.

The purpose here is not to draw conclusions as much as it is to start a conversation that looks beyond the individuals involved. My concern is not with the woman in the *Ally McBeal* situation, or about my friends and colleagues, or even about myself. My anxiety is with the signals this sort of behavior sends, and about the very real effects it has on society—on the workplace and on families.

In businesses, individuals are expected to wear many "hats" to adopt and satisfy the requirements of different roles. Businesspeople are not simply functionaries of the firm, however; they are also children, spouses, and parents. Firms are wise to recognize these competing and often complementary roles, and they do well not to force a separation between the various relationships the individual has when he or she walks through the office door in the morning. Clearly, a stronger, richer paradigm recognizes those relationships and helps people draw and build upon them, inside and outside the workplace. Such a paradigm would not only come closer to capturing reality, but it also holds tremendous potential for moving firms forward as successful and positive contributors to society.

Reading **6-3**

Employment-at-Will, Employee Rights, and Future Directions for Employment

Tara J. Radin and Patricia H. Werhane

Abstract

During recent years, the principle and practice of employment-at-will have been under attack. While progress has been made in eroding the practice, the principle still governs the philosophical assumptions underlying employment practices in the United States, and, indeed.

Note: In-text references have been deleted, but they are available from the authors.

EAW has been promulgated as one of the ways to address economic ills in other countries. This paper will briefly review the major critiques of EAW. Given the failure of these arguments to erode the underpinnings of EAW, we shall suggest new avenues for approaching employment issues to achieve the desirable goal of employee dignity and respect.

Private employment in the United States has traditionally been governed by "employment-at-will" (EAW), which provides for minimal regulation of employment practices. It allows either the employer or the employee to terminate their employment relationship at any time for virtually any reason or for no reason at all. At least 55 percent of all employees and managers in the private sector of the workforce in the United States today are "at-will" employees.

During recent years, the principle and practice of employment-at-will have been under attack. While progress has been made in eroding the practice, the principle still governs the philosophical assumptions underlying employment practices in the United States, and, indeed, EAW has been promulgated as one of the ways to address economic ills in other countries. In what follows, we will briefly review the major critiques of EAW. Given the failure of these arguments to erode the underpinnings of EAW, we shall suggest new avenues for approaching employment issues to achieve the desirable end of employee dignity and respect.

Critiques of EAW

Attacks have been levied against EAW on numerous fronts for generations. While it remains the default rule for the American workplace, a variety of arguments have been made that employees should not be treated "at will." Most of these arguments fall within two broad categories: those that relate to rights and those that relate to fairness.

Rights Talk

The first set of arguments critiquing the principle of EAW is grounded on a commonly held theory of moral rights, that is, the claim that human beings have moral claims to a set of basic rights vis-à-vis their being *human*. This set of arguments makes three points. First, principles governing employment practices that interfere with commonly guaranteed political rights, such as free speech (including legitimate whistle blowing), privacy, due process, and democratic participation, would therefore appear to be questionable principles and practices from a rights perspective. Second, justifiable rights claims are generalizable. It thus follows that, if employers and managers have certain rights, say, to respect, free speech, and choice, employees should also have equal claims to those rights. Third, if property rights are constitutionally guaranteed, it would appear to follow that employees should have some rights to their work contributions, just as managers, as representatives of companies, have rights to exercise property claims.

There are at least three countervailing arguments against these conclusions, however. In the United States, constitutional guarantees apply to interactions between persons or institutions and the state, but they do not extend to the private sector or to the home, except in cases of egregious acts. Claims to employee rights are not, therefore, guaranteed by the Constitution. Second, employment agreements are contractual agreements between consenting adults. Unless a person is forced to work or to perform a particular task, EAW thus protects liberty rights in allowing a person freely to enter into and leave contracts of his or her own choosing. Third, property rights protect companies and their owners, and companies and their managers should be free to hire and fire as they see fit. Indeed, Christopher McMahon, a defender of employee rights, argues that although, as property owners or agents for companies, employers and managers have rights to hire and fire "at will," this does not provide them with moral justification for ignoring other employee rights claims, including, for example, rights to participate in corporate decision making.

Fairness

A second set of arguments against EAW stems from fairness concerns regarding employment-at-will agreements and practices. EAW has, on numerous occasions, seemingly translated into a license for employers and employees to treat one another *amorally*, if not *immorally*. " 'Why are you firing me, Mr. Ford?' asked Lee Iacocca, president of Ford Motor Company. Henry, looking at Iacocca, said: 'I just don't like you!' " While EAW demands ostensibly *equal* treatment of both employers and employees, the result is often not inherently *fair* to either. A requirement of "equal" treatment, therefore, is not sufficient. Good employment practices should aim for equality, while, at the same time, allowing for different, though comparable, treatment where relevant differences exist. For example, while it would not necessarily represent a good, or sound, employment practice to demand *equal* pay for all employees and managers, a good practice would be to demand *equal* pay for employees in similar positions doing similar tasks, and *comparable* pay for others, after taking into account relevant differences, such as in experience, position, tenure at the company, and special skills.

Except under conditions of very low unemployment, employers ordinarily stand in a position of power relative to prospective employees, and most employees, at any level, are replaceable with others. At a minimum, though, employees deserve to be given reasons for employment decisions that involve them. Unjustified dismissals are not appropriate in light of employees' considerable investment of time and effort. Employees are human beings, with dignity and emotional attachments, not feelingless robots. This is not to say that inadequate employees should not be replaced with better performers. but employees at least deserve to find out the reasons underlying employment changes. And if employees are to take charge of their careers, they should receive good reasons for employment decisions and full information. From a management point of view as well, employees should be given *good* reasons for employment decisions, or it appears that management decisions are arbitrary, and this sort of behavior is not in keeping with good management practice. Even if it were possible to defend EAW on the basis of freedom of contracts, in practice, EAW supports inconsistent, even irrational, management behavior by permitting arbitrary, not work-related, treatment of employees—behavior that is not considered a best management practice. Since arbitrary accounting, marketing, and investment practices are not tolerated, arbitrary human resource practices should be considered equally questionable.

We have therefore concluded that due process procedures should be instituted as mandatory procedures in every workplace. On the other side, employers suffer when employees simply walk off jobs without notice. In a much earlier work. Werhane therefore has argued that employees *and* employers have equal rights, rights that would entail reciprocal obligations to inform each other about firing or quitting and to give justifiable reasons for these actions.

Interestingly, due process procedures have become mandatory guarantees for employees in the public sectors of the economy, on the federal, state, and local levels, but not in the private sector. Again, on the basis of the fairness of equal treatment for *all* workers, this appears to be unfair. The inapplicability of constitutional guarantees in the private sector of the economy nevertheless prevails in employment. This is not to suggest that there are no relevant differences between employment in the public and private sector. In fact, there are a number of significant variations, including, but not limited to, salary differentials. Considering the degree of similarity between public and private work, though, it only makes sense that due process be afforded to employees in both sectors.

Erosion of EAW: Law and Public Policy

Despite these and other arguments, there is evidence that the principle, if not the practice, of EAW is alive and well: people are still losing jobs for seemingly arbitrary reasons. Rather than attacking the principle directly, legislatures and courts have created ways to reduce the impact of the practice through narrowly carved-out exceptions, and Congress has chosen to control the scope of EAW through limiting legislation. A wave of federal legislation has also had a significant impact on private employment, beginning with the passage of Title VII of the Civil Rights Act of 1964, which prohibits the discrimination of employees on the basis of "race, color, religion, sex, or national origin." It has been followed by the Age Discrimination in Employment Act, the Pregnancy Discrimination Act, and the employment provisions of the Americans with Disabilities Act. Together, such legislation demonstrates Congress's recognition that there are limits to EAW, and that the default rule cannot, and should not, be used as a license to disregard fundamental rights.

Even greater limiting power lies in the hands of state and local legislatures. Many have sidestepped EAW to recognize employee rights, such as in the area of privacy, by passing statutes on issues ranging from workplace discrimination to drug testing. A few states, such as Colorado, North Dakota, and Nevada, have enacted statutes barring employers from firing employees for legal off-work activity. In 1987, Montana became the first state to pass a comprehensive statute rejecting EAW in favor of "just cause" terminations.[1] Contrary to EAW, the "just cause" standard requires that the reasons offered in termination decisions be defensible.[2] Montana currently stands alone in demanding "just cause" dismissals. Although it is too early to know whether one state's move in this direction signals a trend toward the increasing state challenges to EAW, there is currently no evidence that this is the case.

Courts have also begun to step in and carve out exceptions to EAW as a default rule. Many employers and employees have opted to alter the employment relationship through contractual agreements. Since evidence of such agreements is not always lodged in an explicit arrangement, courts often find it necessary to delve further in order to determine the reasonable assurances and expectations of employers and employees. For example, some courts have held that an employment contract exists, even where it exists only as a result of assumed behavior, through a so-called "implied-in-fact" contract. In *Pugh v. See's Candies, Inc.*, an employee was fired after 32 years of service without explanation. Although no contract existed that specified the duration of employment, the court determined that the implied corporate policy was not to discharge employees without good reasons. The court in *Pugh* determined:

> [T]here were facts in evidence from which the jury could determine the existence of such an implied promise: the duration of appellant's employment, the commendations and promotions he received, the apparent lack of any direct criticism of his work, the assurances he was given, and the employer's acknowledged policies.

Where an employer's behavior and/or policies encourage an employee's reliance upon employment, the employer cannot dismiss that employee without a good reason.

In some states, it can be considered a breach of contract to fire a long-term employee without sufficient cause, under normal economic conditions, even when the implied contract is only a verbal one. In California, for example, the majority of recent implied contract cases have been decided in favor of the employee. Reliance upon employee manuals has also been determined to give rise to reasonable employment expectations. In *Woolley* v. *Hoffmann-La Roche, Inc.*, the court held that companies are contractually bound by the statements in their employment manuals. In *Woolley,* the employment manual implicitly provided that employees would not be terminated without good cause:

> It is the policy of Hoffmann-La Roche to retain to the extent consistent with company requirements, the services of all employees who perform their duties efficiently and effectively.

The court thus held that an employee at Hoffmann-La Roche could not be dismissed without good cause and due process. *Woolley* is but one of many decisions that demonstrate that employers are accountable to employees for what is contained in employment manuals, as if the manual is part of an implicit employment contract.

Courts also have been known to override EAW in order to respond to or deter tortuous behavior. Out of this has arisen the "public policy" exception to EAW. The court has carved out the "public policy" exception to handle situations where employers attempt to prevent their employees from exercising fundamental liberties, such as the rights to vote, to serve on a jury, and to receive state minimum wages. In *Frampton* v. *Central Indiana Gas Company*, the court found in favor of an employee who was discharged for attempting to collect worker compensation:

> If employers are permitted to penalize employees for filing workmen's compensation claims, a most important public policy will be undermined. The fear of discharge would have a deleterious effect on the exercise of a statutory right. Employees will not file claims for justly deserved compensation … [and] the employer is effectively relieved of his obligation …
> Since the Act embraces such a fundamental … policy, strict employer adherence is required.

Such decisions clearly demonstrate the court's unwillingness to stand by without doing anything as employers attempt to interfere with fundamental liberties.

The public policy exception is also used in order to discourage fraudulent or wrongful behavior on the part of employers, such as in situations where employees are asked to break a law or to violate state public policies. In *Petermann* v. *International Brotherhood of Teamsters*, the court confronted a situation where an employee refused to perjure himself to keep his job. The court held that compelling an employee to commit perjury "would encourage criminal conduct … and … serve to contaminate the honest administration of public affairs." Then, in *Palmateer* v. *International Harvester Corporation*, the court reinstated an employee who was fired for reporting theft at his plant on the grounds that criminal conduct requires such reporting.

Whistleblower protection is also provided as a result of tort theory. In *Pierce* v. *Ortho Pharmaceutical Corporation*, the court reinstated a physician who was fired from a company for refusing to seek approval to test a certain drug on human subjects. The court held that safety clearly lies in the interest of public welfare, and that employees are not to be fired for refusing to jeopardize public safety.

Similarly, in *Bowman* v. *State Bank of Keysville*, a Virginia court asserted its refusal to condone retaliatory discharges. In *Bowman*, a couple of employee-shareholders of a bank voted for a merger at request of the bank's officers. After the vote was counted, the employee-shareholders subsequently retracted their votes and contended that their vote had been coerced. They alleged that the bank officers had warned them that they would lose their jobs if they did not vote in favor of the merger. They were then fired. The court in *Bowman* found in favor of the employee-shareholders. According to the *Bowman* court, "Virginia has not deviated from the common law doctrine of employment-at-will . . . And we do not alter the traditional rule today. Nonetheless, the rule is not absolute." In this way, the *Bowman* court demonstrated that EAW is subject to limitations and exceptions. Even where the EAW doctrine still appears to "thrive," it does so within definite restrictive legal and policy constraints.

Rethinking Employment Relationships

Without attacking or circumventing EAW, it is possible to discern signs of a changing mindset about employment, a mindset that values the competitive advantage of the contributions of good employees and managers. The extensive work of scholars, such as Jeffrey Pfeffer, illustrates this change. Pfeffer, a management professor at Stanford, has argued in a series of books and articles that a "people first" strategy can serve as an economic advantage for companies. In other words, it is not just for the benefit of *employees*, but also for the benefit of *firm employers*, to treat employees with respect. To provide evidence for his point, Pfeffer has studied a number of North American and international companies and amassed a great deal of data that demonstrates that economic success is linked to fair labor practices when employees and managers are considered critical stakeholders for the long-term viability of their companies. According to Pfeffer, the most successful companies—those that have sustained long-term economic profitability and growth—work carefully to engage in employment practices that include selective hiring, employment security, high compensation, decentralization, empowerment and self-managed teams, training, open information, and fair treatment of all of their employees.

From an organizational perspective, contrary to some points of view, it is a mistake to sort out employees, customers, products, services, shareholders, and so on, as if each represented an autonomous set of concerns. For example, a firm cannot do business without people, products, finance and accounting, markets, and a strategy. In times of economic exigency, a merger, or corporate change, it is, therefore, generally *not* to the advantage of a company merely to lop off employees (even if they are the "low hanging [most easily disposable] fruit"), without thinking carefully about their employees *as people*, and recognizing those *people's* contributions to the long-term survival and success of the company. In uncertain times, no company would simply quit doing accounting, and it would be to its peril to quit marketing its products and services. Similarly, to get rid of too many employees would not serve a company's long-term viability very well.

Similarly, Rosebeth Moss Kanter argues that it is in the firm's interest to take care of employees. Kanter contends that it is both desirable and obligatory for companies to give their employees what she calls "employability security": abilities and skills that are transferable to other jobs and other situations in that company or elsewhere so that employees are adaptable in a world of technological and economic change. Today, while some companies engage in layoffs to change employee skills, many managers and companies are training and retraining old workers, giving them new skills. Kanter would argue, with Pfeffer, that it is valuable, in terms of both economics and respect for workers, to have a workforce that is comprised of a collection of highly skilled and employable people who would be desirable assets in a number of employment settings, both within a particular company and among industries.

Linking Pfeffer's and Kanter's findings with a notion of employee rights makes it possible to re-envision the mindset of employment to consider each job applicant, employee, manager, or CEO as a unique individual. In addition, it prompts us to begin to rethink employment, not in terms of employees as merely economic value added, but in terms of employees as *individuals*—unique and particularized *individuals*.

A "Citizen" Metaphor

One way of developing an individualized analysis of employment is through a citizen metaphor. "Citizenship" is a designation that links people to rights and duties relative to their membership in a larger community, such as a political community. There is a growing body of literature addressing this notion of "corporate citizenship." According to Waddock,

> Good corporate citizens live up to clear constructive visions and core values. They treat well the entire range of stakeholders who risk capital in, have an interest in, or are linked to the firm through primary and secondary impacts through developing respectful, mutually beneficial operating practices and by working to maximize sustainability of the natural environment.

Replacing the view that corporations are, or should be, socially responsible, the corporate citizenship model argues that a firm's membership in complex cultural, national, and global communities accords them, like individuals, rights and responsibilities comparable to those accorded to individuals through national citizenship. The belief is that, if corporations are to enjoy operational privileges, they must then honor as well their responsibilities to the communities to which they belong. The model of corporate citizenship is used both to describe corporate relationships with external stakeholders, such as customers, communities, governmental entities, and the environment, and to address corporate responsibilities to internal stakeholders, such as managers and employees.

The citizen metaphor can be applied to managerial-employee relationships as well. This process of portraying employees as citizens is not complicated; it requires, simply, "treating workers like adults." Treating people as adults translates into acknowledging their dignity and respecting their relevant legal and moral rights and duties. Rights and duties connected to "citizenship" reflect the coexistence of people in a common space and help delineate how people can best interact with the fewest conflicts. This space does not have to be a global or semi-global community but could also refer to the context of a firm. Within the firm context, the citizen metaphor links people to one another in such a way that they inevitably take responsibility for working together for the benefit of the firm. At the same time, the metaphor of citizenship requires that each "citizen" has equal rights, and requires that all citizens be treated with respect and dignity. According to such a model, employees thus serve as participants in, and members of, a firm community.

As applied to employment, a citizenship model would take into account productivity and performance, and it would also require rethinking hiring in terms of long-time employment. This would not entail keeping every employee hired, or even guaranteeing lifetime employment. It would, however, at a minimum, require due process for all employment changes, employability training, protection of fundamental rights such as free speech and privacy, and the provision of adequate information to employees about their future and the future of the company. The employability requirement would require employees to serve as good corporate citizens in the broad sense of being able to contribute in a number of areas in the economy, and, if Pfeffer's data is correct, such measures add economic value to shareholders as well. At the same time productivity, loyalty, and good performance would be expected from all employees just as they are expected from citizens in a community.

In sum, if a company's core values were to drive the assumption that each employee is a corporate citizen analogous to a national citizen with similar rights and duties, then the way we would think about employment would change.

Employees and Systems

Systems thinking, a way of looking at business that is becoming increasingly popular, operates similarly to the citizenship model in challenging traditional views of employment. According to systems thinking, employment is a phenomenon embedded in a complex set of interrelationships, between employees and managers or employers, between workers and labor organizations such as unions, and between employment and public policy. It involves customer relationships, human resource policies, and, given pensions plans, often employee/owner relationships with management. Employees are just one of many stakeholders who affect, and are affected by, the companies in which they work. Moreover, companies, and, indeed, industries and the system of commerce, are embedded within a complex structure of laws, regulations, regulatory agencies, public policy, media interaction, and public opinion. And this system—employment—is part of a global economy of exchange, ownership, and trade.

Employees, as "players" in these overlapping sets of systems, are at the same time individuals, members of a company, and factors embroiled in a system of commerce. Their interests are important, but they are not the only interests that must be taken into account. Like the phenomenon of employment, employee rights and responsibilities are embedded in a complex social system of rights and responsibilities. Employee rights claims, thus, are not merely individual manifesto claims to certain privileges, but also entail reciprocal respect for others' rights and responsibilities.

If employment relationships are embedded in a set of systems or subsystems, then it is important—strategically important—for managers and employees to attack employment issues systemically from a fact-finding perspective, from an organizational or social perspective, and from the perspective of the individuals involved, in this case, employees and managers. Conceptualizing employment systemically may help both employees and managers to reconsider their importance in the underlying system of which they are a contributing part. This sort of analysis will neither eliminate nor replace the principle of EAW, but it does represent another step in the process of reconceptualizing employment.

Pfeffer's conclusion, that employees are critical to corporate success, is grounded in a systems approach, which views employees, as well as products, services, and customers, as part of the strategic advantage of the company. By analyzing corporate results, he demonstrates that, without good employees, a company will fail, just as it will fail without customers, and fail if it does not think strategically about its products and services.

In thinking about employment and employees, it is tempting to become preoccupied with managerial/employer responsibilities to employees, as if employees were merely pawns in the system. It is, though, important to note that a systems approach does not preclude individual autonomy. No individual in a free commercial society is defined completely by the set of systems in which he or she participates. Interestingly, a systematic approach actually looks beyond protection of employee rights and emphasizes employee responsibilities as well—to themselves as well as to the firm. As part of the workforce, each of us has claims to certain rights, such as free choice, free speech, rights to strike, rights to work contributions or compensation for those contributions, rights to information, and rights to a safe workplace. As a consequence of claiming such rights, every worker, employee, or manager, in every sector of the economy, has responsibilities as well—responsibilities not merely to employers, but to him- or herself and his or her future, and to manage that future as he or she is able and sees fit.

In other words, systems thinking indicates that employees are, or should be, responsible for their own lives and careers, and they need to take the steps necessary to research and explore mobility options. Thinking about employment systemically and thinking about personal responsibilities as well as responsibilities to others within that system can help employees take charge of their own working lives, professions, and careers.

The view of employment as a system is consistent with the notion of corporate citizenship. The systemic conceptualization of employment gives rise to employee rights and duties that animate the employment system. In other words, the rights employees enjoy, and the duties they must bear, are those that ensure the continued existence of the system. Similarly, through the lens of corporate citizenship, employee rights and duties include those that contribute to the firm. Employees have rights to engage in behavior that allows for their development within the system, or firm, and have duties to enable others to develop as well.

A Professional Model for Employees

Despite developments in eroding EAW through law and public policy, changing mindsets regarding the value of employment and employment practices, the work of Pfeffer, Kanter, and others demonstrating the worth of good employment practices for long-term profitability and success, and the systemic citizen model we propose, the principle of EAW continues to underlie North American management practice, and the language of rights, or employee rights, still evades popular management thinking about employment, at least in the private sectors of the economy. This is most clearly demonstrated by three sets of phenomena. First, there has been a consistent demise of unions and unionism in this country. Since the 1950s, union membership has dropped from about 33 percent of all workers to barely 10 percent today. This demise not only reflects the philosophy of corporations, but it is also the result of a series of public policy initiatives. In addition, it reflects interests of workers, even low-wage workers who toil under strenuous or dangerous conditions, who are nevertheless reluctant to unionize.[3]

Second, despite the enlightened focus on employability and despite an almost full employment economy, layoffs still dominate the ways in which corporations think about employees and employment when making changes in their strategic direction. In 1999 alone, more than a million workers were laid off.[4] Admittedly, given low unemployment, most of these people found new jobs, but this often required relocation and, sometimes, even in this economy, taking less desirable jobs for lower wages. This is particularly true for unskilled workers.

Third, one of the criticisms of Northern Europe's high unemployment and Japan's recent economic difficulties is that these countries have massive legal restrictions on the ability of their companies to engage in flexible employment practices. We are thus exporting our EAW mindset, sometimes as a panacea for economic difficulties that are not always traceable to overemployment. It is important for us to think carefully about the practices we export, particularly considering their questionable success here.

A systems approach, while serving as an obvious description of the complex nature of employment in advanced political economies such as our own, is not internalized in employment thinking today—at least not in the United States. The citizen metaphor requires an expansion of notions of trust and solidarity within firms, and, considering the mobility of the workforce, the ease with which companies can lay off employees and hire new ones, and the preoccupation with short-term bottom lines, it is unlikely that this metaphor will be universally adapted. Given these seemingly contradictory conclusions, then, namely, the persistence of the principle of EAW, the argument that employees have rights and that employees and managers have moral responsibilities to each other, the economic value added of employees to firms, and the questionable adaptability of the citizen metaphor, we are challenged to try to reformulate the notion of employment proactively from an employee perspective—that of the employee as a *professional.*

The popular literature is replete with laments that the "good old days" of alleged employee–employer lifetime employment contracts, company paternalism, and lifetime benefits are under threat of extinction. So, too, are the expectations of loyalty, total commitment, company-first sacrifices, and perhaps, even, obedience and trust. Whether or not there ever were "good old days," such laments could be used to change thinking in a positive way, in that they indicate we have alternatives—the way that we view work is not necessarily the only way. This realization should prompt employees and managers to rethink who they are—to manage their own careers within the free enterprise system and to rejoice in the demise of paternalism such that they no longer can even imagine that a person is dependent upon, or co-dependent upon, a particular employer, training program, or authority. It demands changes in what we have called elsewhere the "boss" mental model, so aptly exploited by Dilbert, and to alter our vision of ourselves from that of "just an employee" to that of an independent worker or manager with commitments to self-development.

While all of this might seem farfetched, particularly for unskilled and uneducated workers, this sort of thinking dates back at least two centuries. As Adam Smith, and later Karl Marx argued, the Industrial Revolution provided the opportunity for workers to become independent of landholder serfdom and free from those to whom they had been previously apprenticed. This occurred because, by providing workers opportunities to choose and change jobs and to be paid for their productivity, people were able to trade their labor without chatteling themselves. This sense of economic independence was never fully realized because, in fact, circumstances often prevent most of us from achieving Smith's ideal "where every man was perfectly free both to chuse what occupation he thought proper, and to change it as often as he thought proper."

During and after the Industrial Revolution, one of the great debates about labor was the status of "free labor" versus "wage labor." Free labor was "labor carried out under conditions likely to cultivate the qualities of character that suits citizens to self-government." These conditions included being economically independent, and indeed Thomas Jefferson associated free labor with property ownership and farming. Wage earning was thought by some to be equivalent to slavery since it "denied [workers] economic and political independence essential to republican citizenship." Even the authors of *Rerum Novarum* (1892), the first Papal social encyclical, argue that wage labor should be paid enough to enable each worker to become a property owner and thus gain some degree of independence.

A question remains: How, in the 21st century, is a person to develop this sort of independence and independent thinking about work, when the vast majority of us work for others? A new model of employment is required, and this model requires developing different mindsets about work and working that draw from Smith's and Jefferson's ideas, and, at the same time, take into account the fact that most of us are, and will be, employees.

The model is that of employees as *professionals*. "Profession" refers to "any group of individuals with particular skills who work from a shared knowledge base." A professional is a person who has trained skills in certain areas that position that person as employable in his or her area of expertise. A professional is identified with, and has a commitment to, his or her professional work, and to the ability to be versatile. It is the work and its achievements that are important, even more important, for some professionals, than its monetary reward. Additionally, most professionals belong to independent associations that have their own codes of professional ethics and standards for expertise and certification or licensure.

The responsibilities of a professional are first to his or her expertise, second to his or her profession and the code of that profession, and only third to his or her employer. This is not a model of the "loyal servant," but, rather, of a person who manages him- or herself with employable and retrainable skills that he or she markets, even as he or she may simultaneously be in the employment of others. This is a person who commits to excellence in whatever employment situations he or she encounters, but is not wedded to one employer or one particular job. Further, in some professions, such as law and health care, professionals are encouraged—if not required—to participate in work solely for community benefit.

The professional model is one that has developed primarily in the high tech and dot. com industries, as people with specialized skills have built firms around those skills. While the model has developed within a particular context, it is one that easily could, and should, be emulated elsewhere. The growth of dot.com firms offers an excellent example because through these ventures people have been able to focus on their talents, even as employees have moved from company to company, because employees are valued for their skills rather than their loyalty. Dot.com firms are not models for all employment since they are often narrowly tailored to offering particularized products and services, but they do stand as potential models for a number of companies or divisions within companies.

There are other opportunities for professionalism as well, particularly with regard to contingent workers. For the past 20 years we have witnessed what some label as an alarming trend—the increase in contingent workers—workers who work part-time, or full-time on a contract basis without insurance, pensions, or other benefits. Contingent workers include self-employed, voluntary part-time workers, contract workers and consultants, and home-bound workers. These workers range from dishwashers to professionals and managers. Many have chosen this sort of employment arrangement. Some of these people have benefits independently or through spouses, and they thus appreciate the enhanced flexibility and higher salaries as compared to their full-time counterparts. The problem is that many others resent their "contingency." There are many, who, according to Brockner and Wiesenfeld, see themselves as "peripheral" to the organization, particularly those who are part-time, contract, short-term, or "disposable" workers.

These workers are independent contractors—"free labor"—even though many of them do not revel in that. They are disposable, and some are involuntarily contingent workers, subject to a number of injustices: (1) the involuntary nature of the employment position; (2) the two-tier wage system (a) with unequal compensation, and (b) where many of these workers are psychologically, economically, and socially treated as, and feel themselves to be, second class workers; (3) the fact that women and minorities account for a greater percentage of contingent workers than white males, even taking into account skills, those who opt for part-time and mommy-track employment, and those who cannot speak English or are otherwise disadvantaged. The further decline in union membership and the shift in the composition of the workforce indicate that, by the year 2005, nearly 20 percent of new hires will be white males. This appears to suggest that we will see increased exploitation of new labor and greater utilization of contingent workers.

There is yet another dimension to what might already be considered a gloomy picture. Given the psychological pressures and perception of second class citizenry, involuntary contingent workers in companies tend to be less loyal, less productive, and exhibit lower morale—all of which hurts the long-term productivity and well-being of the company for which they work.

At the same time, contingent workers are not as vulnerable to some of the problems that hinder full-time workers. Contingent workers are less likely to be absent, drink or use drugs on the job, complain, snooze, schmooze, or engage in time-consuming office or work floor politics. Moreover, without the shadow of union protection they are unencumbered by work rules or traditions. They are, therefore, more flexible.

As the number of contingent workers increases, those who choose this path, as well as those who are involuntarily forced into it, should be able to develop a sense of independence, engendered by redefining themselves in relation to their work. This could translate into a rise of professionalism. Because contingent workers are no longer linked to particular companies, it could lead to a shift of loyalty from the company to work and to the profession. In addition, it could lead to the formation of new professional associations—associations, not necessarily industry- or position-specific, which develop guidelines for skills, licensing, and conduct, form employment contracts, develop codes of conduct, and protect members, just as the legal, medical, academic, and, to some extent, the engineering professions do today. These professions, then, could gain leverage with employers, just as unions have done in the past, with leverage translated into equal pay for equal work and professionally provided benefits and pensions.

But what about unskilled low-wage workers? As Barbara Ehrenreich points out in her provocative book, *Nickel and Dimed*, one of the indignities suffered by allegedly "unskilled" work is that their skills are not treated as such. Virtually all work entails some sort of skills—it is just that the "skills" required by this sort of work are not respected by many of us. Another indignity associated with much of low-wage work is that the workers tend not to be respected or treated with dignity, even by their employers. Professionalism of these workers might alleviate this treatment and also help to raise their wages.[5]

Ehrenreich herself recognizes that offering incentives to low-wage workers to take control of their lives and their careers is not easy. Unskilled workers, like many managers today, would have to rethink of themselves as independent contractors with trained or trainable skills that are transferable to a number of job settings, rather than as mere wage earners. By taking their work and productivity contributions seriously, workers with such mindsets would create economic value added for firms and a sense of self-worth. There is little in our backgrounds that assists us in thinking of ourselves as free laborers rather than wage earners. But if George Washington could take scruffy groups of farmers and laborers from thirteen independent colonies each with its own culture and customs, and transform that motley crew into the Revolutionary Army that eventually defeated the British, and if union organizers in the late nineteenth and early twentieth centuries could organize wage laborers to strike, then a revolution of the mental model of employment, from wage earners to free professionals, is not impossible.

Conclusion

We are a country that has thrived on individualism in our political democracy. Although we have made progress in dispelling the public/private division, it will undoubtedly continue to influence the protection of Constitutional rights. We have failed, and probably will continue to fail, to adapt new metaphors that challenge that individualism, such as a systems approach or a citizen metaphor for employment.

This is not where the story ends, though. While EAW remains the default rule for employment in most of the United States, new models are emerging that encourage and motivate both employers and employees to rise above the default rule in order to create a more satisfying workplace, which, at the same time, can boast higher performance.

Hope for a workplace that respects both employers and employees lies in variations of models such as the professional model. Interestingly, the professional model serves as a link between the individualism that cripples other models and the fair employment principles espoused by all of these models. The professional model is a form of, and reinforcement for, individualism. It will be interesting to see how that individualism plays out in the workplace. The model of the worker, the employee, the manager, and the executive as professionals, offers a paradigm for thinking about oneself as *both* independent and part of a political economy. With the pending end of implied job security in every sector of the economy, with global demands on management skills, and with the loss of union representation, this is a model for the future—a model that would circumvent EAW and take us fittingly into a new millennium of global capitalism.

Ironically, recent events surrounding the horrific destruction of the twin towers of the World Trade Center on September 11, 2001, underscore the values that underlie the American workplace, which are about professionals, not robots engaged in routine tasks. Although terrorists attempted to attack capitalism, they were only able to break apart the buildings that housed the tremendous values. As Howard Lutnick, CEO of Cantor Fitzgerald, explained, even in the wake of disaster, his people were anxious to get back to work. They felt a need to be part of something, and that something was work. And Lutnick, like many of the surviving business executives was, and is, struggling to find ways to help support the survivors and the families of those lost—not because they have to, but because they want to do something to assist those who were part of their workplaces.

The time has thus come to look past what our default rule says, in order to pay attention to what the reality is. It no longer makes sense to waste words arguing against EAW. The reality is that, regardless of what the default rule says, there are values embedded in the American workplace that elevate it above that default and point to inherent respect for both employers and employees. It is important for us now to accept EAW for what it is—a mere default—and to move forward by emphasizing models, such as that of professionalism, that help show where the desirable values already exist, and to motivate more employers and employees to adopt similar practices. The firms that not only *survive*, but *succeed*, in the decades to come are going to be those that adopt such models.

Source: *Business Ethics Quarterly* 13, no. 2. ISSN 1052-150X, pp. 113–130. Reprinted by permission.

Notes

1. In 1991, the Commissioners on Uniform State Laws passed the Model Employment Termination Act, which offers a framework for "just-cause" regimes. State legislatures have looked toward this Act as a model, but no state has yet adopted it.

2. "Just cause" advocates differ as to whether or not they define the standard as demanding merely "fair and honest" reasons or "good" reasons.

3. For example, less than 40 percent of all chicken catchers are unionized, despite the fact that they are exposed to pecking and chicken feather dust all day and work under very dangerous and stressful conditions.

4. According to "Extended Mass Layoffs in the Second Quarter of 2000," USDL 00–266. released September 20, 2000, http://stats.bls.gov/newsrels.htm. 1,099,267 people were separated from their jobs for more than 30 days in 1999, and 971,612 people filed initial claims for unemployment insurance during a consecutive five-week period. During the second quarter of 2000, there were 227,114 separations, and 162,726 initial claimants.

5. As Ehrenreich points out, most people cannot live on a minimum-wage salary so that those working at minimum wage usually have two jobs or a supporting family.

7.

Ethical Decision Making: Technology and Privacy in the Workplace

We must adjust to changing times and still hold to unchanging principles.
Former U.S. President Jimmy Carter

You say you want a revolution? Well, you know, we all want to change the world.
John Lennon and Paul McCartney

Things do not change; we change.
Henry David Thoreau

In his article "Code of Ethics for Programmers?" Jon Katz proposes the following list as broad ethical principles for computer users and builders:

- *Opportunity.* People who work in computers might work for the equitable distribution of technology, so that computer users don't become a powerful elite in control of a culture that excludes the technologically illiterate, a social nightmare already well under way.
- *Responsibility.* People who make technology need to consider its social implications, applications, and consequences.
- *Access.* Programmers and computer users should promote unfettered access to the Internet, its information unrestricted and unregulated by corporations or government except in the most dire circumstances.
- *Civics.* Programmers should foster democracy and inclusion, using network computing to break down elites, to bring more people into the political process, provide them with more information, and give them new ways to express their opinions and attitudes.
- *Civility.* Another ethical goal might be a civil society online—especially a new kind of media—where information is gathered and shared openly, solutions are approached rationally rather than ideologically, facts replace confrontation and dogma, and argument is encouraged but personal attacks are viewed as the unethical assaults on the free movement of ideas that they are.

Do you believe these goals are attainable from a pragmatic perspective? Why or why not? To what extent does one have a responsibility to adhere to them when (at least some) others might be unlikely to do so?

- What are the key facts relevant to your decision regarding the practicality of these standards?
- What are the ethical issues involved? What incentives would actively support or pose challenges to your response above?
- Who are the stakeholders in connection with computer use?
- What alternative or additional standards might you suggest?
- How would adherence to these standards (or their disregard) affect the stakeholders you have identified?

Source: http://slashdot.org/features/99/09/02/2038236.shtml.

Chapter Objectives

After reading this chapter, you should be able to:

1. Explain and distinguish the two definitions of privacy.
2. Describe the ethical sources of privacy as a fundamental value.
3. Identify the three legal sources of privacy protection.

4. Discuss the concept of a "reasonable expectation of privacy."
5. Discuss recent development in connection with employee monitoring.
6. Explain the risks involved in a failure to understand the implications of technology and its use.
7. Identify additional ethical challenges posed by technology use.
8. Articulate the manner in which employee monitoring works.
9. Enumerate the reasons why employers choose to monitor employees' work.
10. Explain why monitoring might also pose some costs for the employer and for the employee.
11. Discuss the elements of a monitoring program that might balance the interests of the employee and the employer.
12. Discuss the ethics of monitoring as it applies to drug testing.
13. Discuss the ethics of monitoring as it applies to polygraphs, genetic testing, and other forms of surveillance.
14. Explain the interests of an employer in regulating an employee's activities outside of work.
15. Discuss the implications of September 11, 2001, on privacy rights.

Introduction

In his best-selling book, *The World is Flat,* Thomas Friedman describes the hastening pace of globalization and how significantly the business, economic, and political landscape has changed in just the first decade of the 21st century. Friedman employs the image of a "flat world" to convey the idea that neither distance, time, geography, nor national boundaries still create artificial barriers to business and trade. Nine of the 10 forces that Friedman identifies as creating this flat world are the direct result of computer and Internet-related technologies. Even the tenth, the fall of the Berlin Wall and opening of Eastern Europe, is attributed in part to the information revolution that began in the years leading up to the fall of the wall.

There can be no doubt that the business world today is global, nor that a technological revolution is largely responsible for this fact. Not surprisingly, that technological revolution has brought with it as many challenges as opportunities. Many of these challenges raise ethical questions, particularly as this technology impacts employee and consumer privacy. This chapter will review some of the key ethical issues of technology and privacy, with a particular focus on privacy in the workplace.

Privacy issues in the workplace raise ethical issues involving individual rights as well as those involving utilitarian consequences. Workplace privacy issues evoke an inherent conflict (or some might call it a delicate balance) between what some may consider to be a fundamental right of the employer to protect its interests and the similarly grounded right of the employee to be free from wrongful intrusions into her or his personal affairs. This conflict can arise in the workplace environment through the regulation of personal activities or personal choices, or through various forms of monitoring. Some forms of monitoring, such as drug testing, may occur after a job offer has been made but even before the individual begins working. Other forms might also occur once the individual begins to work, such as electronic surveillance of e-mail.

Similarly, contrasting utilitarian arguments can be offered on the ethics of monitoring employees. The employer can argue that the only way to manage the workplace effectively and efficiently is to maintain knowledge about and control over all that takes place within it. The employee can simultaneously contend that she or he will be most productive in a supportive environment based on trust, respect, and autonomy. In any case, the question of balance remains—whose rights should prevail or which consequences take precedent?

This chapter will examine technology and its impact on these several issues. We will explore the origins of the right to privacy as well as the legal and ethical limitations on that right. We will also explore the means by which employers monitor performance and the ethical issues that arise in connection with these *potential* technological invasions to privacy. We will then connect these issues of technology and privacy to the balance of rights and responsibilities between employers and employees.

Because of the extraordinary breadth of the technology's reach, this chapter could not possibly address all issues under its umbrella. We have therefore sought to limit our coverage in this chapter to issues of technology and privacy *in the workplace* and related arenas. For instance, the intersection between ethics, intellectual property, the law, and technology open far too many doors for the survey anticipated by this text and will therefore not be examined within this overview. Similarly, though a phone company's decision whether to comply with the government's request to turn over phone records certainly raises issues of both technology and privacy, it is not necessarily related to issues of employment, so we will not be examining that decision. However, readers should be aware of these issues and seek to apply the lessons of this chapter to wider issues of privacy and technology in business.

The Right to Privacy

Privacy is a surprisingly vague and disputed value in contemporary society. With the tremendous increase in computer technology in recent decades, calls for greater protection of privacy rights have increased. Yet there is widespread confusion concerning the nature, extent, and value of privacy. Some Western countries, for example, do not acknowledge a legal right to privacy as recognized within the United States, while others such as New Zealand and Australia seem far more sophisticated in their centralized and consistent approaches to personal privacy issues. Even within the United States, there is significant disagreement about privacy. The U.S. Constitution, for example, makes no mention of a right to privacy and the major Supreme Court decisions that have relied on a fundamental right to privacy, *Griswold* v. *Connecticut* and *Roe* v. *Wade,* remain highly contentious and controversial.

Defining Privacy

OBJECTIVE

Two general and connected understandings of privacy can be found in the legal and philosophical literature on this topic: privacy as a *right to be "let alone"* within a personal zone of solitude, and privacy as the *right to control information about oneself.* It is valuable to consider the connection between these two senses of privacy. Certain decisions that we make about how we live our lives, as well as the control of personal information, play a crucial role in defining our own personal identity. Privacy is important because it serves to establish the boundary between individuals and thereby serves to define one's individuality. The right to control certain extremely personal decisions and information helps determine the kind of person we are and the person we become. To the degree that we value the inherent dignity of each individual and the right of each person to be treated with respect, we must recognize that certain personal decisions and information are rightfully the exclusive domain of the individual.

Many people believe that a right to be let alone is much too broad to be recognized as a moral right. It would be difficult for employees, for example, to claim that they should be totally left alone in the workplace. This has led some people to conclude that a better understanding focuses on privacy as involving the *control* of personal information. From this perspective, the clearest case of an invasion of privacy occurs when others come to know personal information about us, as when a stranger reads your e-mail or eavesdrops on a personal conversation. Yet, the claim that a *right* of privacy implies a right to control all personal information might also be too broad. Surely, there are many occasions when others, particularly within an employment context, can legitimately know or need to know even quite personal information about us.

Philosopher George Brenkert has argued that the informational sense of privacy involves a relationship between two parties, A and B, and personal information X about A. Privacy is violated only when B comes to know X, and no relationship exists between A and B that would justify B knowing X. Thus, whether my privacy is violated or not by a disclosure of personal information depends on my relationship with the person or persons who come to know that information. My relationship with my mortgage company, for example, would justify that company's having access to my credit rating, while my relationship with students would not justify their accessing that information. Limiting access of personal information to only those with whom one has a personal relationship is one important way to preserve one's own personal integrity and individuality.

Ethical Sources of a Right to Privacy

OBJECTIVE

The right to privacy is founded in the individual's fundamental, universal right to autonomy, in our right to make decisions about our personal existence without restriction. This right is restricted by a social contract in our culture that prevents us from infringing on someone else's right to her or his personal autonomy. Philosopher Patricia Werhane describes this boundary as a "reciprocal obligation"; that is, for an individual to expect respect for her or his personal autonomy, that individual has a reciprocal obligation to respect the autonomy of others.[1]

Applied to the workplace, Werhane's concept of reciprocal obligation implies that, while an employee has an obligation to respect the goals and property of the employer, the employer has a reciprocal obligation to respect the rights of the employee as well, including the employee's right to privacy. In other work, Werhane has asserted that a bill of rights for the workplace would therefore include both the right of the employee to privacy and confidentiality, and the right of employers to privacy in terms of confidentiality of trade secrets and so on. This contention is supported throughout traditional philosophical literature. Kant links the moral worth of individuals to "the supreme value of their rational capacities for normative self-determination" and considers privacy a categorical moral imperative.[2]

Ethicists Thomas Donaldson and Thomas Dunfee have developed an approach to ethical analysis that seeks to differentiate between those values that are fundamental across culture and theory ("hypernorms") and those values that are determined within "moral free space" and that are not hypernorms. Donaldson and Dunfee propose that we look to the convergence of religious, cultural, and philosophical beliefs around certain core principles as a clue to the identification of hypernorms. Donaldson and Dunfee include as examples of hypernorms freedom of speech, the right to personal freedom, the right to physical movement, and informed consent. Individual privacy is at the core of many of these basic minimal rights and is, in fact, a necessary prerequisite to many of them. Indeed, a key finding of one survey of privacy in 50 countries around the world found the following:

> Privacy is a fundamental human right recognized in all major international treaties and agreements on human rights. Nearly every country in the world recognizes privacy as a fundamental human right in their constitution, either explicitly or implicitly. Most recently drafted constitutions include specific rights to access and control one's personal information.[3]

Accordingly, the value of privacy to civilized society is as great as the value of the various hypernorms to civilized existence. Ultimately, the failure to protect privacy may lead to an inability to protect personal freedom and autonomy.

Finally, legal analysis of privacy using a property rights perspective yields additional insight. "Property" is an individual's life and all nonprocreative derivatives of her or his life. Derivatives may include thoughts and ideas, as well as personal information. The concept of property *rights* involves a determination of who maintains control over tangibles and intangibles, including, therefore, personal information. Property rights relating to personal information thus define actions that individuals can take in relation to other individuals regarding their personal information. If one individual has a *right* to her or his personal information, someone else has a commensurate duty to observe that right.

Why do we assume that an individual has the unfettered and exclusive right to her or his personal information? Private property rights depend upon the existence and enforcement of a set of rules that define who has a right to undertake which activities on their own initiative and how the returns from those activities will be allocated. In other words, whether an individual has the exclusive right to her or his personal information depends upon the existence and enforcement of a set of rules giving the individual that right. Do these rules exist in our society, legal or otherwise? In fact, as we will discuss below, the legal rules remain vague. Many legal theorists contend that additional or clearer rules regarding property rights in personal information would lead to an improved and more predictable market for this information, thus ending the arbitrary and unfair intrusions that may exist today as a result of market failures.

Legal Sources of a Right to Privacy

OBJECTIVE

As with others areas of lightning-quick advances, the law has not yet caught up with the technology involved in employee privacy. Many recent advances, thus much recent case law, and therefore much of our discussion in this chapter, will focus on employee monitoring, which we will cover in detail shortly. As a result, this is one area where simply obeying the law may fall far short of responsible management practice. While the law might be clear with regard to tapping a worker's telephone, it is less clear in connection with monitoring a worker's e-mail or text messages on a handheld device.

Privacy can be legally protected in three ways: by the *constitution* (federal or state), by federal and/or state *statutes*, and by the *common law*. Common law refers to the body of law comprised of the decisions handed down by courts, rather than specified in any particular statutes or regulations.

The Constitution's Fourth Amendment protection against an unreasonable search and seizure governs only the public sector workplace because the Constitution applies only to state action. Therefore, unless the employer is the government or other representative of the state, the Constitution generally will not apply.

Statutes also offer little, if any, protection from workplace intrusions. The Electronic Communications Privacy Act of 1986 (ECPA) prohibits the "interception" or unauthorized access of stored communications. However, courts have ruled that "interception" applies only to messages in transit and not to messages that have actually reached company computers. Therefore, the impact of the EPCA is to punish electronic monitoring only by third parties and not by employers. Moreover, the ECPA allows interception where consent has been granted. Therefore, a firm that secures employee consent to monitoring at the time of hire is immune from ECPA liability. The following Reality Check provides examples of how these issues might arise in the technology environment.

Some states rely on statutory protections rather than common law. Other states provide state constitutional recognition and protection of privacy rights, including Alabama, Arizona, Florida, Hawaii, Illinois, Louisiana, Montana, South Carolina, and Washington. However, in all states except California, application of this provision to *private* sector organizations is limited, uncertain, or not included at all.

The "invasion of privacy" claim with which most people are familiar is one that developed through case law called "intrusion into seclusion." This legal violation occurs when someone intentionally intrudes on the private affairs of another when the intrusion would be "highly offensive to a reasonable person." As we begin to live more closely with technology, and the intrusions it allows, we begin to accept more and more intrusions in our lives as reasonable; as privacy invasions become more common, they begin to be closer to what is normal and expected. It may no longer be reasonable to be offended by intrusions into one's private life that used to be considered unacceptable. It is important to be aware

Reality Check *Privacy and Technology*

In an Arizona case, a husband and wife who worked as nurses were fired from a hospital after hospital officials learned that they ran a pornographic Web site when not at work. The couple explained that they engaged in this endeavor in order to save more money for their children's college education. "We thought we could just do this and it really shouldn't be a big deal," said the husband.[4] Though their dismissal attracted the attention of the American Civil Liberties Union for what it considered was at-will gone awry, the nurses had no recourse. In another case, a police office was docked three days' pay when his wife posted nude pictures of herself on the Internet as a surprise to her husband. The pay suspension was justified by the department in that case since police officers could arguably be held to a higher standard of conduct than average citizens.

OBJECTIVE

that, while Georgia was the first jurisdiction whose courts recognized a common law—or court-created—right to privacy, two states, North Dakota and Wyoming, do not recognize any privacy claims generally accepted by the courts.[5]

Most recent court decisions with regard to monitoring specifically seem to depend on whether the worker had *notice* that the monitoring might occur. Since the basis for finding an invasion of privacy is often the employee's legitimate and reasonable expectation of privacy, if an employee has actual notice, then there truly is no real expectation of privacy. This conclusion was supported in *K-Mart* v. *Trotti,* where the court held that search of an employee's company-owned locker was unlawful invasion since the employee used his own lock. However, in a later landmark case, *Smyth* v. *Pillsbury,* Smyth sued after his manager read his e-mail, even though Pillsbury had a policy saying that e-mails would not be read. The court concluded, "we do not find a reasonable expectation of privacy in the contents of email communications voluntarily made by an employee to his supervisor over the company email system, *notwithstanding any assurances that such communications would not be intercepted by management*" (emphasis added). The end result of *Smyth,* then, is to allow for monitoring even when a firm promises not to monitor. Evidence of the impact of this decision is the fact that only one state, Connecticut, requires employers to notify workers when they are being monitored.

Courts have often supported reasonable monitoring of employees in open areas as a method of preventing and addressing employee theft. For example, in *Sacramento County Deputy Sheriff's Ass'n* v. *County of Sacramento,*[6] a public employer placed a silent video camera in the ceiling overlooking the release office countertop in response to theft of inmate money. The California Court of Appeals determined that the county had engaged in reasonable monitoring because employee privacy expectations were diminished in the jail setting.[7] See Table 7.1 for an overview of how the courts have tended to treat the legality of monitoring from a general perspective.

Global Applications

This somewhat unpredictable regime of privacy protection is all the more problematic to maintain when one considers the implications of the European Union's

TABLE 7.1
Legal Status of Employee Monitoring

Telephone calls	Monitoring is permitted in connection with quality control. Notice to the parties to the call is often required by state law, though federal law allows employers to monitor work calls without notice. If the employer realizes that the call is personal, monitoring must cease immediately.
E-mail messages	Under most circumstances, employers may monitor employee e-mails. Even in situations where the employer claims that it will not, its right to monitor has been upheld. However, where the employee's reasonable expectation of privacy is increased (such as a password-protected account), this may impact the court's decision.
Voice-mail system messages	Though not yet completely settled, the law here appears to be similar to the analysis of e-mail messages.
Internet use	Where the employer has provided the equipment and/or access to the Internet, the employer may track, block, or review Internet use.

Directive on Personal Data Protection.[8] The directive strives to harmonize all the various means of protecting personal data throughout the European Union, where each country originally maintained myriad standards for information gathering and protection. In addition, the directive also prohibits E.U. firms from transferring personal information to a non-E.U. country unless that country maintains "adequate protections" of its own; in other words, protections equivalent to those the directive guarantees in E.U. countries.[9] Because the United States would not qualify as having adequate protection, the U.S. Department of Commerce negotiated a *"Safe Harbor exception"* for firms that maintain a certain level of protection of information.[10] If a firm satisfies these requirements, the directive allows the information transfer. If not, both firms can be held liable. (See Table 7.2).

Given the nature of the legal uncertainty or instability concerning these challenging areas of information gathering, perhaps the only source of an answer is ethics. Yet, "the development of our moral systems has not been able to keep pace with technological and medical developments, leaving us prey individually and societally to a host of dangers."[11] As a court put it in regard to the legitimacy of police use of infrared thermal detection devices aimed at an individual's home without a warrant or notification,

> As technology races with ever increasing speed, our subjective expectations of privacy may be unconsciously altered . . . our legal rights to privacy should reflect thoughtful and purposeful choices rather than simply mirror the current state of the commercial technology industry.[12]

Reality Check *New Job Discovered!*

Evidently, the ethical and legal challenges that the issues addressed in this chapter pose are perceived as tremendously complicated and also vital to employers worldwide. As of 2004, there were more than 2,000 "CPOs" (chief privacy officers) in businesses around the world, more than 10 times the estimate three years ago.

Source: Steve Ulfelder, "CPOs on the Rise?" *Computerworld*, March 15, 2004, http://www.computerworld.com/securitytopics/security/story/0,10801,91166,00.html, quoting Alan F. Westin, president of the nonprofit Privacy & American Business.

Perhaps the more personalized response of Northrup Grumman Corporation's ethics officer, Frank Daly, sums it up better: "Can this characteristic of speed drive us and have a negative effect upon how we treat other people? You can't rush love or a soufflé."[13]

What are the implications of this definition or understanding of privacy for businesses and for business ethics analysis? (For one implication, please see the Reality Check, above.) In general, one would argue that personal information should remain private unless a relationship exists between the business and the individual that legitimates collecting and using personal information about that individual. For example, to determine the range of employee privacy, we would have to specify the nature of the relationship between employer and employee. The nature of the employment relationship will help determine the appropriate boundary between employers and employees and therefore the information that ought to remain rightfully private within the workplace. (See the following Decision Point in considering information reasonably related to the job.) If we adopt something like a contractual model of employment, where the conditions and terms of employment are subject to the mutual and informed consent of both parties, then employee consent would become one major condition on what information employers can collect.

TABLE 7.2   The Safe Harbor Exception

The Safe Harbor requires that the receiving firm provide the following:

- Clear and conspicuous notice about the personal information collected.
- Choice to opt out of information collection or dissemination.
- Transfer of information to other firms only if they also demonstrate that they maintain the same level of adequate protections.
- Reasonable measures to ensure reliability of the information and protection from disclosure or loss of the information.
- Limitation to information that is relevant to the purpose for which it was gathered; that is, the firm does not access any information that is unrelated to its purposes.
- Access by the subject of the information, who then has the ability to correct any misinformation.
- Mechanisms for ensuring compliance and consequences for noncompliance.

The following information is sometimes requested on standard employment applications, though candidates might consider some of it to be private or personal. Which of the following items about an employee might an employer have a legitimate claim to know, and why?

A job applicant's social security number

An applicant's arrest record

An employee's medical records

An employee's marital status

Whether a job applicant smokes

An employee's political affiliation

An employee's sexual orientation

An employee's credit rating

- What facts are relevant to your decisions?
- What would the consequences be of refusing to answer any questions on an employment application?
- Are you basing your decision on particular rights of the employee or the employer?
- Are there people other than the employer and employee who might have a stake in what information is released to employers?

We might summarize our above examination by saying that employee privacy is violated whenever (a) employers infringe upon personal decisions that are not relevant to the employment contract (whether the contract is implied or explicit); or (b) personal information that is not relevant to that contract is collected, stored, or used without the informed consent of the employee. Further, since consent plays a pivotal role in this understanding, the burden of proof rests with the employer to establish the relevancy of personal decisions and information at issue.

Linking the Value of Privacy to the Ethical
Implications of Technology

OBJECTIVE

The advent of new technology challenges privacy in ways that we could never before imagine. For example, consider the implications of new technology on employee and employer expectations regarding the use of time; the distinction between work use and personal use of technology; the protection of proprietary information, performance measurement, and privacy interests; or accessibility issues related to the digital divide. Technology allows for in-home offices, raising both extraordinary opportunities and challenges, issues of safety, and privacy concerns (there are now more than 15.7 million U.S. telecommuters). Because each of us is capable of much greater production through the use of technology,

technology not only provides benefits but also allows employers to ask more of each employee.

Following is an overview of the implications of the technology economy as reported in the *World Employment Report 2001,* issued by the International Labour Office:

> More and more, boundaries are dissolving between leisure and working time, the place of work and place of residence, learning and working . . . Wherever categories such as working time, working location, performance at work and jobs become blurred, the result is the deterioration of the foundations of our edifice of agreements, norms, rules, laws, organizational forms, structures and institutions, all of which have a stronger influence on our behavioral patterns and systems of values than we are aware.[14]

New technology, however, does not necessarily impact our value judgments but instead simply provides new ways to gather the information on which to base them. Sorting through these issues is challenging nevertheless. Consider the impact of the attacks of September 11, 2001, on an employer's decision to share personal employee information or customer information with law enforcement. Private firms may be more willing—or less willing—today to share private information than they would have been previously.

Firms often experience, and often find themselves ill prepared for, unanticipated challenges stemming from new technology. Consider the lesson one firm learned about how problems with e-mail use and abuse might extend beyond the end of the employment relationship. After Intel Corporation fired an employee, he began to use e-mail to express some complaints about the company. He repeatedly flooded his former employer's e-mail system with mass communications that the firm's security department was unable to block. Intel took the former employee to court and was successful in blocking any further e-mails on the basis of a legal theory called "trespass to chattels" (a "chattel" refers to an item of personal property as opposed to a piece of real property or real estate). Even after the former employee appealed, claiming that blocking his e-mails violated free speech principles, a California appellate court disagreed and held in favor of Intel.

Do we need "new ethics" for this "new economy?" Perhaps not, since the same values one held under previous circumstances should, if they are true and justified, permeate and relate to later circumstances.[15] However, the perspective one brings to each experience is impacted by the understanding and use of new technology and other advances. As economist Antonio Argandona cautions, there has been a change in values "that may be caused by the opportunities created by the technology."[16] On the other hand, he points to the possibility that new technology may also do much good, including development of depressed regions, increased citizenship participation, defense of human rights, and other potential gains.

Information and Privacy

A business needs to be able to anticipate the perceptions of its stakeholders in order to be able to make the most effective decisions for its long-term sustainability.

New technological advancements are often difficult for the public to understand and therefore ripe for challenge. How do you best manage the entrepreneurial passion for forward momentum with stakeholder comfort and security?

The motto at Google, the Internet-based search engine, is the deontological imperative: "don't do evil." Its founders describe that imperative by striving to "define precisely what it means to be a force for good—always do the right, ethical thing. Ultimately, 'don't do evil' seems the easiest way to summarize it."[17] For instance, Google does not allow gun ads, which admittedly upset the gun lobby. So one might expect that Google would be especially sensitive to stakeholder concerns as it develops new technology. Google believed it was providing a value to society when it created an e-mail system called "Gmail." Yet, critics charge that Gmail violates Google's own principles. This free e-mail system provides a free gigabyte of e-mail storage to anyone in the world—200 times more storage than other free e-mail services. However, there was one catch: Google scans user e-mail in order to target advertisements based on the contents. The company explained, "When people first read about this feature, it sounded alarming, but it isn't. The ads correlate to the message you're reading at the time. We're not keeping your email and mining it or anything like that. . . You should trust whoever is handling your email"[18]

That trust is truly the crux of the issue with the introduction of new technology, isn't it? When consumers rely on technology provided by a business—from e-mail to Internet access and from cell phones to medical labs—they might easily assume that the business will respect their privacy. Most average e-mail users do not understand the technology behind the process. One would like to believe that those responsible for the technology are, themselves, accountable to the user. That would be the ideal.

However, the Electronic Privacy Information Center, a consumer advocacy group, considered Google's marketing plan to be equivalent to a telephone operator who listens in on conversations and then pitches advertisements where relevant. Scanning e-mail violates the two fundamental elements of privacy: the right to be left alone and the right to control information about oneself. Moreover, since the scanning and targeting of advertisements takes place without the user's original knowledge or consent, it violates the ethical foundations of autonomy in the user's right to make decisions about her or his "personal existence." Finally, if one's personal information is respected as property, Google uses individual property without consent.

Google responded that it was not doing anything more than other e-mail services (which also include advertisements) except that its advertising was more relevant to the user's interests. In fact, Google's research showed that people actually followed many of those advertisements and ultimately made purchases. "It's an example of the way we try to do good. It's a high quality product. I like using it. Even if it seems spooky at first, it's useful and it's a good way to support a valuable service," says Google founder Larry Page.[19]

To the contrary, however, by failing to fully comprehend and plan for its stakeholders' perceptions of the program, Google not only breached ethical boundaries but also suffered public backlash. It did not anticipate concerns over privacy or the controversy the program would engender. Critics argued that Google should have consulted with stakeholders, determined the best way to balance their interests, and then considered these interests as they introduced the new program, all of which might have precluded the negative impact on its reputation. The lesson learned is that, notwithstanding even reasonable justification (which remains arguable in this case), people are simply not comfortable with an involuntary loss of control over these personal decisions. Google failed to consider the perspectives of its stakeholders, the impact of its decisions on those stakeholders, and the fundamental values its decision implied. Consider the discomfort evidenced in the following Decision Point.

Economist Antonio Argandona contends that, if new technology is dependent on and has as its substance information and data, significant moral requirements should be imposed on that information. He suggests the following as necessary elements:

- **Truthfulness and accuracy:** The person providing the information must ensure that it is truthful and accurate, at least to a reasonable degree.
- **Respect for privacy:** The person receiving or accumulating information must take into account the ethical limits of individuals' (and organizations') privacy. This would include issues relating to company secrets, espionage, and intelligence gathering.
- **Respect for property and safety rights:** Areas of potential vulnerability, including network security, sabotage, theft of information and impersonation, are enhanced and must therefore be protected.
- **Accountability:** Technology allows for greater anonymity and distance, requiring a concurrent increased exigency for personal responsibility and accountability.[20]

Imagine how firms may respond to this call for responsibility in the development, manufacture, marketing, and service related to new production or other corporate activities. What ethical issues does Argandona's proposal raise, and how will stakeholders be impacted if firms respond positively to this call?

Let us take a look at another example in which consumers were surprised to learn about a business activity that some activists considered a violation of privacy. *Reason* magazine decided to include a customized cover on its June 2004 issue of a satellite picture of the recipient's neighborhood with the individual's home circled.[21] Of course, a magazine will have its recipients' home addresses, but the magazine chose to use the image to illustrate its cover article on the power and importance of databases, illustrating a "we know where you live" mentality. The article focused on the balance between the possible invasions of privacy information that database management affords and the realistic benefits the technology could bring, such as instant credit, customized advertisements, and personalized mortgage offers. Nick Gillespie, *Reason's* editor-in-chief, asks, "what if you received a magazine that only had stories and ads that you were interested in

Questions about using technology for "good" or "evil," from an anonymous Web posting:

Management wants me to spy.

"Management wants me to spy on a colleague. I'll be using [a spying program] that is 100% hidden, does screen captures, etc. Is there a document out there that I can have management sign to limit my liability? I want signatures from all management stating that they are authorizing me to spy. Thoughts? I have done this before, but this is the first time that they have asked me to compile data against a user for possible use in court. Thanks."

What are some of the questions or concerns you might raise in an answer and what would you suggest this individual do to respond to them?

- What are the key facts relevant to your response?
- What is the ethical issue involved in peer spying in the workplace?
- Who are the stakeholders?
- What alternatives would you suggest to this individual, and what alternatives exist for employers who wish to gather information about employees surreptitiously?
- How do the alternatives compare; how do the alternatives affect the stakeholders?

and pertained to you? That would be a magazine everyone would want to read." Is he right? Perhaps. The ethical question is what we are willing to, or what we can be forced to, give up of our personal information, privacy, and autonomy in order to get it.

Managing Employees through Monitoring

OBJECTIVE 5

One of the most prevalent forms of information gathering in the workplace, in particular, is monitoring employees' work, and technology has afforded employers enormous abilities to do so effectively at very low costs. The American Management Association has conducted surveys of mid- to large-sized U.S. firms over the past few years that show an increasing trend with regard to employee **e-mail monitoring.** While its 2003 survey reported that 52 percent of firms monitored e-mail communications, up from 47 percent in 2001, its 2005 survey reported that 55 percent engaged in monitoring (see Figure 7.1). The 2005 survey also found that 42 percent of these firms have a policy that covers its employees' instant message use.[22] Much of this monitoring is on an occasional basis rather than by regular routine.

The most prevalent subject of monitoring is Internet use monitoring (76 percent) followed by e-mail monitoring (55 percent) and videotaping (10 percent).[23]

FIGURE 7.1

Percent of Large U.S. Companies That Monitor E-Mail

Adapted by the authors from data from the American Management Association.

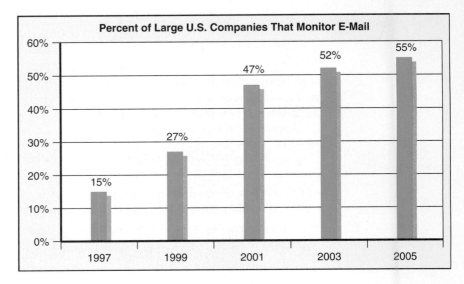

Of firms that monitor, 86 percent notify their workers that they do so. Notably, 14 percent of firms do not notify their workers of e-mail monitoring and 20 percent do not tell them that they are monitoring content of Web sites visited. In actual numbers, estimates regarding the number of workers subject to surveillance are difficult to measure. One estimate contends that the e-mail or Internet use of 14 million U.S. workers is under constant surveillance each day, increasing to 27 million workers around the globe.[24]

More than 80 percent of mid- to large-sized firms in the United States have Internet access policies. More than 60 percent of these companies have disciplined employees for violations of these policies (with 26 percent reporting that they have terminated an employee for a violation). The leading violations include access to pornography, online chat forums, gaming, investing, or shopping at work.[25]

OBJECTIVE

Unfortunately, many of the ethical issues that arise in the area of managing information are not readily visible. When we do not completely understand the technology, we might not understand the ethical implications of our decisions. When that occurs, we are not able effectively to protect our own information because we may not understand the impact on our autonomy, the control of our information, our reciprocal obligations, or even what might be best for our personal existence. For example, do you always consider all the people who might see the e-mails you send? Can your employer read your e-mail? Your first response might be "no, my boss doesn't have my secret password." However, experts tell us that any system is penetrable. Employers have been known to randomly read e-mails to ensure that the system is being used for business purposes. Is this ethical? Does it matter if there is a company policy that systems must only be used for business purposes, or that the employees are given notice that their e-mail will be read?

How do you know that your boss will not forward your disparaging remarks about a colleague directly to that colleague? It can be done with the touch of a key. Are different issues raised by that concern from those that arose with a traditional written letter? People could always send or show your letter to someone. When we mistakenly believe that no one is watching, we may engage in activities that we would otherwise refrain from doing. For instance, you may believe that hitting the "delete" key actually deletes an e-mail message. But it does not always delete that message from the server, so it might be retrieved by your supervisor or have a negative impact in a lawsuit.

These ethical issues may be compounded by the fact that a knowledge gap exists between people who *do* understand the technology and others who are unable to protect themselves precisely because they do *not* understand. You might not expect to be fired for sending out an e-mail—but if you thought about it a bit, you might have known what to expect.

OBJECTIVE

Technology allows for access to information that was never before possible. Under previous circumstances, one could usually tell if someone had steamed open a letter over a teapot. Today, you usually cannot discover if someone reads the e-mail you sent to your best friend yesterday. Access can take place unintentionally, as well. In doing a routine background check, a supervisor may unintentionally uncover information of an extremely personal nature that may bear absolutely no relevance to one's work performance. This occurs because the information, though previously unavailable or too burdensome to uncover, is now freely available from a variety of sources.

Moreover, because technology allows us to work from almost anywhere on this planet, we are seldom out of the boundaries of our workplace. For instance, just because you are going to your sister's wedding does not mean that your supervisor cannot reach you. This raises a tough question: *Should* your supervisor try to reach you just because she has the ability to do so? Our total accessibility creates new expectations, and therefore conflicts. How long is reasonable to wait before responding to an e-mail? If someone does not hear from you within 24 hours of sending an e-mail, is it unreasonable for them to resend it? Continuous accessibility blurs the lines between our personal and professional lives.

Another challenge posed by the new technology accessible in the workplace is the facelessness that results from its use. If we have to face someone as we make our decisions, we are more likely to care about the impact of that decision on that person. Conversely, when we don't get to know someone because we don't have to see that person in order to do our business, we often don't take into account the impact of our decisions on him or her. It's merely a name at the other end of an e-mail correspondence, rather than another human being's name. Given the ease and informality of electronic communications, we often "say" (write, e-mail, and the like) things to each other that we would never say to someone's face, precisely because we don't have to consider the impact of what we're saying. We are more careless with our communications because they are easier to conduct—just hit a button and they are sent.

TABLE 7.3
Public Access to
Personal Information

Tracing America (www.tracingamerica.com) provides the following personal information at the listed prices:
- Social security numbers, $25
- General all-around background search, $39
- Countywide search for misdemeanors and felonies, $35
- Whether subject has ever spent time in prison, $25
- Whether subject has ever served time in a federal prison, $50
- National search for outstanding warrants for subject, $50
- Countywide search for any civil filings filed by or against subject, $50
- Subject's driving record at least three years back, $30

To address some of the ethical issues computers present, the Computer Ethics Institute has created "The Ten Commandments of Computer Ethics," which include these imperatives: "Thou shalt not snoop around in other people's computer files; Thou shalt think about the social consequences of the program you are writing or the system you are designing; and Thou shalt always use a computer in ways that insure consideration and respect for your fellow humans." Of course, such guidelines have no enforcement mechanism and are little more than suggestions. To see the types of additional information available through other Web services, see Table 7.3.

Why do firms monitor technology usage?

OBJECTIVE

A firm chooses to monitor its employees and collect the information discussed above for numerous reasons. Employers need to manage their workplaces to place workers in appropriate positions, to ensure compliance with affirmative action requirements, or to administer workplace benefits. Monitoring also allows the manager to ensure effective, productive performance by preventing the loss of productivity to inappropriate technology use. Research evidences a rise in personal use of technology, with 86 percent of employees admitting sending or receiving personal e-mails at work and 55.1 percent admitting to having received politically incorrect or offensive e-mails at work. Among employers, 62 percent of firms find employees accessing sex sites during the workday.[26] In fact, 10 percent of employees spend more than half the workday on e-mail or surfing nonbusiness sites.[27]

Beyond the management of its human resources, monitoring offers an employer a method by which to protect its others resources. Employers use monitoring to protect proprietary information and to guard against theft, to protect their investment in equipment and bandwidth, and to protect against legal liability (more than 20 percent of firms have been ordered to produce employee e-mail in legal proceedings as of 2005).

In the American Management Association's 2005 survey, employer respondents reported that they engaged in monitoring as a result of their concerns for legal liability. Given the courts' focus in many cases on employer response to claims of sexual harassment or unethical behavior, among other complaints, firms believe they need a way to uncover these inappropriate activities. One-fourth of

Reality Check *Immoral Mail?*

A survey in the United Kingdom. reports that 53 percent of the workers surveyed behave "immorally" in e-mail; 38 percent have used e-mail in the pursuit of political gain within their company, at the expense of others; and 30 percent admit to having sent racist,

pornographic, sexist, or otherwise discriminatory e-mails while at work.

Source: Institute for Global Ethics, "U.K. Survey Finds Many Workers Are Misusing E-mail," *Newsline* 5, no. 10 (March 11, 2002).

the largest firms report firing employees for inappropriate e-mail.[28] (See the Reality Check above for a quantification regarding "inappropriate" e-mails.) Without monitoring, how would they know what occurs? Moreover, as courts maintain the standard in many cases of whether the employer "knew or should have known" of wrongdoing, the state-of-the-art definition of "should have known" becomes all the more vital. If most firms use monitoring technology to uncover this wrongdoing, the definition of "*should have* known" will begin to include an expectation of monitoring.

Business Reasons to Limit Monitoring

OBJECTIVE

Notwithstanding these persuasive justifications for monitoring in the workplace, employee advocates suggest limitations on monitoring for several reasons. First, there is a concern that monitoring may create a suspicious and hostile workplace. By reducing the level of worker autonomy and respect, as well as workers' right to control their environment, the employer has neglected to consider the key stakeholder critical to business success in many ways—the worker. Another concern demonstrates the problem. Monitoring may arguably constrain effective performance since it can cause increased stress and pressure, negatively impacting performance and having the potential to cause physical disorders such as carpal tunnel syndrome.[29] One study found monitored workers suffered more depression, extreme anxiety, severe fatigue or exhaustion, strain injuries, and neck problems than unmonitored workers. Stress might also result from a situation where workers do not have the opportunity to review and correct misinformation in the data collected. These elements will lead not only to an unhappy, disgruntled worker who perhaps will seek alternative employment but also to lower productivity and performance that will lead to higher costs and fewer returns to the employer. Finally, employees claim that monitoring is an inherent invasion of privacy that violates their fundamental human right to privacy.

Balancing Interests

Therefore, where should the line be drawn between employer and employee rights? Most of us would agree that installing video cameras in the washrooms of the workplace in order to prevent theft may be going a bit too far, but knowing where to draw the line before that might be more difficult. As long as technology exists to allow for privacy invasions, should the employer have the right to use it?

Consider whether monitoring could be made ethical or humane. One suggestion is to give due notice to employees that they will be monitored, plus the opportunity to avoid monitoring in certain situations. For instance, if an employer chooses to monitor random phone calls of its customer service representatives, it could notify the workers that certain calls may be monitored and these calls would be signified by a "beep" on the line during the monitoring. In addition, if workers make a personal call, they may use a nonmonitored phone to avoid a wrongful invasion of privacy.

However, such an approach may not solve all the concerns about monitoring. Suppose you are the employer and you want to make sure your service representatives handle calls in a patient, tolerant, and affable manner. By telling the worker which calls you are monitoring, your employees may be sure to be on their best behavior during those calls. This effect of employer monitoring is termed the "Hawthorne Effect": Workers are found to be more productive based on the psychological stimulus of being singled out, which makes them feel more important. In other words, merely knowing one is being studied might make one a better worker. Random, anonymous monitoring may better resolve your concerns (but not those of the worker).

Perhaps the most effective means to achieve monitoring objectives while remaining sensitive to the concerns of employees is to strive towards a balance that respects individual dignity while also holding individuals accountable for their particular roles in the organization. Ann Svendsen, director of the Center for Innovation in Management, studied the link between high-trust stakeholder relationships and business value creation. Svendsen concludes that "trust, a cooperative spirit and shared understanding between a company and its stakeholders, creates greater coherence of action, better knowledge sharing, lower transaction costs, lower turnover rates and organizational stability. In the bigger picture, social capital appears to minimize shareholder risk, promote innovation, enhance reputation and deepen brand loyalty."[30]

OBJECTIVE

A monitoring program developed according to the mission of the organization (for example, with integrity), then implemented in a manner that remains accountable to the impacted employees, approaches that balance. Consider the following parameters for a monitoring policy that endeavors to accomplish the goals described above:

- No monitoring in private areas (e.g., restrooms).
- Monitoring limited to within the workplace.
- Employees should have access to information gathered through monitoring.
- No secret monitoring—advance notice required.
- Monitoring should only result in attaining some business interest.
- Employer may only collect job-related information.

Agreement regarding disclosure of information gained through monitoring.

- Prohibition of discrimination by employers based on off-work activities.

The above parameters allow the employer to effectively and ethically supervise the work employees do, to protect against misuse of resources, and to have an appropriate mechanism by which to evaluate each worker's performance, thus respecting the legitimate business interest of the employer. They are also supported by global organizations such as the International Labour Organization (ILO) (see Table 7.4).

Philosopher William Parent conceives the right to privacy more appropriately as a right to liberty and therefore seeks to determine the potential affront to liberty from the employer's actions. He suggests the following six questions to determine whether those actions are justifiable or have the potential for an invasion of privacy or liberty:

1. For what purpose is the undocumented personal knowledge sought?
2. Is this purpose a legitimate and important one?
3. Is the knowledge sought through invasion of privacy relevant to its justifying purpose?

TABLE 7.4
ILO Principles for Protecting Workers' Personal Data

In 1997, the International Labour Organization published a Code of Practice on the Protection of Workers' Personal Data. Though not binding on employers, it serves to help codify ethical standards in connection with the collection and use of employee personal information. The code includes, among others, the following principles:

5.1   Personal data should be processed lawfully and fairly, and only for reasons directly relevant to the employment of the worker.

5.4   Personal data . . . should not be used to control the behavior of workers.

5.6   Personal data collected by electronic monitoring should not be the only factors in evaluating worker performance. . . .

5.8   Workers and their representatives should be kept informed of any data collection process, the rules that govern that process, and their rights. . . .

5.10   The processing of personal data should not have the effect of unlawfully discriminating in employment or occupation. . . .

5.13   Workers may not waive their privacy rights.

6.5   An employer should not collect personal data concerning a worker's: sex life; political, religious or other beliefs; or criminal convictions. In exceptional circumstances, an employer may collect personal data concerning those in named areas above, if the data are directly relevant to an employment decision and in conformity with national legislation.

6.6   Employers should not collect personal data concerning the worker's membership in a workers' organization or the worker's trade union activities, unless obliged or allowed to do so by law or a collective agreement.

4. Is invasion of privacy the only or the least offensive means of obtaining the knowledge?

5. What restrictions or procedural restraints have been placed on the privacy-invading techniques?

6. How will the personal knowledge be protected once it has been acquired?[31]

Both of these sets of guidelines may also respect the personal autonomy of the individual worker by providing for personal space within the working environment, by providing notice of where that "personal" space ends, and by allowing access to the information gathered, all designed toward achievement of a personal and professional development objective.

Monitoring Employees through Drug Testing

OBJECTIVE

Drug testing is one area in which employers have had a longer history of monitoring employees. The employer has a strong argument in favor of drug or other substance testing based on the law. Since the employer is often responsible for legal violations its employees committed in the course of their job, the employer's interest in retaining control over every aspect of the work environment increases. On the other hand, employees may argue that their drug usage is only relevant if it impacts their job performance. Until it does, the employer should have no basis for testing.

Consider the possibilities of incorrect presumptions in connection with drug testing. For instance, in *Drug Abuse in The Workplace: An Employer's Guide for Prevention,* Mark de Bernardo suggests that possessing crudely wrapped cigarettes, razor blades, or eye droppers; making frequent trips to the bathroom; or dressing inappropriately for the season may be warning signs of drug use.[32] On the other hand, it does not take a great deal of imagination to come up with other, more innocuous alternative possibilities. Yet, an employer may decide to test based on these "signs." Is it ethical to presume someone is guilty based on these signs? Does a person have a fundamental right to be presumed innocent? Or, perhaps, do the risks of that presumption outweigh the individual's rights in this situation and justify greater precautions?

In a study examining the attitudes of college students to drug testing programs, researchers found that "virtually all aspects of drug testing programs are strongly accepted by some individuals and strongly rejected by others." Not surprisingly, the only variable that the researchers found indicative of a student's attitude was whether the student had ever used drugs in the past. Where a student had never used drugs, she or he was more likely to find drug testing programs acceptable.[33] In general, the following factors contribute to greater acceptance and approval by workers: programs that use a task force made up of employees and their supervisors, a completely random program, effective communication of procedures, programs that offer treatment other than termination for first-time offenders, and programs with no distinction between supervisory and other workers.

In the seminal legal case on the issue, *Skinner* v. *Railway Labor Executives' Ass'n*,[34] the Court addressed the question of whether certain forms of drug and alcohol testing violate the Fourth Amendment. In *Skinner,* the defendant justified testing railway workers based on safety concerns: "to prevent accidents and casualties in railroad operations that result from impairment of employees by alcohol or drugs." The court held that "[t]he Government's interest in regulating the conduct of railroad employees to ensure safety, like its supervision of probationers or regulated industries, or its operation of a government office, school, or prison, likewise presents 'special needs' beyond normal law enforcement that may justify departures from the usual warrant and probable-cause requirements."

It was clear to the Court that the governmental interest in ensuring the safety of the traveling public and of the employees themselves "plainly justifies prohibiting covered employees from using alcohol or drugs on duty, or while subject to being called for duty." The issue then for the Court was whether, absent a warrant or individualized suspicion, the means by which the defendant monitored compliance with this prohibition justified the privacy intrusion. In reviewing the justification, the Court focused on the fact that permission to dispense with warrants is strongest where "the burden of obtaining a warrant is likely to frustrate the governmental purpose behind the search," and recognized that "alcohol and other drugs are eliminated from the bloodstream at a constant rate and blood and breath samples taken to measure whether these substances were in the bloodstream when a triggering event occurred must be obtained as soon as possible." In addition, the Court noted that the railway workers' expectations of privacy in this industry are diminished given its high scrutiny through regulation to ensure safety. The court therefore concluded that the railway's compelling interests outweighed privacy concerns since the proposed testing "is not an undue infringement on the justifiable expectations of privacy of covered employees."

Where public safety is at risk, there is arguably a compelling public interest claim from a utilitarian perspective that may be sufficiently persuasive to outweigh any one individual's right to privacy or right to control information about oneself. However, what about jobs in which public safety is not at risk? Is it justifiable to test all employees and job applicants? Is the proposed benefit to the employer sufficiently valuable in your perspective to outweigh the employee's fundamental interest in autonomy and privacy? Should a utilitarian viewpoint govern or should deontological principles take priority? Should we consider a distributive justice perspective and the fairest result—does distributive justice apply under these circumstances?

Several major retail employers, including Home Depot, Ikea, and Wal-Mart, have comprehensive drug-testing policies for both job applicants and employees. Many stores also promote their "drug-free" workplace policy as a marketing strategy. With just a few exceptions, such policies are legal throughout the United States. The question is, "Are they ethically appropriate?" The following Decision Point explores these issues.

What limits should be placed on the grounds on which employment can be denied to a job applicant? The law prohibits denying someone a job on the basis of race, religion, ethnicity, gender, or disability. The law generally allows denial of a job on the basis of drug use. Like employment at will, the burden of proof lies with the job applicant to demonstrate that the denial was based on the prohibited categories; otherwise employers need no reason to deny someone a job. Suppose a business wanted to ensure not only a drug-free workplace, but also an alcohol-free workplace. Would a business have the ethical right to deny a job, or dismiss an employee, for drinking alcohol? Courts have been asked to decide the legitimacy of dismissals for cigarette smoking, for political beliefs, and for having an abortion. Which of these do you think is legitimate grounds for dismissal? Many businesses have also used personality tests and psychological profiling to evaluate potential employees. Such tests ask many personal questions, including some that concern a person's sexual life. Would a business have an ethical right to deny employment to someone on the basis of the results of a personality test?

What are some of the questions or concerns you might raise in trying to answer the above challenge? What would you suggest a business do to respond to them?

- What are the key facts relevant to your response?
- What are the ethical issues involved in basing hiring decisions on personal information?
- Who are the stakeholders?
- What alternatives would you suggest to business in considering personal information in hiring, and what alternatives exist for employers?
- How do the alternatives compare for business and for the stakeholders?

Other Forms of Monitoring

OBJECTIVE

Employers are limited in their collection of information through other various forms of testing, such as polygraphs or medical tests. Employers are constrained by a business necessity and relatedness standard or, in the case of polygraphs, by a requirement of reasonable suspicion. With regard to medical information specifically, employers' decisions are not only governed by the Americans with Disabilities Act but also restricted by the Health Insurance Portability and Accountability Act (HIPAA). HIPAA stipulates that employers cannot use "protected health information" in making employment decisions without prior consent. Protected health information includes all medical records or other individually identifiable health information.

In recent years polygraph and drug testing, physical and electronic surveillance, third-party background checks, and psychological testing have all been used as means to gain information about employees. More recently, electronic monitoring and surveillance are increasingly being used in the workplace. Where might this practice develop in the future? One area that is sure to provide new questions about privacy is genetic testing. Genetic testing and screening, of both employees and consumers, is another new technology that will offer businesses a wealth of information about potential employees and customers. Though Executive Order 13145, signed by then-President Clinton, prohibits discrimination in employment based on genetic information, this order applies only to the federal workplaces.

Similar restraint in the private sector is represented both by certain individual state restrictions on the use of genetic information and by voluntary corporate efforts such as the statement by IBM in 2005 of a privacy policy that will exclude the use of genetic information from potential or current employees for hiring or employment purposes. Because of the significant costs associated with sequencing a person's DNA, few companies currently use genetic information for these purposes, but the potential remains, nonetheless. Using genetic information is not unheard of—insurance companies, for example, already inquire about diseases in family history. Since some diseases are more prevalent among certain groups, genetic discrimination is a risk that has not yet been resolved. On the other hand, with increased knowledge comes the possibility of preventing the onset or further development of a disease, or the opportunity of placing employees in a position more appropriate for their physical well-being, thus creating extraordinary value. The balance between the value in information, employees' right to privacy, and the risk of information sharing remains the unsettled issue. (See the following Decision Point for examples of just how difficult the balancing efforts can be.) Such developments will keep employee privacy concerns in the public eye for many years to come.

The following section, Regulation of Off-Work Acts, will provide some guidance regarding how far the employer is permitted to go in directing the activities of its workers while not at work.

Regulation of Off-Work Acts

OBJECTIVE

The regulation of an employee's activities when she or he is away from work is an interesting issue, particularly in at-will environments. However, as discussed throughout this chapter, even employers of at-will employees must comply with a variety of statutes in imposing requirements and managing employees. For instance, New York's lifestyle discrimination statute prohibits employment decisions or actions based on four categories of off-duty activity: legal recreational activities, consumption of legal products, political activities, and membership in a union.

Across the nation, there are other less broad protections for off-work acts. A number of states have enacted protections about the consumption or use of legal products off the job, such as cigarettes.[35] These statutes originated from the narrower

Decision Point

My Information or Yours?

Review the following scenarios and reach a conclusion about whether the employee or the employer has the stronger *ethical* position. In reaching your conclusion, consider the following:

- What are the key facts relevant to your response?
- What are the ethical issues involved in this particular scenario?
- Who are the stakeholders?
- What alternatives might exist for the employee or for the employer that might otherwise resolve the conflict presented, if any? Is there any other way, for instance, to gather information about employees, to protect employees from a particular harm, or to protect employers from a cost that concerns them?
- How do the alternatives compare, and how do the alternatives affect the stakeholders?

■ An employee is fired when a mandatory urinalysis test detects nicotine in her urine. Her company prohibits smoking by all employees. The company argues that increasing health care costs due to smoking justifies the action.

■ An employee is fired when her employer learns that she has had an abortion. The employer is a strong antiabortion, prolife advocate who believes that abortion is equivalent to murder.

■ An employee is denied health care coverage offered to all other employees when his employer switches health care providers to one that requires a medical examination before offering coverage. The employee is diagnosed as HIV positive during the examination. Rising health care costs under the previous provider, attributed to a large extent to costs associated with this employee, were the reason for the switch in providers.

■ As part of a preemployment psychological test administered to all applicants for security guard positions, a major department store asks potential employees to respond to the following statements: "I feel very strongly attracted to members of my own sex. . . . I have never indulged in any unusual sex practices. . . . I feel sure that there is only one true religion. . . . I go to church almost every week. . . . I wish that I was not bothered by thoughts about sex. . . . I have had no difficulty starting or holding my urine. . . . I believe that my sins are unpardonable." The store received reports on the evaluation but not responses to individual questions. A group of job applicants sued the store, claiming that the tests violated their privacy rights.

protection for workers who smoked off-duty. Currently, abstention from smoking cannot be a condition of employment in at least 29 states and the District of Columbia (and those states provide antiretaliation provisions for employers who violate the prohibition). In fact, instead of simply identifying the right to use lawful products outside of work, Rhode Island goes further by specifically prohibiting an employer from banning the use of tobacco products while not at work.

On the other hand, employers are not prohibited from making employment decisions on the basis of weight, as long as they are not in violation of the American with Disabilities Act (ADA) when they do so. The issue depends on whether the employee's weight is evidence of or results from a disability. If so, the employer must explore whether the worker is otherwise qualified for the position. Under the ADA, the individual is considered "otherwise qualified" if she or he can perform the essential functions of the position with or without reasonable accommodations. If the individual cannot perform the essential functions of the position, the employer is not subject to liability for reaching an adverse employment decision. However, employers should be cautious since the ADA also protects workers who are not disabled but who are *perceived* as being disabled, a category into which someone might fall based on his or her weight.

Laws that protect against discrimination based on marital status exist in just under half of the states. However, though workers might be protected based on marital *status,* they are not necessarily protected against adverse action based on *the identity of the person* they married. For instance, some companies might have an antinepotism policy under which an employer refuses to hire or terminates a worker on the basis of the spouse's working at the same firm, or a conflict-of-interest policy under which the employer refuses to hire or terminates a worker whose spouse works at a competing firm.

Since about one-third of workers have dated an office colleague, policies and attitudes on workplace dating have an especially strong potential impact.[36] Though only about 12 percent of workplaces have policies prohibiting workplace dating,[37] a New York decision reaffirms the employer's right to terminate a worker on the basis of romantic involvement. In *McCavitt* v. *Swiss Reinsurance America Corp.,*[38] the court held that an employee's dating relationship with a fellow officer of the corporation was not a "recreational activity," within the meaning of a New York statute that prohibited employment discrimination for engaging in such recreational activities. The employee contended that, even though "[t]he personal relationship between plaintiff and Ms. Butler has had no repercussions whatever for the professional responsibilities or accomplishments of either" and "Swiss Re (sic) . . . has no written anti-fraternization or anti-nepotism policy," he was passed over for promotion and then discharged from employment largely because of his dating. The court agreed with the employer and found that dating was not a recreational activity.

The majority of states protect against discrimination on the basis of political involvement, though states vary on the type and extent of protection. Finally, lifestyle discrimination may be unlawful if the imposition of the rule treats one protected group differently than another. For instance, if an employer imposes a rule restricting the use of peyote in Native American rituals that take place during off-work hours, the rule may be suspect and may subject the employer to liability. Similarly, the rule may be unlawful if it has a different impact on a protected group than on other groups.

Most statutes or common law decisions, however, provide for employer defenses for those rules that (a) are reasonably and rationally related to the employment activities of a particular employee, (b) constitute a "bona fide occupational requirement," meaning a rule that is reasonably related to that particular position, or (c) are necessary to avoid a conflict of interest or the appearance of conflict of interest.

The Reality Check on the following page provides an overview of the intersection of the discussions of the prior two sections in its evaluation of privacy, testing, and off-work acts. While our analysis to this point has addressed the regulation of behavior during employment, perhaps it is important to consider your choices preemployment and the impact they will have on an employer's later decisions about hiring you. Alternatively, from the employer's perspective, it is important to understand when it is valuable to test prospective employees or why it might be effective to refrain from testing in the hiring process.

Privacy Rights since September 11, 2001

OBJECTIVE

The events of September 11, 2001, have had a major impact on privacy within the United States, and on the employment environment in particular. The federal government has implemented widespread modifications to its patchwork structure of privacy protections since the terror attacks of September 11, 2001. In particular, proposals for the expansion of surveillance and information-gathering authority were submitted and, to the chagrin of some civil rights attorneys and advocates, many were enacted.

The most public and publicized of these modifications was the adoption and implementation of the Uniting and Strengthening America by Providing Appropriate Tools Required to Intercept and Obstruct Terrorism (USA PATRIOT) Act of 2001. The USA PATRIOT Act expanded states' rights with regard to Internet surveillance technology, including workplace surveillance, and amended the Electronic Communications Privacy Act. The act also grants access to sensitive data with only a court order rather than a judicial warrant and imposes or enhances civil and criminal penalties for knowingly or intentionally aiding terrorists. In addition, the new disclosure regime increased the sharing of personal information between government agencies in order to ensure the greatest level of protection.

Title II of the act provides for the following enhanced surveillance procedures that have a significant impact on individual privacy and may impact an employer's effort to maintain employee privacy:

• Expands authority to intercept wire, oral, and electronic communications relating to terrorism and to computer fraud and abuse offenses.

Reality Check *The Employment Relationship Begins Preemployment*

by Tara J. Radin and Martin Calkins

Society has traditionally treated the employment relationship as beginning and ending with the start and end dates of the employment appointment. In fact, the relationship begins prior to hiring and ends, often, only with death.

PREEMPLOYMENT PRACTICES

The importance of the preemployment relationship is commonly overlooked. In spite of this, preemployees (i.e., job candidates) today have few if any legally recognized rights. This is becoming increasingly problematic because of widespread advances in technology and the virtual lack of respect afforded the personal privacy of job-seekers.

A number of companies have recently emerged and are taking advantage of new information-gathering technologies by offering these services to employers in the process of hiring new employees. These companies contract with organizations (and individuals) to gather personal information about potential new hires. They gather any information that is requested about job candidates—from credit histories to their driving records.

While collecting data on people prior to their employment is nothing new, the methods used today lack the transparency of the past and skew the balance of power even more toward the employer and away from the employee. Further, employers do not always ask permission or even inform job candidates that they are doing background checks and are often unwilling to reveal to applicants the specific information that has influenced their hiring decisions.

Firms support this sort of information gathering on the basis that it enables them to make better hiring decisions. Even so, the practice is not without serious drawbacks—even from the perspective of the hiring firms. For one reason, the accuracy of third-party information is not always assured. In addition, there are no guarantees that the data collected is complete. Background checks can result in inaccurate or downright erroneous candidate profiles. While employers assume they are finding out relevant information to enhance their hiring decisions, the reality is that the information they are obtaining might be distorted without their

knowledge; instead of eliminating certain risky candidates, they might unknowingly be overlooking "diamonds in the rough."

From the perspective of job applicants, the practice of preemployment information-gathering is particularly insidious. Job candidates are not always given notice that they are being scrutinized and that the material being collected is highly personal. In addition, job candidates are generally not offered the opportunity to provide any sort of rebuttal to the reports generated by information-gathering agencies. This is especially problematic in situations where candidates are rejected on the basis of background checks.

IMPACT OF PREEMPLOYMENT PRACTICES

To see how this testing can have a negative impact on the hiring process, take the example of Maria, a fictitious job candidate. Maria applies for a job in marketing for a regional department store. She is asked to take a prescreening drug test and, through this and the personal information she provides as part of a general background check, the potential employer gains access to Maria's credit report. This report reveals that she has a judgment pending against her. Fearing that Maria is an employment risk, the company decides not to hire her.

While the credit report's data might be accurate, it does not tell the complete story about Maria. It does not indicate, for example, that Maria was the victim of identity fraud. In addition, the report might be inaccurate without her knowledge. While Maria should be aware of the credit information in her report, she has not looked at it in some time and the collecting agency has included some incorrect information. The fact that Maria has an unpaid debt does not provide information inherently relevant to the particular job for which she has applied.

The employer considering Maria's application might rationalize that the background check is necessary to assess her general suitability. Many employers consider this a legitimate purpose and argue that there is a relationship between a candidate's responsibility in handling client affairs and her manner of dealing with personal finances. Although such an argument is not without merit,

(continued)

the result seems somewhat excessive. Consider, for example, the relevance of the driving record of a candidate for a bus driver position: it would seem almost counterintuitive not to inquire into that sort of information. There are meaningful differences, however, between this situation and that of Maria. Where work is of a particularly sensitive nature or where the level of the open position is high within a company, background checks directly related to performance might be appropriate when linked to a legitimate business purpose. In addition, the type of company or potential liability for the company could also warrant specific checks. In Maria's situation, none of these circumstances are present.

ARGUMENTS AGAINST EXCESSIVE PREEMPLOYMENT TESTING

There are many arguments against preemployment testing, particularly when used indiscriminately. Excessive preemployment testing can be attacked on moral grounds. First, it undermines the dignity of the individual by strengthening the notion of the person as a mere factor of production. It effectively enables employers to treat people as a means to achieving profitable ends without regard for the individual as a person valuable in and of him- or herself. In addition, it creates a climate of suspicion that undermines trust and loyalty and encourages duplicity and insincerity. Finally, it affects the character of the companies and individuals who work there. Companies become secretive and manipulative through such information-gathering and candidates, in turn, do what they can to conceal information they consider potentially unfavorable to their acceptance or advancement. This sort of behavior is to the detriment of the character of both employers and potential employees.

In addition to these sorts of ethical considerations, there are strong business arguments against excessive use of preemployment testing. Unfettered collection of personal information disregards property interests associated with that personal information. Hiring practices involving background checks ignore a person's ownership of information about him- or herself. It also erodes the privacy expectations a person has in his or her personal information. Moreover, it creates a bad first impression for potential employees and detracts from general morale. During bad economic times, this might not matter, but when times

are good and employment rates are high, potential job candidates are likely to seek out opportunities with employers who do not utilize such intrusive methods. In addition, current employees—those who stay by necessity or choice—will see themselves in a relationship with an employer who does not trust them or respect individual privacy. In other words, the practice used in hiring spills over and effectively becomes the tenor of the overall employment relationship, and this can prove demoralizing to employees and result in an underlying tone of distrust.

RESPONSIBLE USE OF PERSONAL INFORMATION

Although abundant information is readily available to employers, this does not mean that they have to use all of it. Ideally, personal information should remain personal and, at the very least, the individual should have the ability to determine who gains access to his or her personal information and to know when someone obtains that information. It is important here to keep in mind that the availability of access is not the same as the moral right to access information or to use that information in a hiring decision.

As employers consider how to use the information they gather, they should consider "legitimate business purpose" as a guiding principle. Where there is a legitimate business purpose (defined generally to be applied to job function, type of company, and so on) and an identifiable direct correlation between that information and the job candidate, it would then seem appropriate for personal information to be solicited.

At the same time and as Maria's situation illustrates, it now becomes incumbent upon individuals to keep better track of their personal information. Now that individuals are aware that credit checks can be performed and used against them, they need to make sure that the credit bureaus have accurate information. In addition, individuals need to be prepared to respond to anomalies that might exist in their personal information. It is no longer an issue of what is right and what is wrong, but what is going to happen. If we know that employers have access to this information, it is for us to determine what we are going to do about it for ourselves.

Source: Copyright © Tara Radin and Martin Calkins; adapted for this publication and used by permission of the authors.

- Provides roving surveillance authority under the Foreign Intelligence Surveillance Act of 1978 (FISA) to track individuals. (FISA investigations are not subject to Fourth Amendment standards but are instead governed by the requirement that the search serve "a significant purpose.")
- Allows nationwide seizure of voice-mail messages pursuant to warrants (i.e., without the previously required wiretap order).
- Broadens the types of records that law enforcement may obtain, pursuant to a subpoena, from electronic communications service providers.
- Permits emergency disclosure of customer electronic communications by providers to protect life and limb.
- Provides nationwide service of search warrants for electronic evidence.

These provisions allow the government to monitor anyone on the Internet simply by contending that the information is "relevant" to an ongoing criminal investigation. In addition, the act includes provisions designed to combat money laundering activity or the funding of terrorist or criminal activity through corporate activity or otherwise. All financial institutions must now report suspicious activities in financial transactions and keep records of foreign national employees, while also complying with the antidiscrimination laws discussed throughout this text.

Though some of its surveillance and information sharing provisions were set to expire (or "sunset") in 2005, President George W. Bush reauthorized the act in March 2006, which made permanent or extended many of these authorities. In addition, the USA PATRIOT Act was not the only legislative response. By September 2002, the Office of Management and Budget had recorded 58 new regulations responding to terrorism[39] and both federal and state agencies have passed a number of new pieces of legislation. Not everyone is comfortable with these new protections. Out of concern for the USA PATRIOT Act's newly permitted investigatory provisions, some librarians now warn computer users in their libraries that their computer use could be monitored by law enforcement agencies. *The Washington Post* reports that some librarians are even ensuring privacy by destroying records of sites visited, books checked out, and logs of computer use.[40] The American Civil Liberties Union reports that a number of communities have passed resolutions against the USA PATRIOT Act.[41]

While the Patriot Act has implications for all citizens, it also has direct implications for business since it relies on employers for information gathering, among other requests. Employers have three choices in terms of their response to a governmental request for information. They may opt to voluntarily cooperate with law enforcement by providing confidential employee or customer information upon request and as part of an ongoing investigation. They may instead choose to cooperate by asking for permission to seek employee authorization to release the requested information. Or, finally, they may request to receive a subpoena, search warrant, or FISA order from the federal agency before disclosing an employee's confidential information.[42]

Opening Decision Point Revisited

The opening Decision Point presented Jon Katz's proposal for ethical principles for computer users and builders. The Decision Point asked whether you believe that his principles are attainable from a pragmatic perspective and to what extent one has a responsibility to adhere to them when (at least some) others might be unlikely to do so.

To determine whether Katz's list of ethical principles for computer users and builders is attainable, we first must determine whether we need additional facts before we can reach a judgment. In addition, are we clear on all of the possible ethical issues involved? As mentioned in the chapter, as technology advances, we might not necessarily be prepared for the ethical dilemmas we could face. Would you have considered, for instance, whether an individual computer programmer is responsible for the end result of what someone ultimately does with her or his program? If the programmer fails to protect the code sufficiently, and therefore someone is able to hack into the code and use the program for unethical purposes, does the programmer bear any responsibility? You have to determine how far you are going to take the responsibility.

Have you considered all the stakeholders in connection with computer use? Of course, by now we are used to considering employees, consumers, clients, investors, and even competitors. But have you thought about governments and their interest in protecting or accessing data? What about a data owner? Are there others? Additional research is likely to uncover additional or alternative standards surrounding these issues as well. On the basis of your analysis, do Katz's standards or principles seem to be reasonable, practical, and possible?

Questions, Projects, and Exercises

1. Marriott Resorts had a formal company party for more than 200 employees. At one point during the party, the company aired a videotape that compiled employees' and their spouses' comments about a household chore they hated. However, as a spoof, the video was edited to make it seem as if they were describing what it was like to have sex with their partner. One employee's wife was very upset by the video and sued Marriott for invasion of privacy. Evaluate her argument, focusing on the ethical arguments for a violation of her rights.

2. Richard Fraser, an at-will independent insurance agent for Nationwide Mutual Insurance Company, was terminated by Nationwide and the parties disagree on the reason for Fraser's termination. Fraser argues that Nationwide terminated him because he filed complaints regarding Nationwide's allegedly illegal conduct, for criticizing Nationwide to the Nationwide Insurance Independent Contractors Association, and for attempting to obtain the passage of legislation in Pennsylvania to ensure that independent insurance agents could be terminated only for "just cause." Nationwide argues, however, that it terminated Fraser because he was disloyal. Nationwide points out that Fraser drafted a letter to two competitors saying that policy holders were not happy with Nationwide and asking whether the competitors would be interested in acquiring them. (Fraser claims that the letters were drafted only to get Nationwide's attention and were not sent.)

   When Nationwide learned about these letters, it claims that it became concerned that Fraser might also be revealing company secrets to its competitors. It therefore searched its main file server—on which all of Fraser's e-mail was lodged—for any e-mail to or from Fraser that showed similar improper behavior. Nationwide's general counsel testified that the e-mail search confirmed Fraser's disloyalty. Therefore, on the basis of the two letters and the e-mail search, Nationwide terminated Fraser's employment agreement. The search of his e-mail gives rise to Fraser's claim for damages under the Electronic Communications Privacy Act of 1986 (ECPA). Do you believe the employer was justified in monitoring the employee's e-mail and then terminating him? What ethical arguments do you believe either side could use in this case?

3. A customer service representative at an electronics store is surfing the Internet using one of the display computers. She accesses a Web site that shows graphic images of a crime scene. A customer in the store who notices the images is offended. Another customer service representative is behind the counter, using the store's computer to access a pornographic site, and starts to laugh. A customer asks him why he is laughing. He turns the computer screen around to show her the images that are causing him amusement. Is there anything wrong with these activities?

4. The term *cybersquatting* refers to the practice of: registering a large number of Web site domain names hoping to sell them at huge prices to others who may want the URL or who are prepared to pay to get rid of a potentially confusing domain name. For instance, People for the Ethical Treatment of Animals, which operates www.peta.org, was able to shut down www.peta.com, a prohunting Web site that dubbed itself "People Eating Tasty Animals." Cybersquatters often determine possible misspellings or slightly incorrect Web sites with the hopes that the intended Web site will pay them for their new domain. For example, someone paid over $7 million for the address www.business.com. In one case, one day after a partnership was announced that would result in an online bookstore for the Toronto *Globe & Mail* newspaper, with the domain name www.chaptersglobe.com, Richard Morochove, a technology writer, registered the domain chapters-globe.com. When the partnership demanded that he stop using the name, he promptly agreed, as long as he received a percentage of the sales from the Chapters/Globe Web site. The case went to trial. In situations such as these, do you believe the cybersquatter is doing anything wrong? What options might the "intended Web site" owner have?

5. Spam, or spamming, refers to the use of mailing lists to blanket usenets or private e-mail boxes with indiscriminate advertising messages. Some people believe that spamming should be protected as the simple exercise of one's First Amendment right to free speech while others view it as an invasion of privacy or even theft of resources or trespass to property, as Intel argued when a disgruntled ex-employee spammed more than 35,000 Intel employees with his complaints. In that case, the court agreed, considering his e-mail spamming equivalent to trespassing on Intel's property and recognizing that Intel was forced to spend considerable time and resources to delete the e-mail messages from its system.

It is amusing to note that the source of the term *spam* is generally accepted to be the Monty Python song, "Spam spam spam spam, spam spam spam spam, lovely spam, wonderful spam . . . "Like the song, spam is an endless repetition of worthless text. Others believe that the term came from the computer group lab at the University of Southern California, which gave it the name because it has many of the same characteristics as the lunchmeat Spam:

- Nobody wants it or ever asks for it.
- No one ever eats it; it is the first item to be pushed to the side when eating the entree.

- Sometimes it is actually tasty, like 1 percent of junk mail that is really useful to some people.[43]
- Using stakeholder analysis, make an argument that spamming is either ethical or unethical.

6. Term papers on practically every subject imaginable are available on the Internet. Many of those who post the papers defend their practice in two ways: (1) These papers are posted to assist in research in the same way any other resource is posted on the Web and should simply be cited if used; and (2) these papers are posted in order to encourage faculty to modify paper topics and/or exams and not to simply bring back assignments that have been used countless times in the past. Are you persuaded? Is there anything unethical about this service in general? If so, who should be held accountable, the poster, the ultimate user, or someone else?

7. A college provided its security officers with a locker area in which to store personal items. The security officers occasionally used the area as a dressing room. After incidents of theft from the lockers and reports that the employees were bringing weapons to campus, the college installed a video surveillance camera in the locker area. Did the employees have a reasonable expectation of privacy that was violated by the video surveillance? Explain.

8. You work in the information technology area of a large U.S. corporation. After a rash of mass sexually explicit e-mails were sent from an inside source to the entire corporate e-mail list, your supervisor asked you to draft a technology usage policy. What are some of the issues you will need to consider?

Key Terms

After reading this chapter, you should have a clear understanding of the following Key Terms. The page numbers refer to the point at which they were discussed in the chapter. For a more complete definition, please see the Glossary.

Electronic Communications Privacy Act of 1986, *p. 259*
e-mail monitoring, *p. 267*
European Union Directive on Personal Data Protection, *p. 260*
Fourth Amendment protections, *p. 259*
HIPAA, *p. 276*
hypernorms, *p. 258*

Internet use monitoring, *p. 267*
intrusion into seclusion, *p. 259*
moral free space, *p.258*
personal data, *p. 261*
privacy, *p. 255*
privacy rights, *p. 256*
property rights in information, *p. 258*
reasonable expectation of privacy, *p. 260*

reciprocal obligation, *p. 257*
Safe Harbor exception, *p. 261*
Uniting and Strengthening America by Providing Appropriate Tools Required to Intercept and Obstruct Terrorism (USA PATRIOT) Act of 2001, *p. 280*

Endnotes

1. Patricia Werhane, *Persons, Rights, and Corporations* (Englewood Cliffs, NJ: Prentice Hall, 1985), p. 94.
2. Gerald Doppelt, "Beyond Liberalism and Communitarianism: Towards a Critical Theory of Social Justice," Philosophy and Social Criticism 14 (1988), pp. 271, 278.
3. Global Internet Liberty Campaign, "Privacy and Human Rights: An International Survey of Privacy Laws and Practice," http://www.gilc.org/privacy/survey/exec-summary.html (1998).
4. Mike Brunker, "Cyberporn Nurse: I Feel Like Larry Flynt," MSNBC, July 16, 1999.

5. *Lake* v. *Wal-Mart Stores, Inc.*, 582 N.W.2d 231 (Minn. 1998).

6. 59 Cal.Rptr.2d 834 (Cal.Ct.App., 1996).

7. See "Ted Clark's Legal Corner: Monitoring Employee Activities: Privacy Tensions in the Public Workplace," *NPLERA Newsletter,* June 1999, http://www.seyfarth.com/ practice/labor/articles/II_1393.html.

8. Formally known as "Directive 95/46/EC of the European Parliament and of the Council of 24 October 1995 on the Protection of Individuals with Regard to the Processing of Personal Data and on the Free Movement of Such Data, Council Directive 95/46," 1995 O.J. (L281).

9. Council Directive 95/46, 1995 O.J. (L281) at arts, 25–26.

10. Pamela Samuelson, "Data Privacy Law: A Study of United States Data Protection," *California Law Review* 87, no. 3 (May 1999), p. 751.

11. John Haas, "Thinking Ethically about Technology," http://www.nd.edu/~rbarger/haas. ethic.

12. *State of Washington* v. *Young*, 123 Wash.2d 173 (1994).

13. Frank Daly, "Reply, Delete . . . or Relate? IT's Human Dimension," Lecture as Verizon Professor in Business Ethics and Technology, Bentley College, March 31, 2004.

14. U. Klotz, "The Challenges of the New Economy" (October 1999), cited in *World Employment Report 2001: Life at Work in the Information Economy* (Geneva: International Labour Office, 2001), p. 145.

15. For a similar interpretation, see B. Kracher and C. Corritore, "Is There a Special E-Commerce Ethics?" *Business Ethics Quarterly* 14, no. 1 (2004), pp. 71–94.

16. Antonio Argandona, "The New Economy: Ethical Issues," *Journal of Business Ethics* 44 (2003), pp 3–22, 26.

17. Google S-1, filed with the Securities and Exchange Commission, http://www.sec.gov/ Archives/edgar/data/1288776/000119312504139655/ds1a.htm, appendix B (2004).

18. Google S-1, *infra*, note 17.

19. Google S-1, *infra*, note 17.

20. Antonio Argandoña, "The New Economy: Ethical Issues," *Journal of Business Ethics* 44 (2003), pp 3–22, 28.

21. David Carr, "Putting 40,000 Readers, One by One, on a Cover," *The New York Times* (April 5, 2004).

22. American Management Association Workplace Email and Instant Messaging Survey (2005).

23. *CSO Magazine* Survey of 520 Chief Security Officers and Senior Security Executives (January 2004).

24. American Management Association Workplace Email and Instant Messaging Survey (2005). Andrew Schulman, "One-third of U.S. Online Workforce under Internet/Email Surveillance," *Workforce Surveillance Project*, Privacy Foundation, July 9, 2001, http://www.privacyfoundation.org/workplace/business/biz_show.asp?id=70&ac. Schulman reports that, of the 140 million workers in the U.S., 40 million are online. Of that 40 million, 14 million are subject to monitoring (35 percent). Worldwide, 100 million of 3 billion workers are online and 27 million (27 percent) are subject to monitoring (p. 2). See also Linda Rosencrance, "Study: Monitoring of Employee Email, Web Use Escalates," *Computerworld*, July 9, 2001.

25. Vasant Raval, "Ethical Behavior in the Knowledge Economy," *Information Strategy* 16, no. 3 (Spring 2000), p. 45.

26. Elron Software, "Guide to Internet Usage and Policy" (2001), pp. 7, 17; and American Management Association Workplace Email and Instant Messaging Survey (2004).

27. American Management Association Workplace Email and Instant Messaging Survey (2005); Alan Cohen, "Worker Watchers," *Fortune/CNET Technology Review* (Summer 2001) pp. 70, 76.

28. American Management Association Workplace Email and Instant Messaging Survey (2005).

29. Stephen Hawk, "The Effects of Computerized Performance Monitoring: An Ethical Perspective," *Journal of Business Ethics* 13, pp. 949–957 (1994).

30. Ann Svendsen and David Wheeler, *Measuring the Business Value of Stakeholder Relationships (Part 1)* (Toronto CICA, 2001).

31. Miriam Schulman, "Little Brother Is Watching You," *Issues in Ethics* 9, no. 2 (Spring 1998).

32. Mark A. de Bernardo, *Drug Abuse in the Workplace: An Employer's Guide for Prevention*, available from the U.S. Chamber of Commerce, 1615 H Street, NW, Washington, DC 20062.

33. Murphy, Thornton, and Reynolds, "College Students' Attitudes."

34. 109 S.Ct. 1402 (1989).

35. As of publication, these included Arizona, Connecticut, Washington, DC, Illinois, Indiana, Kentucky, Louisiana, Maine, Mississippi, New Jersey, New Mexico, Oklahoma, Oregon, Rhode Island, South Carolina, South Dakota, Virginia, West Virginia, and Wyoming. See also John Pearce and Dennis Kuhn, "The Legal Limits of Employees' Off-Duty Privacy Rights," *Organizational Dynamics* 32, no. 4 (2003), pp. 372–383.

36. American Management Association Survey on Workplace Dating (2003).

37. American Management Association Survey on Workplace Dating (2003).

38. 37 237 F.3d 166 (2nd Cir. 2001).

39. Office of Management and Budget, "Stimulating Smarter Regulation, 2002: Report to Congress on the Costs and Benefits of Regulations and Unfunded Mandates on State, Local, and Tribal Entities" (Washington, DC: Office of Information and Regulatory Affairs, March 2003), www.whitehouse.gov/omb/inforeg/2002_report_to_congress.pdf.

40. Rene Sanchez, "Librarians Make Some Noise over Patriot Act," *Washington Post* (April 10, 2003), p. A20.

41. http://www.aclu.org/SafeandFree/SafeandFree.cfm?ID=11256&c=206.

42. Vance Knapp, "The Impact of the Patriot Act on Employers," http://www.rothgerber.com/newslettersarticles/le0024.asp (2003).

42. http://www.webopedia.com/TERM/s/spam.html.

Readings

Reading **7-1**

The New Economy: *Ethical Issues*

Antonio Argandoña

Abstract

The new economy is a technological revolution involving the information and communication technologies that affects almost all aspects of the economy, business, and our personal lives. The problems it raises for businesses are not radically new, and even less so from an ethical viewpoint. However, they deserve particular attention, especially now, in the first years of the 21st century, when we are feeling the full impact of the changes brought about by this technological revolution. In this article, I will try to draw a "map" of the main positive and negative ethical challenges raised by the new economy, concentrating on its three basic features: (1) a knowledge- and information-based technological change, (2) which is taking place in real time on a planetary scale (globalization), and (3) which entails a new, flexible, network-based business organization.

Introduction

The new economy is a technological revolution involving the information and communication technologies that affects almost all aspects of the economy, business, and our personal lives. The economic or management problems it raises are not radically new, and even less so from an ethical viewpoint. However, they deserve particular attention, especially now, in the first years of the 21st century, when we are feeling the full impact of the changes brought about by this technological revolution.

In this article, I will try to draw a "map" of the main ethical challenges raised by the new economy, concentrating on its three basic features: (1) a knowledge- and information-based technological change, (2) which is taking place in real time on a planetary scale (globalization), and (3) which entails a new, flexible, network-based business organization.

First of all, I will discuss what the new economy is and whether a "new" ethics is needed to address the challenges it raises. I will then discuss the main economic, social, human, and business ethics issues raised by the new information and communication technologies, by the development of a planetary-scale economy (globalization), and by the changes this brings about in companies (flexible, networked organizations), closing with the conclusions.

The New Economy

It seems that the term "new economy" was proposed for the first time by *BusinessWeek* in 1994. However, it was generalized immediately to designate a series of interrelated and not always well-defined phenomena, such as these:

1. A temporary but long-lasting period of high growth in the United States' productivity, particularly in the second half of the nineties. This period was interrupted by the recession of 2001, but seems likely to resume in the near future.

Note: In-text references and reference list have been removed and are available from the author.

2. Perhaps a temporary but long-lasting period of prosperity made possible by the "virtuous cycle" created by high productivity growth rates, low inflation, contained macroeconomic disequilibria and full employment, which lasted at least until the recession of 2001 and goes beyond the technological change that concerns us here.

3. The impact of the production and widespread use of the so-called information and communication technologies (ICT). This, in my view, lies at the heart of the new economy.

4. A presumed change in the rules by which the economy operates, some of which may have ceased to apply (for example, the rule that high growth leads to inflation).

5. The explosion of the prices of equities on the United States and other countries' capital markets, to the point of stating that the traditional rules used to value shares were no longer valid—based on the fact that companies that had never earned any profits and which foreseeably would not earn them in many years attained very high values. With the benefit of hindsight, we can say that this is not an inherent feature of the new economy, and it seems to have been due more to a speculative bubble than to any lasting change in the capital markets.

The experts have argued at length on the meaning, content and impact of the new economy. And it is logical that they should, because the term is appealing to the man in the street and the media, but it does not have a defined economic meaning. And any attempt to give it one requires establishing a delimiting criterion that will inevitably be debatable.

Strictly speaking, the new economy expresses the impact of the technological revolution developed around information and communications, first in the industry that produces ICT goods and services; second, in the industries that use these goods as production capital; and third, in the other industries and in the economy as a whole.

However, the key to the new economy is not in the silicon chips but knowledge: the fact that it is based on the acquisition, processing, transformation, and distribution of knowledge and information (hence the name of information and communication technologies, ICT). In a word, the distinguishing feature of the new economy is not merely a change in production and costs, or the use of the new technologies throughout the economy, but rather the nature of the "new" knowledge-intensive goods. In a strict sense, it is concerned with

1. The hardware (particularly computers) that processes and stores the information.

2. The communication system that receives and sends it.

3. The software that controls the entire system.

Obviously, we are not talking about new industries (the calculator and the telephone belong to previous technological revolutions), but it [the new economy] has certain features that give it particular significance:

1. The generalized use of software (which is, to a certain degree, a surrogate for human intelligence).

2. A high speed of technological progress.

3. Certain economic features that, without being radically new, interfere with the markets' competitive functioning, such as the fact that they are "experience goods," which are bought without sufficient knowledge of them and which cease to hold any interest when they are known. Or the presence of high, sunk entry costs, almost zero marginal production costs, and the virtual nonexistence of capacity constraints.

4. The possibility of working in a network, with high adoption externalities, effects of being "locked in" to a certain technology, the tendency towards market domination by one or a few companies, and the like.

5. The diffusion of its effects throughout the economy, affecting consumption and work decisions, how companies are run and government policies are implemented, and so on.

Does the new economy exist? This question continues to be the subject of discussion between economists, among other reasons because, as we have already pointed out, there is no agreement about what this new economy is, what its effects are, whether they are permanent or temporary, and so on; because the time that has passed is too short to be certain whether the changes observed are real or whether they are just a statistical mirage, and whether they are passing or look like becoming permanent. Our (tentative) opening thesis can be presented as follows:

1. The degree of technological progress experienced by the ICTs has been considerable since the 50s. Initially, the change was not revolutionary because the "new" products (mainly the computer and the cellular phone) were only variants of the "old" products (the calculator, the typewriter, and the telephone). However, eventually, technological progress significantly increased total factor productivity in the ICT-producing industries (computers, software, telecommunications, and the like).

   As a result, the quality, speed, capacity, and similar characteristics of the hardware, software and communication media increased, and their cost fell. This led to increased demand for their products and increased output, so that the weight of the industry in the economy as a whole has become progressively greater.

2. The ICTs are general purpose technologies, which are used as factors in the production of many goods and services, and which are combined with currently used technologies in other industries, giving rise to new products, processes, and organization forms. The reduced cost of the ICTs led to a high demand for their products from other industries, which replaced conventional capital and labor with computers, robots, new communication systems, and the like, or created new goods and services using these technologies. This led to a rapid increase in the productivity of the other factors, particularly labor, as a result of the more intensive vise of the capital related with the new technologies (capital deepening).

3. In turn, the new technologies' specifications altered the demand for the other production factors: new labor skills, new management systems, need for support infrastructures, and so on. And this also increased the productivity of the information and communication capital.

4. As technological progress spreads from one industry to another, spillover effects are generated that increase the total factor productivity in industries that are not directly related to the use of the new technologies' capital goods and, eventually, in the economy as a whole.

5. All of these effects have occurred or are currently occurring, first in the U.S. economy and then in the other countries, which are acting in this case as followers.

6. There is not a new-economy-linked "new" economic theory. The economic laws continue to be the same, although certain specific problems, linked with network economies, high entry costs and virtually zero marginal costs, new competitive models, and the like are raised.

Is the New Economy a Challenge for Ethics?

However, it is not the new economy we are interested in but the ethical problems that it poses for companies. Is a new brand of ethics needed for the new economy? And what are the main ethical issues facing companies as a result of the new economy?

The viewpoint we are interested in here is that of business ethics. The subject has already been discussed elsewhere, but we feel that the magnitude of the changes that are taking place requires a more detailed analysis. Also, although there are many studies that discuss the ethical problems of the new economy, there are not so many on the ethical problems of the companies operating in the new economy—in other words, the level of discussion is macro rather than micro.

Is a new brand of ethics needed for the new economy? The answer seems to be no. The new technological revolution does not raise any new ethical problems nor does it require the adoption of new criteria or principles. And the fact that the new economy does not require a distinct technical-economic treatment gives rise to the following thesis: if the economic problems are not different, it is unlikely that the moral problems will be.

However, there are powerful reasons for studying the ethical problems raised by the new economy; these for example:

1. The negative side of ethics ("don't do bad") becomes important in the new economy, because the new technologies create the opportunity for immoral conducts. Examples are legion: not respecting copyright of software or information, malicious entry into computers and networks (hackers), violation of privacy rights, creation of information monopolies, falsification of information (informational cheating) and creation of false information (information pollution), loss of security in public information, and so on.

2. One variant of this problem is the change in values that may be caused (or, at least, facilitated) by the opportunities created by the technology. For example, the new technologies' potential may lead to aggressive conducts to enter a new market as quickly as possible, corner competitors, acquire size, reduce competition, and make it difficult for customers to change to other suppliers. Also, there may be changes in personal conducts (computer addiction, for example, or the appearance of more individualistic personalities).

3. For some authors, the problem goes beyond specific behaviors and even beyond values and is, in fact, a systemic problem: it is the whole capitalist system that is immoral or, at least, suspect. And the new economy, like globalization, simply adds new dimensions to this problem.

4. The speed of change hampers ethical learning processes—the speeding up of processes is, in itself, an ethical problem. New companies with young staff in industries where it has not been possible to develop an adequate culture may facilitate nonethical conducts. The process is probably temporary, until society develops defense mechanisms, but the cost of acquiring the necessary virtues and culture may be very high.

5. The positive side ("do good") also has new aspects, because the new technologies provide opportunities for the economic development of depressed areas, increased participation, going beyond national barriers, defending human rights, and the like.

In the following pages, I will review a number of defining features of the new economy, from the business viewpoint, with a view to drawing a "map" of the main ethical problems that are appearing. To do this, I will develop my analysis following the three basic features of the new economy:

1. A knowledge- and information-based technological change;

2. which operates in real time on a planetary scale (globalization); and

3. with a new, flexible, network-based business organization.

* * * *

The Ethical Problems of the Information and Communication Technologies

The first ethical problem we face lies precisely in the field of technological innovation. The idea of the ethical neutrality of technological progress is not a new one and it has been criticized from many quarters. "Technology" is intended here not in the strict sense (knowledge, machines, capacity, production), but in a broader sense, with cultural (ends, values, beliefs) and organizational connotations (structures, users, companies, etc.).

One could argue that the ICTs do not create any moral problems that have not already been encountered in the old technologies (the calculator, the typewriter, or the telephone). But this is not true, because opening up new possibilities for action may change the problems' nature. A typical example would be the invasion of privacy that is now easier with the new technologies: spying on people in the street or in their homes; "infiltrating" their computer, monitoring their movements, compiling information on their health, their political ideas or their religious beliefs. It is true that this invasion has always been possible but now we can control practically all facets of a person's life, at any time and without that person knowing. And this must necessarily create more serious problems with a greater social, psychological and political impact. This is why some authors prefer to talk of "information ethics" rather than "computer ethics."

Obviously, when faced with this type of problem, we can always argue that technology (its creation and development) is neutral, and any problems will lie with the user. But this too is questionable. Any technology that can be used immorally must be developed with caution. A case in point here could be the destruction of barriers to information acquisition: the hackers have developed an undoubtedly interesting technology, which on occasions can be used legally and ethically, but which is more likely to be used for illicit purposes.

A final argument applied to technology is the legitimacy of progress in general: what technology can do, should be done, because it leads to progress, and progress is always desirable, even if it entails costs. This thesis also accepts the opposite argument: any decision, in technology too, has a number of dimensions—not only technical but also economic, cultural, social, organizational and ethical—and it must be judged taking all of them into account.

All of these are old problems and they are usually more acute in other fields of technological progress, such as the biotechnologies or the nuclear industry. However, the people and organizations involved in the research, development, and application of the ICTs must also be able to ask themselves ethical questions such as those we have mentioned.

The Ethical Problems of Information

If the new technologies revolve around information, then this information's moral requirements will hold a prominent position. Here are a few:

- Truthfulness and accuracy: the person providing the information must ensure that it is truthful and accurate, at least to a reasonable degree.
- Respect for privacy: the person receiving or accumulating information must take into account the ethical limits of individuals' (and organizations') privacy.
- The same can be said about company secrets, industrial espionage, and so on.
- Network security problems: sabotage, removal of information, impersonation, and the like.

- Irresponsibility, under the coverage of the anonymity allowed by some of the new technologies.
- How the recipient uses the information.

Admittedly, these are not new ethical problems: the propagation of false news, stealing information, industrial espionage, and misuse of staff surveillance are well-known problems. But, as we have said, the new technologies make them easier, more widespread or more serious.

The Economic Problems of the New Technologies

The ICTs have a number of economic features that have attracted the attention of the experts and which may also give rise to ethical problems. Here are some of these problems:

1. The ICTs' goods or services are "experience goods": they must be known to be appreciated, but their value falls sharply when they are known. For example, a new software program may be very useful for a prospective buyer. If her knowledge about the program is insufficient, she cannot appreciate it or make a decision about purchasing it. But knowing the software means having it and, therefore, being able to copy it, which destroys the program's economic value.

   The problem can be palliated by segmenting the market (so that only those who appreciate the product pay for it), such as, for example, by offering an incomplete product free (a software with few applications) and charging for providing the final product; offering a basic version for free and charging for later releases, and the like. However, all this may also give rise to moral problems: trust (in the product's quality, in that the other party will keep his word, etc.), deceit or lack of transparency in the information (sometimes, as a defensive weapon, but also as an opportunistic behavior), and so on. In addition, this type of relationship may lead to a "gift culture," in which certain individuals "give" something to others (a computer program, or a file with information, etc.), hoping perhaps that the other person will become a customer, or pay a quantity of money for the good or service, or give in turn information to the other party (about her buying habits, tastes, etc.).

2. The ICTs usually entail high sunk fixed entry costs, very low (even zero) marginal production costs, and no capacity constraints. For example, starting up a portal is enormously expensive and the investment is virtually irrecoverable if the project fails, while the cost of attending to a new visitor to the portal is virtually zero.

   From the economic viewpoint, this implies that the best strategy is to become big as quickly as possible. But is this compatible with competition? The economic (and ethical) problem lies in the fact that the traditional concept of what a competitive market is may not be valid in the new economy: for example, the important issue is not the market share controlled by a company but the ease with which new competitors can enter the market, the pace of technological development, the existence of countervailing forces in the market, and so on. None of this prevents the existence of practices that may be considered unfair or incompatible with competition.

3. The ICTs have significant "network effects": a network's value depends primarily on the number of subscribers (telephone or the Internet services offer little interest if they can only connect a handful of users, but their value increases exponentially with the number of customers connected).

Faced with these effects, companies try to be the first to start a network, increase the network's size at any price (to attract more users), seek allies and partners (to extend the network and make it stronger) and make it difficult for members to leave the network.

And this is where, without doubt, major moral issues come into play. Being the first may mean launching a new product without adequate testing and guaranteeing that it will operate satisfactorily, or offering certain benefits that it will not be possible to maintain. Increasing the network's size may also entail limited competition. Likewise, the search for allies and partners requires generating trust in the relationship, and expanding networks enormously increases the number of interpersonal and intercompany contacts (with positive and negative effects).

* * * *

Conclusions

The new economy is not radically new. No new economic theory is needed to understand it, nor new rules for running companies nor, therefore, new ethical principles to govern it. But we do need to understand the specific ways in which ethical problems arise in the new economy. And this must be done from within each decision, in its different dimensions: technical-economic, socio-political and moral.

Not everything is new in the new economy nor is everything undergoing hectic change. The old economy is still alive and kicking, and for millions of people, earning a living continues to be linked with working methods, tools, and machines in which the new technologies are perhaps present but which they have not transformed entirely. It may be that, in the long run, our lives will change completely. But, leaving to one side the innovational frenzy of the 90s, this change will probably be gradual and, foreseeably, also subject to a certain degree of backtracking, as we are currently observing.

Above and beyond semantic issues, the new economy has become a factor of many specific problems of companies and it must be studied together with them. The sweeping condemnations are ideological, not ethical, and, in my opinion, any serious ethical analysis of the new economy should not let itself by influenced by them.

In the course of this article, we have brought to light a broad range of technological, economic, social, managerial, and moral problems associated with the appearance and implementation of the ICTs. In all likelihood, many of these problems are temporary and they will lose their uniqueness, or even perhaps disappear, when full adaptation to the ICTs has been achieved. But this does not make the ethical analysis we must now perform any less important:

1. Because at stake is the happiness of millions of people, who are suffering these problems now and will continue to suffer them for a lot longer yet.
2. Because we are lacking in experience and perspective to understand, diagnose, and solve them—also from the sociological, political, economic, and technological viewpoints.
3. Because many corporate cultures have been lost, with the argument (probably mistaken) that that particular culture was no longer valid in the new economy. Consequently, many people are trying to address serious moral problems without an adequate cultural base.
4. Because moral learning takes place during the decision and action process itself, and, with the accumulation of errors, this learning process may become much more laborious and lengthy.

The new economy in itself is neither good nor bad. It is laden with opportunities: for improving the standard of living, for creating an environment in which sharing, trusting, and serving others is easier, for furthering transparency and increasing empowerment, with individual dignity as the ultimate beneficiary. However, it also holds dangers: unnecessary destruction of opportunities, encouraging disloyalty and opportunistic conducts, violating copyright or privacy rights, increased insecurity and uncertainty. But whatever may be the final outcome, it will not be a consequence of the new technologies but of the decisions made by the people who invent, develop, distribute and use them.

Source: A. Argandona, "The New Economy: Ethical Issues," *Journal of Business Ethics* 44, no. 1 (April 2003), pp. 3–22. Copyright © 2003 Kluwer Academic Publishers. Printed in the Netherlands. Reprinted by permission. All rights reserved.

Reading **7-2**

Gene Machine: *Keep Your Hands off Our Genes*

Rory O'Neill, Hazards.org

Not perfect? One day soon it might cost you your job. The U.K. government has refused to rule out for good genetic testing at work. Hazards editor Rory O'Neill warns that as the gene test gizmos and gadgets make genetic screening a wrong-headed but cheap choice for companies, we may find perfectly capable workers are discarded because of unsound and unsafe workplace gene tests.

Employers Want Gene Tests

In recent years, genetic testing has become an affordable option, unregulated and used routinely by the police and increasingly common in our hospitals.

At work—where being at risk of an occupational disease isn't a crime or a personal trait, but the result of an exposure to an occupational risk—many, maybe most, U.K. employers are interested in using genetic screening as a scientific shortcut that could weed out the weak and cut compensation and sick leave.

An Institute of Directors report in 2000 found that 50 percent of employers responding to a questionnaire thought it would be appropriate to conduct genetic testing "to see if employees are at risk of developing an occupation-related disease due to exposure in the workplace" and 34 percent thought it would be appropriate "to see if they will develop heart disease which might affect sickness or early retirement".

One problem. They are wrong—where genetic testing has been used at work, it has been a disaster. In the United States, where employers and insurers have been most enthusiastic for the tests—a 1997 survey found up to 10 percent of firms might already be using gene screening—equality chiefs have ruled it out of order and the government is on the verge of outlawing the practice entirely.

Stop the Gene Testers

U.K. law needs to be changed to prevent employers from refusing people jobs on the basis of genetic test results, campaigners have warned.

Note: Endnotes have been removed.

In September 2003 TUC teamed up with GeneWatch UK and the British Council of Disabled People (BCODP) to call for legal measures to block genetic discrimination at work.

A GeneWatch report, *Genetic Testing in the Workplace*, published on 25 September 2003, the day the Human Genetics Commission (HGC) met to consider the UK government's response to its recommendations on genetic discrimination, reveals that genetic tests cannot accurately predict which workers will suffer future disability or illness.

Despite this, many employers wish to use genetic test results and many research projects are seeking to identify people who are "genetically susceptible" to workplace hazards. It adds that workplace hazards affect everyone—not just people with "bad genes"—so the remaining workers would still be at risk.

"Some employers might see selecting workers on the basis of genetic tests simply as a more economic and efficient means of employee selection," says the report.

"Picking and choosing workers to suit hazardous environments or cut pensions costs is totally unacceptable," said Dr Helen Wallace, deputy director of GeneWatch UK. "The government should act now to close the loophole in the law. Worker exclusion must not replace employers' obligations to clean up workplaces for all."

Andy Rickell, director of the BCODP, said: "We are very concerned about this pernicious means of disability discrimination and totally oppose it."

And TUC general secretary Brendan Barber said: "We want the government to make sure everyone has an equal right to succeed at work, whatever their genetic inheritance. We should be promoting opportunities for all, not penalizing people because of their genes."

In January 2002 TUC's own report, *Ban Unfair Screening*, said "we oppose susceptibility screening as this will remove the emphasis on an employer's legal duties to make the workplace safe for all."

It added "first and foremost employers must provide a safe working environment . . . this type of genetic screening is about eliminating the worker rather than the hazard which is simply unacceptable."

Without exposure to hazards, we can all work safely, regardless of our alleged genetic foibles, said the TUC.

The June 2003 government White Paper on genetics in the NHS, however, made no commitment to legislation to prevent genetic discrimination. Instead, the government has since 1991 opted for a "moratorium," a watching brief that leaves hope for the biotech, business, and insurance industry lobby . . .

Gene Tests Don't Work

In 2001, *Hazards* warned of serious dangers in the use of genetic screening at work.

IT NEVER WORKED: Attempts in the 1960s to introduce workplace genetic screening were soundly rejected because occupational and environmental factors were a far more productive focus of preventive action.

IT STILL DOESN'T WORK: Efforts over 30 years to push gene screens for sensitivity to the potent workplace asthma cause TDI and other substances have failed.

IT MISSES THE POINT: Genetic screening tended to give some—often dubious—protection from one risk. Many targeted substances including benzene, beryllium, lead, and cadmium had many more and more serious risks for the entire workforce that would have been a better focus for "preventive" efforts.

IT IS DISCRIMINATORY: The markers chosen were often linked to race—sickle cell, Tay Sachs, Glucose-6-phosphate dehydrogenase (G-6-PD) deficiency—or gender, which could have led to something uncomfortably close to workplace eugenics.

Everybody Loses

The GeneWatch report warns that efforts to winnow out the weak or the susceptible are "fundamentally flawed."

The report says: "Genetic tests could result in many—perhaps hundreds—of workers being excluded to prevent one case of a workplace-related disease. The majority of those excluded would suffer the ill-effects of unemployment on their health and finances, even though they might not actually belong to a higher risk group." The report argues:

- There are more effective ways of improving employees' health—for example, meeting legal duties and ensuring risks are "eliminated, reduced or, at the every least, effectively controlled."
- The imbalance of power between employer and employee makes it difficult to ensure that the employee is giving voluntary consent to a genetic test—job applicants could face discrimination and existing workers might not be able to walk away from a high risk job, but could have the test used against them if they didn't leave the job and went on to develop an occupational disease.
- A genetic test could have wider implications—for blood relatives who might have a similar genetic trait, or when applying for other jobs or for insurance.
- The use of genetic tests is unethical—excluding people from employment on the basis of their genetic makeup would constitute a violation of their fundamental human rights.
- There is potential for discrimination—tests are complex and open to misinterpretation, can lead to "false positive" results, and lead to a generally unemployable "genetic underclass."

For those with something to gain—the plethora of firms flogging testing kits for example, or the employers looking for a cut-price alternative to safe work—the your-money-or-your-life argument might have its attractions.

It seems unethical at best that 21st century workplaces, where there is the capability to cheaply obtain a person's genetic fingerprint, can argue they can't make their workplaces safe.

Testers Face Legal Pitfalls

Where tests have been used, employers have sometimes found themselves on the wrong side of the law. In the United States, legal, equal opportunity, and governmental bodies have acted to curtail the practice.

In 2002, the U.S. Equal Employment Opportunity Commission told Burlington Northern Santa Fe Railroad that its use of secret genetic testing of some employees violated federal law.

An EEOC official said Burlington Northern broke the Americans with Disabilities Act by treating employees with carpal tunnel syndrome as disabled and then discriminating against them, and should pay compensation.

In December 2000, a U.S. federal court approved a $2.2 billion settlement to thousands of employees of Lawrence Berkeley Laboratories who had been secretly tested for decades for syphilis, pregnancy, and the genetic trait for sickle cell disease.

The only possible justification for genetic testing in the U.K. would seem to be a cut-price alternative to compliance with health and safety laws.

Gene tests have never had the approval of the U.K. safety establishment. A 1995 Health and Safety Commission working group concluded genetic science was not a reliable and accurate predictor of a predisposition to occupational ill health.

Tests Fail the Test

GeneWatch argues that your genetic fingerprint is personal, and not personnel, information. This argument appears to be winning in the United States too where, despite the support of a powerful business and biotech lobby, genetic screening's days could be numbered.

In October 2003 the U.S. Senate voted by overwhelming majority to approve legislation that would prohibit companies from using genetic test results to make employment decisions, deny health coverage, or raise insurance premiums.

The measure, which will now move forward for consideration by the House of Representatives, would bar insurers from requiring genetic tests, from obtaining test results, and from using the results of tests to increase insurance premiums or deny coverage.

Employers would be barred from seeking most genetic information and from using any such information to influence hiring or promotion decisions.

Employers could, however, require testing to monitor potential ill effects from workplace exposure to hazardous substances. And disability and workers' advocates warn that the proposed U.S. law has employer-friendly loopholes—it would not, for example, rule out gene tests in occupational disease compensation cases, so the gene testers could still have a route into the workplace.

Positive Approaches

Europe's top union body called on 29 October 2003 for a ban on genetic testing in the workplace. ETUC said a prohibition should be included explicitly in a European Commission directive on the protection of workers' personal data.

The proposed Europe-wide law is opposed by European employers' groups and strongly supported by unions.

ETUC said gene testing would distract attention from efforts to remedy occupational hazards "in particular in the chemical field" and it could "introduce discrimination among workers according to certain genetic characteristics.

"The United States' experience shows that genetic screening could lead to indirect forms of racial discrimination."

ETUC added: "From the prevention point of view, nothing justifies a genetic screening compared to risks at work." Austria, Belgium, and Finland have already prohibited genetic screening in the workplace, it said.

The European Group on Ethics in Science and New Technology, a European Commission advisory panel, issued a 28 July 2003 opinion on the ethical aspects of genetic testing in the workplace which concluded "employers should not in general perform genetic screening nor ask employees to undergo tests."

It added: "The use of genetic screening in the context of the medical examination . . . is not ethically acceptable. The legitimate duties and right of employers concerning the protection of health and the assessment of ability can be fulfilled through medical examination but without performing genetic screening."

Danger Signs

Elsewhere, developments have given the gene test lobby more reason to be cheerful, despite enforced union contributions and compelling arguments.

In January 2002, Australian unions said employers should "be prohibited from requiring, requesting, collecting or disclosing information derived from genetic testing of current or potential employees."

WE DON'T LIKE IT

The 2003 GeneWatch report concludes that

- Genetic tests cannot accurately predict which workers will suffer future disability or illness. Many false test results are likely.

- Despite their poor predictive value, many employers wish to use genetic test results and many research projects are seeking to identify people who are "genetically susceptible" to workplace hazards.

- If genetic tests were used, large numbers of people would need to be excluded from employment to try to prevent a single case of workplace illness. Workplace hazards affect everyone—not just people with "bad genes"—so the remaining workers would still be at risk.

- People with adverse genetic test results but no symptoms are not protected by the existing Disabilities Discrimination Act.

AND WE WON'T HAVE IT

The TUC has called for strict genetic screening safeguards to protect workers from unscrupulous, discriminating employers. In its 2001 submission to the Human Genetics Commission, TUC

- Opposed susceptibility screening as it removes the emphasis on an employer's legal duties to make the workplace safe for all.

- Called for an amendment to the Disability Discrimination Act 1995 to include asymptomatic (symptom-free) employees, or prospective employees, who have tested positive to a genetic mutation. Preemployment screening may be appropriate in rare occasions but employers carrying out such tests should still be subject to disability discrimination laws.

- Demanded employers be prohibited from using genetic information to affect the terms, conditions, privileges, and benefits of employment.

- Insisted an individual should never be forced to take a genetic test for employment purposes.

Source: "Ban Unfair Screening: TUC Response to the Human Genetics Commission," January 2002 (see *Hazards* 74).

In submission to an official Australian Law Reform Commission (ALRC) enquiry, union federation ACTU said: "Although sometimes justified in terms of protecting workers' health and safety at work, the ACTU submits that this is an inversion of the fundamental principles; employers are responsible for providing employees with a safe and healthy workplace, while work-related illnesses and injuries are caused by hazards in the workplace, not by employees' genetic make-up."

The ACTU submission added, "the focus in workplace health and safety needs to be on hazard removal, not on a mathematical calculation of risk based on genetic testing."

In May 2003, the ALRC report, *Essentially Yours: The Protection of Human GeneticInformation in Australia*, concluded "it is not appropriate to impose a complete prohibition on the use of genetic information by employers to screen for work-related susceptibilities."

The ALRC rationale is straight out of the employer-insurer-biotech play book.

An accompanying news release concluded "the arguments in favour of genetic screening for work-related susceptibilities include its potential to protect susceptible employees from avoidable risk to their health and safety, and to protect employers from potential legal liability and financial costs for illness suffered by susceptible employers."

It says that gene screening should "generally" be conducted only on a voluntary basis, but adds in certain circumstances "it may be reasonable to implement a mandatory screening programme."

Findings like this will give the biotech companies hope there is a market out there for the test kits, and will give employers a glimmer of hope that they will be able to reduce their risks without reducing the risks at work. It is a dangerous development.

For you—it is your body, your genes, your future. When the boss sends in the gene testers, remember it may be their company, but your genetic fingerprint is your business.

Source: Copyright © Hazards.org. Reprinted from the Web site *www.hazards.org* by permission of the author, Rory O'Neill. Further reproduction prohibited.

Reading 7-3

Drug Testing and the Right to Privacy: *Arguing the Ethics of Workplace Drug Testing*

Michael Cranford

In other work, author Cranford argues that drug testing is ethically justified within the terms of the employment agreement, and therefore does not amount to a violation of an employee's right to privacy. In the following article, which is an excerpt from a longer piece, "The Ethics of Privacy," he expands the contention to include an obligation to test in certain employment contexts.

Drug Testing and the Obligation to Prevent Harm

The argument over the ethical justification for drug testing takes a different turn when we consider drug testing, not as an employer's right under the terms of an employment contract, but as a means by which an employer may prevent harms committed by employees who abuse drugs. By "harms" I mean actual or probable dangers to the safety and health of employees (other than the one impaired by drugs) and of persons outside the workplace. At issue are two related arguments, either of which may provide adequate justification for workplace drug testing. The first argument assumes that an employer has a general obligation to prevent harm. This obligation requires an employer to utilize reasonable means to prevent or mitigate potential harms committed in connection with workplace activities. To the extent that drug testing is such a reasonable means, the employer is obligated to test for employee drug abuse.

A primary assumption in this argument is that employees who are drug users pose a threat to the safety and well-being of themselves and others. That alcohol and drug abuse are connected with significant work-related harms is reasonably established, however. For example, the National Transportation Safety Board found that marijuana used by a Conrail engineer was a major contributing factor to the Conrail-Amtrak collision in January 1987, which killed 16 people and injured 170. An earlier study by the Federal Railroad Administration (FRA) determined that between 1969 and 1979 48 major train accidents, 37 deaths, and 80 injuries could be directly connected with alcohol and drug abuse. A similar study concluded that between 1975 and 1983 at least 45 significant train accidents, resulting in 34 fatalities, 66 injuries and over $28 million in property damage, could be directly linked to the errors of alcohol- and drug-impaired employees. Without the benefit of regular post-accident testing, these figures probably amount to less than half of the total drug- or alcohol-related accidents during that period.

Note: Notes and references removed for publication here, but are available from the author.

The second argument is that employers have not only an obligation to prevent harm, but a responsibility for harms committed by their employees. This responsibility justifies an employer in obtaining information pertaining to employee drug abuse if by acquiring such information the employer can mitigate potential harms. It is this second phase of the argument that has drawn the greatest attention and criticism, though my analysis is ultimately grounded on the corporation's obligation to prevent harm.

Unlike the argument based on performance of contract, drug testing as a means to prevent harm does not entail a devaluation of human beings by considering them as means to purely economic ends. Rather, the purpose of drug testing affirms the essential value and dignity of human beings by subjugating technique and economic efficacy to human safety and well-being. The fact that preventing harms may also be in a company's best economic interests is a conclusion resulting from cost-benefit analysis that has no immediate bearing on a mandatory drug testing program.[1] Drug testing and employee assistance programs themselves place significant financial burdens on corporations that cannot always be rationalized as offsetting accident settlements that only *might* have been paid out.

Responsibility to Drug Test and Questions of Justification

Jennifer Moore addresses the second argument listed, that "because corporations are responsible for harms committed by employees while under the influence of drugs, they are entitled to test for drug use." She invokes Kant's "ought implies can" principle, which states that if a person is obligated to do X then they must have the capacity to do X (i.e., they must be free to do or not do X). In assigning corporations a responsibility for harms caused by employees who abuse drugs, it follows that they must have the capacity to prevent these harms. Specifically, they must have the freedom to test for drug use. Moore then explores the meaning of the statement that corporations are "responsible" for harms committed by employees to determine if drug testing is, in fact, warranted.

Moore's first point is that, whatever is meant by "responsible," it cannot mean *legally* responsible. Legally, the doctrine of *respondeat superior* makes a corporation vicariously liable for an employee's action, regardless of whether or not the corporation was at fault. Legal liability, in this case, does not imply a capacity to have prevented harm. Moore concludes that holding corporations legally liable for harms committed by employees who abuse drugs while at the same time forbidding drug testing is not inconsistent.

Moore seems to think that just because legal liability applies when a corporation cannot prevent harm, a corporation should not attempt to prevent harm to the greatest degree possible, either on the basis of an obligation to beneficence or, in the very least, to minimize its liability. Certainly a corporation can be held liable when it is not at fault, but nothing follows from this with regard to its obligation to public safety when it *is* at fault. To the degree that a corporation *can* be at fault, it should be allowed the ability to prevent harms. Legal liability does imply a justification for drug testing.

Moore then addresses corporate responsibility as a *moral* obligation to prevent harm caused by employees who abuse drugs. The argument goes as follows:

[1]Though it might have a bearing on a drug testing program that was only enacted for certain projects that were assessed as cost-prohibitive on the basis of potential harms. Consequently, drug testing will only be justified under this argument if it is effected uniformly and mandatorily without regard for such assessments.

1. If corporations have obligations, they must be capable of carrying them out, on the principle of "ought implies can."
2. Corporations have an obligation to prevent harm from occurring in the course of conducting their business.
3. Drug use by employees is likely to lead to harm.
4. Corporations must be able to take steps to eliminate (or at least reduce) drug use by employees.
5. Drug testing is an effective way to eliminate/reduce employee drug use.
6. Therefore corporations must be permitted to test for drugs.

Moore claims that this conclusion (6) does not follow, since it is not clear that the obligation to prevent harm justifies drug testing:

> Of course this does not necessarily mean that drug testing is *unjustified*. But it does mean that before we can determine whether it is justified, we must ask what is permissible for one person or group of persons to do to another to prevent harm for which they are responsible.

Moore offers a number of examples to show that the obligation to prevent harm cannot justify just any action. In none of her examples, however, does she actually counterpose the act of preventing harm with a right to privacy. For example, her first case is of a hostess who is responsible for a drunken guest leaving her party. Moore argues that she is perhaps allowed to take the guest's car keys away from her, but is not entitled to knock her out and lock her in the bathroom. Moore is relying on the difficulty in discerning between these actions to argue that drug testing is not obviously justified simply because it prevents harm.

While testing impairment by a battery of eye-hand coordination and reflex exercises might detect the most seriously impaired employees at the precise moment of testing, it would not detect employees who remained sober only during the time frame immediately preceding such tests. Such testing is also indeterminate, as anyone can vouch who has successfully passed a field sobriety test while legally intoxicated. Even if some degree of impairment were indicated, the employer is left with no means by which she may evaluate the significance of the employee's failure to pass the test. The difference between an employee who is impaired due to lack of sleep and an employee who is under the influence of an illegal substance is morally significant.[2]

Finally, testing impairment fails to detect habitual users of drugs who, while not noticeably impaired at the precise moment of testing, nonetheless may constitute a significant and ongoing risk. Consequently, testing for impairment is not "just more effective in all ways" than drug testing. Drug testing is not directed at identifying impairment, which (as I have pointed out) is rather difficult to quantify or detect by any means, but at (1) identifying employees who abuse drugs, and (2) deterring habitual users from becoming impaired

---

[2]My point here is best explained by way of an example. Let us say that a young employee dances all night for several nights in a row, and therefore shows up for work impaired due to lack of sleep. The difference between this individual and someone who is impaired because of substance abuse is at least that the latter admits of an addictive and increasingly significant (and ultimately self-destructive) condition, whereas the former is at worst compulsive, and is therefore unlikely to continue for more than a few nights (even the best of us dancers eventually find ourselves nodding off). There is also the legality of purchasing and using illicit substances, not to mention driving under the influence of illicit substances. Breaking those laws is ethically significant, whereas dancing all night is just dumb—but completely legal.

at the workplace. Toward these ends, drug testing is the most effective and direct means currently available.

In response to Moore, I agree that drug testing is neither necessary nor sufficient for ridding the workplace of drug abuse. Consequently, she is correct in stating that the conclusion to the present argument (6) does not follow. But this is only if we allow her to define what it means for drug testing to be an "effective" way to eliminate or reduce employee drug abuse (5). If by "effective" we understand that drug testing prevents or eliminates harms that would not, in its absence, be prevented or eliminated by some other measure, then it follows that corporations must be permitted to test for drugs. Corporations must be permitted to undertake any reasonable measures for preventing workplace harms when no equally effectual measures are available. I will refer to all such measures as *measures of last resort*. In this understanding of "effective," the conclusion (6) does follow.

But in this case, however, our conclusion (6) is not strong enough. Referring back to our original argument, I asserted that an employer has a general obligation to prevent harm, and that this obligation requires an employer to utilize reasonable means to prevent or mitigate potential harms committed in connection with workplace activities. But if drug testing is necessary in that process as a measure of last resort, then it not only follows that corporations must be permitted to test for drugs, but that corporations are obligated to do so. It is for this reason that a corporation is responsible to take on the "Protector of Harms" role in its relationship with an employee even when such a role is not inherent in the employment contract.

The Kew Gardens Principle and the Obligation to Prevent Harm

There are two elements in my analysis to this point which I have offered without any accompanying substantiation. The first is the claim that an employer has a general obligation to prevent harm. The second is the claim that drug testing is a measure of last resort, as I have defined it. It is only if these assertions are reasonable that it would follow that corporations are obligated to test for drugs.

In defense of both these points I would like to introduce four criteria which together indicate a moral obligation to prevent harm. This combination of features governing difficult cases of assessing moral responsibility has elsewhere been termed the "Kew Gardens Principle."

1. *Need.* A corporation's responsibility to test for drugs, or take any other appropriate measures to reduce the occurrence of harms, is a function of the extent of the harms which may result. In cases where the other three factors are constant, increased need indicates increased responsibility. In reference to his engineering company, Lewis Maltby states that "a single Drexelbrook employee working under the influence of drugs could cause a disaster as tragic as occurred in Bhopal." If true, this would suggest a significant responsibility to prevent such harms.

2. *Proximity.* Proximity is less a function of distance and more a function of awareness. We hold a person blameworthy if she knows of a crisis or a potential crisis and does not do what she can to prevent it. "When we become aware of a wrongdoing or a social injury, we take on obligations that we did not have while ignorant." Greater responsibility exists in situations where one would expect a heightened awareness of need as a consequence of civic duty, duties to one's family, and so on. In other words, we would hold a family member more blameworthy than a stranger for not being aware of a person's critical plight.

Proximity becomes important in the case of workplace drug abuse because the network of social relationships involved in a daily, cooperative setting, combined with the social and legal perception that an employer is responsible for the activities of her employees, entail a high degree of expectation that the employer not only will learn of a potential harm caused by drug abuse, but *should* learn of it. A corporation delegates its employees to act on its behalf and, in fact, acts only through its employees. This integral and intimate relationship whereby the employees act on behalf of the corporation obligates the corporation to become aware of potential dangers which could result from drug abuse.

While a variety of measures can and have been used that locate and address the problem of workplace drug abuse (such as direct observation of employees, hidden cameras, mandatory educational programs in dealing with drug abuse, and basic dexterity/reflexivity/judgment testing), none of these programs has the same certainty of screening out drug abusers as does drug testing. Direct observation and dexterity tests can be beaten (and are, routinely). While education is an effective counterpreventative, it does not screen out users who are resistant to receiving help—the individuals most likely to place others at risk. On the other hand, it can be argued that drug testing also is falsifiable. If given advance notice of testing, drug users can abstain long enough to pass the test. Or, they can procure a sample of "clean" urine from another individual and substitute it for their own.

At most, these examples argue against regularly scheduled testings—not against random, unannounced testings. These examples also overlook the fact that the time necessary for drug metabolites to become absent from the urine varies from individual to individual and from use to use. Serious and habitual users (who are the most likely to commit harms) would probably be unable to abstain from use long enough even to pass an announced test. And while drug testing is not unfalsifiable, it is more difficult to falsify than other options for testing. Consequently, while not a perfect instrument for the detection of drug abuse, drug testing has an effectiveness and specificity that remain unparalleled.

Since drug testing is the most effective technology currently available to make the employer aware of potential dangers by locating habitual users, and without which many such users will likely not be identified, use of drug testing is obligatory as a measure of last resort. Since no one other than the employer is more aware of the potential for an employee committing work-related harms, a significant moral responsibility to prevent such harms follows.

This responsibility could be mitigated if the employer has a reasonable certainty that an employee (or all employees) does not abuse drugs. Thus, drug testing is not only essential to the employer's obligation to come to know of potential harms, but it reduces a corporation's moral responsibility for harms committed by ruling out drug abuse as a contributing factor.

3. *Capability.* Even if there is a need to which someone has proximity, that person cannot be held morally responsible unless she has the capacity to meet the need. As I have discussed at length, not just any action offered to prevent a harm is necessarily reasonable. What is reasonable is that action which is least intrusive or harmful, most efficient and specific, and with the highest probability of achieving its goals (thus, my principles for what constitutes a reasonable means of coming to know private information). Drug testing, in combination with a counseling and rehabilitation program that relieves employees of hazardous duty, meets these criteria. In most cases, as will be noted below, no other agent has the capability of performing this combination of actions.

4. *Last Resort.* In situations where the other three features are present, one becomes more responsible the less likely it is that someone else will prevent the harm in question. While it is often difficult to assess whether one alone has knowledge of a potential harm, to

the degree that one can be certain that one does, and that no one else has the proximity or capacity for intervening, significant responsibility is entailed.

In the case of harms caused by drug abuse, it is rarely the case that an agency outside the workplace will possess the means to either assess the potential for harm (thus need and proximity) or be able to prevent the harm from being realized (by possessing the capacity to locate and remove employees who abuse drugs from hazardous duty). When there is no agency beyond the employer which can effectively prevent harms, the employer becomes the agent of last resort. When there is no method of identifying drug abusers more effective than drug testing, it becomes a method of last resort in the process of preventing drug-related harms in the workplace. Consequently, the criterion of last resort, in connection with the other three features of the Kew Gardens Principle, assign a corporation a high degree of moral responsibility to prevent drug-related harms, and obligate it to make use of reasonable methods for identifying such harms, particularly when more effective methods are unavailable.

The actual degree of responsibility turns on the level of need (criterion #1), however. To the degree that harms are improbable or of little consequence to human life and safety, a corporation's obligation to prevent such harms is diminished. Drug testing is not justified under this argument if the condition it is testing for has little potential to result in any real danger. The difficulty arises in attempting a risk analysis when the effects of impairment remain hypothetical. For example, one might argue that the condition of increased need exists in the case of railroad engineers who control the velocity and breaking of high-speed locomotives. Similarly, a condition of increased need exists in the case of factory workers who operate heavy machinery in a crowded work setting. It is less clear, though, that a condition of increased need arises among clerks at the same railroad, who could potentially create disaster through an error in paper work that goes unnoticed by field operatives. Nor is it clear that a condition of increased need arises in the case of the janitorial staff at a factory, who might perhaps leave a bit too much water on the floor if they were impaired while mopping a hallway. Of these latter examples, the first is improbable, and the last is insignificant (or at least, not significant enough to justify drug testing the entire janitorial staff). While many cases can be cited that are problems in risk assessment, it is critical to note that nothing follows with regard to the obligation to prevent harms in cases that are not problematic. In such cases (like the two listed first), corporations can and should use reasonable means to prevent drug related harms.

* * * *

Conclusions and Policy Recommendations

It is the position adopted in this paper that (1) a corporation is entitled to drug test its employees to determine employee capacity to perform according to the terms of the employment contract, and (2) a corporation is morally obligated to test employees for drug and alcohol abuse when a condition of impairment would place the safety and health of other human beings at risk. The first of these two justifications, I have argued, quantifies human beings under a measure of efficiency, treating them as means to a purely economic end (i.e., the corporation's profitability). Drug testing does not, in the large majority of cases, benefit the employee's best interests, and is therefore directed at effecting extrinsic goods only (as opposed to respecting the employee's intrinsic value and dignity). This criticism fails in the latter justification, however, since the ultimate end of drug testing *is* the preservation of human life as an intrinsic good. In this case, a corporation is not only entitled to use toxicological testing, but is obligated to do so, to the degree that a critical need to prevent drug-related harms is actually present.

Source: Copyright © Michael Cranford. Excerpted by permission of the author from the forthcoming publication *The Ethics of Privacy*. All rights reserved.

Reading **7-4**

Alternative Explanations for Drug Testing— Blaming the Individual

Michelle R. Greenwood, Peter Holland, and Karen Choong

* * * *

Thus far this chapter has presented the traditional arguments for and against drug testing in the workplace. In doing so, it has been argued that workplace drug testing serves neither the interests of the employees nor the employers, and that fitness for duty testing offers employers a viable alternative. Given that such an alternative is available, why do employers continue to employ workplace drug testing? One possible explanation advanced here is that employers pursue drug testing in order to place the onus and responsibility for any drug abuse in the workplace solely on the individual employees. Blaming the employee has the added feature of being a means of diverting attention away from their own role in creating working conditions that may induce employees to use drugs to cope:

> Holding the view that drug use is a problem for the individual worker is functional from the employer's point of view because it avoids any exploration of how the workplace, and management's support of such an environment, may contribute to the problem.

Focusing on fitness for duty would have the opposite effect. By testing for actual work performance, fitness for duty assessment would not exclude impairment caused by work related factors. As such, work conditions that are under the control of the company such as overtime, stressful work conditions, and poor training could be identified through such testing.

Ironically, these very work conditions may be complicit in employee drug use. It has been argued that drug use may be symptomatic of issues of control, alienation, and stress due to underlying structural problems such as hazardous work, a poor work environment, unrealistic deadlines, lack of job satisfaction, lack of participation and control, perceptions of powerlessness, inadequate training and supervision, shift work and the culture of the industry. Charlton acknowledges that problems in the workplace that lead to stress and fatigue should be eliminated where possible, as these contribute directly to drug use. He suggests such problems include excessive overtime, boring repetitive tasks and poorly planned shift work. Evidence also suggests that fatigue, rather than impairment from drug abuse, leads to the majority of workplace accidents. Maltby thus dismissed drug testing as fundamentally flawed as it tests for the wrong thing. He claims that to be effective in detecting employees whose impairment presents potential harm, the initiative would test for the underlying conditions that actually creates the danger rather than merely identification of the symptoms.

Drug testing is becoming increasingly prevalent in a time of decreasing union control and the increasing use of casual and contract employees (and the simultaneous reduction of management responsibility to these employees). Understandably, employees and unions have questioned why drug testing has assumed such priority in an industrial climate where increasing demands have been placed upon workers. These endless pressures of working longer and harder are rarely linked to illicit drug use that may be sustaining these work patterns. Thus by focusing on drug use as the individual's problem, it absolves management from any responsibility and ignores their contributing role in creating stressful and unsustainable working conditions.

Symbolic and Moral Control

Another explanation for the practice of drug testing is that the employer undertakes this activity as a way of enforcing a form of indirect or symbolic control over employees. Drug taking tends to be seen in our society as an irrational and anarchistic activity pursued by deviants. In modern organizations, drug use and the presence of drug using employees threatens to undermine organizational rationality by introducing elements of disorder and deviance. More than endangering productivity and performance, drug use threatens the fundamental "rational" foundations of organizations by undermining the work ethic and promoting an immoral disregard for the collective well-being of the organization. Such irrationality cannot be controlled through the use of traditional managerial techniques but requires control through the management of more abstract and emotional elements of the organization. Cavanaugh and Prasad posit that drug testing offers three interrelated "symbolic" functions for employers: as means for restoring or creating the image of managerial control; as providing management a scientific and rational response to an irrational and chaotic situation; and, as providing management moral legitimation in the eyes of its constituents and stakeholders.

Creating the Image of Control

In the perceived volatile and chaotic environment created by drug use, managers symbolically demonstrate through workplace drug testing that they are nevertheless in control and taking action. Otherwise, in failing to act, management may be perceived as being passive and futile, and the situation as being out of its control, leading to authority being undermined. Hence despite the controversy surrounding drug testing, the existence of such testing programs focuses attention on the fact that at least something is being done to combat the drug problem in the workplace.

Pfeffer has suggested that persistent management behavior that is ineffective in pursuing stated organizational goals is best understood as "symbolic" behavior. Such behavior, rather than being aimed at achieving organization goals, is aimed at reinforcing power and control relationships in the organization. Because of our focus on the rational and the analytic, we tend to downplay the potency of symbolic action. Language, ceremonies, and settings are important in the exercise of influence because we are rarely conscious of their effects on us. Indeed, "the effectiveness of this symbolic action is enhanced by the confusion of all involved between substantive and symbolic results."

Trade unions often see the introduction of activities such as drug testing as management exercising control under the guise of its "right" to manage. Such actions are also seen as strategies to marginalize the countervailing power of unions, limiting their effectiveness while significantly increasing managerial control, particularly where there has been no consultation. This view is particularly salient as many policy issues associated with employer directed substance testing can result in employee-union conflict.

The continued use of workplace drug testing suggests that privacy rights do not seem to be included in the negotiated terms of employment. This omission may be due to the acceptance of the invasion of information privacy rights as being less intuitively "wrong" than invasions of other rights. However, the fundamental issue underlying such disregard of individual privacy rights is the reluctance for employers to sacrifice their management prerogative to run their workplace in order to protect these rights. It is argued that when employers are prevented from performing monitoring such as drug testing, they are effectively being prevented from controlling their own workplace. Thus retaining management control may be considered an underlying motivation for the overriding of employee privacy rights. The changing nature of the employment relationship, and consequent increasing support of management prerogative, may provide some indication as to why drug testing is continuing.

Scientific Response

Drug testing further can demonstrate that a neutral, scientific response is being employed. Sonnenstuhl observes that historically management has often introduced a number of policies designed to set work standards, motivate workers, and control deviants under the guise of science. Modern-day drug testing is historically and ideologically consistent with previous managerial responses to lack of order and rule adherence. It is intended to strengthen management's symbolic control over employees by responding rationally and scientifically.

American sociologist Robert Merton argued in 1947 that science and technology was not benign and neutral as it is often represented. He argued that the use of technology in corporations has significant social implications and, as such, should be regarded as a political tool. The scientific management of Taylorism has been identified as an ideological effort to establish managerial legitimacy and control over the workforce. The ideology of technocracy with "its attendant insistence on neutrality and inevitability of modern, scientific, rational technologies and social structures" is said to have significantly influenced employees' attitudes.

Scientific and rational language is used in organizational discourse in order to form arguments in a manner as to make it hard to rebut or undermine them by presenting them as "objective" or "fact" and, by inference, fair and rational. Managers may be able to manipulate employees through the use of science and technology by appealing to the technological determinist argument "We have to do this because the technology demands it." Consequently, technological determinism is often used to justify unpopular management decisions.

Moral Legitimation

The prevalence of drug testing has further been strengthened out of concern for maintaining the organization's reputation, as no organization wants to be perceived as being "soft on drugs." The moral legitimacy of an organization is understood as the acceptability of the organization, the product it supplies and the manner in which the product is created, as to whether its activities promote social welfare. Moral legitimacy "reflects the positive normative evaluation of an organization and its activities" based on "judgments about whether the activity is "the right thing to do." Hence, the moral legitimacy of an organization is based to a large extent on the projected image or reputation of that organization. Legitimacy is not considered a characteristic of the organization per se but rather a measure of societal perceptions of the adequacy of corporate behavior compared to societal expectation of corporate activity.

Organizations seek to influence stakeholders' behavior by demonstrating that they are morally legitimate. Organizational activities such as drug testing are undertaken to legitimate the organization in the eyes of its constituents and stakeholders. Organizational responsiveness to social problems such as drug use can be understood as strategically appealing to stakeholders to further the interests of the company. In this pursuit of maximizing shareholder value, community perceptions of zero tolerance against drugs are incorporated into the organization's own stance, translated into drug testing practices. The organization is seen to be reflecting and supporting the community's values.

There is corporate peer pressure to be perceived as responsive to drug issues. This sense of corporate peer pressure echoes Aldrich who argued that among "the major factors that organizations must take into account are other organizations." Organizations compete not just for resources and customers, but also on the basis of political power and institutional legitimacy and social acceptance.

Furthermore, when one organization publicly takes this stance many others are likely to follow. This process of homogenization is consistent with DiMaggio and Powell's concept of institutional isomorphism. Hawley describes isomorphism as a constraining process which forces one unit in a population to resemble other units that face the same set of environmental conditions. DiMaggio and Powell's description of mimetic isomorphic processes is consistent with the conditions surrounding drug testing. They claim uncertainty is a powerful force that encourages imitation. When the environment creates symbolic uncertainty, organizations tend to model themselves on other organizations. Isomorphism may explain why so many organizations continue to adopt drug testing procedures.

* * * *

Conclusion

What then is the attraction for employers to drug test? Two related alternatives have been posited. One explanation is that by focusing blame on individual employees for socially unacceptable drug use, the spotlight is drawn away from the contributing role of the employer, which may in fact cause and sustain such deviant behavior. These might include the imposition of intense rosters and long hours, alienation, high pressure, the stress of job insecurity, poor working conditions, and the lack of adequate training and supervision. Indeed, these factors may have been complicit in creating a problem for the employee in the first place. The second explanation is that in an environment where traditional forms of control may not be effective, managers may seek more abstract and symbolic forms of control. Drug testing may provide symbolic control through a number of mechanisms. A common theme in these alternative explanations is that drug testing allows management to "seize the moral high ground."

Source: Excerpted from "Re-evaluting Drug Testing: Questions of Moral and Symbolic Control," in John Deckop, Bob Giacalone, and Carole L. Jurkiewicz (eds.), *Human Resource Management Ethics* (Greenwich, CT: Information Age Publishers). Copyright © Information Age Publishers. Reprinted with permission from Information Age Publishers.

Chapter 8

Ethics and Marketing

Reality is how we felt and saw events, not events as they appeared objectively, because we are not objective.

Anaïs Nin

A magazine is simply a device to induce people to read advertising.

James Collins

I am the world's worst salesman; therefore, I must make it easy for people to buy.

F. W. Woolworth (1852–1919)

Opening Decision Point
Marketing to the Base of the Pyramid

In a recent book, business scholar C.K. Prahalad details the business opportunities that exist for firms that are creative and resourceful enough to develop markets among the world's poorest people.[1]

Done correctly, marketing to the 4 billion people at the base of the global economic pyramid would employ market forces in addressing some of the greatest ethical and environmental problems of the 21st century.

Obviously, helping to meet the needs of the world's poorest people would be a significant ethical contribution. The strategy involves another ethical consideration as well: A market of this size requires environmentally sustainable products and technologies. If everyone in the world used resources and created wastes at the rate Americans do, the global environment would suffer immeasurably. Businesses that understand this fact face a huge marketing opportunity.

Accomplishing such goals will require a significant revision to the standard marketing paradigm. Business must, in Prahalad's phrase, "create the capacity to consume" among the world's poor. Creating this capacity to consume among the world's poor would create a significant win–win opportunity from both a financial and an ethical perspective.

Prahalad points out that the world's poor do have significant purchasing power, albeit in the aggregate rather than on a per capita basis. Creating the capacity to consume among the world's poor will require a transformation in the conceptual framework of global marketing and some creative steps from business. Prahalad mentions three principles as key to marketing to the poor: affordability, access, and availability.

Do you think that business firms and industries have an ethical responsibility to address global poverty by creating the capacity to consume among the world's poor? Do you think that this can be done? What responsibilities, ethical and economic, do firms face when marketing in other countries and among different cultures? Imagine that you are in the marketing department of a firm that manufacturers a consumer product such as laundry detergent or shampoo. Describe how it might be marketed differently in India.

- What are the key facts relevant to your judgment?
- What ethical issues are involved in a firm's decision to market its products among the world's poor by creating the capacity to consume?
- Who are the stakeholders?
- What alternatives does a firm have with regard to the way in which it markets its products?
- How do the alternatives compare; how do the alternatives you have identified affect the stakeholders?

 ## Chapter Objectives

After reading this chapter, you will be able to:

1. Understand the application of the ethical decision-making framework to ethical issues in marketing.

2. Describe the three key concerns of ethical analysis of marketing issues.

3. Describe three interpretations of responsibility and apply them to the topic of product safety.

4. Explain contractual standards for establishing business's responsibilities for safe products.

5. Articulate the tort standards for establishing business's responsibilities for safe products.

6. Analyze the ethical arguments for and against strict product liability.

7. Discuss how to evaluate both ethical and unethical means by which to influence people through advertising.

8. Explain the ethical justification for advertising.

9. Trace debates about advertising's influence on consumer autonomy.

10. Distinguish ethical from unethical target marketing, using marketing to vulnerable populations as an example.

11. Discuss business's responsibilities for the activities of its supply chain.

Introduction

Some believe that the very purpose of business is found within the marketing function. The description of business's purpose offered by marketing scholar Theodore Levitt is a case in point. Levitt suggests that:

> The purpose of a business is to create and keep a customer. To do that you have to produce and deliver goods and services that people want and value at prices and under conditions that are reasonably attractive relative to those offered by others. . . . It was not so long ago that a lot of companies assumed something quite different about the purpose of business. They said quite simply that the purpose is to make money. But that is as vacuous as to say that the purpose of life is to eat. Eating is a prerequisite, not a purpose of life . . . Profits can be made in lots of devious and transient ways. For people of affairs, a statement of purpose should provide guidance to the management of their affairs. To say that they should attract and hold customers forces facing the necessity of figuring out what people really want and value, and then catering to those wants and values. It provides specific guidance, and has moral merit.[2]

Similarly, the American Marketing Association defines **marketing** in a way that suggests marketing is at the heart of business activity: "an organizational function and a set of processes for creating, communicating, and delivering value to customers and for managing customer relationships in ways that benefit the organization and its stakeholders."[3]

The concept of an exchange between a seller and a buyer is central to the "market" and is the core idea behind marketing. Marketing involves all aspects of creating a product or service and bringing it to market where an exchange can take place. Marketing ethics therefore examines the responsibilities associated with bringing a product to the market, promoting it to buyers, and exchanging it with them. But this simple model of a seller bringing a product to the marketplace, and the ethics implicit within it, gets complicated fairly quickly.

Even before a product is created, a producer might first consider who, if anyone, is interested in purchasing it. The product might then be redesigned or changed in light of what is learned about potential buyers. Once the product is ready for market, the producer must decide on a price that will be mutually acceptable. At first glance, the minimal asking price should be the production cost plus some reasonable profit. But the producer might also consider who the buyers are and what they can afford, how price might influence future purchases, how the price might affect distributors and retailers, and what competitors are charging before settling on a price. The producer might also consider advertising the product to attract new potential purchasers and offer incentives to promote the product among buyers.

The producer might also consider the lost production that results from the trip to the market and therefore consider hiring someone else, a salesperson, or delegating someone, a "retailer," to handle the actual exchange itself. Producers might be more concerned with cash flow than profit and therefore be willing to ask a price that is below production costs. They might consider where and under what conditions the product is sold, and they might decide that the best chance for a sale will occur only among certain people. The producer might also consider issues of volume and price the product in such a way to insure profit only after certain sales targets are met. The producer might also consider how such factors as price, convenience, reliability, and service might contribute to sustaining an ongoing relationship with the customer. Finally, throughout this entire process the producer might conduct market research to gather information and use that information in production, pricing, promotion, and placement decisions.

All of the factors considered and each decision made throughout this process are elements of marketing. What, how, why, and under what conditions is something *produced*? What *price* is acceptable, reasonable, fair? How can the product be *promoted* to support, enhance, and maintain sales? Where, when, and under what conditions should the product be *placed* in the marketplace? These four general categories—*product, price, promotion, placement*—are sometimes referred to as the "Four Ps" of marketing.

Each of the Four Ps also raises important ethical questions. What responsibilities do producers have for the quality and safety of their products? Who is responsible for harms caused by a product? Are there some products that should not be produced, or does consumer demand decide all production questions? Is the consumer's willingness to pay the only ethical constraint on fair pricing? Should the ability to pay be a factor in setting price? Do all customers deserve the same price, or can producers discriminate in favor of, or against, some consumers? What effects will price have on competitors? On retailers? Are deceptive or misleading ads ethical? What ethical constraints should be placed on sales promotions? Is the information gathered in market research the property of the business that conducts the research? What privacy protections should be offered for marketing data? Is it ethical to target vulnerable populations such as children or the elderly? What responsibilities does a producer have when marketing in foreign countries? What responsibilities do producers have to retailers? To competitors? To suppliers?

Ethical Issues in Marketing: A Framework

OBJECTIVE

We can take the simple model of a single exchange between two individuals as a useful way to introduce an ethical framework for marketing ethics (see Table 8.1). As in previous chapters, this framework will provide insights to assist the decision maker in arriving at an ethical decision but will not point to the "correct" decision since this is not a normative framework—in other words, it does not determine the right answer but instead identifies rights, responsibilities, duties and obligations, causes and consequences. Once these parameters are clarified, the decision maker uses the framework to effectively analyze the scenario and arrive at the decision that best reflects her or his person and professional value structure.

This simple situation in which two parties come together and freely agree to an exchange is *prima facie* ethically legitimate. The deontological ethical tradition described in Chapter 3 would see it as upholding respect for individuals by treating them as autonomous agents capable of pursuing their own ends. This tradition presumes that each individual will abide by fundamental principles. The utilitarian ethical tradition would take the two parties' agreement as evidence that both are better off than they were prior to the exchange and thus conclude that overall happiness has been increased.

This assessment is only *prima facie* because, like all agreements, certain conditions must be met before we can conclude that autonomy has in fact been respected

TABLE 8.1

Ethical Issues in Marketing: A Framework

Market Exchange is *prima facie* ethically legitimate because of
- Kantian respect for autonomy
- Utilitarian mutual benefit

This ethical judgment is conditional because
- Informed consent is needed
- Benefits might not occur
- Other values might conflict

Is consent "voluntary"?
- *Windows* operating system?
- Anxiety and stress in some purchasing situations
- Price-fixing, monopolies, price gouging, etc.
- Targeted and vulnerable consumers

Is it "informed"?
- Lack of information
- Deception
- Complicated information

Are people truly benefited?
- Impulse buying, "affluenza," consumerism
- Injuries, unsafe products
- "Contrived" wants

Competing Values
- Justice—e.g., "redlining" mortgages
- Market failures (externalities)

Quality → Safety.

Warranty
Express → written oral

and mutual benefit has been achieved. Thus, for example, we would need to establish that the agreement resulted from an informed and voluntary consent, and that there was no fraud, deception, or coercion involved. When these conditions are violated, autonomy is not respected, and mutual benefit is not attained. Furthermore, even when such conditions are met, other values may override the freedom of individuals to contract for mutually beneficial purposes. Thus, for example, the freedom of drug dealers to pursue mutually agreeable ends is overridden by society's concern to maintain law and order.

OBJECTIVE

In general, therefore, it will be helpful to keep three concerns in mind as we approach any ethical issue in marketing: The Kantian ethical tradition would ask to what degree the participants are respected as free and autonomous agents rather than treated simply as means to the end of making a sale. The utilitarian tradition would want to know the degree to which the transaction provided actual as opposed to merely apparent benefits. Every ethical tradition would wonder what other values might be at stake in the transaction. Let us consider these three issues in more detail.

It is not always easy to determine if someone is being treated with respect in marketing situations. As a first approximation we might suggest two conditions. First, the person must freely consent to the transaction. But how free is "free"? Surely transactions completed under the threat of force are not voluntary and therefore are unethical. But there are many degrees of voluntariness. For example, the more consumers need a product, the less free they are to choose and therefore the more protection they deserve within the marketplace. Consider the use of the *Windows* operating system by the overwhelming majority of computer users. How voluntary is the decision to use *Windows*? Do most people even make a decision to use *Windows*? Or, consider the anxiety and stress that many consumers experience during a car purchase. When an automobile dealer exploits that anxiety to sell extended warranty insurance, it is not at all clear that the consumer has made a fully voluntary decision. More dramatic cases of price gouging, price-fixing, and monopolistic pricing clearly raise the issue of freedom in marketing. Practices aimed at vulnerable populations such as children and the elderly also raise questions of voluntariness. Thus, an adequate analysis of marketing ethics challenges us to be sensitive to the many ways in which consumer choice can be less than fully voluntary. (To explore what it means to engage in "voluntary" purchasing decisions, review the following Reality Check.)

A second condition for respect requires that the consent be not only voluntary, but also informed. Informed consent has received a great deal of attention in the medical ethics literature because patients are at a distinct informational disadvantage when dealing with health care professionals. Similar disadvantages can occur in marketing situations. Outright deception and fraud clearly violate this condition and are unethical. A consumer's consent to purchase a product is not informed if that consumer is being misled or deceived about the product. But there can also be many more nuanced cases of deception and misleading marketing practices.

The complexity of many consumer products and services can mean that consumers may not understand fully what they are purchasing. Consider, as an example, all that would be involved for a consumer to determine which fuel tank design was

Article
↳ Baby Slings
↳ 3 baby killed ↳ Recall.

Reality Check *Impulse Buying*

Though the cartoon to the right pokes fun at the ability of marketing professionals to "make" us buy certain items, not everyone exercises similar levels of effective judgment necessary to protect themselves from poor decisions about credit and debt, good and bad spending choices. Young spenders in particular may not yet be sufficiently experienced—with shopping, spending or responding to sophisticated marketing campaigns—to adequately protect themselves against strategies designed to encourage impulse buying.

Sales pitches that hype the latest and trendiest items, those that must be purchased today and worn tonight, are difficult to resist for some purchasers, who buy in haste and perhaps regret it later. Marketing campaigns are also chastised for creating needs where the purchaser may originally have only sensed a desire. Purchases on impulse are often not reversible, but because they are often so hastily made that the purchaser fails to notice that the product is imperfect or does not match a personal style, they are perhaps most in need of later returns.

In the same way that a hungry person is more likely to buy groceries on impulse than one who has just had her or his meal, we are better off engaging in our purchasing efforts when we are capable of evaluating our options with a clear head (and a full stomach!).

Yeah, the features are nice... how do you think it'll look in the garage draped with laundry and stuff?

Source: Copyright © cartoonstock.com. Reprinted with permission.

most safe for subcompact cars, or which tire design is least likely to cause blow-outs. Consider also the many people who have very weak mathematical skills. Imagine such a person trying to decide on the economic benefits of whole-life versus term insurance, or a 48-month auto lease versus a five-year purchase loan at 2.9 percent financing. In general, while some businesses claim that an "informed consumer is our best customer," many others recognize that an uninformed consumer can be an easy target for quick profits.[4] Serious ethical questions should be raised whenever marketing practices either deny consumers full information or rely on the fact that they lack relevant information or understanding.

The second ethical concern looks to the alleged benefits obtained through market exchanges. Economics textbooks commonly assume that consumers benefit, almost by definition, whenever they make an exchange in the marketplace. But this assumption won't bear up under close scrutiny. Many purchases do not result in actual benefit.

For example, impulse buying, and the many marketing techniques used to promote such consumer behavior, cannot be justified by appeal to satisfying consumer interests. (See the preceding Reality Check.) The ever-increasing number of individual bankruptcies suggests that consumers cannot purchase happiness. Empirical studies provide evidence that suggests that greater consumption can lead to unhappiness, a condition called by some "affluenza."[5] So, if simple consumer satisfaction is not a conclusive measure of the benefits of market exchanges, one must always ask about the ends of marketing. What goods are attained by successfully marketing this product or service? How and in what ways are individuals and society benefited from the product?

Both parties to the marketing exchange are also not benefited in situations in which one party is injured by the product. Unsafe products do not further the utilitarian goal of maximizing overall happiness. It would also be the case that consumers are not benefited if the desires that they seek to satisfy in the market are somehow contrived or manipulated by the seller.

The third set of factors that must be considered in any ethical analysis of marketing are values other than those served by the exchange itself. Such primary social values as fairness, justice, health, and safety are just some of the values that can be jeopardized by some marketing practices. For example, a bank that offers lower mortgage rates in affluent neighborhoods than it does in inner-city neighborhoods might be involved only in deals that are mutually beneficial since they do not, in fact, sell mortgages in the inner city. But such contracts would violate important social norms of equal treatment and fairness.

There may be a very strong market for such things as certain body parts of endangered species. There is also, unfortunately, a market for children. But just because someone wants to buy something and someone else is willing to sell it does not mean that the transaction is ethically legitimate. An adequate ethical analysis of marketing must ask who else might be affected by the transaction. How, if at all, are the interests of these others represented? What social goods are promoted, and which are threatened, by marketing this product?

One must also ask what the true costs of production are. An adequate ethical analysis of marketing must consider externalities, those costs that are not integrated within the exchange between buyer and seller. Externalities show that even if both parties to the exchange receive actual benefits from the exchange, other parties external to the exchange might be adversely affected. One thinks of the environmental or health impact of marketing products such as SUVs, pesticides, and tobacco as examples in which a simple model of individual consumer exchange would ignore significant social costs. With these general issues in mind, we can now turn to a closer examination of several major aspects of marketing ethics.

Responsibility for Products: Safety and Liability

OBJECTIVE

The general category of business's responsibility for the products and services it sells includes a wide range of topics. Few issues have received as much scrutiny in law, politics, and ethics as has the responsibility of business for the harms caused by its products. Business has an ethical responsibility to design, manufacture, and promote its products in ways that avoid causing harm to consumers.

It will be helpful to review here several different meanings of the word *responsibility* that were introduced in the discussion of corporate social responsibility in Chapter 5. In one sense, to be responsible is to be identified as the *cause* of something. (See the following Reality Check, which is related to the "cause" of obesity and the possible "responsibility" of soft drinks for childhood obesity.) Thus, we say that Hurricane Katrina was responsible for millions of dollars in property damages in New Orleans. In another sense, responsibility involves accountability. When we ask who will be responsible for the damages caused by Katrina, we are asking who will pay for the damages. A third sense of responsibility, connected to but different from the sense of accountability, involves assigning fault or liability for something.

negligence

The hurricane example demonstrates how these three meanings can be distinguished. Katrina was responsible for (caused) the damage, but cannot be held responsible (accountable for paying for the damages), nor can it be faulted for it. Yet, many think that those who designed, built, or managed the levees in New Orleans were at fault and should be made to pay because their negligence caused much of the harm. In other situations, an automobile crash, for example, a careless driver would be identified as the cause of the accident and held accountable because he was at fault.

Both law and ethics rely on a similar framework when evaluating cases in which business products or services cause harm in the marketplace. The focus for much of the discussion of business's responsibility for product safety is on assigning liability (fault) for harms caused by unsafe products. The legal doctrine of strict liability is ethically controversial exactly because it holds a business accountable for paying damages whether or not it was at fault. In a strict liability case, no matter how careful the business is in its product or service, if harm results from use, the business is liable. We will consider the case of strict liability in more detail in the following section. For the present, let us examine the various standards for holding business liable for its products.

Contractual Standards for Product Safety

OBJECTIVE 4

It is fair to say that the standard of *caveat emptor* (let the buyer beware) is in the background to many discussions of product safety. The ***caveat emptor*** **approach** understands marketing on a simple model of a contractual exchange between a buyer and seller. This perspective assumes that every purchase involves the informed consent of the buyer and therefore it is assumed to be ethically legitimate. Buyers have the responsibility to look out for their own interests and protect their own safety when buying a product. From this perspective, business has only the responsibility to provide a good or service at an agreed-upon price.

The social contract tradition in ethics holds that all ethical responsibilities can be understood with this contractual model, and that the only duties we have are those that we have freely taken on within a social contract. Individual contracts and promises are the basis of ethical duties. The implication of this within the business sphere is that unless a seller explicitly warrants a product as safe, unless, in other words, the seller promises otherwise, buyers are liable for any harms they suffer.

Reality Check   *The "Cause" of Obesity?*

Scholar Regina Lawrence explored where we actually place the responsibility for obesity in our society.[6] Her research sought to determine who is "blamed and burdened in the public debate" surrounding obesity and divided the options between individuals and systemic or environmental causes. Individual causes would limit the causes of the problem to particular individuals, such as eating too much or a lack of exercise, while environmental causes would broaden the focus to government, business, and larger social forces, such as marketing campaigns, a lack of safe places to exercise, or unhealthy food choices in school cafeterias.

To answer the question of where we place responsibility for obesity, Lawrence reviewed the content of *New York Times* page-one stories (from all sections of the paper) and editorials that mentioned obesity over a select period of years. She found that, in 1990, the articles analyzed most often discussed obesity as caused by the individuals themselves (86 percent compared to 14 percent discussing environmental issues as a cause). However, by 2003, only 54 percent discussed individuals as potential causal factors, while 46 percent discussed environmental issues with possible causal links. In other words, our assessment of "fault" for obesity has shifted from a discussion of individual fault to a discussion of responsibility that includes a variety of possible factors. We have shifted the responsibility for obesity from solely those who are obese to a broader view that also includes business, the government and other external forces.

Tara Radin and Martin Calkins explore a similar question in the article "Stakeholders Influence Sales: Soda Companies Stop Selling in Schools," which follows (*adapted with permission of the authors*):

The largest soft drink companies in the United States recently announced that they will stop selling regular soft drinks in school vending machines and cafeterias. By 2008, Coca-Cola, PepsiCo, and Cadbury Schweppes will replace the high-calorie sodas they have been selling with bottled water, natural fruit juice, and diet soda. Specifically targeted are carbonated beverages containing more than 100 calories per serving. While parents and health advocates are thrilled with the success of

their concerted efforts, this decision is nothing short of shocking to teenagers around the country.

The decision was motivated in large part by increasing concerns about childhood obesity. It is somewhat myopic, in that it selectively addresses a single possible problem, when there are so many health challenges that children and young adults confront—lack of exercise, smoking, drugs and alcohol, and so on. The decision is also relatively paternalistic in that it effectively removes this temptation from the easy access of children and young adults.

Ironically, this decision runs counter to many past predatory marketing practices. Vulnerable groups, such as children, have traditionally been easy targets for many types of companies. Even though alcohol cannot be sold legally to individuals under the age of 21, it has been claimed time and again that beer manufacturers have featured teenage female models in order to appeal to the young adult market. In the 1970s and 1908s, cigarette companies allegedly focused aggressive marketing campaigns on low-income black males. They initially sold cigarettes with high levels of nicotine to increase their addictiveness, and then gradually reduced the nicotine levels to keep the young men buying more and more cigarettes.

At the same time, this decision calls into question underlying assumptions about freedom of choice. By exerting excessive pressure on soft drink manufactures with threats of litigation, interest groups have removed choice from children and young adults. Is this a positive step? By removing the temptation, are not we in fact depriving children and young adults of a valuable learning? Would it not be preferable for us to teach them moderation and resistance to temptation?

The reality is that this is not expected to affect the soft drink industry dramatically—at least not in the short run—considering that the affected sales have accounted for only about 1% of total industry revenues. From a business perspective, however, it is somewhat alarming to see the extent of stakeholder control over companies. In this situation, parents and health advocates have effectively put an end to a distribution channel for a popular product.

Interestingly, it has been labeled a "voluntary" change. This is a shift from customers exercising influence by choosing the products to support through their individual purchases, to interest groups and other stakeholders influencing access to products.

What does this mean for companies? Perhaps this is a signal that, to remain competitive, companies in the 21st century are going to have to pay closer attention to the concerns of stakeholders, and they are going to have to cast a wider net around which stakeholders they consider relevant. We are seeing this in the health arena—not just with sodas, but also with the struggles of Krispy Kreme, for example. Other markets, too, are likely vulnerable.

At the same time, however, this also reinforces the value of ethics and social responsibility, in that vigilant businesspeople and entrepreneurs are likely going to be able to identify more growth niches providing products that service socially conscious stakeholders.

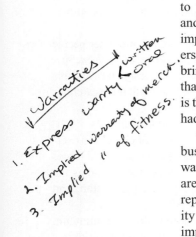

But even this simple model of a contractual market exchange would place ethical constraints on the seller. Sellers have a duty not to coerce, defraud, or deceive buyers, for example. Consumers who were injured by a product that was deceptively or fraudulently marketed would have legal recourse to recover damages from the seller.

Even in the early years of product safety law, courts recognized an implicit promise, or implied warranty, that accompanies any product that is marketed. What the law refers to as the **"implied warranty of merchantability,"** holds that in selling a product a business implicitly offers assurances that the product is reasonably suitable for its purpose. Even without a verbal or written promise or contract, the law holds that business has a duty to insure that its products will accomplish their purpose. How far does this duty reach? See the preceding Reality Check for a discussion of that responsibility.

The ethics implicit within the contract approach assumes that consumers adequately understand products well enough that they can reasonably be expected to protect themselves. But consumers don't always understand products fully and they are not always free to choose not to purchase some things. In effect, the implied warranty standard shifts the burden of proof from consumers to producers by allowing consumers to assume that products were safe for ordinary use. By bringing goods and services to the market, producers were implicitly promising that their products were safe under normal use. The ethical basis for this decision is the assumption that consumers would not give their consent to a purchase if they had reason to believe that they would be harmed by it when used in a normal way.

Of course, if law will hold business liable for implicit promises, a prudent business will seek to limit its liability by explicitly disowning any promise or warranty. Thus, many businesses will issue a disclaimer of liability (e.g., products are sold "as is"), or offer an expressed and limited warranty (e.g., the seller will replace the product but neither offers any other guarantees nor seeks to cap liability damages). Most courts will not allow a business to completely disclaim the implied warranty of merchantability.

Tort Standards for Product Safety

OBJECTIVE

The use of an implied warranty solved one set of problems with the contract law approach to product liability. Consumers wouldn't need complex contracts in order to protect themselves from all possible harms that products might cause. But a

Reality Check *Responsibility beyond Direct Contracts*

The classic 1916 legal case of *MacPherson* v. *Buick* established the principle that manufacturers could be held responsible for damages caused by their products even when no direct contract existed between the manufacturer and the injured party.

Like all automobile companies, Buick assembled automobiles at its manufacturing plant from parts manufactured by a chain of suppliers. In turn, Buick sold these cars to local automobile dealers who then resold them to consumers. Soon after purchasing a Buick, Donald MacPherson was injured in an accident caused when a defective wheel collapsed.

Buick argued that it was not liable since it had not manufactured the wheel and had no contractual relationship with Mr. MacPherson. The courts rejected these arguments and held Buick liable. The court concluded that Buick could be held liable for defective products it used in automobiles because by selling this product the company was implicitly promising that it was safe for use as intended. Further, by selling it to a retailer, Buick knew the product would be resold and therefore the court did not require an explicit and direct contract with MacPherson to determine Buick's responsibilities.

second problem remains. If we hold business liable for only those promises made during the market exchange, then as the consumer gets further separated from the manufacturer by layers of suppliers and retailers, there may be no relationship at all between the consumer who gets harmed and the ultimate manufacturer or designer who was at fault. (See the following Decision Point for a discussion of the concept of causation or "at fault.")

Negligence, a concept from the area of law known as torts, provides a second avenue for consumers to hold producers responsible for their products. The distinction between contract law and tort law also calls attention to two different ways to understand ethical duties. Under a contract model, the only duties that a person owes are those that have been explicitly promised to another party. Otherwise, I owe nothing to anyone.

The ethical perspective that underlies tort law holds that we all owe other people certain general duties, *even if we have not explicitly and voluntarily assumed them.* Specifically, I owe other people a general duty not to put them at unnecessary and avoidable risk. Thus, although I have never explicitly promised anyone that I will drive carefully, I have an ethical duty not to drive recklessly down the street.

Negligence is a central component of tort law. As the word suggests, negligence involves a type of ethical neglect, specifically neglecting one's duty to exercise reasonable care not to harm other people. Many of the ethical and legal issues surrounding manufacturers' responsibility for products can be understood as the attempt to specify what constitutes negligence in their design, production, and sale. What duties, exactly, do producers owe to consumers?

One can think of possible answers to this question as falling along a continuum. On one extreme is the social contract answer: Producers owe only those things promised to consumers in the sales agreement. At the other extreme is something closer to **strict liability:** Producers owe compensation to consumers for any harm caused by their products. In between these extremes is a range of answers that vary with different interpretations of negligence. We have already suggested why

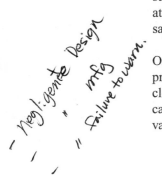

(handwritten margin notes)

Unintentional tort.

√ 5 elements of neg.

Duty
Breached Duty
Injury / Damage
Actual Cause
proximate cause
(Forseeability)

Negligente Design
' " mfg
" " failure to warn.

Decision Point

When Has a Company's Action Caused Injuries to Its Customers?

Agency law

One of the most influential cases in U.S. tort law involved a railroad company being sued by a customer who was injured while waiting for a train. In *Palsgraf v. Long Island Railroad*, Helen Palsgraf was standing at a train station awaiting the arrival of her train. As an earlier train was leaving the station, another passenger ran to catch the moving train. Railroad employees helped the man onto the moving train. In the process of being jostled by the employees, the man dropped his package onto the tracks. The package contained fireworks for the upcoming 4th of July celebration, and they exploded, setting off a chain of events. In the mayhem that followed, a scale at the end of the platform was knocked over, striking Helen Palsgaf and causing her injuries. Palsgraf sued to recover damages for her injuries.

The court in this case faced two basic questions: Did the actions of the railroad employees cause her injuries? Were the railroad employees negligent in the way they treated customers and, if so, were they negligent to Mrs. Palsgraf? How would you have decided this case?

- What facts would you want to know before deciding this case?
- What alternatives would a jury face in deciding this case?
- Who are the stakeholders of your decision? What is the impact of each alternative decision on each stakeholder you have identified?
- What rights and duties are involved?
- How would you decide the case? Is it mostly a matter of consequences, or are there important principles involved?

the strict contract approach is incomplete. In the next section we shall examine the pros and cons of strict product liability. The remainder of this section will examine the important concept of negligence.

Negligence can be characterized as a failure to exercise reasonable care or ordinary vigilance that results in an injury to another. In many ways, negligence simply codifies two fundamental ethical precepts: "ought implies can" (we cannot reasonably oblige someone to do what they cannot do) and "one ought not harm others." People have done an ethical wrong when they cause harm to others in ways that they can reasonably be expected to have avoided. Negligence includes acts of both commission and omission. One can be negligent by doing something that one ought not (e.g., speeding in a school zone) or by failing to do something that one ought to have done (e.g., neglecting to inspect a product before sending it to market).

Negligence involves the ability to forsee the consequences of our acts and failing to take steps to avoid the likely harmful consequences (see the following Decision Point). The standards of foreseeability, however, raise interesting challenges. One standard would hold people liable only for those harms they actually foresaw occurring (actual foreseeability). Thus, for example, they would be acting negligently if (as was alleged in the famous Ford Pinto case), on the basis of engineering tests, they concluded that a fuel tank placed behind the rear axle would puncture and explode during crashes at speeds below 30 miles per hour, yet still brought the car to market.

In 1992 a 70-year-old woman was severely burned when a cup of coffee she had just purchased at a McDonald's drive-through window spilled on her lap. She apparently held the cup between her legs and tried to pry off the lid as she drove away. The coffee was hot enough (185 degrees) to cause third-degree burns that required skin grafts and long-term medical care. A jury awarded this woman $2.86 million, $160,000 for compensatory damages and $2.7 million in punitive damages. Should McDonald's be held liable for these injuries? Was the restaurant negligent in serving such hot coffee at a drive-through window? Was the consumer negligent in her own actions?

- What facts would you want to know before deciding whether this settlement was fair?
- What alternatives would a jury face in deciding this case?
- Who are the stakeholders of your decision? What is the impact of each alternative mentioned above on each stakeholder you have identified?
- Should *caveat emptor* govern the situation?
- What are the consequences of the jury's decision?
- What rights and duties are involved?
- How would you decide the case? Is it mostly a matter of consequences, or are there important principles involved?

In an interesting 2006 case with somewhat related facts, a woman was awarded more than $300,000 by a jury when a Starbucks Coffee employee caused a cup of coffee to spill on to the woman's foot. In fact, the *barista* (the coffee server at Starbucks) slid the coffee toward the woman; the coffee slipped over the edge of the counter; the top fell off; and the coffee spilled onto the woman's sneaker-covered foot. Her foot suffered nerve damage from the scalding liquid. Starbucks' public statement explained that, while it regrets any injury to Griffin, "we do not believe we are responsible for her injury."

- Do you see a distinction between these two cases?
- Is there any difference between the responsibility McDonald's owes the woman in the first instance and the responsibility Starbucks owes the woman in the second situation, as described above?
- Are the principles involved in the two cases any different?
- Will the decisions in the two cases lead to different consequences?

But this standard of actual foreseeability is too restricted. If someone actually thinks that harms are likely to result from his acts and proceeds nonetheless, he has committed a serious wrong and deserves harsh punishment. Such a case seems more akin to recklessness, or even intentional harm, than negligence. But this standard would also imply that unthoughtful people cannot be negligent, since one escapes liability by not actually thinking about the consequences of one's acts. "I never thought about that" would be an adequate defense if we used this standard of negligence. Yet this surely is part of what we are after with the concept of negligence. We want to encourage people to be thoughtful and hold them liable when they are not.

Manufacturers can be held legally and ethically negligent if they fail to foresee harms that could reasonably be anticipated in the normal use of a product. Consider this case with the design of a kitchen stove.

A young child is curious about what her mother is cooking on top of the kitchen stove. In order to gain a better view, she opens the oven door and steps up on it to look into the pans on the stovetop. Her weight causes the stove to tip over, spilling the hot food on her and causing severe burns. Was the manufacturer at fault for not designing a stove that would not tip with the weight of a child on the oven door?

Could the stove design team have foreseen a child using the oven door as a stepladder? Could the designers foresee the use of the oven door as a work surface on which to place heavy roasting pans, for example, a turkey pan while basting? If the weight of such a large oven pan is comparable to the weight of a young child, should the oven have been designed to withstand a foreseeable weight being placed on the door? If you were on a jury and had to decide this case, would you hold the manufacturer accountable for the child's injuries?

- What facts would you want to know before deciding this case?
- What alternatives would a jury face in deciding this case?
- Who are the stakeholders of such your decision? What is the impact of each alternative decision on each stakeholder you have identified?
- What rights and duties are involved?
- How would you decide the case? Is it mostly a matter of consequences, or are important principles involved?

A preferable standard would require people to avoid harms that, even if they haven't actually thought about, they *should* have thought about had they been reasonable. For example, in the Decision Point on page 324 presumably McDonald's did not actually anticipate that customers would be severely burned by coffee. But, had its managers thought about what people who are served coffee at drive-through windows might do to hold their cups when they drive away from the window, they could have foreseen the likelihood of spills. Moreover, the fact that McDonald's had received over 700 prior burn claims involving coffee over a 10-year period suggests that a reasonable person would have concluded that this was a dangerous practice. This "reasonable person" standard is the one most often used in legal cases and seems to better capture the ethical goals of the very concept of negligence. People are expected to act reasonably and are held liable when they are not. In addition, when one has actual notice of a likelihood of harm, such as in this case, the reasonable person expectation is increased. An issue arises surrounding foreseeability when a product might be misused, as in the Decision Point above.

But even the reasonable person standard can be interpreted in various ways. On one hand, we expect people will act in ways that would be normal or average.

A "reasonable" person does what we could expect the ordinary, average person to do. There are problems using this standard for both consumer and producer behavior. It may turn out that the ordinary average consumer is not as smart as we might hope. The average person doesn't always read, or understand, warning labels, for example. The ordinary and average person may thoughtlessly place a cup of very hot coffee between her legs as she drives out of a parking lot and into traffic. The average person standard when applied to consumers risks exempting many consumers from taking responsibility for their own acts. When applied to producers, the average person standard sets the bar too low. We can expect more from a person who designs, manufacturers, and sells a product than average and ordinary vigilance.

Reasons such as these can lead us to interpret the reasonable person standard more normatively than descriptively. In this sense, a "reasonable" person assumes a standard of thoughtful, reflective, and judicious decision making. The problem with this, of course, is that we might be asking more of average consumers than they are capable of giving. Particularly if we think that the disadvantaged and vulnerable deserve greater protection from harm, we might conclude that this is too stringent a standard to be applied to consumer behavior. On the other hand, given the fact that producers do have more expertise than the average person, this stronger standard seems more appropriate when applied to producers than to consumers.

Strict Product Liability

OBJECTIVE

The negligence standard of tort law focuses on the sense of responsibility that involves liability or fault. As such, it asks what the business or person involved had foreseen or should have foreseen. But there are also cases in which consumers can be injured by a product in which no negligence was involved. In such cases where no one was at fault, the question of accountability remains. Who should pay for damages when consumers are injured by products and no one is at fault? The legal doctrine of strict product liability holds manufacturers accountable in such cases.

One classic strict product liability case involved the synthetic estrogen hormone diethylstilbestrol (DES). In the late 1940s, DES was approved for use in the prevention of miscarriages and was widely prescribed for problem pregnancies until the early 1970s. The drug had been widely tested in clinical trials and proved quiet successful in reducing the number of miscarriages. However, in the early 1970s a connection was discovered between the use of DES during pregnancy and certain forms of vaginal cancer in the female children of women who used the drug. These cancers did not typically appear until more than a decade after the drug was used. In 1972 the FDA prohibited all marketing of the drug for use during pregnancy. For the experience of another manufacturer, see the Decision Point that follows.

Ethical Debates on Product Liability

OBJECTIVE

It is fair to say that the business community is a strong critic of much of the legal standards of product liability. Liability standards, and the liability insurance costs in which they have resulted, have imposed significant costs on contemporary business. In particular, these critics single out the strict product liability standard as

Another major strict product liability case involves asbestos, a fibrous mineral used for decades for insulation and fire prevention in homes, industry, and consumer products. When inhaled through long-term exposure, asbestos dust causes a variety of lung and respiratory diseases, including mesothelioma, a particularly fatal form of cancer. Millions of workers have been exposed to asbestos, especially during the middle decades of the 20th century. However, many of the diseases associated with asbestos, including mesothelioma, might take decades before they appear. Thus, it is often difficult if not impossible to identify the exact source of the asbestos that caused the disease. In such cases, the liability focuses on any and all manufacturers of asbestos products. They brought the product to market, the product proved defective, therefore they ought to be held accountable for the damages.

One estimate suggests that 700,000 people have been involved in lawsuits against 8,000 corporations for asbestos-related injuries. Asbestos liability lawsuits have bankrupted several corporations, including the high-profile Johns-Manville. As much as $70 billion has been paid in asbestos claims, and lawsuits continue in every state.

Should manufacturers of asbestos be held accountable for the damages caused by the product they brought to market, even if no direct link can be established between the injury and any specific product they manufactured?

- What facts would you need to know to make a fully informed judgment in this case?
- What alternatives are available? If not the manufacturer, who should be accountable to pay for the damages caused by asbestos?
- Who are the stakeholders who should be involved in this case?
- What are the likely consequences of holding manufacturers strictly liable? Of holding the injured consumer accountable? Of having the government pay?
- What duties do the manufacturers of asbestos have? What does the principle of fairness require in this case?
- If you were on a jury and had to decide who should pay the costs of a worker's mesothelioma, how would you decide?

especially unfair to business because it holds business responsible for harms that were not the result of business negligence.

In fact, the rationale often used to justify strict product liability is problematic. Defenders of the strict product liability standard, including juries who decide in favor of injured consumers, often reply with two major claims. First, by holding business strictly liable for any harms their products cause, society creates a strong incentive for business to produce safer goods and services. Second, given that someone has to be accountable for the costs of injuries, holding business liable allocates the costs to the party best able to bear the financial burden. Each rationale is open to serious objections.

First, the incentive argument seems to misunderstand the nature of strict liability. Holding someone accountable for a harm can provide an incentive only if they could have done otherwise. But this means that the harm was foreseeable and the failure to act was negligent. Surely this is a reasonable justification for the tort standard of negligence. But strict liability is not negligence and the harms caused by such products as DES and asbestos were not foreseeable. Thus, holding business liable for these harms cannot provide an incentive to better protect consumers in the future.

The second rationale also suffers a serious defect. This argument amounts to the claim that business is best able to pay for damages. Yet, as the asbestos case indicates, many businesses have been bankrupted by product liability claims.

If it is unfair to hold business accountable for harms caused by their products, however, it is equally if not more unfair to hold injured consumers accountable. Neither party is at fault, yet someone must pay for the injuries. A third option would be to have government, and therefore all taxpayers, accountable for paying the costs of injuries caused by defective products. But this, too, seems unfair.

A third argument for holding business accountable might be more persuasive. Accountability, after all, focuses on those situations where no one is at fault, yet someone has to pay. This might be another way of saying that accountability is not a matter of ethical principle in that no one deserves to pay for damages. But perhaps accountability is best understood as a matter of utilitarian efficiency rather than principle. When business is held accountable, the costs for injuries will eventually fall on those consumers who buy the product through higher costs, especially higher insurance costs to business. This amounts to the claim that external costs should be internalized and that the full costs of a product should be paid for by those who use the product. Products that impose a cost on society through injuries will end up costing more to those who purchase them. Companies that cannot afford to remain in business when the full costs of its products are taken into account perhaps ought not remain in business.

Responsibility for Products: Advertising and Sales

Along with product safety, the general area of advertising ethics has received significant legal and philosophical attention within business ethics. The goal of all marketing is the sale, the eventual exchange between seller and buyer. A major element of marketing is sales promotion, the attempt to influence the buyer to complete a purchase. (See the Decision Point that follows.) Target marketing and marketing research are two important elements of product placement, seeking to determine which audience is most likely to buy, and which audience is mostly likely to be influenced by product promotion.

There are, of course, ethically good and bad ways for influencing others. Among the ethically commendable ways to influence another are persuading, asking, informing, and advising. Unethical means of influence would include threats, coercion, deception, manipulation, and lying. Unfortunately, all too often sales and advertising practices employ deceptive or manipulative means of influence, or are aimed at audiences that are susceptible to manipulation or deception. Perhaps the most infamous and maligned of all marketing fields is automotive sales, especially in used car markets. The concept of manipulation, and its subset of deception,

"Below invoice prices." "Cash-back incentives." "Low monthly lease rate." "Late model close-outs." "$500 cash back." "Manufacturer's suggested retail price." "Sticker price." "Factory rebates." "Absolute lowest price guaranteed." "0% interest on selected vehicles." "Factory authorized clearance." "Extended service contracts." "No money down." "Certified preowned vehicles." "No reasonable offer refused." "Huge discounts. Save thousands." "We sell wholesale to the public!" "We are dealing. Save $$$." "Credit problems? No problem. Your approval is guaranteed or we'll give you $1,000." "No games, no gimmicks."

All of these claims were found in just a few pages of one local Sunday newspaper. They point to the extraordinary difficulty that consumers face in purchasing a car. Perhaps no other industry suffers as bad a reputation in pricing and sales as the automobile industry.

Do you find any of these claims misleading? Confusing? Deceptive? Which are easily understood? Which are least clear? Who is being targeted by these ads?

- What facts would you want to know before making a judgment about these ads?
- Which ads, if any, raise ethical questions?
- Who are the stakeholders in automobile advertising? What are the potential benefits and potential harms of such advertising?
- What ethical principles have you used in making your judgments?
- What type of people do you think are involved in automobile advertising and automobile sales?

is central to the ethical issues explored in this chapter and can help organize the following sections.

To manipulate something is to guide or direct its behavior. Manipulation need not involve total control, and in fact it more likely suggests a process of subtle direction or management. Manipulating people implies working behind the scenes, guiding their behavior without their explicit consent or conscious understanding. In this way, manipulation is contrasted with persuasion and other forms of rational influence. When I manipulate someone, I explicitly do not rely on their own reasoned judgment to direct their behavior. Instead, I seek to bypass their autonomy (although successful manipulation can be reinforced when the person manipulated *believes* she acted of her own accord).

One of the ways in which we can manipulate someone is through deception, one form of which is an outright lie. I need not deceive you to manipulate you, although I would be happy if you falsely believed that you were not being manipulated. We can manipulate someone without deception, as when I get my sons to mow the lawn by making them feel guilty about not carrying their share of family responsibilities. Or I might manipulate my students into studying more diligently by hinting that there may be a quiz during the next class. These examples raise a very crucial point because they suggest that the more I know about your psychology—your motivations, interests, desires, beliefs, dispositions, and so forth—the better able I will be to manipulate your behavior. Guilt, pity, a desire to please, anxiety, fear, low self-esteem, pride, and conformity can all be powerful motivators. Knowing such things about another person provides effective tools for manipulating their behavior.

We can see how this is relevant to marketing ethics. Critics charge that many marketing practices manipulate consumers. Clearly, many advertisements are deceptive, and some are outright lies. We can also see how marketing research plays into this. The more one learns about customer psychology, the better able one will be to satisfy their desires, but the better able one will also be to manipulate their behavior. Critics charge that some marketing practices target populations that are particularly susceptible to manipulation and deception.

Ethical Issues in Advertising

OBJECTIVE

The general ethical defense of advertising reflects both utilitarian and Kantian ethical standards. Advertising provides information for market exchanges and therefore contributes to market efficiency and to the overall happiness. Advertising information also contributes to the information necessary for autonomous individuals to make informed choices. But note that each of these rationales assumes that the information is true and accurate.

The deontological tradition in ethics would have the strongest objections to manipulation. When I manipulate someone I treat them as a means to my own ends, as an object to be used rather than as an autonomous person in his or her own right. Manipulation is a clear example of disrespect for persons since it bypasses their own rational decision making. Because the evil rests with the intention to use another as a means, even unsuccessful manipulations are guilty of this ethical wrong.

As we might expect, the utilitarian tradition would offer a more conditional critique of manipulation, depending on the consequences. There surely can be cases of paternalistic manipulation, in which someone is manipulated for their own good. But even in such cases, unforeseen harms can occur. Manipulation tends to erode bonds of trust and respect between persons. It can erode one's self-confidence and hinder the development of responsible choice among those manipulated. In general, because most manipulation is done to further the manipulator's own ends at the expense of the manipulated, utilitarians would be inclined to think that manipulation lessens overall happiness. A general practice of manipulation, as critics would charge occurs in many sales practices, can undermine the very social practices (e.g., sales) that it is thought to promote as the reputation of sales is lowered. The example of used car sales, once again, is a good example of such a situation.

A particularly egregious form of manipulation occurs when vulnerable people are targeted for abuse. Cigarette advertising aimed at children is one example that has received major criticism in recent years. Marketing practices targeted at elderly populations for such goods and services as insurance (particularly Medicare supplemental insurance), casinos and gambling, nursing homes, and funerals have been subjected to similar criticisms. (See the following Reality Check.)

We can suggest the following general guidelines. Marketing practices that seek to discover which consumers might already and independently be predisposed

Reality Check *Winners and Losers*

The Illinois Lottery Commission came under fire in 2005 for a billboard marketing campaign in downtown Chicago that included signs that read, "How to go from Washington Street to Easy Street —Play the Illinois State Lottery." A boycott of the lottery was organized, claiming that the lottery took advantage of the poor of the inner city. The claim is that the lottery is actually an unfair form of a regressive tax because it draws a disproportionate amount of its revenues from the poor by preying on unrealistic hopes.

To the contrary, argues Edward J. Stanek, the president of the North American Association of State and Provincial Lotteries:

> Big jackpot games are equalizers. Those who were not fortunate in the drawing of genes and inheritance can venture a chance equal to everyone else to benefit financially . . . Lotteries don't discriminate among their customers. . . . If there is something inherently wrong with allowing less prosperous people the choice to buy a ticket, then the protectionists should seek legislation to prohibit low-income citizens from taking a chance. Why haven't they? Because the folly of their self-righteous protectionism would be exposed. . . .

> For a lottery to take "advantage" of the poor would imply that the poor have a "disadvantage." Obviously they have less money, which means that lotteries can benefit them more relative to helping those of greater means. The only way that the poor can be at a disadvantage is if they don't have the same mental capacity to make $1 decisions as those who are wealthier. It follows that those who make such claims are assuming that the poor have a diminished intellectual capacity. But economic status is not a measure of intelligence. Saying that the poor are taken advantage of in this context is an insult to the intelligence of those who play lottery games.

With which side do you agree?

Source: E. Stanek, "Take the High Road and Keep the Upper Hand: A Critique of Lottery Critics," speech to North American Association of State and Provincial Lotteries (Sept. 29, 1997), http://www.nmlottery.com/Miscellaneous/CRITIQUE.HTM.

to purchasing a product are ethically legitimate. So, for example, an automobile dealership learns from its manufacturer's marketing department that the typical buyer of its car is a college-educated female between the ages of 25 and 30 who enjoys outdoors activities and earns more than $30,000. Sending targeted direct mail pieces to everyone within an area who matches these criteria seems an ethically legitimate marketing practice. Marketing practices that seek to identify populations that can be easily influenced and manipulated, on the other hand, are not. Sales and marketing that appeal to fear, anxiety, or other nonrational motivations are ethically improper. For example, an automobile dealer who knows that an unmarried or widowed woman is anxious about the purchase and who uses this anxiety as a way to sell extended warranty insurance, disability insurance, theft protection products, and the like is unethical. (The manner in which this or other information is collected is also subject to ethical concerns; see the following Reality Check.)

Marketing research seeks to learn something about the psychology of potential customers. But not all psychological categories are alike. Some are more cognitive and rational than others. Targeting the considered and rational desires of consumers is one thing; targeting their fears, anxiety, and whims is another.

Reality Check *New Challenges to Old Problems: From Redlining to E-Lining*

by Tara J. Radin, Martin Calkins, and Carolyn Predmore

Today, more than a decade since the Internet became widely and publicly available, we still lack consensus about the degree of ownership and acceptable limits of data gathering and use. In fact, Richard De George's 1999 remark is arguably more valid now than previously: "The U.S. is schizophrenic about information privacy, wanting it in theory and giving it away in practice."[7] Such schizophrenia is problematic in itself, but it has been exacerbated by the questionable applications of data collection that have occurred. E-lining (electronic redlining) represents one glaring example of how data gathering crosses moral boundaries.

Redlining is the practice of denying or increasing the cost of services to residents of certain geographic locations. In the United States, it has been deemed illegal when the criteria involve race, religion, or ethnic origin. The term came to prominence with the discussions that led to the Housing Act of 1934, which established the Federal Housing Authority, which later became the Department of Housing and Urban Development. It occurs when financial institutions (banks, brokerages, and insurance companies) literally draw red lines on maps to distinguish between creditworthy and financially risky neighborhoods.

Although illegal, redlining has not died out completely. It reemerged recently when MCI removed international long distance service via calling cards from pay phones in poorer communities in the suburbs of Los Angeles. It reappeared also in retail sales when Victoria's Secret allegedly tailored its catalog prices along customer demographics (specifically, ethnicity). In this case, two sisters living in different parts of town discovered price differences when discussing items from seemingly identical catalogs. As the two compared prices on the phone, they found that the cost of some items varied by as much as 25 percent. A subsequent and more thorough investigation revealed that Victoria's Secret had been engaging in an extensive practice of price variation according to gender, age, and income. In the end, although Victoria's Secret was

vindicated in the court of law, it lost in the court of public opinion.

Finally, it resurfaced when Kozmo.com, an online provider of one-hour delivery services, used zip codes to refuse to deliver merchandise to customers in predominantly black neighborhoods. In all of these cases, companies (to different degrees) "exclude(d) classes of individuals from full participation in the marketplace and the public sphere."

E-lining differs from these more traditional forms of redlining by not drawing a red line on a map, but by using information that Internet users unwittingly leave behind as they surf Web sites. E-liners use "spyware" programs embedded in Web pages to collect information surreptitiously and with little or no outside oversight. They are able to "spy on" surfers in this way without much challenge because, at present, there are few limits on what companies can do with the information they gather.

In recent years companies have used customer information to direct customers to particular products or services. In this way, they have used information in much the same way high-end clothing stores use a Rolodex of customer phone numbers to alert customers about newly arrived items that match or complement prior purchases. At other times, businesses have not acted so benevolently. They have used the data they collected in a discriminatory way to direct customers to particular products or services that fit a profile based on demographics. Amazon has received significant criticism for its use of historical purchase information to tailor Web offerings to repeat customers. Amazon allegedly used data profiling in order to set prices. In September 2000, Amazon customers determined that they were charged different prices for the same CDs. Although Amazon claimed that the price differentiation was part of a randomized test, the result was price discrimination that appeared to be based on demographics.

This sort of discrimination and deprivation of financial opportunities according to demographics is exactly what the rules against redlining are intended to prevent. The absence of comparable rules against e-lining is not, as some firms might like to argue, an indication that this sort of behavior is acceptable in e-commerce, but, rather, is a reflection of the lag in time it is taking for the legal infrastructure to catch up with e-commerce. Our current legal infrastructure, particularly in the United States, which is aimed almost exclusively toward brick-and-mortar enterprises, does not account for the tremendous amount of information available through e-commerce or for the numerous ways in which e-merchants are able to exploit customers through misuse of that information. The unfortunate reality is that there is not a clear distinction between acceptable and unacceptable forms of information gathering, use, and market segmentation, and e-commerce provides a cloak that insulates from detection many firms engaging in inappropriate behavior.

There are few if any obstacles to firms engaging in questionable e-commerce business practices in the first place. Public outcries are generally short-lived and do not appear to have a significant impact on e-shopping. If anything, e-commerce continues to attract an increasing number of customers. In the meantime, few generally agreed-upon standards exist regarding the acceptable limits of information gathering via the Internet. Instead, businesses are shaping the expectations of Web users and society in general as they implicitly set standards to guide future marketers through their irresponsible behavior. They are sending the message: "Internet user beware!" to Internet surfers and potential e-customers. As long as the legal infrastructure remains underdeveloped, society remains vulnerable to an increasing number of potential electronic abuses.

Marketing Ethics and Consumer Autonomy

OBJECTIVE

Defenders of advertising argue that despite cases of deceptive practices, overall advertising contributes much to the economy. The majority of advertisements provide information to consumers, information that contributes to an efficient function of economic markets. These defenders argue that over time, market forces will weed out deceptive ads and practices. They point out that the most effective counter to a deceptive ad is a competitor's ad calling attention to the deception.

Beyond this question of what advertising does *for* people, a second important ethical question asks what advertising, specifically, and marketing in general, does *to* people. People may well benefit from business's marketing of its products. People learn about products they may need or want, they get information that helps them make responsible choices, they even sometimes are entertained. But marketing also helps shape culture and the individuals who develop and are socialized within that culture, some would say dramatically so. Marketing can have direct and indirect influence on the very persons we become. How it does that, and the kind of people we become as a result, is of fundamental ethical importance. Critics of such claims either deny that marketing can have such influence or maintain that marketing is only a mirror of the culture of which it is a part.

The initial proposal in this debate was offered by economist John Kenneth Galbraith in his 1958 book, *The Affluent Society*. Galbraith claimed that advertising and marketing were creating the very consumer demand that production then aimed to satisfy. Dubbed the "dependence effect," this assertion held that consumer demand depended upon what producers had to sell. This fact had three major and unwelcome implications.

First, by creating wants advertising was standing the "law" of supply and demand on its head. Rather than supply being a function of demand, demand turns out to

Reality Check *Advertising Spending*

Total spending on advertising in all media for 2005 was estimated by one marketing group to exceed $275 billion. Worldwide, advertising was a $560 billion industry.[8]

In terms of direct marketing, alone, companies spent more than $160 billion in the United States, which, measured against total U.S. sales, generated an estimated $1.85 trillion in increased sales in 2005, or 7 percent of the $26 trillion in total sales in the U.S. economy, and accounted for 10.3 percent of total U.S. GDP in that year.[9]

be a function of supply. Second, advertising and marketing tend to create irrational and trivial consumer wants and this distorts the entire economy. The "affluent" society of consumer products and creature comforts is in many ways worse off than so-called undeveloped economies because resources devoted to contrived, private consumer goods are therefore denied to more important public goods and consumer needs. Taxpayers deny school districts small tax increases to provide essential funding while parents drop their children off at school in $40,000 SUVs. A society that cannot guarantee vaccinations and minimal health care to poor children spends millions annual for cosmetic surgery to keep its youthful appearance. Finally, by creating consumer wants, advertising and other marketing practices violate consumer autonomy. Consumers who consider themselves free because they are able to purchase what they want are not in fact free if those wants are created by marketing. In short, consumers are being manipulated by advertising.

Ethically, the crucial point is the assertion that advertising violates consumer autonomy. The law of supply and demand is reversed, and the economy of the affluent society is contrived and distorted, only if consumer autonomy can be violated, and consumers manipulated, by advertising's ability to create wants. But can advertising violate consumer autonomy and, if it can, does this occur? Consider the annual investment in this effort (see the preceding Reality Check). Given this investment, what does advertising do *to* people and *to* society?

An initial thesis in this debate claims that advertising controls consumer *behavior*. Autonomy involves making reasoned and voluntary choices, and the claim that advertising violates autonomy might mean that advertising controls consumer choice. Psychological behaviorists and critics of subliminal advertising, for example, would claim that advertising can control consumer behavior in this way. But this seems to be an empirical claim and the evidence suggests that it is false. For example, some studies show that more than half of all new products introduced in the market fail, a fact that should not be true if consumer behavior could be controlled by marketing. Consumers certainly don't seem controlled by advertising in any obvious sense of that word.

But consumer autonomy might be violated in a more subtle way. Rather than controlling behavior, perhaps advertising creates the wants and desires on the basis of which consumers act. The focus here becomes the concept of *autonomous desires* rather than *autonomous behavior*. This is much closer to the original assertion by Galbraith and other critics of advertising. Consumer autonomy is violated by advertising's ability to create nonautonomous desires.

Advertisements promoting prescription drugs have increased significantly since the FDA changed regulations in 1997 to allow direct to consumer (DTC) advertising. Among the most widely marketed drugs have been Lipitor, Zocor, Prilosec, Prevacid, Nexium, Celebrex, Vioxx, Zoloft, Paxil, Prozac, Viagra, Cialis, Levitra, Propecia, and Zyban. These drug names, literally household words today, were unheard of or nonexistent even 10 years ago. Together, they accounted for over $21 billion in sales in 2002.

These drugs treat the following conditions: ulcers and acid-reflux (Prilosec, Prevacid, Nexium), high cholesterol (Lipitor, Zocor), arthritis pain (Celebrex, Vioxx), depression, panic attacks, and anxiety (Zoloft, Paxil, Prozac), "erectile dysfunction" (Viagra, Cialis, and Levitra), hair loss (Propecia), and cigarette and nicotine withdrawal (Zyban).

Ads for these drugs often appeal to such emotional considerations as embarrassment; fear; shame; social, sexual, and romantic inferiority; helplessness; vulnerability; and vanity. Many of these drugs are heavily advertised in women's magazines and during televised sporting events.

Perhaps no marketing campaign has received as much critical attention as the Viagra, Cialis, and Levitra campaign to counteract erectile dysfunction. Much of the criticism has focused on the ad placements, particularly in places where young children would see them such as during prime time television and during high-profile sporting events. Other criticisms suggest that although these drugs can be used to treat real medical conditions, they are being marketed as little more than sex toys. Erectile dysfunction can be a problem for older men and especially for men recovering from such medical treatments as prostate surgery. But for younger and otherwise healthy men, the primary causes of erectile dysfunction are alcohol consumption, obesity, lack of exercise, smoking, and the use of other prescription drugs. All these causes are either easily addressed without reliance on pharmaceuticals or, as in the case of alcohol abuse, use of erectile dysfunction drugs is potentially unsafe with them.

Arguments in support of this type of marketing are that they provide information to consumers, respect consumer choice, encourage those who are reluctant to seek medical care to do so, get more people into the health care system, address real public health issues, and increase competition and efficiency in the pharmaceutical industry. Opponents claim that these ads increase the unnecessary use of drugs; that because all drugs have harmful side effects, the ads increase public harms; that the ads increase reliance on pharmaceutical health care treatments and discourage alternative therapies and treatments, many of which have fewer side effects; that these ads manipulate and exploit vulnerable consumers; that they often provide misleading and incomplete information; that they alienate patients from physicians by bypassing the gatekeeper function of medical professionals; and that they treat social and behavior problems with medical and chemical solutions. What is your judgment about the ethics of advertising prescription drugs?

What facts would you want to know before deciding this case?

- What alternatives exist for marketing prescription drugs?
- Who are the stakeholders of drug marketing?
- What are the consequences of alternative marketing strategies?
- What rights and duties are involved?
- How would you decide the case? Is it mostly a matter of consequences, or are important principles involved?

A helpful exercise to understand how desires might be nonautonomous is to think of the many reasons people buy the things they buy and consume the things they do, and why, in general, people go shopping. After certain basic needs are met, there is a real question of why people consume the way they do. People buy things for many reasons, including the desire to appear fashionable, for status, to feel good, because everyone else is buying something, and so forth. The interesting ethical question at this point is where did *these* desires originate, and how much has marketing influenced these non-necessity purchases. These questions and issues are addressed in the preceding Decision Point.

Marketing to Vulnerable Populations

OBJECTIVE

Consider two examples of target marketing. In one case, based on market research supplied by the manufacturer, an automobile retailer learns that the typical customer is a single woman, between the ages of 30 and 40 years old with annual income over $30,000, who enjoys outdoor sports and recreation. Knowing this information, the dealer targets advertising and direct mail to this audience. Ads depict attractive and active young people using their product and enjoying outdoors activities. A second targeted campaign is aimed at selling an emergency call device to elderly widows who live alone. This marketing campaign depicts an elderly woman at the bottom of a stairway crying out "I've fallen and can't get up!" These ads are placed in media that elderly women are likely to see or hear. Are these marketing campaigns on an equal ethical footing?

The first marketing strategy appeals to the considered judgments which consumers, presumably, have settled on over the course of their lives. People with similar backgrounds tend to have similar beliefs, desires, and values and often make similar judgments about consumer purchases. Target marketing in this sense is simply a means for identifying likely customers based on common beliefs and values. On the other hand, there does seem to be something ethically offensive about the second case. This campaign aims to sell the product by exploiting the real fear and anxiety that many older people experience. This marketing strategy tries to manipulate people by appealing to nonrational factors such as fear or anxiety rather than relying on straightforward informative ads. Is there anything to the claim that elderly women living alone are more "vulnerable" than younger women and that this vulnerability creates greater responsibility for marketers? In general, do marketers have special responsibility to the vulnerable?

Are elderly people living alone particularly vulnerable? The answer to this depends on what we mean by particularly vulnerable. In one sense, a person is vulnerable as a consumer by being unable in some way to participate as a fully informed and voluntary participant in the market exchange. Valid market exchanges make several assumptions about the participants: They understand what they are doing, they have considered their choice, they are free to decide, and so forth. What we can call *consumer vulnerability* occurs when a person has an impaired ability to make an informed consent to the market exchange. A vulnerable consumer lacks

The *Boston Globe* reported one controversial attempt to market pharmaceuticals in 2002. The *Globe* reported that sales representatives for TAP Pharmaceuticals, makers of Lupron Depot, an analgesic for treating pain associated with prostate cancer, were instructed to attend meetings of a prostate cancer support group to promote the drug directly to cancer patients. While pharmaceutical companies often provide support groups with financial assistance and informational materials, many critics believed that this action crossed the line of acceptable marketing.

A second case of marketing drugs to targeted populations involves the drug Strattera, Eli Lilly's prescription medication that controls attention deficit disorder and hyperactivity (ADHD) in children. This ad ran in magazines such as *Family Circle* (September 2003) under the simple title "Welcome to Ordinary." The ad pictures two boys holding up a model airplane that they have finished building, a challenging task for a child with ADHD. The ad reads: "4:30 p.m. Tuesday. He started something you never thought he'd finish. 5:20 p.m. Thursday. He's proved you wrong." The ad suggests that, if a child with ADHD is not "ordinary," it is the parents who are "wrong" because all it would take would be Strattera to solve their problem. The same issue of *Family Circle* contained ads for McNeil Pharmaceutical's Concerta and Shire Pharmaceutical's Adderall, the two major competitors to Strattera.

Are these marketing practices ethically responsible?

- What facts would you want to know before deciding this case?
- What alternative marketing practices were open to these companies?
- Who are the stakeholders of your decision? What is the impact of each alternative decision on each stakeholder you have identified?
- What rights and duties are involved?
- How would you decide the case? Would you primarily consider consequences, or are important principles involved?

the intellectual capacities, psychological ability, or maturity to make informed and considered consumer judgments. Children would be the paradigmatic example of consumer vulnerability. The harm to which such people are susceptible is the harm of not satisfying one's consumer desires and/or losing one's money. Elderly people living alone are not necessarily vulnerable in this sense.

There is a second sense of vulnerability in which the harm is other than the financial harm of an unsatisfactory market exchange. Elderly people living alone are susceptible to injuries from falls, from medical emergencies, from expensive health care bills, from loneliness. Alcoholics are susceptible to alcohol abuse, the poor are susceptible to bankruptcy, single women walking alone at night are vulnerable to sexual assault, accident victims are susceptible to high medical expenses and loss of income, and so forth. What we can call *general vulnerability* occurs when someone is susceptible to some specific physical, psychological, or financial harm.

From this we can see that there can be two types of marketing that targets vulnerable populations. Some marketing practices might target those consumers who are likely to be uninformed and vulnerable as consumers. Marketing aimed at children, for example, aims to sell products to customers who are unable to make thoughtful and informed consumer decisions. Other marketing practices might target populations that are vulnerable in the general sense as when, for example, an insurance company markets flood protection insurance to homeowners living in a river's floodplain. Are either, or both, types of targeting ethically legitimate?

As an initial judgment, we must say that marketing that is targeted at those individuals who are vulnerable as consumers is unethical. This is a case of taking advantage of someone's frailty and manipulating it for one's own advantage. Clearly a portion of marketing and sales targets people who are vulnerable as consumers. Just as clearly such practices are wrong.

One way that this issue plays out involves groups who are vulnerable in both senses. Oftentimes people can become vulnerable as a consumer *because* they are vulnerable in some more general sense. The vulnerability that many elderly have with respect to injuries and illness might cause them to make consumer choices based on fear or guilt. A family member grieving over the death of a loved one might make choices in purchasing funeral services based on guilt or sorrow, rather than on a considered judgment. A person with a medical condition or disease is vulnerable, and the anxiety or fear associated with this vulnerability can lead to uninformed consumer choices. An inner city resident who is poor, uneducated, and chronically unemployed is unlikely to weigh the full consequences of the choice of alcoholic beverage.

A number of marketing campaigns seem to fit this model. The most abhorrent (and stereotypical) example is the ambulance-chasing attorney seeking a client for a personal-injury lawsuit. An accident victim is vulnerable to many harms and, while experiencing the stress of this situation, is unlikely to make a fully informed choice about legal representation. Marketing campaigns that target the elderly for such products as supplemental medical insurance, life insurance, emergency call devices, funeral services, and insurance often play on the fears, anxiety, and guilt that many elderly people experience. (See preceding and following Decision Points to consider examples of marketing to particular populations.)

But just as people can be made vulnerable as consumers because they are vulnerable to other harms, there can also be cases in which people become vulnerable to other harms because they are vulnerable as consumers. Perhaps this strategy is the most abhorrent case of unethical marketing. Certain products—tobacco and alcohol are the most obvious examples—can make an individual vulnerable to a wide range of health risks. Marketing campaigns for products that target people who are vulnerable as consumers seem ethically repugnant. This explains the particular public outrage directed at tobacco and alcohol companies that target young people. Companies that market alcoholic beverages in poor inner-city neighborhoods must take this ethical guideline into account. Marketing malt beverages, fortified wines, and other alcoholic drinks to poor inner-city residents must acknowledge that many people in such situations are not fully autonomous consumers. Many people in such situations drink to get drunk; they drink to escape; they drink because they are alcoholics.

→ Principles of scientific management

Is there an age below which marketers ought not to target commercial products? Is every person, regardless of age, a potential consumer? The market potential of young people is huge. According to one 2001 report, children's spending tripled in the 1990s. Children between the ages of 4 and 12 spent $2.2 billion in 1968, $4.2 billion in 1984, $17.1 billion in 1994, and more than $40 billion by 2002. Estimates are that direct buying by children is expected to exceed $51.8 billion by 2006. This makes young people an attractive target for marketers, and where better to target marketing than in schools?

Commercials in schools occur in many forms. Products are directly advertised in a variety of formats and circumstances, including on school busses and through Channel One, a for-profit media company that produces news programming shown daily in thousands of middle and high school classrooms. Indirect advertising occurs with sponsorships of school activities and supplies. Many products are sold in and by schools and many schools participate in a variety of marketing research studies. In every case, schools provide the occasion for students to learn about some commercial product.

Hawthorne Studies — more attention, ↑ productivity.

- Should advertising be allowed in schools?
- What facts would you want to know before deciding this question?
- What alternative marketing practices are open to companies that sell products to children? If some school districts propose advertising on and in buses, which are public property paid for by tax dollars, does that raise additional issues?
- Who are the stakeholders of your decision? What is the impact of each alternative decision on each stakeholder you have identified?
- What rights and duties are involved?
- How would you decide the case? Is it mostly a matter of consequences, or are important principles involved?

Frank Gilbreth? Time + Motion Studies.

One final form of marketing to a vulnerable population involves potentially all of us as consumer targets. We are each vulnerable when we are not aware that we are subject to a marketing campaign. This type of campaign is called "stealth" or "undercover" marketing and refers to those situations where we are subject to directed commercial activity without our knowledge. Certainly we are subjected to numerous communications on a regular basis without paying much attention, such as the billboards at which we might glance sideways as we speed past on a highway. That is not undercover marketing. Instead, undercover marketing is an intentional effort to hide the true marketing element of the interaction. For example, Sony Ericsson Mobile Communications hired 60 actors to pose as tourists in New York City's Empire State Building. The actor/tourists were supposed to pretend they were tourists and to ask passersby if they would mind taking their pictures. In doing so, the unsuspecting passersby had a chance to see how easy the new Ericsson mobile phone cameras were to operate. The actors praised the phones and said how much they loved them, and the passersby left having had a good experience with the new product, unaware they were just involved in a product test!

Reality Check *Word-of-Mouth Marketing*

The above practices should not be confused with "word-of-mouth marketing," which refers to those efforts by companies to generate personal recommendations by users. The Word of Mouth Marketing Association (WOMMA, www.womma.org) produced a Code of Ethics in 2005 which sought to distinguish word-of-mouth marketing from stealth and buzz marketing, both of which had received a great deal of press at that time. The WOMMA explained that "this is a first step in the complicated process of building an industry based on consumer respect and fundamental ethical principles."

The essence of the WOMMA Code comes down to the Honesty ROI:

- **Honesty of Relationship:** You say who you're speaking for
- **Honesty of Opinion:** You say what you believe
- **Honesty of Identity:** You never obscure your identity

THE WOMMA CODE OF ETHICS: SUMMARY

1. Consumer protection and respect are paramount.

2. We uphold the Honesty ROI: Honesty of Relationship, Opinion, and Identity.
3. We respect the rules of the venue.
4. We manage relationships with minors responsibly.
5. We promote honest downstream communications.
6. We protect privacy and permission.

WOMMA CODE OF ETHICS: FUNDAMENTAL PRINCIPLES

1. Happy, interested people will say good things about you.
2. Honest, genuine opinion is our medium.
3. We start, support, and simplify the sharing.
4. Word of mouth cannot be faked.
5. Word of mouth marketing empowers the consumer.

Source: From www.womma.org. Reprinted by permission of Word of Mouth Marketing Association.

With the advent of blogs, stealth marketing has hit the Internet, as well. Internet users reading a product review cannot know if the individual posting the review is a user, the product's manufacturer, or even a competitor posting a negative review just to sway consumers away from the product. "Buzz marketing," where people are paid to create a "buzz" around a new product by using it or discussing in ways that create media or other attention, also creates the potential for unspoken conflicts of interest. See the preceding Reality Check for the distinction between buzz marketing and **word-of-mouth marketing** practices.

Marketing experts consider stealth marketing extraordinarily effective because the consumer's guard is down; she is not questioning the message as she might challenge a traditional advertising campaign. Consumers do not seek out the communicator's vested interest; they see the communication as more personal and often tend to trust the communicator much more than they would trust an advertisement or other marketing material.

Where these practices simply involve the use of a product and the honest response to that use, arguably there is no deception. However, where the practice—however termed—involves subversion and deception to encourage a product's use, or deception surrounding the fact that a practice is part of a marketing campaign, it is challenging to argue that the practice remains ethical. From a universalist perspective, there is a violation of trust in the communication, which could also lead to a sense of betrayal so the consumer may no longer trust the company itself. In addition, the consumer is no longer being treated as an end in itself but instrumentally only as a means to the manufacturer's end. Further, if stealth marketing becomes the universal practice, the erosion of trust could become so significant that our commercial interactions would disintegrate under burdens of disclosures that would then be necessary.

Utilitarian analysis also does not support the ethics of these types of practices. When a consumer cannot trust the company's communication, the consumer may also lose faith in the company as a whole and will choose to purchase products and services elsewhere. Neither the company nor the consumer benefits from this result, and a product or service that might otherwise be the most effective or efficient solution may cease production because of a faulty marketing campaign.

Supply Chain Responsibility

OBJECTIVE

In creating a product, promoting it, and bringing it to the market, the marketing function of business involves a wide range of relationships with other commercial entities. In recent decades, the ethical spotlight has focused on the responsibility that a firm has for the activities of these other entities, what we shall refer to as supply chain responsibility. Few businesses have received as much attention in this regard as Nike.

Nike is the world's largest athletic shoe and apparel maker. In 1999, Nike held over 30 percent of the world's market share for athletic footwear, and along with Adidas (15 percent) and Reebok (11 percent) controls more than half of the world market. Nike began business in 1964 as Blue Ribbon Sports, an importer and marketer of low-priced Japanese sport shoes. As sales increased, the company began to design its own line of shoes and subcontract the manufacturing of the shoes to Japanese firms, eventually changing its name to Nike. Nike's Web site described its business philosophy decades later in the following words:

> Our business model in 1964 is essentially the same as our model today: We grow
> by investing our money in design, development, marketing and sales and then
> contract with other companies to manufacture our products.

In the late 1990s, as discussed in Chapter 6, Nike was subjected to intense international criticism for the working conditions in the factories where its products were manufactured. Critics charged that Nike relied on child labor and sweatshops in producing their shoes. They charged that workers in these factories were paid pennies a day, were subjected to cruel, unhealthy, and inhumane working conditions, were harassed and abused, and were prohibited from any union or collective bargaining activities.

Nike initially seemed to ignore the critics and deflect any criticism by denying responsibility for the behavior of its suppliers. If local manufacturers treated their workers poorly, that was beyond Nike's responsibility. At one point, Nike's vice president for Asia claimed that Nike did not "know the first thing about manufacturing. We are marketers and designers." Nike soon learned that the public was not persuaded by this response.

Ordinarily, we do not hold a person responsible for the actions of someone else. Assuming that the other person is an autonomous agent, we believe that each person is responsible for her or his own actions. But this is not always the case. There is a legal parallel to the idea that a business should be held responsible for the actions of its suppliers. The doctrine of *respondent superior,* Latin for "let the master answer," holds a principal (e.g., an employer) responsible for the actions of an agent (e.g., an employee) when that agent is acting in the ordinary course of his or her duties to the principal.[10] Thus, in the standard example, an employer can be held liable for damages caused by an accident involving an employee driving the company car on company business.

The justification for doing what might otherwise be considered unfair is that the agent is acting on the principal's behalf, at the principal's direction, and that the principal has direct influence over the agent's actions. Thus, if someone is doing something for you, at your direction, and under your influence, then you must take at least some responsibility for that person's actions. Most of the ethical rationale for business's responsibility for the actions of its suppliers stems from two of these conditions: Suppliers often act at the direction of business, and business often exercises significant influence over the actions of its suppliers.

However, in the multinational apparel and footwear industry, historically the corporate brands accepted responsibility only for their own organizations and specifically did not regard themselves as accountable for the labor abuses of their contractors (see Figure 8.1). This conception changed as multinationals and others became more aware of working conditions in these factories and the lack of legal protections for workers. Today, multinationals customarily accept this responsibility and use their leverage to encourage suppliers to have positive working environments for workers. The new concept of responsibility travels far deeper throughout the entire supply chain system, as is depicted in Figure 8.2. Each

FIGURE 8.1
Historical Responsibility

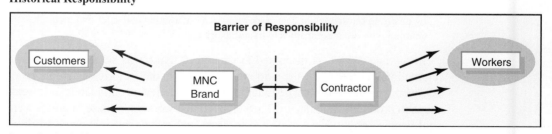

Source: Reprinted with permission from D. Arnold and L. Hartman, "Moral Imagination and the Future of Sweatshops,"
Business & Society Review 108, no. 4 (2003).

FIGURE 8.2   **Evolved Concept of Responsibility**

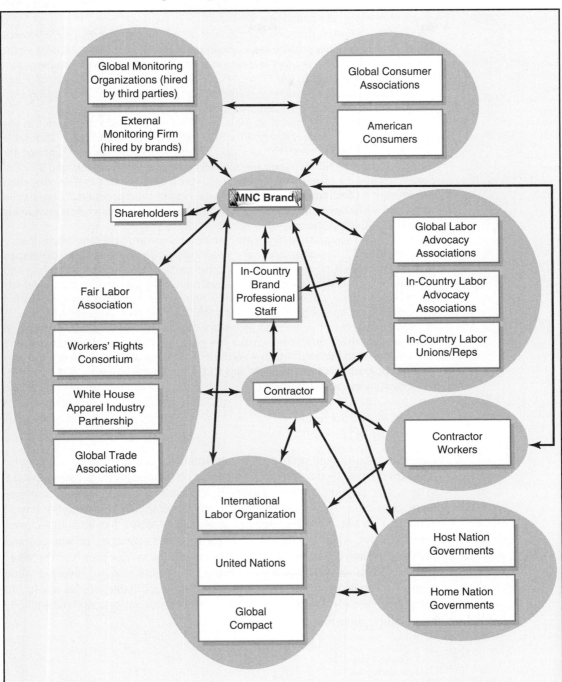

Source: Reprinted with permission from D. Arnold and L. Hartman, "Moral Imagination and the Future of Sweatshops,"
Business & Society Review 108, no. 4 (2003).

Consider how a firm might market such household products as laundry soap differently in India than in the United States. Marketing in the United States can involve large plastic containers, sold at a low per-unit cost. Trucks transport cases from manufacturing plant to wholesale warehouses to giant big-box retailers where they can sit in inventory until purchase. Consumers wheel the heavy containers out to their cars in shopping carts and store them at home in the laundry room.

The aggregate soap market in India could be greater than the market in the United States, but Indian consumers would require smaller and more affordable containers. Prahalad therefore talks about the need for single-size servings for many consumer products. Given longer and more erratic work hours and a lack of personal transportation, the poor often lack access to markets. Creative marketing would need to find ways to provide easier access to their products. Longer store hours and wider and more convenient distribution channels can reach consumers otherwise left out of the market.

So, too, can imaginative financing, credit, and pricing schemes. Microfinance and microcredit arrangements are developing throughout less developed economies as creative means to support the capacity of poor people to buy and sell goods and services. Finally, innovative marketing can ensure that products are available where and when the world's poor need them. Base-of-the-pyramid consumers tend to be cash customers with incomes that are unpredictable. A distributional system that ensures product availability at the time and place when customers are ready and able to make the purchase can help create the capacity to consume. Prahalad's approach—tied to moral imagination discussed previously —responds both to the consumers and to the corporate investors and other for-profit multinational stakeholders.

element of what should strike you as a tremendously complicated set of interrelationships is based on the potential to influence or exercise leverage throughout the system. The question, however, relates back to our earlier discussion of responsibility. How far down—or across—the supply chain should responsibility travel? Should a firm like Nike truly be responsible for the entire footwear and apparel system? If not, where would you draw the line as a consumer, or where would you draw the line if you were the corporate responsibility vice president for Nike? What response will most effectively protect the rights of those involved while creating the most appropriate incentives to achieve profitable, ethical results? In today's increasingly complicated, globalized multinational systems, stakeholders have yet to resolve this challenging dilemma.

Questions, Projects, and Exercises

1. Are some products too dangerous to be marketed in any circumstance? What regulations, if any, would you place on marketing cigarettes? Handguns? Prescription drugs?

2. Conduct a classroom debate on the McDonald's spilt coffee case. Conduct an Internet search for this case (*Liebeck* v. *McDonald's*) to find both legal and journalistic comments on this case. One-third of the class should play the role of Mrs. Liebeck's attorneys, one-third the role of McDonald's attorneys, and one-third the role of the judge and jury.

3. Research the case *Pelman* v. *McDonald's* in which it was alleged that McDonald's was partially responsible for the health problems associated with the obesity of children who eat McDonald's fast food. Should McDonald's and other fast-food restaurants be judged negligent for selling dangerous products, failing to warn consumers of the dangers of a high-fat diet, and deceptive advertising?

4. The Federal Trade Commission regulates advertising on the basis of two criteria: deception and unfairness. How can an ad be unfair? Who gets hurt by deceptive advertising?

5. Collect several sample prescription drug ads from magazines, newspapers, and television. On the basis of location of the ad, what do you think is the intended target audience? Are the ads in any way misleading? Are the required side-effect warnings deceptive in any way? Do you believe that health care professionals provide adequate screening to ensure that prescription drugs are not misused?

6. Review the Decision Point concerning marketing in the schools and Channel One and reflect on your own educational experience. Assume you were offered a laptop computer as long as you understood that you would see a commercial every time you turned it on and for two minutes for every fifteen minutes of use. How would you feel about this arrangement from a gut perspective? As you consider it in greater detail, what types of restrictions on advertisements do you think the laptop manufacturer (or service provider who is responsible for managing the advertising messages) should impose if the laptops will be given to college-aged students? How would you develop standards for these restrictions?

7. Many salespeople are compensated predominantly on a commission basis. In other words, though the salesperson receives a small base hourly rate, most of her or his compensation derives from a percentage of the price of items sold. Since basically the salesperson makes money only if you buy something and he or she makes more money if you spend more money, do you ever trust a salesperson's opinion? What would make you more likely to trust a commission-based salesperson, or less likely? Is there anything a commissioned salesperson could do to get you to trust her or him? Best Buy, the consumer electronics store, communicates to consumers that it does *not* pay its salespeople on the basis of commissions in order to encourage objectivity. Are you more likely to go to Best Buy as a result?

8. In 2001 TAP Pharmaceuticals pled guilty to participating in a criminal conspiracy with doctors by providing free samples of Lupron for which the doctors later billed Medicare and patients. Federal prosecutors also charged TAP executives and midlevel managers with fraud, alleging that TAP employees bribed doctors and hospitals with cash, free vacations, and free samples as an incentive for them to prescribe Lupron. Defendants argued that the samples and gifts were standard industry practice and did not amount to a bribe. In December 2004, a jury acquitted the individuals involved. TAP itself settled its case with the government by agreeing to pay $150 million restitution to consumers and insurance companies for what the government charged were artificially inflated drug prices. The prices were inflated because of the alleged bribes paid to doctors. TAP

did not admit to any wrongdoing, claiming that it settled to avoid further legal costs. Studies have shown that samples, as well as small gifts and lunches, can lead doctors to prescribe more expensive brand names when cheaper generic drugs would be as effective. What additional facts might you need to know to make a fully informed judgment in this case? What outcome do you believe the pharmaceutical companies are striving to achieve through these practices? What alternatives might be available to pharmaceutical companies to serve a similar outcome without incurring legal liability or crossing ethical lines? Do the doctors or hospitals bear any ethical responsibility under these circumstances? What duties do the pharmaceutical companies, doctors, or hospitals have? What does the principle of fairness require in this case? What rights are implicated?

Key Terms

After reading this chapter, you should have a clear understanding of the following Key Terms. The page numbers refer to the point at which they were discussed in the chapter. For a more complete definition, please see the Glossary.

caveat emptor approach, *p. 319*

"Four Ps" of marketing, *p. 314*

implied warranty of merchantability, *p. 321*

marketing, *p. 313*

negligence, *p. 322*

prima facie, *p. 315*

stealth marketing, *p. 339*

strict liability, *p. 322*

word-of-mouth marketing, *p. 340*

Endnotes

1. C.K. Prahalad, *The Fortune at the Bottom of the Pyramid* (Upper Saddle River, NJ: Wharton Publishing, 2005)

2. The Levitt quote is taken from Theodore Levitt, "Marketing and the Corporate Purpose: The Purpose Is to Create and Keep a Customer," a speech delivered at New York University, March 2, 1977, available from Vital Speeches of the Day. Similar claims can be found in Theodore Levitt, "Marketing and the Corporate Purpose," Chapter 1 of *The Marketing Imagination* (New York: Free Press, 1983), pp. 5 and 7.

3. The American Marketing Association definition is taken from its Web site: http://www.marketingpower.com/

4. An informal Internet search found over a hundred companies advertising with this slogan. They ranged from real estate companies to antique dealers, and from long-distance phone providers to water filtration systems dealers. Presumably those who disagree do not advertise that fact.

5. See, for example, the PBS video *Affluenza,* produced by KCTS/Seattle and Oregon Public Broadcasting. See also Juliet Shor, "Why Do We Consume So Much?", the Clemens Lecture at St. John's University, in *Contemporary Issues in Business Ethics,* Joseph DesJardins and John McCall, eds., (Belmont, CA. Wadsworth Publishing, 2005); and Jim Pooler, *"Why We Shop: Emotional Rewards and Retail Strategies"* (Westport, CT: Praeger Publishing, 2003).

6. Regina Lawrence, "Framing Obesity: The Evolution of News Discourse on a Public Health Issue," Harvard University Working Paper No. 2004-5, 2004, http://www.ksg.harvard.edu/presspol/Research_Publications/Papers/Working_Papers/2004_5.pdf.

7. References have been removed but are available from the authors.

8. McCann-Erickson U.S. Advertising Volume Reports and Bob Coen's Insider's Report for December 2005, http://www.mccann.com/news/pdfs/insiders05.pdf, accessed 6/16/06.

9. Direct Marketing Association, http://www.the-dma.org/cgi/disppressrelease?article=787 (May 2006).

10. This parallel is explained in Michael Santoro, *Profits and Principles: Global Capitalism and Human Rights in China* (Ithaca, NY: Cornell University Press, 2000), p. 161, and is cited as well by Denis Arnold and Norman Bowie, "Sweatshops and Respects for Persons," *Business Ethics Quarterly* 13, no. 2 (2003), pp. 221–242.

Readings

Reading 8-1: "An Interview with Alex Molnar," by Jay Huber, *p. 347.*

Reading 8-2: "Sony Online Entertainment: EverQuest® or EverCrack?" by Laura P. Hartman and Moses L. Pava, *p. 351.*

Reading 8-3: "Everquest®: A Rejoinder to Hartman and Pava," by Tara Radin, *p. 361.*

Reading 8-4: "Wrestling with Ethics: Is Marketing Ethics an Oxymoron?" by Philip Kotler, *p. 362.*

Reading **8-1**

An Interview with Alex Molnar*

Jay Huber

Stay Free!: Early in the book you bring up the Apples program, where people, by buying stuff at sponsoring stores, help schools get Apple computers. Does your criticism of that program boil down to it not being generous enough? Because you bring up the actual percentage of the amount that was set aside and take issue with that.

Molnar: It's pretty much just a straightforward marketing scam. It's an attempt to get parents to purchase products at stores that they might or might not otherwise patronize, on the grounds that they're somehow improving the chances that their children will have access to computer technology. But you gotta spend an awful lot of money to get any computer technology, because the way the rules are rigged, the people who make the most from the Apples for Computers game are the people who buy the computers from the manufacturer and then sell them to the marketers that run the contest. For a store that participates it's neither here nor there; they have a marketing budget and they spend it on this instead of something else. So, a marketer goes to them and says, Spend your advertising dollars this way. For the store, it doesn't make any difference at all. The big bucks are really for the people who inflate the cost of the computers to make their profit. Instead of being something that's really win-win for the kids, it's nothing more than a very large money-making operation for the middle people. If computer technology is important, I'm trying to imagine a stupider way of equipping schools with computers. If children need access to computer technology, then it ought to be a fundamental part of the school program. It ought to be paid for with tax dollars and every child ought to have equal access to that technology. It shouldn't be dependent on whether a parent can afford to buy $150 worth of flank steak at Cole's.

Looking at it from a local level, with locally owned companies, can the desire to help out the local school system and the desire to get a good marketing push or a bit of goodwill out of it, can those desires coexist in any productive way?

No. First of all, although the Supreme Court at the end of the nineteenth century established the Constitutional fiction that corporations are legal individuals and that therefore
they have constitutional protections that individuals have, that was kind of a nutty decision
that has cast a long shadow over a lot of things. Quite apart from the legal consequences
of it, it's led to a kind of assumption that we can talk about corporations the same way we
can talk about individuals in everyday life. In fact, corporations are special interests. They
have a legal obligation to promote the welfare of the people that own them. Simple as that,
whether it's a closely held corporation owned by private individuals, or whether it's a publicly traded corporation. Any kind of scheme that involves a corporation will be held to one
test, and that test is: does this benefit the corporation? Any other benefit that may accrue
is tangential to that, is secondary to that. So any relationship with a business that a school
enters into is characterized by the business first and foremost serving itself. Those interests
may or may not coincide with the interests of the school. Most often they don't.

The other problem of thinking about corporations as individuals is that at a practical level, people tend to talk about corporate involvement and corporate citizenship with
regard to schools and think about it the same way in which they think about a local PTO
member (Parent-Teacher Organization) volunteering to do something for the schools. And
it's absurd. Can you imagine in your wildest dreams that a father or mother volunteering
to tutor children in a school would only do so if they were allowed to promote the business
they worked for? People would say, What a reprehensible parent.

**On the other hand, I could see the example of a fairly conscientious executive or a
local CEO who says, "Hmm, you know, I really want to tutor poor kids who are reading several grades below level, and gosh, we can get our name out there at the same
time." Does that latter motivation ultimately trump the former motivation?**

Absolutely it does. If a business executive wants to tutor children, what's wrong with
that? That's a wonderful and laudable thing to do. Why should that carry any other freight?

* * * *

**... A recent educational supplement of *The New York Times* talked about how Colo-
rado Springs and Seattle were examples of school systems that accept advertising
dollars. The ostensible motivation for that is that they are cash-strapped and in places
where any sort of tax revenue increase is highly unlikely.**
Actually, in Washington state, it is possible.

I guess the way the writer couched it ...

That's the rhetoric that's coming out of the school board. Certainly in a place like Colorado Springs, which is very conservative, it's probably not very likely that they're going to
be able to raise tax revenue, or there's a strong public resistance to it ... Since you read
that, Jay, you realize that the amount of money that's even going full-tilt boogie ... Colorado Springs is raising peanuts. About $68,000.

* * * *

**So the notion that this money can somehow be a necessary evil to alleviate cash short-
ages is a joke because it won't even come close to serving that function.**

If you're going to discuss it within that frame of reference, then that's right: it's a joke.
However, even if it would raise the necessary money, I'd say you shouldn't do it. Even if
you accepted the premises of the argument, it's a wrong-headed argument. I don't accept
the premises of the argument because I don't think that advertising, which is in essence
propaganda, is consistent with the purposes of education. It's like matter and antimatter.
They don't fit together.

Let's talk about that. A libertarian [Nick Gillespie] proposed to me the idea that classrooms are not uncontested space. There's ideology and agendas coming from various angles, even if you exclude commercials. In one sense, you can't really say that you can make the classroom a commercial-free zone, because there's all kinds of competing agendas already taking place.

I'd regard that as kind of a nutty argument, too. And the reason I say *nutty* is because *of course* it's a contested space. But the point is that it's contested explicitly with reference to public pedagogical, educational, and civic values. And that's very different than inserting propaganda, which is incomplete, misleading, and whose explicit purpose is not to promote the best interests of the children, but the welfare of the corporation. I mean that's an absolute given. And that's uncontested.

So of course classrooms and curriculum are contested space. What does it mean to promote the welfare of children? That's a question that contains all shades of meaning and is subject to all kinds of different interpretations. I think it should be that way. I agree with that. The question is: What is legitimate to contest and what isn't? Would your libertarian friend say that the most important contest that goes on in the classroom is the duel between Pepsi and Coke? Is that what we reduce our civic dialogue to?

He seems to think that some of these commercial inroads into the classrooms can be used for purposes of media critique.

Yeah, but you can't turn the whole school curriculum into media criticism. The problem is, most teachers are not trained in media criticism, they're trained in English or social studies or whatever. So, as a practical matter, that's not gonna happen.

Secondly, since most advertising propaganda is good propaganda, it never literally lies. It's either empty, in an appeal to the emotions: "Pepsi's cool," "Sprite is what's happening." And so on. It's empty, it means nothing. I was in Germany and I saw a commercial for Pepsi, and the whole tagline of the commercial was "Pepsi *is* America." Well, what's that? It's either empty or, it's really good propaganda in the sense that it doesn't tell you the complete story. In other words, it lies by omission. And most teachers are not able to be well-enough trained, or have the time, to say, "Look at all the things that are omitted. Look at all the things that weren't said."

I guess I was going to get into Channel One in that regard, too, because this educational supplement in *The New York Times* said that Channel One is now in almost 40 percent of the secondary schools in the country.

According to them, it's in about 12,000 [schools], but then they want to pump up their numbers to get advertising bucks. According to the NEA, it's in about 8,000. The figure's probably somewhere in between.

It's still fairly extraordinary. Given that, is it even a possible way to salvage the use of the thing with media critique. I mean, if it's going to be in the school already ...

Not really, because of the contract terms. The terms have varied somewhat over the years; sometimes an individual school could negotiate a slightly different contract. But, in essence, 90 percent of the children need to be watching the program 90 percent of the time. In most schools, that means that those programs are broadcast in any class the child happens to be in when the program is broadcast. That might be homeroom, that might be science, it might be math, it might be anything. It might be gym. The idea that this is somehow going to be subject to media scrutiny is nonsense.

I hadn't realized that the element of control was so completely removed from the school.

Oh, the school has no control at all. None at all. Channel One is the antithesis of local control of curriculum. Nobody at the school knows what the content of that program is going to be until it appears on their screen.

Given that, you don't think that the North Carolina Supreme Court decision was correct? That is, you don't think the control should remain local.

Channel One would use whatever argument it can to make its tawdry bucks. The question of whether or not it's constitutional, despite their motives and intentions, is an entirely different thing. I think the North Carolina Supreme Court was led astray in the arguments. Schools are a creature of the state, not of local school districts. School districts are created as administrative contrivances of the state. If North Carolina wanted to disband all of its school districts tomorrow, it could. The ability of the state to regulate the schools strikes me as unassailable. Obviously the North Carolina Supreme Court disagrees. But I'm not sure constitutionally that's the final word on it. The federal Constitution reserves to the states all powers not explicitly granted to the federal government and education is not explicitly granted to the federal government; it's therefore state responsibility. It is not the primary responsibility of some school district which is itself a creature of the state. The federal government can't devolve powers that the Constitution reserves to it. It's like you can't sell your right to vote.

You bring up the *Nation at Risk* report at the beginning of the book, and you talk about how that led to this wave of corporate activism, and all the market ideas started flowering out of that. One thing that the corporate world certainly has is money. And this sort of touches on the later chapters on charter schools and privatization and that is: Are the public schools suffering from a huge PR problem? Is the crisis in education in some large way a huge corporate PR boondoggle to allow the public opinion to be more sympathetic to all these market ideas?

Corporate executives are all over on public education. Again, what corporate executives do best is serve their own purposes. I mean, we are fast evolving in this country a kind of mandarin class of wildly overpaid prima donnas called CEOs. So the first people they serve is themselves, the second people they serve are their corporate shareholders or owners, and so on. I think schools figure in some of this thought but only insofar as they might be able to use the schools to solve a public relations problem. Like Waste Management provides college scholarships to students at Carver High School in Chicago because they had this huge fine for dumping toxic waste in that neighborhood. That really doesn't have anything to do with education per se, it's just, "What the hell can we do to get out from under this public relations blemish?"

Some corporate executives are fairly enlightened. If I had to choose the educational values that they express personally, I would support them as opposed to many other folks. And other corporate executives see education as either a market to be exploited—I think Louis Gerstner, Jr. [CEO of IBM], is a prime example of that—or they see education as a cost to be contained. So I think corporate executives are just all over the map. These market-based school reforms are gaining adherence because anybody who's taken a look at the demographics at all realizes that with public education setting record enrollments—and it will continue to increase for about the next eight years—the potential tax liability is enormous. So the question is how do you contain the cost of that? If you look at the tax structure of most states, it doesn't take a genius to realize that corporations are going to have to pay more. Unless something gives, they gotta pay more because the people who had been footing the bill can't afford to anymore.

I think a lot of this sympathy is based on a fairly straightforward calculus as: this is a way of reducing our tax liability. These reforms are not only consistent with our basic ideological predisposition–I mean, I kind of like the idea of "the market," I like the sound of "competition," and all of this other stuff–but, Christ, they probably cost less. There's a lot of things that go into building corporate support or consensus about so-called market-based school reforms, privatization.

Source: Copyright © Stay Free! #13. Excerpted from original article and reprinted with permission of *Stay Free* magazine, www.stayfreemagazine.org.

*Alex Molnar is a professor at the University of Wisconsin–Milwaukee, author of *Giving Kids the Business: The Commercialization of America's Schools,* and one of the nation's leading experts on the commercialization of public education.

* * * *

Reading **8-2**

Sony Online Entertainment: *EverQuest® or EverCrack? Oxford-Style Debate Presented at Tenth Annual International Conference Promoting Business Ethics*

Laura P. Hartman and Moses L. Pava

Abstract

This Oxford-style debate was held at the Tenth Annual International Conference Promoting Business Ethics between Laura Hartman, J.D., and Dr. Moses Pava. . . . In a traditional Oxford-style debate, two debaters take opposing viewpoints and the third debater argues the neutral position. At the Conference, the modified format featured the two debaters presenting diametrically opposing views—corporate responsibility versus personal responsibility. This modified format was also used during the Ethics Awareness Week, with University professors presenting the debate before the student body. Ms. Hartman's position focused on the personal responsibility by Mr. Woolley while Dr. Pava opined that Sony Online Entertainment had corporate responsibility toward Mr. Woolley and all other individuals similarly situated.

Ms. Hartman's Presentation

The question put to our debate today is who shall bear the responsibility for the death of young Mr. Wooley. Personally, I believe that we're here arguing this issue, not because of a responsibility of Sony Online Entertainment, but instead simply because we have a need in our society to blame. By validating our blame, we then feel better able to prevent harm in the future. If we can find the cause, we can prevent the damage next time.

But, unfortunately, this is not always the case—and certainly not the case in this particular instance. As stated by Judge Nelson in the seminal case on this topic, "tragedies such as this simply defy rational explanation, and courts should not pretend otherwise." Nor should my esteemed colleague from the East and nor should we all.

Note: Citations and references have been deleted, but are available from the authors.

In my allotted time, I will set forth my plea that we not extend liability—whether legal or ethical—to Sony for the unforeseen death of Mr. Wooley. If we were to do so, we would have no choice but to barrel down the slippery slope of responsibility in connection with everything from a child's television addiction to Teletubbies and Clifford, to those who overeat because of tantalizing candy packaging.

Consider the possibilities of a slippery slope if we impose liability—in any manner—on the supplier of entertainment for the implications of enjoying the entertainment. For example, there is extraordinarily more evidence of a real addiction to television among children. We allow significantly more violence—and in fact more widespread addiction—in our television and film media environments notwithstanding evidence that violence in the media begets violence in reality. Remarkably, the evidence is uncontroverted.

The question is this: if the general public and the Hollywood machine itself acknowledge that graphical violence in the media is bad for the individual and bad for society as a whole, why does it continue to grow and flourish?

The answer is simple: addiction.

A *New York Times* article reports the following:

> One study found that self-described [television] addicts watched an average of 56 hours a week; the A.C. Nielsen Company reports the average for adults is just above 30 hours a week. Recent studies have found that 2–12% of viewers see themselves as addicted to television; they feel unhappy watching as much as they do, yet seem powerless to stop themselves. . . .

> For compulsive viewers, inertia becomes extreme, so that the longer they watch, the more passive and less discriminating they become.

Similarly, a *Scientific American* article reported that 40 percent of adults and 70 percent of children surveyed said that they were watching more television than they would like. What is to blame here for any unfortunate implications? Our society has concluded that the networks, producers, and other providers of this entertainment are certainly not responsible. Instead, the responsibility lies flatly on the user. Though we wish there was someone else who could pay a price, the responsibility for Mr. Wooley's death also lies with Mr. Wooley and not Sony Online Entertainment.

My argument will focus on three areas, two teleological contentions and one deontological: (1) the lack of foreseeability of harm, (2) Mr. Wooley's assumption of risk in violating reasonable use expectations, and (3) Sony's right to freedom of speech. In considering the underlying claims with regard to Mr. Wooley's demise, perhaps we can learn from this third inquiry based on individual rights and responsibilities. What are Sony's rights in connection with this complaint? Freedom of expression and the right to product commercialization in a free market. What then are Sony's responsibilities with regard to the Wooley complaint? Our discussion of foreseeability and of assumption of risk will address this arena.

The overriding theme of this discussion is the nature of personal accountability itself. As stated by Judge Posner of the 7th Circuit, "people are unlikely to become well-functioning, independent-minded adults and responsible citizens if they are raised in an intellectual bubble." In that case, the video games involved were perceived as tremendously violent and inappropriate for children. Judge Posner held that preventing children from this type of exposure—certainly more insightful of violence to self and/or others than EverQuest®— was not warranted and in fact may be harmful in other ways, as he explains in his above comments. Besides, as has been stated in multiple arenas also in support of this concept of accountability, it is a significant challenge to blame another for an individual's suicide.

This accountability is reiterated in a statement by the Commission on Marketing and Advertising of the International Chamber of Commerce:

> Marketers and advertisers must market and sell their products to children in a responsible manner. It is equally important that other parties, such as parents, educators, the media, entertainment content providers and both governmental and non-governmental organizations should also play a role in helping children develop a critical understanding of advertising and other media messages.

Nowhere in the ICC's regulations relating to marketing is there any prohibition of marketing a product such as EverQuest®. In particular, the only prohibitions articulated under "social responsibility" include a proscription against discrimination, against unjustifiably playing on fear, inciting violence or encouraging reprehensible behavior, and against playing on superstition.

If we protect our children from exposure to experiences derived from video games that are so involving as to be considered addicting, how will these same children learn self-control, self-discipline and discrimination between and among the vast multitude of media experiences they are destined to have as adolescents and adults?

Lack of Foreseeability

The first basis on which I will argue against liability is the lack of foreseeability. The key to any responsibility here of any sort must first be premised on Sony's ability to have actually foreseen the potential death of Mr. Wooley. There is absolutely no evidence nor barely a reason to believe that Mr. Wooley's death was proximately related to Sony's game. Mrs. Wooley insists that it is simply her "guess" that something terrible in the game prompted Mr. Wooley's choice to commit suicide. Even if there were some evidence of proximate cause (which there is not), if the company could not possibly have anticipated the death, how can it be expected to prevent it?

In a similar case involving a youth who committed suicide after becoming engrossed in the role-playing game, Dungeons and Dragons, the conclusion was that a responsibility would only arise if the resulting harm could have reasonably been anticipated. In that case, the youth's mother asserted that Johnny had "never caused his mother any problems," and that "no one had any reason to know that Johnny Burnett was going to take his own life." The court explained that, if Johnny's own mother could not foresee the possible harm, how could the game manufacturer possibly have known?

If we conclude that Sony is responsible for the death of Mr. Wooley, aren't we then concluding as well that any manufacturer of a product that people enjoy and from which they simply "just cannot pull themselves away" is accountable for any resulting harm? Mark misses his children at the school bus because he can't pull himself away from his favorite soap opera? Is the broadcasting station responsible for resulting harm? Of course not. But it would be counterintuitive to claim that the producer is not striving for soap opera addiction, wouldn't it? Yet we would never consider that same producer responsible for the results of that addiction such as eating disorders, lack of attention to work, and so on.

In addition, also highly relevant to the concept of foreseeability—or lack thereof—is the fact that Mr. Wooley suffered from depression and a schizoid personality disorder. These aggravating factors could not possibly have been anticipated by Sony. Consider the following language from Watters:

> The defendant [game manufacturer] cannot be faulted, obviously, for putting its game on the market without attempting to ascertain the mental conditions of each

and every prospective player. The only practicable way of insuring that the game would never reach a "mentally fragile" individual would be to refrain from selling it at all.

This dicta was later used to support the successful defense of an entertainment firm that marketed the movie, *The Basketball Diaries,* against the claim that the movie incited the violence of several youths in the Columbine tragedy. As the court explained in *Watters,* "we are not dealing here with the kind of violence or depravity to which children can be exposed when they watch television, or go to the movies, or read the fairy tales of the Brothers Grimm, for example." Similarly the benign EverQuest® does not rise to those levels.

In the alternative, if the harm was foreseeable to any extent, shouldn't the weight of the responsibility fall on those who were most likely to be able to influence his actions? *48 Hours* explained that Mr. Wooley quit his job late the previous autumn, he stopped seeing his family, and he ceased to take care of himself and his apartment. His mother then realized that "he was completely addicted, playing all night and day." In fact, he was prone to epileptic seizures which were aggravated by the game; yet his mother permitted him to continue without intervention. Notwithstanding any responsibility of Sony to know that Mr. Wooley might have ill effects from playing the game, might not his mother have sensed a problem of some sort whatsoever at these admittedly abnormal occurrences?

Assumption of Risk and Reasonable Use

The next basis for Sony's defense is the concept of "assumption of risk." In this case, Mr. Wooley and his parents assumed a risk that was known—"Shawn was playing 12 hours a day, and he wasn't supposed to because he was epileptic and the game would cause seizures." In addition to the epilepsy, there remains the question of how a reasonable person would experience this game. Similar to the Watters case, there is no question but that Ever-Quest® is a "let's pretend" game—not an incitement to do anything more than exercise the imagination.

If Mr. Wooley chose to abuse the game by exceeding a reasonable playing time, with full knowledge of his epileptic risk, Sony should not bear responsibility for the results of his recklessness. It is neither Sony's legal nor ethical obligation to police all of its users as would, say, a parent.

Reasonable use of EverQuest® has never been shown to be harmful. Sony cannot be held responsible because certain individuals choose to use the product in an unreasonable manner.

It should be noted that this was a rare and individual case. To claim that addiction to EverQuest® was the decisive factor in his suicide is no more accurate than saying purchasing a computer drove his life to a premature end.

First Amendment Freedom of Speech

In considering Sony's affirmative defenses, it appears that Sony would have both a legal and an ethical defense to any responsibility based on the First Amendment. From a legal perspective, Sony might bear responsibility only if its expression (EverQuest®) was "directed to inciting or producing imminent lawless action and likely to incite or produce that action." Nowhere in any of the Wooley claims is there a contention that Sony's actions were "directed" to inciting or producing Mr. Wooley's suicide.

Significantly, not only has there been no contention in the literature that freedom of speech *should* be curtailed except in instances of violence, but the courts have not been willing to constrain speech even where it is contended that the expression *does* incite violence. In the case where a 13-year-old hung himself after watching a mock hanging on television, the court barred recovery against the broadcaster (even where the court found a negligent failure to give adequate warnings). In another case where a youth hurt himself while trying to duplicate a sound effect demonstrated on television, the court barred recovery on First Amendment grounds. In the name of the First Amendment, the courts have even precluded recovery in a case filed on behalf of a nine-year-old victim of a bizarre sexual crime committed by minors allegedly copying a similar crime seen on television! In Mr. Wooley's case, the facts are far less persuasive that Sony's expression (EverQuest®) somehow incited violence than the convincing, credible, and disturbing facts cited above.

From an ethical perspective, the freedom of speech is one of the most oft-cited hypernorms in the consideration of fundamental rights. In order to suggest this constraint on Sony's expression, the protection of its free expression must constitute an overwhelming violation of a countervailing value. Since prior arguments do not support this countervailing value, Sony's right to free expression would prevail.

Therefore, not only does the constraint hold no water from a legal perspective, but restricting this expression also violates fundamental concepts of human rights and hypernorms.

In conclusion, though in troubling times we strive to find someone to blame, someone to "pay," there remain those circumstances where we can look no further than the individual who engaged in the damaging act. In this case, that individual was Mr. Wooley, and Mr. Wooley alone. Sony Entertainment could not possibly have foreseen that harm would result from playing its game. In fact, the person best positioned to have foreseen the harm and perhaps even to have prevented it was Mr. Wooley's mother. She noticed his personality changes and changes in their relationship—factors of which Sony had no knowledge, of course. One hates to place an additional burden on an otherwise grieving mother in this circumstance. Perhaps pursuing this complaint in part helps her feel as if she is doing everything that she can since his death to reach peace.

Accountability also falls on Mr. Wooley for using the game in a manner that presented some risk to himself. By assuming this risk, Mr. Wooley violated Sony's expectations of reasonable use, thus preventing the aforementioned foreseeability. Finally, Sony's expression in EverQuest® is protected as free speech and our slippery slope argument has evidenced the ludicrousness of constraining this type of entertainment. What is next? A claim that someone is addicted to the *Lord of the Rings* trilogy and therefore was "forced" to spend their money to see the last installment?

Recall Judge Posner's caution that "people are unlikely to become well-functioning, independent-minded adults and responsible citizens if they are raised in an intellectual bubble." Let us not all sacrifice our adult capabilities and exposure simply because one man's behavior warrants it.

Dr. Pava's Presentation

Resolved: Sony bears no responsibility, whether ethically or legally, for damages incurred as a result of playing EverQuest®.

"Only a cheesy company can make real cheesy hamburgers." So goes the corporate motto of the hypothetical company Cheesy Cheese Hamburgers.

Cheesy Cheese is one of the leading purveyors of fast food in the world and is an American icon recognized across the globe.

Two years ago, though, things began to unravel for the fast food giant. The company was losing market share, and quarterly profits were down for the first time in anyone's memory. That's when the board hired Laura Headman. An attorney by training, Ms. Headman had gained a reputation over the years as a hard-nosed, no-nonsense hamburger wiz!

As Laura took over the reigns at Cheesy Cheese Hamburgers, she was concerned about the increasing popularity of some of the new restaurant chains that were attracting some of Cheesy Cheese's more upscale customers. Laura was also informed by her lawyers about a number of recent legal suits filed against the company claiming that Cheesy Cheese Hamburgers was responsible for their obesity problems. These legal suits had captured the imagination of the media, and some of the corporate giants in the industry had taken notice and action.

CEO Headman, however, was certain that these legal claims were just a frivolous nuisance. In fact, Laura believed strongly in the doctrine of the consumer as king. She was so convinced of Cheesy Cheese Hamburgers' right to sell as many hamburgers as it possibly could that she actually decided to increase the fat content in the company's fries and shakes after her research department informed her that the new recipes scored higher in head-to-head taste tests, especially among children and young teenagers.

Laura Headman also decided to refocus the chain's advertising, targeting the company's efforts directly to children and teenagers through clever television ads making use of well-known cartoon characters, movie-placements, and cereal tie-ins. Headman even has plans for a theme park built around Cheesy Cheese's corporate logo—the cheesy cow.

"This company got its start by inventing the idea of serving the best tasting fast food at very reasonable prices. I see no reason to deviate from this formula," said Laura. "We sell what families want, and that's what we're going to continue to do—only better and even more efficiently."

When asked about health concerns Laura laughed and said, "we're a fast food company for God's sake, and not a healthcare company. It is the consumers' responsibility to eat a well-balanced diet, not big brother's responsibility to make sure that they do."

Laura Headman's strategy is short-sighted. To claim that a company bears no responsibility for the effects of its product on consumer health is bad ethics and bad business. Sooner or later, as has happened in the tobacco industry, alcohol industry, and chemical and oil industries, Cheesy Cheese Hamburgers and its shareholders will need to rethink core business objectives and strategies, but by then it might be too late.

Even if it's too late for Cheesy Cheese Hamburgers, it's not too late yet for Sony Online Entertainment. Though I don't think anyone believes that Sony is legally liable for the death of Shawn Wooley—the 21-year-old young man, who quit his job, holed up in his apartment for a week, and whose body was found in a rocking chair at his computer desk with EverQuest® still playing on his computer screen—I do think that this case should serve as a shrill wake-up call to the industry.

Unlike Laura Headman in the Cheesy Cheese case, Scott McDaniel, VP of Marketing for Sony Online Entertainment, and John Smedley, President, are real flesh and blood executives and not products of someone's imagination. As high-level executives in the new and emerging industry of online fantasy games, they, like all of us, own a degree of responsibility for the products they invent, manufacture, and market.

It should go without saying that Mr. McDaniel is surely correct when he states that "There's a duty on the consumer to use it [the product] responsibly." Even more so, I would think it should go without saying that there is a duty on the part of the manufacturer to act responsibly. This is what is called corporate social responsibility, an idea endorsed at least in words by almost all major corporations in the world today including Sony.

EverQuest® players enter into an enormous virtual world called Norrath "with its own species, economic systems, alliances, and politics." Players create their own characters. They might choose to be elves, trolls, knights, or even monsters. What many game players find so exciting and liberating is, as the case states, that once the players choose a character, they are then "free to roam the fantasy world," slaying other monsters, forming guilds, and becoming the powerful rulers of Norrath.

Even Milton Friedman, the economist famous for endorsing the magical benefits of the free market system, would surely recognize the difference between the fantasy world of Norrath and the real world of corporate America.

In the case at hand, Sony is not operating in a virtual world with its own economic and political system. Scott McDaniel and John Smedley are neither gnomes nor monsters "free to roam the fantasy world" and to choose whether to be human or not, as game players are, but are high level business leaders morally responsible to a host of diverse stakeholders.

Like the hypothetical company Cheesy Cheese Hamburgers, Sony Online Entertainment is producing a product that is highly desirable and harmless to many and perhaps most consumers, but is also potentially dangerous to a significant number of them.

Consider some of the following facts:

- EverQuest® is so addictive that the average player spends 20 hours per week online. As the magazine, *Business 2.0*, calculates it, that's more man-hours per week than it took to build New York City's Empire State Building.
- One-third of players 18 and older spend more time playing EverQuest® than they do their real jobs.
- About two-thirds of players self-report that they are probably addicted to the game.
- About 5 percent of players play for more than 50 hours per week.
- About one out of five players self-report that they would spend all of their time online if they could.

There is some preliminary evidence that video games increase the production of dopamine, the molecular neurotransmitters of the brain that has been found to play a major role in other addictions like cocaine use.

As one player puts it, "I call myself an addict because I share the same symptoms as someone who's addicted to smoking, or alcohol, or some other substance. I think about EverQuest® when I'm not playing, I get stressed when I have to go 24 hours without logging on for a fix, and I wasn't able to quit when I tried. If that's not an addiction, I don't know what is."

If one defines an addiction as "a recurring behavior that is unhealthy or self-destructive which the individual has difficulty ending" as one researcher has, then there can be little doubt that EverQuest® is highly addictive for some players.

According to Addictions Counselor Jay Parker here are just some of the symptoms of computer game addiction:

- Failed attempts to control personal computer use for an extended period of time.
- Neglecting family and friends.
- Lying to employers and family about computer activity.
- Problems with school or job performance.
- Feelings of guilt, shame, anxiety, or depression.
- Obsessing about sexual acting out through the use of the Internet.
- Withdrawal from real life hobbies and social interactions.
- Denials, rationalizations, and minimization of adverse consequences stemming from computer use.

It appears that just as some addicts have a hard time admitting that a problem really exists, so too do Sony and its top executives. I don't think that Sony should stop producing its popular on-line games like Ever-Quest®, but I do believe that in the long run it is in the company's own interest to recognize its corporate social responsibilities. These responsibilities derive from Sony's huge information advantage over consumers and from the fact that its product, when used correctly, may be harmfully addictive to a minority of players.

Here are four simple ideas for meeting its obligations to its most vulnerable consumers:

- Sony should fund third-party research to determine the precise effects of its game. Although, as mentioned above, there is some preliminary research on the effects of computer games, more rigorous studies are needed, especially research on neurotransmitters and their relationship to computer game addiction.
- Sony should strongly consider putting on warning labels informing customers of the possibility of online addiction, even if Sony considers the probability of addiction to be quite low.
- Sony should stop marketing the game to children and young teenagers. Even the most staunch free-marketers recognize the limitations of children to make rational choices.
- Finally, Sony should change the incentives of the game. As it is currently set up, the longer one is online the more likely one's characters will be successful. In fact, the game continues even when one is not online and one's characters are at risk. In addition, because of the formation of teams, there is strong peer pressure to stay online as long as possible. Sony should also consider putting on a time limit on weekly play.

Let me conclude with a short quote from Nobuyuki Idei, Chairman and Chief Executive Officer of Sony:

Creating successful businesses in the short term is a goal of management. But I also feel that management must look beyond this to conduct corporate activities in a way that strikes a harmonious balance with diverse communities over the long term.

Ms. Hartman's Rebuttal Response to Dr. Pava

Did Sony have any responsibility at all for the death of Mr. Wooley?

Dr. Pava mentions our protagonist just ONCE in his argument, evidencing the lack of ANY link between Sony and Mr. Wooley at all!!

Instead, he found it necessary to make up a hypothetical that goes far beyond the facts of the current case. Evidently, he needed to do so since the current facts do not actually support a claim of Sony responsibility. It is completely understandable since I have found myself using the exact same ploy in class sometimes when I am struggling to make a point.

But, for better or worse, the slippery slope from manufacturing a video entertainment game to abetting obesity or heart disease from eating a high-fat diet is simply nonexistent. (Though I do not actually buy in to his contention that a company is responsible in any way for the eating habits of its consumers, either! What did YOU have for lunch today and did someone make you do it??)

In addition, I do not think even Dr. Pava's extensive research in this area could uncover a link between his hypothetical company's financial challenges and its subsequent intent to create an addiction to cheeseburgers, and Sony's current extraordinary financial comfort level. Sony has posted operating revenues of $62 billion and net income of $963 million for fiscal year 2003.

Instead, Dr. Pava chooses not to respond at all to the far more appropriate comparison between entertainment through a video game and entertainment through a sitcom or other television show. Dr. Pava bases his argument for Sony responsibility on a claim that "there is a duty on the part of the manufacturer to act responsibly." Of course Sony would agree that manufacturers have a duty to act responsibly—and THEY DID DO. Dr. Pava in fact fails to identify any standard of practice that Sony has not met or any way in which he could claim that they have been irresponsible.

Instead, he bases his entire argument on his contention that Sony is "producing a product that is highly desirable and harmless to many and perhaps most consumers." Well, of course, I would agree. He then offers a number of interesting facts about addiction. Also interesting. However, HE FAILS TO LINK THESE TWO DISCUSSIONS! There is absolutely nothing offered to you by my colleague that even begins to suggest medical evidence that Sony has encouraged an addiction to EverQuest®. And, without that link, a manufacturer has never been held liable for a customer's addiction to a product!

Further, he fails to cite even one case in the world that finds a manufacturer liable—legally or ethically—for an addiction to a video game (or to a television show, or cheeseburger, for that matter). Do you not think he would have told you about one if he could only have found one?

He has told you all that he could, and it is not enough to change the facts.

Dr. Pava's Rebuttal Response to Ms. Hartman

Let me begin this second part of the debate by noting my agreement with Laura.

I don't believe that Sony should be held legally responsible for the death of Shawn Wooley, As an aside, I should point out, in the interest of full disclosure, that if I were ever to get into the kind of trouble that Sony is in, I'd love to get Laura on my side as my defense attorney.

Unfortunately there is little else I can agree with in her presentation. Most importantly, *I would suggest that there is a stark difference between legal and ethical responsibilities.* In fact, this is what makes this case so interesting and important in the first place.

So, unlike Laura, I don't think that the only reason we're debating this case is because "we have a need in our society to blame." Rather, I believe the reason for engaging in this debate is to underscore the importance of corporate social responsibility to our society. Perhaps by raising these issues here and in the classroom, we can begin to protect the most vulnerable members of society (like Shawn Wooley) from being the victims of corporate manipulation.

This case demonstrates exactly why the concept of social responsibility is so important. Here is a situation where the legal remedy is probably too costly from society's point of view (Laura's right about that), but where a real sense of social responsibility just might make a difference (this is where Laura's mistake lies).

From a legalistic perspective, it may be true that Sony could not have *foreseen the death* of Shawn Wooley. But, from an ethical point of view, I'm not sure that this is the real issue. Could Sony have foreseen the possibility that some players might become addicted to their game, especially when the game never ends and the longer you play the better your odds are? And, further, doesn't Sony have an obligation to study the effects of its product on consumers, especially if these effects are unknown? These are not legal questions, of course, but are nothing more than a matter of common sense.

Laura also suggests that a basis for Sony's defense is the concept of the "*assumption of risk.*" She says, "Mr. Wooley assumed a risk that was known." This is a view that only a lawyer could love.

It misses the entire point of what addiction is all about. Addiction means you want to stop but you *can't*. Mr. Wooley didn't assume a risk that was known as if he was an economist specializing in rational choice theory. Mr. Wooley started playing a game that looked innocent enough but once he got started he couldn't stop.

Of course, we don't know whether or not EverQuest® is truly addictive from a scientific point of view or whether or not Mr. Wooley's death really had anything to do with his addiction, but minimally the case does demonstrate that Sony has a responsibility to its game players to find out. There is already enough evidence to make one extremely suspicious.

Laura believes in freedom of speech and so do I.

But when looked at from a social responsibility perspective and not from a legalistic perspective, this case shows how precarious this right is. The only way such a right can be maintained in a democracy such as ours is if citizens, including corporate executives, use the right constructively.

To the extent that a company exploits its right to freedom of speech in order to produce and market a game that is potentially dangerous to a sizeable group of consumers, it is acting in an irresponsible way, especially when it is marketing the game to children and young teenagers. Further, this kind of behavior makes it *more* difficult for proponents of free speech like Laura and myself to defend it not less difficult.

"If we protect our children from exposure to experiences derived from video games that are so involving as to be considered addicting, how will these same children learn self-control and self-discipline?" asks Laura.

Hmm. I don't know, but I'm sure if we all put on our thinking caps we could figure out a way to teach our children self-control in a world without EverQuest®. If nothing else works, we could always put them in front of the TV, buy them a Big Mac, pour them a Bud, and offer them a cigarette. That should do the trick!

Rushword Kidder recently identified the universities from which 13 executives graduated. These executives were drawn from the leadership ranks of firms such as Imclone, Tyco, Enron, Arthur Andersen and so on. Their alma mater(s) included Harvard, NYU, Ohio State, University of Houston, Northwestern, Tufts, SMU, Barnard, and other fine institutions. He then asked "how can you hold those schools accountable for the deviance of a few, when so many of their graduates care deeply about ethics?"

One might even add, certainly these universities could not have foreseen what these graduates would do in the future. And, these universities more than any other institution enjoy the protection of the First Amendment's right to freedom of speech.

But a recent President of the Business Ethics Society took Kidder to task. She asked, and I think correctly, "How can you hold those schools accountable? I ask how can we not? Consider the alternative. If we are not responsible for the impact (or lack thereof) that we have on our students, then what is our purpose? Doesn't each of us seek to leave an imprint on our students? And if that imprint is irrelevant to their later decisions, what is our value as educators?"

The President of the Business Ethics Society, Laura Hartman, was not suggesting that these schools bear a legal responsibility: she was suggesting that they bear a social responsibility.

Let me take Laura's own words and apply them to the case at hand.

How can we hold Sony accountable? I ask how can we not? Consider the alternative. If Sony is not responsible for the impact that it has on consumers, then what is its purpose? Certainly, Sony must have an obligation beyond its own self-interest.

Source: *Journal of Business Ethics,* vol. 58, no. 1 (2005), pp. 17–26.

Reading **8-3**

Everquest®: *A Rejoinder to Hartman and Pava*

Tara Radin

Interestingly, the popular TV drama *Boston Legal* recently featured an episode in which this very issue was addressed. In the episode, a mother sued a video game company when her son died from a heart attack after playing their game for two days straight, barely eating or drinking. The fictional TV show mentioned some very real studies that indicate that video gaming causes an adrenaline rush and an increase in dopamine levels, also linked to the reinforcing effects of drugs like cocaine. The assumption by many people tends to be that the fault here lies with the individual, and this was also the decision of the fictitious judge in *Boston Legal*, who ruled that there was insufficient evidence linking the dead child to any fault on the part of the video game company.

It is perhaps important to separate the intricacies of our legal system from the social and/or moral responsibility of corporations. In this situation, members of corporations are aware that intense video gaming has an effect on the brain similar to that of drugs—it can be called "addictive." This causes changes in some people who play video games, in that it has been observed that they stop taking care of themselves, in terms of regular sleep, eating, attention to work, and so on. In fact, the people who make these games know this and actually prey upon it, if indirectly, in that they endeavor to keep people engaged in their games as much as possible for as long as possible.

From a business perspective, Sony's strategy is ingenious. The more a person plays, the more he or she has to play in order to reach higher levels. In addition, there is an advantage to playing the game for multiple consecutive hours in terms of the progress the player is able to make. The very nature of the game therefore compounds any other addictive qualities of the game. The significant effect of Everquest® is manifest in the incredible community—even offline—that has developed around the game. Through eBay, Everquest® fans can bid on hundreds of weapons and characters that players have acquired—some that sell for more than a thousand dollars.

While the slippery slope to which Hartman refers is of very real concern, it is important to distinguish a product known to affect the brain in an addictive fashion from other sorts of potentially undesirable products. And while Mr. Wooley's death might have been unanticipated, it was not unforeseeable—the negative effect the game had on his life was entirely consistent with the strategy Sony set out to achieve. If we did not have sufficient evidence of this at the time of Mr. Wooley's death, we certainly do now.

Aside from the legal implications, what about Sony's moral responsibility? What about Abercrombie and Fitch, a clothing company that distributed a catalogue targeted to children and young adults, which featured provocative, explicit photos of group of scantily clad young people (labeled as pornography by some critics)? Should we have to rely on our legal system to send the message that this sort of predatory behavior is unacceptable? Or should not businesses be willing to take that responsibility on themselves?

Hartman's argument that excessive paternalism prevents vital learning is an important message, consistent with concern expressed regarding the decision by soft drink companies to remove most of their products from schools. It is essential, however, not to allow the power of that argument to blur the difference between sodas and physically addictive products and, arguably, pornography. Again, there are studies that suggest that video games are like drugs. If these studies are accurate, how can we ignore that reality?

The purpose here is not to advocate a particular course of action, but to emphasize how important it is that we not treat this too casually. It is about very real harm that is happening as a result of altered brain activity, intentionally being caused by video game manufacturers. Should not it bother us that manufacturers are preying on our physical weaknesses? Moreover, should not manufacturers, as members of society, care about the effect of their products on stakeholders? Perhaps the issue is not the inability of the legal system to address this situation adequately, but, rather, the unwillingness of people in companies independently to recognize their own moral and/or social responsibilities to their own families and communities. In a sense, then, perhaps the societal reaction to sodas in schools is a positive step.

Source: Copyright © Tara Radin. Reprinted with permission of the author.

Reading **8-4**

Wrestling with Ethics: *Is Marketing Ethics an Oxymoron?*

Philip Kotler

Every profession and business has to wrestle with ethical questions. The recent wave of business scandals over inaccurate reporting of sales and profits and excessive pay and privileges for top executives has brought questions of business ethics to the fore. And lawyers have been continuously accused of "ambulance chasing," jury manipulation, and inflated fees, leaving the plaintiffs with much less than called for in the judgment. Physicians have been known to recommend certain drugs as more effective while receiving support from pharmaceutical companies.

Marketers are not immune from facing a whole set of ethical issues. For evidence, look to Howard Bowen's classic questions from his 1953 book, *Social Responsibilities of the Businessman:*

> Should he conduct selling in ways that intrude on the privacy of people, for example, by door-to-door selling? Should he use methods involving ballyhoo, chances, prizes, hawking, and other tactics which are at least of doubtful good taste? Should he employ "high pressure" tactics in persuading people to buy? Should he try to hasten the obsolescence of goods by bringing out an endless succession of new models and new styles? Should he appeal to and attempt to strengthen the motives of materialism, invidious consumption, and keeping up with the Joneses? (Also see N. Craig Smith and Elizabeth Cooper-Martin, "Ethics and Target Marketing: The Role of Product Harm and Consumer Vulnerability," *Journal of Marketing* (July 1997), pp. 1–20.)

The issues raised are complicated. Drawing a clear line between normal marketing practice and unethical behavior isn't easy. Yet it's important for marketing scholars and those interested in public policy to raise questions about practices that they may normally endorse but that may not coincide with the public interest.

We will examine the central axiom of marketing: Companies that satisfy their target customers will perform better than those that don't. Companies that satisfy customers can expect repeat business; those that don't will get only one-time sales. Steady profits come from holding onto customers, satisfying them, and selling them more goods and services.

This axiom is the essence of the well-known marketing concept. It reduces to the formula "Give the customer what he wants." This sounds reasonable on the surface. But notice that it carries an implied corollary: "Don't judge what the customer wants."

Marketers have been, or should be, a little uneasy about this corollary. It raises two public interest concerns: (1) What if the customer wants something that isn't good for him or her? (2) What if the product or service, while good for the customer, isn't good for society or other groups?

When it comes to the first question, what are some products that some customers desire that might not be good for them? These would be products that can potentially harm their health, safety, or well-being. Tobacco and hard drugs such as cocaine, LSD, or ecstasy immediately come to mind.

As for the second question, examples of products or services that some customers desire that may not be in the public's best interest include using asbestos as a building material or using lead paint indiscriminately. Other products and services where debates continue to rage as to whether they are in the public's interest include the right to own guns and other weapons, the right to have an abortion, the right to distribute hate literature, and the right to buy large gas guzzling and polluting automobiles.

We now turn to three questions of interest to marketers, businesses, and the public:

1. Given that expanding consumption is at the core of most businesses, what are the interests and behaviors of companies that make these products?
2. To what extent do these companies care about reducing the negative side effects of these products?
3. What steps can be taken to reduce the consumption of products that have questionable effects, and is limited intervention warranted?

Expanding Consumption

Most companies will strive to enlarge their market as much as possible. A tobacco company, if unchecked, will try to get everyone who comes of age to start smoking cigarettes. Given that cigarettes are addictive, this promises the cigarette company "customers for life." Each new customer will create a 50-year profit stream for the cigarette company if the consumer continues to favor the same brand—and lives long enough. Suppose a new smoker starts at the age of 13, smokes for 50 years, and dies at 63 from lung cancer. If he spends $500 a year on cigarettes, he will spend $25,000 over his lifetime. If the company's profit rate is 20 percent, that new customer is worth $5,000 to the company (undiscounted). It is hard to imagine a company that doesn't want to attract a customer who contributes $5,000 to its profits.

The same story describes the hard drug industry, whose products are addictive and even more expensive. The difference is that cigarette companies can operate legally but hard drug companies must operate illegally.

Other products, such as hamburgers, candy, soft drinks, and beer, are less harmful when consumed in moderation, but are addictive for some people. We hear a person saying she has a "sweet tooth." One person drinks three Coca-Colas a day, and another drinks five beers a day. Still another consumer eats most of his meals at McDonald's. These are the "heavy users." Each company treasures the heavy users who account for a high proportion of the company's profits.

All said, every company has a natural drive to expand consumption of its products, leaving any negative consequences to be the result of the "free choice" of consumers. A high-level official working for Coca-Cola in Sweden said that her aim is to get people to start drinking Coca-Cola for breakfast (instead of orange juice). And McDonald's encourages customers to choose a larger hamburger, a larger order of French fries, and a larger cola drink. And these companies have some of the best marketers in the world working for them.

Reducing Side Effects

It would not be a natural act on the part of these companies to try to reduce or restrain consumption of their products. What company wants to reduce its profits? Usually some form of public pressure must bear on these companies before they will act.

The government has passed laws banning tobacco companies from advertising and glamorizing smoking on TV. But Philip Morris's Marlboro brand still will put out posters showing its mythical cowboy. And Marlboro will make sure that its name is mentioned in sports stadiums, art exhibits, and labels for other products.

Tobacco companies today are treading carefully not to openly try to create smokers out of young people. They have stopped distributing free cigarettes to young people in the United States as they move their operations increasingly into China.

Beer companies have adopted a socially responsible attitude by telling people not to over-drink or drive during or after drinking. They cooperate with efforts to prevent underage people from buying beer. They are trying to behave in a socially responsible manner. They also know that, at the margin, the sales loss resulting from their "cooperation" is very slight.

McDonald's has struggled to find a way to reduce the ill effects (obesity, heart disease) of too much consumption of their products. It tried to offer a reduced-fat hamburger only to find consumers rejecting it. It has offered salads, but they weren't of good quality when originally introduced and they failed. Now it's making a second and better attempt.

Limited Intervention

Do public interest groups or the government have the right to intervene in the free choices of individuals? This question has been endlessly debated. On one side are people who resent any intervention in their choices of products and services. In the extreme, they go by such names as libertarians, vigilantes, and "freedom lovers." They have a legitimate concern about government power and its potential abuse. Some of their views include:

- The marketer's job is to "sell more stuff." It isn't the marketer's job to save the world or make society a better place.
- The marketer's job is to produce profits for the shareholders in any legally sanctioned way.
- A high-minded socially conscious person should not be in marketing. A company shouldn't hire such a person.

On the other side are people concerned with the personal and societal costs of "unregulated consumption." They are considered do-gooders and will document that Coca-Cola delivers six teaspoons of sugar in every bottle or can. They will cite statistics on the heavy health costs of obesity, heart disease, and liver damage that are caused by failing to reduce the consumption of some of these products. These costs fall on everyone through higher medical costs and taxes. Thus, those who don't consume questionable products are still harmed through the unenlightened behavior of others.

Ultimately, the problem is one of conflict among different ethical systems. Consider the following five:

Ethical egoism. Your only obligation is to take care of yourself (Protagoras and Ayn Rand).

Government requirements. The law represents the minimal moral standards of a society (Thomas Hobbes and John Locke).

Personal virtues. Be honest, good, and caring (Plato and Aristotle).

Utilitarianism. Create the greatest good for the greatest number (Jeremy Bentham and John Stuart Mill).

Universal rules. "Act only on that maxim through which you can at the same time will that it should become a universal law" (Immanuel Kant's categorical imperative).

Clearly, people embrace different ethical viewpoints, making marketing ethics and other business issues more complex to resolve.

Let's consider the last two ethical systems insofar as they imply that some interventions are warranted. Aside from the weak gestures of companies toward self-regulation and appearing concerned, there are a range of measures that can be taken by those wishing to push their view of the public interest. They include the following six approaches:

1. **Encouraging these companies to make products safer.** Many companies have responded to public concern or social pressure to make their products safer. Tobacco companies developed filters that would reduce the chance of contracting emphysema or lung cancer. If a leaf without nicotine could give smokers the same satisfaction, they would be happy to replace the tobacco leaf. Some tobacco companies have even offered information or aids to help smokers limit their appetite for tobacco or curb it entirely.

   Food and soft drink companies have reformulated many of their products to be "light," "nonfat," or "low in calories." Some beer companies have introduced nonalcoholic beer. These companies still offer their standard products but provide concerned consumers with alternatives that present less risk to their weight or health.

   Auto companies have reluctantly incorporated devices designed to reduce pollution output into their automobiles. Some are even producing cars with hybrid fuel systems to further reduce harmful emissions to the air. But the auto companies still insist on putting out larger automobiles (such as Hummers) because the "public demands them."

   What can we suggest to Coca-Cola and other soft drink competitors that are already offering "light" versions of their drinks? First, they should focus more on developing the bottled water side of their businesses because bottled water is healthier than sugared soft drinks. Further, they should be encouraged to add nutrients and vitamins in standard drinks so these drinks can at least deliver more health benefits, especially to those in undeveloped countries who are deprived of these nutrients and vitamins. (Coca-Cola has some brands doing this now.)

   What can we suggest to McDonald's and its fast food competitors? The basic suggestion is to offer more variety in its menu. McDonald's seems to forget that, while parents bring their children to McDonald's, they themselves usually prefer to eat healthier food, not to mention want their children eating healthier foods. How about a first-class salad bar? How about moving more into the healthy sandwich business? Today more Americans are buying their meals at Subway and other sandwich shops where they feel they are getting healthier and tastier food for their dollar.

There seems to be a correlation between the amount of charity given by companies in some categories and the category's degree of "sin." Thus, McDonald's knows that overconsumption of its products can be harmful, but the company is very charitable. A cynic would say that McDonald's wants to build a bank of public goodwill to diffuse potential public criticism.

2. **Banning or restricting the sale or use of the product or service.** A community or nation will ban certain products where there is strong public support. Hard drugs are banned, although there is some debate about whether the ban should include marijuana and lighter hard drugs. There are even advocates who oppose banning hard drugs, believing that the cost of policing and criminality far exceeds the cost of a moderate increase that might take place in hard drug usage. Many people today believe that the "war on drugs" can never be won and is creating more serious consequences than simply dropping the ban or helping drug addicts, as Holland and Switzerland have done.

Some products carry restrictions on their purchase or use. This is particularly true of drugs that require a doctor's prescription and certain poisons that can't be purchased without authorization. Persons buying guns must be free of a criminal record and register their gun ownership. And certain types of guns, such as machine guns, are banned or restricted.

3. **Banning or limiting advertising or promotion of the product.** Even when a product isn't banned or its purchase restricted, laws may be passed to prevent producers from advertising or promoting the product. Gun, alcohol, and tobacco manufacturers can't advertise on TV, although they can advertise in print media such as magazines and newspapers. They can also inform and possibly promote their products online.

Manufacturers get around this by mentioning their brand name in every possible venue: sports stadiums, music concerts, and feature articles. They don't want to be forgotten in the face of a ban on promoting their products overtly.

4. **Increasing "sin" taxes to discourage consumption.** One reasonable alternative to banning a product or its promotion is to place a "sin" tax on its consumption. Thus, smokers pay hefty government taxes for cigarettes. This is supposed to have three effects when done right. First, the higher price should discourage consumption. Second, the tax revenue could be used to finance the social costs to health and safety caused by the consumption of the product. Third, some of the tax revenue could be used to counteradvertise the use of the product or support public education against its use. The last effect was enacted by California when it taxed tobacco companies and used the money to "unsell" tobacco smoking.

5. **Public education campaigns.** In the 1960s, Sweden developed a social policy to use public education to raise a nation of nonsmokers and nondrinkers. Children from the first grade up were educated to understand the ill effects of tobacco and alcohol. Other countries are doing this on a less systematic and intensive basis. U.S. public schools devote parts of occasional courses to educate students against certain temptations with mixed success. Girls, not boys, in the United States seem to be more prone to taking up smoking. The reason often given by girls is that smoking curbs their appetite for food and consequently helps them avoid becoming overweight, a problem they consider more serious than lung cancer taking place 40 years later.

Sex education has become a controversial issue, when it comes to public education campaigns. The ultra-conservative camp wants to encourage total abstinence until marriage. The more liberal camp believes that students should be taught the risks of early sex and have the necessary knowledge to protect themselves. The effectiveness of both types of sex education is under debate.

6. **Social marketing campaigns.** These campaigns describe a wide variety of efforts to communicate the ill effects of certain behaviors that can harm the person, other persons, or society as a whole. These campaigns use techniques of public education, advertising and promotion, incentives, and channel development to make it as easy and attractive as possible for people to change their behavior for the better. (See Philip Kotler, Philip, Eduardo Roberto, and Nancy Lee, *Social Marketing: Improving the Quality of Life,* 2nd ed., London: Sage Publications, 2002.) Social marketing uses the tools of commercial marketing—segmentation, targeting, and positioning, and the four Ps (product, price, place, and promotion)—to achieve voluntary compliance with publicly endorsed goals. Some social marketing campaigns, such as family planning and anti-littering, have achieved moderate to high success. Other campaigns including anti-smoking, anti-drugs ("say no to drugs"), and seat belt promotion have worked well when supplemented with legal action.

Social Responsibility and Profits

Each year *Business Ethics* magazine publishes the 100 best American companies out of 1,000 evaluated. The publication examines the degree to which the companies serve seven stakeholder groups: shareholders, communities, minorities and women, employees, environment, non-U.S. stakeholders, and customers. Information is gathered on lawsuits, regulatory problems, pollution emissions, charitable contributions, staff diversity counts, union relations, employee benefits, and awards. Companies are removed from the list if it has significant scandals or improprieties. The research is done by Kinder, Lydenberg, Domini (KLD), an independent rating service. (For more details see the Spring 2003 issue of *Business Ethics.*)

The 20 best-rated companies in 2003 were (in order): General Mills, Cummins Engine, Intel, Procter & Gamble, IBM, Hewlett-Packard, Avon Products, Green Mountain Coffee, John Nuveen Co., St. Paul Companies, AT&T, Fannie Mae, Bank of America, Motorola, Herman Miller, Expedia, Autodesk, Cisco Systems, Wild Oats Markets, and Deluxe.

The earmarks of a socially responsible company include:

- Living out a deep set of company values that drive company purpose, goals, strategies, and tactics.
- Treating customers with fairness, openness, and quick response to inquiries and complaints.
- Treating employees, suppliers, and distributors fairly.
- Caring about the environmental impact of its activities and supply chain.
- Behaving in a consistently ethical fashion.

The intriguing question is whether socially responsible companies are more profitable. Unfortunately, different research studies have come up with different results. The correlations between financial performance (FP) and social performance (SP) are sometimes positive, sometimes negative, and sometimes neutral, depending on the study. Even when FP and SP are positively related, which causes which? The most probable finding is that high FP firms invest slack resources in SP and then discover that SP leads to better FP, in a virtuous circle. (See Sandra A. Waddock and Samuel B. Graves, "The Corporate Social

Performance-Financial Performance Link," *Strategic Management Journal* 18 (4) (1997), pp. 303–319.)

Marketers' Responsibilities

As professional marketers, we are hired by some of the aforementioned companies to use our marketing toolkit to help them sell more of their products and services. Through our research, we can discover which consumer groups are the most susceptible to increasing their consumption. We can use the research to assemble the best 30-second TV commercials, print ads, and sales incentives to persuade them that these products will deliver great satisfaction. And we can create price discounts to tempt them to consume even more of the product than would normally be healthy or safe to consume.

But, as professional marketers, we should have the same ambivalence as nuclear scientists who help build nuclear bombs or pilots who spray DDT over crops from the airplane. Some of us, in fact, are independent enough to tell these clients that we will not work for them to find ways to sell more of what hurts people. We can tell them that we're willing to use our marketing toolkit to help them build new businesses around substitute products that are much healthier and safer.

But, even if these companies moved toward these healthier and safer products, they'll probably continue to push their current "cash cows." At that point, marketers will have to decide whether to work for these companies, help them reshape their offerings, avoid these companies altogether, or even work to oppose these company offerings.

Remember Marketing's Contributions

Nothing said here should detract from the major contributions that marketing has made to raise the material standards of living around the world. One doesn't want to go back to the kitchen where the housewife cooked five hours a day, washed dishes by hand, put fresh ice in the icebox, and washed and dried clothes in the open air. We value refrigerators, electric stoves, dishwashers, washing machines, and dryers. We value the invention and diffusion of the radio, the television set, the computer, the Internet, the cellular phone, the automobile, the movies, and even frozen food. Marketing has played a major role in their instigation and diffusion. Granted, any of these are capable of abuse (bad movies or TV shows), but they promise and deliver much that is good and valued in modern life.

Marketers have a right to be proud of their field. They search for unmet needs, encourage the development of products and services addressing these needs, manage communications to inform people of these products and services, arrange for easy accessibility and availability, and price the goods in a way that represents superior value delivered vis-à-vis competitors' offerings. This is the true work of marketing.

Source: Copyright © Philip Kotler. Used by permission of the author.

About the Author

Philip Kotler is S.C. Johnson and Son Distinguished Professor of International Marketing, Kellogg School of Management, Northwestern University. He may be reached at pkotler @nwu.edu.

Author's Note: The author wishes to thank Professor Evert Gummesson of the School of Business, Stockholm University, for earlier discussion of these issues.

Chapter 9

Business, the Environment, and Sustainability

A thing is right when it tends to preserve the integrity, stability and beauty of the biotic community. It is wrong when it does otherwise.

Aldo Leopold

Growth for the sake of growth is the ideology of the cancer cell.

Edward Abbey

Waste equals food.

William McDonough

Tons of toxic wastes are created every day in the production and disposal of countless goods and services. Business and government must decide what to do with such leftovers as the radioactive wastes created in nuclear power plants, the fly ash from industrial and municipal incinerators, chemical residues from industrial processes and consumer goods, and heavy metals in computers and other consumer electronics. Consumers are challenged to find ways to dispose of toxic chemicals in household cleaners, lawn and garden pesticides, home appliances, and consumer electronics.

Ordinary waste disposal is a serious enough public policy challenge for every level of government. Newer landfills soon reach their capacity; many older and closed landfills contaminate groundwater; and incinerators spew noxious pollutants. But the challenge is compounded when the wastes entering into the disposal system are themselves highly toxic and dangerous.

Historically, industry has disposed of wastes into the easiest and least desirable sites. For decades, industry simply dumped waste into the air and water or buried it underground. Landfills, trash dumps, incinerators, and other socially undesirable activities were located either in out-of-the-way and unattractive locations, or in the most convenient location to ease disposal. Such decisions seemed to make economic sense; if land values would be degraded because of proximity to a toxic waste dump, it makes most sense to choose a location that already has the lowest valued property.

One result of this dumping is that domestic waste disposal often creates a cycle of decreasing land values that seem clearly to harm the poorest and most disenfranchised citizens. Areas with the lowest land values, and therefore areas targeted as the location for socially undesirable activities, tend to be the areas in which a society's poorest citizens live. As those areas accept more of the undesirable wastes and industries, they became even less attractive locations in which to live, thereby making them poorer and poorer, as those who are able to move away leave behind those who are less able to do so. This practice raises fundamental questions of social justice when society's least advantaged citizens pay the highest costs for the social benefits of industrial society.

In recent decades, this same economic logic has created a market for toxic wastes among the world's poorest countries. The incentive to send toxic wastes offshore increases as waste disposal has become more expensive domestically. The world's less developed countries need the income and, because they are less developed, often do not have the industrial pollution problems that plague developed countries.

Should waste disposal be treated simply as an economic issue, to be resolved through private market exchanges, or should government regulations place greater responsibility on producers for the entire life cycle of products?

- What facts do you need to know to form an opinion on the practice of exporting toxic wastes to foreign countries?
- What values are implicit in the economic reasoning that leads to the decision to export such wastes?
- Does it matter if the countries that accept such wastes are democratic?

(continued)

- How should the decision to locate toxic wastes sites be made?
- What are the consequences of making this decision on the basis of costs?
- What principles are relevant to this decision?
- Can you think of undesirable land uses (trash dumps, incinerators, smokestack industries) in your own region? Describe the neighborhoods in which they are located.

✴ Chapter Objectives

After reading this chapter, you will be able to:

1. Describe a range of values that play a role in environmental decision making.
2. Explain the difference between market-based and regulatory-based environmental policies.
3. Describe business's environmental responsibilities that flow from each approach.
4. Identify the inadequacies of sole reliance on a market-based approach.
5. Identify the inadequacies of regulatory-based environmental policies.
6. Define and describe sustainable development and sustainable business.
7. Highlight the business opportunities associated with a move towards sustainability.
8. Describe the sustainable principles of ecoefficiency, biomimicry, and service.

Introduction

Cradle to Cradle

There is a tendency to believe that environmental issues have been a concern only in recent times. Environmentalism flourished in the latter half of the twentieth century: Issues such as air and water pollution and the protection of endangered species became public policy concerns only in the 1970s. Certainly few businesses gave the natural environment much thought at all prior to this time. But environmental degradation has been a part of human history forever. In the recent best-selling book *Collapse*, geographer Jared Diamond documents numerous cultures that suffered and collapsed as a result of environmental degradation.

The Industrial Revolution of the 18th and 19th centuries, however, brought with it the ability to degrade the natural environment to a greater extent and at a faster rate than ever before. By the start of the 21st century, the earth was experiencing the greatest period of species extinction since the end of the dinosaurs 65 million years ago. Humans are also threatened by global climate change. Each of these monumental environmental events is largely due to human activity, and specifically to our present arrangements of modern industrial society. Simply put, the way we have done business over the last two centuries has brought us up against the biophysical limits of the earth's capacity to support human life, and it has already crossed those limits in the case of countless other forms of life. Thus, the

Reality Check *Do Business Leaders Think There Is an Environmental Crisis?*

In a 1997 speech that attracted worldwide attention, John Browne, chief executive of BP, announced:

> [T]he time to consider the policy dimensions of climate change is not when the link between greenhouse gases and climate change is conclusively proven . . . but when the possibility cannot be discounted and is taken seriously by the society of which we are part. We in BP have reached that point . . . there is now an effective consensus among the world's leading scientists and serious and well informed people outside the

scientific community that there is a discernible human influence on the climate, and a link between the concentration of carbon dioxide and the increase in temperature. . . . Those are wide margins of error, and there remain large elements of uncertainty—about cause and effect . . . and even more importantly about the consequences. But it would be unwise and potentially dangerous to ignore the mounting concern.

Source: John Browne, group chief executive, British Petroleum (BP America) in a speech at Stanford University, May 19, 1997.

major ethical question of this chapter is what responsibilities contemporary businesses have regarding the natural environment. For a business leader's perspective on this question, see the Reality Check above.

It is fair to say that, throughout the history of industrial economies, business most often looked at environmental concerns as unwanted burdens and barriers to economic growth. Nonetheless, there is some evidence that, at the start of the 21st century, a new model of business is emerging, perhaps first initiated in Europe and followed by North America and Asia. Sustainable business and sustainable economic development seek to create new ways of doing business in which business success is measured in terms of economic, ethical, and environmental sustainability, often called the Triple Bottom Line approach. The sustainability paradigm sees environmental responsibilities as a fundamental part of basic business practice. Indeed, sustainable business ventures may find that environmental considerations offer creative and entrepreneurial businesses enormous opportunities.

This chapter will introduce a range of ethical issues that will accompany this transition to an environmentally sustainable future. Environmental issues are no longer at the periphery of business decisions, as burdens to be managed if not avoided altogether. Environmental sustainability must accompany financial sustainability for business to survive in the 21st century. For reasons of both deontological principles and for the overall social good, sustainable business is the wave of the future.

Business Ethics and Environmental Values

OBJECTIVE

The opening chapters of this text introduced ethics in terms of practical reasoning. Deciding what we should do is the ultimate goal of practical reason and our values are those standards that encourage us to act one way rather than another. Given this objective, what values does the natural environment support? Why should we act in ways that protect the natural environment from degradation? Why should business be concerned with, and value, the natural world?

Reality Check *Breast Milk Toxins*

Pollutants in the biosphere will tend to accumulate in the fatty tissue of species at the top of the food chain. In mammals, fatty tissue is broken down as a source of energy during lactation. As a result, breast milk is a particularly significant resource for studying toxins that the body has absorbed. The following is a list of synthetic toxins that one study found in human breast milk.

Chlordane (a compound used in pesticides)

DDT (a pesticide that has been banned in the United States for decades)

Dieldrin, Aldrin, and Endrin (insecticides)

Hexachlorobenzene (a pesticide and an industrial chemical)

Hexachlorocyclohexane (insecticide)

Heptachlor (insecticide)

Mirex (insecticide)

Nitro musks (used as a fragrance in household products such as detergents and soaps)

Toxaphene (agricultural insecticide)

Dioxins and furans (any of a number of polychlorinated compounds produced as by-products from industry and combustion)

PBDEs (used as flame retardants in clothes and other fabrics)

PCBs (no longer manufactured, but persistent toxins that were used for a wide variety of industrial purposes)

Solvents (any of a number of chemical compounds used to dissolve or stabilize other complex chemical compounds)

Lead, mercury, cadmium, and other metals (can be especially toxic to the developing brain)

Human self-interest is the most obvious answer to these questions. All human beings depend on the natural environment in order to survive. Humans need clean water to drink, healthy air to breathe, fertile soil and oceans to produce food, an ozone layer to screen out solar radiation, and a biosphere that maintains the delicate balance of climate in which human life can exist. Two aspects of contemporary environmental realities underscore the importance of self-interested reasoning.

As documented in *Collapse*, past human societies have often run up against the limits of the local environment's ability to sustain human life. In these historical cases, environmental degradation has been localized to a particular region and has seldom affected more than a generation. In contrast, some contemporary environmental issues have the potential to adversely affect the entire globe and change human life forever. Global climate change, species extinction, soil erosion and desertification, and nuclear wastes will threaten human life into the indefinite future.

Second, the science of ecology and its understanding of the interrelatedness of natural systems have helped us understand the wide range of human dependence on ecosystems. Where once we might have thought that buried wastes were gone forever, we now understand how toxins can seep into groundwater and contaminate drinking water across great time and distances. We now understand how pesticides accumulate throughout the food chain and pose greatest dangers not only to top predators such as bald eagles, but to human beings as well. (Consider the basic issue of the environment's impact on breast milk, discussed in the preceding Reality Check.) Where once we thought that ocean fisheries were inexhaustible and the atmosphere too big to be changed by humans, we now understand that a precise environmental balance is necessary to maintain life-supporting systems.

Is the market, what people are most willing to pay, the best means to determine land and resource use? Consider the case of a proposed development in Virginia.

The city of Manassas is today a suburb of Washington, DC, in northern Virginia. During the U.S. Civil War, it was the site of two historic battles, the first and second Battle of Bull Run. Thousands of soldiers were killed during these battles and many more thousands injured. Today, Manassas Battlefield National Park and several Civil War cemeteries are located at the site.

In the late 1980s developers announced plans to build a large shopping mall on the land that had once served as Robert E. Lee's headquarters during the battle. Significant public opposition led to a public purchase of the land and its incorporation into the national park. A few years later, Disney Company announced plans to develop a large theme park called Disney's America on land adjacent to the National Park. Disney's America would have included a theme park that would be a tribute to the Civil War, as well as residential subdivisions and commercial developments including hotels and restaurants. Eventually, the national park would have been surrounded by commercial development.

The plan met with vociferous opposition from a coalition of environmentalists, preservationists, historians, and Civil War authorities. Although it was convinced that the project would have been a tremendous commercial success, Disney eventually abandoned its plans to develop this site. Should the company have abandoned these plans?

- What facts would be helpful to know before making a decision?
- What values are in conflict in this case? Take a look at Disney's "environmentality" mission statement at http://corporate.disney.go.com/environmentality/mission_history.html. How might its mission guide its decisions or present conflicts in the current dilemma?
- Who are the stakeholders in this case?
- What would be the consequences if all public land uses were decided by the market?
- What are the rights and duties involved in this case?

By the late 19th century, humans came to recognize the self-interested reasons for protecting the natural environment. The conservation movement, the first phase of modern environmentalism, advocated a more restrained and prudent approach to the natural world. From this perspective, the natural world was still valued as a resource, providing humans with both direct benefits (air, water, food), and indirect benefits (the goods and services produced by business). Conservationists argued against the exploitation of natural resources as if they could provide an inexhaustible supply of material. They made the case that business had good reasons for conserving natural resources, reasons that paralleled the rationale to conserve financial resources. The natural world, like capital, had the productive capacity to produce long-term income but only if managed and used prudently.

Reality Check *Treatment of Animals in Agriculture*

Some animal farming practices, especially within large-scale industrial factory farms, have been criticized as cruel and heartless. Calves are prevented from exercising and intentionally malnourished so that consumers can enjoy tender and pink veal. Chickens are tightly packed in cages with their beaks cut off to prevent them from pecking each other. Cattle are raised in giant feed lots where they spend their time walking in their own manure.

Opponents have organized boycotts against such fast-food chains as McDonald's and KFC (formerly called Kentucky Fried Chicken) to protest how animals in their supply chain are treated. In response to this criticism, McDonald's has become an industry leader in creating policies to ensure the humane treatment of animals. As part of this effort, McDonald's has adopted a set of guiding principles, including the following:

> McDonald's commitment to animal welfare is global and guided by the following principles.

These principles apply to all the countries in which McDonald's does business.

Safety. First and foremost, McDonald's will provide its customers with safe food products. Food safety is McDonald's number one priority.

Quality. McDonald's believes treating animals with care and respect is an integral part of an overall quality assurance program that makes good business sense.

Animal Treatment. McDonald's supports that animals should be free from cruelty, abuse and neglect while embracing the proper treatment of animals and addressing animal welfare issues.

Source: McDonald's Corporation, "2006 Worldwide Corporate Responsibility Report; Products: Responsible Purchasing Guiding Principles," http://www.mcdonalds.com/corp/values/purchasing/animalwelfare/guiding_principles.html.

Besides these reasons to protect human life and health, the natural environment is essential and valuable for many other reasons. Often, these other values conflict with the more direct instrumental value that comes from treating the natural world as a resource. The beauty and grandeur of the natural world provide great aesthetic and inspirational value. Many people view the natural world as a manifestation of religious and spiritual values. Parts of the natural world can have symbolic value, historical value, and such diverse psychological values as serenity and exhilaration. These values can clearly conflict with the use of the earth itself as a resource to physically, as opposed to spiritually, sustain those who live on it. Consider that balance as you review the preceding Decision Point.

The moral status of animals has been the environmental value that, arguably, has raised the greatest challenge to business. Variously referred to as the animal rights, animal liberation, or animal welfare movement, this approach attributes a moral standing to animals. Such a status would create a wide variety of distinctive ethical responsibilities concerning how we treat animals and would have significant implications for many businesses. Two versions of this perspective are worth mentioning.

The first approach emphasizes the fact that many animals, presumably all animals with a central nervous system, have the capacity to feel pain. Reminiscent of the utilitarian tradition described in Chapter 3, this view asserts an ethical responsibility to minimize pain. Inflicting unnecessary pain is taken to be an ethical wrong; therefore, acts that inflict unnecessary pain on animals are ethically

To distinguish these two approaches to the ethical treatment of animals, consider a case in which veal calves are spared the pain of their confinement by being raised in more humane circumstances. Even if they feel no pain, is it still cruel to slaughter a young calf in order to eat its flesh? Similarly, as explained above, McDonald's has gone to great lengths to ensure that the animals their suppliers slaughter are treated in ways that are "free from cruelty, abuse and neglect." Is it possible to treat animals humanely while they are being raised and led to slaughter for the purpose of being used as food?

- What facts would be relevant to your decision?
- What are the ethical issues involved in this situation?
- Who are the stakeholders for the issues of the ethical treatment of animals?
- What alternatives are available for businesses like McDonald's that rely on animals?
- What are the consequences of various alternatives?
- What ethical principles are involved?

wrong. Raising and slaughtering animals for food, particularly in the way industrial farming enterprises raise poultry, hogs, and cattle, would be an obvious case in which business would violate this ethical responsibility, as one side argues in the preceding Reality Check.

A second approach argues that at least some animals have the cognitive capacity to possess a conscious life of their own. Reminiscent of the Kantian ethical tradition described in Chapter 3, this view asserts that we have a duty not to treat these animals as mere objects and means to our own ends. Again, businesses that use animals for food, entertainment, or pets would violate the ethical rights of these animals. Let's explore the humane treatment of animals in more detail through the Decision Point above.

Business's Environmental Responsibility: The Market Approach

While significant debate surrounds some environmental values, an overwhelming consensus exists about the prudential reasons for protecting the natural environment—humans have a right to be protected from harm. What controversy remains has more to do with the best means for achieving this goal. Historically, this debate has focused on whether efficient markets or government regulation is the most appropriate means for meeting the environmental responsibilities of business. Each of these two approaches has significant implications for business.

OBJECTIVE

From one perspective, if the best approach to environmental concerns is to trust them to efficient markets, then the responsible business manager simply ought to seek profits and allow the market to allocate resources efficiently. By doing this, business fills its role within a market system, which in turn serves the greater overall (utilitarian) good. On the other hand, if government regulation is a more adequate approach, then business ought to develop a compliance structure to ensure that it conforms to those regulatory requirements.

Defenders of the market approach contend that environmental problems are economic problems that deserve economic solutions. Fundamentally, environmental problems involve the allocation and distribution of limited resources. Whether we are concerned with the allocation of scarce nonrenewable resources such as gas and oil, or with the earth's capacity to absorb industrial by-products such as CO_2 or PCBs, efficient markets can address environmental challenges.

OBJECTIVE

Consider the implications of this model for pollution and resource conservation. In his well-known book, *People or Penguins: The Case for Optimal Pollution,* William Baxter argued that there is an optimal level of pollution that would best serve society's interests.[1] This optimal level is best attained, according to Baxter, by leaving it to a competitive market. (The reasoning here is identical to the reasoning we described in Chapter 6 in connection with a market-based approach for protecting employee health and safety.)

Denying that there is any "natural" or objective standard for clean air or water (as this view would deny there is an objective state of perfect health), Baxter begins with a goal of "safe" air and water quality, and translates this goal to a matter of balancing risks and benefits. Society *could* strive for pure air and water, but the costs (lost opportunities) that this would entail would be too high. A more reasonable approach is to aim for air and water quality that is safe enough to breathe and drink without costing too much. This balance, the "optimal level of pollution" can be achieved through competitive markets. Society, through the activities of individuals, will be willing to pay for pollution reduction as long as the perceived benefits outweigh the costs.

The free market also provides an answer for resource conservation. From a strict market economic perspective, resources are "infinite." Julian Simon, for example, has argued that resources should not be viewed as material objects but simply as any means to our ends.[2] History has shown that human ingenuity and incentive have always found substitutes for any shortages. As the supply of any resources decreases, the price increases, thereby providing a strong incentive to supply more or provide a less costly substitute. In economic terms, all resources are "fungible." They can be replaced by substitutes, and in this sense resources are infinite. Resources that are not being used to satisfy consumer demand are being wasted.

A similar case can be made for the preservation of environmentally sensitive areas. Preservation for preservation's sake would be wasteful since it would use resources inefficiently. Thus, to return to the Manassas Battlefield development plan described previously, preserving open space surrounding the area rather than developing the land as a theme park should be done only if people are willing to pay more for open space than for a park. Since the Disney plan would have been financially very profitable, leaving it undeveloped would be wasting these valuable resources.

OBJECTIVE

Challenges to this narrow view of corporate social responsibility are familiar. A variety of market failures, many of the best known of which involve environmental issues, point to the inadequacy of market solutions. One example is the existence of externalities, the textbook example of which is environmental pollution. Since the "costs" of such things as air pollution, groundwater contamination and depletion, soil erosion, and nuclear waste disposal are typically borne by parties "external" to the economic exchange (e.g., people downwind, neighbors, future generations), free market exchanges cannot guarantee optimal results.

A second type of market failure occurs when no markets exist to create a price for important social goods. Endangered species, scenic vistas, rare plants and animals, and biodiversity are just some environmental goods that typically are not traded on open markets (or, when they are, they are often traded in ways that seriously threaten their viability as when rhinoceros horns, tiger claws, elephant tusks, and mahogany trees are sold on the black market). Public goods such as clean air and ocean fisheries also have no established market price. With no established exchange value, the market approach cannot even pretend to achieve its own goals of efficiently meeting consumer demand. Markets alone fail to guarantee that such important public goods are preserved and protected. The case study discussed in the next Decision Point explores whether market incentives always lead to the decisions that we might prefer in these particular conflicts.

A third way in which market failures can lead to serious environmental harm involves a distinction between individual decisions and group consequences. We can miss important ethical and policy questions if we leave policy decisions solely to the outcome of individual decisions. Consider the calculations that an individual consumer might make regarding the purchase of an SUV and the consequences of that decision on global warming. The additional CO_2 that would be emitted by a single SUV is miniscule enough that an individual would likely conclude that her decision will make no difference. However, if every consumer made exactly the same decision, the consequences would be significantly different.

This example demonstrates that the overall social result of individual calculations might be significant increases in pollution and such pollution-related diseases as asthma and allergies. A number of alternative policies (e.g., restricting SUV sales, increasing taxes on gasoline, treating SUVs as cars instead of light trucks in calculating Corporate Automotive Fuel Efficiency [CAFE] Standards) that could address pollution and pollution-related disease would never be considered if we relied only on market solutions. Because these are important ethical questions, and because they remain unasked from within market transactions, we must conclude that markets are incomplete (at best) in their approach to the overall social good. In other words, what is good and rational for a collection of individuals is not necessarily what is good and rational for a society.

Such market failures raise serious concerns for the ability of economic markets to achieve a sound environmental policy. Defenders of a narrow view of corporate social responsibility have responses to these challenges of course. Internalizing external costs and assigning property rights to unowned goods such as wild species are two responses to market failures. But there are good reasons for thinking that such ad hoc attempts to repair market failures are environmentally inadequate. One important reason is what has been called the first-generation problem. Markets can work to prevent harm only through information supplied by the existence of market failures. Only when fish populations in the North Atlantic collapsed,

The Pacific Lumber Corporation, based in Humboldt County in northern California, a major timber and wood products corporation, was a publicly traded company run by the same family for most of its history.

Pacific Lumber managed natural resources in a manner that protected the long-term sustainability of its tree harvest. Its forests, some of which contained old-growth redwood trees, were harvested at a rate of 2 to 3 percent a year, about equal to the annual growth rate of the trees. The company was known for treating its employees very responsibly. It paid employees relatively well, provided financial support during periods of economic decline, guaranteed jobs for family members of employees, established scholarships for the children of employees, and implemented a generous pension plan. By all accounts, the company was a good corporate citizen contributing in many ways to the life of the community.

Pacific Lumber appeared to be well managed financially as well. The company was debt free and profitable, and it provided a steady rate of return to its investors. But this management philosophy changed dramatically when the company became a takeover target in 1986.

Through the late 1980s and early 1990s, outside buyers took over many corporations. The takeover mania that characterized these years was financed largely through so-called junk bonds. These bonds are higher-risk loans that financial investors make on the promise of a high rate of return. Takeover specialists, generally with expertise in finance and law but seldom in the particular industry being purchased, identify a corporation that appears to be undervalued. That is, its assets appear to be worth more than the "book value" of its stock. Armed with cash from the high-interest junk bonds, takeover specialists are able to purchase a controlling interest in the corporation at a price above the present trading price of its stock. They then either manage the corporation more efficiently than the present management or sell off the undervalued assets. Because the high-interest loans provide a strong incentive to produce immediate income, the most common strategy is to sell off the company's assets. Such "leveraged buyouts" create the potential of immense profits in a very short period of time.

Pacific Lumber was a target for such a leveraged buyout. Because it was debt free and because it was not optimally using many of its resources (the 97 to 98 percent of its trees that were not harvested each year, for example), the financial value of Pacific Lumber seemed much higher than its stock value. From a financial point of view, these unused resources seemed to be wasted. Armed with $800 million in high-interest junk bonds managed by Drexel Burnham Lambert, corporate raider Charles Hurwitz succeeded in a leveraged buyout of Pacific Lumber.

Predictably, the new owners immediately established plans to increase the rate of its timber harvest, including previously preserved old-growth redwood trees, to raise cash to pay off its debt. Pacific Lumber was split into three separate companies and much of the debt was transferred to these new companies and refinanced with lower interest loans secured with the forest lands as collateral. The company pension plan was terminated and its funds used to repay debt and purchase retirement annuities from an insurance company that Hurwitz owned. Due to the increased logging, employment in the Humboldt County area increased slightly after the takeover.

Pacific Lumber provides an interesting case study of two competing managerial philosophies. The managerial philosophy that guided Pacific Lumber prior to

(continued)

the takeover directed management to balance a diverse group of interests. This management team kept Pacific Lumber operating as a profitable and stable business. Customers had a steady source of timber products at a price they were willing to pay. Employees had stable and well-paying jobs with generous benefits. Investors received a return on their investment favorable enough to keep their money in the firm. The firm provided the community with a stable economic base and an acceptable balance of environmental protection and economic activity. Any additional benefits that could be given to one group would come as a cost to another. Investors could have received a higher rate of return, but only at the cost of lowering employee wages or benefits, increased environmental destruction, or higher prices. Employees could have received higher wages, but at a cost of lower stock value, higher prices, and so on. On this model, managerial expertise involves finding and maintaining a stable balance between these competing interests.

After the takeover, the managerial philosophy was to maximize profit. From this perspective, the company's resources should be organized in a way that most efficiently produces profit. Unused resources, for example the 98 percent of the forests not harvested, were wasted resources. Capital sitting in a pension plan was a wasted resource. Wages and benefits above what was needed to maintain a stable supply of labor were wasted. Wasted resources indicate that people are losing opportunities and not getting all they want. In particular, as owners of the firm, stockholders deserve to have priority over the interests of employees, customers, and the community.

Both of these managerial philosophies are deeply rooted in contemporary managerial practice. Each can appeal to long ethical traditions for support as well.

1. Evaluate the management philosophy of the original managers of Pacific Lumber from the point of view of stockholders, employees, the local community, environmentalists, the company's financial institutions, and customers.

2. Were the 97 to 98 percent of company resources that were not harvested each year being wasted? Was this rate of use fair to stockholders? Who should decide such questions?

3. Was the buyout a reasonable thing to do from a financial perspective? From an ethical perspective? Were there any other options?

4. Should business management always seek the highest rate of return on investment? What reasons might there be for seeking something less?

5. Would your views change if instead of a lumber company harvesting old-growth forests, this case involved a mining company mining coal or other minerals?

for example, did we learn that free and open competition among the world's fishing industry for unowned public goods failed to prevent the decimation of cod, swordfish, Atlantic salmon, and lobster populations. That is, we learn about market failures and thereby prevent harms in the future only by sacrificing the "first generation" as a means of gaining this information. When public policy involves irreplaceable public goods such as endangered species, rare wilderness areas, and public health and safety, such a reactionary strategy is ill advised. (See the following Reality Check for a call for public policy in connection with energy.)

Reality Check   *Supply and Demand for Energy*

A recent call from the chairman and CEO of Chevron-Texaco for changes in U.S. energy policy emphasizes the need for partnership between government and business to address the energy market. In a speech delivered in February 2005, David J. O'Reilly claimed that we are now in the midst of what he called a "new energy equation" requiring a broad-based energy policy.

The most visible element of this new equation is that relative to demand, oil is no longer in plentiful supply. The time when we could count on cheap oil and even cheaper natural gas is clearly ending. Why is this happening now? . . . Demand from Asia is one fundamental reason for this new age of more volatile and higher prices. The Chinese economy alone is a roaring engine whose thirst for oil grew by more than 15 percent last year and will double its need for imported oil between 2003 and 2010—just seven years. This new Asian demand is reshaping the marketplace. And we're seeing the center of gravity of global petroleum markets shift to Asia and, in particular, to China and India. . . . But demand isn't the only factor at play. Simply put,

the era of easy access to energy is over. In part, this is because we are experiencing the convergence of geological difficulty with geopolitical instability. Although political turmoil and social unrest are less likely to affect long-term supplies, the psychological effect of those factors can clearly have an impact on world oil markets, which are already running at razor-thin margins of capacity. Many of the world's big production fields are maturing just as demand is increasing. The U.S. Geological Survey estimates the world will have consumed one-half of its existing conventional oil base by 2030. Increasingly, future supplies will have to be found in ultradeep water and other remote areas, development projects that will ultimately require new technology and trillions of dollars of investment in new infrastructure.

Source: David J. O'Reilly, chairman and CEO, Chevron-Texaco Corporation, "U.S. Energy Policy: A Declaration of Interdependence," keynote address to the 24th annual CERA Week Conference, Houston, Texas, February 15, 2005. Available on the Chevron-Texaco Web site: http://www.chevrontexaco.com/news/speeches/2005/2005-02-15_oreilly.asp.

Business's Environmental Responsibility: The Regulatory Approach

OBJECTIVE

A broad consensus emerged in the United States in the 1970s that unregulated markets are an inadequate approach to environmental challenges. Instead, governmental regulations were seen as the better way to respond to environmental problems. Much of the most significant environmental legislation in the United States was enacted during the 1970s. The Clean Air Act of 1970 (amended and renewed in 1977), Federal Water Pollution Act of 1972 (amended and renewed as the Clean Water Act of 1977), and the Endangered Species Act of 1973 were part of this national consensus for addressing environmental problems. Each law was originally enacted by a Democratic Congress and signed into law by a Republican president.

These laws share a common approach to environmental issues. Before this legislation was enacted, the primary legal avenue open for addressing environmental concerns was tort law. Only individuals who could prove that they had been harmed by pollution could raise legal challenges to air and water pollution.

That legal approach placed the burden on the person who was harmed and, at best, offered compensation for the harm only after the fact. Except for the incentive provided by the threat of compensation, U.S. policy did little to prevent the pollution in the first place. Absent any proof of negligence, public policy was content to let the market decide environmental policy. Because endangered species themselves had no legal standing, direct harm to plant and animal life was of no legal concern and previous policies did little to prevent harm to plant and animal life.

The laws enacted during the 1970s established standards that effectively shifted the burden from those threatened with harm to those who would cause the harm. Government established regulatory standards to try to prevent the occurrence of pollution or species extinction rather than to offer compensation after the fact. We can think of these laws as establishing minimum standards to ensure air and water quality and species preservation. Business was free to pursue its own goals as long as it complied with the side constraints these minimum standards established.

The consensus that emerged was that society had two opportunities to establish business's environmental responsibilities. As consumers, individuals could demand environmentally friendly products in the marketplace. As citizens, individuals could support environmental legislation. As long as business responded to the market and obeyed the law, it met its environmental responsibilities. If consumers demand environmentally suspect products, such as large gas-guzzling SUVs, and those products are allowed by law, then we cannot expect business to forgo the financial opportunities of marketing such products.

Philosopher Norman Bowie (in an essay reprinted at the end of this chapter) defended a modified version of this narrow view of corporate social responsibility. Bowie argued that, apart from the duties to cause no avoidable harm to humans and to obey the law, business has no special environmental responsibility. Business may voluntarily choose to do environmental good, but it has no obligation to do so. Business should be free to pursue profits by responding to the demands of the economic marketplace without any particular regard to environmental responsibilities. In so far as society desires environmental goods (for example, lowering pollution by increasing the fuel efficiency of automobiles), it is free to express those desires through legislation or within the marketplace. Absent those demands, business has no special environmental responsibilities.

OBJECTIVE

Several problems suggest that this approach will prove inadequate over the long term. First, it underestimates the influence that business can have in establishing the law. The Corporate Automotive Fuel Efficiency (CAFE) standards mentioned previously provide a good example of how this can occur. A reasonable account of this law suggests that the public very clearly expressed a political goal of improving air quality by improving automobile fuel efficiency goals (and thereby reducing automobile emissions). However, the automobile industry was able to use its lobbying influence to exempt light trucks and SUVs from these standards. It should be no surprise that light trucks and SUVs at the time represented the largest selling, and most profitable, segment of the auto industry.

Second, this approach also underestimates the ability of business to influence consumer choice. To conclude that business fulfills its environmental responsibility when it responds to the environmental demands of consumers is to underestimate the role that business can play in shaping public opinion. Advertising is a $200 billion a year industry in the United States alone. It is surely misleading to claim that business passively responds to consumer desires and that consumers are unaffected by the messages that business conveys. Assuming that business is not going to stop advertising its products or lobbying government, this model of corporate environmental responsibility is likely to prove inadequate for protecting the natural environment.

Further, if we rely on the law to protect the environment, environmental protection will extend only as far as the law extends. Yet, most environmental issues, pollution problems especially, do not respect legal jurisdictions. New York State might pass strict regulations on smokestack emissions, but if the power plants are located downwind in Ohio or even further west in the Dakotas or Wyoming, New York State will continue to suffer the effects of acid rain. Similarly, national regulations will be ineffective for international environmental challenges. While hope remains that international agreements might help control global environmental problems, the failure of the Kyoto agreement suggests that this might be overly optimistic.

Finally, and perhaps most troubling from an environmental standpoint, this regulatory model assumes that economic growth is environmentally and ethically benign. Regulations establish side constraints on business's pursuit of profits and, as long as they remain within those constraints, accept as ethically legitimate whatever road to profitability management chooses. What can be lost in these discussions is the very important fact that there are many different ways to pursue profits within the side constraints of law. Different roads towards profitability can have very different environmental consequences.

Business's Environmental Responsibilities: The Sustainability Approach

6

OBJECTIVE

Beginning in the 1980s, a new model for environmentally responsible business began to take shape, one that combines financial opportunities with environmental and ethical responsibilities. The concept of sustainable development and sustainable business practice suggests a radically new vision for integrating financial and environmental goals, compared to the growth model that preceded it (as explored in the Reality Check that follows). These three goals, economic, environmental, and ethical sustainability, are often referred to as the three pillars of sustainability.

The concept of sustainable development can be traced to a 1987 report from the United Nations' World Commission on Environment and Development (WCED), more commonly known as the Brundtland Commission, named for its chair, Gro Harlem Brundtland. The commission was charged with developing

Reality Check *Why Sustainability?*

Three factors are most often cited to explain and justify the need for a model of economic development that stresses sustainability rather than growth.

First, billions of human beings live in severe poverty and daily face real challenges associated with the lack of food, water, health care, and shelter. Addressing these challenges will require significant economic activity.

Second, world population continues to grow at a disturbing rate, with projections of an increase from 6 billion people in 1998 to 7 billion shortly after 2010 and 8 billion before 2030. Most of this population growth will occur within the world's poorest regions, thereby only intensifying the first challenge. Even more economic activity will be needed to address the needs of this growing population.

Third, all of this economic activity must rely on the productive capacity of the earth's biosphere. Unfortunately, there is ample evidence that the type

and amount of economic activity practiced by the world's economies have already approached if not overshot the earth's ability to support human life.

Given these realities, citizens within developed economies have three available paths. We can believe that developing economies in places such as China, India, and Indonesia cannot, will not, or should not strive for the type of economic prosperity enjoyed in developed economies. Second, we could believe, optimistically, that present models of business and economic growth can be extended across the globe to an expanding population without degrading the natural environment beyond its limits. Third, we can search for new models of economic and business activity that provide for the needs of the world's population without further degrading the biosphere. Sustainable development and the connected model of sustainable business choose this third path.

recommendations for paths towards economic and social development that would not achieve short-term economic growth at the expense of long-term environmental and economic sustainability. The Brundtland Commission offered what has become the standard definition of sustainable development. "Sustainable development is development that meets the needs of the present without compromising the ability of future generations to meet their own needs."

Economist Herman Daly has been among the leading thinkers who have advocated an innovative approach to economic theory based on the concept of sustainable development. Daly makes a convincing case for an understanding of economic *development* that transcends the more common standard of economic *growth*. Unless we make significant changes in our understanding of economic activity, unless quite literally we change the way we do business, we will fail to meet some very basic ethical and environmental obligations. According to Daly, we need a major paradigm shift in how we understand economic activity.

We can begin with the standard understanding of economic activity and economic growth found in almost every economics textbook. What is sometimes called the "circular flow model" (Figure 9.1) explains the nature of economic transactions in terms of a flow of resources from businesses to households and back again. Business produces goods and services in response to the market demands of households, then ships the goods and services to households in exchange for payments back to business. These payments are in turn sent back to households in the form of wages, salaries, rents, profits, and interests. Households receive the

FIGURE 9.1 **The Circular Flow Model**

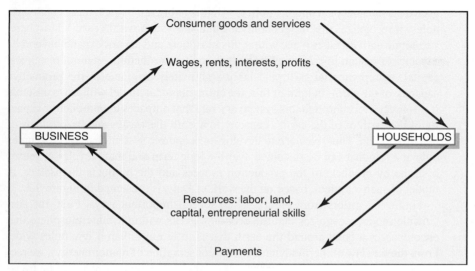

payments in exchange for the labor, land, capital, and entrepreneurial skills business uses to produce goods and services.

Two aspects of this circular flow model are worth noting. First, it does not differentiate natural resources from the other factors of production. This model does not explain the origin of resources. They are simply owned by households from which they, like labor, capital, and entrepreneurial skill, can be sold to business. As economist Julian Simon has argued, "As economists or consumers, we are interested in the particular services that resources yield, not in the resources themselves." Those services can be provided in many ways and by substituting different factors of production. In Simon's terms, resources can therefore be treated as "infinite."

A second observation is that this model treats economic growth as both the solution to all social ills and also as boundless. To keep up with population growth, the economy must grow. To provide for a higher standard of living, the economy must grow. To alleviate poverty, hunger, and disease, the economy must grow. The possibility that the economy cannot grow indefinitely is simply not part of this model.

The three points summarized in the previous Reality Check suggest why this growth-based model will be inadequate. According to some estimates, the world's economy would need to grow by a factor of five- to tenfold over the next 50 years in order to bring the standard of living of present populations in the developing world into line with the standard of living in the industrialized world. Yet, within those 50 years, the world's population will increase by more than 3 billion people, most of whom will be born in the world's poorest economies. Of course, the only source for all this economic activity is productive capacity of the earth itself.

Daly argues that neoclassical economics, with its emphasis on economic growth as the goal of economic policy, will inevitably fail to meet these challenges unless it recognizes that the economy is but a subsystem within earth's biosphere. Economic activity takes place within this biosphere and cannot expand beyond its capacity to sustain life. All the factors that go into production—natural resources, capital, entrepreneurial skill, and labor—ultimately originate in the productive capacity of the earth. In light of this, the entire classical model will prove unstable if resources move through this system at a rate that outpaces the productive capacity of the earth or of the earth's capacity to absorb the wastes and by-products of this production. Thus, we need to develop an economic system that uses resources only at a rate that can be sustained over the long term and that recycles or reuses both the by-products of the production process and the products themselves. A model of such a system, based on the work of Daly, is presented in Figure 9.2.

Figure 9.2 differs from Figure 9.1 in several important ways. First, the sustainable model recognizes that the economy exists within a finite biosphere that encompasses a band around the earth that is little more than a few miles wide. From the first law of thermodynamics (the conservation of matter/energy), we recognize that neither matter nor energy can truly be "created," it can only be transferred from one form to another. Second, energy is lost at every stage of economic activity. Consistent with the second law of thermodynamics (entropy increased within a closed system), the amount of usable energy decreases over time. "Waste energy" is continuously leaving the economic system and thus new low-entropy energy must constantly flow into the system. Ultimately, the only source for low-entropy energy is the sun. Third, this model no longer treats natural resources as

FIGURE 9.2   **A Model of the Economy (or Economic System) as a Subset of the Biosphere (or Ecosystem)**

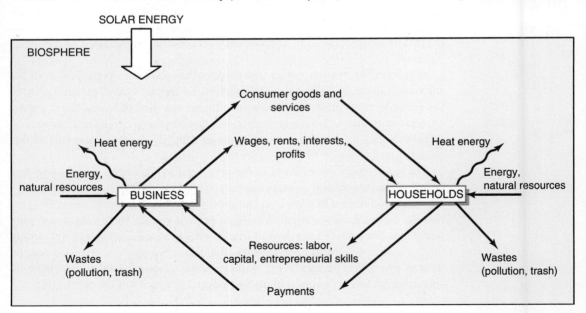

an undifferentiated and unexplained factor of production emerging from households. Natural resources come from the biosphere and cannot be created ex nihilo. Finally, it recognizes that wastes are produced at each stage of economic activity and these wastes are dumped back into the biosphere.

The conclusion that should be drawn from this new model is relatively simple. Over the long term, resources and energy cannot be used, nor waste produced, at rates at which the biosphere cannot replace or absorb them without jeopardizing its ability to sustain (human) life. These are what Daly calls the "biophysical limits to growth.[3] The biosphere can produce resources indefinitely, and it can absorb wastes indefinitely, but only at a certain rate and with a certain type of economic activity. This is the goal of sustainable development. Finding this rate and type of economic activity, and thereby creating a sustainable business practice, is the ultimate environmental responsibility of business.

Business Opportunities in a Sustainable Economy

OBJECTIVE

While the regulatory and compliance model tends to interpret environmental responsibilities as constraints upon business, the sustainability model is more forward looking and may present business with greater opportunities than burdens. Indeed, it offers a vision of future business that many entrepreneurial and creative businesses are already pursuing.

The environmental research and consulting group The Natural Step uses an image of a funnel, with two converging lines, to help business understand these opportunities. The resources necessary to sustain life are on a downward slope. While there is disagreement about the angle of the slope (are we at the start, with only a mild slope, or further along, with a sharper downward slope?), there is widespread consensus that available resources are in decline. The second line represents aggregate worldwide demand, accounting for both population growth and the increasing demand of consumerist lifestyles. Barring an environmental catastrophe, many but not all industries will emerge through the narrowing funnel into an era of sustainable living. Businesses unable to envision that sustainable future will hit the narrowing wall. Innovative and entrepreneurial business will find their way through. The Natural Step's funnel is illustrated in Figure 9.3.

The Natural Step then challenges business to "backcast" a path towards sustainability. We are all familiar with forecasting, in which we examine present data and predict the future. "**Backcasting**" examines what the future will be when we emerge through the funnel. Knowing what the future must be, creative businesses then look backwards to the present and determine what must be done to arrive at that future.

Why ought a business pursue a strategy of sustainability? For reasons of business self-interest alone, a strong case can be made for taking steps now to achieve a sustainable future. At least five reasons establish a persuasive case for concluding that it is almost always in business's self-interest to pursue a strategy of sustainability. (For some clarity on the circumstances under which it is not, take a look at the Reality Check on page 389.)

FIGURE 9.3
The Natural Step Funnel

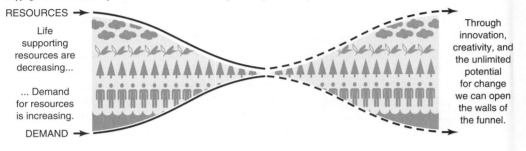

RESOURCES →

Life supporting resources are decreasing...

... Demand for resources is increasing.

DEMAND →

Through innovation, creativity, and the unlimited potential for change we can open the walls of the funnel.

First, sustainability is a prudent long-term strategy. As the Natural Step's funnel image suggests, business will need to adopt sustainable practices to ensure long-term survival. Firms that fail to adapt to the converging lines of decreasing availability of resources and increasing demand risk their own survival. One can look to the ocean fishing industry as an example.

Second, the huge unmet market potential among the world's developing economies can only be met in sustainable ways. Enormous business opportunities exist in serving the billions of people who need, and are demanding, economic goods and services. The base of the economic pyramid represents the largest and fastest-growing economic market in human history. Yet, the sheer size of these markets alone makes it impossible to meet this demand with the environmentally damaging industrial practices of the 19th and 20th centuries. For example, if China were to consume oil at the same rate as the United States, it alone would consume more than the entire world's daily production and would more than triple the emission of atmospheric carbon dioxide. It is obvious that new sustainable technologies and products will be required to meet the Chinese demand.

Third, significant cost savings can be achieved through sustainable practices. Business stands to save significant costs in moves towards ecoefficiency. Savings on energy use and materials will reduce not only environmental wastes, but spending wastes as well. Minimizing wastes makes sense on financial grounds as well as on environmental grounds.

Fourth, competitive advantages exist for sustainable businesses. Firms that are ahead of the sustainability curve will both have an advantage serving environmentally conscious consumers and enjoy a competitive advantage attracting workers who will take pride and satisfaction in working for progressive firms.

Finally, sustainability is a good risk management strategy. Refusing to move towards sustainability offers many downsides that innovative firms will avoid. Avoiding future government regulation is one obvious benefit. Firms that take the initiative in moving towards sustainability will also likely be the firms that set the standards of best practices in the field. Thus, when regulation does come, these firms will likely play a role in determining what those regulations ought to be. Avoiding legal liability for unsustainable products is another potential benefit. As

Reality Check   *Is Everything Sustainable?*

"Sustainability" has become a somewhat trendy term and can seem to mean all things to all people. When we hear talk about "sustainability," we should always be prepared to ask "*What* is being sustained?" "*For whom* is it being sustained?" "*How* is it being sustained?" and "What *should* be sustained?"

The language of sustainability can be especially attractive to those of us living comfortably in developed economies if it is interpreted to mean maintaining the status quo over the long term. But, not every industry, nor every firm, nor every business practice, nor every consumer product is sustainable. Industrial fishing practices in the North Atlantic have already proven unsustainable, as has or soon will be many agricultural practices such as burning rain forests to increase cropland, tapping underground aquifers for irrigation, and burning fossil fuels to power personal transportation.

social consciousness changes, the legal system may soon begin punishing firms that are now negligent in failing to foresee harms caused by their unsustainable practices. Consumer boycotts of unsustainable firms are also a risk to be avoided.

We can summarize these previous sections by reflecting on the ethical decision-making model used throughout this text. The facts suggest that the earth's biosphere is under stress and that much of this comes from the type of global economic growth that has characterized industrial and consumerist societies. The ethical issues that develop from these facts include fairness in allocating scare resources, justice in meeting the real needs of billions of present and future human beings, and the values and rights associated with environmental conservation and preservation. The stakeholders for these decisions include, quite literally, all life on earth. Relaying on our own moral imagination, we can envision a future in which economic activity can meet the real needs of present generations without jeopardizing the ability of future generations to meet their own needs. Sustainability seems to be just this vision. The next section describes directions in which business might develop towards this sustainable model.

Principles for a Sustainable Business

OBJECTIVE

Figure 9.2 provides a general model for understanding how firms can evolve towards a sustainable business model. In the simplest terms, resources should not enter into the economic cycle from the biosphere at rates faster than they are replenished. Ideally, waste should be eliminated or, at a minimum, not produced at a rate faster than the biosphere can absorb it. Finally, the energy to power the economic system should be renewable, ultimately relying on the sun, the only energy that is truly renewable.

The precise implications of sustainability will differ for specific firms and industries, but three general principles will guide the move towards sustainability. Firms and industries must become more efficient in using natural resources; they should model their entire production process on biological processes; and they should emphasize the production of services rather than products.

Versions of the first principle, sometimes called **ecoefficiency,** has long been a part of the environmental movement. "Doing more with less" has been an environmental guideline for decades. On an individual scale, it is environmentally better to ride a bike than to ride in a bus, to ride in a fuel-cell or hybrid-powered bus than in a diesel bus, to ride in a bus than to drive a personal automobile, and to drive a hybrid car than an SUV. Likewise, business firms can improve energy and materials efficiency in such things as lighting, building design, product design, and distribution channels. Some estimates suggest that with present technologies alone, business could readily achieve at least a fourfold increase in efficiency and perhaps as much as a tenfold increase. Consider that a fourfold increase, called "Factor-Four" in the sustainability literature, would make it possible to achieve double the productivity from one-half the resource use.[4]

The second principle of business sustainability can be easily understood by reference to Figure 9.2. Imagine that the waste leaving the economic cycle is being turned back into the cycle as a productive resource. "Closed-loop" production seeks to integrate what is presently waste back into production. In an ideal situation, the waste of one firm becomes the resource of another, and such synergies can create ecoindustrial parks. Just as biological processes such as photosynthesis cycle the "waste" of one activity into the resource of another, this principle is often referred to as **biomimicry.** The following Reality Check provides an example of biomimicry.

The ultimate goal of biomimicry is to eliminate waste altogether rather than reducing it. If we truly mimic biological processes, the end result of one process (e.g., leaves and oxygen produced by photosynthesis) is ultimately reused as the productive resources (e.g., soil and water) of another process (plant growth) with only solar energy added.

The evolution of business strategy towards biomimicry can be understood along a continuum. The earliest phase has been described as "take-make-waste." Business takes resources, makes products out of them, and discards whatever is left over. A second phase envisions business taking responsibility for its products from "cradle to grave." Sometimes referred to as "life-cycle" responsibility, this approach has already found its way into both industrial and regulatory thinking. Cradle-to-grave, or life-cycle, responsibility holds that a business is responsible for the entire life of its products, including the ultimate disposal even after the sale. Thus, for example, a cradle-to-grave model would hold a business liable for groundwater contamination caused by its products even years after they had been buried in a landfill.

Cradle-to-cradle responsibility extends this idea even further and holds that a business should be responsible for incorporating the end results of its products back into the productive cycle. This responsibility, in turn, would create incentives to redesign products so that they could be recycled efficiently and easily.

The environmental design company McDonough and Braungart, founded by architect William McDonough and chemist Michael Braungart, has been a leader in helping businesses reconceptualize and redesign business practice to achieve sustainability. Their book, *Cradle to Cradle,* traces the life cycle of several products, providing case studies of economic and environmental benefits attainable when business

Reality Check   *Corn from Coal?*

Large-scale production of agricultural fertilizer has relied on natural gas as its feedstock. The gas is processed into its chemical components to produce high-nitrogen fertilizers. As the price of natural gas has increased significantly in recent years, the cost of producing fertilizers in this way has created a severe financial burden on farmer and fertilizer companies alike. One company, Royster-Clark, was driven to sell its fertilizer plant in Illinois.

As it turns out, parts of Illinois sit atop large reserves of coal, but it is a type of high-sulfur coal that, because of environmental regulations, is inappropriate for burning in electric power plants. Rentech, a small energy company with an innovative technology for converting coal and other hydrocarbons into liquids, bought the Royster-Clark plant. Rentech's process converts the coal into ultraclean fuels, nitrogen, and electric power. The plant now produces fertilizer at lower costs than it could have with natural gas, and as its by-products it produces sulfur-free diesel fuel, other industrial chemicals, and power. Reduced-sulfur diesel fuel, newly required by federal regulations, can play a major role in increasing fuel efficiency with fewer of the pollution problems of traditional diesel.

While the process also produces carbon dioxide, it does so in such a way that the gas can be separately collected rather than discharged into the atmosphere. Long-term plans would be to sequester the carbon dioxide deep underground.

takes responsibility for the entire life cycle of products. Among their projects is the redesign of Ford Motor Company's Rouge River manufacturing plant.

Beyond ecoefficiency and biomimicry, a third sustainable business principle involves a shift in business model from products to services. Traditional economic and managerial models interpret consumer demand as the demand for products—washing machines, carpets, lights, consumer electronics, air conditioners, cars, computers, and so forth. A service-based economy interprets consumer demand as a demand for services—for clothes cleaning, floor covering, illumination, entertainment, cool air, transportation, word processing, and so forth.

The book *Natural Capitalism* provides examples of businesses that have made such a shift in each of these industries.[5] This change produces incentives for product redesigns that create more durable and more easily recyclable products.

One well-known innovator in this area is Interface Corporation and its CEO, Ray Anderson. Interface has made a transition from selling carpeting to leasing floor-covering services. On the traditional model, carpet is sold to consumers who, once they become dissatisfied with the color or style or once the carpeting becomes worn, dispose of the carpet in landfills. There is little incentive here to produce long-lasting or easily recyclable carpeting. Once Interface shifted to leasing floor-covering services, it created incentives to produce long-lasting, easily replaceable and recyclable carpets. Interface thereby accepts responsibility for the entire life cycle of the product it markets. Because the company retains ownership and is responsible for maintenance, Interface now produces carpeting that can be easily replaced in sections rather than in its entirety, that is more durable, and that can eventually be remanufactured. Redesigning carpets and shifting to a service lease has also improved production efficiencies and reduced material and energy costs significantly. Consumers benefit by getting what they truly desire at lower costs and fewer burdens.

Should toxic wastes be exported? In the early 1990s, an internal World Bank memo discussing the export of toxic wastes was leaked to the public. The memo was written by then–World Bank chief economist Lawrence Summers. Summers later became secretary of the Treasury under President Clinton and, after that, president of Harvard University. Summers makes the economic case for exporting wastes in this memo.

DATE: December 12, 1991

TO: Distribution

FR: Lawrence H. Summers

Subject: GEP

'Dirty' Industries: Just between you and me, shouldn't the World Bank be encouraging MORE migration of the dirty industries to the LDCs [Less Developed Countries]? I can think of three reasons:

1) The measurements of the costs of health impairing pollution depends on the forgone earnings from increased morbidity and mortality. From this point of view a given amount of health impairing pollution should be done in the country with the lowest cost, which will be the country with the lowest wages. I think the economic logic behind dumping a load of toxic waste in the lowest wage country is impeccable and we should face up to that.

2) The costs of pollution are likely to be non-linear as the initial increments of pollution probably have very low cost. I've always thought that under-populated countries in Africa are vastly UNDER-polluted, their air quality is probably vastly inefficiently low compared to Los Angeles or Mexico City. Only the lamentable facts that so much pollution is generated by non-tradable industries (transport, electrical generation) and that the unit transport costs of solid waste are so high prevent world welfare enhancing trade in air pollution and waste.

3) The demand for a clean environment for aesthetic and health reasons is likely to have very high income elasticity. The concern over an agent that causes a one in a million change in the odds of prostate cancer is obviously going to be much higher in a country where people survive to get prostate cancer than in a country where under 5 mortality is 200 per thousand. Also, much of the concern over industrial atmosphere discharge is about visibility impairing particulates. These discharges may have very little direct health impact. Clearly trade in goods that embody aesthetic pollution concerns could be welfare enhancing. While production is mobile the consumption of pretty air is a non-tradable.

The problem with the arguments against all of these proposals for more pollution in LDCs (intrinsic rights to certain goods, moral reasons, social concerns, lack of adequate markets, etc.) could be turned around and used more or less effectively against every Bank proposal for liberalization.

During the controversy that followed the release of this memo, defenders of Summers and the World Bank alleged that this memo was intended as ironic and tongue-in-cheek. Whether this was true or not, the memo does provide a clear description of some ethical and environmental implications of a fairly common

(continued)

pattern of economic thinking. If we were to apply the principles of free market economic thinking to business decision making and corporate social responsibility, we would seek to put a price on everything, including "increased morbidity and mortality" (illness and death). This economic way of thinking then advises that we make decisions by applying a utilitarian calculus: act in whichever way will maximize overall happiness. In the case of exporting toxic waste, "the economic logic behind dumping a load of toxic waste in the lowest wage country is impeccable and we should face up to that."

On the other hand, deontological principles of justice would seem to imply that economic benefits and burdens be distributed fairly and that those who reap the benefits of industrial economies ought to be the same people who bear the burdens created by that economy. Justice would require that that we not burden the least advantaged people in the world with the additional harms that industrial wastes create.

Of course, the ideal would be to create industrial processes that do not produce toxic wastes in the first place. "Take-back" regulations that many European countries are developing will produce incentives for business to ensure that the by-products of industrial processes are benign.

Questions, Projects, and Exercises

1. As a research project, choose a product with which you are familiar (one with local connections is best), and trace its entire life cycle. From where does this product originate? What resources go into its design and manufacture? How is it transported, sold, used, and disposed of? Along each step in the life cycle of this product, analyze the economic, environmental, and ethical costs and benefits. Consider if a service could be exchanged for this product. Some examples might include your local drinking water, food items such as beef or chicken, any product sold at a local farmer's market, or building materials used in local projects.

2. Conduct a Web search for ecological footprint analysis. You should be able to find a self-administered test to evaluate your own ecological footprint. If everyone on earth lived as you do, how many earths would be required to support this lifestyle?

3. Research corporate sustainability reports. How many corporations can you find that issue annual reports on their progress towards sustainability? Can you research a company that does not and explore why not (perhaps through its critics), or whether it has plans to change?

4. A movement within the European Union requires that business take back its products at the end of their useful life. Can you learn the details of such laws? Discuss whether or not you believe such a law could be passed in the United States. Should the United States have similar laws?

5. Apply the concept of sustainability to a variety of businesses and industries. What would sustainable agriculture require? What are sustainable energy sources? What would sustainable transportation be? What would be required to turn your hometown into a sustainable community?

6. Investigate what is involved in an environmental audit. Has such an audit been conducted at your own college or university? In what ways has your own school adopted sustainable practices? In what ways would your school need to change to become more sustainable?

7. Do you believe that business has any direct ethical duties to living beings other than humans? Do animals, plants, or ecosystems have rights? What criteria have you used in answering such questions? What is your own standard for determining what objects count, from a moral point of view?

8. Investigate LEED (Leadership in Energy and Environmental Design) building designs. If possible, arrange a visit to a local building designed according to LEED principles. Should all new buildings be required by law to adopt LEED design standards and conform to the LEED rating system?

Key Terms

After reading this Chapter, you should have a clear understanding of the following Key Terms. The page numbers refer to the point at which they were discussed in the chapter. For a more complete definition, please see the Glossary.

backcasting, *p. 387*
biomimicry, *p. 390*
Corporate Automotive
Fuel Efficiency (CAFE)
Standards, *p. 378*

cradle-to-cradle
responsibility, *p. 390*
ecoefficiency, *p. 390*
service-based economy,
p. 391

sustainable development,
p. 383
sustainable business
practice, *p. 383*
three pillars of
sustainability, *p. 383*

Endnotes

1. William Baxter, *People or Penguins: The Case for Optimal Pollution* (New York: Columbia University Press, 1974).

2. Julian Simon, *The Ultimate Resource* (Princeton, NJ: Princeton University Press, 1983).

3. Herman Daly, *Beyond Growth* (Boston: Beacon Press, 1996), pp. 33–35.

4. For the Factor Four claim, see Ernst von Weizacker, Amory B. Lovins, L. Hunter Lovins, and Kogan Page, "Factor Four: Doubling Wealth—Halving Resource Use: A Report to the Club of Rome" (1998), and for Factor 10, see Friedrich Schmidt-Bleek, Factor 10 Institute, http://www.factor10-institute.org/.

5. Paul Hawken, Amory Lovins, and Hunter Lovins, *Natural Capitalism* (Boston: Little Brown, 1999).

Readings

Reading 9-1: "Morality, Money, and Motor Cars," by Norman Bowie, *p. 395*

Reading 9-2: "The Next Industrial Revolution," by William McDonough and Michael Braungart, *p. 401*

Reading 9-3: "Taking Sustainability Seriously: An Argument for Managerial Responsibility," by Tara. Radin, *p. 410*

Morality, Money, and Motor Cars

Norman Bowie

Environmentalists frequently argue that business has special obligations to protect the environment. Although I agree with the environmentalists on this point, I do not agree with them as to where the obligations lie. Business does not have an obligation to protect the environment over and above what is required by law; however, it does have a moral obligation to avoid intervening in the political arena in order to defeat or weaken environmental legislation. In developing this thesis, several points are in order.

First, many businesses have violated important moral obligations, and the violation has had a severe negative impact on the environment. For example, toxic waste haulers have illegally dumped hazardous material, and the environment has been harmed as a result. One might argue that those toxic waste haulers who have illegally dumped have violated a special obligation to the environment. Isn't it more accurate to say that these toxic waste haulers have violated their obligation to obey the law and that in this case the law that has been broken is one pertaining to the environment? Businesses have an obligation to obey the law—environmental laws and all others. Since there are many well-publicized cases of business having broken environmental laws, it is easy to think that business has violated some special obligations to the environment. In fact, what business has done is to disobey the law. Environmentalists do not need a special obligation to the environment to protect the environment against illegal business activity; they need only insist that business obey the laws.

Business has broken other obligations beside the obligation to obey the law and has harmed the environment as a result. Consider the grounding of the Exxon oil tanker *Valdez* in Alaska. That grounding was allegedly caused by the fact that an inadequately trained crewman was piloting the tanker while the captain was below deck and had been drinking. What needs to be determined is whether Exxon's policies and procedures were sufficiently lax so that it could be said Exxon was morally at fault. It might be that Exxon is legally responsible for the accident under the doctrine of respondent superior, but Exxon is not thereby morally responsible. Suppose, however, that Exxon's policies were so lax that the company could be characterized as morally negligent. In such a case, the company would violate its moral obligation to use due care and avoid negligence. Although its negligence was disastrous to the environment, Exxon would have violated no special obligation to the environment. It would have been morally negligent.

A similar analysis could be given to the environmentalists' charges that Exxon's cleanup procedures were inadequate. If the charge is true, either Exxon was morally at fault or not. If the procedures had not been implemented properly by Exxon employees, then Exxon is legally culpable, but not morally culpable. On the other hand, if Exxon lied to government officials by saying that its policies were in accord with regulations and/or were ready for emergencies of this type, then Exxon violated its moral obligation to tell the truth. Exxon's immoral conduct would have harmed the environment, but it violated no special obligation to the environment. More important, none is needed.

Environmentalists, like government officials, employees, and stockholders, expect that business firms and officials have moral obligations to obey the law, avoid negligent behavior, and tell the truth. In sum, although many business decisions have harmed the environment, these decisions violated no environmental moral obligations. If a corporation is negligent in providing for worker safety, we do not say the corporation violated a special obligation to employees; we say that it violated its obligation to avoid negligent behavior.

The crucial issues concerning business obligations to the environment focus on the excess use of natural resources (the dwindling supply of oil and gas, for instance) and the externalities of production (pollution, for instance). The critics of business want to claim that business has some special obligation to mitigate or solve these problems. I believe this claim is sadly mistaken. If business does have a special obligation to help solve the environmental crisis, that obligation results from the special knowledge that business firms have. If they have greater expertise than other constituent groups in society, then it can be argued that, other things being equal, business's responsibilities to mitigate the environmental crisis are somewhat greater. Absent this condition, business's responsibility is no greater than and may be less than that of other social groups. What leads me to think that the critics of business are mistaken?

William Frankena distinguished obligations in an ascending order of the difficulty in carrying them out: avoiding harm, preventing harm, and doing good. The most stringent requirement, to avoid harm, insists no one has a right to render harm on another unless there is a compelling, overriding moral reason to do so. Some writers have referred to this obligation as the moral minimum. A corporation's behavior is consistent with the moral minimum if it causes no avoidable harm to others.

Preventing harm is a less stringent obligation, but sometimes the obligation to prevent harm may be nearly as strict as the obligation to avoid harm. Suppose you are the only person passing a two-foot-deep [wading] pool where a young child is drowning. There is no one else in the vicinity. Don't you have a strong moral obligation to prevent the child's death? Our obligation to prevent harm is not unlimited, however. Under what conditions must we be good Samaritans? Some have argued that four conditions must exist before one is obligated to prevent harm: capability, need, proximity, and last resort. These conditions are all met with the case of the drowning child. There is obviously a need that you can meet since you are both in the vicinity and have the resources to prevent the drowning with little effort; you are also the last resort.

The least strict moral obligation is to do good—to make contributions to society or to help solve problems (inadequate primary schooling in the inner cities, for example). Although corporations may have some minimum obligation in this regard based on an argument from corporate citizenship, the obligations of the corporation to do good cannot be expanded without limit. An injunction to assist in solving societal problems makes impossible demands on a corporation because at the practical level, it ignores the impact that such activities have on profit.

It might seem that even if this descending order of strictness of obligations were accepted, obligations toward the environment would fall into the moral minimum category. After all, the depletion of natural resources and pollution surely harm the environment. If so, wouldn't the obligations business has to the environment be among the strictest obligations a business can have?

Suppose, however, that a businessperson argues that the phrase "avoid harm" usually applies to human beings. Polluting a lake is not like injuring a human with a faulty product. Those who coined the phrase *moral* minimum for use in the business context defined harm as "particularly including activities which violate or frustrate the enforcement of rules of domestic or institutional law intended to protect individuals against prevention of health, safety or basic freedom." Even if we do not insist that the violations be violations of a rule of law, polluting a lake would not count as a harm under this definition. The environmentalists would respond that it would. Polluting the lake may be injuring people who might swim in or eat fish from it. Certainly it would be depriving people of the freedom to enjoy the lake. Although the environmentalist is correct, especially *if* we grant the legitimacy of a human right to a clean environment, the success of this reply is not enough to establish the general argument.

Consider the harm that results from the production of automobiles. We know statistically that about 50,000 persons per year will die and that nearly 250,000 others will be seriously injured in automobile accidents in the United States alone. Such death and injury, which is harmful, is avoidable. If that is the case, doesn't the avoid-harm criterion require that the production of automobiles for profit cease? Not really. What such arguments point out is that some refinement of the moral minimum standard needs to take place. Take the automobile example. The automobile is itself a good producing instrument. Because of the advantages of automobiles, society accepts the possible risks that go into using them. Society also accepts many other types of avoidable harm. We take certain risks—ride in planes, build bridges, and mine coal—to pursue advantageous goals. It seems that the high benefits of some activities justify the resulting harms. As long as the risks are known, it is not wrong that some avoidable harm be permitted so that other social and individual goals can be achieved. The avoidable-harm criterion needs some sharpening.

Using the automobile as a paradigm, let us consider the necessary refinements for the avoid-harm criterion. It is a fundamental principle of ethics that "ought" implies "can." That expression means that you can be held morally responsible only for events within your power. In the ought-implies-can principle, the overwhelming majority of highway deaths and injuries is not the responsibility of the automaker. Only those deaths and injuries attributable to unsafe automobile design can be attributed to the automaker. The ought-implies-can principle can also be used to absolve the auto companies of responsibility for death and injury from safety defects that the automakers could not reasonably know existed. The company could not be expected to do anything about them.

Does this mean that a company has an obligation to build a car as safe as it knows how? No. The standards for safety must leave the product's cost within the price range of the consumer ("ought implies can" again). Comments about engineering and equipment capability are obvious enough. But for a business, capability is also a function of profitability. A company that builds a maximally safe car at a cost that puts it at a competitive disadvantage and hence threatens its survival is building a safe car that lies beyond the capability of the company.

Critics of the automobile industry will express horror at these remarks, for by making capability a function of profitability, society will continue to have avoidable deaths and injuries; however, the situation is not as dire as the critics imagine. Certainly capability should not be sacrificed completely so that profits can be maximized. The decision to build products that are cheaper in cost but are not maximally safe is a social decision that has widespread support. The arguments occur over the line between safety and cost. What we have is a classical trade-off situation. What is desired is some appropriate mix between engineering safety and consumer demand. To say there must be some mix between engineering safety and consumer demand is not to justify all the decisions made by the automobile companies. Ford Motor Company made a morally incorrect choice in placing Pinto gas tanks where it did. Consumers were uninformed, the record of the Pinto in rear-end collisions was worse than that of competitors, and Ford fought government regulations.

Let us apply the analysis of the automobile industry to the issue before us. That analysis shows that an automobile company does not violate its obligation to avoid harm and hence is not in violation of the moral minimum if the trade-off between potential harm and the utility of the products rests on social consensus and competitive realities.

As long as business obeys the environmental laws and honors other standard moral obligations, most harm done to the environment by business has been accepted by society. Through their decisions in the marketplace, we can see that most consumers are unwilling to pay extra for products that are more environmentally friendly than less friendly competitive products. Nor is there much evidence that consumers are willing to conserve resources, recycle, or tax themselves for environmental causes.

Consider the following instances reported in *The Wall Street Journal.* The restaurant chain Wendy's tried to replace foam plates and cups with paper, but customers in the test markets balked. Procter & Gamble offered Downey fabric softener in concentrated form that requires less packaging than ready-to-use products; however the concentrated version is less convenient because it has to be mixed with water. Sales have been poor. Procter & Gamble manufactures Vizir and Lenor brands of detergents in concentrate form, which the customer mixes at home in reusable bottles. Europeans will take the trouble; Americans will not.

Kodak tried to eliminate its yellow film boxes but met customer resistance. McDonald's has been testing mini-incinerators that convert trash into energy but often meets opposition from community groups that fear the incinerators will pollute the air. A McDonald's spokesperson points out that the emissions are mostly carbon dioxide and water vapor and are "less offensive than a barbecue." Exxon spent approximately $9,200,000 to "save" 230 otters ($40,000 for each otter). Otters in captivity cost $800. Fishermen in Alaska are permitted to shoot otters as pests. Given these facts, doesn't business have every right to assume that public tolerance for environmental damage is quite high, and hence current legal activities by corporations that harm the environment do not violate the avoid-harm criterion?

Recently environmentalists have pointed out the environmental damage caused by the widespread use of disposable diapers. Are Americans ready to give them up and go back to cloth diapers and the diaper pail? Most observers think not. Procter & Gamble is not violating the avoid-harm criterion by manufacturing Pampers. Moreover, if the public wants cloth diapers, business certainly will produce them. If environmentalists want business to produce products that are friendlier to the environment, they must convince Americans to purchase them. Business will respond to the market. It is the consuming public that has the obligation to make the trade-off between cost and environmental integrity.

Data and arguments of the sort described should give environmental critics of business pause. Nonetheless, these critics are not without counter-responses. For example, they might respond that public attitudes are changing. Indeed, they point out, during the Reagan deregulation era, the one area where the public supported government regulations was in the area of environmental law. In addition, *Fortune* predicts environmental integrity as the primary demand of society on business in the 1990s. More important, they might argue that environmentally friendly products are at a disadvantage in the marketplace because they have public good characteristics. After all, the best situation for the individual is one where most other people use environmentally friendly products but he or she does not, hence reaping the benefit of lower cost and convenience. Since everyone reasons this way, the real demand for environmentally friendly products cannot be registered in the market.

Everyone is understating the value of his or her preference for environmentally friendly products. Hence, companies cannot conclude from market behavior that the environmentally unfriendly products are preferred.

Suppose the environmental critics are right that the public goods characteristic of environmentally friendly products creates a market failure. Does that mean the companies are obligated to stop producing these environmentally unfriendly products? I think not, and I propose that we use the four conditions attached to the prevent-harm obligation to show why not. There is a need, and certainly corporations that cause environmental problems are in proximity. However, environmentally clean firms, if there are any, are not in proximity at all, and most business firms are not in proximity with respect to most environmental problems. In other words, the environmental critic must limit his or her argument to the environmental damage a business actually causes. The environmentalist might argue that Procter & Gamble ought to do something about Pampers; I do not see how an environmentalist can use the avoid-harm criterion to argue that Procter & Gamble should do something about acid rain. But even narrowing the obligation to damage actually caused will not be sufficient to establish an obligation to pull a product from the market because it damages the environment or even to go beyond what is legally required to protect the environment. Even for damage actually done, both the high cost of protecting the environment and the competitive pressures of business make further action to protect the environment beyond the capability of business. This conclusion would be more serious if business were the last resort, but it is not.

Traditionally it is the function of the government to correct for market failure. If the market cannot register the true desires of consumers, let them register their preferences in the political arena. Even fairly conservative economic thinkers allow government a legitimate role in correcting market failure. Perhaps the responsibility for energy conservation and pollution control belongs with the government.

Although I think consumers bear a far greater responsibility for preserving and protecting the environment than they have actually exercised, let us assume that the basic responsibility rests with the government. Does that let business off the hook? No. Most of business's unethical conduct regarding the environment occurs in the political arena.

Far too many corporations try to have their cake and eat it too. They argue that it is the job of government to correct for market failure and then use their influence and money to defeat or water down regulations designed to conserve and protect the environment. They argue that consumers should decide how much conservation and protection the environment should have, and then they try to interfere with the exercise of that choice in the political arena. Such behavior is inconsistent and ethically inappropriate. Business has an obligation to avoid intervention in the political process for the purpose of defeating and weakening environmental regulations. Moreover, this is a special obligation to the environment since business does not have a general obligation to avoid pursuing its own parochial interests in the political arena. Business need do nothing wrong when it seeks to influence tariffs, labor policy, or monetary *policy.* Business does do something wrong when it interferes with the passage of environmental legislation. Why?

First, such a noninterventionist policy is dictated by the logic of the business's argument to avoid a special obligation to protect the environment. Put more formally:

1. Business argues that it escapes special obligations to the environment because it is willing to respond to consumer preferences in this matter.
2. Because of externalities and public goods considerations, consumers cannot express their preferences in the market.

3. The only other viable forum for consumers to express their preferences is in the political arena.

4. Business intervention interferes with the expression of these preferences.

5. Since point 4 is inconsistent with point 1, business should not intervene in the political process.

The importance of this obligation in business is even more important when we see that environmental legislation has special disadvantages in the political arena. Public choice reminds us that the primary interest of politicians is being reelected. Government policy will be skewed in favor of policies that provide benefits to an influential minority as long as the greater costs are widely dispersed. Politicians will also favor projects where benefits are immediate and where costs can be postponed to the future. Such strategies increase the likelihood that a politician will be reelected.

What is frightening about the environmental crisis is that both the conservation of scarce resources and pollution abatement require policies that go contrary to a politician's self-interest. The costs of cleaning up the environment are immediate and huge, yet the benefits are relatively long range (many of them exceedingly long range). Moreover, a situation where the benefits are widely dispersed and the costs are large presents a twofold problem. The costs are large enough so that all voters will likely notice them and in certain cases are catastrophic for individuals (e.g., for those who lose their jobs in a plant shutdown).

Given these facts and the political realities they entail, business opposition to environmental legislation makes a very bad situation much worse. Even if consumers could be persuaded to take environmental issues more seriously, the externalities, opportunities to free ride, and public goods characteristics of the environment make it difficult for even enlightened consumers to express their true preference for the environment in the market. The fact that most environmental legislation trades immediate costs for future benefits makes it difficult for politicians concerned about reelection to support it. Hence it is also difficult for enlightened consumers to have their preferences for a better environment honored in the political arena. Since lack of business intervention seems necessary, and might even be sufficient, for adequate environmental legislation, it seems business has an obligation not to intervene. Nonintervention would prevent the harm of not having the true preferences of consumers for a clean environment revealed. Given business's commitment to satisfying preference, opposition to having these preferences expressed seems inconsistent as well.

The extent of this obligation to avoid intervening in the political process needs considerable discussion by ethicists and other interested parties. Businesspeople will surely object that if they are not permitted to play a role, Congress and state legislators will make decisions that will put them at a severe competitive disadvantage. For example, if the United States develops stricter environmental controls than other countries do, foreign imports will have a competitive advantage over domestic products. Shouldn't business be permitted to point that out? Moreover, any legislation that places costs on one industry rather than another confers advantages on other industries. The cost to the electric utilities from regulations designed to reduce the pollution that causes acid rain will give advantages to natural gas and perhaps even solar energy. Shouldn't the electric utility industry be permitted to point that out?

These questions pose difficult questions, and my answer to them should be considered highly tentative. I believe the answer to the first question is *"yes"* and the answer to the second is *"no."* Business does have a right to insist that the regulations apply to all those in the industry. Anything else would seem to violate norms of fairness. Such issues of fairness do not arise in the second case. Since natural gas and solar energy do not contribute to acid rain and since the costs of acid rain cannot be fully captured in the market, government intervention through regulation is simply correcting a market failure. With respect to acid rain, the electric utilities do have an advantage they do not deserve. Hence they have no right to try to protect it.

Source: Copyright © Norman Bowie. Used by permission of the author.

The Next Industrial Revolution

William McDonough and Michael Braungart

In the spring of 1912 one of the largest moving objects ever created by human beings left Southampton and began gliding toward New York. It was the epitome of its industrial age—a potent representation of technology, prosperity, luxury, and progress. It weighed 66,000 tons. Its steel hull stretched the length of four city blocks. Each of its steam engines was the size of a townhouse. And it was headed for a disastrous encounter with the natural world.

This vessel, of course, was the *Titanic*—a brute of a ship, seemingly impervious to the details of nature. In the minds of the captain, the crew, and many of the passengers, nothing could sink it. One might say that the infrastructure created by the Industrial Revolution of the nineteenth century resembles such a steamship. It is powered by fossil fuels, nuclear reactors, and chemicals. It is pouring waste into the water and smoke into the sky. It is attempting to work by its own rules, contrary to those of the natural world. And although it may seem invincible, its fundamental design flaws presage disaster. Yet many people still believe that with a few minor alterations, this infrastructure can take us safely and prosperously into the future.

During the Industrial Revolution resources seemed inexhaustible and nature was viewed as something to be tamed and civilized. Recently, however, some leading industrialists have begun to realize that traditional ways of doing things may not be sustainable over the long term. "What we thought was boundless has limits," Robert Shapiro, the chairman and chief executive officer of Monsanto, said in a 1997 interview, "and we're beginning to hit them."

The 1992 Earth Summit in Rio de Janeiro, led by the Canadian businessman Maurice Strong, recognized those limits. Approximately 30,000 people from around the world, including more than a hundred world leaders and representatives of 167 countries, gathered in Rio de Janeiro to respond to troubling symptoms of environmental decline. Although there was sharp disappointment afterward that no binding agreement had been reached at the summit, many industrial participants touted a particular strategy: eco-efficiency. The machines of industry would be refitted with cleaner, faster, quieter engines. Prosperity would remain unobstructed, and economic and organizational structures would remain intact. The hope was that eco-efficiency would transform human industry from a system that takes, makes, and wastes into one that integrates economic, environmental, and ethical concerns. Eco-efficiency is now considered by industries across the globe to be the strategy of choice for change.

What is eco-efficiency? Primarily, the term means "doing more with less"—a precept that has its roots in early industrialization. Henry Ford was adamant about lean and clean operating policies; he saved his company money by recycling and reusing materials, reduced the use of natural resources, minimized packaging, and set new standards with his timesaving assembly line. Ford wrote in 1926, "You must get the most out of the power, out of the material, and out of the time"—a credo that could hang today on the wall of any eco-efficient factory. The linkage of efficiency with sustaining the environment was perhaps most famously articulated in *Our Common Future,* a report published in 1987 by the United Nations' World Commission on Environment and Development. *Our Common Future* warned that if pollution control were not intensified, property and ecosystems would be threatened, and existence would become unpleasant and even harmful to human health in some cities. "Industries and industrial operations should be encouraged that are more efficient in terms of resource use, that generate less pollution and waste, that are based on the use of renewable rather than nonrenewable resources, and that minimize irreversible adverse impacts on human health and the environment," the commission stated in its agenda for change.

The term "eco-efficiency" was promoted five years later, by the Business Council (now the World Business Council) for Sustainable Development, a group of 48 industrial sponsors including Dow, Du Pont, Con Agra, and Chevron, who brought a business perspective to the Earth Summit. The council presented its call for change in practical terms, focusing on what businesses had to gain from a new ecological awareness rather than on what the environment had to lose if industry continued in current patterns. In *Changing Course,* a report released just before the summit, the group's founder, Stephan Schmidheiny, stressed the importance of eco-efficiency for all companies that aimed to be competitive, sustainable, and successful over the long term. In 1996 Schmidheiny said, "I predict that within a decade it is going to be next to impossible for a business to be competitive without also being 'eco-efficient'—adding more value to a good or service while using fewer resources and releasing less pollution."

As Schmidheiny predicted, eco-efficiency has been working its way into industry with extraordinary success. The corporations committing themselves to it continue to increase in number, and include such big names as Monsanto, 3M, and Johnson & Johnson. Its famous three *R*s—reduce, reuse, recycle—are steadily gaining popularity in the home as well as the workplace. The trend stems in part from eco-efficiency's economic benefits, which can be considerable: 3M, for example, has saved more than $750 million through pollution-prevention projects, and other companies, too, claim to be realizing big savings. Naturally, reducing resource consumption, energy use, emissions, and wastes has implications for the environment as well. When one hears that Du Pont has cut its emissions of airborne cancer-causing chemicals by almost 75 percent since 1987, one can't help feeling more secure. This is another benefit of eco-efficiency: it diminishes guilt and fear. By subscribing to eco-efficiency, people and industries can be less "bad" and less fearful about the future. Or can they?

Eco-efficiency is an outwardly admirable and certainly well-intended concept, but, unfortunately, it is not a strategy for success over the long term, because it does not reach deep enough. It works within the same system that caused the problem in the first place, slowing it down with moral proscriptions and punitive demands. It presents little more than an illusion of change. Relying on eco-efficiency to save the environment will in fact achieve the opposite—it will let industry finish off everything quietly, persistently, and completely.

We are forwarding a reshaping of human industry—what we and the author Paul Hawken call the Next Industrial Revolution. Leaders of this movement include many people in diverse fields, among them commerce, politics, the humanities, science, engineering, and education. Especially notable are the businessman Ray Anderson; the philanthropist Teresa Heinz; the Chattanooga city councilman Dave Crockett; the physicist Amory Lovins; the environmental-studies professor David W. Orr; the environmentalists Sarah Severn, Dianne Dillon Ridgley, and Susan Lyons; the environmental product developer Heidi Holt; the ecological designer John Todd; and the writer Nancy Jack Todd. We are focused here on a new way of designing industrial production. As an architect and industrial designer and a chemist who have worked with both commercial and ecological systems, we see conflict between industry and the environment as a design problem—a very big design problem.

Any of the basic intentions behind the Industrial Revolution were good ones, which most of us would probably like to see carried out today: to bring more goods and services to larger numbers of people, to raise standards of living, and to give people more choice and opportunity, among others. But there were crucial omissions. Perpetuating the diversity and vitality of forests, rivers, oceans, air, soil, and animals was not part of the agenda.

If someone were to present the Industrial Revolution as a retroactive design assignment, it might sound like this: Design a system of production that

- Puts billions of pounds of toxic material into the air, water, and soil every year.
- Measures prosperity by activity, not legacy.
- Requires thousands of complex regulations to keep people and natural systems from being poisoned too quickly.
- Produces materials so dangerous that they will require constant vigilance from future generations.
- Results in gigantic amounts of waste.
- Puts valuable materials in holes all over the planet, where they can never be retrieved.
- Erodes the diversity of biological species and cultural practices.

Eco-efficiency instead

- Releases *fewer* pounds of toxic material into the air, water, and soil every year.
- Measures prosperity by *less* activity.
- *Meets or exceeds* the stipulations of thousands of complex regulations that aim to keep people and natural systems from being poisoned too quickly.
- Produces *fewer* dangerous materials that will require constant vigilance from future generations.
- Results in *smaller* amounts of waste.
- Puts *fewer* valuable materials in holes all over the planet, where they can never be retrieved.
- Standardizes and homogenizes biological species and cultural practices.

Plainly put, eco-efficiency aspires to make the old, destructive system less so. But its goals, however admirable, are fatally limited.

Reduction, reuse, and recycling slow down the rates of contamination and depletion but do not stop these processes. Much recycling, for instance, is what we call "downcycling," because it reduces the quality of a material over time. When plastic other than that found in such products as soda and water bottles is recycled, it is often mixed with different plastics to produce a hybrid of lower quality, which is then molded into something amorphous and cheap, such as park benches or speed bumps. The original high-quality material is not retrieved, and it eventually ends up in landfills or incinerators.

The well-intended, creative use of recycled materials for new products can be misguided. For example, people may feel that they are making an ecologically sound choice by buying and wearing clothing made of fibers from recycled plastic bottles. But the fibers from plastic bottles were not specifically designed to be next to human skin. Blindly adopting superficial "environmental" approaches without fully understanding their effects can be no better than doing nothing.

Recycling is more expensive for communities than it needs to be, partly because traditional recycling tries to force materials into more lifetimes than they were designed for—a complicated and messy conversion, and one that itself expends energy and resources. Very few objects of modern consumption were designed with recycling in mind. If the process is truly to save money and materials, products must be designed from the very beginning to be recycled or even "upcycled"—a term we use to describe the return to industrial systems of materials with improved, rather than degraded, quality.

The reduction of potentially harmful emissions and wastes is another goal of eco-efficiency. But current studies are beginning to raise concern that even tiny amounts of dangerous emissions can have disastrous effects on biological systems over time. This is a particular concern in the case of endocrine disrupters—industrial chemicals in a variety of modern plastics and consumer goods which appear to mimic hormones and connect with receptors in human beings and other organisms. Theo Colborn, Dianne Dumanoski, and John Peterson Myers, the authors of *Our Stolen Future* (1996), a groundbreaking study on certain synthetic chemicals and the environment, assert that "astoundingly small quantities of these hormonally active compounds can wreak all manner of biological havoc, particularly in those exposed in the womb."

On another front, new research on particulates—microscopic particles released during incineration and combustion processes, such as those in power plants and automobiles—shows that they can lodge in and damage the lungs, especially in children and the elderly. A 1995 Harvard study found that as many as 100,000 people die annually as a result of these tiny particles. Although regulations for smaller particles are in place, implementation does not have to begin until 2005. Real change would be not regulating the release of particles but attempting to eliminate dangerous emissions altogether—by design.

Applying Nature's Cycles to Industry

"Produce more with less," "Minimize waste," "Reduce," and similar dictates advance the notion of a world of limits—one whose carrying capacity is strained by burgeoning populations and exploding production and consumption. Eco-efficiency tells us to restrict industry and curtail growth—to try to limit the creativity and productiveness of humankind. But the idea that the natural world is inevitably destroyed by human industry, or that excessive demand for goods and services causes environmental ills, is a simplification. Nature—highly industrious, astonishingly productive and creative, even "wasteful"—is not efficient but *effective*.

Consider the cherry tree. It makes thousands of blossoms just so that another tree might germinate, take root, and grow. Who would notice piles of cherry blossoms littering the ground in the spring and think, "How inefficient and wasteful"? The tree's abundance is useful and safe. After falling to the ground, the blossoms return to the soil and become nutrients for the surrounding environment. Every last particle contributes in some way to the health of a thriving ecosystem. "Waste equals food"—the first principle of the Next Industrial Revolution.

The cherry tree is just one example of nature's industry, which operates according to cycles of nutrients and metabolisms. This cyclical system is powered by the sun and constantly adapts to local circumstances. Waste that stays waste does not exist.

Human industry, on the other hand, is severely limited. It follows a one-way, linear, cradle-to-grave manufacturing line in which things are created and eventually discarded, usually in an incinerator or a landfill. Unlike the waste from nature's work, the waste from human industry is not "food" at all. In fact, it is often poison. Thus the two conflicting systems: a pile of cherry blossoms and a heap of toxic junk in a landfill.

But there is an alternative—one that will allow both business and nature to be fecund and productive. This alternative is what we call "eco-effectiveness." Our concept of eco-effectiveness leads to human industry that is regenerative rather than depletive. It involves the design of things that celebrate interdependence with other living systems. From an industrial-design perspective, it means products that work within cradle-to-cradle life cycles rather than cradle-to-grave ones.

Waste Equals Food

Ancient nomadic cultures tended to leave organic wastes behind, restoring nutrients to the soil and the surrounding environment. Modern, settled societies simply want to get rid of waste as quickly as possible. The potential nutrients in organic waste are lost when they are disposed of in landfills, where they cannot be used to rebuild soil; depositing synthetic materials and chemicals in natural systems strains the environment. The ability of complex, interdependent natural ecosystems to absorb such foreign material is limited if not nonexistent. Nature cannot do anything with the stuff *by design*: many manufactured products are intended not to break down under natural conditions. If people are to prosper within the natural world, all the products and materials manufactured by industry must after each useful life provide nourishment for something new. Since many of the things people make are not natural, they are not safe "food" for biological systems. Products composed of materials that do not biodegrade should be designed as technical nutrients that continually circulate within closed-loop industrial cycles—the technical metabolism.

In order for these two metabolisms to remain healthy, great care must be taken to avoid cross-contamination. Things that go into the biological metabolism should not contain mutagens, carcinogens, heavy metals, endocrine disrupters, persistent toxic substances, or bio-accumulative substances. Things that go into the technical metabolism should be kept well apart from the biological metabolism.

If the things people make are to be safely channeled into one or the other of these metabolisms, then products can be considered to contain two kinds of materials: *biological nutrients* and *technical nutrients.*

Biological nutrients will be designed to return to the organic cycle—to be literally consumed by microorganisms and other creatures in the soil. Most packaging (which makes up about 50 percent by volume of the solid-waste stream) should be composed of biological nutrients—materials that can be tossed onto the ground or the compost heap to biodegrade. There is no need for shampoo bottles, toothpaste tubes, yogurt cartons, juice containers, and other packaging to last decades (or even centuries) longer than what came inside them.

Technical nutrients will be designed to go back into the technical cycle. Right now anyone can dump an old television into a trash can. But the average television is made of hundreds of chemicals, some of which are toxic. Others are valuable nutrients for industry, which are wasted when the television ends up in a landfill. The reuse of technical nutrients in closed-loop industrial cycles is distinct from traditional recycling, because it allows materials to retain their quality: high-quality plastic computer cases would continually circulate as high-quality computer cases, instead of being downcycled to make soundproof barriers or flowerpots.

Customers would buy the *service* of such products, and when they had finished with the products, or simply wanted to upgrade to a newer version, the manufacturer would take back the old ones, break them down, and use their complex materials in new products.

First Fruits: A Biological Nutrient

A few years ago we helped to conceive and create a compostable upholstery fabric—a biological nutrient. We were initially asked by Design Tex to create an aesthetically unique fabric that was also ecologically intelligent—although the client did not quite know at that point what this would mean. The challenge helped to clarify, both for us and for the company we were working with, the difference between superficial responses such as recycling and reduction and the more significant changes required by the Next Industrial Revolution.

For example, when the company first sought to meet our desire for an environmentally safe fabric, it presented what it thought was a wholesome option: cotton, which is natural, combined with PET (polyethylene terephthalate) fibers from recycled beverage bottles. Since the proposed hybrid could be described with two important eco-buzzwords, "natural" and "recycled," it appeared to be environmentally ideal. The materials were readily available, market-tested, durable, and cheap. But when the project team looked carefully at what the manifestations of such a hybrid might be in the long run, we discovered some disturbing facts. When a person sits in an office chair and shifts around, the fabric beneath him or her abrades; tiny particles of it are inhaled or swallowed by the user and other people nearby. PET was not designed to be inhaled. Furthermore, PET would prevent the proposed hybrid from going back into the soil safely, and the cotton would prevent it from re-entering an industrial cycle. The hybrid would still add junk to landfills, and it might also be dangerous.

The team decided to design a fabric so safe that one could literally eat it. The European textile mill chosen to produce the fabric was quite "clean" environmentally, and yet it had an interesting problem: although the mill's director had been diligent about reducing levels of dangerous emissions, government regulators had recently defined the trimmings of his fabric as hazardous waste. We sought a different end for our trimmings: mulch for the local garden club. When removed from the frame after the chair's useful life and tossed onto the ground to mingle with sun, water, and hungry microorganisms, both the fabric and its trimmings would decompose naturally.

The team decided on a mixture of safe, pesticide-free plant and animal fibers for the fabric (ramie and wool) and began working on perhaps the most difficult aspect: the finishes, dyes, and other processing chemicals. If the fabric was to go back into the soil safely, it had to be free of mutagens, carcinogens, heavy metals, endocrine disrupters, persistent toxic substances, and bio-accumulative substances. Sixty chemical companies were approached about joining the project, and all declined, uncomfortable with the idea of exposing their chemistry to the kind of scrutiny necessary. Finally one European company, Ciba-Geigy, agreed to join.

With that company's help the project team considered more than 8,000 chemicals used in the textile industry and eliminated 7,962. The fabric—in fact, an entire line of fabrics—was created using only 38 chemicals.

The director of the mill told a surprising story after the fabrics were in production. When regulators came by to test the effluent, they thought their instruments were broken. After testing the influent as well, they realized that the equipment was fine—the water coming out of the factory was as clean as the water going in. The manufacturing process itself was filtering the water. The new design not only bypassed the traditional three-R responses to environmental problems but also eliminated the need for regulation.

In our Next Industrial Revolution, regulations can be seen as signals of design failure. They burden industry by involving government in commerce and by interfering with the marketplace. Manufacturers in countries that are less hindered by regulations, and whose factories emit *more* toxic substances, have an economic advantage: they can produce and sell things for less. If a factory is not emitting dangerous substances and needs no regulation, and can thus compete directly with unregulated factories in other countries, that is good news environmentally, ethically, and economically.

A Technical Nutrient

Someone who has finished with a traditional carpet must pay to have it removed. The energy, effort, and materials that went into it are lost to the manufacturer; the carpet becomes little more than a heap of potentially hazardous petrochemicals that must be toted to a landfill. Meanwhile, raw materials must continually be extracted to make new carpets.

The typical carpet consists of nylon embedded in fiberglass and PVC. After its useful life a manufacturer can only downcycle it—shave off some of the nylon for further use and melt the leftovers. The world's largest commercial carpet company, Interface, is adopting our technical-nutrient concept with a carpet designed for complete recycling. When a customer wants to replace it, the manufacturer simply takes back the technical nutrient —depending on the product, either part or all of the carpet—and returns a carpet in the customer's desired color, style, and texture. The carpet company continues to own the material but leases it and maintains it, providing customers with the *service* of the carpet. Eventually the carpet will wear out like any other, and the manufacturer will reuse its materials at their original level of quality or a higher one.

The advantages of such a system, widely applied to many industrial products, are twofold: no useless and potentially dangerous waste is generated, as it might still be in eco-efficient systems, and billions of dollars' worth of valuable materials are saved and retained by the manufacturer.

Selling Intelligence, Not Poison

Currently, chemical companies warn farmers to be careful with pesticides, and yet the companies benefit when more pesticides are sold. In other words, the companies are unintentionally invested in wastefulness and even in the mishandling of their products, which can result in contamination of the soil, water, and air. Imagine what would happen if a chemical company sold intelligence instead of pesticides—that is, if farmers or agro-businesses paid pesticide manufacturers to protect their crops against loss from pests instead of buying dangerous regulated chemicals to use at their own discretion. It would in effect be buying crop insurance. Farmers would be saying, "I'll pay you to deal with boll weevils, and you do it as intelligently as you can." At the same price per acre, everyone would still profit. The pesticide purveyor would be invested in *not* using pesticide, to avoid wasting materials. Furthermore, since the manufacturer would bear responsibility for the hazardous materials, it would have incentives to come up with less-dangerous ways to get rid of pests. Farmers are not interested in handling dangerous chemicals; they want to grow crops. Chemical companies do not want to contaminate soil, water, and air; they want to make money.

Consider the unintended design legacy of the average shoe. With each step of your shoe the sole releases tiny particles of potentially harmful substances that may contaminate and reduce the vitality of the soil. With the next rain these particles will wash into the plants and soil along the road, adding another burden to the environment.

Shoes could be redesigned so that the sole was a biological nutrient. When it broke down under a pounding foot and interacted with nature, it would nourish the biological metabolism instead of poisoning it. Other parts of the shoe might be designed as technical nutrients, to be returned to industrial cycles. Most shoes—in fact, most products of the current industrial system—are fairly primitive in their relationship to the natural world. With the scientific and technical tools currently available, this need not be the case.

Respect Diversity and Use the Sun

The leading goal of design in this century has been to achieve universally applicable solutions. In the field of architecture the International Style is a good example. As a result of the widespread adoption of the International Style, architecture has become uniform in many settings. That is, an office building can look and work the same anywhere. Materials such as steel, cement, and glass can be transported all over the world, eliminating dependence on a region's particular energy and material flows. With more energy forced into the heating and cooling system, the same building can operate similarly in vastly different settings.

The second principle of the Next Industrial Revolution is "Respect diversity." Designs will respect the regional, cultural, and material uniqueness of a place. Wastes and emissions will regenerate rather than deplete, and design will be flexible, to allow for changes in the needs of people and communities. For example, office buildings will be convertible into apartments, instead of ending up as rubble in a construction landfill when the market changes.

The third principle of the Next Industrial Revolution is "Use solar energy." Human systems now rely on fossil fuels and petrochemicals, and on incineration processes that often have destructive side effects. Today even the most advanced building or factory in the world is still a kind of steamship, polluting, contaminating, and depleting the surrounding environment, and relying on scarce amounts of natural light and fresh air. People are essentially working in the dark, and they are often breathing unhealthful air. Imagine, instead, a building as a kind of tree. It would purify air, accrue solar income, produce more energy than it consumes, create shade and habitat, enrich soil, and change with the seasons.

Oberlin College is currently working on a building that is a good start: it is designed to make more energy than it needs to operate and to purify its own wastewater.

Equity, Economy, Ecology

The Next Industrial Revolution incorporates positive intentions across a wide spectrum of human concerns. People within the sustainability movement have found that three categories are helpful in articulating these concerns: equity, economy, and ecology.

Equity refers to social justice. Does a design depreciate or enrich people and communities? Shoe companies have been blamed for exposing workers in factories overseas to chemicals in amounts that exceed safe limits. Eco-efficiency would reduce those amounts to meet certain efficiency would reduce those amounts to meet certain standards; eco-effectiveness would not use a potentially dangerous chemical in the first place. What an advance for humankind it would be if no factory worker anywhere worked in dangerous or inhumane conditions.

Economy refers to market viability. Does a product reflect the needs of producers and consumers for affordable products? Safe, intelligent designs should be affordable by and accessible to a wide range of customers, and profitable to the company that makes them, because commerce is the engine of change.

Ecology, of course, refers to environmental intelligence. Is a material a biological nutrient or a technical nutrient? Does it meet nature's design criteria: Waste equals food, Respect diversity, and Use solar energy?

The Next Industrial Revolution can be framed as the following assignment: Design an industrial system for the next century that

- Introduces no hazardous materials into the air, water, or soil.
- Measures prosperity by how much natural capital we can accrue in productive ways.
- Measures productivity by how many people are gainfully and meaningfully employed.
- Measures progress by how many buildings have no smokestacks or dangerous effluents.
- Does not require regulations whose purpose is to stop us from killing ourselves too quickly.
- Produces nothing that will require future generations to maintain vigilance.
- Celebrates the abundance of biological and cultural diversity and solar income.

Albert Einstein wrote, "The world will not evolve past its current state of crisis by using the same thinking that created the situation." Many people believe that new industrial revolutions are already taking place, with the rise of cybertechnology, biotechnology, and nanotechnology. It is true that these are powerful tools for change. But they are only tools—hyperefficient engines for the steamship of the first Industrial Revolution. Similarly, eco-efficiency is a valuable and laudable tool, and a prelude to what should come next. But it, too, fails to move us beyond the first revolution. It is time for designs that are creative, abundant, prosperous, and intelligent from the start. The model for the Next Industrial Revolution may well have been right in front of us the whole time: a tree.

Source: Published in the *Atlantic Monthly*, October 1998. Reproduced with permission of the authors. See http://www.mcdonough.com.

Taking Sustainability Seriously: *An Argument for Managerial Responsibility*

Tara J. Radin

I. Sustainability and Stakeholders

Concern for the natural environment has become a pivotal issue for businesses today. Companies have found that legal approaches only go so far in helping managers deal with the complexity of the environment and they have come to rely more heavily on managerial discretion in dealing with it and the laws governing it. Managers, in turn, increasingly need to be able to interpret and apply laws appropriately. Moreover, they need to develop discretion because there is no formula—no single, universal rule—that will enable them to deal effectively with their problems. Managers must navigate uncharted territory by weighing competing interests to determine the best way to address complex business issues involving the natural world. All this means is that there is less need for regulation and more need for managers to have a clear understanding of ethics and a sense of responsibility for the influence of their businesses on the natural environment. It seems then that responsible organization decision making in response to concerns relating to the natural environment is critical.

During the last 20 years, a number of arguments have emerged in support of the responsibility of business for the natural environment. Throughout this period, appeals have been made to both moral and economic considerations. One of the chief concerns has involved the legitimacy and standing of the natural environment as a stakeholder and the ways the environment relates to business and its various constituents. While the status of the environment as a stakeholder has not been fully resolved, a view of the firm emphasizing the interconnected relationship is helpful in addressing some of the more pressing concerns surrounding the interaction between human beings and the biosphere.

Addressing environmental concerns from a stakeholder perspective demands addressing the so-called "separation thesis," or notion that business and ethics are distinct functions. The term derives from an article by R. Edward Freeman published a decade after his seminal book, *Stakeholder Management*. In the article he asserted that one of the problems in business thinking is the view that functional areas can be isolated (made separate) from one another. In business, for example, marketing is thought to be separate from finance, which is separate from operations, and so on. The result is a mindset that views these entities as discrete and decisions made in each domain as isolated from each another.

While, in many instances, an approach that compartmentalizes the functional areas of business seems to enhance the efficiency of the organization, it nevertheless misses the big picture. More troubling, it can leave out altogether certain functional areas that do not make obvious contributions to the bottom line. One of these is ethics. In terms of business and ethics, the separation thesis would have business and ethics as distinct and non-overlapping, with business concerned with the financial bottom line without consideration of ethics, and ethics concerned with the individual's adherence to moral norms devoid of the contingencies of business.

The separation thesis in regard to business and ethics is mistaken chiefly because the firm's bottom line is influenced by a multitude of interrelated decisions and effects, most of which are embedded with ethical concerns. The same holds true for issues involving the natural environment, where, again, the effects of decisions are multiple, interrelated, and embedded with ethical concerns.

This is particularly relevant as it pertains to the natural environment and concerns for sustainability. As businesses rely on the natural environment, deplete its resources, and interact with the biosphere, it becomes increasingly difficult to separate business concerns from concerns relating to the natural environment. Many of the effects might not be felt on the firm's short-term bottom line, but they nevertheless represent a very real challenge to the firm's long-term stability and success.

A. Three Fundamental Questions

If the separation thesis is false and business and the natural environment are as tightly conjoined as business and ethics, then at least three questions about how firms can and/or should address the environment in their business decision-making arise. Consider the following questions:

Question 1: Is it permissible for firms to contribute resources to environmental efforts?

This question addresses the permissibility of firms considering the environment in their strategic planning, in particular in regard to the environment's influence on short-term profitability. It also introduces topics such as the legitimacy of redirecting funds that would otherwise be channeled toward stockholders or other direct business purposes, as well as the permissibility of investing in research for alternative energy sources, engaging in costly waste reduction procedures, manufacturing lower margin environmentally friendly products, and so forth.

While a stockholder approach to this question might simply focus on the bottom line, a relational stakeholder approach devoid of the separation thesis would charge that firms are morally responsible for the environment as a legitimate stakeholder. It would claim, moreover, that a firm has reciprocal relationships with a wide range of stakeholders who care about the environment and that these concerns warrant the firm's attention to environmental issues.

Question 2: Is it consistent with existing laws for firms to contribute resources to environmental efforts?

This question asks whether or not it is legal for firms to contribute resources to environmental efforts. In doing so, it draws attention to laws related to corporate governance that allow for and require significant managerial discretion.

Since companies hire managers in lieu of robots to access the complex set of values and talents they possess, it is beneficial for the firm's bottom line for decision-makers to be empowered to respond to their inherent moral and strategic intuitions. Firms have found that attention to such concerns is not inconsistent with profit-generation. To the contrary, as numerous examples illustrate, firms increase their profitability and place themselves at a competitive advantage when they take such considerations into account. As George W. Merck stated in 1950: "We try never to forget that medicine is for the people. It is not for the profits. The profits follow, and if we have remembered that, they have never failed to appear. The better we have remembered that, the larger they have been." The same holds true for their concern for the natural environment: it makes good business sense to support laws that encourage managerial discretion and creativity in regard to environmental responsibility.

Question 3: Could it be considered mandatory for firms to contribute resources to environmental efforts?

This question explores the difference between permissibility and obligation. It asks whether or not firms are obliged to support or enhance the environment and whether or not firms need to support other stakeholders who are concerned about the environment.

Again, firms are morally and legally responsible to stakeholders based, at least in part, on reliance considerations. Because society relies upon the natural environment and because some natural resources are finite, it is incumbent upon society to carefully steward natural resources. Since firms as an aggregate use substantial amounts of natural resources and because they often have the power, control, and finances to protect natural resources, they are obliged to use their wherewithal to protect natural resources for the benefit of the societies in which the firms are embedded.

B. Three Guiding Principles

The answers to questions such as those above indicate that environmental responsibility on the part of firms is desirable. These answers do not, however, specify how it should manifest itself or to what degree.

Principle 1: Firms are obliged to attend to the natural environment.

The first principle is straightforward: Firms are obligated to pay attention to the environment. How they do this is their choice. At a minimum, they must comply with existing rules, regulations, and industry requirements. The reasons for this mandate are twofold.

First, the pragmatic view: It is important for firms to attend to stakeholder concern to maintain satisfied stakeholders with whom they are engaged in relationships. Second, they have moral duties based on a principle of "do no harm." Since firms are aware of their potential for causing harm and because they typically have the resources to mitigate that harm, they are required to do so.

Principle 2: The nature of a firm's obligation is generally discretionary.

According to this principle, the nature and extent of a firm's obligations beyond compliance is largely discretionary. The manner in which a firm responds to environmental concerns is therefore voluntary. Environmentally responsible efforts on the part of firms tend to be categorized along a spectrum, as displayed in Figure A, which is both normative and descriptive. At a minimum, firms are morally obliged to "do no harm" and remain in compliance with the law. While not specifically definite, this position encompasses the sort of exploitation that leads to tragedies such as Love Canal. It does not mean that firms are not permitted to partake in the earth's resources, but that they should do so moderately and consistent with existing laws.

In the indeterminate middle is the notion that some firms choose to be proactive in deciding to prevent harm while others are merely reactive. The proactive approach considers

FIGURE A
Shades of Green

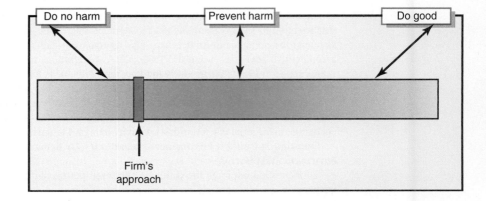

Do no harm   Prevent harm   Do good

Firm's
approach

investments in research, waste management, development of environmentally responsible products, and so forth. A number of companies have engaged in this approach, adopting systemic product and/or process redesigns to make positive contributions to society and the environment. While some companies engage in such undertakings because they consider it their moral obligation, others do so for self-interested reasons, finding that doing so gives them a competitive advantage.

Principle 3: There are circumstances that create mandatory obligations for firm behavior toward the environment beyond mere compliance.

The third principle suggests that there are situations where a firm's obligation could be considered mandatory. Such situations are not the norm, but occur where a particular firm is specially suited for the role.

In general, it is unusual for positive obligations to be assigned—particularly to firms. Firms represent a voluntary contribution to the economy, that is, investors and owners are motivated to participate generally because of the opportunity to profit from certain enterprises. It is therefore generally considered inappropriate to impose correlative burdens that might detract from investment in such enterprises and thereby interfere with the economy.

At the same time, someone must be made responsible when there is harm or potential harm. Economists such as Ronald Coase and Guido Calebresi have argued in favor of efficiency. Coase has argued that firms exist only because of their inherent efficiency. It would seem, then, that coordinated and/or collective corporate initiatives will and should arise when they are recognized as more efficient than costly alternatives. Further, Calebresi has argued that an effective and efficient way of dealing with harm is to impose the burden on the individual or entity who or which is in best position to discover the problem and most cheaply avoid harm. In fact, while it can be argued that we are all aware of the harm, corporations are in the best position to avoid the harm since they are the ones on the front line engaging in the most destructive behavior. It would thus seem logical and appropriate to impose on corporations a mandatory obligation beyond mere compliance when they are specifically in the best position to avoid the harm.

This leads to a set of criteria that can frame those situations in which there can be construed a mandatory obligation for environmental responsibility. First, there must be a specific need for change as manifest in actual or foreseeable harm. Second, there must be proximity through a direct or indirect link. The firm must be a participant in the problem or a direct beneficiary. Third is capability. The firm must have the ability to change products or processes without it becoming overly cumbersome to the firm. Fourth and finally, there exists some sort of comparative advantage. The firm must be particularly situated to address the harm. When these four criteria are met, it can be said that a firm has a specific obligation to engage in environmentally responsible behavior to address harm with regard to the natural environment.

C. Sustainability and Fiduciary Duties

Corporations are often resistant to the imposition of mandatory duties, particularly those that could be construed as conflicting with their other obligations—particularly their fiduciary duty to shareholders. For this reason, it is important to emphasize the connection between sustainability and fiduciary duty. Although it is possible to construe fiduciary duties narrowly in terms of profit-maximization, the reality is that there are many factors that can affect a firm's bottom line—in the long if not short term. Further, shareholders can be held accountable for corporate violations or neglect. On this basis, Professor Cynthia A. Williams and Professor John M. Conley have argued that managers are responsible to consider human rights. In the context of the natural environment, added to this is the recognition that shareholders can be held legally liable for negligence. Since the 1990s, there has been criminal enforcement of American environmental statutes.

The inescapable reality is that corporate responsibilities to the natural environment can no longer be viewed as anything but mandatory—the environment is a business concern. If for no other reasons, corporations have to be mindful of sustainability concerns in light of their reliance on the natural environment. As Bruce Ledewitz warns, "The state of the world is not good, or, since the world will be here long after we are gone, I should say the state of the world upon which people depend is not good. Long predicted and feared environmental problems are now cascading upon us. Not a day goes by, it seems, without news of catastrophic global warming or collapsed fisheries or depleted resources or diminished topsoil or lack of fresh water or diminished biological diversity—and on and on."

While the manner in which a corporation responds to these responsibilities remains voluntary, the presence of a duty must be viewed as mandatory. It can be argued that there is a moral duty to the environment. Beyond that, failure to address environmental concerns can result in financial distress for the firm, including bankruptcy. If it is the fiduciary responsibility of managers to protect the interests (and profits) of shareholders, the only way they can do that is to consider how it affects and is affected by the natural environment because stakeholders affect and are affected by the natural environment. Not only can the corporation's approach to sustainability influence short- and long-term profits, the corporation faces expensive tort litigation and shareholders face criminal sanctions if the corporation does not behave responsibly.

D. Stakeholders, Sustainability, and Citizenship

In addressing environmental responsibility, the term most commonly used today is *sustainability*. Sustainability refers to the integrated, systemic, lasting effect of attention to the natural environment and encompasses everything from the local neighborhood to the planet and the well-being of all living things. The emphasis lies on investments in the future rather than on one-time actions. Sustainability is a process; environmental responsibility is about beginning or participating in this process of addressing environmental concerns. Sustainability is inherently connected to stakeholder thinking (particularly the relationship view) in that both build upon existing relationships, interconnectedness, and synergies.

The key here lies in the notion of "systems thinking," which has recently taken hold in contemporary business scholarship. Systems thinking provides both the rationale for why corporations should be paying attention to sustainability and how they should go about doing so. Each corporation is itself embedded in a web of relationship and at the same time part of a "networked economy."

Stakeholder thinking and sustainability are also connected to the concept of "citizenship." Citizenship emphasizes the responsibilities of individuals in social (community-based) and political systems. An individual derives both rights and responsibilities from his or her affiliation with particular communities or social systems. The protection of the nonhuman, natural environment, as a resource shared by a social system or social systems, becomes a shared responsibility.

Individual citizenship has given way to corporate citizenship. Borrowing from common understandings of individual citizenship, the notion of corporate citizenship suggests that business organizations have rights and responsibilities comparable to those of individuals. This means that corporate citizens are expected to contribute to the communities in which they operate and to be considerate of their interaction with other community members. By implication, this means that, since community members share the environment, corporate citizens should be respectful of them in their use of natural resources and reliance on the environment—if not because of their own feelings toward the environment, then as a result of their community's interdependent and respect for the environment. Progressive interpretations of the law are increasingly reflecting consideration of stakeholder interests.

II. Stakeholders, the Environment, and Good Business Decision Making

The contribution of stakeholder thinking to developing an approach to environmental responsibility is to show how obligations can be assigned to firms. Specifically, firms have legal duties to some stakeholders in some specified circumstances. They have moral responsibilities to stakeholders in general. Whereas it is left to the discretion of firms to determine how they will handle these responsibilities, there is evidence that attention to stakeholders can contribute to profitability.

Specific examples illustrate how environmental responsibility can turn into a competitive advantage. Unpacking fundamental assumptions about business, humanity, and the environment reveals how shifting mental models can open up tremendous new opportunities for business.

A. The Bottom of the Pyramid

C.K. Prahalad argues that the often assumed target of business has been misplaced. He points out that most businesses focus on providing goods and services to the middle and upper class, whereas the poorest socioeconomic group holds the key to tremendous opportunity. In economic terms, the pyramid, as illustrated in Figure B, refers to the distribution of wealth in society. According to Prahalad, the poor represents a virtually untapped resource:

> If we stop thinking of the poor as victims or as a burden and start recognizing them as resilient and creative entrepreneurs and value-conscious consumers, a whole new world of opportunity will open up. Four billion poor can be the engine of the next round of global trade and prosperity…. What is needed is a better approach to help the poor, an approach that involves partnering with them to innovate and achieve sustainable win-win scenarios where the poor are actively engaged and, at the same time, the companies providing products and services to them are profitable.

First, there are many more members of this class at the bottom of the pyramid than of the class of wealthy people at the top. Second, particularly from a global perspective, many

FIGURE B
Economic Pyramid

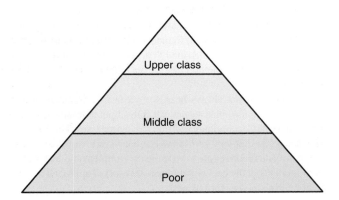

of the poorest people have fundamental needs that can be addressed without huge capital investments. Third, elevating the standards of the socioeconomic disadvantaged can help to transform societal drains into societal contributions.

Muhammad Yunus has demonstrated the tremendous power of this proposition. In the 1970s, Yunus found the Grameen Bank, a microfinance organization that started in Bangladesh. The purpose of this enterprise is to elevate the status of the impoverished by making small loans without requiring collateral. The underlying premise is that the poor have skills that are underutilized because of their lack of capital.

By infusing capital into poor communities, the Grameen Bank has both elevated local conditions and profited significantly. The bank's assets are experiencing tremendous growth—in the three years between 2002 and 2005 the bank's assets nearly doubled from $391 million to $678 million. The bank boasts 5.58 million borrowers, 1,735 branches, and a 21.22 percent return on equity.

B. Cradle-to-Cradle

William McDonough offers an alternative perspective on how organizations can approach sustainability with an eye toward profits. He advocates what he calls a "cradle-to-cradle" approach. This translates into comprehensive redesign of products and/or processes. The result is far-reaching. In contrast with the traditional "cradle-to-grave" perspective whereby resources are used once and then discarded, the cradle-to-cradle approach advocates the use of perpetually recyclable or compostable materials. According to McDonough, "Pollution is a symbol of design failure."

Small and large companies alike have adopted McDonough's approach to sustainable business. One of his most famous projects in which he was involved was a site restoration of Ford Motor Co.'s historic River Rouge Complex in Michigan. Kodak's single-use camera is another example of cradle-to-cradle product design. Kodak controls the entire lifecycle of the cameras and, even through recovery, keeps most of the materials traveling in a continuous loop.

Cradle-to-cradle design reflects a reconceptualization of what an externality is. Traditional manufacturing has emphasized cost reduction by externalizing nonessential processes. Waste, for example, has traditionally been externalized as pollution. McDonough espouses the exact opposite: he argues that companies should take ownership of their processes and invest in ways to internalize processes so as to minimize waste. Whereas companies fear short-term costs, McDonough argues that long-term profits will follow in addition to positive contributions toward sustainability.

C. Restorative Commerce

An arguably even more dramatic approach lies in aiming for "restorative" commerce. According to Ray Anderson, founder and former CEO of Interface, Inc., a global leader in the design, production, and sale of carpeting, "[B]eing restorative means to put back more than we take, and to do good to the Earth, not just no harm." This is his long-term goal for Interface.

Interface has not always been so "green." Although Interface today is recognized as a leader in sustainable business, it was only about a decade ago that Anderson spearheaded an effort to harness technology and transform processes. The catalyst for this initiative was Paul Hawken's *The Ecology of Commerce*. Hawken's words stunned him into recognizing his company's destructive role toward the environment and he set about reducing his company's petroleum dependence. For Anderson, this sort of approach is not just the morally right thing to do; it is also good for business.

In 2005, Interface introduced a production process that enables the company to recycle old carpeting. Interface considers it a "dream come true.... We can now mine the landfill instead of siphoning off more oil. But it's also good business. Now, we're not just willing to take back old carpet, we're eager to take it because Cool Blue [the production equipment responsible for the recycling process] can turn it into profit."

This is Anderson's legacy for Interface: his company has turned a product into a service. Instead of selling carpet tiles, Interface now leases them; as they wear down, they are replaced and the old tiles are remanufactured, as part of an endless loop. Waste has been reduced and this has dramatically decreased the company's reliance on raw materials.

The experience at Interface has been tremendously positive. In the five years between 2000 and 2005, Interface tripled its use of recycled or biobased raw materials and grew its use of renewable energy from 6.4 percent to 21.7 percent. At the same time, it cut its waste (sent to a landfill) by 50 percent. Net sales are growing and the company is looking healthier and healthier.

The experience at Interface underscores the tremendous value—psychically, environmentally, and financially—of the greening of business.

D. Bottom Line

All of these examples reflect the value of sustainable business to the financial bottom line of organizations, communities, and the globe. The bottom line for us is that our businesses do not need laws in order to provide for sustainability; they need good business sense. While laws might have failed businesses, the inherent problem is not the law—it is the reliance of businesses upon laws and the expectation that legislation can and should determine what responsible decision making entails.

Moving forward, it is possible to continue to strive to improve the legal framework, but there will virtually always be an inevitable "lag effect." An alternative is thus to endeavor to influence the norms of acceptable and expected business behavior. Fiduciary duties, prescribed by law, are interpreted according to existing norms. In affecting these norms, then, the fiduciaries of corporations become responsible for living up to and abiding by current societal standards and expectations.

Environmental responsibility is about justice not charity. As a corporate citizen that can and does affect the lives of others, the firm has an obligation to act as a citizen by acting responsibly vis-à-vis the environment. Further, good business decision making (that can translate into profits) demands attention to stakeholder concerns about issues such as the environment.

It is important to keep in mind that, while corporations are legal fiction, the individuals who populate them are very real. While the corporation might not "care" about the environment, its stakeholders are dependent upon its survival. Sustainability is not just the way of the future; it is what will provide a future.

Source: Copyright © Tara Radin. Reprinted by permission of the author.

10

Ethical Decision Making: Corporate Governance, Accounting, and Finance

Did you ever expect a corporation to have a conscience, when it has no soul to be damned and no body to be kicked?

Edward Thurlow (1731–1806), Lord Chancellor of England

Whenever an institution malfunctions as consistently as boards of directors have in nearly every major fiasco of the last forty or fifty years, it is futile to blame men. It is the institution that malfunctions.

Peter Drucker

Earnings can be as pliable as putty when a charlatan heads the company reporting them.

Warren Buffet

Consider a decision that faced the board of directors of Hershey Foods, headquartered in Hershey, Pennsylvania. Hershey had $4.4 billion in sales in 2004, and had as its majority shareholder the $5.4 billion Milton Hershey Trust.

The Trust in 2002 decided that it wanted to put Hershey up for sale in order to diversify its assets. The residents of Hershey were extremely concerned as they envisioned job loss, reduced support of the community through fewer taxes and other financial impacts, and a weakened tourism industry, especially if the company were sold to a foreign investor. Since the board did not represent the stakeholders who would be impacted by this decision, an ethical decision that considered all stakeholder perspectives was less likely (though not impossible). Contrary to some Western European countries, the United States does not require stakeholder representation, such as employees or local citizenry, on corporate boards.

What do you think the board should have done?

- What are the key facts relevant to your decision regarding the sale of Hershey?
- What is the ethical issue involved in the sale and the decision process?
- Who are the stakeholders?
- What alternatives do you have in situations such as the one above?
- How do the alternatives compare, and how do the alternatives affect the stakeholders?

Management Controls
B of Directors

✳ Chapter Objectives

After reading this chapter, you will be able to:

1. Describe the environment for corporate governance prior and subsequent to the Sarbanes-Oxley Act.
2. Explain the role of accountants and other professionals as "gatekeepers."
3. Describe how conflicts of interest can arise for business professionals.
4. Outline the requirements of the Sarbanes-Oxley Act.
5. Describe the COSO framework.
6. Define the "control environment" and the means by which ethics and culture can impact it.
7. Discuss the legal obligations of a member of a board of directors.
8. Explore the obligations of an ethical member of a board of directors.
9. Highlight conflicts of interest in financial markets and discuss the ways in which they may be alleviated.
10. Describe conflicts of interest in governance created by excessive executive compensation.
11. Define insider trading and evaluate its potential for unethical behavior.

Consider the following:

> The jury is still out on the costs to corporations of Sarbanes-Oxley compliance, but it's a safe guess that it's already in the billions of dollars and millions of person-hours. No one doing Sarbanes-Oxley work adds value to any company. They design nothing, make nothing, and sell nothing. They make no improvements to management, marketing, or morale. They meet no demands, satisfy no necessities, create no opportunities. They simply report.[1]

If Sarbanes-Oxley has these challenges, are there alternatives to address wrongdoing in corporate governance? Is Sarbanes-Oxley the best alternative? What other suggestions might you offer?

- What else might you need to know to determine how to prevent mismanagement of this type?
- What ethical issues are involved?
- Who are the stakeholders in financial mismanagement?
- Whose rights are protected by Sarbanes-Oxley's implementation? What are the consequences of Sarbanes-Oxley's implementation? Is it the fairest option? Is it regulating companies to act in the way a virtuous company would act?
- What alternatives have you compiled?
- How do the alternatives compare; how do the alternatives affect the stakeholders?

Many of the companies mentioned in the opening pages of this book were involved in financial corruption. Recall those company names—whether from this text or from the headlines of the national press—such as Enron, World-Com, Tyco, Adelphia, Cendant, Rite Aid, Sunbeam, Waste Management, Health-South, Global Crossing, Arthur Andersen, Ernst &Young, ImClone, KPMG, J.P.Morgan, Merrill Lynch, Morgan Stanley, Citigroup Salomon Smith Barney, Marsh & McLennan, Credit Suisse First Boston, and even the New York Stock Exchange itself. In the past few years, each of these companies, organizations, accounting firms, and investment firms has been implicated in some ethically questionable activity that has resulted in fines or criminal convictions. Most of the unethical behavior involved some aspect of finance, from manipulating special purpose entities in order to evidence growth, to cooking the books, to instituting questionable tax dodges, to allowing investment decisions to warp the objectivity of investment research and advice. Ethics in the governance and financial arenas has been perhaps the most visible issue in business ethics during the first years of the new millennium. Accounting and investment firms that were looked upon as the guardians of integrity in financial dealings have now been exposed in violation of the fiduciary responsibilities entrusted to them by their stakeholders. Many analysts contend that this corruption is evidence of a complete failure in corporate governance structures; could better governance and oversight have prevented these ethical disgraces?

Reality Check   *What Did They Say, Again?*

According to a report from PricewaterhouseCoopers, more than 1,000 public companies have had to restate their financial statements over the past five years due to accounting irregularities, with the average company losing approximately 6 percent of its revenue to fraud and abuse. Historically, more than 50 percent of CFOs report that they were pressured by their CEOs to misrepresent accounting or otherwise engage in fraud.

This chapter will address the cultural elements that led to the Enron Corporation debacle, as well as others during the end of the 20th and beginning of the 21st centuries. Though the Sarbanes-Oxley Act is one response to these corporate governance failures, others exist, such as adherence to the elements of the control environment framework advocated by the Committee of Sponsoring Organizations of the Treadway Commission. (See the Decision Point on the previous page and the above Reality Check to consider other alternatives.) Perhaps, however, many of these challenges could be avoided by having more accountable and responsible boards of directors. The chapter will outline board member roles and responsibilities and discuss specifically pervasive issues such as conflicts of interest, insider trading, and leveraged buyouts and mergers. We will explore the impact that corporate institutions have on the social fabric and how corporate issues connect with the global environment in the first decades of the 21st century.

Professional Duties and Conflicts of Interest

OBJECTIVE

The watershed event that brought the ethics of finance to prominence at the beginning of the 21st century was the collapse of Enron and its accounting firm Arthur Andersen. William Thomas's essay "The Rise and Fall of Enron" details the steps that led to the downfall of those companies, including using complex special purpose entities to access capital or hedge risk. The Enron case "has wreaked more havoc on the accounting industry than any other case in U.S. history,"[2] including the demise of Arthur Andersen. Of course, ethical responsibilities of accountants were not unheard of prior to Enron, but the events that led to Enron's demise brought into focus the necessity of the independence of auditors and the responsibilities of accountants like never before.

Accounting is one of several professions that serve very important functions within the economic system itself. Remember that even Milton Friedman, a staunch defender of free market economics, believes that markets can function only when certain conditions are met. It is universally recognized that markets must function within the law; they must assume full information; and they must be free from fraud and deception. Ensuring that these conditions are met is an important internal function for market-based economic systems. Several important business professions, for example, attorneys, auditors, accountants, and financial analysts, function in just this way. Just as the game of baseball requires umpires who act with integrity and fairness, business and economic markets require these professionals to operate in a similar manner.

Such professions can be thought of as "gatekeepers" or "watchdogs" in that their role is to ensure that those who enter into the marketplace are playing by the rules and conforming to the very conditions that ensure the market functions as it is supposed to function. Recall from Chapter 3 the critical importance of role identities in determining ethical duties of professionals. These roles offer us a source of rules from which we can determine universal values to apply under deontological and Kantian analysis. We accept responsibilities based on our roles. Therefore, in striving to define the rules that we should apply, we see that the ethical obligations of accountants originate in part from their roles as accountants.

These professions can also be understood as intermediaries, acting between the various parties in the market, and they are bound to ethical duties in this role as well. All the participants in the market, especially investors, boards, management, and bankers, rely on these gatekeepers. Auditors verify a company's financial statements so that investors' decisions are free from fraud and deception. Analysts evaluate a company's financial prospects or creditworthiness, so that banks and investors can make informed decisions. Attorneys ensure that decisions and transactions conform to the law. Indeed, even boards of directors can be understood in this way. Boards function as intermediaries between a company's stockholders and its executives and should guarantee that executives act on behalf of the stockholders' interests.

The most important ethical issue facing professional gatekeepers and intermediaries in business contexts involves conflicts of interest. A **conflict of interest** exists where a person holds a position of trust that requires that she or he exercise judgment on behalf of others, but where her or his personal interests and/or obligations conflict with those of others. For instance, a friend knows that you are heading to a flea market and asks if you would keep your eyes open for any beautiful quilts you might see. She asks you to purchase one for her if you see a "great buy." You are going to the flea market for the purpose of buying your mother a birthday present. You happen to see a beautiful quilt at a fabulous price. In fact, your mother would adore the quilt. You find yourself in a conflict of interest—your friend trusted you to search the flea market on her behalf. Your personal interests are now in conflict with the duty you agreed to accept on behalf of your friend.

Conflicts of interest can also arise when a person's ethical obligations in her or his professional duties clash with personal interests. Thus, for example, in the most egregious case, a financial planner who accepts kickbacks from a brokerage firm to steer clients into certain investments fails in her or his professional responsibility by putting personal financial interests ahead of client interest. Such professionals are said to have **fiduciary duties**—a professional and ethical obligation—to their clients, duties that override their own personal interests. (For another example of a conflict of interest, see the Decision Point on page 425.)

Unfortunately, and awkwardly, many of these professional intermediaries are paid by the businesses over which they keep watch, and perhaps are also employed by yet another business. For example, David Duncan was the principal accounting professional employed by Arthur Andersen, though he was hired by and assigned to work at Enron. As the Arthur Andersen case so clearly demonstrated, this situation

FIGURE 10.1   **Conflicts of Interest in Public CPA Activity**

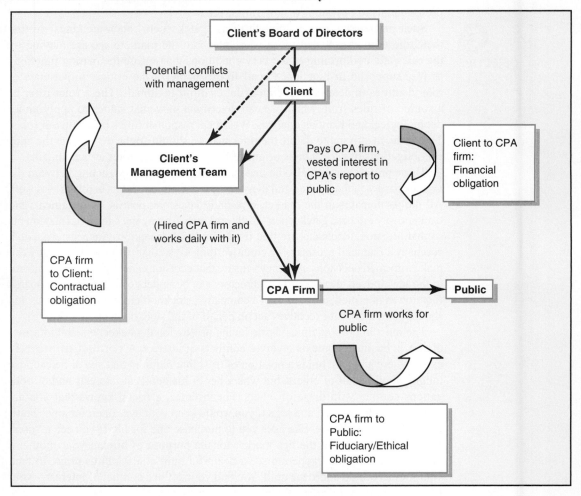

can create real conflicts between a professional's responsibility and his or her financial interests. Certified *public* accountants (CPAs) have a professional responsibility to the public. But they work for clients whose financial interests are not always served by full, accurate, and independent disclosure of financial information. Even more dangerously, they work daily with and are hired by a management team that itself might have interests that conflict with the interests of the firm represented by the board of directors. Thus, real and complex conflicts can exist between professional duties and a professional's self-interest. We will revisit conflicts in the accounting profession later in the chapter.

In one sense, the ethical issues regarding such professional responsibilities are clear. Because professional **gatekeeper** duties are necessary conditions for economic legitimacy, they should trump other responsibilities an employee might have. David Duncan's responsibilities as an auditor should have overridden his

Decision Point

When Does Financial Support Become a Kickback?

Consider the case of what is referred to as "soft money" within the securities industry. According to critics, a common practice in the securities industry amounts to little more than institutionalized kickbacks. "Soft money" payments occur when financial advisors receive payments from a brokerage firm to pay for research and analyst services that, in theory, should be used to benefit the clients of those advisors. Such payments can benefit clients if the advisor uses them to improve the advice offered to the client. Conflicts of interest can arise when the money is used for the personal benefit of the advisor. In 1998, the Securities and Exchange Commission released a report that showed extensive abuse of soft money. Examples included payments used for office rent and equipment, personal travel and vacations, memberships at private clubs, and automobile expenses. If you learned that your financial advisor received such benefits from a brokerage, could you continue to trust the financial advisor's integrity or professional judgment?

- What facts do you need to know to better judge this situation?
- What values are at stake in this situation? Who gets harmed if a financial advisor accepts payments from a brokerage? What are the consequences?
- For whom does a financial advisor work? To whom does she have a professional duty? What are the sources of these obligations?
- Does accepting these soft money payments violate any individual's rights? What would be the consequence if this practice were allowed and became commonplace?
- Can you think of any public policies that might prevent such situations? Is this a matter for legal solutions and punishments

role as an Andersen employee. But knowing one's duties and fulfilling those duties are two separate issues.

This common situation has many ethical implications. If we recognize that the gatekeeper function is necessary for the very functioning of economic markets, and if we also recognize that it can be difficult for individuals to fulfill their gatekeeper duties, then society has a responsibility to make changes to minimize these conflicts. For example, as long as auditors are paid by the clients on whom they are supposed to report, there will always be an apparent conflict of interest between their duties as auditors and their personal financial interests. This conflict is a good reason to make structural changes in how public accounting operates. Perhaps boards rather than management ought to hire and work with auditors since the auditors are more likely reporting on the management activities rather than those of the board. Perhaps public accounting somehow ought to be paid by public fees. Perhaps legal protection or sanctions ought to be created to shield professionals from conflicts of interests. These changes would remove both the apparent and the actual conflicts of interest created by the multiple roles—and therefore multiple responsibilities—of these professionals. From the perspective of social ethics, certain structural changes would be an appropriate response to the accounting scandals of recent years.

Perhaps the most devastating aspect of the Enron case was the resulting deterioration of trust that the public has in the market and in corporate America. Decision makers at Enron ignored their fiduciary duties to shareholders, employees, and the public in favor of personal gain, a direct conflict of interest leading not only to extraordinary personal ruin but also to its own demise: Enron filed for bankruptcy in December 2001. In an effort to prevent these conflicts in the future, Congress enacted legislation to mandate independent directors and a host of other changes discussed below.

However, critics contend that these rules alone will not rid society of the problems that led to this tragedy. Instead, they argue, extraordinary executive compensation and conflicts within the accounting industry itself have created an environment where the watchdogs have little ability to prevent harm. Executive compensation packages based on stock options create huge incentives to artificially inflate stock value. (You might wish to review the reading on executive compensation in Chapter 3 to consider this issue in more detail.) Changes within the accounting industry stemming from the consolidation of major firms and avid "cross-selling" of services such as consulting and auditing within single firms have virtually institutionalized conflicts of interest.

Answers to these inherent challenges are not easy to identify. Imagine that an executive is paid based on how much she or he impacts the share price and will be ousted if that impact is not significantly positive. A large boost in share price—even for the short term—serves as an effective defense to hostile takeovers and boosts a firm's equity leverage for external expansion. In addition, with stock options as a major component of executive compensation structures, a higher share price is an extremely compelling quest to those in leadership roles. That same executive, however, has a fiduciary duty to do what is best for the stakeholders in the long term, an obligation that is often at odds with that executive's personal interests. Not the best environment for perfect decision making, or even for basically decent decision making.

The Sarbanes-Oxley Act of 2002

The string of corporate scandals since the beginning of the millennium has taken its toll on investor confidence. The more it is clear that deceit, chicanery, evasiveness, and cutting corners go on in the markets and in the corporate environment, the less trustworthy those engaged in financial services become. Because reliance on corporate boards to police themselves did not seem to be working, Congress passed the Public Accounting Reform and Investor Protection Act of 2002, commonly known as the Sarbanes-Oxley Act, which is enforced by the Securities and Exchange Commission (SEC). The act applies to over 15,000 publicly held companies in the United States and some foreign issuers. In addition, a number of states have enacted legislation similar to Sarbanes-Oxley that apply to private firms, and some private for-profits and nonprofits have begun to hold themselves to Sarbanes-Oxley standards even though they are not necessarily subject to its requirements.

Reality Check *A Perfect Ten*

Governance Metrics International produces an annual ranking of global companies based on their governance standards. In its 2004 results of 2,588 companies, GMI reported that 26 firms received a score of 10 points, its highest rating. As a group, these companies outperformed the Standard & Poor's 500 Index by 10 percent over the last five years. "This suggests a correlation between corporate governance prac-

tices and portfolio returns when measured across a number of variables across a multiyear period," said GMI's CEO. In addition, he notes, U.S. companies' overall ratings increased based, in part, he posits, on the impact of Sarbanes-Oxley.

Source: Governance Metrics International, "GMI Releases New Global Governance Ratings," press release, September 7, 2004.

OBJECTIVE

Sarbanes-Oxley strived to respond to the scandals by regulating safeguards against unethical behavior. Because one cannot necessarily predict each and every lapse of judgment, no regulatory "fix" is perfect. However, the act is intended to provide protection where oversight did not previously exist. Some might argue that protection against poor judgment is not possible in the business environment but Sarbanes-Oxley seeks instead to provide oversight in terms of direct lines of accountability and responsibility. The following provisions have the most significant impact on corporate governance and boards:

- *Section 201:* Services outside the scope of auditors (prohibits various forms of professional services that are determined to be consulting rather than auditing).
- *Section 301:* Public company audit committees (requires independence), mandating majority of independents on any board (and all on audit committee) and total absence of current or prior business relationships.
- *Section 307:* Rules of professional responsibility for attorneys (requires lawyers to report concerns of wrongdoing if not addressed).
- *Section 404:* Management assessment of **internal controls** (requires that management file an internal control report with its annual report each year in order to delineate how management has established and maintained effective internal controls over financial reporting).
- *Section 406:* Codes of ethics for senior financial officers (required).
- *Section 407:* Disclosure of audit committee financial expert (requires that they actually have an expert).

Sarbanes-Oxley includes requirements for certification of the documents by officers. When a firm's executives and auditors are required to literally *sign off* on these statements, certifying their veracity, fairness, and completeness, they are more likely to personally ensure their truth. The Reality Check above explores other possible positive consequences of Sarbanes-Oxley.

One of the most significant criticisms of the act is that it imposes extraordinary financial costs on the firms; and the costs are apparently even higher than anticipated. A 2005 survey of firms with average revenues of $4 billion conducted by Financial Executives International reports that section 404 compliance averaged

The **European Union's 8th Directive,** effective in 2005 (though member states have two years to integrate it into law), covers many of the same issues as Sarbanes-Oxley but applies these requirements and restrictions to companies traded on European Union exchanges. The directive mandates external quality assurances through audit committee requirements and greater auditing transparency. The directive also provides for cooperation with the regulators in other countries, closing a gap that previously existed. However, contrary to Sarbanes-Oxley, the directive does not contain a whistleblower protection section, does not require similar reporting to shareholders, and has less detailed requirements compared to Sarbanes-Oxley's section 404.

$4.36 million, which is 39 percent more than those firms thought it would cost in 2004. However, the survey also reported that more than half the firms believed that section 404 gives investors and other stakeholders more confidence in their financial reports—a valuable asset, one would imagine. The challenge is in the balance of costs and benefits. "Essentially section 404 is well intentioned, but the implementation effort is guilty of overkill," says one CEO.[3] In response, one year after its implementation, in May 2005, the Public Company Accounting Oversight Board (PCAOB) released a statement publicly acknowledging the high costs and issuing guidance for implementation "in a manner that captures the benefits of the process without unnecessary and unsustainable costs."[4] The PCAOB now advocates a more risk-based approach where the focus of internal audit assessments is better aligned with high-risk areas than those with less potential for a material impact. For a comparison of the application of Sarbanes in the European Union, see the Reality Check above.

The Internal Control Environment

5
OBJECTIVE

Sarbanes-Oxley and the European Union's 8th Directive are external mechanisms that seek to ensure ethical corporate governance, but there are internal mechanisms as well. One way to ensure appropriate controls within the organization is to utilize a framework advocated by the **Committee of Sponsoring Organizations (COSO).** COSO is a voluntary collaboration designed to improve financial reporting through a combination of controls and governance standards called the Internal Control—Integrated Framework. It was established in 1985 by five of the major professional accounting and finance associations, originally to study fraudulent financial reporting and later to develop standards for publicly held companies. COSO describes "control" as encompassing "those elements of an organization that, taken together, support people in the achievement of the organization's objectives."[5] The elements that comprise the control structure will be familiar as they are also the essential elements of culture discussed in Chapter 5. They include:

- *Control environment*—the tone or culture of a firm: "the control environment sets the tone of an organization, influencing the control consciousness of its people."

- *Risk assessment*—risks that may hinder the achievement of corporate objectives.

- *Control activities*—policies and procedures that support the control environment.

- *Information and communications*—directed at supporting the control environment through fair and truthful transmission of information.

- *Ongoing monitoring*—to provide assessment capabilities and to uncover vulnerabilities.

OBJECTIVE

Control environment refers to cultural issues such as integrity, ethical values, competence, philosophy, operating style. Many of these terms should be reminiscent of issues addressed in Chapter 4 during our discussion of corporate culture. COSO is one of the first efforts to address corporate culture in a quasi-regulatory framework in recognition of its significant impact on the satisfaction of organizational objectives. Control environment can also refer to more concrete elements (that can better be addressed in an audit) such as the division of authority, reporting structures, roles and responsibilities, the presence of a code of conduct, and a reporting structure.

The COSO standards for internal controls moved audit, compliance, and governance from a *numbers orientation* to concern for the *organizational environment* (see Figure 9.1). In recognition of the interplay between the COSO control environment and the Sarbanes-Oxley requirements with the discussion of culture in Chapter 5, it is critical to influence the *culture* in which the control environment develops in order to impact both sectors of this environment described above. In fact, these shifts impact not only executives and boards; internal audit and compliance professionals also are becoming more accountable for financial stewardship, resulting in greater transparency, greater accountability, and a greater emphasis on effort to prevent misconduct. In fact, all the controls one could implement have little value if

TABLE 10.1   **COSO Definition of Internal Control**

Internal control is a process, effected by an entity's board of directors, management and other personnel, designed to provide reasonable assurance regarding the achievement of objectives in the following categories:

- Effectiveness and efficiency of operations.
- Reliability of financial reporting.
- Compliance with applicable laws and regulations.

Key Concepts

- Internal control is a *process*. It is a means to an end, not an end in itself.
- Internal control is affected by *people*. It's not merely policy manuals and forms, but people at every level of an organization.
- Internal control can be expected to provide only *reasonable assurance*, not absolute assurance, to an entity's management and board.
- Internal control is geared to the achievement of *objectives* in one or more separate but overlapping categories.

Source: Committee of Sponsoring Organizations, "Key Concepts," http://www.coso.org/key.htm. Copyright © 1985–2005 by the Committee of Sponsoring Organizations of the Treadway Commission. Reproduced by permission from the AICPA acting as the authorized copyright administrator for COSO.

there is no unified corporate culture to support it or mission to guide it. As philosopher Ron Duska noted in the Mitchell Forum on Ethical Leadership in Financial Services, "If you don't have focus and you don't know what you're about, as Aristotle says, you have no limits. You do what you have to do to make a profit."[6]

More recently, COSO developed a new system, Enterprise Risk Management—*Integrated Framework,* to serve as a framework for management to evaluate and improve their firms' prevention, detection, and management of risk. This system expands on the prior framework in that it intentionally includes "objective setting" as one of its interrelated components, recognizing that both the culture and the propensity toward risk are determined by the firm's overarching mission and objectives. Enterprise risk management, therefore, assists an organization or its governing body in resolving ethical dilemmas based on the firm's mission, its culture, and its appetite and tolerance for risk.

Going beyond the Law: Being an Ethical Board Member

As discussed above, perhaps the most effective way to avoid the corporate failures of recent years would be to impose high expectations of accountability on boards of directors. After all, it is the board's fiduciary duty to guard the best interests of the firm itself. However, much of what Enron's board did that caused its downfall was actually well within the law. For instance, it is legal to vote to permit an exception to a firm's conflicts of interest policy. It may not necessarily be ethical or best for its stakeholders, but it is legal nonetheless. So what does it take to be an ethical board member, to govern a corporation in an ethical manner, and why is governance so critical? The law offers some guidance on minimum standards for board member behavior.

Legal Duties of Board Members

OBJECTIVE

The law imposes three clear duties on board members, the duties of care, good faith, and loyalty. The **duty of care** involves the exercise of reasonable care by a board member to ensure that the corporate executives with whom she or he works carry out their management responsibilities and comply with the law in the best interests of the corporation. Directors are permitted to rely on information and opinions only if they are prepared or presented by corporate officers, employees, a board committee, or other professionals the director believes to be reliable and competent in the matters presented. Board members are also directed to use their "business judgment as prudent caretakers": the director is expected to be disinterested and reasonably informed, and to rationally believe the decisions made are in the firm's best interest. The bottom line is that a director does not need to be an expert or actually run the company!

The **duty of good faith** is one of obedience, which requires board members to be faithful to the organization's mission. In other words, they are not permitted to act in a way that is inconsistent with the central goals of the organization. Their decisions must always be in line with organizational purposes and direction, strive towards corporate objectives, and avoid taking the organization in any other direction.

The **duty of loyalty** requires faithfulness; a board member must give undivided allegiance when making decisions affecting the organization. This means that conflicts of interest are always to be resolved in favor of the corporation. A board member may never use information obtained through her or his position as a board member for personal gain, but instead must act in the best interests of the organization.

Board member conflicts of interest present issues of significant challenges, however, precisely because of the alignment of their personal interests with those of the corporation. Don't board members usually have *some* financial interest in the future of the firm, even if it is only through their position and reputation as a board member? Consider whether a board member should own stock. If the board member does own stock, then her or his interests may be closely aligned with other stockholders, removing a possible conflict there. However, if the board member does not hold stock, perhaps he or she is best positioned to consider the long-term interests of the firm in lieu of a sometimes enormous windfall that could occur as the result of a board decision. In the end, a healthy board balance is usually sought. Consider the impact that the composition and training of a board might have on board decision making as you review the following Reality Check.

The **Federal Sentencing Guidelines** (FSG), promulgated by the United States Sentencing Commission and (since a 2005 Supreme Court decision) discretionary in nature, do offer boards some specifics regarding ways to mitigate eventual fines and sentences in carrying out these duties by paying attention to ethics and compliance. In particular, the board must work with executives to analyze the incentives for ethical behavior. It must also be truly knowledgeable about the content and operation of the ethics program. "Knowledgeable" would involve a clear understanding of the process by which the program evolved, its objectives, its process and next steps, rather than simply the mere contents of a training session. The FSG also suggest that the board exercise "reasonable oversight" with respect to the implementation and effectiveness of the ethics/compliance program by ensuring that the program has adequate resources, appropriate level of authority, and direct access to the board. In order to ensure satisfaction of the FSG and the objectives of the ethics and compliance program, the FSG discuss periodic assessment of risk of criminal conduct and of the program's effectiveness. In order to assess their success, boards should evaluate their training and development materials, their governance structure and position descriptions, their individual evaluation processes, their methods for bringing individuals onto the board or removing them, and all board policies, procedures, and processes, including a code of conduct and conflicts policies. Though the above FSG recommendations seem intuitive to some extent, see the following Reality Check for the actual numbers of firms that implement training on these issues for their boards of directors.

Beyond the Law, There Is Ethics

OBJECTIVE

The law answers only a few questions with regard to boards of directors. Certainly Sarbanes-Oxley has strived to answer several more, but a number of issues remain open to board discretionary decision making. One question we would expect the law to answer, but that instead remains somewhat unclear, is whom the board

Reality Check *Do As I Say, Not As I Do . . .*

Board Ethics Training? A 2003 Conference Board report found that 81 percent of firms represented at their conferences had conducted ethics and compliance training, perhaps a good sign. However, only 27 percent of these same firms had held similar training sessions or other opportunities for learning for members of their boards of directors.

Board Diversity? A 2006 report by Catalyst found that women held 14.7 percent of board seats in the *Fortune* 500 in 2005. Though some might contend that this is the result of the fact that women did not enter the executive suites in significant numbers until the latter part of the 20th century, Catalyst's report points out that, at current growth rates, women in board rooms will not reach parity with men for another 70 years.[7] Women of color are progressing at an even slower pace, holding only 3.4 percent of board seats in the *Fortune* 500.

represents. Who are its primary stakeholders? By law, the board of course has a fiduciary duty to the owners of the corporation—the stockholders. However, many scholars, jurists, and commentators are not comfortable with this limited approach to board responsibility and instead contend that the board is the guardian of the firm's social responsibility as well.

Bill George, former chairman and CEO of Medtronic and a recognized expert on governance, contends that there are 10 basic tenets that boards should follow to ensure appropriate and ethical governance:

1. *Standards:* There should be publicly available principles of governance for the board created by the independent directors.
2. *Independence:* Boards should ensure their independence by requiring that the majority of their members be independent.
3. *Selection:* Board members should be selected based not only on their experience or the role they hold in other firms but also for their value structures.
4. *Selection, number 2:* The board's governance and nominating committees should be staffed by independent directors to ensure the continuity of independence.
5. *Executive sessions:* The independent directors should meet regularly in executive sessions to preserve the authenticity and credibility of their communications.
6. *Committees:* The board must have separate audit and finance committees that are staffed by board members with extensive expertise in these arenas.
7. *Leadership:* If the CEO and the chair of the board are one and the same, it is critical that the board select an alternative lead director as a check and balance.
8. *Compensation committee outside expert:* The board should seek external guidance on executive compensation.
9. *Board culture:* The board should not only have the opportunity but be encouraged to develop a culture including relationships where challenges are welcomed and difference can be embraced.

10. *Responsibility:* Boards should recognize their responsibility to provide oversight and to control management through appropriate governance processes.[8]

Some executives may ask whether the board even has the legal right to question the ethics of its executives and others. If a board is aware of a practice that it deems to be unethical but that is completely within the realm of the law, on what basis can the board require the executive to cease the practice? The board can prohibit actions to protect the long-term sustainability of the firm. Notwithstanding the form of the unethical behavior, unethical acts can negatively impact stakeholders such as consumers or employees who can, in turn, negatively impact the firm, which could eventually lead to a firm's demise. (And good governance can have the opposite effect—see the Reality Check that follows!) It is in fact the board's fiduciary duty to protect the firm and, by prohibiting unethical acts, it is doing just that.

As author Malcolm Salter warned, perhaps one of the most important lessons form Enron was that "corporate executives can be convicted in a court of law for a pattern of deception that may or may not be illegal."[9] The critical distinction Salter identifies in the Enron jury decision is that "at the end of the day, we are a principles-based society rather than a rules-based society, even though rules and referees are important." Therefore, though our rules and processes offer guidance in terms of corporate decision making from a teleological, utilitarian perspective, if corporate executives breach common principles of decency and respect for human dignity, society will exact a punishment, nonetheless. Accordingly, a board has an obligation to hold its executives to this higher standard of ethics rather than simply following the legal rules.

Fortune journalists Ram Charan and Julie Schlosser[10] suggest that board members have additional responsibilities beyond the law to explore and to investigate the organizations that they represent, and they suggest that an open conversation is the best method for understanding, not just what board members know, but also what they do not know. They suggest that board members often ignore even the most basic questions such as how the firm actually makes its money and whether customers and clients truly do pay for products and services. That is rather basic, but the truth is that the financial flow can explain a lot about what moves the firm. Board members should also be critical in their inquiries about corporate vulnerabilities—what could drag the firm down and what could competitors do to help it along that path? You do not know where to make the incision (or even just apply a Band-Aid) unless you know where the patient is hurting. Ensuring that information about vulnerabilities is constantly and consistently transmitted to the executives and the board creates effective prevention. Board members need to understand where the company is heading and whether it is realistic that it will get there. This is less likely if it is not living within its means or if it is paying out too much of its sustainable growth dollars to its chief executives in compensation.

Failing in any of these areas creates pressures on the firm and on the board to take up the slack, to manage problems that do not have to exist, to be forced to make decisions that might not have had to be made if only the information systems were working as they should. It is the board members' ultimate duty to provide oversight, which is impossible without knowing the answers to the above questions.

Reality Check *Does Good Governance Mean Good Business?*

Researchers Roberto Newell and Gregory Wilson examined 188 companies from India, Korea, Malaysia, Mexico, Taiwan, and Turkey to determine whether good corporate governance practices resulted in a higher market valuation. They found that companies with better corporate governance had 10 percent to 12 percent higher price-to-book ratios than those with poor practices, indicating that investors do actually reward efforts in these arenas.

Source: Roberto Newell and Gregory Wilson, "A Premium for Good Governance," *The McKinsey Quarterly*, no. 3 (2002), pp. 20–23.

Conflicts of Interest in Accounting and the Financial Markets

OBJECTIVE

Conflicts of interest, while common in many situations among both directors and officers as discussed above, also extend beyond the board room and executive suite throughout the financial arena. In fact, trust is an integral issue for all involved in the finance industry. After all, what more can an auditor, an accountant, or an analyst offer than her or his integrity and trustworthiness? There is no real, tangible product to sell, nor is there the ability to "try before you buy." Therefore, treating clients fairly and building a reputation for fair dealing may be a finance professional's greatest assets. Conflicts—real or perceived—can erode trust, and often exist as a result of varying interests of stakeholders. As discussed earlier in this chapter, public accountants are accountable to their stakeholders—the stockholders and investment communities who rely on their reports—and therefore should always serve in the role of independent contractor to the firms whom they audit. In that regard, companies would love to be able to direct what that outside accountant says because people believe the "independent" nature of the audit. On the other hand, if accountants were merely rubber stamps for the word of the corporation, they would no longer be believed or considered "independent."

If you were to look in a standard business textbook, you might find the following definition of accounting: "the process by which any business keeps track of its financial activities by recording its debits and credits and balancing its accounts." Accounting offers us a system of rules and principles that govern the format and content of financial statements. Accounting, by its very nature, is a system of principles applied to present the financial position of a business and the results of its operations and cash flows. It is hoped that adherence to these principles will result in fair and accurate reporting of this information. Now, would you consider an accountant to be a watchdog or a bloodhound? Does an accountant stand guard or instead seek out problematic reporting? The answer to this question may depend on whether the accountant is employed internally by a firm or works as outside counsel.

Linking public accounting activities to those conducted by investment banks and securities analysts creates tremendous conflicts between one component's duty to audit and certify information with the other's responsibility to provide guidance on future prospects of an investment. Perhaps the leading example of the unethical effects of conflicts of interest is manifested in the shocking fact that 10 of the top investment firms in the country had to pay fines for actions that involved conflicts of interest between research and investment banking. Companies that engaged in investment banking pressured their research analysts to give high ratings to companies whose stocks they were issuing, whether those ratings were deserved or not. William H. Donaldson, the chairman of the SEC, spelled out the problem on the occasion of a global settlement between those companies and the SEC, NASAA, NASD, and NYSE of approximately $1.5 billion for such breaches.

The ethical issues and potential for conflicts surrounding accounting practices go far beyond merely combining services. They may include underreporting income, falsifying documents, allowing or taking questionable deductions, illegally evading income taxes, and engaging in fraud. In order to prevent accountants from being put in these types of conflicts, the American Institute of CPAs publishes professional rules. In addition, accounting practices are governed by generally accepted accounting principles (GAAP) established by the Financial Accounting Standards Board that stipulate the methods by which accountants gather and report information. However, the International Accounting Standards Committee, working with the U.S. SEC, is in the process of creating "convergence" between the International Financial Reporting Standards and the GAAP, with compliance required by 2009.[11] It is not an insignificant task; indeed, it poses daunting challenges. Beyond the prospect of the standards simply being translated appropriately and effectively, the standards themselves can be complex, modifying the standards becomes infinitely more complicated, small global firms may realize a greater burden than larger multinationals, and differences in knowledge bases between countries may pose strong barriers. Accountants are also governed by the American Institute of Certified Public Accountants' (AICPA) Code of Professional Conduct. The code relies on the judgment of accounting professionals in carrying out their duties rather than stipulating specific rules.

But can these standards keep pace with readily changing accounting activities in newly emerging firms such as what occurred with the evolution of the dot.coms of a decade or more ago? *Fortune* magazine devoted an entire cover story at the time to the accounting "sleight of hand" in which dot.coms were engaging to "pull revenues out of thin air."[12] Similar to the slow speed at which the courts caught up to emerging technology such as employee monitoring, accountants need to be on the lookout for the evolutionary tendencies of these sleight of hands.

In any case, would standards be enough? The answers to ethical dilemmas are not always so easily found within the deontological rules and regulations governing the industry. Scholar Kevin Bahr identifies a number of causes for conflicts in the financial markets that may or may not be resolved through simple rule-making:

1. *The financial relationship between public accounting firms and their audit clients:* Since audits are paid for by audited clients, there is an inherent conflict found simply in that financial arrangement.

2. *Conflicts between services offered by public accounting firms:* Since many public accounting firms offer consulting services to their clients, there are conflicts in the independence of the firm's opinions and incentives to generate additional consulting fees.

3. *The lack of independence and expertise of audit committees.*

4. *Self-regulation of the accounting profession*: Since the accounting industry has historically self-regulated, oversight has been lax, if any.

5. *Lack of shareholder activism:* Given the diversity of ownership in the market based on individual investors, collective efforts to manage and oversee the board are practically nonexistent.

6. *Short-term executive greed versus long-term shareholder wealth:* Executive compensation packages do not create appropriate incentive systems for ethical executive and board decision making. "Enron paid about $681 million in cash and stock to its 140 senior managers, including at least $67.4 million to former chairman and chief executive Kenneth Lay, in the year prior to December 2, 2001, when the company filed for bankruptcy. Not bad for a company that saw its stock decline from $80 in January of 2001 to less that $1 when filing for bankruptcy."[13]

7. *Executive compensation schemes:* Stock options and their accounting treatment remain an issue for the accounting profession and the investment community since, though meant to be an incentive to management and certainly a form of compensation, they are not treated as an expense on the income statement. They also tend to place the incentives, again, on short-term growth rather than long-term sustainability.

8. *Compensation schemes for security analysts:* Investment banking analysts have an interest in sales; this is how they generate the commissions or fees that support their salaries. However, the sale is not always the best possible transaction for the client, generating potential conflicts.[14]

Similarly, scholar Eugene White contends that, in part based on the above challenges, markets are relatively ineffective and the only possible answer is additional regulation. Though Bahr argues that there may be means by which to resolve the conflicts, such as due notice and separation of research and auditing activities, White instead maintains that these conflicts cannot in fact be eliminated.[15] "Financial firms may hide relevant information and disclosure may reveal too much proprietary information." There remains no perfect solution; instead the investment community has no choice but to rely in part on the ethical decision making of the agent who acts within the market, constrained to some extent by regulation.

Executive Compensation

Few areas of corporate governance and finance have received as much public scrutiny in recent years as executive compensation. A *Fortune* cover exclaimed: "Inside the Great CEO Pay Heist," and the article inside detailed how many top corporate executives now receive "gargantuan pay packages unlike any seen before." In the words of *Fortune*'s headline: "Executive compensation has become highway robbery—we all know that."

In 1960, the after-tax average pay for corporate chief executive officers (CEO) was 12 times the average pay earned by factory workers. By 1974, that factor had risen to 35 times the average, but by 2000, it had risen to a high of 525 times the average pay received by factory workers! (See Figure 10.2.) The most recent figure reports an estimated ratio of 411 times a worker's average pay for 2005. Importantly, these numbers address only the *average* pay; the differences would be more dramatic if we compared the top salary for CEOs and minimum-wage workers. In two of the more well-publicized cases of the past decade, Sandy Weill, the CEO of Travelers Insurance, received over $230 million in compensation for 1997 and Michael Eisner of Walt Disney received $589 million in 1998. These numbers continue to rise. In 2005, total direct compensation for CEOs rose by 16 percent to reach a median figure of $6.05 million, not including pensions, deferred compensation, and other perks.[16] Let's take another look at the salary of former New York Stock Exchange Chairman Richard Grasso's salary, which we discussed in Chapter 2.

Forbes reported that the CEOs of 800 major corporations received an average 23 percent pay raise in 1997 while the average U.S. worker received around 3 percent. The median total compensation for these 800 CEOs was reported as $2.3 million. Half of this amount was in salary and bonuses, and 10 percent came from such things as life insurance premiums, pension plans and individual retirement accounts, country club memberships, and automobile allowances. Slightly less than half came from stock options.

It is relevant to note in Figure 10.2 that CEO pay and the S&P 500 Index seem to follow similar trajectories. One might expect something along these lines since "pay for performance" is often based on stock price as one element of measurable performance. However, notice that actual corporate profits, not to mention worker pay, have not increased at the same rate as CEO pay. So, though CEOs have seen an increase, the corporations themselves—and the workers who contribute to their successes—have not reaped equivalent benefits. This lack of balance in the distribution of value has led to the perception of unfairness with regard to executive compensation, as we will discuss below. (See the following Decision Point for a review of the fairness of Richard Grasso's compensation during his work with the New York Stock Exchange.)

More recently, compensation packages paid to the top executives of Exxon-Mobil drew harsh public criticism amid rising gas prices and soaring profits. Exxon-Mobil CEO Lee Raymond received total compensation of $28 million, including $18 million in stock in 2003 and $38 million, of which $28 million was in Exxon-Mobile stock, in 2004. In 2005, the year in which he retired, Raymond received $51 million in salary. The interest alone on this three-year salary would, at a modest 5 percent rate of return, forever produce $5.85 million annually. Apparently this was not sufficient for Raymond's needs because he also received an additional retirement package with a combined worth of $400 million. When he succeeded Raymond, new CEO Rex Tillerson's salary increased 33 percent to a total of $13 million including $8.75 million in stock. The combined compensation

In Chapter 2, a Decision Point discusses the fact that Richard Grasso, during his last year as chairman of the New York Stock Exchange, received total compensation of $140 million and was slated to receive approximately another $48 million in retirement benefits. At the same time, the average starting salary of a trader on an exchange is $90,000.[17] Grasso therefore was paid at a ratio of approximately 1,555 to 1. Considering this figure, how would you suggest the level of compensation for chief executives be determined? What could an individual possibly do to warrant a salary of 1,555 times what you might be able to accomplish during the course of your workday?

just for these two executives in 2004 and 2005 was in excess of $500 million. During the same period, Exxon-Mobil also achieved record profits, earning more than $25 billion in 2004 and $36 billion in 2005.

The relationship between profits and executive compensation, however, is not always as direct as this. In 1998, *Forbes* also reported that there was little correlation between CEO pay and performance. Comparing CEO compensation to stock performance over a five-year period, *Forbes* described 15 CEOs who earned over $15 million while their company's stock lagged well behind the market average of 23 percent. One CEO, Robert Elkins of Integrated Health Systems, received over $43 million during this five-year period while his company's stock valued *declined* by 36 percent. Another report, based on data for 1996, showed that the top executives of firms that laid off more than 3,000 workers in the previous

FIGURE 10.2   Average CEO to Average Worker Pay Ratio, 1990–2005

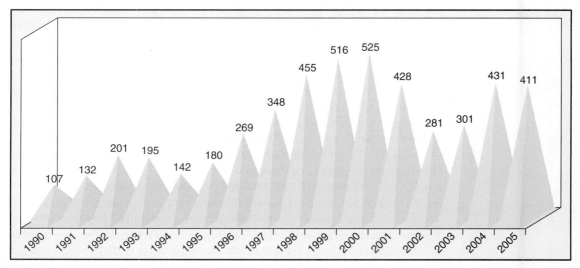

Source: Copyright © United for a Fair Economy, www.faireconomy.org. Reprinted by permission.

FIGURE 10.3   **Cumulative Percent Change in Economic Indicators, from 1990 (in 2005 dollars)**

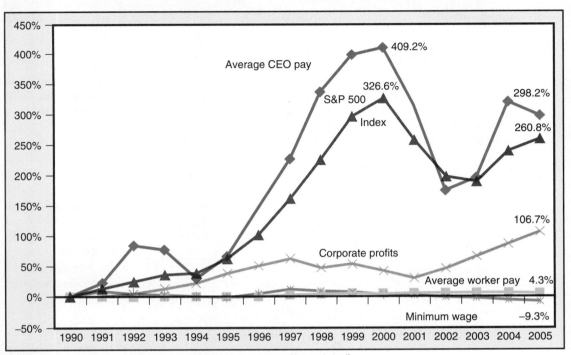

Source: Copyright © United for a Fair Economy, www.faireconomy.org. Reprinted by permission.[18]

year received an average 67 percent increase in their total compensation package for the year. In 1996, the average gap between CEO pay and the wages for the lowest-paid worker for the top 12 job-cutting companies was 178 to 1. Finally, Pfizer's stock price decreased by more than 40 percent since 2001 when McKinnell became CEO though he has received $79 million in pay during that same period and has a guaranteed pension of $83 million when he retires.

These gaps continue to increase. For the decade ending in 2000, the U.S. minimum wage increased 36 percent, from $3.80 per hour to $5.15 per hour. The median household income in the United States increased 43 percent, from $29,943 to $42,680. The average annual salary for a tenured New York City teacher increased 20 percent, from $41,000 to $49,030. During this same decade the total compensation for the Citicorp CEO increased 12,444 percent from $1.2 million to $150 million dollars annually. General Electric CEO Jack Welch's salary increased 2,496 percent, from $4.8 million to $125 million.

Skyrocketing executive compensation packages raise numerous ethical questions. Greed and avarice are the most apt descriptive terms for the moral character of such people from a virtue ethics perspective. Fundamental questions of distributive justice and fairness arise when these salaries are compared to the pay of average workers or to the billions of human beings who live in abject poverty on a global level.

OBJECTIVE

But serious ethical challenges are raised against these practices even from within the business perspective. The reading by Jeffery Moriarty in Chapter 3 details the shortcomings of attempted justifications for such excessive pay packages. Both *Fortune* and *Forbes* magazines have been vocal critics of excessive compensation while remaining staunch defenders of corporate interests and the free market. Beyond issues of personal morality and economic fairness, however, excessive executive compensation practices also speak to significant ethical issues of corporate governance and finance.

In theory, lofty compensation packages are thought to serve corporate interests in two ways. They provide an incentive for executive performance, and they serve as rewards for accomplishments. (See the Reality Check above.) In terms of ethical theory, they have a utilitarian function when they act as incentives for executives to produce greater overall results, and they are a matter of ethical principle when they compensate individuals on the basis of what they have earned and deserve.

In practice, reasonable doubts exist about both of these rationales. First, as suggested by Moriarty's essay and the *Forbes* story mentioned previously, there is much less correlation between pay and performance than one would expect. At least in terms of stock performance, executives seem to reap large rewards regardless of business success. Of course, it might be argued that in difficult financial times, an executive faces greater challenges and therefore perhaps deserves his salary more than in good times. But the corollary of this is that in good financial times, as when Exxon-Mobil earns a $30 billion profit, the executives have less to do with the success.

More to the point of governance, there are several reasons why excessive compensation may evidence a failure of corporate boards to fulfill their fiduciary duties. First, as mentioned before, is the fact that in many cases there is no correlation between executive compensation and performance. Second, there is also little evidence that the types of compensation packages described above are actually needed as incentives for performance. The fiduciary duty of boards ought to involve approving high enough salaries to provide adequate incentive, but not more than what is needed. Surely there is a diminishing rate of return on incentives beyond a certain level. Does a $40 million annual salary provide twice the incentive of $20 million, 4 times the incentive of $10 million, and 40 times the return of a $1 million salary?

Another crucial governance issue is the disincentives that compensation packages, and in particular the heavy reliance on stock options, provide. When executive compensation is tied to stock price, executives have a strong incentive to focus on short-term stock value rather than long-term corporate interests. One of the fastest ways to increase stock price is through layoffs of employees. This may not always be in the best interests of the firms, and there is something perverse about basing the salary of an executive on how successful they can be in putting people out of work.

Further, a good case can be made that stock options have also been partially to blame for the corruption involving managed earnings. Two academic studies concluded that there is a strong link between high levels of executive compensation and the likelihood of misstating or falsely reporting financial results.[20] When huge amounts of compensation depend on quarterly earning reports, there is a strong incentive to manipulate those reports in order to achieve the money.

Excessive executive compensation can also involve a variety of conflicts of interests and cronyism. The board's duties should include ensuring that executives are fairly and not excessively paid. They also have a responsibility to evaluate the executive's performance. However, all too often, the executive being evaluated and paid also serves as chair of the board of directors. The board is often comprised of members hand-selected by the senior executives. In addition, the compensation board members receive is determined by the chief executive officer, creating yet another conflict of interest. (See Figure 10.4.)

FIGURE 10.4   **Duties of the Board and Senior Executives That May Give Rise to Conflicts of Interest**

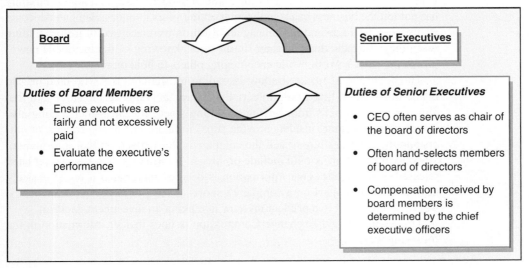

The cronyism does not end at the boardroom door. One of the larger concerns to have arisen in recent years has been the cross-fertilization of boards. The concern spawned a Web site called www.theyrule.net, which allows searching for links between any two given companies. A search for a connection, for instance, between Coca-Cola and PepsiCo uncovers within seconds the fact that PepsiCo board member Robert Allen sits on the Bristol-Myers Squibb board alongside Coca-Cola board member James D. Robinson III. Though sitting on a board together does not necessarily mean Pepsi's board member will gain access to Coke's secret recipe, it does lend itself to the appearance of impropriety and give rise to a question of conflicts.

In another case involving lesser-known companies, three individuals served on the boards of three companies, with each serving as CEO and chairman of one of the companies, Brocade, Verisign, and Juniper. Unfortunately, the companies were found to have backdated stock options, and each firm found itself subject to either Securities and Exchange Commission inquiries or criminal or civil legal proceedings. Cronyism or basic occurrences of overlapping board members might occur, of course, simply because particular individuals are in high demand as a result of their expertise. However, where the overlap results in a failure of oversight and effective governance—the primary legal and ethical responsibility of board members—the implications can be significant to all stakeholders involved.

Insider Trading

OBJECTIVE

No discussion of the ethics of corporate governance and finance would be complete without consideration of the practice of **insider trading** by board members, executives, and other insiders. The issue became front page news in the 1980s when Ivan Boesky was sent to prison for the crime of insider trading. Though it certainly has not left the business pages in the intervening years, it once again gained iconic status when Ken Lay and his colleagues at Enron were accused of insider trading when they allegedly dumped their Enron stock, knowing of the inevitable downturn in the stock's worth, while encouraging others to hold on to it.

The definition of insider trading is trading by shareholders who hold private inside information that would materially impact the value of the stock and that allows them to benefit from buying or selling stock. Illegal insider trading also occurs when corporate insiders provide "tips" to family members, friends, or others and those parties buy or sell the company's stock based on that information. "Private information" would include privileged information that has not yet been released to the public. That information is deemed material if it could possibly have a financial impact on a company's short- or long-term performance or if it would be important to a prudent investor in making an investment decision.

The Securities and Exchange Commission defines insider information in the following way:

"Insider trading" refers generally to buying or selling a security, in breach of a fiduciary duty or other relationship of trust and confidence, while in possession of material, nonpublic information about the security. Insider trading violations may also include "tipping" such information, securities trading by the person "tipped" and securities trading by those who misappropriate such information. Examples of insider trading cases that have been brought by the Commission are cases against: corporate officers, directors, and employees who traded the corporation's securities after learning of significant, confidential corporate developments; friends, business associates, family members, and other "tippees" of such officers, directors, and employees, who traded the securities after receiving such information; employees of law, banking, brokerage and printing firms who were given such information in order to provide services to the corporation whose securities they traded; government employees who learned of such information because of their employment by the government; and other persons who misappropriated, and took advantage of, confidential information from their employers.[21]

Because insider trading undermines investor confidence in the fairness and integrity of the securities markets, the commission has treated the detection and prosecution of insider trading violations as one of its enforcement priorities.[22]

Accordingly, if an executive gets rid of a stock he knows is going to greatly decrease in worth because of bad news in the company that no one knows except a few insiders, he takes advantage of those who bought the stock from him without full disclosure.

Insider trading may also be based on a claim of unethical misappropriation of proprietary knowledge, that is, knowledge only those in the firm should have, knowledge owned by the firm and not to be used by abusing one's fiduciary responsibilities to the firm. The law surrounding insider trading therefore creates a responsibility to protect confidential information, proprietary information, and intellectual property. That responsibility also exists based on the fiduciary duty of "insiders" such as executives. Misappropriation of this information undermines the trust necessary to the proper functioning of a firm and is unfair to others who buy the stock. Though one might make the argument that, in the long run, insider trading is not so bad since the inside information will be discovered shortly and the market will correct itself, this contention does not take account of the hurt to those who completed the original transactions in a state of ignorance.

Insider trading is considered patently unfair and unethical since it precludes fair pricing based on equal access to public information. If market participants know that one party may have an advantage over another via information that is not available to all players, pure price competition will not be possible and the faith upon which the market is based will be lost.

On the other hand, trading on inside information is not without its ethical defense. If someone has worked very hard to obtain a certain position in a firm and, by virtue of being in that position, the individual is privy to inside information, isn't it just for that person to take advantage of the information since she or he has worked so hard to obtain the position? Is it really wrong? Unethical?

Where does a private investor find information relevant to stock purchases? Barring issues of insider trading, do all investors actually have equivalent access to information about companies?

- What are the ethical issues involved in access to corporate information?
- Where do private investors go to access information about stock purchases? On whose opinion do they rely? Does everyone have access to these same opinions? If not, what determines access to information in an open market? Instead, is there equal opportunity to have access to information?
- Who are the stakeholders involved in the issue of access? Who relies on information relevant to stock purchases? Who has an interest in equal access to information?
- What alternatives are available when considering access to information? How can we perhaps best ensure equal access?
- How do the alternatives compare, and how do the alternatives affect the stakeholders?

Consider an issue that might be closer to home. If your brother has always been successful in whatever he does in the business world, is it unethical to purchase stock in the company he just acquired? Others don't know quite how successful he has been, so are you trading on inside information? Would you tell others? What about officers in one company investing in the stocks of their client companies? No legal rules exist other than traditional SEC rules on insider trading, but isn't there something about this that simply doesn't feel "right?" Consider the ethical issues surrounding access to information in the Decision Point above.

Some people do seem to have access to more information than others, and their access does not always seem to be fair. Let's take a look at what landed Martha Stewart in jail. Stewart was good friends with Sam Waksal, who was the founder and CEO of a company called ImClone. Waksal had developed a promising new cancer drug and had just sold an interest in the drug to Bristol Myers for $2 billion. Unfortunately, though everyone thought the drug would soon be approved, Waksal learned that the Food and Drug Administration had determined that the data were not sufficient to allow the drug to move to the next phase of the process. When this news became public, ImClone's stock price was going to fall significantly.

On learning the news (December 26, 2001), Waksal contacted his daughter and instructed her to sell her shares in ImClone. He then compounded his violations by transferring 79,000 of his shares (worth almost $5 million) to his daughter and asking her to sell those shares, too. Though the Securities and Exchange Commission would likely uncover these trades, given the decrease in share price, it was not something he seemed to consider. "Do I know that, when I think about it? Absolutely," says Waksal. "Did I think about it at the time? Obviously not. I just acted irresponsibly."[23] Waksal eventually was sentenced to more than seven years in prison for these actions.

In evaluating the causes of the Enron debacle and its implications for change, scholar Lisa Newton analyzes the possible responses we could utilize as a society.[24] Contemplate her arguments that some responses *will not work* and consider whether you agree or disagree:

More regulation: "The people who are making the money eat regulations for breakfast. You can't pass regulations fast enough to get in their way." Regulations are bad business, she states; they do not have sufficient foresight; and virtual and global business leaves us with little to grasp in terms of regulation.

Business ethics courses: Newton contends that they are ineffective in guiding future action, and they do not sufficiently impact motivations.

Changes in corporate cultures: "What the company's officers do, when they act for good or (more likely) evil, does not *proceed from* the corporate culture, as if the corporate culture *caused* their actions. . . . What people do, habitually, just *is* their character, which they create by doing those things. What a corporation does, through its officers, just *is* its culture, created by that behavior. To say that if we change the culture we'll change the behavior is a conceptual mistake—trivial or meaningless."

Does anything work? "Back to those other eras: this is not the first time that, up to our waists in the muck of corporate dishonesty, we have contemplated regulations and ethics classes and using large rough weapons on the corporate culture. And nothing we did in the past worked."

Instead, Newton posits, "capitalism was always known not to contain its own limits; the limits were to be imposed by the democratic system, whose representatives were the popularly elected watchdogs of the economy." Business crime comes not from "systemic capitalist contradictions" or sin; instead it

> . . . arises from a failure of the instruments of democracy, which have been weakened by three decades of market fundamentalism, privatization ideology and resentment of government. Capitalism is not too strong; democracy is too weak. We have not grown too hubristic as producers and consumers [as if the market were, when working right, capable of governing itself]; we have grown too timid as citizens, acquiescing to deregulation and privatization (airlines, accounting firms, banks, media conglomerates, you name it) and a growing tyranny of money over politics.[25]

Newton then explains that "we need, as Theodore Roosevelt well knew (20 years before his cousin presided over the aftermath of the 1929 disaster), democratic oversight of the market, or it will run amok. As it has.

Her conclusion? "Ultimately, our whining and hand-wringing about corporate culture, or executive incentives, or other technicalities of the way businesses run themselves, is useless. Business was never supposed to run itself, at least not for long. We the people were supposed to be taking responsibility for its operations as a whole. We have evaded this responsibility for almost a quarter of a century now, and that's long enough. It is time to remember that we have a public responsibility hat as well as a private enterprise hat, to put it on and put the country back in order."

(continued)

Is taking public responsibility the answer to ethical lapses in business ?

- What else might you need to know in order to effectively evaluate Professor Newton's conclusion?
- What ethical issues are involved in the challenges she addresses?
- Who are the stakeholders?
- What do you think about her evaluation of the alternatives above?
- How do the alternatives compare? How do the alternatives affect the stakeholders?

Elements adapted by the authors with permission of Dr. Lisa Newton. For a more in-depth analysis, see also Reading 10-1.

How does Stewart fit into this picture? The public trial revealed that Stewart's broker ordered a former Merrill Lynch & Co. assistant to tell her that Waksal was selling his stock, presumably so that she would also sell her stock. Stewart subsequently sold almost 4,000 shares on December 27, 2001, one day after Waksal sold his shares and one day prior to the public statement about the drug's failed approval.

Stewart successfully avoided prison for several years, and on November 7, 2003, she explained that she was scared of prison but "I don't think I will be going to prison."Nevertheless she was convicted on all counts except securities fraud and sentenced to a five-month prison term, five months of home confinement, and a $30,000 fine, the minimum the court could impose under the Federal Sentencing Guidelines.

During the trial, the public heard the testimony of Stewart's friend, Mariana Pasternak, who reported that Stewart told her several days after the ImClone sale that she knew about Waksal's stock sales and that Stewart said, "Isn't it nice to have brokers who tell you those things?" So, to return to the issue with which we began this tale, it appears that some investors do seem to have access to information not necessarily accessible to all individual investors. Though Stewart, Waksal, and others involved in this story were caught and charged with criminal behavior, many believe they were identified and later charged because they were in the public eye. If others are not in the public eye and also engage in this behavior, can the SEC truly police all inappropriate transactions? Is there a sufficient deterrent effect to discourage insider trading in our markets today? If not, what else can or should be done? Or, to the contrary, is this simply the nature of markets, and those who have found access to information should use it to the best of their abilities? What might be the consequences of this latter, perhaps more Darwinian, approach to insider trading, and whose rights might be violated if we allow it?

What should the board of directors of Hershey Foods have done in connection with Hershey's possible sale?

In evaluating the key facts relevant to your decision, are you persuaded by the concerns of the residents? Do you agree with the source of their concerns, the presumed consequences of the sale? Could alternate consequences occur? In other words, the residents claim that the sale will result in these negative circumstances. Do you agree? Does the board have any ethical obligations to the residents of Hershey, Pennsylvania? What other ethical obligations might the board have? To whom does it owe a responsibility; who are its stakeholders?

Can you imagine any possible alternatives to serve the Trust's interests, the board's obligations, the residents' concerns, and any other issues you anticipate the stakeholders will raise? How will each of your alternatives impact each of the stakeholders you have identified? How will you reach this decision?

RESOLUTION

The Trust received two significant offers for Hershey. The first was from Chicago-based Wrigley Chewing Gum and the second was a joint offer from Nestlé and Cadbury. Though both included plans to keep all factories open and running, the community continued its vociferous protests and the Trust rejected both offers.

The chairman and CEO of the Hershey Trust, Robert Vowler, explained, however, that the Trust's decision was based solely on the failure to receive satisfactory offers rather than being in response to any protest. He explained that the Trust's original purpose was to diversify the Trust's assets to protect its beneficiary and the Wrigley offer would not have achieved this goal. The Nestlé/Cadbury offer was evidently too low.

Following is the press release the Hershey Company issued on the day of the Trust's decision:

Hershey Foods Reaffirms Its Strength

HERSHEY, Pa., Sep 18, 2002. The Board of Directors, management and employees of Hershey Foods Corporation today reaffirmed their commitment to the long-term, value-enhancing strategy embarked upon earlier this year. The company affirmed the termination of the sale process and also stated that its Board of Directors has not been approached by the Milton Hershey School Trust regarding repurchasing stock from the Trust, nor does it have any intention of renewing the stock repurchase proposal previously rejected by the Trust prior to the commencement of the sale process.

Richard H. Lenny, Chairman, President and Chief Executive Officer, said, "There has been significant disruption to our company, employees and the communities in which we live and work over the past few months. However, Hershey Foods remains a competitively advantaged market leader in an attractive category. We also have a truly outstanding workforce, one that consistently has maintained focus and shown courage in the face of significant uncertainty about our future as an independent company. Our mission, as always, is to bring our energy and attention to the task of building our brands and capitalizing on the immense strengths that were so clearly evident to potential acquirers."[26]

Questions, Projects, and Exercises

1. You have been asked by the board of a large corporation to develop a board assessment and effectiveness mechanism, which could be a survey, interviews, an appraisal system, or other technique that will allow you to report back to the board on both individual and group effectiveness. What would you recommend?

2. You have been asked to join the board of a large corporation. What are some of the first questions that you should ask and what are the answers that you are seeking?

3. Scholars have made strong arguments for required representation on boards by stakeholders beyond stockholders such as employees, community members, and others, depending on the industry. What might be some of the benefits and costs of such a process?

4. You are an executive at a large nonprofit. Some of your board members suggest that perhaps the company should voluntarily comply with Sarbanes-Oxley. What are some of the reasons the company might consider doing so or not doing so?

5. You are on the compensation committee of your board and have been asked to propose a compensation structure to be offered to the next CEO. Explore some of the following Web sites on executive compensation and then propose a structure or process for determining CEO compensation at your corporation.

   http://www.aflcio.org/corporateamerica/paywatch/ceou/database.cfm
   http://www.ecomponline.com/
   http://www.rileyguide.com/execpay.html
   http://www.sec.gov/investor/pubs/execomp0803.htm
   http://www.eri-executive-compensation.com/?TrkID=479-82
   http://bwnt.businessweek.com/exec_comp/2002/index.asp
   http://www.tgci.com/magazine/97fall/exec.asp

6. What are the strongest, most persuasive arguments in favor of a board's consideration of its social responsibility when reaching decisions?

7. A press release has a significant negative impact on your firm's stock price, reducing its value by more than 50 percent in a single day of trading! You gather from conversations in the hallway that the company's fundamentals remain strong, aside from this one-time event. You see this as a great opportunity to buy stock. Is it appropriate to act on this and to purchase company stock? Does it make a difference whether you buy 100 shares or 1,000 shares? Is it OK to discuss the "dilemma" with family members and friends? What should you do if you do mention it to family and friends but then later feel uncomfortable about it?

8. Modify slightly the facts of the previous question. Assume that you are also privy to the annual forecast of earnings, which assures you that the fundamentals remain strong. Stock analysts and investors are also provided this same information. Do your answers change at all?

9. In connection with the two previous questions, assume instead that you think something significant is about to be made public because all officers have consistently stayed late, a special board meeting has been called, you and your boss have been advised to be on call throughout the weekend, and various rumors have been floating throughout the company. You are not aware of the specifics, but you can reasonably conclude that it's potentially good or bad news. You decide to call a friend in the accounting department

who has been staying late to find out what she knows. In this situation, do your answers about what you might do change? Is it appropriate to partake in the "rumor mill"? Is it appropriate to discuss and confide your observations with family and friends? Is it appropriate to buy or sell company stock based upon these observations (you may rationalize that it is only speculation and you do not know the facts)?

Key Terms

After reading this chapter, you should have a clear understanding of the following Key Terms. The page numbers refer to the point at which they were discussed in the chapter. For a more complete definition, please see the Glossary.

Committee of Sponsoring Organizations (COSO), *p. 428*

conflict of interest, *p. 423*

control activities, *p. 429*

control environment, *p. 429*

corporate governance, *p. 421*

duty of care, *p. 430*

duty of good faith, *p. 430*

duty of loyalty, *p. 431*

Enron Corporation, *p. 427*

European Union 8th Directive, *p. 428*

Federal Sentencing Guidelines, *p. 431*

fiduciary duties, *p. 423*

gatekeeper, *p. 424*

insider trading, *p. 442*

internal control, *p. 429*

Sarbanes-Oxley Act, *p. 422*

Endnotes

1. Rushworth Kidder, "Combating Ethical Lapses: Why Compliance Is Not the Answer," *Ethics Newsline* 8, no. 16 (April 25, 2005).
2. C. William Thomas, "The Rise and Fall of Enron," *Journal of Accountancy* (April 2002), p. 7.
3. "Recent Survey Results from the Financial Executives Institute," *NACD Director's Monthly,* March 2005, p. 6.
4. Public Company Accounting Oversight Board, "PCAOB Issues Guidance on Audits of Internal Control," Press Release, May 16, 2005.
5. Criteria of Control, Board Guidance on Control.
6. Ron Duska, "Perspectives in Ethical Leadership," *Mitchell Forum on Ethical Leadership in Financial Services*, January 10, 2004, p. 35.
7. Catalyst, "2005 Catalyst Census of Women Board Directors of the *Fortune* 500," 2006.
8. William W. George, "Restoring Governance to Our Corporations," address given to the Council of Institutional Investors, September 23, 2002, http://www.authenticleaders. org/articles/restoringgovernancetocorp.htm.
9. Malcolm S. Salter, "Enron Jury Sent the Right Message," *Harvard Business School Working Knowledge for Business Leaders Series,* July 21, 2006, http://hbswk.hbs.edu/ item/5456.html.
10. Ram Charan and Julie Schlosser, "Ten Questions Every Board Member Should Ask; And for That Matter, Every Shareholder Too," *Fortune*, November 10, 2003, p. 181.
11. International Accounting Standards Board, "Accounting Standards: EU Commissioner McCreevy Sees Agreement with S.E.C. as Progress toward Equivalence," Press Release, April 22, 2005, http://www.iasb.org/news/index.asp?showPageContent=no &xml=10_380_25_22042005_22042006.htm.

12. Jeremy Kahn, "Presto Chango! Sales are Huge!" *Fortune*, March 20, 2000, http://www.fortune.com/fortune/2000/03/20/net.html.

13. Kevin Bahr, "Conflicts of Interest in the Financial Markets" (Stevens Point, WI: Central Wisconsin Economic Research Bureau, 2002), http://www.uwsp.edu/business/cwerb/4thQtr02/SpecialReportQtr4_02.htm.

14. Kevin Bahr, "Conflicts of Interest in the Financial Markets," (Stevens Point, WI: Central Wisconsin Economic Research Bureau, 2002), http://www.uwsp.edu/business/cwerb/4thQtr02/SpecialReportQtr4_02.htm.

15. Eugene White, "Can the Market Control Conflicts of Interest in the Financial Industry?" presentation at the International Monetary Fund, June 4, 2004, http://www.imf.org/external/np/leg/sem/2004/cdmfl/eng/enw.pdf.

16. Carol Hymowitz, "Sky-High Payouts to Top Executives Prove Hard to Curb," *The Wall Street Journal*, June 26, 2006, p. B1.

17. *The Princeton Review*, 2006, http://www.princetonreview.com/cte/profiles/facts.asp?careerID=213.

18. Data sources for Figures 10.2 and 10.3: Total executive compensation: 2005 data based on a *Wall Street Journal* survey, April 10, 2006; all other years based on similar sample in *BusinessWeek* annual compensation surveys (now discontinued). Includes salary, bonus, restricted stock, payouts on other long-term incentives, and the value of options exercised. S&P 500 Index: "Economic Report of the President," 2006 Table B-96; 1997, 2000 Table B-93; average of daily closing prices. Corporate Profits: U.S. Department of Commerce, Bureau of Economic Analysis, National Income and Product Accounts, Table 6.16, with inventory valuation and capital consumption adjustments. Average worker pay: Based on U.S. Department of Labor, Bureau of Labor Statistics, Employment, Hours, and Earnings from the Current Employment Statistics Survey (average hourly earnings of production workers × average weekly hours of production workers × 52). Minimum wage: Lowest mandated federal minimum wage, nominal; U.S. Dept. of Labor, Employment Standards Administration, Wage and Hour Division. Adjustment for inflation: BLS, Average Annual CPI-U, all urban consumers, all items.

19. Quoted in "Justice, Incentives, and Executive Compensation," by William Shaw, in *The Ethics of Executive Compensation*, edited by Robert Kolb (Malden, MA: Blackwell, 2006), p. 93.

20. J. Harris and P. Bromiley, *Incentives to Cheat: Executive Compensation and Corporate Malfeasance*, and O'Conner et al., "Do CEO Stock Options Prevent or Promote Corporate Accounting Irregularities?" as quoted in Jared Harris, "How Much Is Too Much?" in *The Ethics of Executive Compensation*, pp. 67–86.

21 U.S. Securities and Exchange Commission, "Key Topics: Insider Trading," http://www.sec.gov/answers/insider.htm(2001).

22. http://www.sec.gov/divisions/enforce/insider.htm.

23. CBS News, "Sam Waksal: I Was Arrogant," June 27, 2004, http://www.cbsnews.com/stories/2003/10/02/60minutes/main576328.shtml.

24. Adapted and quoted from Lisa Newton, "Enron and Andersen: Guideposts for the Future," presentation to the Society for Business Ethics, Annual Meeting, August 2002.

25. Benjamin Barber, "A Failure of Democracy, Not Capitalism," *The New York Times*, July 29, 2002, Op-Ed. (A-19).

26. The Hershey Company, "Hershey Reaffirms Its Strength," September 18, 2002, http://www.thehersheycompany.com/news/release.asp?releaseID=335032

Readings

Reading **10-1**

"Enron: The Parable"

Lisa H. Newton   Director, Program in Applied Ethics, Fairfield University

1. Pipes to Riches in Wonderland

Beginnings: Enron had its humble beginnings as a natural gas company. When Kenneth L. Lay became chairman and COO of Houston Natural Gas in June 1984, the company owned pipelines, and it transported natural gas to customers. Utilities of all sorts had always been highly regulated, and the industry wasn't very interesting. But Ken Lay's vision had its origin in President Ronald Reagan's deregulation agenda, which Lay had helped to further, and drew its operating practices from the mergers and acquisitions habits of the 1980s business community. He set out to grow the company into the biggest and most profitable energy company in the world, which, eventually, he almost did, at least on paper. He snapped up a small pipeline company in Florida, then merged with InterNorth, Inc. in July 1985, to give him 40,000 miles of pipeline. Such size required a catchier name, so in 1986 Enron was born. (He'd thought of "Enteron" first, but changed it to "Enron" when he found out that *enteron* is another word for the digestive tract.)

Largely due to the lobbying efforts of Lay and others who shared his vision of unfettered utilities, most of the regulations came off the production and sale of energy in the last years of the 1980s. By 1989, Enron was trading natural gas on the commodities market. The next year Lay hired Jeffrey K. Skilling, a Harvard MBA, away from his consulting job at McKinsey & Co., to head up the new energy-trading operations. Skilling transformed the operation from a simple transportation service to an immense trading center, a "gas bank" purchasing large amounts of natural gas from the producers and reselling it to customers here and abroad on long-term contracts. After that, market innovation and company growth outpaced each other through the decade. The company began trading online, increasing by orders of magnitude the speed with which its deals could be completed.

Deals: And what deals they were! If you could name it, you could buy and sell it. It wasn't just that Enron had turned natural gas into a commodity, a move that rapidly expanded to energy futures contracts. By the end, Enron was selling broadband, water, and weather derivatives—hedges against bad weather that might affect business operations.

But the major innovations were financial. Federal regulators permitted Enron to use "mark-to-market" accounting, a way of evaluating future income that works reasonably

Note: Some references and citations have been deleted, but are available from the author.

well in securities trading. In Enron's case, it allowed the company to calculate projected income as present profit, a practice that can be taken to extremes; in 1999, for instance, the company claimed a $65 million profit "based on its projections of natural-gas sales from a South American pipeline project. The pipeline had yet to be built."

It should be noted that Enron was not the only company turning itself from a company that dealt with things to a company that made financial deals. All through the deregulatory 1990s, law firms and banks were selling their clients "structured" deals, setting up new companies and partnerships to move assets or debts off the books and preferably off the continent. It's just that Enron became more dependent on these deals than the others, because it set such high earnings targets (to keep the investors happy) and because there was by now so little of the original enterprise to rely on. These deals are not always lucky. By the Fall of 2000, two of the Enron investment vehicles called the Raptors were failing; Enron solved the problem by having the two solvent Raptors pick up the debt of the two insolvent ones. Another rescue had to be engineered in March 2001. This time $700 million of Enron stock had to be transferred in from another partnership. At this point Arthur Andersen protested strongly. Enron's threat to take its business elsewhere worked once more to keep its auditors cooperative.

Throughout these years, Enron wasn't paying taxes. Enron had paid no income taxes in four of the last five years, making good use of about 900 subsidiaries in tax-haven countries to cover its revenues (this according to an analysis of its financial reports to its shareholders). It even collected $382 million in tax refunds. The subsidiaries chose prime vacation spots for their services: there were 692 in the Cayman Islands, 119 in the Turks and Caicos Islands, 43 on Mauritius, 8 in Bermuda, 6 in Barbados, 4 in Puerto Rico, 2 in Hong Kong, 2 in Panama, and one each in Aruba, the British Virgin Islands, Guam, Guernsey, and Singapore. In the year 2000, the company got $278 million in refunds. (Stock options, with which they were very generous, do not have to be reported to the shareholders as an expense, but are deducted from company income for tax purposes.) Even Robert Hermann, the company's general tax counsel, wondered about this apparent exemption from the U.S. Internal Revenue requirements; by his own account, he asked Skilling at a 2000 meeting why it was that the company seemed to be doing so well, but paid so little in taxes! The answer, of course, was in his own division. Enron's skill in locating its partnerships offshore and keeping cash flow small had made the tax division a significant "profit center" for the company, saving $1 billion over the previous five years.

Strategy: The impression left by all of the above is that Enron was in constant motion, always innovating, always daring, always out in front of some field, but also doing rather little to earn a living. Shortly into its meteoric course into the hearts and purses of investors, Enron's financial activities well outstripped its pipelines and its natural gas trade in the amount of money generated. And the financial activities' profits were, as the world would soon find out, bogus. Why were they playing this game? What were they thinking?

They were trying to please Wall Street. In order to secure a "buy" recommendation from investment analysts, a company must report ever higher earnings every quarter, and in these days of deregulation, there are many fewer restrictions on how it does it. That doesn't sound like Adam Smith's description of a business enterprise, but it is an accurate description of the kinds of pressures placed on any business today by the investment community. Now that aggressively managed funds have largely taken the place of the wealthy individual at the stock counters (or computers), every publicly traded firm must expect to be held accountable for pleasing numbers four times a year. (In order to keep the corporate executives' minds focused on this accounting, they are paid largely in stock options— another reason for issuing lots of stock options—which will make them millionaires and more if the stock goes up, nothing if it goes down.) If the price of a company's stock should nonetheless go down for any reason, it can expect to be rejected by stock analysts (so the price will decline even more) downgraded by credit raters (seriously impacting its ability to do business), and sued by Bill Lerach, who brings class-action suits against companies whose stocks go south. Accountability is not entirely bad, but the focus on quarterly earnings can create distortions in the best run companies. In the case of Enron, whose stock had to maintain its price or expose the entire pyramid of interlocked obligations to horrible collapse, it dictated the multiplication of the special purpose entities and secret loans. The basic business was long forgotten. (In the end, Enron was selling pipelines in order to raise quarterly earnings.) When the business itself takes a back seat, and only the numbers count, distortion is bound to follow. In Enron's case, it followed immediately; the tangled web of deception required earnings, which it had not, or at least the illusion of earnings, which it could produce, so Enron became a master illusionist.

2. Where Are We Going and Why Am I in This Handbasket?

Enron's singular rise and fall resulted from a confluence of several factors.

The New Economy: When Enron approached its peak in mid-2000, the country had had 20 years of deregulation, beginning in the administration of President Ronald Reagan, continued in the administration of George H. W. Bush, not reversed in the centrist administrations of William J. Clinton, and taking off at a wild gallop when George W. Bush entered the White House. Even as the new century opened and the Bush Recession set in, the "most admired" CEO in America was Jack Welch of General Electric, whose personal greed and self-indulgence, in combination with callousness toward his employees, was legendary. It is significant that in the face of the truly baffling financial deals that Enron undertook, almost no one asked publicly where all the money was supposed to come from if some of their bets didn't work out. Blind trust replaced the healthy suspicion on which the conduct of business depends. Dazzled, investors, regulators, and auditors watched in admiration as the swiftly moving shells in Enron's game twinkled across the business world. The general public sat mesmerized, as at a fireworks display; criticism of the corporations was silenced across the land.[1]

The New Culture: The Enron "culture" has received a good deal of attention—perhaps too much. There is broad agreement on its nature: ambition, greed, and contempt for everyone who wasn't part of the cheering section. Nothing mattered except getting rich, very rich, and the company was led by people (see next point) who were completely convinced that rich was what they deserved to be. Convinced of their natural superiority, Enron's day-to-day managers sent clear signals to ignore the law, the rules, the accounting practices, and all other manifestations of the lesser breeds without the New Economy. Their highest virtue was that they could break the rules and get away with it—in the face of the incredulity of their own more experienced colleagues. They could pull off deals that would enrich the shareholders, enrich themselves, and keep the company strong. Questions were not permitted. Those who stood in the way of the top people were quickly silenced, transferred, fired. When banks hesitated to invest in the new funds, they were given to understand that their continued opportunity to do business with Enron required that they overcome their hesitations. When Arthur Andersen auditors objected to keeping those new funds off the books, they were warned that Enron might take its lucrative consulting business to another auditing firm. Even at the end, in August 2001, when Chung Wu, a broker at UBS PaineWebber from

Houston, e-mailed his clients to consider selling their Enron shares, given the difficulties that the company was experiencing, his employer rapidly reversed his recommendation—and fired him. There is no indication, anywhere, that any other banks, or other auditors, would have put up more resistance to the glamorous and admired schemes of the mighty Enron, ranked in March 2000 as the sixth largest energy company in the world (seventh in the Fortune 500). (That rank, of course, was part of the history of misrepresentation at Enron. It was never profitable—even its energy trading in California brought in only .5 percent on sales.)[2]

What is less clear is the origin and support for this "culture." Cultures do not make themselves. Logically, a "culture," in the sense intended, is no more than the cumulative accustomed acts of all the people who claim it as their own. Yet while the key players in the Enron debacle surely embodied the culture, they came aboard too late to have created it. More likely, they were recruited because they already fit it—they were entirely prepared to engage in the single-minded effort to raise earnings and keep them high, only on condition that they too could become rich, and had the ability and imagination both to create the financial instruments that made Enron's earnings possible and to sell the ideas to the appropriate clients. It is significant that the "culture" claimed for Enron happens to be identical with the national culture where money is concerned: admiration for the rich, tolerance for innovative rule-breakers, and an unshakeable conviction that government has no right to stand in the way of any person's efforts to get fabulously wealthy.

The New Accounting: When the van crashes into the retaining wall at 120 mph, at least three causal factors are present: the driver who lost control (was he paying attention?) the engine that brought the van to that speed (was it operating properly?), and the brakes that failed. In this particular crash, the drivers were the managers of Enron, who were apparently zipping along without a roadmap with little regard to the safety of the passengers (let alone the pedestrians), the engine was the unrestrained culture of greed and confidence in the business community that permeated the nation as a whole, and the brakes were the bankers and auditors who were supposed to be making good business judgments about the soundness of Enron's decision making. In this case, "market discipline"—that is, the need to satisfy customers or go out of business—had put a fatal wound in the brakes, all of whom needed, or felt they needed, Enron as a customer.

Endgame: . . . It wasn't exactly a whistle that Enron Vice President Sherron S. Watkins blew. Hers was not (initially) a principled stance. She wanted the career and the money as much as anyone, but confronted with reality, she decided to tell Ken Lay about it instead of pretending it wasn't there. That alone makes her exceptional. She had gotten a temporary assignment to look into the LJM partnerships, including the Raptors, and was horrified by what she saw. On August 15, the day after Skilling resigned, Watkins wrote a long anonymous letter to Lay suggesting that Skilling knew what he was running away from. The letter spoke of the danger that "we will implode in a wave of accounting scandals," when the problems with Condor and Raptor came out. There would be "suspicions of accounting improprieties," because of Enron's "aggressive accounting." In this memo, she coolly estimates the appropriate course of action according to the "probability of discovery" of the improper accounting for these SPEs; she concludes that the probability of discovery is high; therefore the company should "quantify [the losses], develop damage containment plans and disclose." She followed up with a memo suggesting damage containment activity. That sounds more like your cell-phone ringing than a whistle to stop play.

Then September 11, 2001, arrived, the terrorist attack with fuel-laden 747 aircraft, the collapse of the twin towers of the World Trade Center. The radical drop in the stock market in the week following that attack brought Enron stock down to $28.08, eight dollars from that disaster point where its obligations to the Raptors would become so great that the company would not have enough available shares to meet them. "For every dollar the stock dropped below $20, Enron would be facing $124 million in losses," according to an internal Enron document. Enron was hanging on by its fingernails.

On September 26, when the stock fell to $25 per share, Lay had an Internet "chat" with Enron employees. They had watched their 401(k) plans, stuffed with Enron stock, plunge to that level from $90 a year ago. Lay assured the employees that he, personally, was buying more Enron stock, which he characterized as an "incredible bargain," and he urged them to do the same. As the end of the third quarter became imminent, the habits acquired in previous years reasserted themselves. Enron worked out one more "prepay" deal for $350 million on September 28; Enron and Qwest arranged a purchase of networks for another $112 million, a deal that made very little business sense. With all that cash to pump up earnings, third-quarter losses still had to be admitted, and somehow spun to the Wall Street analysts on whose approval the company depended. On October 8, Lay addressed the company's outside board of directors with the same bad news. But how bad was it? When the meeting was over, in which the demise of the Raptors had been cheerfully described as a one-time setback, the directors left thinking the company was basically in good shape. There were claims of future profitability, even as the company was on the ropes.

Enron's October 16 news release on its third-quarter problems had much the same message; the losses were one-time, nonrecurring, and the company's future was rosy. An accounting error, he told a reporter on the phone, resulted in a $1.2 billion loss in equity. Where had all that money gone? It seems that Enron had counted a Raptors' acknowledgement of $1.2 billion transferred from Enron to the SPEs as "shareholder equity." On October 18, when *The Wall Street Journal* found out about that assignment, it wrote a sharp article calling for better explanations. When Lay addressed investment fund managers later that day, trying to get them to hold their stock, or even buy more, he responded to their concerns, and the questions triggered by the article, by attacking the press and promising, over and over, that the loss was a one-time thing, that there were no more write-offs hiding in the books.

Not quite satisfied with that explanation, on October 22 the SEC launched an investigation into Enron. By the end of the day the stock stood at $20.65. On October 28, Lay announced the formation of a special investigative committee, headed up by the Dean of the University of Texas Law School, William Powers, who hired William R. McLucas, former SEC enforcement chief and currently with the law firm of Wilmer, Cutler & Pickering to do the actual investigating. McLucas hired some accountants from Deloitte & Touche to look into the books. They found all those hidden debts and all those cover-ups and all those overstatements of profits, and there was no longer any chance of keeping them hidden. When McLucas issued his report, the company was essentially finished.

There was one more attempt to save the company, by selling it to its smaller rival Dynegy. But, Dynegy had seen enough. On November 26, the deal officially died. Six days later, on December 2, 2001, Enron filed for bankruptcy.

Just in summary, to keep the moral point in focus: who ended up with the money? On October 22, the day that the stock plunged to $20.65, Lay convened the Enron employees, several thousand strong, and commiserated with them about the loss of their investments. He promised, even as he knew that bankruptcy was inevitable, that Enron would get it all back for them. That day he took a $4 million cash advance from the company. Over the next three days he took $19 million more, repaying $6 million by transferring Enron stock, which by then he was very glad to unload. In the end, Ken Lay sold $37,683,887 in stock just before the crash came; Jeff Skilling cashed out $14,480,755. Andrew Fastow had made $45 million, at least as far as anyone has been able to determine. Employees were in "lockdown," not permitted to sell their stock, between October 29 (about the time the employees would have figured that it would never go up again) and November 12, when it stood at $9.98. Effectively they were barred from selling until the bankruptcy, when it was worth nothing. Employees in their 50s and 60s saw retirement funds go from millions of dollars to nothing, and there was nothing they could do about it. Many of those who lost were involved in the trading scams, one way or another, but many others, who had done nothing to deserve it and everything not to deserve it, were mortally hurt.

* * *

4. The Shredding of Arthur Andersen

Accounting firm Arthur Andersen has to take some of the responsibility for that hurt. Andersen had signed off on all of the deals that Enron had made, sometimes under pressure, but it had signed off. Moreover, despite doubts and periodic whimpering about the risk of it all, Andersen had profited from its participation; Enron was one of its biggest clients. Now the firm stood to lose badly.

It wasn't just the money. When the accounting profession had assumed the role of corporate honesty guarantors, the company's founder, Arthur Andersen himself, had been one of the most powerful arguers, and arguments, for trusting the profession with the job of telling the truth to the public. A man of unquestionable integrity, he had argued that the moral integrity of accountants could be counted on to protect the investors from the tendencies of businesses to cut corners. Through its 88-year history, Arthur Andersen especially, among the large accounting firms, had stood for that integrity. Everything rested on that reputation, and once lost, it would not be recovered. Extraordinary pressures had descended upon Arthur Andersen and its competitors during the 1980s and 1990s. Accounting firms discovered, in the rapid growth of technology-based industry, that they could sell their technology consulting services to the very firms they had been auditing for very attractive prices. Both stood to gain: the accounting firm suddenly had a new and major source of income, and the hiring firm had, beside the value of the consulting services, an interesting source of influence with the watchdog supposedly scrutinizing it. As the Enron case illustrates, that influence could be very great indeed. But there was a downside to the new mixture of revenues. Recall the discussion of "the New Culture." Accounting had always been a gray and lumpishly unattractive profession, guaranteeing a safe income and a good retirement, but nothing glamorous. Now suddenly the Big Five had moved from the wallflower auditing culture to the swinging consultant culture, and all their people began to demand big bucks—really big bucks—to enjoy the lifestyles practiced by the investment bankers and their audit clients. Andersen had done very well; its consulting arm brought in barrels of money, divided among all the partners and associates, and everyone was happy.

But not for long. Greed, as Plato pointed out so long ago, is essentially unlimited. If I am enjoying a comfortable existence now, I immediately see that with more money I could enjoy a luxurious existence, and I want it, also immediately. Andersen's consultants were not happy sharing their huge earnings with the old-fashioned stick-in-the-mud rain-on-your-parade auditors. In a brutal divorce, they separated themselves as a unit from the company, and formed a new company (Accenture) to earn their money far away from all the poor relations. But by now the auditors had got used to that larger income, and they put pressure on the senior partners to get it back for them. So they started recruiting consulting clients all over again, built the business quickly, and secured Enron as their largest client, one they could not afford to lose. (According to *Forbes,* Enron was paying Andersen, by the end, $1 million a week in auditing and consulting fees.)

5. The Ultimate Failure of the System

The events narrated here meant the end of Enron. They might mean the end of business as we know it. There seems to be general, if muted, agreement, that the Enron case has shown us a terrible, possibly lethal, weakness in our business system. When wrongdoing is this extensive, long-lived, and shockingly serious, we know well that whether it be the Roman Catholic Diocese of Boston or the high-flying New Economy businesses, the problem goes beyond the "few bad apples." Unlike the Roman Catholic Diocese of Boston, the regulatory institutions of the U.S. government cannot cure souls, but they can change the institutions, the laws and the practices and the expectations governing the practice of business. Does Enron demonstrate that the current practices of the business world lead straight to the impoverishment of the citizens and, most likely, the ultimate demise of capitalism itself? Quite possibly.

Notes

1. ". . . the euphoria that characterized investing in the late 1990's is gone; that wide-eyed acceptance of every word corporate executives uttered, of every financial statement they released, of every outlandish projection an analyst made has been replaced by a sense that trust must once again be earned, that skepticism is a worthy trait, that the advice of analysts can be costly." Gretchen Morgenson, "Rebound from Ruin, if Not from Distrust," *The New York Times* Section 3, Money & Business, Sunday, September 8, 2002.

2. Gretchen Mergenson, "How 287 Turned into 7: Lessons in Fuzzy Math," *New York Times* January 20, 2002, Money & Business 1, 12. "Another half-truth concerned Enron's appearance last year at No. 7 on the Fortune 500 list of largest American companies. The company's $101 billion in revenue placed it between the powerhouses Citigroup and I.B.M. on the list. But rising to that level occurred only because energy trading companies can record as revenue the total amount of their transactions, rather than the profits made on each trade as is typical at brokerage firms. If viewed this way, Enron's revenue would have been $6.3 billion last year, pushing it to the bottom half of the list, at No. 287, wedged between Automatic Data Processing and Campbell Soup."

Source: Copyright © Dr. Lisa H. Newton. Reprinted by permission of the author.

Reading 10-2

WorldCom

Dennis Moberg and Edward Romar

2002 saw an unprecedented number of corporate scandals: Enron, Tyco, Global Crossing. In many ways, WorldCom is just another case of failed corporate governance, accounting abuses, and outright greed. But none of these other companies had senior executives as colorful and likable as Bernie Ebbers. A Canadian by birth, the six-foot, three-inch former basketball coach and Sunday School teacher emerged from the collapse of WorldCom not only broke but with a personal net worth as a negative nine-digit number.[1] No palace in a gated community, no stable of racehorses, or multimillion-dollar yacht to show for the

Note: References and citations have been deleted but are available from the authors.

telecommunications giant he created. Only debts and red ink—results some consider inevitable given his unflagging enthusiasm and entrepreneurial flair. There is no question that he did some pretty bad stuff, but he really wasn't like the corporate villains of his day: Andy Fastow of Enron, Dennis Koslowski of Tyco, or Gary Winnick of Global Crossing.

Personally, Bernie is a hard guy not to like. In 1998 when Bernie was in the midst of acquiring the telecommunications firm MCI, Reverend Jesse Jackson, speaking at an all-black college near WorldCom's Mississippi headquarters, asked how Ebbers could afford $35 billion for MCI but hadn't donated funds to local black students. Businessman LeRoy Walker, Jr., was in the audience at Jackson's speech, and afterwards set him straight. Ebbers had given over $1 million plus loads of information technology to that black college. "Bernie Ebbers," Walker reportedly told Jackson, "is my mentor." Rev. Jackson was won over, but who wouldn't be by this erstwhile milkman and bar bouncer who serves meals to the homeless at Frank's Famous Biscuits in downtown Jackson, Mississippi, and wears jeans, cowboy boots, and a funky turquoise watch to work.

It was 1983 in a coffee shop in Hattiesburg, Mississippi, that Mr. Ebbers first helped create the business concept that would become WorldCom. "Who could have thought that a small business in itty bitty Mississippi would one day rival AT&T?" asked an editorial in Jackson, Mississippi's *Clarion-Ledger* newspaper. Bernie's fall and the company's was abrupt. In June, 1999 with WorldCom's shares trading at $64, he was a billionaire, and WorldCom was the darling of the New Economy. By early May of 2002, Ebbers resigned his post as CEO, declaring that he was "1,000 percent convinced in my heart that this is a temporary thing." Two months later, in spite of Bernie's unflagging optimism, WorldCom declared itself the largest bankruptcy in American history.

This case describes three major issues in the fall of WorldCom, the corporate strategy of growth through acquisition, the use of loans to senior executives, and threats to corporate governance created by chumminess and lack of arm's length dealing. The case concludes with a brief description of the hero of the case—whistle blower Cynthia Cooper.

The Growth through Acquisition Merry-Go-Round

From its humble beginnings as an obscure long distance telephone company WorldCom, through the execution of an aggressive acquisition strategy, evolved into the second largest long distance telephone company in the United States and one of the largest companies handling worldwide Internet data traffic. According to the WorldCom website, at its high point the company:

- Provided mission-critical communications services for tens of thousands of businesses around the world.
- Carried more international voice traffic than any other company.
- Carried a significant amount of the world's Internet traffic.
- Owned and operated a global IP (Internet Protocol) backbone that provided connectivity in more than 2,600 cities, and in more than 100 countries.
- Owned and operated 75 data centers . . . on five continents." [Data centers provide hosting and allocation services to businesses for their mission critical business computer applications.]

WorldCom achieved its position as a significant player in the telecommunications industry through the successful completion of 65 acquisitions. Between 1991 and 1997, WorldCom spent almost $60 billion in the acquisition of many of these companies and accumulated $41 billion in debt. Two of these acquisitions were particularly significant. The

MFS Communications acquisition enabled WorldCom to obtain UUNet, a major supplier of Internet services to business, and MCI Communications gave WorldCom one of the largest providers of business and consumer telephone service. By 1997, WorldCom's stock had risen from pennies per share to over $60 a share. Through what appeared to be a prescient and successful business strategy at the height of the Internet boom, WorldCom became a darling of Wall Street. In the heady days of the technology bubble, Wall Street took notice of WorldCom and its then visionary CEO, Bernie Ebbers. This was a company "on the move," and Wall Street investment banks, analysts and brokers began to discover WorldCom's value and make "strong buy recommendations" to investors. As this process began to unfold, the analysts' recommendations, coupled with the continued rise of the stock on the stock market, made WorldCom stock desirable and the market's view of the stock was that it could only go up. As the stock value went up, it was easier for WorldCom to use stock as the vehicle to continue to purchase additional companies. The acquisition of MFS Communications and MCI Communications were, perhaps, the most significant in the long list of WorldCom acquisitions. With the acquisition of MFS Communications and its UUNet unit, "WorldCom (s)uddenly had an investment story to offer about the value of combining long distance, local service and data communications." In late 1997, British Telecommunications Corporation made a $19 billion bid for MCI. Very quickly, Ebbers made a counter offer of $30 billion in WorldCom stock. In addition, Ebbers agreed to assume $5 billion in MCI debt, making the deal $35 billion or 1.8 times the value of the British Telecom offer. MCI took WorldCom's offer making WorldCom a truly significant global telecommunications company.

All this would be just another story of a successful growth strategy if it wasn't for one significant business reality—mergers and acquisitions, especially large ones, present significant managerial challenges in at least two areas. First, management must deal with the challenge of integrating new and old organizations into a single smooth functioning business. This is a time-consuming process that involves thoughtful planning and a considerable amount of senior managerial attention if the acquisition process is to increase the value of the firm to both shareholders and stakeholders. With 65 acquisitions in six years and several of them large ones, WorldCom management had a great deal on its plate. The second challenge is the requirement to account for the financial aspects of the acquisition. The complete financial integration of the acquired company must be accomplished, including an accounting of asset, debts, good will, and a host of other financially important factors. This must be accomplished through the application of generally accepted accounting practices (GAAP).

WorldCom's efforts to integrate MCI illustrate several areas senior managers did not address well. In the first place, Ebbers appeared to be an indifferent executive who "paid scant attention to the details of operations." For example, customer service deteriorated. One business customer's service was discontinued incorrectly, and when the customer contacted customer service, he was told he was not a customer. Ultimately, the WorldCom representative told him that if he was a customer, he had called the wrong office because the office he called only handled MCI accounts. This poor customer stumbled "across a problem stemming from WorldCom's acquisition binge: For all its talent in buying competitors, the company was not up to the task of merging them. Dozens of conflicting computer systems remained, local systems were repetitive and failed to work together properly, and billing systems were not coordinated."

Poor integration of acquired companies also resulted in numerous organizational problems. Among them were:

1. Senior managers made little effort to develop a cooperative mindset among the various units of WorldCom.
2. Interunit struggles were allowed to undermine the development of a unified service delivery network.

3. WorldCom closed 3 important MCI technical service centers that contributed to network maintenance only to open 12 different centers that, in the words of one engineer, were duplicate and inefficient.

4. Competitive local exchange carriers (clercs) were another managerial nightmare. WorldCom purchased a large number of these to provide local service. According to one executive, "(t)he WorldCom model was a vast wasteland of clercs, and all capacity was expensive and very underutilized . . . There was far too much redundancy, and we paid far too much to get it."

Regarding financial reporting, WorldCom used a liberal interpretation of accounting rules when preparing financial statements. In an effort to make it appear that profits were increasing, WorldCom would write down in one quarter millions of dollars in assets it acquired while, at the same time, it "included in this charge against earnings the cost of company expenses expected in the future. The result was bigger losses in the current quarter but smaller ones in future quarters, so that its profit picture would seem to be improving." The acquisition of MCI gave WorldCom another accounting opportunity. While reducing the book value of some MCI assets by several billion dollars, the company increased the value of "good will," that is, intangible assets, a brand name, for example, by the same amount. This enabled WorldCom each year to charge a smaller amount against earnings by spreading these large expenses over decades rather than years. The net result was WorldCom's ability to cut annual expenses, acknowledge all MCI revenue and boost profits from the acquisition.

WorldCom managers also tweaked their assumptions about accounts receivables, the amount of money customers owe the company. For a considerable time period, management chose to ignore credit department lists of customers who had not paid their bills and were unlikely to do so. In this area, managerial assumptions play two important roles in receivables accounting. In the first place, they contribute to the amount of funds reserved to cover bad debts. The lower the assumption of noncollectable bills, the smaller the reserve fund required. The result is higher earnings. Secondly, if a company sells receivables to a third party, which WorldCom did, then the assumptions contribute to the amount of receivables available for sale.

So long as there were acquisition targets available, the merry-go-round kept turning, and WorldCom could continue these practices. The stock price was high and accounting practices allowed the company to maximize the financial advantages of the acquisitions while minimizing the negative aspects. WorldCom and Wall Street could ignore the consolidation issues because the new acquisitions allowed management to focus on the behavior so welcome by everyone, the continued rise in the share price. All this was put in jeopardy when, in 2000, the government refused to allow WorldCom's acquisition of Sprint. The denial stopped the carousel and put an end to the acquisition-without-consolidation strategy and left management a stark choice between focusing on creating value from the previous acquisitions with the possible loss of share value, or trying to find other creative ways to sustain and increase the share price.

In July 2002, WorldCom filed for bankruptcy protection after several disclosures regarding accounting irregularities. Among them was the admission of improperly accounting for operating expenses as capital expenses in violation of generally accepted accounting practices (GAAP). WorldCom has admitted to a $9 billion adjustment for the period from 1999 thorough the first quarter of 2002.

Sweetheart Loans to Senior Executives

Bernie Ebbers's passion for his corporate creation loaded him up on common stock. Through generous stock options and purchases Ebbers's WorldCom holdings grew and grew, and he typically financed these purchases with his existing holdings as collateral.

This was not a problem until the value of WorldCom stock declined, and Bernie faced margin calls (a demand to put up more collateral for outstanding loans) on some of his purchases. At that point he faced a difficult dilemma. Because his personal assets were insufficient to meet the substantial amount required to meet the call, he could either sell some of his common shares to finance the margin calls or request a loan from the company to cover the calls. Yet, when the board learned of his problem, it refused to let him sell his shares on the grounds that it would depress the stock price and signal a lack of confidence about WorldCom's future.

Had he pressed the matter and sold his stock, he would have escaped the bankruptcy financially whole, but Ebbers honestly thought WorldCom would recover. Thus, it was enthusiasm and not greed that trapped Mr. Ebbers. The executives associated with other corporate scandals sold at the top. In fact, other WorldCom executives did much, much better than Ebbers. Bernie borrowed against his stock. That course of action makes sense if you believe the stock will go up, but it's the road to ruin if the stock goes down. Unlike the others, he intended to make himself rich taking the rest of the shareholders with him. In his entire career, Mr. Ebbers sold company shares only half a dozen times. Detractors may find him irascible and arrogant, but defenders describe him as a principled man.

The policy of boards of directors authorizing loans for senior executives raises eyebrows. The sheer magnitude of the loans to Ebbers was breathtaking. The $341 million loan the board granted Mr. Ebbers is the largest amount any publicly traded company has lent to one of its officers in recent memory. Beyond that, some question whether such loans are ethical. "A large loan to a senior executive epitomizes concerns about conflict of interest and breach of fiduciary duty," said former SEC enforcement official Seth Taube. Nevertheless, 27 percent of major publicly traded companies had loans outstanding for executive officers in 2000 up from 17 percent in 1998 (most commonly for stock purchase but also home buying and relocation). Moreover, there is the claim that executive loans are commonly sweetheart deals involving interest rates that constitute a poor rate of return on company assets. WorldCom charged Ebbers slightly more than 2 percent interest, a rate considerably below that available to "average" borrowers and also below the company's marginal rate of return. Considering such factors, one compensation analyst claims that such lending "should not be part of the general pay scheme of perks for executives . . . I just think it's the wrong thing to do."

What's a Nod or Wink among Friends?

In the autumn of 1998, Securities and Exchange Commission's Arthur Levitt, Jr. uttered the prescient criticism, "Auditors and analysts are participants in a game of nods and winks." It should come as no surprise that it was Arthur Andersen that endorsed many of the accounting irregularities that contributed to WorldCom's demise. Beyond that, however, were a host of incredibly chummy relationships between WorldCom's management and Wall Street analysts.

Since the Glass-Steagall Act was repealed in 1999, financial institutions have been free to offer an almost limitless range of financial services to its commercial and investment clients. Citigroup, the result of the merger of Citibank and Travelers Insurance Company, which owned the investment bank and brokerage firm Salomon Smith Barney, was an early beneficiary of investment deregulation. Citibank regularly dispensed cheap loans and lines of credit as a means of attracting and rewarding corporate clients for highly lucrative work in mergers and acquisitions. Since WorldCom was so active in that mode, their senior managers were the target of a great deal of influence peddling by their banker, Citibank. For example,

Travelers Insurance, a Citigroup unit, lent $134 million to a timber company Bernie Ebbers was heavily invested in. Eight months later, WorldCom chose Salomon Smith Barney, Citigroup's brokerage unit to be the lead underwriter of $5 billion of its bond issue.

The entanglements, however, went both ways. Since the loan to Ebbers was collateralized by his equity holdings, Citigroup had reason to prop up WorldCom stock. No one was better at that than Jack Grubman, Salomon Smith Barney's telecommunication analyst. Grubman first met Bernie Ebbers in the early 1990s when he was heading up the precursor to WorldCom, LDDS Communications. The two hit it off socially, and Grubman started hyping the company. Investors were handsomely rewarded for following Grubman's buy recommendations until stock reached its high, and Grubman rose financially and by reputation. In fact, *Institutional Investing* magazine gave Jack a Number 1 ranking in 1999, and *BusinessWeek* labeled him "one of the most powerful players on Wall Street."

The investor community has always been ambivalent about the relationship between analysts and the companies they analyze. As long as analyst recommendations are correct, close relations have a positive insider quality, but when their recommendations turn south, corruption is suspected. Certainly Grubman did everything he could to tout his personal relationship with Bernie Ebbers. He bragged about attending Bernie's wedding in 1999. He attended board meeting at WorldCom's headquarters. Analysts at competing firms were annoyed with this chumminess. While the other analysts strained to glimpse any tidbit of information from the company's conference call, Grubman would monopolize the conversation with comments about "dinner last night."

It is not known who picked up the tab for such dinners, but Grubman certainly rewarded executives for their close relationship with him. Both Ebbers and WorldCom CFO Scott Sullivan were granted privileged allocations in IPO (Initial Public Offering) auctions. While the Securities and Exchange Commission allows underwriters like Salomon Smith Barney to distribute its allotment of new securities as it sees fit among its customers, this sort of favoritism has angered many small investors. Banks defend this practice by contending that providing high net worth individuals with favored access to hot IPOs is just good business. Alternatively, they allege that greasing the palms of distinguished investors creates a marketing "buzz" around an IPO, helping deserving small companies trying to go public get the market attention they deserve. For the record, Mr. Ebbers personally made $11 million in trading profits over a four-year period on shares from initial public offerings he received from Salomon Smith Barney. In contrast, Mr. Sullivan lost $13,000 from IPOs, indicating that they were apparently not "sure things."

There is little question but that friendly relations between Grubman and WorldCom helped investors from 1995 to 1999. Many trusted Grubman's insider status and followed his rosy recommendations to financial success. In a 2000 profile in *BusinessWeek*, he seemed to mock the ethical norm against conflict of interest: "what used to be a conflict is now a synergy," he said at the time. "Someone like me . . . would have been looked at disdainfully by the buy side 15 years ago. Now they know that I'm in the flow of what's going on." Yet, when the stock started cratering later that year, Grubman's enthusiasm for WorldCom persisted. Indeed, he maintained the highest rating on WorldCom until March 18, 2002 when he finally raised its risk rating. At that time, the stock had fallen almost 90 percent from its high two years before. Grubman's *mea culpa* was to clients on April 22 read, "In retrospect the depth and length of the decline in enterprise spending has been stronger and more damaging to WorldCom than we even anticipated." An official statement from Salomon Smith Barney two weeks later seemed to contradict the notion that Grubman's analysis was conflicted, "Mr. Grubman was not alone in his enthusiasm for the future prospects of the company. His coverage was based purely on information yielded during his analysis and was not based on personal relationships." Right.

On August 15, 2002, Jack Grubman resigned from Salomon where he had made as much as $20 million/year. His resignation letter read in part, "I understand the disappointment and anger felt by investors as a result of [the company's] collapse, I am nevertheless proud of the work I and the analysts who work with me did." On December 19, 2002, Jack Grubman was fined $15 million and was banned for securities transactions for life by the Securities and Exchange Commission for such conflicts of interest.

The media vilification that accompanies one's fall from power unearthed one interesting detail about Grubman's character—he repeatedly lied about his personal background. A graduate of Boston University, Mr. Grubman claimed a degree from MIT. Moreover, he claimed to have grown up in colorful South Boston, while his roots were actually in Boston's comparatively bland Oxford Circle neighborhood. What makes a person fib about his personal history is an open question. As it turns out, this is probably the least of Jack Grubman's present worries. New York State Controller H. Carl McCall sued Citicorp, Arthur Andersen, Jack Grubman, and others for conflict of interest. According to Mr. McCall, "this is another case of corporate coziness costing investors billions of dollars and raising troubling questions about the integrity of the information investors receive."

The Hero of the Case

No integrity questions can be raised about Cynthia Cooper, whose careful detective work as an internal auditor at WorldCom exposed some of the accounting irregularities apparently intended to deceive investors. Originally charged with responsibilities in operational audit, Cynthia and her colleagues grew suspicious of a number of peculiar financial transactions and went outside their assigned responsibilities to investigate. What they found was a series of clever manipulations intended to bury almost $4 billion in misallocated expenses and phony accounting entries.

A native of Clinton, Mississippi, where WorldCom's headquarters was located, Ms. Cooper's detective work was conducted in secret, often late at night to avoid suspicion. The thing that first aroused her curiosity came in March, 2002 when a senior line manager complained to her that her boss, CFO Scott Sullivan, had usurped a $400 million reserve account he had set aside as a hedge against anticipated revenue losses. That didn't seem kosher, so Cooper inquired of the firm's accounting firm, Arthur Andersen. They brushed her off, and Ms. Cooper decided to press the matter with the board's audit committee. That put her in direct conflict with her boss, Sullivan, who ultimately backed down. The next day, however, he warned her to stay out of such matters.

Undeterred and emboldened by the knowledge that Andersen had been discredited by the Enron case and that the SEC was investigating WorldCom, Cynthia decided to continue her investigation. Along the way, she learned of a WorldCom financial analyst who was fired a year earlier for failing to go along with accounting chicanery. Ultimately, she and her team uncovered a $2 billion accounting entry for capital expenditures that had never been authorized. It appeared that the company was attempting to represent operating costs as capital expenditures in order to make the company look more profitable. To gather further evidence, Cynthia's team began an unauthorized search through WorldCom's computerized accounting information system. What they found was evidence that fraud was being committed. When Sullivan heard of the ongoing audit, he asked Cooper to delay her work until the third quarter. She bravely declined. She went to the board's audit committee and in June, Scott Sullivan and two others were terminated. What Ms. Cooper had discovered was the largest accounting fraud in U. S. history.

As single-minded as Cynthia Cooper appeared during this entire affair, it was an incredibly trying ordeal. Her parents and friends noticed that she was under considerable stress and was losing weight. According to *The Wall Street Journal*, she and her colleagues worried "that their findings would be devastating to the company [and] whether their revelations would result in layoffs and obsessed about whether they were jumping to unwarranted conclusions that their colleagues at WorldCom were committing fraud. Plus, they feared that they would somehow end up being blamed for the mess."

It is unclear at this writing whether Bernie Ebbers will be brought to bear for the accounting irregularities that brought down his second in command. Jack Grubman's final legal fate is also unclear. While the ethical quality of enthusiasm and sociability are debatable, the virtue of courage is universally acclaimed, and Cynthia Cooper apparently has it. Thus, it was not surprising that on December 21, 2002, Cynthia Cooper was recognized as one of three "Persons of the Year" by *Time* magazine.

WorldCom Update

Edward Romar and Martin Calkins

In December 2005, two years after this case was written, the telecommunications industry consolidated further. Verizon Communications acquired MCI/WorldCom and SBC Communications acquired AT&T Corporation, which had been in business since the 19th century. The acquisition of MCI/WorldCom was the direct result of the behavior of WorldCom's senior managers as documented above. While it can be argued that the demise of AT&T Corp. was not wholly attributable to WorldCom's behavior, AT&T Corp.'s decimation certainly was facilitated by the events surrounding WorldCom, since WorldCom was the benchmark long distance telephone and Internet communications service provider. Indeed, the ripple effect of WorldCom's demise goes far beyond one company and several senior managers. It had a profound effect on an entire industry.

This postscript will update the WorldCom story by focusing on what happened to the company after it declared bankruptcy and before it was acquired by Verizon. The postscript also will relate subsequent important events in the telecommunications industry, the effect of WorldCom's problems on its competitors and labor market, and the impact WorldCom had on the lives of the key players associated with the fraud and its exposure.

From Benchmark to Bankrupt

Between July 2002 when WorldCom declared bankruptcy and April 2004 when it emerged from bankruptcy as MCI, company officials worked feverishly to restate the financials and reorganize the company. The new CEO Michael Capellas (formerly CEO of Compaq Computer) and the newly appointed CFO Robert Blakely faced the daunting task of settling the company's outstanding debt of around $35 billion and performing a rigorous financial audit of the company. This was a monumental task, at one point utilizing an army of over 500 WorldCom employees, over 200 employees of the company's outside auditor, KPMG, and a supplemental workforce of almost 600 people from Deloitte & Touche. As Joseph McCafferty notes, "(a)t the peak of the audit, in late 2003, WorldCom had about 1,500 people working on the restatement, under the combined management of Blakely and five controllers . . . (the t)otal cost to complete it: a mind-blowing $365 million"(McCafferty, 2004).

In addition to revealing sloppy and fraudulent bookkeeping, the post-bankruptcy audit found two important new pieces of information that only served to increase the amount of fraud at WorldCom. First, "WorldCom had overvalued several acquisitions by a total of $5.8 billion." In addition, Sullivan and Ebbers "had claimed a pretax profit for 2000 of $7.6 billion." In reality, WorldCom lost "$48.9 billion (including a $47 billion write-down of impaired assets)." Consequently, instead of a $10 billion profit for the years 2000 and 2001, WorldCom had a combined loss for the years 2000 through 2002 (the year it declared bankruptcy) of $73.7 billion. If the $5.8 billion of overvalued assets is added to this figure, the total fraud at WorldCom amounted to a staggering $79.5 billion.

Although the newly audited financial statements exposed the impact of the WorldCom fraud on the company's shareholders, creditors, and other stakeholders, other information made public since 2002 revealed the effects of the fraud on the company's competitors and the telecommunications industry as a whole. These show that the fall of WorldCom altered the fortunes of a number of telecommunications industry participants, none more so than AT&T Corporation.

The CNBC news show, "The Big Lie: Inside the Rise and Fraud of WorldCom," exposed the extent of the WorldCom fraud on several key participants, including the then-chairmen of AT&T and Sprint (Faber, 2003). The so-called "big lie" was promoted through a spreadsheet developed by Tom Stluka, a capacity planner at WorldCom, that modeled in Excel format the amount of traffic WorldCom could expect in a best-case scenario of Internet growth. In essence, "Stluka's model suggested that in the best of all possible worlds Internet traffic would double every 100 days." In working with the model, Stluka simply assigned variables with various parameters to "whatever we think is appropriate."

This was innocent enough, had it remained an exercise. A problem emerged when the exercise was extended and integrated into corporate strategy, when it was adopted and implemented by WorldCom and then by the telecommunications industry. Within a year, "other companies were touting it" and the model was given credibility it should not have been accorded. As Stluka explains, "there were a lot of people who were saying 10X growth, doubling every three to four months, doubling every 100 days, 1,000 percent, that kind of thing." But it wasn't true. "I don't recall traffic . . . in fact growing at that rate . . . still, WorldCom's lie had become an immutable law." Optimistic scenarios with little foundation in reality began to spread and pervade the industry. They became emblematic of the "smoke and mirrors" behavior not only at WorldCom prior to its collapse, but the industry as a whole.

Fictitious numbers drove not just WorldCom, but also other companies as they reacted to WorldCom's optimistic projections. According to Michael Armstrong, then chairman and CEO of AT&T, "For some period of time, I can recall that we were back-filling that expectation with laying cable, something like 2,200 miles of cable an hour." He adds: "Think of all the companies that went out of business that assumed that that was real."

The fallout from the WorldCom debacle was significant. Verizon obtained the freshly minted MCI for $7.6 billion, but not the $35 billion of debt MCI had when it declared bankruptcy. Although WorldCom was one of the largest telecommunications companies with nearly $160 billion in assets, shareholder suits obtained $6.1 billion from a variety of sources including investment banks, former board members and auditors of WorldCom. If this sum were evenly distributed among the firm's 2.968 billion common shares, the payoff would (have been) well under $1 a share for a stock that peaked at $49.91 on Jan. 2000.

There are more losers in the aftermath of the WorldCom wreck. The reemerged MCI was left with about 55,000 employees, down from 88,000 at its peak. Since March 2001, however, "about 300,000 telecommunications workers have lost their jobs. The sector's total employment—1.032 million—is at an eight year low." The carnage does not stop there.

Telecommunications equipment manufacturers such as Lucent Technologies, Nortell Networks, and Corning, while benefiting initially from WorldCom's groundless predictions, suffered in the end with layoffs and depressed share prices. Perhaps most significant, in December 2005, the venerable AT&T Corporation ceased to exist as an independent company.

The Impact on Individuals

The WorldCom fiasco had a permanent effect on the lives of its key players as well. Cynthia Cooper, who spearheaded the uncovering of the fraud, went on to become one of *Time* Magazine's 2002 Persons of the Year. She also received a number of awards, including the 2003 Accounting Exemplar Award, given to an individual who has made notable contributions to professionalism and ethics in accounting practice or education. At present, she travels extensively, speaking to students and professionals about the importance of strong ethical and moral leadership in business. Even so, as Dennis Moberg points out, "After Ebbers and Sullivan left the company, ". . . Cooper was treated less positively than her virtuous acts warranted. In an interview with her on 11 May 2005, she indicated that, for two years following their departure, her salary was frozen, her auditing position authority was circumscribed, and her budget was cut."

As far as the protagonists are concerned, in April 2002, CEO Bernie Ebbers resigned and two months later, CFO Scott Sullivan was fired. Shortly thereafter, in August 2002, Sullivan and former Controller David Myers were arrested and charged with securities fraud. In November 2002, former Compaq chief Michael Capellas was named CEO of WorldCom and in April 2003, Robert Blakely was named the company's CFO.

In March 2004, Sullivan pleaded guilty to criminal charges. At that time, too, Ebbers was formally charged with one count of conspiracy to commit securities fraud, one count of securities fraud, and seven counts of fraud related to false filings with the Security and Exchange Commission. Two months later, in May of 2004, Citigroup settled class action litigation for $1.64 billion after-tax brought on behalf of purchasers of WorldCom securities. In like manner, JPMorgan Chase & Co. agreed to pay $2 billion to settle claims by investors that it should have known WorldCom's books were fraudulent when it helped sell $5 billion in company bonds.

On March 15, 2005, Ebbers was found guilty of all charges and on July 13th of that year, sentenced to 25 years in prison, which was possibly a life sentence for the 63-year-old. He was expected to report to a federal prison on October 12, but remained free while his lawyers appealed his conviction.

At the time of his conviction, Ebbers's lawyers claimed the judge in the case gave the jury inappropriate instructions about Ebbers's knowledge of WorldCom's accounting fraud. By January of 2006, Reid Weingarten, Ebbers's lawyer, was claiming that the previous trial was manipulated against Ebbers because three high level WorldCom executives were barred from testifying on Ebbers's behalf. At that time, too, Judge Jose Cabranes of the US Second Circuit Court of Appeals commented, "There are many violent criminals who don't get 25 years in prison. Twenty years does seem an awfully long time."

Weingarten went on to assert that the government "should have charged the three former WorldCom employees that could have helped exonerate Ebbers or let them go." He charged, too, that "the jury was wrongly instructed that it could convict Ebbers on the basis of so-called "conscious avoidance" of knowledge of the fraud at WorldCom." Perhaps most compellingly, Weingarten called into question the fairness of Ebbers's sentence that was five times as long as that given to ex-WorldCom financial chief Scott Sullivan.

Weingarten's claims are not without merit. In August 2005, former CFO Sullivan was sentenced to five years in prison for his role in engineering the $11 billion accounting fraud. His relatively light sentence was part of a bargain wherein he agreed to plead guilty to the charges filed against him and to cooperate with prosecutors as they built a case against Ebbers. In doing so, Sullivan became the prosecution's main witness against Ebbers and the only person to testify that he discussed the WorldCom fraud directly with Ebbers. Others involved in the scandal were also treated less harshly than Ebbers. In September 2005, judgments were rendered approving settlement and dismissing action against David Myers and a number of others associated with WorldCom.

Despite Weingarten's claims, on July 28, 2006, the courts rejected Ebbers's contention that his trial was "fundamentally flawed" and concluded that his sentence was "harsh but not unreasonable." In doing so, the courts upheld Ebbers's conviction and prison sentence and cleared the way for the start of his 25-year prison term. It also ended, what is to date, the largest corporate fraud in history.

Notes

1. This is only true if he is liable for the loans he was given by WorldCom. If he avoids those somehow, his net worth may be plus $8.4 million according to *The Wall Street Journal* (see S. Pulliam & J. Sandberg, "Worldcom Seeks SEC Accord As Report Claims Wider Fraud," November 5, 2002, p. A-1).

Source: "WorldCom," Copyright © 2003 by Dennis Moberg, Santa Clara University, and Edward Romar, University of Massachusetts-Boston. Reprinted by permission. This case was made possible by a Hackworth grant from the Markkula Center for Applied Ethics, Santa Clara University. Reprinted with permission.

"WorldCom Update," Copyright © 2006 by Edward Romar and Martin Calkins, University of Massachusetts-Boston. Reprinted by permission of the authors.

Will the SEC Ever Get Serious about Making Corporate Insiders Pay for Fraud?

Mark Pincus, on Mark Pincus Blog

Tuesday, March 29, 2005

We are all watching yet another venerable old company (AIG) blow up over corporate accounting fraud and investor misrepresentation. Same old story, investors lose billions, often everything, while corporate insiders say "I'm sorry." Then the SEC tries to go after a small few with expensive criminal proceedings that rarely yield much. In this case, the chairman, Maurice Greenberg, has decided to "retire" and to walk away with $2.8 billion, in addition to the millions he's already sold. Maybe there'll be a whistleblower. Maybe, in five years, he'll face trial after an Enron-style bottom-up investigation. This white collar crime has become the norm and the SEC is useless in correcting it.

Here's the easy solution—MAKE THEM PAY! It would be so simple. Just create a rule that says that any insider who sold during a time of accounting fraud (or any restatement) has to disgorge all profits. This would immediately make every insider liable for the billions they made without bothering proving any knowledge of wrongdoing. The rationale is that they didn't deserve the profit, that they were selling a "lemon." California has this for cars, why can't the SEC have it for stocks? Instead, we punish all companies (especially small ones) with Sarbanes-Oxley, one of the dumbest laws our country has ever produced. It makes about as much sense as asking people to swear on the Bible before testifying.

Last year, over 400 public companies restated earnings. Think about the billions that would have been recaptured for the injured investors. Think about AOL where the insiders walked with billions, virtually unscathed, while the poor saps who owned stock in Time-Warner were left with a billions dollar tab to the SEC over fraudulent accounting. How about Gary Winnick who sold $600m at Global Crossing before it blew up? He chose to give back $30m to former employees. With this rule, he would have returned the whole boot. John Moores sold $600m too in his company, Peregrine Systems, before it too went bankrupt for fraudulent filings. Maybe these guys Didn't know about it. WHO CARES? Just make them give back the ill-gotten gains, and the SEC can still go after any of these people in the current long drawn-out criminal process and nab one out of 400 or less at a huge tab to the taxpayers.

We're all disgusted with Ken Lay and the insanity they brewed at Enron. Maybe a few of these guys will see jail time, but even then they'll keep the loot.

So why doesn't the SEC enact this obvious rule? I don't know. Maybe the same Wall Street guys who run the stock exchange that regulates them have a hand here. Maybe this would go too far in causing some real pain to a group that is a massive political donor.

Btw, there is a clear precedent for this in the current $16B short swing profit rule that says that, if an insider buys and sells in a six-month period, they have to disgorge the profit. I'm sure that this was enacted after realization that the criminal laws were ineffective.

If anyone has ideas on how we push the SEC to enact real dollar regulations that will start to protect investors and not whitewash the same old game, let me know.

Source: Copyright © Mark Pincus, http://markpincus.typepad.com. Reprinted by permission.

Mark Pincus is Chairman, Co-Founder and former CEO of Tribe Networks, Inc., a venture-backed startup to enable individuals and communities to connect and transact; Co-Founder and former Chairman and CEO of SupportSoft, Inc., a publicly traded enterprise software company, formerly known as Support.com; and former CEO of Freeloader.com, the first Web-based push service, acquired after seven months by Individual, Inc. for $38 million, among other ventures.

Reading **10-4**

Three Women's Moral Courage: *Why We Care*

Rushworth Kidder

Time magazine's writers duly noted similarities among the three ["People of the Year" for 2002]: Each worked from within to expose wrongdoing—financial mismanagement at Enron and WorldCom, a culture of nonresponse at the Bureau. Each worked in high-profile organizations—Enron known for its devastating corporate collapse, WorldCom for its record bankruptcy filing of $3.8 billion, and the FBI for charges that it failed to investigate leads that might have helped prevent the 9/11 attacks.

What's more, each woman worked in relative obscurity, neither at the top nor
limelight. Each, by filing a complaint, was seeking to reform an organization she dea
loved, not setting out to destroy something she despised. Each depended on her job for a
livelihood. And each was a woman.

For their part, these three told *Time* they don't think gender has much to do with their
actions. They can't abide the term "whistleblower." They remain emotionally attached to
their organizations: Of the three, only Watkins has since left her employer—and has taken
serious flak, initially for failing to go public with her accusations, and now for capitalizing
on her experiences through her share of a half-million-dollar book advance. Still, she and
her co-awardees are acutely aware of the stresses that whistleblowing involves.

At bottom, however, there's another overriding commonality: moral courage, a term
strangely muted in the *Time* account. In varying degrees, each of these women understood
the danger they faced, found the will to endure the risk, and based her action on clear moral
principle. These three characteristics—awareness, endurance, and principle—are the defining features of moral courage.

And that helps us answer the big question surrounding *Time*'s choice: Why, this year,
give an award for moral courage? What is it in our culture, the ethos of our time, our zeit-
geist that makes it so important to honor the courage to be moral?

In part, of course, it's our want of heroes, our longing for bold leadership in an age of
insecurity. The tragedy of 9/11 supplied us with a few heroes in the form of firefighters.
Now the pendulum has swung to a different sort of courage, where what's endangered is not
life and limb but reputation, ethical standards, and the need for principle.

And in part, it's just the reverse: our desire for something to moderate the glut of executive swashbuckling. Weary of the excesses of corporate rapacity, we reach out for the mod-
esty and humility of a moral leadership that carefully tracks the right numbers, establishes
a culture of trust, subordinates style to substance, and tells the truth.

But there's something else, I think, driving this thirst for moral courage. Call it the
Age of Disjunction. These days there's an unusual disconnect between words and action,
theory and practice, assertion and demonstration. Increasingly, it seems, there's an inertia
that keeps goodness in a state of suspended animation while badness rolls on of its own
momentum. It's an age fixed on show and surface, a two-dimensional televisual culture that
militates against depth and penetration. Result: an almost hypnotic inability to bring things
to conclusion. Perhaps that's what T. S. Eliot had in mind when, in "The Hollow Men," he
noted that "Between the motion / And the action / Falls the Shadow."

In a fascinating moment in their *Time* interview, these women glimpsed that shadow. "In
this country," said Watkins, "we have a vacuum in leadership. . . . We value splashy leaders."

"People who move to the top," added Cooper, "are typically racehorses, not workhorses.
And they're very charismatic."

"And the dark side of charisma," replied Watkins, "is narcissism."

That's not your usual whistleblower talk. But it speaks to a key point about moral courage. Because it seeks truth, moral courage probes for depth. In the end, what unites these
three women is their discomfort with the superficial. For them, neither the glitz of World-
Com, the bland denials of Enron, nor the veneer of old traditions at the FBI was compelling. They wanted something more profound.

So, ultimately, do we. Sobered by 9/11, rocked by corporate scandals, clouded by rumors
of war, we long to unite motion and action, dissolve the shadow, and connect our ideas and
our lives. That can be hard, discomforting work. That three women did it—and that some
editors thought what they did was supremely important—is a sign of hope for the new year.

Source: Excerpted from *Ethics Newsline*, 6, no. 1 (January 6, 2003), a publication of the
Institute for Global Ethics, www.globalethics.com. Copyright © 2003 Institute for Global
Ethics. Reprinted by permission.

Glossary

A

accountability As a first step in making ethically responsible decisions, requires a justification or reason to support decisions.

affirmative action A policy or a program that strives to redress past discrimination through the implementation of proactive measures to ensure equal opportunity. In other words, affirmative action is the intentional inclusion of previously excluded groups. Affirmative action efforts can take place in employment environments, education, or other arenas.

autonomy From the Greek for "self-ruled," autonomy is the capacity to make free and deliberate choices. The capacity for autonomous action is what explains the inherent dignity and intrinsic value of individual human beings.

B

backcasting As developed as part of the Natural Step, involves imagining what a sustainable future must hold. From that vision, creative businesses then look backwards to the present and determine what must be done to arrive at that future.

biomimicry ("closed-loop" production) Seeks to integrate what is presently waste back into production in much the way that biological processes turn waste into food.

C

categorical imperative An imperative is a command or duty; "categorical" means that it is without exception. Thus a categorical imperative is an overriding principle of ethics. Philosopher Immanual Kant offered several formulations of the categorical imperative: act so as the maxim implicit in your acts could be willed to be a universal law; treat persons as ends and never as means only; treat others as subjects, not objects.

***caveat emptor* approach:** *Caveat emptor* means "buyer beware" in Latin and this approach suggests that the burden of risk of information shall be placed on the buyer. This perspective assumes that every purchase involves the informed consent of the buyer and therefore it is assumed to be ethically legitimate.

character The sum of relatively set traits, dispositions, and habits of an individual. Along with rational deliberation and choice, a person's character accounts for how she or he makes decisions and acts. Training and developing character so that it is disposed to act ethically is the goal of virtue ethics.

child labor Though the term literally signifies children who work, it has taken on the meaning of exploitative work that involves some harm to a child who is not of an age to justify his or her presence in the workplace. The elements of that definition—harm, age of the child, justification to be in the workplace relative to other options—remain open to social and economic debate. UNICEF's 1997 State of the World's Children Report explains, "Children's work needs to be seen as happening along a continuum, with destructive or exploitative work at one end and beneficial work—-promoting or enhancing children's development without interfering with their schooling, recreation and rest—-at the other. And between these two poles are vast areas of work that need not negatively affect a child's development."

code of conduct A set of behavioral guidelines and expectations that govern all members of a business firm.

compliance based culture A corporate culture in which obedience to laws and regulations is the prevailing model for ethical behavior.

Committee of Sponsoring Organizations (COSO) COSO is a voluntary collaboration designed to improve financial reporting through a combination of controls and governance standards called the Internal Control–Integrated Framework. It was established in 1985 by five of the major professional accounting and finance associations originally to study fraudulent financial reporting and later developed standards for publicly held companies. It has become one of the most broadly accepted audit systems for internal controls.

conflict of interest A conflict of interest exists where a person holds a position of trust that requires that she or he exercise judgment on behalf of others, but where her/his personal interests and/or obligations conflict with those others.

consequentialist theories Ethical theories, such as utilitarianism, that determine right and wrong by calculating the consequences of actions.

control activities Policies and procedures that support the control environment.

control environment   One of the five elements that comprise the control structure, similar to the culture of an organization, and support people in the achievement of the organization's objectives. The control environment "sets the tone of an organization, influencing the control consciousness of its people."

Corporate Automotive Fuel Efficiency (CAFE) Standards   Established by the Energy Policy Conservation Act of 1975, Corporate Average Fuel Economy (CAFE) is the sales-weighted average fuel economy, expressed in miles per gallon (mpg), of a manufacturer's fleet of passenger cars or light Trucks. The U.S. federal government establishes CAFE standards as a means of increasing fuel efficiency of automobiles.

corporate citizenship model of CSR   Environment in which a company engages in CSR efforts solely for the public good and does not expect a commercial return on its contributions. These organizations believe that they play a particular role in the community and that their ability to do good creates a responsibility to do good.

corporate governance   The structure by which corporations are managed, directed, and controlled towards the objectives of fairness, accountability, and transparency. The structure generally will determine the relationship between the board of directors, the shareholders or owners of the firm, and the firm's executives or management.

corporate social responsibility   The responsibilities that businesses have to the societies within which they operate. In various contexts, it may also refer to the voluntary actions that companies undertake to address economic, social, and environmental impacts of its business operations and the concerns of its principal stakeholders. The European Commission defines CSR as "a concept whereby companies decide voluntarily to contribute to a better society and a cleaner environment." Specifically, CSR suggests that a business identify its stakeholder groups and incorporate its needs and values within its strategic and operational decision-making process.

cradle-to-cradle responsibility   Holds that a business should be responsible for incorporating the end results of its products back into the productive cycle.

culture   A shared pattern of beliefs, expectations, and meanings that influences and guides the thinking and behaviors of the members of a particular group.

D

deontological ethics   Derived from the Greek word for "duty," deontological ethics stresses the ethical centrality of such things as duties, principles, and obligations. It denies that all ethical judgments can be made in terms of consequences.

descriptive ethics   As practiced by many social scientists, provides a descriptive and empirical account of those standards that actually guide behavior, as opposed to those standards that should guide behavior. Contrast with *normative ethics,* below.

discrimination   Discrimination refers to the act of discernment or the ability to make fine distinctions. It is an important element in both personal and professional decision making. However, when this ability is used to distinguish on the basis of classifications that are prohibited by law, discrimination may be the basis for legal liability. Where discrimination is used to infringe upon the fundamental rights of other humans, to treat people unfairly, to achieve unjust results, or to achieve unfair advantage over others, it may be considered unethical.

diversity   Diversity refers to the presence of differing cultures, languages, ethnicities, races, affinity orientations, genders, religious sects, abilities, social classes, ages, and national origins of the individuals in a firm. When used in connection with the corporate environment, it often encompasses the values of respect, tolerance, inclusion, and acceptance.

downsize   The reduction of human resources at an organization through terminations, retirements, corporate divestments, or other means.

due process   The right to be protected against the arbitrary use of authority. In legal contexts, due process refers to the procedures that police and courts must follow in exercising their authority over citizens. In the employment context, due process specifies the conditions for basic fairness within the scope of the employer's authority over its employees.

duties   Those obligations that one is bound to perform, regardless of consequences. Duties might be derived from basic ethical principles, from the law, or from one's institutional or professional role.

duty of care   Involves the exercise of reasonable care by a board member to ensure that the corporate executives with whom she or he works carry out their management responsibilities and comply with the law in the best interests of the corporation.

duty of good faith   Requires obedience, compelling board members to be faithful to the organization's mission. In other words, they are not permitted to act in a way that is inconsistent with the central goals of the organization.

duty of loyalty   Requires faithfulness; a board member must give undivided allegiance when making decisions affecting the organization. This means that conflicts of interest are always to be resolved in favor of the corporation.

E

ecoefficiency   Doing more with less. Introduced at the Rio Earth Summit in 1992, the concept of eco-efficiency is a way business can contribute to sustainability by reducing resource usage in its production cycle.

egoism   As a psychological theory, egoism holds that all people act only from self-interest. Empirical evidence strongly suggests that this is a mistaken account of human motivation. As an ethical theory, egoism holds that humans ought to act for their own self-interest. Ethical egoists typically distinguish between one's perceived best interests and one's true best interests.

Electronic Communications Privacy Act of 1986   The United States statute that establishes the provisions for access, use, disclosure, interception, and privacy protections relating to electronic communications.

e-mail monitoring   The maintenance and either periodic or random review of e-mail communications of employees or others for a variety of business purposes.

employment at will (EAW)   The legal doctrine that holds that, absent a particular contractual or other legal obligation that specifies the length or conditions of employment, all employees are employed "at will." Unless an agreement specifies otherwise, employers are free to fire an employee at any time and for any reason. In the same manner, an EAW worker may opt to leave a job at any time for any reason, without offering any notice at all; so the freedom is *theoretically* mutual.

enlightened self-interest model of CSR   A belief that the incorporation of CSR can lead to differentiation and competitive market advantage for the business, something that can be branded for the present and future. This model is supported by arguments based in the reduction of risk, market reputation, brand image, stakeholder relationships, and long-term strategic interests.

Enron Corporation   An energy company based in Houston, Texas, that *Fortune* magazine named America's most innovative company for six consecutive years before it was discovered to have been involved in one of the largest instances of accounting fraud in world history. In 2001, with over 21,000 employees, it filed the largest bankruptcy in United States history and disclosed a scandal that resulted in the loss of millions of dollars, thousands of jobs, the downfall of Big Five accounting firm Arthur Andersen LLP, at least one suicide, and several trials and convictions, among other consequences. Enron remains in business today as it continues to liquidate its assets.

ethical custom   Along with law, one of the restraints on business's pursuit of profits advocated by Milton Friedman.

ethical decision-making process   Requires a persuasive and rational justification for a decision. Rational justifications are developed through a logical process of decision making that gives proper attention to such things as facts, alternative perspectives, consequences to all stakeholders, and ethical principles.

ethical relativism   An important perspective within the philosophical study of ethics, which holds that ethical values and judgments are ultimately dependent upon, or relative to, one's culture, society, or personal feelings. Relativism denies that we can make rational or objective ethical judgments.

ethical values   Those properties of life that contribute to human well-being and a life well lived. Ethical values would include such things as happiness, respect, dignity, integrity, freedom, companionship, health.

ethics   Derived from the Greek word *ethos*, which refers to those values, norms, beliefs, and expectations that determine how people within a culture live and act. Ethics steps back from such standards for how people *do* act, and reflects on the standards by which people *should* live and act. At its most basic level, ethics is concerned with how we act and how we live our lives. Ethics involves what is perhaps the most monumental question any human being can ask: How *should* we live? Following from this original Greek usage, ethics can refer to both the standards by which an individual chooses to live her/his own personal life, and the standards by which individuals live in community with others (see *morality* below). As a branch of philosophy, ethics is the discipline that systematically studies questions of how we ought to live our lives.

ethics officers   Individuals within an organization charged with managerial oversight of ethical compliance and enforcement within the organization.

European Union Directive on Personal Data Protection   E.U. legislation seeking to remove potential obstacles to cross-border flows of personal data, to ensure a high level of protection within the European Union, and to harmonize protections across the European continent and with those countries with whom E.U. countries do business.

European Union 8th Directive   Covers many of the same issues as Sarbanes-Oxley but applies these requirements and restrictions to companies traded on European Union exchanges. The updates to the directive in 2005 clarified required duties, independence, and ethics of statutory auditors and called for public oversight of the accounting profession and external quality assurance of both audit and financial reporting processes. In addition, the directive strives to improve cooperation between E.U. oversight bodies and provides for effective and balanced international regulatory cooperation with oversight bodies outside the E.U. regulatory infrastructure (e.g., the U.S. Public Company Accounting Oversight Board).

F

Federal Sentencing Guidelines (FSG)   Developed by the United States Sentencing Commission and implemented in 1991, originally as mandatory parameters for judges to use during organizational sentencing cases. By connecting punishment to prior business practices, the guidelines establish legal norms for ethical business behavior. However, since a 2005 Supreme Court decision, the FSG are now considered to be discretionary in nature and offer some specifics for organizations about ways to mitigate eventual fines and sentences by integrating bona fide ethics and compliance programs throughout their organizations.

fiduciary duties   A legal duty to act on behalf of or in the interests of another.

four Ps of marketing   Production, price, promotion, and placement.

Fourth Amendment protections   The U.S. Constitution's Fourth Amendment protection against unreasonable search and seizure extends privacy protections to the public sector workplace through the Constitution's application to state action.

G

gatekeepers   Some professions, such as accountant, that act as "watchdogs" in that their role is to ensure that those who enter into the marketplace are playing by the rules and conforming to the conditions that ensure the market functions as it is supposed to function.

H

HIPAA Health Insurance Portability and Accountability Act (HIPAA) (Pub. L. 104-191)   HIPAA stipulates that employers cannot use "protected health information" in making employment decisions without prior consent. Protected health information includes all medical records or other individually identifiable health information.

hypernorms   Values that are fundamental across culture and theory.

I

implied warranty of merchantability   Implied assurances by a seller that a product is reasonably suitable for its purpose.

insider trading   Trading of securities by those who hold private inside information that would materially impact the value of the stock and that allows them to benefit from buying or selling stock.

internal control   A process, effected by an entity's board of directors, management, and other personnel, designed to provide reasonable assurance regarding the achievement of objectives in the following categories: effectiveness and efficiency of operations, reliability of financial reporting, and compliance with applicable laws and regulations.

Internet use monitoring   The maintenance and either periodic or random review of the use of the Internet by employees or others based on time spent or content accessed for a variety of business purposes.

intrusion into seclusion   The legal terminology for one of the common law claims of invasion of privacy. Intrusion into seclusion occurs when someone intentionally intrudes on the private affairs of another when the intrusion would be "highly offensive to a reasonable person."

J

just cause   A standard for terminations or discipline that requires the employer to have sufficient and fair cause before reaching a decision against an employee.

L

loyalty   A character trait that involves the disposition to make sacrifices for the well-being of the object of loyalty, whether it be one's friend, country, or employer.

M

marketing   Defined by the American Marketing Association as "an organizational function and a set of processes for creating, communicating, and delivering value to customers and for managing customer relationships in ways that benefit the organization and its stakeholders."

mission statement   A formal summary statement that described the goals, values, and institutional aim of an organization.

moral free space   That environment where hypernorms or universal rules do not govern or apply to ethical decisions but instead culture or other influences govern decisions, as long as they are not in conflict with hypernorms. In other words, as long as a decision is not in conflict with a hypernorm, it rests within moral free space and reasonable minds may differ as to what is ethical.

moral imagination   When one is facing an ethical decision, the ability to envision various alternative choices, consequences, resolutions, benefits, harms.

morality   Sometimes used to denote the phenomena studied by the field of ethics. This text uses *morality* to refer to those aspects of ethics involving personal, individual decision making. "How should I live my life?" or "What type of person ought I be?" is taken to be the basic question of morality. Morality can be distinguished from questions of *social justice*, which address issues of how communities and social organizations ought to be structured.

multiculturalism   Similar to diversity, refers to the principle of tolerance and inclusion that supports the coexistence of multiple cultures, while encouraging each to retain that which is unique or individual about that particular culture.

N

negligence   Unintentional failure to exercise reasonable care not to harm other people. Negligence is considered to be one step below "reckless disregard" for harm to others and two steps below intentional harm.

norms   Those standards or guidelines that establish appropriate and proper behavior. Norms can be established by such diverse perspectives as economics, etiquette, or ethics.

normative ethics   Ethics as a *normative* discipline that deals with norms, those standards of appropriate and proper (or "normal") behavior. Norms establish the guidelines or standards for determining what we should do, how we should act, what type of person we should be. Contrast with *descriptive ethics,* above.

normative myopia   The tendency to ignore, or the lack of the ability to recognize, ethical issues in decision making.

O

OSHA   – The United States Occupational Safety and Health Administration, an agency of the federal government that publishes and enforces safety and health regulations for U.S. businesses.

P

perceptual differences   Psychologists and philosophers have long recognized that individuals cannot perceive the world independently of their own conceptual framework. Experiences are mediated by and interpreted through our own understanding and concepts. Thus, ethical disagreements can depend as much on a person's conceptual framework as on the facts of the situation. Unpacking our own and others' conceptual schema plays an important role in making ethically responsible decisions.

personal and professional decision making   Individuals within a business setting are often in situations in which they must make decisions both from their own personal point of view and from the perspective of the specific role they fill within an institution. Ethically responsible decisions require an individual to recognize that these perspectives can conflict and that a life of moral integrity must balance the personal values with the professional role-based values and responsibilities.

personal data   Any information relating to an identifiable person, directly or indirectly, in particular by reference to one or more factors specific to her or his physical, physiological, mental, economic, cultural, or social identity.

practical reasoning   Involves reasoning about what one ought to do, contrasted with *theoretical reasoning*, which is concerned with what one ought to believe. Ethics is a part of practical reason.

prima facie   Legal term that literally means "at first sight," used to designate the burden of proof in a legal case. It refers to the elements of a case that would be sufficient to state a claim if one's legal opponent does not rebut them. If one fails to state a *prima facie* case, the case will be dismissed.

privacy   The right to be "let alone" within a personal zone of solitude, and/or the right to control information about oneself.

privacy rights   The legal and ethical sources of protection for privacy in personal data.

property rights in information   The boundaries defining actions that individuals can take in relation to other individuals regarding their personal information. If one individual has a *right* to her or his personal information, someone else has a commensurate duty to observe that right.

R

reasonable expectation of privacy   The basis for some common law claims of invasion of privacy. Where an individual is notified that information will be shared or space will not be private, there is likely no reasonable expectation of privacy.

reciprocal obligation   The concept that, while an employee has an obligation to respect the goals and property of the employer, the employer has a *reciprocal obligation* to respect the rights of the employee as well, including the employee's right to privacy.

reputation management   The practice of caring for the "image" of a firm.

reverse discrimination   Decisions made or actions taken against those individuals who are traditionally considered to be in power or the majority, such as white men, or in favor of a historically nondominant group.

rights   Function to protect certain central interests from being sacrificed for the greater overall happiness. According to many philosophers, rights entail obligations: your rights create duties for others either to refrain from violating your rights ("negative" duties) or to provide you with what is yours by right ("positive" duties).

S

Safe Harbor exception   Considered "adequate standards" of privacy protection for U.S.-based companies under the European Union's Data Protection Directive.

Sarbanes-Oxley Act (Public Accounting Reform and Investor Protection Act of 2002)   Implemented on July 30, 2002, and administered by the Securities and Exchange Commission to regulate financial reporting and auditing of publicly traded companies in the United States. SOX or SarbOx (popular shorthands for the act) was enacted very shortly following and directly in response to the Enron scandals of 2001. One of the greatest areas of consternation and debate that has emerged surrounding SOX involves the high cost of compliance and the challenging burden therefore placed on smaller firms. Some contend that SOX was the most significant change to the corporate landscape to occur in the second half of the 20th century.

service-based economy   Interprets consumer demand as a demand for services, for example, for clothes cleaning, floor covering, cool air, transportation, or word processing, rather than as a demand for products such as washing machines, carpeting, air conditioners, cars, and computers.

social contract model of CSR   Environment in which a company engages in CSR on the basis of a reciprocal obligation to that community generated by the benefits received from serving as a community citizen. The moral rights that various stakeholders possess create responsibilities on the part of the corporation to respect those rights.

social contract theory   In general, the theory that the rights and responsibilities of individuals are derived from a hypothetical contract between all members of that society. As a model of corporate social responsibility within business ethics, it argues that the responsibilities of business and management are derived from a hypothetical social contract between business institutions and society.

social ethics   The area of ethics that is concerned with how we should live together with others and social organizations ought to be structured. Social ethics involves questions of political, economic, civic, and cultural norms aimed at promoting human well-being.

social justice   Addresses questions of how the benefits and burdens of living in community ought to be distributed

stakeholders   In a general sense, a stakeholder is anyone who can be affected by decisions made within a business. More specifically, stakeholders are considered to be those people who are necessary for the functioning of a business.

stakeholder theory   A model of corporate social responsibility that holds that business managers have ethical responsibilities to a range of stakeholders that goes beyond a narrow view that the primary or only responsibility of managers is to stockholders.

stealth marketing   Also called undercover marketing. Marketing campaigns that are based on environments or activities where the subject is not aware that she or he is the target of a marketing campaign; those situations where one is subject to directed commercial activity without knowledge or consent.

strict liability   A legal doctrine that holds an individual or business accountable for damages whether or not it was at fault. In a strict liability case, no matter how careful the business is in its product or service, if harm results from use, the individual or business is liable.

sustainable business practice   A model of business practice in which business activities meet the standards of sustainability.

sustainable development   Development that meets the needs of the present without compromising the ability of future generations to meet their own needs as defined by the Brundtland Commission in 1987.

sweatshops   A term that remains subject to debate. Some might suggest that all workplaces with conditions that are below standards in more developed countries are sweatshops since all humans have a right to equally decent working conditions. (See the discussion in Chapter 6 and D. Arnold and L. Hartman, "Beyond Sweatshops: Positive Deviancy and Global Labor Practices," *Business Ethics: A European Review* 14, no. 3 (July 2005).) In this text we use the following definition: any workplace in which workers are typically subject to two or more of the following conditions: systematic forced overtime, systematic health and safety risks that stem from negligence or the willful disregard of employee welfare, coercion, systematic deception that places workers at risk, underpayment of earnings, and income for a 48-hour workweek less than the overall poverty rate for that country (one who suffers from overall poverty lacks the income necessary to satisfy one's basic nonfood needs such as shelter and basic health care).

T

three pillars of sustainability   Three factors that are often used to judge the adequacy of sustainable practices. Sustainable development must be (1) economically, (2) environmentally, and (3) ethically satisfactory.

theoretical reasoning   Involves reasoning that is aimed at establishing truth and therefore at what we ought to believe. Contrast with practical reasoning, which aims at determining what is reasonable for us to do.

U

United States Sentencing Commission   An independent agency in the United States judiciary created in 1984 to regulate sentencing policy in the federal court system.

Uniting and Strengthening America by Providing Appropriate Tools Required to Intercept and Obstruct Terrorism United States (USA PATRIOT) Act of 2001   A U.S. statute designed to increase the surveillance and investigative powers of law enforcement agencies in the United States in response to the terrorist attacks of September 11, 2001. The act has been lauded as a quick response to terrorism (it was introduced less than a week after the attacks) and for implementing critical amendments to more than 15 important statutes; it also has been criticized for failing to include sufficient safeguards for civil liberties.

utilitarianism   An ethical theory that tells us that we can determine the ethical significance of any action by looking to the consequences of that act. Utilitarianism is typically identified with the policy of "maximizing the overall good" or, in a slightly different version, of producing "the greatest good for the greatest number."

V

values   Those beliefs that incline us to act or to choose in one way rather than another. We can recognize many different types of values: financial, religious, legal, historical, nutritional, political, scientific, and aesthetic. Ethical values serve the ends of human well-being in impartial, rather than personal or selfish ways.

values-based culture   A corporate culture in which conformity to a statement of values and principles rather than simple obedience to laws and regulations is the prevailing model for ethical behavior.

veil of ignorance   A heuristic device developed by philosopher John Rawls to ensure that decision making is done in impartial and fair ways. Rules accepted by parties behind a veil of ignorance are those made without knowledge of one's own characteristics, interests, and desires.

virtue ethics   An approach to ethics that studies the character traits or habits that constitute a good human life, a life worth living. The virtues provide answers to the basic ethical question "What kind of person should I be?"

W

whistleblowing   A practice in which an individual within an organization reports organizational wrongdoing to the public or to others in position of authority.

word-of-mouth marketing   Efforts by companies to generate personal recommendations by users.

Index